Featuring over 1,000 Hotels & Guesthouses

as well as details on Golfing, Angling, Conference, Spa & Leisure Facilities and Touring Maps

irelandhotels.com
Official Website of the Irish Hotels Federation

One source - Endless possibilities

IRISH HOTELS FEDERATION

13 Northbrook Road, Dublin 6, Ireland
Telephone +353 1 497 6459   Fax: +353 1 497 4613

The Irish Hotels Federation does not accept any responsibility for errors, omissions or any information whatsoever in the Guide and members and users of the Guide are requested to consult page 10 hereof for further information.

N.B. Some telephone/fax numbers and codes will change during 2006. If you experience any difficulty, please contact the operator. When dialling Ireland from abroad, please use the following codes: Republic of Ireland: 00 353 + local code (drop the 0). Northern Ireland: 00 44 + local code (drop the 0). If dialling Northern Ireland directly from the Republic of Ireland replace the prefix code 028 with the code 048.

Design & Database published by Neogen, Dublin. Tel: +353 1 810 2043 Fax: +353 1 838 8260

SELECTING YOUR HOTEL AND GUESTHOUSE

REGIONS
Begin by selecting the Region(s) you wish to visit. This guide divides into **8** separate Regions –
South West, Shannon, West, North West, North, Dublin & East Coast, Midlands & Lakelands and South East –
and they are represented in that order.

COUNTIES
Within each Region, Counties are presented alphabetically.

LOCATIONS – CITIES, TOWNS, VILLAGES
Within Counties, Locations are also presented alphabetically, see Index to Locations on Pages 12 & 13.

PREMISES
Within Locations Hotels and Guesthouses are also presented in alphabetical order, see Index of Hotels and
Guesthouses on Pages 493 to 512.

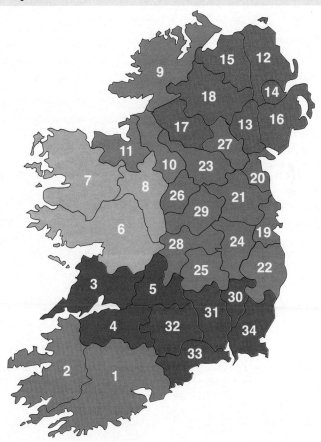

FACILITIES - KEY TO SYMBOLS

- Total Number of Bedrooms
- Number of Bedrooms with Bath/Shower and Toilet
- Direct Dial Facilities
- TV in All Bedrooms
- Elevator/Lift
- Can be Booked Through Travel Agent/ Tourist Office and Commission Paid
- Childrens Playground
- Childrens Playroom
- C Price Reduction for Children
- Babysitter Service
- CM Childrens Meals
- CS Crèche
- Garden for Visitors Use
- Indoor Swimming Pool
- Outdoor Swimming Pool
- Sauna
- Gym
- Leisure Complex (Including Sauna / Swimming Pool / Gym)
- Tennis Court - Hard/Grass
- Games Room
- Squash Court
- Horse Riding/Pony Trekking On Site or Nearby
- 9-Hole Golf Course On Site
- 18-Hole Golf Course On Site

- Angling on Site or Nearby
- Evening Entertainment
- P Car Parking
- Facilities for Pets
- S Price Reduction for Senior Citizens excl. July/August and Subject to Availability
- Wine Licence
- Dispense Bar Service
- Licensed to Sell All Alcoholic Drink
- alc À la Carte Meals Provided
- Tea/Coffee Making Facilities in Bedroom
- Inet Modem Access in Bedroom
- WiFi Wireless Internet Access
- Guide Dogs Welcome
- 1. Accessible to Ambulant People Capable of Climbing Flights of Steps with a Maximum Height Between Landings of 1.8 Metres.
- 2. Accessible to Ambulant People with Mobility Impairments but Capable of Climbing Three Steps.
- 3. Accessible to Wheelchair Users Including those who can Transfer Unaided to and from the Wheelchair.
- 4. Accessible to All Wheelchair Users Including those Requiring Assistance to Transfer to and from the Wheelchair e.g. Carer/Partner.

IRISH HOTELS FEDERATION — *Denotes that premises are members of the Irish Hotels Federation as at 16 September 2005.*

NIHF — *Denotes that premises are members of the Northern Ireland Hotels Federation as at 16 September 2005.*

ACTIVITY SECTIONS

Green symbols Illustrated below denote that the hotel or guesthouse is included in a particular Activity Section. Further details of the facilities available and the arrangements made on behalf of guests for participation in these activities are shown on pages 407 to 475.

 Golf   Angling   Conference   Spa & Leisure

SAMPLE ENTRY

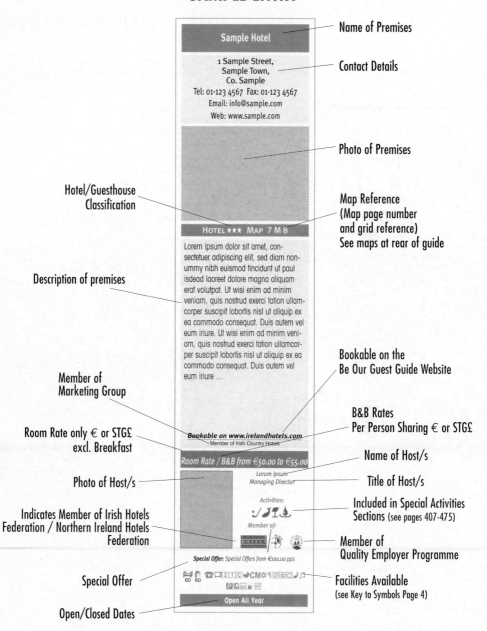

Name of Premises

Contact Details

Photo of Premises

Hotel/Guesthouse Classification

Map Reference
(Map page number
and grid reference)
See maps at rear of guide

Description of premises

Bookable on the
Be Our Guest Guide Website

Member of
Marketing Group

B&B Rates
Per Person Sharing € or STG£

Room Rate only € or STG£
excl. Breakfast

Name of Host/s

Photo of Host/s

Title of Host/s

Included in Special Activities
Sections (see pages 407-475)

Indicates Member of Irish Hotels
Federation / Northern Ireland Hotels
Federation

Member of
Quality Employer Programme

Special Offer

Facilities Available
(see Key to Symbols Page 4)

Open/Closed Dates

Sample Hotel

1 Sample Street,
Sample Town,
Co. Sample
Tel: 01-123 4567 Fax: 01-123 4567
Email: info@sample.com
Web: www.sample.com

HOTEL ★★★ MAP 7 M 8

Lorem ipsum dolor sit amet, consectetuer adipiscing elit, sed diam nonummy nibh euismod tincidunt ut paul isdead laoreet dolore magna aliquam erat volutpat. Ut wisi enim ad minim veniam, quis nostrud exerci tation ullamcorper suscipit lobortis nisl ut aliquip ex ea commodo consequat. Duis autem vel eum iriure. Ut wisi enim ad minim veniam, quis nostrud exerci tation ullamcorper suscipit lobortis nisl ut aliquip ex ea commodo consequat. Duis autem vel eum iriure ...

Bookable on www.irelandhotels.com
Member of Irish Country Hotels

Room Rate / B&B from €50.00 to €55.00

Lorum Ipsum
Managing Director

Activities:

Member of:

Special Offer: Special Offers from €100.00 pps

Open All Year

Fáilte Ireland

'Who made a difference?'

Help us **recognise** those who have made a difference to your holiday & you could win the Irish holiday of your dreams

• A kindness above and beyond the call of duty
• The laughter generated by a fantastic story
• Exceptional service with a personal touch ...... and more

Help us find the true **tourism champions**.
The people you want to tell your family and friends about.
Those who made a **difference**.

Nominate online
www.**irishwelcomeawards**.com
Or fill in the Irish Welcome Awards Nomination form

OUR QUALITY TEAM MAINTAINS 100,000 LINES.

WHAT FLOWS IS POETRY.

NO WONDER THE GUINNESS IS GREAT

It is essential that when booking your accommodation you request the "Be Our Guest 2006" Rate

Our Guide features a broad selection of Irish Hotels and Guesthouses, from ultra modern buildings to stately Country Houses, luxurious Castles and old-world Inns. The majority of these Hotels and Guesthouses are members of the Irish Hotels Federation or the Northern Ireland Hotels Federation and we hope that the illustrations and descriptions of these premises and the amenities they offer will help you to choose the most suitable premises for your holiday.

All of the Hotels and Guesthouses featured in the Guide at the time of going to print (10th Oct 2005) have been registered or are awaiting registration by Fáilte Ireland or by the Northern Ireland Tourist Board, in accordance with the Statutory Registration Regulations which they administer.

B&B AND ROOM RATES

The only rates featured in this publication relate to either **a Bed & Breakfast Per Person Sharing or a Room Rate only**. These are Guideline Rates, please ensure that you contact the premises to vertify the rates applicable to your reservation. **Supplements may be payable for suites or superior/de luxe rooms. Also, where single or double/twin bedded rooms are occupied by one person, a supplement may be payable. Correspondingly, if more than two persons share a family room, special reduced rates may be arranged.**

Per Person Sharing: relates to the cost of Bed & Full Breakfast per person per Night, on the basis of two persons occupying a Standard Double/Twin Bedded Room, most having private bath/shower.
Room Rate: relates to the cost of a Standard Room per Night. There may be a restriction on the number of persons allowed to share the room. It is advisable to check this when making your reservation.

The rates range from minimum to maximum and are those generally in operation throughout the year, but may not apply during special occasions such as Public Holiday Weekends, Christmas and New Year, International Events, Major Festivals and Sporting Fixtures, or on such other occasions as individual premises may decide. Note: The Ryder Cup 2006 will take place in Ireland in September.

Rates are inclusive of Value Added Taxes at current (2005) rates and Services Charges (if any).

In the case of Hotels and Guesthouses in the Republic of Ireland, rates are quoted in € (Euro), whereas in Northern Ireland rates are quoted in STG£.

STANDARD SPECIAL OFFERS (Per Person Sharing)
Many of the Hotels / Guesthouses in the Guide feature special offers :
- Standard Weekend Specials include 2 nights' accommodation, 2 Breakfasts and 1 Dinner.
- Standard Midweek Specials include 3 nights' accommodation and 3 breakfasts.
- Standard Weekly Partial Board includes 7 nights' accommodation, 7 breakfasts and 7 dinners.
Alternative Special Offers may also be featured

OPENING DATES FOR PREMISES UNDER CONSTRUCTION OR REFURBISHMENT

Some of the premises featured in the guide were not open at the guide print date (10 October 2005). The planned date of opening as supplied by these premises is displayed on the premises photograph.

EXPLANATION OF CLASSIFICATIONS GUINNESS.

HOTEL CLASSIFICATIONS

ONE STAR ★

Here you can enjoy the comforts of a pleasantly simple hotel where a warm welcome prevails. These premises offer all the mandatory services and facilities to a satisfactory standard, which are necessary for a most enjoyable and relaxed visit. Some guest rooms have a private bathroom with a bath or a shower.

TWO STAR ★★

These are more likely to be family operated premises, selected for their charm and their comfortable facilities. All guest rooms have a telephone and most have a private bathroom with a bath and/or shower. Full dining facilities are available with good wholesome food, representing excellent value.

THREE STAR ★★★

These range from small, family operated premises to larger, modern hotels. Guest rooms are well decorated with the emphasis on comfort and all have a private bathroom with a bath and/or shower. Some rooms may also have colour TV, direct dial phones, hairdryers, tea/coffee facilities and room service. Many hotels also have leisure facilities, car parking and safety deposit boxes. Restaurants offer high standards of cuisine in relaxed and hospitable surroundings. Table d'hôte and/or à la carte dinner menus are available.

FOUR STAR ★★★★

These include contemporary hotels of excellent quality and charming period houses renovated to very high standards, complete with all modern comforts. All guest accommodation is luxurious with suites and half suites available in most cases. Restaurant facilities provide excellent cuisine and service for the discerning diner. Table d'hôte and/or à la carte lunch and dinner menus are available.

FIVE STAR ★★★★★

These include Ireland's most luxurious hotels, all of which are of high international standard. They range from elegant, stately castles to prestigious country clubs and top class city hotels catering for both the business and tourist visitor. All guest accommodation is luxurious and spacious suites are also available. These fine hotels boast of some of the country's best restaurants and offer table d'hôte and/or à la carte lunch and dinner menus. Exceptional service and a personalised welcome are the norm in these hotels.

GUESTHOUSE CLASSIFICATIONS

ONE STAR ★

These premises meet all the mandatory requirements for guesthouses and offer simple accommodation, facilities and services to a satisfactory standard. Restaurant facilities are available in some guesthouses.

TWO STAR ★★

Half or more of the guest rooms have private bathroom with bath and/or shower. Guesthouse facilities include a reading/writing room or lounge area for residents' use. Restaurant facilities are available in some guesthouses.

THREE STAR ★★★

All guest rooms have private bathroom with bath and/or shower and direct dial telephone. Guesthouse facilities include a TV lounge, travellers cheques are exchanged and major credit cards are accepted. Restaurant facilities are available in some guesthouses.

FOUR STAR ★★★★

This is the top classification for guesthouses in Ireland. Guest accommodation includes half suites and all guest rooms have private bathroom with bath and/or shower, direct dial telephone, colour TV and radio. Room service offers full breakfast. Many premises provide dinner, with table d'hôte and/or à la carte menus. Guesthouse facilities include car parking, safety deposit boxes, fax.

Hotels and Guesthouses may have the symbols: U, N, R, P, CR for the following reasons:

U Under the terms of the classification scheme a premises may opt to remain unclassified and will be shown U in this guide. Of course these premises meet all the mandatory requirements for hotel/guesthouse registration.

N These are premises that have recently registered with Fáilte Ireland/Northern Irish Tourist Board but, at the time of going to print, have not been long enough in operation for their standards to be fully assessed.

R These premises were undergoing major refurbishment at the time of printing this guide. Their classification will be assessed when the work is completed.

P These premises had applied to Fáilte Ireland/Northern Ireland Tourist Board for registration at time of going to print and are pending registration.

CR Classification Rescinded - At the time of going to print (10 October 2005) the classification of these properties had been rescinded and the registration was under review by Fáilte Ireland.

9

RESERVATIONS

Courtesy Onward Reservations

If you are moving around the country, the premises in which you are staying will be delighted to help you select your next accommodation from the Be Our Guest Guide and make your reservation.

The following are other ways in which a booking can be made:

1. Advance enquiries and reservations may be made directly to the premises by phone, fax, e-mail or letter and details of the reservation should be confirmed by both parties. A deposit should be forwarded if requested.

2. Book your accommodation online at:

irelandhotels.com
Official Website of the Irish Hotels Federation

IRISH
HOTELS
FEDERATION

Irelandhotels.com features all premises listed in the Be Our Guest Guide.

www.irelandhotels.com
One source - Endless possibilities

3. Some of the hotels and guesthouses in the Guide participate in a Central Reservations system which may be indicated in their entry.

4. Travel Agent - your travel agent will normally make a booking on your behalf without extra charge where the premises pays travel agents' commission (this is indicated by the symbol ⊤ in the Guide). In other cases, agents will usually charge a small fee to cover the cost of telephone calls and administration.

5. Some local tourist information offices listed in this guide (see pages 29-30) operate an enquiry and booking service and will make an accommodation reservation on your behalf.

COMPLAINTS

Should there be cause for complaint, the matter should be brought to the notice of the Management of the premises in the first instance. Failing satisfaction, the matter should be referred to the Tourist Information Office concerned (see list on page 29-30) or Fáilte Ireland, Baggot Street Bridge, Dublin 2. In the case of Northern Ireland premises, complaints should be addressed to the Customer Relations Section, Northern Ireland Tourist Board, 59 North Street, Belfast BT1 1NB.

ERRORS AND OMISSIONS

The information contained in the accommodation section has been supplied by individual premises. While reasonable care has been taken in compiling the information supplied and ensuring its accuracy and compliance with consumer protection laws, the Irish Hotels Federation cannot accept any responsibility for any errors, omissions or misinformation regarding accommodation, facilities, prices, services, classification or any other information whatsover in the Guide and shall have no liability whatsoever and howsoever arising to any person for any loss, whether direct, indirect, economic or consequential, or damages, actions, proceedings, costs, claims, expenses or demands arising therefrom. The listing of any premises in this guide is not and should not be taken as a recommendation from the IHF or a representation that the premises will be suitable for your purposes.

THINK ABOUT INSURANCE

We strongly advise you to take out an insurance policy against accidents, cancellations, delays, loss of property and medical expenses. Such travel and holiday insurance policies are available quite cheaply and are worth every penny for peace of mind alone.

CANCELLATIONS

Should it be necessary to amend or cancel your reservation, please advise the premises immediately, as there may be a cancellation penalty. Please establish, when making a reservation, what cancellation policy applies.

the soul...
...OF IRELAND

AN GHAELTACHT

*Fascinating landscapes, seascapes,
culture, song and language.....
and of course, fascinating people.*

*For activity holidays,
cultural breaks, the chance to relax
and de-stress,
or just a breath of fresh air,
the Gaeltacht has it all...
Don't miss out!*

Dún na nGall
Donegal

Maigh Eo
Mayo

Gaillimh
Galway

An Mhí
Meath

Ciarraí
Kerry

Port Láirge
Waterford

Corcaigh
Cork

■ GAELTACHT

Éire i mbláth a maitheasa!

INDEX TO LOCATIONS · GUINNESS

INDEX TO LOCATIONS   GUINNESS.

13

Dick Bourke
President, Irish Hotels Federation

Hotels and Guesthouses in Ireland are very special. The majority are family owned with the proprietor and members of the family there to welcome guests and to extend to them renowned Irish hospitality. Even when they are owned by a company, or are part of a group, they still retain the character and ambience of a family premises - a place where you will be truly welcome.

The Irish hotel is unique, in that more often than not, it acts as a social centre for the community. Hotels offer a lot more than just a bed and a meal - they are fully fledged social, leisure, business and community centres with every imaginable facility and amenity, providing food, accommodation, sports, leisure facilities, entertainment and other attractions.

If you are moving around the country, you'll find that "Be Our Guest" is an invaluable help in choosing your next location.

Ireland's hoteliers and guesthouse owners want to welcome you and want to play their part in ensuring that your stay in Ireland is a happy one. We hope that you will stay with us and that you will use this guide to select the hotel or guesthouse of your choice, so that we can personally invite you to -

Ní haon ní coitianta é an Óstlann nó an Teach Lóistín in Éirinn. Is i seilbh teaghlaigh iad a bhformhór acu agus bíonn an t-úinéir agus baill den teaghlach romhat chun fáilte Uí Cheallaigh a chur romhat. Fiú nuair is le comhlacht iad, nó is cuid de ghrúpa iad, baineann meon agus atmaisféar áitreabh teaghlaigh leo – áiteanna ina gcuirfí fíorchaoin fáilte romhat.

Rud ar leith is ea an óstlann in Éirinn agus is dócha nach a mhalairt go bhfeidhmíonn sí mar lárionad sóisialta don phobal. Cuireann an óstlann i bhfad níos mó ná leaba agus béile ar fáil - is lárionad sóisialta,a siamsaíochta, gnó agus pobail ar fheabhas í chomh maith agus gach aon áis faoin spéir aici, a chuireann bia, lóistín, imeachtaí spóirt, áiseanna siamsíochta agus só agus tarraingtí nach iad ar fáil.

Agus tú ag taisteal timpeall na tíre gheobhaidh tú amach go mbeidh "Bí i d'Aoi Againn" an-áisiúil agus an chéad suíomh eile á roghnú agat. Is mian le hóstlannaithe agus le lucht tithe lóistín na hÉireann fáilte a chur romhat agus a bheith in ann a dheimhniú go mbainfidh tú sult as do sheal in Éirinn. Tá súil againn go bhfanfaidh tú linn agus go mbainfidh tú leas as an treoir seo chun do rogha óstlann nó teach lóistín a aimsiú, i dtreo is go mbeimid in ann a rá leat go pearsanta -

Les hôtels et les pensions en Irlande sont d'un caractère particulier.

Ils sont très souvent gérés par le propriétaire et des membres de sa famille, présents pour accueillir les visiteurs et leur faire découvrir la célèbre hospitalité irlandaise. Même s'ils appartiennent à une entreprise ou font partie d'un groupe de sociétés, ils possèdent toujours ce caractère et cette ambiance des lieux familiaux - un endroit où vous serez sincèrement bien accueillis.

L'hôtel irlandais est unique en ce qu'il joue très souvent le rôle de centre social pour la communauté. Les hôtels offrent beaucoup plus qu'un lit et un repas - ce sont, pour la communauté, de véritables centres sociaux, de loisirs et d'affaires, équipés de toutes les infrastructures et installations imaginables. Ils vous proposent le gîte et le couvert, mais aussi activités sportives et de loisir, divertissements et autres attractions.

Si vous voyagez dans le pays, vous trouverez que le guide "Be Our Guest" est d'une aide précieuse pour vous aider à choisir votre prochaine destination.

Les hôteliers et les propriétaires de pensions irlandais veulent vous accueillir et être là pour vous assurer un séjour agréable en Irlande. Nous espérons que vous resterez avec nous et que vous utiliserez ce guide pour sélectionner l'hôtel ou la pension de votre choix, afin que nous ayons le plaisir de vous compter parmi nos visiteurs.

Die Hotels und Pensionen in Irland sind von ganz besonderer Art.

Zum größten Teil handelt es sich dabei um private Familienbetriebe, in denen der Besitzer und die Familienmitglieder ihre Gäste mit der vielgerühmten irischen Gastfreundschaft willkommen heißen. Aber auch wenn sich diese Häuser in Unternehmensbesitz befinden oder einer Kette angehören, strahlen sie dennoch den Charakter und die Atmosphäre von Familienbetrieben aus - ein Ort, an dem Sie immer herzlich willkommen sind.

Hotels in Irland sind einzig in ihrer Art und dienen oftmals als Mittelpunkt geselliger Treffen. Hotels haben viel mehr zu bieten als nur ein Bett und eine Mahlzeit - sie sind Gesellschafts-, Freizeit-, Geschäfts- und öffentlicher Treffpunkt mit allen nur erdenklichen Einrichtungen und Annehmlichkeiten, angefangen bei Essen, Unterkunft, Sport und Freizeitmöglichkeiten bis zur Unterhaltung und anderen Anziehungspunkten.

Auf Ihren Reisen im Land werden Sie feststellen, daß Ihnen der "Be Our Guest"-Führer eine wertvolle Hilfe bei der Suche nach der nächstgelegenen Unterkunft leistet.

Irlands Hotel und Pensionsbesitzer heißen Sie gerne willkommen und möchten ihren Anteil dazu beitragen, daß Ihnen Ihr Aufenthalt in Irland in angenehmer Erinnerung bleibt. Wir hoffen, daß Sie uns besuchen werden und diesen Führer bei der Auswahl Ihres Hotels oder Ihrer Pension zu Rate ziehen, so daß wir Sie persönlich willkommen heißen können.

Be Our Guest

Los hoteles y las pensiones en Irlanda son muy especiales. La mayoría son propiedades familiares habitadas por el mismo propietario junto a los miembros de su familia que se encuentran predispuestos a dar la bienvenida a los huéspedes y, de este modo, contribuir a ampliar su reconocida

hospitalidad irlandesa. Incluso si pertecen a una compañía o forman parte de un grupo, siempre mantendrán el carácter y ambiente de las propiedades familiares, un lugar donde siempre serás bienvenido de corazón. El hotel irlandés es único y se comporta bastante a menudo como el mismo centro social de la comunidad. Estos hoteles ofrecen algo más que una cama y comida, rebozan de centros sociales comunitarios de ocio y negocios con una amplia gama de servicios inimaginables. Ofrece comida, alojamiento, deportes, actividades de ocio, entretenimiento y todo tipo de atracciones.

Si te encuentras viajando por nuestro país, te darás cuenta que la ayuda que te ofrece "Be Our Guest", a la hora de elegir tu próximo destino, no tiene precio. Los hoteleros y propietarios de pensiones de Irlanda quieren darte la bienvenida y quieren contribuir a que tu estancia en Irlanda sea una estancia feliz. Esperamos que te quedes con nosotros y que utilices esta guía para elegir el hotel o pensión que tú elijas y para que nosotros podamos invitarte personalmente a ser nuestro invitado, el invitado de "Be our Guest".

Be Our Guest

Gli hotel e le pensioni in Irlanda sono davvero speciali. Molti sono a conduzione familiare, e gli ospiti vengono accolti dai proprietari e le loro famiglie secondo le famose tradizioni di ospitalità irlandesi. Il

calore e l'ambiente intimo e accogliente si ritrovano persino negli hotel delle grandi compagnie e catene alberghiere: avrete sempre la sensazione di essere ospiti graditi. Una caratteristica unica degli hotel irlandesi è che, molto spesso, fungono anche da centro di aggregazione della comunità. Gli alberghi offrono molto di più di un letto e dei pasti: sono centri per socializzare, divertirsi, fare affari e vivere la dimensione locale. Qui si può trovare ogni attrezzatura e comfort immaginabile: ristoranti, alloggi, impianti sportivi, attività ricreative, divertimento e tante altre attrazioni.

Se prevedete molti spostamenti, scoprirete in "Be Our Guest" uno strumento di valore inestimabile per la scelta delle prossime mete. Gli albergatori e i proprietari delle pensioni irlandesi vi aspettano per darvi il benvenuto e fare la loro parte per rendere piacevole il vostro soggiorno in Irlanda. Ci auguriamo che vogliate viaggiare con noi, usando la nostra guida per scegliere un hotel o una pensione di vostro gusto, così da potervi invitare personalmente a: "Be our Guest".

IRISH HOTELS FEDERATION

Access for Disabled Persons

To assist visitors with mobility impairment, the following 4 symbols are shown on entries for those hotels and guesthouses which have been approved by Failte Ireland and Northern Ireland Tourist Board:

Validated Accessible Scheme (VAS)

Category 1   Accessible to ambulant people capable of climbing flights of steps with a maximum height between landings of 1.8 metres.

Category 2   Accessible to ambulant people with mobility impairments but capable of climbing three steps.

Category 3   Accessible to wheelchair users including those who can transfer unaided to and from the wheelchair.

Category 4   Accessible to all wheelchair users including those requiring assistance to transfer to and from the wheelchair e.g. carer / partner.

These symbols are also explained on page 4 and you will find them amongst the black symbols at the end of relevant premises.

As this is a recent scheme more premises will be approved during 2006, so it is always worthwhile enquiring directly with the hotel and guesthouse. A large number of premises who have not yet been approved under the new scheme at the time of going to print, were approved under a previous scheme and will therefore have good access for the disabled.

Should you require further information on access, please contact Failte Ireland, Baggot Street Bridge, Dublin 2. Tel: +353 1 602 4000 Fax: +353 1 602 4100 or Northern Ireland Tourist Board, 59 North Street, Belfast, BT1 1NB. Tel: +44 28 9023 1221 Fax: +44 28 9024 0960.

Note: Northern Ireland Tourist Board are no longer approving premises for accessibility. Disability Action may be able to provide further information. Please contact them at: Tel: 0044 28 90 297880 Fax: 0044 28 90 297881 Email: hq@disabilityaction.org

All the best from Ireland

Please tick the appropriate boxes - ✓

1. Please rate your overall satisfaction with the Be Our Guest Guide on a scale of 1 to 5 (where 1 is very dissatisfied and 5 is very satisfied).

   1 ☐   2 ☐   3 ☐   4 ☐   5 ☐

2. Please rate your satisfaction with the following features of the Be Our Guest Guide: (where 1 is very dissatisfied and 5 is very satisfied)

Layout   1 ☐   2 ☐   3 ☐   4 ☐   5 ☐
Graphics   1 ☐   2 ☐   3 ☐   4 ☐   5 ☐
Information   1 ☐   2 ☐   3 ☐   4 ☐   5 ☐
Advertisements   1 ☐   2 ☐   3 ☐   4 ☐   5 ☐

3. Did you make a booking with an Irish Hotel or Guesthouse as a result of consulting the Be Our Guest Guide?

   Yes ☐   No ☐

4. Would you consider booking online all or part of your holiday?

   Yes ☐   No ☐

5. Did you visit www.irelandhotels.com as a result of consulting the Be Our Guest Guide?

   Yes ☐   No ☐

6. Did you make a booking with an Irish Hotel or Guesthouse on www.irelandhotels.com as a result of consulting the Be Our Guest Guide?

   Yes ☐   No ☐

7. What improvements would you make to the Be Our Guest Guide? - PLEASE PRINT

   ....

   ....

   ....

8. Any other comments? - PLEASE PRINT

....

....

....

Personal Details - PLEASE PRINT

1. Name: ....

2. Age Group (please circle):   18-30   31-44   45-55   56+

3. Address: ....

....

....

4. Telephone No.: ....

5. Email Address: ....

Would you like to be contacted regarding future promotions from Irelandhotels.com?

Yes ☐   No ☐

All respondents will be entered into a monthly raffle for a short break in one of our featured Hotels and Guesthouses. Winners will be posted monthly on our website **Irelandhotels.com**

Please post this questionnaire to: **Irish Hotels Federation, 13 Northbrook Road, Dublin 6.**

All information supplied by respondents shall remain confidential and will not be supplied to any other sources.

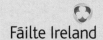

Fáilte Ireland

Optimus
Achieving Business Excellence

○○○
Award of Excellence
BUSINESS EXCELLENCE PROGRAMME

○○
Mark of Best Practice
BEST PRACTICE PROGRAMME

○
Ireland's Best Award
SERVICE EXCELLENCE PROGRAMME

Optimus helps tourism businesses achieve excellence in all aspects of their service to you, the customer.

Optimus – the brand of business excellence. Watch out for it in 2006

Fáilte Ireland
The National Tourism Development Authority
88 – 95 Amiens Street
Dublin 1

GENERAL TOURIST INFORMATION

LANGUAGE

Irish (Gaelic) and English are the two official languages of the Republic of Ireland and street and road signs are all bilingual. In Gaeltacht areas Irish is spoken daily, however English is spoken by everyone.

In Northern Ireland, English is the official language. The Irish Language, Gaelic, is also taught in many schools, and summer schools. Ulster Scots, spoken in Northern Ireland, is on the increase and is being taught to those who are keen to explore another facet of their national identity.

CURRENCY

The Euro is the local currency of the Republic of Ireland. One Euro consists of 100 cent. Notes are €5, €10, €20, €50, €100, €200 and €500. Coins are 1c, 2c, 5c, 10c, 20c, 50c, €1 and €2.

In Northern Ireland (as in the rest of the United Kingdom), Sterling is the local currency. Stg£1 consists of 100 pence. The notes consist of £5, £10, £20, £50 and £100. The coins are 1p, 2p, 5p, 10p, 20p, 50p, £1 & £2.

The Currencies of the Republic of Ireland and Northern Ireland are not interchangeable.

REGULATIONS FOR UNDER 21 YEAR OLDS IN BARS

In the Republic of Ireland the Liquor Licensing Hours provide that persons under the age of 18 are not allowed in the bar areas of licensed premises (including hotels and guesthouses) after 9.00 p.m. (10.00 p.m. May to September)

Persons aged 18 – 21 are required to produce evidence of age in order to be allowed enter or remain in the bar area of licensed premises (including hotels) after 9.00 pm. The acceptable evidence of age may be one of the following: Garda Age Card, a Passport or Identity Card of a EU Member State, a Driver's Licence.

PROHIBITION ON SMOKING

In order to combat the damage to health caused by tobacco smoke and to provide an environment of smoke free air, the Government of the Republic of Ireland introduced, early in 2004, a total ban on smoking in the workplace (indoors). This means that smoking is not permitted in all enclosed areas of hotels and guesthouses with the exception of hotel and guesthouse bedrooms.

DRIVING

Visitors should be in possession of either; a valid full national driving licence, or an international driving permit issued abroad. These are readily available from motoring organisations in the country of origin. If planning to bring your car to Ireland, advise your insurance company before travelling.

Driving in Ireland is on the left and seat belts must be worn at all times in the front and the back of the vehicle; likewise, motorcyclists and their passengers must wear helmets. There are very strict laws on drinking and driving and the best advise is simply 'don't drink and drive'.

In both the Republic of Ireland and Northern Ireland, speed limits are 50kmph/30mph in built-up urban areas, 100kmph/60mph on the open road and 120kmph/75mph on the motorway.

In the Republic of Ireland, the majority of signposts denoting distance are now in kilometres and speed limits are denoted in kilometres per hour. All signposts and place names are displayed bilingually in both Irish (Gaelic) and English.

In Northern Ireland, all signposts and speed limits are in miles and place names are displayed in the English language.

Driving Associations within Ireland include:

The Automobile Association (AA), Tel: 01 617 9977 or visit www.aaireland.ie and the RAC Motoring Services, Tel: 01 412 5500 or visit www.rac.ie.

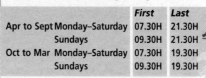

DIAGEO
IRELAND

Diageo is a member of MEAS which promotes responsible drinking

supporting success
through customer
partnership

More than just a supplier of the most important brands, our commitment to growing your business and helping you succeed must surely make us **your partner of choice**

Ireland

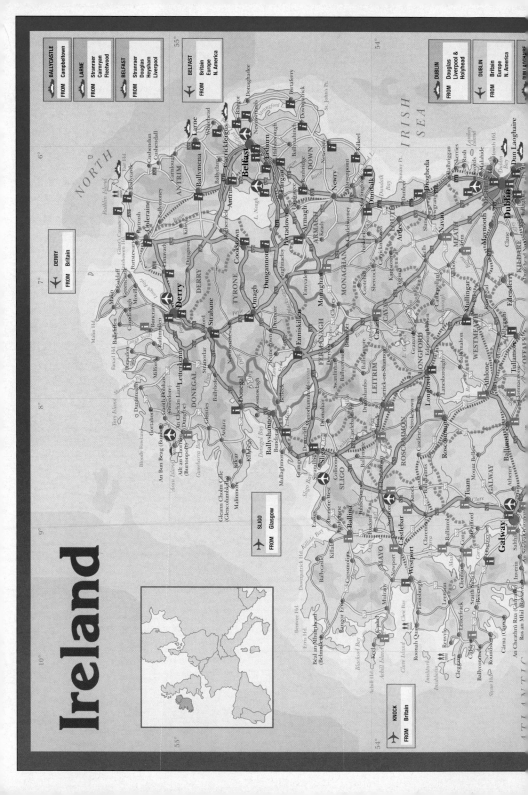

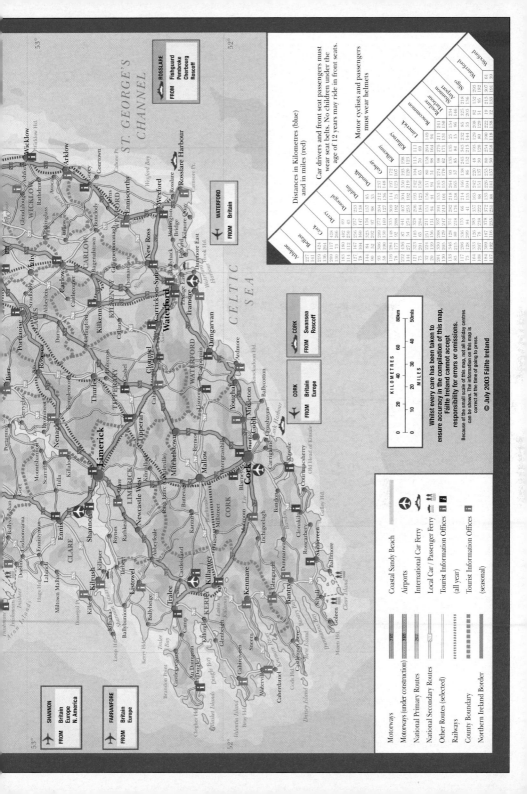

value menu

value menu
V15
UP TO €15

value menu
V25
UP TO €25

value menu
V35
UP TO €35

www.valuemenu.ie

"Good Food, Good Value, Good Times"

TOURIST BOARD OFFICES · GUINNESS.

LOCAL TOURIST INFORMATION OFFICES

The offices below operate throughout the year; approximately one hundred others are open during the summer months.

Antrim
16 High Street
Tel: 028-9442 8331
Email: info@antrim.gov.uk

Aran Islands
Oifig Fáilte, Kilronan
Inis Mór, Co. Na Gaillimhe
Tel: 099-61263
Fax: 099-61420
www.irelandwest.ie

Armagh
40 English Street
Tel: 028-3752 1800
Email: tic@armagh.gov.uk

Ballycastle
7 Mary Street
Tel: 028-2076 2024
Email: tourism@moyle-council.org

Ballymena
76 Church Road
Tel: 028-2563 8494
Email:
tourist.information@ballymena.gov.uk

Banbridge
200 Newry Road
Tel: 028-4062 3322
Email: tic@banbridge.gov.uk

Bangor
34 Quay Street
Tel: 028-9127 0069
Email: tic@northdown.gov.uk

Blarney
Towncentre
Tel: 021-438 1624

Belfast
47 Donegall Place
Tel: 028-9024 6609
Email: info@belfastvisitor.com
Also Belfast International Airport
Arrivals Hall

Bundoran
The Bridge
Tel: 071-984 1350
Email: irelandnorthwest@eircom.net

Carlow
Tullow Street
Tel: 059-913 1554
Fax: 059-917 0776

Carrickfergus
Museum & Civic Centre, Antrim Street
Tel: 028-9336 6455
Email: touristinfo@carrickfergus.org

Clonakilty
Ashe Street
Tel: 023-33226
Email: clonakiltytio@eircom.net

Coleraine
Railway Road
Tel: 028-7034 4723
Email: colerainetic@btconnect.com

Cookstown
The Burnavon, Burn Road
Tel: 028-8676 6727
Email: tic@cookstown.gov.uk

Cork City
Grand Parade
Tel: 021-425 5100
Fax: 021-425 5199
Email: info@corkkerrytourism.ie

Derry
44 Foyle Street
Tel: 028-7126 7284
Email: info@derryvisitor.com

Dingle
The Quay
Tel: 066-915 1188
Fax: 066-915 1270
Email: dingletio@eircom.net

Donegal Town
The Quay
Tel: 074-972 1148
Fax: 074-972 2762
Email: irelandnorthwest@eircom.net

Downpatrick
St. Patrick's Centre, 53A Market Street
Tel: 028-4461 2233
Email: downpatrick.tic@downdc.gov.uk

Dublin
Dublin City
Suffolk Street
O'Connell Street
Baggot Street
Dublin Airport
Arrivals Hall
Dun Laoghaire
Ferryport

For information and reservations
please visit www.visitdublin.com or
contact Dublin Reservations Freephone
Tel: 1800 363 626

Dungannon / Killymaddy
Ballygawley Road (off A4)
Tel: 028-8776 7259
Email: killymaddy@freeuk.com

Dundalk
Jocelyn Street
Tel: 042-933 5484
Fax: 042-933 8070

Dungarvan
The Courthouse
Tel: 058-41741

Ennis
Arthur's Row
Reservations Tel: 1800 200 541
www.shannonregiontourism.ie

Enniskillen
Wellington Road
Tel: 028-6632 3110
Email: tic@fermanagh.gov.uk

Galway
Aras Fáilte, Forster Street
Galway City
Tel: 091-537700
Fax: 091-537733
Email: info@irelandwest.ie
www.irelandwest.ie

29

LOCAL TOURIST INFORMATION OFFICES (CONTINUED)

Giant's Causeway
Causeway Road, Bushmills
Tel: 028-2073 1855
Email: info@giantscausewaycentre.com

Hillsborough
The Square
Tel: 028-9268 9717
Email: tic.Hillsborough@lisburn.gov.uk

Kildare Town
Heritage Centre
Tel: 045-521240

Kilkeel
28 Bridge Street
Tel: 028-4176 2525
Email: kdakilkeel@hotmail.com

Kilkenny
Shee Alms House
Tel: 056-775 1500
Fax: 056-776 3955

Killarney
Beech Road
Tel: 064-31633
Fax: 064-34506
Email:
info@killarney.corkkerrytourism.ie

Kinsale
Pier Road
Tel: 021-477 2234
Email: kinsaletio@eircom.net

Larne
Narrow Gauge Road
Tel: 028-2826 0088
Email: larnetourism@btconnect.com

Letterkenny
Neil T Blaney Road
Tel: 074-912 1160
Fax: 074-912 5180
Email: irelandnorthwest@eircom.net

Limavady
7 Connell Street
Tel: 028-7776 0307
Email: tourism@limavady.gov.uk

Limerick City
Arthur's Quay
Reservations Tel: 1800 200 541
www.shannonregiontourism.ie

Lisburn
Lisburn Square
Tel: 028-9266 0038
Email: tic.lisburn@lisburn.gov.uk

Magherafelt
The Bridwell, 6 Church Street
Tel: 028-7963 1510
Email:
thebridwell@magherafelt.gov.uk

Mullingar
Market Square
Tel: 044-48650
Fax: 044-40413
Email: info@eastcoastmidlands.ie

Newcastle (Co. Down)
10-14 Central Promenade
Tel: 028-4372 2222
Email: newcastle.tic@downdc.gov.uk

Newgrange
Bru na Boinne Visitor Centre
Donore, Co. Meath
Tel: 041-988 0305

Newry City
Town Hall, Bank Parade
Tel: 028-3026 8877
Email:
newrytic@newryandmourne.gov.uk

Newtownards
31 Regent Street
Tel: 028-9182 6846
Email: tourism@ards-council.gov.uk

Omagh
1 Market Street
Tel: 028-8224 7831
Email: omagh.tic@btconnect.com

Oranmore
Co. Galway
Tel: 091 790811
Fax: 091 790812
Email: oranmore@iol.ie

Oughterard
Main Street, Oughterard
Co. Galway
Tel: 091 552808
Fax: 091 552811
Email: oughterardoffice@eircom.net

Shannon Airport
Arrivals Hall
Reservations Tel: 1800 200 541
www.shannonregiontourism.ie

Skibbereen
North Street
Tel: 028-21766
Fax: 028-21353
Email:
skibbereen@skibbereen.corkkerrytourism.ie

Sligo
Temple Street
Tel: 071-916 1201
Fax: 071-916 0360
Email: irelandnorthwest@eircom.net

Tralee
Ashe Memorial Hall
Tel: 066-712 1288
Fax: 066-712 1700
Email: tralee@eircom.net

Waterford City
The Quay
Tel: 051-870800
Fax: 051-876720
Email: info@southeasttourism.ie

Waterford Crystal
Visitor Centre
Tel: 051-358397

Westport
James Street, Westport
Co. Mayo
Tel: 098-25711
Fax: 098-26709
Email: westport@irelandwest.ie
www.irelandwest.ie

Wexford
Crescent Quay
Tel: 053-23111
Fax: 053-41743

Wicklow
Fitzwilliam Square
Tel: 0404-69117
Fax: 0404-69118

Ireland's Welcoming Tourist Information Network

YOUR GATEWAY
to the Holiday Regions of Ireland

Visit our Tourist Information Offices for
detailed information on what to see and
do and what's on. Avail of the popular and
convenient accommodation booking service.

For your convenience we provide

- Instant confirmed
  accommodation booking service
- Guide books for sale
- Local and National Information
- Maps – local and national

- Stamps and postcards
- Itinerary and Route planning service
- Display and sale of local craft items
- Souvenirs and gifts

Be sure to follow the Shamrock

Look for the Shamrock sign on all accommodation. It is
your assurance that this premises provide accommodation
which is inspected and whose standards are fully registered
by agencies supervised by Fáilte Ireland.

TOURIST BOARD OFFICES   GUINNESS.

FÁILTE IRELAND

NATIONAL TOURISM
DEVELOPMENT AUTHORITY

www.ireland.travel.ie

IRELAND
Dublin
Fáilte Ireland,
Baggot Street Bridge, Dublin 2
Tel: 01 - 602 4000
Fax: 01 - 602 4100

NORTHERN IRELAND
Belfast
Fáilte Ireland,
53 Castle Street, Belfast BT1 1GH
Tel: 028 - 9026 5500
Fax: 028 - 9026 5515

Derry
Fáilte Ireland,
44 Foyle Street, Derry BT48 6AT
Tel: 028 - 7136 9501
Fax: 028 - 7136 9501
*If dialling Northern Ireland directly from the
Republic of Ireland the code 048 followed by the
telephone number is sufficient.*

**NORTHERN IRELAND
TOURIST BOARD**
www.discovernorthernireland.com
Belfast
Northern Ireland Tourist Board,
59 North Street, Belfast BT1 1NB
Tel: 028 - 9023 1221
Fax: 028 - 9024 0960

Dublin
Northern Ireland Tourist Board,
16 Nassau Street, Dublin 2
Tel: 01 - 679 1977
Fax: 01 - 679 1863

**TOURISM IRELAND –
EUROPE**
www.tourismireland.com
Austria
Tourism Ireland,
Libellenweg 1, A-1140 Vienna
Tel: 01 - 501 596000
Email: info.at@tourismireland.com
Web: www.tourismireland.com

Belgium/Luxembourg
Tourism Ireland,
Avenue Louise 327, Louizalaan,
1050 Brussels
Tel: 02 - 275 0171
E-mail: info.be@tourismireland.com
Web: www.ireland-tourism.be

Britain-London
Tourism Ireland, Nations House,
103 Wigmore Street,
London W1U 1QS
Tel: 0800-039 7000
Email: info.gb@tourismireland.com
Web: www.tourismireland.com

Britain-Glasgow
Tourism Ireland,
James Miller House,
98 West George Street, (7th Floor),
Glasgow G2 1PJ
Tel: 0800 - 039 7000
Email:
infoglasgow@tourismireland.com
Web: www.tourismireland.com

France
Tourisme Irlandais,
33 Rue de Miromesnil, 75008 Paris
Tel: 01 - 70 20 00 20
Email: info.fr@tourismireland.com
Web: www.irlande-tourisme.fr

Germany
Tourism Ireland,
Gutleustrasse 32,
D-60329 Frankfurt am Main
Tel: 069 668 00950
Email: info@tourismireland.de
Web: www.tourismireland.de

Italy
Tourismo Irlandese,
Piazza Cantore 4,
20123 Milano
Tel: 02 - 4829 6060
Email:
informazioni@tourismireland.com
Web: www.irlanda-travel.com

The Netherlands
Tourism Ireland,
Spuistraat 104, 1012 VA Amsterdam
Tel: 020 - 504 0689
Email: info@ierland.nl
Web: www.ierland.nl

Nordic Region
Tourism Ireland,
Nyhavn 16, (3rd Floor),
DK 1051 Copenhagen K,
Denmark
Tel: 80 60 1518
Email: infonordic@tourismireland.com
Web: www.irland-turisme.dk

Spain
Tourism Ireland,
Paseo de la Castellana 46,
3a Planta, 28046 Madrid
Tel: 91-745 6420
Email: info.sp@tourismireland.com
Web: www.turismodeirlanda.com

Switzerland
Tourism Ireland,
Hindergartenstrasse 36,
CH-8447 Dachsen
Tel: 052-659 4665
Email: info.ch@tourismireland.com
Web: www.tourismireland.com

**TOURISM IRELAND –
REST OF THE WORLD**

USA
Tourism Ireland,
345 Park Avenue, New York NY 10154
Tel: 1800-223 6470
Email: info.us@tourismireland.com
Web: www.tourismireland.com

Canada
Tourism Ireland,
2 Bloor St. West, Suite 3403
Toronto, M4W 3E2
Tel: 1800 - 223 6470
Email: info.ca@tourismireland.com
Web: www.tourismireland.com

South Africa
Tourism Ireland,
c/o Development Promotions
Everite House, Level 7,
20 De Korte Street,
Braamfontein 2001, Gauteng
Tel: 011 - 339 48 65
Email: tourismireland@dpgsa.co.za
Web: www.tourismireland.com

New Zealand
Tourism Ireland,
Level 6, 18 Shortland Street,
Private Bag, 92136, Auckland
Tel: 09 - 977 2255
Email: tourism@ireland.co.nz
Web: www.tourismireland.com

Australia
Tourism Ireland,
Level 5, 36 Carrington Street,
Sydney, NSW 2000
Tel: 02 - 9299 6177
Email: info@tourismireland.com.au
Web: www.tourismireland.com.au

Japan
Tourism Ireland, Woody 21,
23 Aizumi-cho, Shinjuku-ku,
Tokyo 160-0005
Tel: 03 - 5363 6515
Email: sakamoto@marketinggarden.com
Web: www.tourismireland.com

China
Tourism Ireland,
Suite 700A, Shanghai Centre,
1376 Nanjing Road West,
Shanghai 200040, P.R. China
Tel: 021 6279 8788
Fax: 021 6279 7066
Email: sli@tourismireland.com
Web: www.tourismireland.com

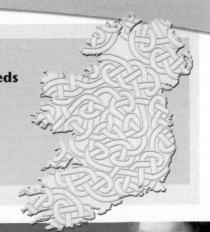

Map of South West Region

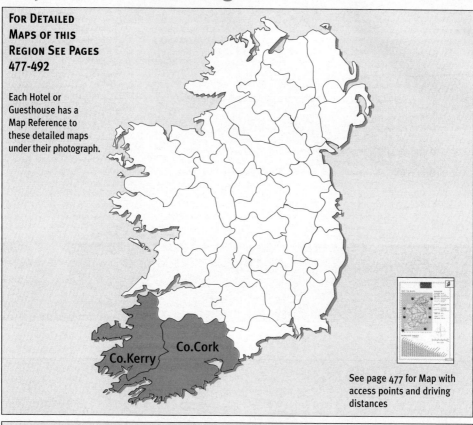

FOR DETAILED MAPS OF THIS REGION SEE PAGES 477-492

Each Hotel or Guesthouse has a Map Reference to these detailed maps under their photograph.

Co.Cork

Co.Kerry

See page 477 for Map with access points and driving distances

Locations listing

irelandhotels.com
Official Website of the Irish Hotels Federation

IRISH HOTELS FEDERATION

INCLUDES DETAILED MAPS & GREAT VALUE SPECIAL OFFERS.

Discover the spectacular South West in the counties of Cork and Kerry. The area is renowned for its scenic contrasts. The long indented coastline blends with spectacular mountains and the many rivers and lakes combine to give a landscape that offers the perfect backdrop for the wide choice of activities on offer- golf, angling, walking, cycling, water sports... the list is endless.

With some of the world's most famous championship golf courses, including Waterville, Ballybunion, Killarney and Fota Island – it is a popular destination for professionals and beginners alike. For those looking for adventure, the region offers some of the most exhilarating outdoor pursuits including kayaking, rock-climbing, horse-riding, diving and much more. Those looking for a different type of adventure can head to Cork City. Natives of Cork proudly boast that their home is the "true capital" of Ireland. Rivalries aside, Ireland's most southerly city can offer visitors an exciting city break with a difference. Cork has established itself as a true European capital of culture, with its trendy cafes and vibrant nightlife, it is also known as the jazz epicenter of Ireland. Or visit West Cork renowned for its spectacular rugged scenery and many visitor attractions.

Kerry is renowned for its magnificent coastline and rich cultural heritage. The region is famous for its restaurants offering the best in fresh seafood and local produce. And if pampering yourself in a gorgeous setting is your idea of a perfect holiday, then Kerry is the ideal location for a break as the region is home to some of the top spa's that specialize in luxury and complete renewal. Natural attractions abound, from the Ring of Kerry, West Cork coast, the Beara and Dingle peninsulas to the Lakes of Killarney and the Bandon, Lee and Blackwater valleys. Cobh, situated on the southern short of the Great Island, lies in one of the world's largest natural harbours. The Queenstown Story in Cobh tells the story of emigration and the history of sail and steam in Cork Harbour. Cobh was the last port of call for the ill-fated Titanic. The coast road from Kinsale to Skibbereen passes through many attractive villages

and towns giving breath-taking views of the south west coastline. Kinsale, a town which has retained its old world charm and character is firmly established as one of Ireland's leading gourmet centres. The Ring of Kerry is a journey through some of the country's most outstanding scenery. With its three famous lakes and great mountain ranges Killarney has been the inspiration of poets and painters over many centuries. A spectacular attraction is the Skellig Experience Centre at Valentia Island which imaginatively tells the story of the history of the Skelligs. The Dingle Peninsula has some of the most interesting antiquities, historic sites and varied scenery in the whole country. Dingle, the most westerly town in Europe is an excellent centre for the visitor. It still retains much of its old-world atmosphere with its many shops and restaurants.

North Kerry is recognized as the literary capital of the south west, it is home to some of Ireland's most famous writers such as John B.Keane, Brendan Kennelly and Bryan MacMahon to name but a few. Annual festivals take place throughout the Cork Kerry region to celebrate the unique culture and heritage of the area. The Cork Kerry region is a fantastic place to visit, no matter what time of year with events such as the Cahersiveen Celtic Festival of Music & The Arts in August. Each season has its own beauty and unique attractions. Whatever time of year you decide to visit, there will always be plenty to see and do. Discover a corner of Ireland that deserves its title – the spectacular South West!
Discover it at: www.corkkerry.ie

For further information contact:
Cork Kerry Tourism, Aras Failte, Grand Parade, Cork.
Tel (021) 4255100
Fax (021) 4255199
email: info@corkkerrytourism.ie

Killarney Tourist Office,
Beech Road, Killarney, Co. Kerry.
Tel. (064) 31633 Fax (064) 34506
email: info@corkkerrytourism.ie

 Calendar of Events

June
Guinness Bandon Music Festival, Bandon, Co. Cork.

July
Killarney SummerFest, Killarney, Co. Kerry.

August
Guinness Puck Fair, Killorglin, Co. Kerry.

September
Listowel Racing Festival, Listowel, Co. Kerry.

October /November
Guinness Jazz Festival, Cork City.

Event details correct at time of going to press.
enjoy Guinness sensibly.

Co. Cork

Allihies / Ballincollig / Ballycotton

Sea View Guest House	Oriel House Hotel & Leisure Centre	Bayview Hotel
Cluin Village, Allihies, Beara, Co. Cork	Ballincollig, Co. Cork	Ballycotton, Co. Cork
Tel: 027-73004 Fax: 027-73211	Tel: 021-487 0888	Tel: 021-464 6746 Fax: 021-464 6075
Email: seaviewg@iol.ie	Email: info@orielhousehotel.ie	Email: res@thebayviewhotel.com
Web: www.seaviewallihies.com	Web: www.orielhousehotel.ie	Web: www.thebayviewhotel.com

UNDER REFURBISHMENT - RE-OPENING DEC 2005

GUESTHOUSE ★★★ MAP 1 C 2 | **HOTEL CR MAP 2 H 3** | **HOTEL ★★★★ MAP 3 J 3**

Sea View Guesthouse is a family-run concern in the remote and unspoilt Beara Peninsula. All bedrooms are en suite with TV and telephone. Situated in the village of Allihies, it is within walking distance of a beach, playground and tennis court. The nearby hills afford excellent opportunities for walking, offering breathtaking views. Traditional Irish music and a friendly welcome can be found in the village pubs.

The newly re-built Oriel House Hotel is conveniently located in Ballincollig, just minutes from Cork City Airport and ferry terminals. The re-developed original Oriel House features 78 uniquely designed luxurious bedrooms, themed restaurant, carvery bar, an events centre to accommodate up to 300 delegates and car parking for up to 250 cars. The leisure centre offers a 25m pool, gym, sauna, steam room, jacuzzi, fitness rooms and health treatments.

The Bayview Hotel is a luxury 35 bedroomed hotel, magnificently situated overlooking Ballycotton Bay and fishing harbour. Private gardens with steps lead to the sea and bathing spot. The Capricho Restaurant produces innovative Irish cuisine and was awarded 2 rosettes by the AA. There are 6 superb golf courses in the area with sea angling, heritage centres and many other activities available. All bedrooms completely refurbished during 2005 to offer complete luxury.

Bookable on www.irelandhotels.com
Member of Manor House Hotels

B&B from €35.00 to €40.00 | *B&B from €70.00 to €130.00* | *B&B from €86.00 to €105.00*

 John & Mary O'Sullivan Proprietors |  *Dudley Fitzell Group General Manager* | *Stephen Belton General Manager*

Activities:

Member of: | | Member of:

Special Offer: Special Offers on www.orielhousehotel.ie | *Special Offer: Weekend Specials from €180.00 pps (2 Nights B&B & 1 Dinner)*

10 10 | 78 78  | 35 35

| Closed 31 October - 01 March | Open All Year | Closed 28 October - 13 April |

36 **South West**

B&B Rates are per Person Sharing per Night incl. Breakfast. or Room Rates are per Room per Night - See also Page 8

Seaview House Hotel

Ballylickey,
Bantry,
Co. Cork
Tel: 027-50073 Fax: 027-51555
Email: info@seaviewhousehotel.com
Web: www.seaviewhousehotel.com

HOTEL ★★★★ MAP 2 E 2

Delightful country house hotel and restaurant, set back in extensive grounds on main Bantry/Glengarriff Road. All bedrooms en suite, D.D. telephone and colour TV. Ideal for touring West Cork & Kerry. Two golf courses nearby. Recommended Egon Ronay, Good Hotel Guide etc. For the restaurant, AA Rosettes & Failte Ireland Awards of Excellence. Seafood a speciality. Member of Manor House Hotels. A wing of new superior rooms was added in Winter 2000 and also a conservatory to the dining room. Special midweek & weekend rates on request, subject to availability.

Bookable on www.irelandhotels.com
Member of Manor House Hotels

B&B from €75.00 to €95.00

Kathleen O'Sullivan
Proprietor

Member of:
IRISH HOTELS FEDERATION

Special Offer: Special Rates Available on Request

25 25

Closed 15 November - 15 March

Abbey Hotel

Ballyvourney,
Co. Cork
Tel: 026-45324 Fax: 026-45830
Email: abbeyhotel@eircom.net
Web: www.theabbeyhotel.net

HOTEL U MAP 2 F 3

Family-run hotel nestles in the valley of the Sullane River among the Cork and Kerry Mountains on the N22. It combines a friendly atmosphere and excellent catering. An ideal base for touring Kerry and Cork. A wide range of activities is available to you at the hotel including fishing, mountaineering, nature walks and golfing. 39 bedrooms with private facilities, direct dial phone & colour TV. Within 20 minutes drive are two 18 hole golf courses and trout fishing on the Sullane River. Fully licensed function room for weddings, dinner dances and parties.

B&B from €50.00 to €60.00

Cornelius Creedon
Proprietor

Member of:
IRISH HOTELS FEDERATION

Special Offer: Weekend Specials from €110.00 pps
(2 Nights B&B & 1 Dinner)

39 39

Closed 30 October - 01 March

B&B Rates are per Person Sharing per Night incl. Breakfast.
or Room Rates are per Room per Night - See also Page 8

Baltimore

Baltimore Bay Guest House

The Waterfront,
Baltimore,
Co. Cork

Tel: 028-20600 Fax: 028-20495
Email: baltimorebay@youenjacob.com
Web: www.youenjacob.com

GUESTHOUSE ★★★ MAP 2 E 1

Baltimore Bay Guesthouse is a superbly appointed new guesthouse with 8 spacious bedrooms. 5 bedrooms have a magnificent view of the sea. Two restaurants are attached to the guesthouse, La Jolie Brise budget restaurant, Egon Ronay listed, and Chez Youen, Egon Ronay Best Irish Fish Restaurant of the Year in 1994 and listed as one of the best places to stay in Ireland. Sawday Guide. Guide du Routard. Youen Jacob and sons, proprietors. Sailing facilities. We have now acquired a pub 'The Waterfront' adjacent to the guesthouse.

Bookable on www.irelandhotels.com

B&B from €40.00 to €60.00

Youen Jacob
Owner-Manager

Member of:

8   8   🕿📠🆃CM🖳🎵🎵🛏️🐕

Open All Year

Baltimore Harbour Hotel & Leisure Centre

Baltimore,
Co. Cork

Tel: 028-20361 Fax: 028-20466
Email: info@baltimoreharbourhotel.ie
Web: www.baltimoreharbourhotel.ie

HOTEL ★★★ MAP 2 E 1

The hotel is situated overlooking the Harbour & Islands in the charming coastal village of Baltimore. It is the ideal haven from which to explore the beauty and wonders of West Cork and the sea and to enjoy the many varied activities available locally, including sailing, golfing, angling, diving, horse riding, walking, cycling and, of course, the Islands. We are especially suited for families and offer childrens' entertainment during peak season. Enjoy our superb indoor leisure centre.

Bookable on www.irelandhotels.com

B&B from €60.00 to €90.00

William Buckley
General Manager

Member of:

Special Offer: *Weekend Specials from €129.00 pps*
(2 Nights B&B & 1 Dinner)

64   64

Closed 20 December - 31 January

Casey's of Baltimore

Baltimore,
Co. Cork

Tel: 028-20197 Fax: 028-20509
Email: info@caseysofbaltimore.com
Web: www.caseysofbaltimore.com

HOTEL ★★★ MAP 2 E 1

A warm welcome awaits you at Casey's of Baltimore. Situated at the entrance to Baltimore with its lovely views overlooking the bay, this superb family-run hotel is the perfect place to spend some time. All rooms feature en suite bathrooms, satellite TV, tea/coffee facility, direct dial phone, hairdryer and trouser press. The traditional pub and restaurant feature natural stone and wood décor, a spectacular view, extensive menu - seafood is our speciality. Activities can be arranged.

Bookable on www.irelandhotels.com
Member of Irish Country Hotels

B&B from €73.00 to €87.00

Ann & Michael Casey
Owners

Member of:

Special Offer: *Please telephone for special offers*

14   14
inet

Closed 20 - 27 December

B&B Rates are per Person Sharing per Night incl. Breakfast.
or **Room Rates** are per Room per Night - See also Page 8

Munster Arms Hotel	Bantry Bay Hotel	Vickery's Inn
Oliver Plunkett Street, Bandon, Co. Cork	Wolfe Tone Square, Bantry, Co. Cork	New Street, Bantry, Co. Cork
Tel: 023-41562 Fax: 023-41562	Tel: 027-50062 Fax: 027-50261	Tel: 027-50006 Fax: 027-50006
Email: info@munsterarmshotel.com	Email: info@bantrybayhotel.net	Email: info@vickerys.ie
Web: www.munsterarmshotel.com	Web: www.bantrybayhotel.net	Web: www.vickerys.ie

HOTEL U MAP 2 G 2	HOTEL ★★ MAP 2 E 2	GUESTHOUSE ★★ MAP 2 E 2

Set at the gateway to West Cork, 30 high quality en suite bedrooms with tea/coffee facilities, direct dial telephone, remote control T.V. radio and hairdryer. Set in beautiful scenic West Cork accessible by the N71 route from Cork City. Renowned for its homely atmosphere and superb quality. Ideal touring base and easily accessible from Kinsale, Cork City, Blarney, Killarney and West Cork. Relax and be pampered! Guests of the Munster Arms Hotel may use the leisure facilities at the local Bandon Leisure Centre for a nominal fee payable direct to the leisure centre.

The Bantry Bay has been operated by the O'Callaghan family for over 50 years in the centre of historic Bantry. Extensively renovated from 1995 to 2005, we offer a choice of family, tourist and commercial accommodation. All rooms are en suite with TV, DD phone, teamaker and hairdryer. They are complemented by our award-winning maritime themed bar and restaurant. Carvery in operation daily. Guests are assured of a hearty O'Callaghan welcome.

Founded by Thomas Vickery in 1850, Vickery's Inn Guesthouse is still managed by the Vickery family. All rooms en suite with T.V., phone and tea-making facilities. Enjoy meals in the restaurant or the 'Hideaway Bar'. With its town centre location, secure car park and covered garage for motor bikes, Vickery's is an ideal choice when visiting scenic West Cork. Walkers, start 'The Sheep's Head Way' here. Luggage transfers arranged. Internet access.

B&B from €50.00 to €70.00	B&B from €60.50 to €66.00	B&B from €35.00 to €50.00

Don O'Sullivan

Vivian O'Callaghan Jnr / Snr Manager / Proprietor

Thomas & Hazel Vickery

Member of:
IRISH HOTELS FEDERATION

Member of:
IRISH HOTELS FEDERATION

Member of:
IRISH HOTELS FEDERATION

Special Offer: www.vickerys.ie/specials

30 30

14 14

13 13

Closed 25 - 26 December	Closed 24 - 27 December	Closed 23 - 30 December

B&B Rates are per Person Sharing per Night incl. Breakfast.
or **Room Rates** are per Room per Night - See also Page 8

Westlodge Hotel

Bantry,
Co. Cork

Tel: 027-50360 Fax: 027-50438
Email: reservations@westlodgehotel.ie
Web: www.westlodgehotel.ie

HOTEL ★★★ MAP 2 E 2

3*** hotel situated in the scenic surroundings of Bantry Bay. Super health & leisure centre including indoor heated swimming pool, childrens' pool, toddlers' pool, sauna, steam room, jacuzzi, gym, aerobics, squash. Outdoor amenities include tennis, pitch & putt, woodland walks. The Westlodge specialises in family holidays with organised activities during Jul & Aug. A warm & friendly welcome awaits you at the Westlodge. Self-catering cottages available. Mighty Duck's Club opens during Jul & Aug. Guaranteed Tee Times at Bantry Bay Golf Club. Themed breaks now available: wellness & golf. Optimus Mark of Best Practice.

Bookable on www.irelandhotels.com
Member of Holiday Ireland Hotels

B&B from €65.00 to €75.00

Eileen M O'Shea FIHI
General Manager

Activities:

Member of:

Special Offer: Weekend Specials from €125.00 pps (2 Nights B&B & 1 Dinner)

90 90

Closed 23 - 28 December

Ashlee Lodge

Tower,
Blarney,
Co. Cork

Tel: 021-438 5346 Fax: 021-438 5726
Email: info@ashleelodge.com
Web: www.ashleelodge.com

GUESTHOUSE ★★★★ MAP 2 H 3

This charming 4**** boutique style property is a rare find striking the perfect balance between traditional comfort and a contemporary atmosphere. A member of the Best Loved Hotels of the World, it holds AA Red Five Diamonds and RAC ♦♦♦♦♦ awards. 10 luxurious bedrooms and suites with all that one expects of a private hotel. Air-conditioning, king sized beds, widescreen TV/CD units and sittingroom areas. Relax in our sauna and Canadian hot tub. RAC Little Gem Award 2005 and National Accommodation Services Award Winner 2004.

Bookable on www.irelandhotels.com
Member of Best Loved Hotels of the World

B&B from €50.00 to €120.00

John & Anne O'Leary
Proprietors

Activities:

Member of:

Special Offer: Weekend Specials from €140.00 pps (2 Nights B&B & 1 Dinner)

10 10

Open All Year

Blarney Castle Hotel

Blarney,
Co. Cork

Tel: 021-438 5116 Fax: 021-438 5542
Email: info@blarneycastlehotel.com
Web: www.blarneycastlehotel.com

HOTEL ★★★ MAP 2 H 3

Established in 1837, still run by the Forrest family. Picturesque inn on a peaceful village green, 5 miles from Cork City. Tastefully appointed spacious bedrooms. Unspoilt traditional bar. Restaurant specialising in finest local produce. Killarney, Kenmare, Kinsale, Cobh, West Cork, Waterford and numerous golf courses all an easy drive. Immediately to the left the magnificent grounds of Blarney Castle guarding that famous stone, to the right, Blarney Woollen Mills. Private car park for hotel guests. Quality entertainment nightly in village.

Bookable on www.irelandhotels.com

B&B from €55.00 to €75.00

Una Forrest / Ian Forrest
Manager / Reservations

Activities:

Member of:

Special Offer: Weekend Specials from €125.00 pps (2 Nights B&B & 1 Dinner)

13 13

Closed 25 - 26 December

B&B Rates are per Person Sharing per Night incl. Breakfast. or <u>Room Rates</u> are per Room per Night - See also Page 8

Blarney Park Hotel and Leisure Centre	Blarney Woollen Mills Hotel	Muskerry Arms

Blarney Park Hotel and Leisure Centre

Blarney,
Co. Cork

Tel: 021-438 5281 Fax: 021-438 1506
Email: info@blarneypark.com
Web: www.blarneypark.com

HOTEL ★★★ MAP 2 H 3

Set on 12 acres in the picturesque village of Blarney with Cork City minutes away. From the moment you arrive, you can be certain of a uniquely warm welcome and pampering. Savour our superb cuisine in the Clancarty Restaurant or relax in the comfort of our residents' lounge. With our excellent supervised playroom and leisure centre with 20m pool, 40m slide, hotrooms and holistic treatments, it makes even a short break seem like a holiday.

Bookable on www.irelandhotels.com
Member of The Blarney Group Hotels

B&B from €60.00 to €110.00

Daire Mannion
Manager

Activities:

🍷

Member of:
IRISH HOTELS FEDERATION

Special Offer: Weekend Specials from €99.00 pps
(2 Nights B&B)

91 91

Closed 24 - 26 December

Blarney Woollen Mills Hotel

Blarney,
Co. Cork

Tel: 021-438 5011 Fax: 021-438 5350
Email: info@blarneywoollenmillshotel.com
Web: www.blarneywoollenmillshotel.com

HOTEL ★★★ MAP 2 H 3

Blarney Woollen Mills 3*** Hotel with 48 beautifully appointed superior rooms and 3 executive suites. Many of the rooms have spectacular views of the famous Blarney Castle. All rooms have been tastefully decorated in the traditional style. All day dining in our self-service restaurant and evening dining in Christys Grill Bar. The hotel boasts one of the finest fitness centres in the area. Located within the old Mill buildings in the famous Blarney Woollen Mills complex where you can enjoy a relaxing drink and experience some Irish hospitality in Christy's Pub.

Bookable on www.irelandhotels.com

B&B from €60.00 to €70.00

Dominic Heaney
General Manager

Member of:
IRISH HOTELS FEDERATION

Special Offer: Weekend Specials from €100.00 pps
(2 Nights B&B & 1 Dinner)

48 48

Closed 21 - 25 December

Muskerry Arms

Blarney,
Co. Cork

Tel: 021-438 5200 Fax: 021-438 1013
Email: info@muskerryarms.com
Web: www.muskerryarms.com

GUESTHOUSE ★★★ MAP 2 H 3

With all the attributes of a small hotel, the Muskerry Arms is ideally central for your stay in Blarney. Stylish, spacious guest rooms offer power showers and all you need for a comfortable stay. Live traditional music every night in season in the Muskerry Bar and delicious menu choices in the popular Muskerry Restaurant. All within a short walk of Blarney Castle and Blarney Woollen Mills.

Bookable on www.irelandhotels.com

B&B from €45.00 to €85.00

Nell O' Connor

Member of:
IRISH HOTELS FEDERATION

Special Offer: Weekend Specials from €130.00 pps
(2 Nights B&B & 1 Dinner)

11 11

Closed 24 - 26 December

B&B Rates are per Person Sharing per Night incl. Breakfast.
or **Room Rates** are per Room per Night - See also Page 8

Co. Cork

Carrigaline

Carrigaline Court Hotel & Leisure Centre

Carrigaline,
Co. Cork

Tel: 021-485 2100 Fax: 021-437 1103
Email: reception@carrigcourt.com
Web: www.carrigcourt.com

HOTEL U MAP 3 H 3

Luxury RAC 4**** hotel, located just minutes from city centre, airport and ferry terminal. Spacious bedrooms with satellite TV, tea/coffee facilities, broadband internet access and all modern comforts as standard. Superb restaurant and traditional Irish bar. Exquisite leisure centre including 20m pool, sauna, jacuzzi, steam room and gym. Golf arranged at Cork's best courses. Local activities include sailing, angling, horse riding and a host of other activities in this beautiful area.

Bookable on www.irelandhotels.com

B&B from €70.00 to €110.00

John O'Flynn
General Manager

Member of:

Special Offer: Weekend Specials from €150.00 pps
(2 Nights B&B & 1 Dinner)

91 91

Closed 25 December

Fernhill Carrigaline Accommodation, Golf & Health Club

Fernhill,
Carrigaline,
Co. Cork

Tel: 021-437 2226 Fax: 021-437 1011
Email: info@fernhillgolfhotel.com
Web: www.fernhillgolfhotel.com

GUESTHOUSE ★★★ MAP 3 H 3

Set on the perimeters of an 80 acre golf course, overlooking the Owenabue Valley. Experience somewhere where you can enjoy golf, dining, tennis and a health and leisure club. Located 20 minutes from the city centre, 10 from the airport and 5 from Cork ferry. Offering 38 spacious guest rooms and 10 holiday houses, designed with your comfort in mind. Fernhill operates with the services of a hotel but with the intimacy and friendliness you would find at a great country house.

Bookable on www.irelandhotels.com

B&B from €55.00 to €99.00

Tom O'Mahony
General Manager

Activities:

Member of:

Special Offer: Weekend Specials from €110.00 pps
(2 Nights B&B & 1 Dinner)

38 38

Closed 25 - 26 December

Glenwood House

Ballinrea Road,
Carrigaline,
Co. Cork

Tel: 021-437 3878 Fax: 021-437 3878
Email: info@glenwoodguesthouse.com
Web: www.glenwoodguesthouse.com

GUESTHOUSE ★★★★ MAP 3 H 3

Glenwood House is a purpose built, self contained guesthouse, designed with all guest requirements in mind. The rooms are large and spacious, offering similar facilities to those of quality hotels, firm orthopaedic beds, heated towel rails, complimentary beverages, trouser press, satellite TV, power shower and many more. Located close to Ringaskiddy Ferry Port (5mins), Cork City (7mins), Kinsale (15mins), Crosshaven (5mins), Airport (10mins). We offer secure car parking, and have facilities to look after disabled guests. All accommodation is of hotel quality.

Bookable on www.irelandhotels.com
Member of Premier Guesthouses

B&B from €45.00 to €55.00

Adrian Sheedy
Proprietor

Member of:

14 14

Closed 09 December - 06 January

42   *South West*

B&B Rates are per Person Sharing per Night incl. Breakfast.
or Room Rates are per Room per Night - See also Page 8

Castle (The)	Dunmore House Hotel	Emmet Hotel

Castle (The)
Castletownshend,
Near Skibbereen,
Co. Cork
Tel: 028-36100 Fax: 028-36166
Email: castle_townshend@hotmail.com
Web: www.castle-townshend.com

Dunmore House Hotel
Muckross,
Clonakilty,
Co. Cork
Tel: 023-33352 Fax: 023-34686
Email: enquiries@dunmorehousehotel.ie
Web: www.dunmorehousehotel.ie

Emmet Hotel
Emmet Square,
Clonakilty,
Co. Cork
Tel: 023-33394 Fax: 023-35058
Email: emmethotel@eircom.net
Web: www.emmethotel.com

GUESTHOUSE ★ MAP 2 F 1

HOTEL ★★★ MAP 2 G 2

HOTEL U MAP 2 G 2

18th century Townshend family home overlooking Castlehaven Harbour. Set in its own grounds at water's edge with access to small beach and woods. Most bedrooms en suite on second floor with excellent sea views. Panelled hall/sitting room with TV and open fire. Breakfast in elegant dining room. Mary Ann's Restaurant and Gallagher's Restaurant close by. Ideal for touring Cork and Kerry. Also self-catering apartments and cottages. For illustrated brochure please apply. Guided tours of The Castle in May, June & September by arrangement.

Situated on the South West coast of Ireland, Dunmore House Hotel is family owned. Rooms are beautifully decorated, with spectacular views of the Atlantic Ocean. Sample a true taste of West Cork with our home-cooked local produce and seafood. Private foreshore available for sea angling. Green fees at the on-site golf club are free to residents. Horse riding available by arrangement. Interesting collection of local and modern Irish art.

The Emmet offers its guests an uncompromising level of service, personal yet efficient. O'Keeffes of Clonakilty Restaurant has established itself as one of the leading restaurants in West Cork, offering innovative menus at very reasonable prices. Facilities in the hotel include restaurant, function facilities, bars, garden patio, and the Bubble Lounge night club. There are 20 bedrooms, all en suite with TV, direct dial telephone and tea/coffee making facilities.

B&B from €50.00 to €80.00

B&B from €75.00 to €85.00

B&B from €40.00 to €70.00

Anne & Malcolm Cochrane
Townshend

Derry & Mary O'Donovan
Proprietors

Activities:

The O'Keeffe Family
Proprietors

Activities:

Member of:
HOTELS

Member of:
HOTELS

Member of:
HOTELS

Special Offer: Seven nights for the cost of 6, 10% off for 3 nights or more

Special Offer: Midweek Specials from €200.00 pps (3 Nights B&B)

Special Offer: Midweek Specials from €110.00 pps (3 Nights B&B)

7 7

29 29

20 20

Closed 15 December - 15 January	Closed 16 January - 14 March	Closed 24 - 26 December

B&B Rates are per Person Sharing per Night incl. Breakfast.
or Room Rates are per Room per Night - See also Page 8

South West 43

Clonakilty

Fernhill House Hotel

Clonakilty,
Co. Cork

Tel: 023-33258 Fax: 023-34003
Email: info@fernhillhousehotel.com
Web: www.fernhillhousehotel.com

HOTEL ★★ MAP 2 G 2

Fernhill House is a family-run old Georgian style hotel located on picturesque grounds 0.8km from Clonakilty. All bedrooms en suite with tea/coffee making facilities, phone, TV and hairdryer. Conference and function facilities available, Par 3 golf on-site and 18 hole Pitch & Putt course. Our hotel offers an intimate homely atmosphere, excellent food and a comfortable bar. Holiday with us and enjoy scenic West Cork from centrally situated Fernhill House Hotel.

B&B from €55.00 to €65.00

Michael & Teresa O'Neill Proprietors

Activities:

Member of:

Special Offer: Midweek Specials from €150.00 pps (3 Nights B&B)

16 16

Closed 23 December - 01 January

Inchydoney Island Lodge & Spa

Clonakilty,
West Cork

Tel: 023-33143 Fax: 023-35229
Email: reservations@inchydoneyisland.com
Web: www.inchydoneyisland.com

HOTEL ★★★★ MAP 2 G 2

Situated on the idyllic island of Inchydoney, between two EU Blue Flag beaches, this luxurious hotel offers de luxe rooms, a fully equipped thalassotherapy (seawater) spa, award-winning restaurant, Dunes Pub and function and meeting facilities. Within a short distance guests can enjoy sailing, golf at the Old Head of Kinsale, riding and deep sea fishing, whale watching and surfing. The style of cooking in the Gulfstream Restaurant reflects the wide availability of fresh seafood and organically grown vegetables.

Bookable on www.irelandhotels.com

B&B from €160.00 to €190.00

The Team at Inchydoney Island Lodge & Spa

Activities:

Member of:

Special Offer: Weekend Specials from €310.00 pps (2 Nights B&B & 1 Dinner)

67 67

Closed 24 - 27 December

O'Donovan's Hotel

Pearse Street,
Clonakilty,
West Cork

Tel: 023-33250 Fax: 023-33250
Email: odhotel@iol.ie
Web: www.odonovanshotel.com

HOTEL ★★ MAP 2 G 2

Charles Stewart Parnell, Marconi and Gen. Michael Collins found time to stop here. This fifth generation, family-run hotel is located in the heart of Clonakilty Town. Abounding in history, the old world charm has been retained whilst still providing the guest with facilities such as bath/shower en suite, TV etc. Our restaurant provides snacks and full meals and is open to non-residents. Ideal for conferences, private functions, meetings etc., with lock up car park.

B&B from €60.00 to €60.00

O'Donovan Family Proprietors

Member of:

Special Offer: Midweek Specials from €120.00 pps (3 Nights B&B for the price of 2)

26 26

Closed 25 - 28 December

B&B Rates are per Person Sharing per Night incl. Breakfast. or **Room Rates** are per Room per Night - See also Page 8

Quality Hotel & Leisure Centre Clonakilty

Clonakilty,
Co. Cork

Tel: 023-36400 Fax: 023-35404
Email: info@qualityhotelclonakilty.com
Web: www.qualityhotelclonakilty.com

HOTEL ★★★ MAP 2 G 2

Clonakilty is a thriving and busy attractive town with a wealth of musical and artistic cultural activities. This unique hotel offers the following excellent facilities, 97 en suite guest rooms, including 17 executive family rooms, 5 executive holiday homes, 12 2-bedroom suites, Lannigans Restaurant, Oscars Bar, an award-winning leisure centre, a 3 screen multiplex cinema, playroom crèche and playground.

Bookable on www.irelandhotels.com
Member of Quality Hotels

B&B from €39.00 to €99.00

David Henry
General Manager

Activities:

Member of:

Special Offer: Weekend Specials from €129.00 pps
(2 Nights B&B & 1 Dinner)

97 97

Closed 20 - 26 December

Randles Clonakilty Hotel

Wolfe Tone Street,
Clonakilty,
West Cork

Tel: 023-34749 Fax: 023-35035
Email: clonakilty@randleshotels.com
Web: www.randleshotels.com

HOTEL ★★★ MAP 2 G 2

Nestled in the beauty and tranquillity of glorious West Cork stands the Randles Clonakilty Hotel. This boutique style hotel is both charming and elegant which is evident in the exquisite furnishings of the lobby. With only 30 bedrooms one can enjoy the intimacy of a smaller hotel backed by a professional team. Maxwell Irwins Bar & Bistro with its wood panelled interior offers traditional and local fayre in attractive surroundings.

Bookable on www.irelandhotels.com

B&B from €40.00 to €85.00

Emma McCarthy
General Manager

Member of:

Special Offer: Weekend Specials from €99.00 pps
(2 Nights B&B & 1 Dinner)

30 30

Closed 21 - 27 December

Commodore Hotel

Cobh,
Co. Cork

Tel: 021-481 1277 Fax: 021-481 1672
Email: commodorehotel@eircom.net
Web: www.commodorehotel.ie

HOTEL ★★ MAP 3 I 3

The Commodore Hotel, owned and managed by the O'Shea family for 37 years - overlooks Cork Harbour. 25 minutes from city centre. Facilities: indoor swimming pool, sauna, snooker - entertainment and roof garden. Locally (subject to availability at clubs) free golf and pitch & putt. Ideal location for visiting Fota Wildlife Park, Fota Golf Course, Blarney etc, The Jameson and Queenstown Heritage Centres. All 42 rooms have full facilities, (21 overlook Cork Harbour supplement applies). Ringaskiddy Ferryport 15 minutes via river car ferry.

Bookable on www.irelandhotels.com

B&B from €50.00 to €70.00

Patrick O'Shea
General Manager

Activities:

Member of:

Special Offer: Weekend Specials from €100.00 pps
(2 Nights B&B & 1 Dinner)

42 42

Closed 24 - 27 December

B&B Rates are per Person Sharing per Night incl. Breakfast.
or Room Rates are per Room per Night - See also Page 8

WatersEdge Hotel	Great Southern Hotel	Abbeypoint House

<table>
<tr>
<td>(Next To Cobh Heritage Centre),
Cobh,
Co. Cork
Tel: 021-481 5566 Fax: 021-481 2011
Email: info@watersedgehotel.ie
Web: www.watersedgehotel.ie</td>
<td>Cork Airport,
Co. Cork

Tel: 021-494 7500 Fax: 021-494 7501
Email: res@corkairport-gsh.com
Web: www.greatsouthernhotels.com</td>
<td>Western Road,
(Opp. UCC),
Cork
Tel: 021-427 5526 Fax: 021-425 1955
Email: info@abbeypoint.com
Web: www.abbeypoint.com</td>
</tr>
</table>

HOTEL ★★★ MAP 3 I 3	HOTEL U MAP 2 H 3	GUESTHOUSE ★★★ MAP 2 H 3

Situated on the waterfront overlooking Cork Harbour. All rooms en suite with satellite TV, tea making facilities, direct dial phone, modem, hairdryer, trouser press. Our restaurant, Jacobs Ladder, is renowned for its seafood, steaks, ambience and friendly staff. Local activities and sightseeing include Cobh Heritage Centre (next door), Cathedral, Titanic Trail, Fota Wildlife Park, Fota House & Gardens, golf, sailing, angling, tennis, horse riding. Ideal touring base for Cork City, Kinsale & Blarney.

The Great Southern Hotel Cork Airport is a stylish contemporary hotel conveniently located within walking distance of the terminal at Cork Airport. With a wide range of meeting rooms, a business centre and a leisure centre with gymnasium, steam room and jacuzzi, it is the perfect base for business meetings or for first or last night stays. Bookable worldwide through Utell International or Central Reservations: 01-214 4800.

A warm welcome and friendly service awaits you at the family-run Abbeypoint House which is located less than 10 minutes walk from Cork City centre and opposite University College Cork. Tastefully decorated, all rooms are en suite with colour TV, direct dial telephone, hairdryers, tea/coffee facilities and we have a private lock-up car park at rear. An ideal base to visit Cork and tour the beautiful South West. AA ♦♦♦ approved.

Bookable on www.irelandhotels.com
Member of Les Routiers

Bookable on www.irelandhotels.com

B&B from €55.00 to €100.00	Room Rate from €89.00 to €160.00	B&B from €35.00 to €50.00

Margaret & Mike Whelan
Proprietors

Activities:

Member of:

Rose O'Donovan
General Manager

Activities:

Member of:

Joy Brazier
Proprietor

Member of:

Special Offer: *Weekend Specials from €140.00 pps (2 Nights B&B & 1 Dinner)*

Special Offer: *Weekend Specials from €125.00 pps (2 Nights B&B & 1 Dinner)*

Closed 01 - 10 January	Closed 23 December - 01 January	Closed 23 December - 06 January

B&B Rates are per Person Sharing per Night incl. Breakfast. or **Room Rates** are per Room per Night - See also Page 8

Achill House

Western Road,
Cork City

Tel: 021-427 9447 Fax: 021-427 9447
Email: info@achillhouse.com
Web: www.achillhouse.com

GUESTHOUSE ★★★ MAP 2 H 3

Stay in luxury, comfort and style at Achill House. This elegant period house is ideally located in the heart of Cork City and opposite UCC. All rooms have de luxe en suite bathrooms with optional jacuzzi. An extensive breakfast menu caters for all tastes, from hearty Irish breakfasts to lighter options. Achill House is convenient to ferry, airport and bus termini, the perfect base for exploring Cork and Kerry. A warm and relaxed atmosphere awaits you, whether on business or pleasure.

Bookable on www.irelandhotels.com

B&B from €35.00 to €60.00

*Helena McSweeney
Proprietor*

Member of:
IRISH HOTELS FEDERATION

Special Offer: Midweek Specials Available

6 6

Open All Year

Ambassador Hotel

Military Hill,
St. Lukes,
Cork

Tel: 021-455 1996 Fax: 021-455 1997
Email: info@ambassadorhotel.ie
Web: www.ambassadorhotel.ie

HOTEL U MAP 2 H 3

Located on a hilltop, the Ambassador Hotel commands spectacular views over Cork City and Harbour. 58 spacious bedrooms luxuriously decorated to the highest standards. A gourmet award-winning "Season's Restaurant", Cocktail Bar, Embassy Bar, Conference Centre and Banqueting facilities, all combine to ensure a memorable stay. New Health Centre (gym, jacuzzi, sauna, steam room) allows guests to unwind at leisure. An excellent base to explore Cork City and county. Wireless Internet Access hotspot.

Bookable on www.irelandhotels.com
Member of Best Western Hotels

B&B from €62.50 to €90.00

Dudley Fitzell

Activities:

Member of:
IRISH HOTELS FEDERATION

Special Offer: Special offers on www.ambassadorhotel.ie

58 58

Closed 24 - 26 December

B&B Rates are per Person Sharing per Night incl. Breakfast. or Room Rates are per Room per Night - See also Page 8

Co. Cork

Cork City

Ashley Hotel

Coburg Street,
Cork City

Tel: 021-450 1518 Fax: 021-450 1178
Email: info@ashleyhotel.com
Web: www.ashleyhotel.com

HOTEL U MAP 2 H 3

The Ashley Hotel is family owned and run with our enthusiastic staff, with all the benefits of a city centre location. Situated north of the River Lee near the bus station and the railway station, and only 8km from the airport. All bedrooms with bathroom en suite, satellite television, tea/coffee making facilities and direct dial telephone. Relax in our very comfortable lounge and enjoy our chef's specials of the day. Private lock up car park. Children welcome.

Bookable on www.irelandhotels.com

B&B from €48.00 to €80.00

Anita Coughlan

Special Offer: Midweek Specials from €165.00 pps
(3 Nights B&B)

27 27

Closed 22 December - 09 January

Blarney Stone

Western Road,
Cork City

Tel: 021-427 0083 Fax: 021-427 0471
Email: bsgh@eircom.net
Web: www.blarneystoneguesthouse.ie

GUESTHOUSE ★★★ MAP 2 H 3

This newly refurbished Victorian residence has character and charm and offers you luxurious accommodation in the heart of the city. Situated opposite University College and within close proximity of a selection of restaurants, bars and entertainment places. Also ideally located for ferry, airport, train and bus. Rooms are tastefully decorated to the highest standard with de luxe en suite optional jacuzzi, TV, DD phone, tea/coffee making facilities. A warm and friendly atmosphere awaits you. Alternative website: www.blarneystoneguesthouse.com

B&B from €35.00 to €70.00

Angela Hartnett
Proprietor

Member of:

8 8

Open All Year

Brookfield Hotel

Brookfield Holiday Village,
College Road,
Cork

Tel: 021-480 4700 Fax: 021-480 4793
Email: brookfieldhotel@eircom.net
Web: www.brookfieldcork.ie

HOTEL ★★★ MAP 2 H 3

Brookfield Hotel, College Road is just 1 mile from Cork City centre. Set on 10 acres of rolling parkland, it is truly a rural setting. *24 bright, modern bedrooms. *Family rooms. *Interconnecting rooms. *Enjoy our leisure and fitness centre which incorporates 25m indoor pool. Kiddies pool, water slide, saunas, steam room, spa jacuzzi, outdoor hot tub, massage, gym, sunbeds, outdoor tennis courts.

B&B from €55.00 to €90.00

Sinead O'Shea
Reservations Manager

24 24

Closed 23 December - 03 January

B&B Rates are per Person Sharing per Night incl. Breakfast. or Room Rates are per Room per Night - See also Page 8

Co. Cork
Cork City

Clarion Hotel

Lapps Quay,
Cork City

Tel: 021-422 4900 Fax: 021-422 4901
Email: info@clarionhotelcorkcity.com
Web: www.clarionhotelcorkcity.com

HOTEL N MAP 2 H 3

Superbly located overlooking Cork's River Lee, the new Clarion Hotel is only 2 minutes walk to the business, shopping and entertainment centre of Cork City. Boasting 191 bedrooms, Sinergie Restaurant with European menu, Kudo's Bar with Asian cuisine, a stunning Atrium Lounge and conference and event suites complimented by SanoVitae Health Club & Spa. The Clarion Hotel is designed to redefine the idea of what a contemporary 4**** hotel should be and is located in the City Quarter which houses a public car park. We look forward to welcoming you to the Clarion Hotel.

Room Rate from €110.00 to €200.00

Charlie Sheil
General Manager

Activities:

Member of:
IRISH HOTELS FEDERATION

191 191

Closed 24 - 26 December

Commons Inn

New Mallow Road,
Cork

Tel: 021-421 0300 Fax: 021-421 0333
Email: info@commonsinn.com
Web: www.commonsinn.com

HOTEL ★★★ MAP 3 H 3

Close to Cork City, on the main Cork to Blarney road, this family-run hotel contains the popular Commons Bar, Baileys Restaurant and the Roebuck Room function centre. All rooms contain two queen sized beds and are priced per room. Enjoy carvery lunch in the bar or dinner in one of Cork's best restaurants. Whether you're in Cork on business or for pleasure we are at your service.

Room Rate from €65.00 to €90.00

Ashley Colson
Accommodation Manager

Activities:

Member of:
IRISH HOTELS FEDERATION

40 40

Closed 24 - 31 December

CORK CITY GAOL

Step back in time to see what 19th & early 20th Century life was like in Cork - inside & outside prison walls! Amazingly lifelike figures, furnished cells, sound effects and fascinating exhibitions.

OPEN 7 DAYS
Throughout the year.
At same location the
RADIO MUSEUM

Sunday's Well, Cork City
Tel: 021-430 50 22
Email: corkgaol@indigo.ie
www.corkcitygaol.com

B&B Rates are per Person Sharing per Night incl. Breakfast.
or Room Rates are per Room per Night - See also Page 8

Co. Cork

Cork City

Country Club Hotel	Crawford Guesthouse	East Village Hotel

Country Club Hotel

Montenotte,
Cork

Tel: 021-450 2922 Fax: 021-450 2082
Email: info@countryclubcork.com
Web: www.countryclubcork.com

UNDER REFURBISHMENT - RE-OPENING AUGUST 2006

HOTEL R   MAP 2 H 3

"Nothing overlooked but the city". The Country Club Hotel is an elegant mansion house which combines old world charm with modern comfort. The ideal base for exploring Cork City, just a stroll from buzzing McCurtain Street and Cork's main thoroughfare, Patrick Street. The stylish Pennant Bar and modern Tivoli Garden Restaurant boast spectacular views of Cork City and harbour. One of Cork's premier venues for your corporate or private event. The hotel will be completely refurbished and extended in early 2006 to include a leisure centre and additional accommodation.

B&B from €60.00 to €90.00

John Gately
Director / Proprietor

Member of:

IRISH HOTELS FEDERATION

60 60

Closed 23 - 29 December

Crawford Guesthouse

Western Road,
Cork

Tel: 021-427 9000 Fax: 021-427 9927
Email: info@crawfordhouse.ie
Web: www.crawfordhouse.ie

GUESTHOUSE ★★★   MAP 3 H 3

One of Cork's finest guesthouses offering bed & breakfast in a contemporary setting. All the bedrooms provide comfort and luxury with oak-wood furniture and orthopaedic 6ft king sized beds. De luxe en suites include jacuzzi baths and power showers. Fax/modem points in all rooms. Located directly across from University College Cork. 10 minutes walk to city centre. Private car park. AA ◆◆◆◆ & RAC ◆◆◆◆ and Sparkling Diamond Award 2005. Recommended by Lonely Planet Guide, Time Out Guide 2005, Bradt City Guide 2005 and Gourmet magazine 2005.

Bookable on www.irelandhotels.com

B&B from €50.00 to €65.00

Cecilia O'Leary
Manager

Member of:

IRISH HOTELS FEDERATION

12 12

Closed 22 December - 15 January

East Village Hotel

Douglas,
Cork

Tel: 021-436 7000 Fax: 021-436 7001
Email: info@eastvillage.ie
Web: www.eastvillage.ie

HOTEL U   MAP 3 H 3

East Village is a welcome addition to the Cork area with a large and vibrant sports bar, award-winning restaurant and just 10 bedrooms. This contemporary hotel provides easy access to all amenities close to Cork City centre, Cork Airport & the Jack Lynch Tunnel. This hotel offers the oft-forgotten personal touch. All rooms have private balcony, en suite, TV etc. and are decorated in a modern fashion.

Room Rate from €60.00 to €120.00

Derry O'Regan
Proprietor

Member of:

IRISH HOTELS FEDERATION

10 10

Closed 24 - 26 December

B&B Rates are per Person Sharing per Night incl. Breakfast. or **Room Rates** are per Room per Night - See also Page 8

Garnish House

Western Road,
Cork

Tel: 021-427 5111 Fax: 021-427 3872
Email: garnish@iol.ie
Web: www.garnish.ie

GUESTHOUSE ★★★ MAP 3 H 3

RAC 4♦♦♦♦ and AA 4♦♦♦♦. A stay in Garnish House is a memorable one. The personal atmosphere & attention instantly make you pleasantly at home. Luxury rooms some with jacuzzi baths offer comfort, are unique and charming. Being welcomed with genuine Irish hospitality - cup of tea and an array of delicacies as featured on National TV. 24hr reception, opposite U.C.C. Awards: Sparkling Diamond, Warm Welcome 1-100 Best Places to Stay. 4**** standard suites and studio accommodation available. Also 4**** self catering properties.

B&B from €50.00 to €100.00

Johanna Lucey
Manageress

Member of:

14 14

Open All Year

Gresham Metropole

Maccurtain Street,
Cork

Tel: 021-464 3789 Fax: 021-450 6450
Email: info@gresham-metropolehotel.com
Web: www.gresham-hotels.com

HOTEL ★★★ MAP 3 H 3

Located in the heart of Cork, the Gresham Metropole has been stylishly refurbished to the highest standards. Facilities include the Riverview Restaurant and Met Bar. There are 12 purpose built meeting rooms and a superb leisure centre which offers three pool areas, a sauna, steam room, aerobics studio and gym. Secure complimentary parking for guests. RAC and AA approved.

Bookable on www.irelandhotels.com
Member of Gresham Hotel Group

B&B from €90.00 to €200.00

Thys Vogels
General Manager

Activities:

Member of:

113 113

Open All Year

Cobh, Co. Cork

Explore Cobh's Fascinating history and the towns' direct links with Titanic! The original Titanic Trail guided walking tour takes place every day all year. Leaving at **11am daily** (time varies off - season) from the Commodore Hotel this famous tour is educational, interesting and fun. Cost is €8.50 per person. Duration is approximately 75 minutes. In June, July, and August additional tours also run at 11am and 2pm.

Contact: Michael Martin Author and Creator Titanic Trail

Tel: +353 (21) 481 5211
Mobile: +353 (87) 276 7218
Email: info@titanic-trail.com
www.titanic-trail.com

B&B Rates are per Person Sharing per Night incl. Breakfast. or Room Rates are per Room per Night - See also Page 8

Co. Cork

Cork City

Hayfield Manor Hotel	Hotel Isaacs	Imperial Hotel with Lifestyle Salon and Spa

Hayfield Manor Hotel

Perrott Avenue,
College Road,
Cork
Tel: 021-484 5900 Fax: 021-431 6839
Email: enquiries@hayfieldmanor.ie
Web: www.hayfieldmanor.ie

HOTEL ★★★★★ MAP 2 H 3

In its own oasis of calm just a mile from the heart of Cork City, 2005 European Capital of Culture. Hayfield Manor is one of Ireland's most elegantly decorated hotels. The superb accommodation is renowned for its antique furniture, authentic fabric designs & marble bathrooms. Enjoy the private leisure centre & unwind with a relaxing treatment. The Manor Room Restaurant offers award-winning cuisine, for a more informal setting try Perrott's Restaurant. AA 4 Red Star, AA Irish Hotel of the Year 03/04, RAC Gold Ribbon Award for Excellence. I.G.T.O.A. Golf Hotel of the Year 2005. Suites also available.

Bookable on www.irelandhotels.com
Member of Small Luxury Hotels of the World

B&B from €120.00 to €200.00

Joe Scally
Proprietor

Member of:

🛏🍴 ☎🖥🚭📺©♨CM✦🐾🅿🛅
88 88
aic Inet WiFi 🐴

Open All Year

Hotel Isaacs

48 MacCurtain Street,
Cork
Tel: 021-450 0011 Fax: 021-450 6355
Email: cork@isaacs.ie
Web: www.isaacs.ie

HOTEL ★★★ MAP 3 H 3

Unique Victorian Hotel tucked away underneath an archway in Cork's city centre. Minutes from bus and train stations. Beautifully furnished standard and air-conditioned superior rooms plus serviced self-catering apartments. Facilities include television, phone, hospitality tray, hairdryer and ironing facilities. Wi-Fi and broadband available throughout the hotel. Greene's Restaurant, overlooking the floodlit waterfall offers modern creative cuisine. Dine al fresco all year in the heated courtyard garden. Limited free parking close to the hotel.

Bookable on www.irelandhotels.com

B&B from €57.50 to €110.00

Paula Lynch
General Manager

Activities:
🏊🎾

Member of:
IRISH HOTELS FEDERATION

Special Offer: *Midweek Specials from €150.00 pps (3 Nights B&B)*

🛏🍴 ☎🖥🚭📺©♨CM✦∪🅿🛅
47 47
🖥 Inet WiFi

Closed 24 - 27 December

Imperial Hotel with Lifestyle Salon and Spa

South Mall,
Cork
Tel: 021-427 4040 Fax: 021-427 5375
Email: reservations@imperialhotelcork.ie
Web: www.flynnhotels.com

HOTEL ★★★ MAP 3 H 3

The Imperial Hotel with Lifestyle Salon & Spa nestled in the heart of Cork City is a truly magical hotel that blends the warmth and intimacy of times past with the style and luxury of a contemporary hotel. Recently refurbished, the Imperial Hotel now boasts 130 fantastic guest rooms including 10 luxurious suites, a penthouse suite, the new Pembroke Restaurant, South's Bar and Ireland's first Aveda Lifestyle Salon & Spa.

Bookable on www.irelandhotels.com
Member of Flynn Hotels

Room Rate from €125.00 to €225.00

Declan Moriarty
General Manager

Activities:
🏊🎾💧

Member of:
IRISH HOTELS FEDERATION

Special Offer: *Weekend Specials from €160.00 pps (2 Nights B&B & 1 Dinner)*

🛏🍴 ☎🖥🚭📺©♨CM∪🎵🅿🅂🛅
130 130
Inet WiFi 🐴

Closed 24 - 27 December

B&B Rates are per Person Sharing per Night incl. Breakfast. or Room Rates are per Room per Night - See also Page 8

Jurys Inn Cork	Killarney Guest House	Kingsley Hotel & Residence

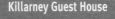

Jurys Inn Cork

Anderson's Quay,
Cork

Tel: 021-494 3000 Fax: 021-427 6144
Email: jurysinncork@jurysdoyle.com
Web: www.jurysinns.com

Killarney Guest House

Western Road,
(Opp. UCC),
Cork City

Tel: 021-427 0290 Fax: 021-427 1010
Email: killarneyhouse@iol.ie
Web: www.killarneyguesthouse.com

Kingsley Hotel & Residence

Victoria Cross,
Cork

Tel: 021-480 0500 Fax: 021-480 0527
Email: resv@kingsleyhotel.com
Web: www.kingsleyhotel.com

HOTEL ★★★ MAP 2 H 3

GUESTHOUSE ★★★ MAP 2 H 3

HOTEL U MAP 2 H 3

Jurys Inn Cork enjoys a superb location right in the heart of Cork City, overlooking the River Lee. Vibrant business and shopping districts and a host of restaurants, bars, museums and galleries are literally within a few minutes' walk. An excellent base to explore the city or the very stunning Co. Cork countryside.

This charming guesthouse is renowned for its unique blend of comfort, style and hospitality. Its sumptuous breakfast menu includes a buffet table laden with fresh produce and home baking. All rooms are en suite with optional jacuzzi bath. A close walk to the city centre and opposite the University College Cork. Large car park for your security. AA acclaimed and RAC ♦♦♦♦ and Sparkling Diamond Award 2005/06.

Nestled on the River Lee, located only minutes from Cork's Airport. An elegant atmosphere and tranquil surroundings. The hotel is being upgraded to 5***** standard and will feature Yauvana Spa and Thermo Suite, 200 seated conference and events centre, private secure parking, health and leisure club, spectacular Riverside Restaurants and walkways. Re-development of hotel - on-going until April 2006.

Bookable on www.irelandhotels.com
Member of Jurys Doyle Hotel Group

Bookable on www.irelandhotels.com

Bookable on www.irelandhotels.com

Room Rate from €65.00 to €155.00

B&B from €45.00 to €65.00

B&B from €85.00 to €120.00

*Julieann Brennan
General Manager*

*Margaret O'Leary
Manageress*

*Michelle Moloney
General Manager*

Activities:

Member of:

Member of:

Member of:

133 133

19 19

69 69

Closed 24 - 26 December	Closed 25 - 26 December	Open All Year

B&B Rates are per Person Sharing per Night incl. Breakfast.
or **Room Rates** are per Room per Night - See also Page 8

Cork City

Lancaster Lodge	Lotamore House	Lough Mahon House

Western Road, Cork	Tivoli, Cork	Tivoli, Cork
Tel: 021-425 1125 Fax: 021-425 1126 Email: info@lancasterlodge.com Web: www.lancasterlodge.com	Tel: 021-482 2344 Fax: 021-482 2219 Email: lotamore@iol.ie Web: www.lotamorehouse.com	Tel: 021-450 2142 Fax: 021-450 1804 Email: info@loughmahon.com Web: www.loughmahon.com

GUESTHOUSE ★★★ MAP 2 H 3 | **GUESTHOUSE ★★★ MAP 3 H 3** | **GUESTHOUSE ★★★ MAP 3 H 3**

Lancaster Lodge, a purpose built 4**** guesthouse, located next to Jury's Hotel and is only a short stroll from the city centre. We provide 24 hour reception, an extensive breakfast menu and our suites each have Jacuzzi bath. Lancaster Lodge is fully wheelchair accessible with lift to all four floors. For the business person on the move we now offer free wireless broadband internet access. With 39 en suite rooms and free parking, it is a natural choice for business people and sophisticated individual travellers. AA 5 ◆◆◆◆◆.

An elegant Georgian residence of outstanding character, Lotamore House is the perfect place to escape from it all to the graciousness of times past. Pleasantly secluded, yet only 5 minutes drive from city centre, welcoming fires, lavish décor and antique furnishings combine to offer the perfect balance of luxury and charm. The stylish elegance in each guest room is individual. Lotamore House offers an uncompromising level of service. Ideally situated, near airport, ferry terminals and golf courses, making it the perfect base when visiting the scenic South West.

Luxurious Georgian house with private parking. Convenient to city centre, bus & rail station.100 metres from Silver Springs Moran Hotel. En suite bedrooms with cable TV, DD phone, hairdryer, tea/coffee making facilities. We offer in-house holistic treatments (integrated energy therapy, reiki, massage & face & body treatments etc.). Close to Fota Wildlife Park, Cobh Heritage Centre, Blarney Castle, golf clubs & ferry terminals. Renowned for our fresh orange juice and extensive breakfast menu, it amounts to a great place to stay.

Member of Premier Guesthouses

B&B from €55.00 to €90.00 | **B&B from €55.00 to €70.00** | **B&B from €35.00 to €44.50**

Susan Leahy
Manageress

Member of:

Geraldine McElhinney
Proprietor / Manager

Pete & Lisa
Proprietors

Activities:

Member of:

🐾 🐕 ☎🖨🛏TC♨∪♩PS 🖥 Inet WiFi
39 39
🐴🐾♿

🐾 🐕 ☎TC✳PS 🖥
20 20

🐾 🐕 ☎🛏TCU♩PS🖥🐴
6 6

Closed 24 - 28 December | **Closed 22 December - 05 January** | **Open all year**

<u>B&B Rates</u> are per Person Sharing per Night incl. Breakfast.
or <u>Room Rates</u> are per Room per Night - See also Page 8

Maryborough House Hotel	**Quality Hotel & Leisure Centre, Cork**	**Radisson SAS Hotel & Spa, Cork**

Maryborough Hill, Douglas, Cork
Tel: 021-436 5555 Fax: 021-436 5662
Email: info@maryborough.ie
Web: www.maryborough.com

John Redmond Street, Cork
Tel: 021-452 9200 Fax: 021-452 9222
Email: info@qualityhotelcork.com
Web: www.qualityhotelcork.com

Ditchley House, Little Island, Cork
Tel: 021-429 7000 Fax: 021-429 7101
Email: info.cork@radissonsas.com
Web: www.radissonsas.com

HOTEL ★★★★ MAP 3 H 3 | **HOTEL U MAP 2 H 3** | **HOTEL P MAP 2 H 3**

Distinctive, delightful and different. Maryborough is set on 24 acres of listed gardens and woodland, located only 10 minutes from Cork City. This charming 18th century house, with its creatively designed extension, features exquisite conference, banqueting and leisure facilities. 79 spacious rooms, some with balconies overlooking the magnificent gardens and orchards. Zing's Restaurant, in contemporary relaxed design, is an exciting mix of modern flavours and styles. 4 minutes from Lee Tunnel. Wheelchair friendly.

A great location for city breaks or an ideal base to explore Cork County. Spacious guest rooms, relaxing surroundings, imaginative menus available at Lannigans Restaurant and Bell's Bar - a perfect place for a relaxing drink, serving bar food daily from 10.30am until 9pm, musical entertainment Wednesday through to Sunday. Club Vitae boasts a superb 20m pool, gym, jacuzzi, steam room, sauna and treatment room. Car parking is subject to availability. Wheelchair accessible.

Nestled on 9 acres of landscaped gardens, the hotel is a fusion of old world charm and new world sophistication offering 129 luxurious guest rooms and suites. Extravagant Retreat Spa & fitness centre includes nine treatment rooms and a hydrotherapy treatment pool. Boasting extensive meeting and events facilities. Dining options include the intimate 'Island Grillroom' and the 'Banks Bar' for lighter meals and cocktails.

Bookable on www.irelandhotels.com

Bookable on www.irelandhotels.com
Member of Quality Hotels

B&B from €85.00 to €150.00 | *B&B from €40.00 to €109.00* | *B&B from €80.00 to €160.00*

Justin McCarthy
General Manager

Activities:

Member of:

Aidan Moynihan
General Manager

Member of:

Ruairi O'Connor
General Manager

Activities:

Member of:

Special Offer: *Weekend Specials from €175.00 pps*
(2 Nights B&B & 1 Dinner)
79 79

Special Offer: *Weekend Specials from €99.00 pps*
(2 Nights B&B & 1 Dinner)
101 101

129 129

Closed 24 - 26 December	**Open All Year**	**Open All Year**

B&B Rates are per Person Sharing per Night incl. Breakfast.
or Room Rates are per Room per Night - See also Page 8

South West 55

Co. Cork

Cork City

Redclyffe Guest House	Rochestown Park Hotel	Rose Lodge Guest House

Redclyffe Guest House

Western Road,
Cork

Tel: 021-427 3220 Fax: 021-427 8382
Email: info@redclyffe.com
Web: www.redclyffe.com

GUESTHOUSE U MAP 2 H 3

Redclyffe is a charming Victorian red brick guesthouse, combining olde world charm with modern elegance. Opposite University College Cork, museum, consultant's clinic and Jurys Hotel. All rooms en suite with TV, hairdryer, direct dial phone, tea and coffee making facilities. Close to city centre, No. 8 bus at door. Easy drive to airport and car ferry. Spacious car park. Be assured of a warm welcome at this family-run guesthouse.

B&B from €30.00 to €45.00

Michael & Maura Sheehan
Proprietors

Member of:
IRISH HOTELS FEDERATION

13 13

Open All Year

Rochestown Park Hotel

Rochestown Road,
Douglas,
Cork

Tel: 021-489 0800 Fax: 021-489 2178
Email: info@rochestownpark.com
Web: www.rochestownpark.com

HOTEL ★★★★ MAP 3 H 3

The Rochestown Park Hotel is a manor style hotel set in mature gardens. Facilities include an award-winning leisure centre and Ireland's premier Thalasso Therapy Centre. A large proportion of our 163 bedrooms are air-conditioned and overlook our gardens and Mahon Golf Club. We cater for weekend breaks, conferences, meetings, as well as groups, families and weddings.

Bookable on www.irelandhotels.com

B&B from €60.00 to €110.00

Liam Lally
General Manager

Activities:

Member of:
IRISH HOTELS FEDERATION

Special Offer: Weekend Specials from €145.00 pps
(2 Nights B&B & 1 Dinner)

163 163

Closed 24 - 26 December

Rose Lodge Guest House

Mardyke Walk,
Off Western Road,
Cork

Tel: 021-427 2958 Fax: 021-427 4087
Email: info@roselodge.net
Web: www.roselodge.net

GUESTHOUSE ★★★ MAP 2 H 3

Rose Lodge is a 10 minute walk from city centre and close to bus and train stations. 16 en suite bedrooms (jacuzzi optional) with direct dial telephone, TV, tea/coffee making facilities, hairdryer and ironing facilities. An ideal base for the busy executive or holidaymaker to explore the South West. Airport and ferry 15 minutes drive. Golf, tennis, cricket, fishing nearby and just minutes from University College Cork.

B&B from €40.00 to €60.00

Paddy Murphy
Proprietor

16 16

Open All Year

B&B Rates are per Person Sharing per Night incl. Breakfast.
or **Room Rates** are per Room per Night - See also Page 8

Silver Springs Moran Hotel

Tivoli,
Cork

Tel: 021-450 7533 Fax: 021-450 7641
Email: silverspringsinfo@moranhotels.com
Web: www.silverspringshotel.ie

HOTEL ★★★★ MAP 3 H 3

This 4**** hotel has been completely
redesigned and re-furbished. The hotel
is located only minutes from Cork City.
109 bedrooms including 5 de luxe
suites all with cable TV, trouser press
and tea/coffee facitlities. Centrally
located only 5 minutes from the city
centre and 7 miles from Cork
Intenational Airport. Excellent base for
touring Cork's many visitor attractions.
Full leisure facilities available include
25m pool. Free parking. A Moran Hotel.

Bookable on www.irelandhotels.com
Member of Moran Hotel Group

B&B from €60.00 to €125.00

*Tom Moran
Managing Director*

Activities:

Member of:
HOTELS

Special Offer: *Weekend Specials from €140.00 pps
(2 Nights B&B & 1 Dinner)*

109 109

Closed 24 - 27 December

Victoria Hotel

Patrick Street,
Cook Street,
Cork

Tel: 021-427 8788 Fax: 021-427 8790
Email: info@thevictoriahotel.com
Web: www.thevictoriahotel.com

HOTEL ★★ MAP 3 H 3

The Victoria Hotel is situated in Cork
City centre. All rooms have bath &
shower, direct dial phone, TV and
hairdryer. Family suites available. Built
in 1810, it was frequented by European
Royalty and was home to some of our
own great political leaders, including
Charles Stewart Parnell who made his
major speeches from its upper balcony.
James Joyce recounts his stay in
Portrait of an Artist. Conference room
available.

Member of MinOtel Hotel Group

B&B from €45.00 to €90.00

*King Family
Managers*

Member of:
HOTELS

Special Offer: *Midweek Specials from €120.00 pps
(3 Nights B&B)*

29 29

Closed 24 - 26 December

Vienna Woods Hotel

Glanmire,
Cork

Tel: 021-482 1146 Fax: 021-482 1120
Email: info@viennawoodshotel.com
Web: www.viennawoodshotel.com

HOTEL ★★★ MAP 3 H 3

This unique country house hotel set in
20 acres of woodland 7 minutes from
Cork City centre. All 50 bedrooms have
been decorated to offer a high standard
of comfort. Food is available throughout
the day, casual dining in the
Conservatory Bar and in the Blue
Room. Ideally placed close to Munster's
finest golf courses, Cobh Titanic
Heritage centre, Fota Wildlife Park &
Kinsale. Leisure Centre due for
completion Summer 2006.

Bookable on www.irelandhotels.com

B&B from €55.00 to €80.00

*John Gately
Managing Director /
Proprietor*

Activities:

Member of:
HOTELS

Special Offer: *Midweek Specials from €145.00 pps
(3 Nights B&B)*

50 50

Closed 24 - 26 December

<u>B&B Rates</u> are per Person Sharing per Night incl. Breakfast.
or <u>Room Rates</u> are per Room per Night - See also Page 8

Whispering Pines Hotel	Casey's Hotel	Glengarriff Blue Pool Lodge
Crosshaven, Co. Cork	The Village, Glengarriff, Co. Cork	The Village, Glengarriff, Co. Cork

Whispering Pines Hotel

Crosshaven,
Co. Cork

Tel: 021-483 1843 Fax: 021-483 1679
Email: reservations@whisperingpineshotel.com
Web: www.whisperingpineshotel.com

HOTEL ★★ MAP 3 I 3

Whispering Pines, personally run by the Twomey Family, is a charming hotel sheltered by surrounding woodland and overlooking the Owenabue River. In this idyllic setting one can enjoy good company, quality home-cooked food and a host of amenities to ensure your stay is a restful and memorable experience. All rooms with direct dial phone, tea/coffee facilities and TV. Our 3 angling boats fish daily from April-October. Ideal base for touring Cork/Kerry Region. Cork Airport 12km and Cork City 19km. AA approved.

Casey's Hotel

The Village,
Glengarriff,
Co. Cork

Tel: 027-63010 Fax: 027-63072
Email: caseyshotel@yahoo.com
Web: www.caseyshotel.ie

HOTEL ★★ MAP 1 D 2

Casey's Hotel is owner managed by the Deasy family. Offering a personal, friendly service with old fashioned courtesy. All our rooms are en suite with telephone, TV and tea/coffee. Private off road car parking and gardens. The perfect base for day trips to Killarney, Sheep's Head and Gougane Barra. Come and discover the unspoilt beauty of the Beara Peninsula. Fine food assured in our bar and à la carte restaurant.

Glengarriff Blue Pool Lodge

The Village,
Glengarriff,
Co. Cork

Tel: 027-63000 Fax: 027-63526
Email: info@glengarrifflodge.com
Web: www.glengarrifflodge.com

GUESTHOUSE P MAP 1 D 2

Perfectly situated in the very heart of beautiful Glengarriff, at the entrance to the Blue Pool Park and Garnish Island. This newly refurbished lodge offers you the opportunity to relax in one of its luxurious rooms, workout or take a rejuvenating treatment in the Health and Beauty Spa or walk through the 60 acres of parks and gardens on the doorstep. With a warm and friendly welcome and staff - always a popular place for visitors.

B&B from €40.00 to €60.00

Norma Twomey
Proprietor

Activities:

Member of:
IRISH HOTELS FEDERATION

15 15

Closed 01 December - 28 February

B&B from €40.00 to €50.00

Donal & Eileen Deasy
Owners

Member of:
IRISH HOTELS FEDERATION

Special Offer: 10% Discount On 3 Nights Stay Or More, Excluding Bank Holidays

19 19

Closed 18 December - 12 February

B&B from €39.00 to €59.00

Maureen McCarthy

Member of:
IRISH HOTELS FEDERATION

Special Offer: Weekend Specials from €69.00 pps (2 Nights B&B)

12 12

Inet

Open All Year

B&B Rates are per Person Sharing per Night incl. Breakfast. or Room Rates are per Room per Night - See also Page 8

Glengarriff Eccles Hotel	Gougane Barra Hotel	Innishannon House Hotel

Glengarriff,
Co. Cork

Tel: 027-63003 Fax: 027-63319
Email: info@eccleshotel.com
Web: www.eccleshotel.com

Gougane Barra,
Ballingeary,
Co. Cork

Tel: 026-47069 Fax: 026-47226
Email: gouganebarrahotel@eircom.net
Web: www.gouganebarra.com

Innishannon,
Co. Cork

Tel: 021-477 5121 Fax: 021-477 5609
Email: info@innishannon-hotel.ie
Web: www.innishannon-hotel.ie

HOTEL ★★★ MAP 2 D 2

HOTEL ★★ MAP 2 E 3

HOTEL ★★★ MAP 2 G 2

Located opposite Garnish Island, in beautiful Bantry Bay. The Glengarriff Eccles Hotel is one of the oldest established hotels in Ireland (1745). Now fully restored this family-run hotel boasts 66 en suite bedrooms, many with panoramic views, restaurant and bar. Ideally situated to explore the beauty of the Beara Peninsula. Golf (3 courses within 20 km), fishing, hill walking, sailing, all nearby. 17km from Bantry.

Situated high up in the mountains between Macroom & Bantry, in its own grounds, overlooking Gougane Barra Lake at the source of the River Lee. This comfortable hotel is nestled in one of the most scenic & romantic glens in Ireland. Freshness of ingredients, locally sourced & generations old recipes served with creativity & the experience of five generations make this hotel a real treat. Ideally situated for touring the beauty spots of Cork & Kerry, 72km west of Cork City & Airport. A walk along the banks of the Lee through the forest park which covers 162 hectares of mystic beauty. GDS Access Code UI Toll Free: 1-800-44-Utell.

The most romantic hotel in Ireland built in 1720 in the Petit Chateau style on the banks of the River Bandon, close to Kinsale. All rooms en suite with TV, DD phone, radio, etc. Award-winning restaurant (AA**, RAC, Egon Ronay) serving fresh fish. Superb wine cellar, stunning views, free salmon and trout fishing from the grounds. Horse riding and golf nearby. GDS code: UI Toll Free 1-800-44 UTELL.

Bookable on www.irelandhotels.com

Bookable on www.irelandhotels.com
Member of Irish Country Hotels

B&B from €55.00 to €130.00

B&B from €60.00 to €70.00

B&B from €70.00 to €90.00

Thos O'Brien
General Manager

Activities:

Member of:

Katy & Neil Lucey

Member of:

David Roche
General Manager

Activities:

Member of:

Special Offer: Weekend Specials from €99.00 pps
(2 Nights B&B & 1 Dinner)

66 66

Special Offer: Weekend Specials from €150.00 pps
(2 Nights B&B & 1 Dinner)

25 25

Special Offer: Weekend Specials from €150.00 pps

12 12

Closed 23 - 28 December	Closed 15 October - 15 April	Closed 23 - 26 December

B&B Rates are per Person Sharing per Night incl. Breakfast.
or **Room Rates** are per Room per Night - See also Page 8

Kinsale

Actons Hotel	Blue Haven Hotel and Restaurant	Captains Quarters
Pier Road, Kinsale, Co. Cork	3 Pearse Street, Kinsale, Co. Cork	5 Dennis Quay, Kinsale, Co. Cork
Tel: 021-477 9900 Fax: 021-477 2231	Tel: 021-477 2209 Fax: 021-477 4268	Tel: 021-477 4549 Fax: 021-477 4944
Email: res@actonshotelkinsale.com	Email: info@bluehavenkinsale.com	Email: captquarters@eircom.net
Web: www.actonshotelkinsale.com	Web: www.bluehavenkinsale.com	Web: www.captains-kinsale.com

HOTEL ★★★ MAP 2 H 2 | **HOTEL U MAP 2 H 3** | **GUESTHOUSE ★★★ MAP 2 H 2**

Superior 3 star hotel located in landscaped gardens overlooking Kinsale's beautiful harbour. Renowned for its welcoming and friendly atmosphere, Actons also features an award-winning restaurant (Kinsale Good Food Circle Member), bar/bistro, and health & fitness club with new lobby, lounges and gardens. Conference and banqueting facilities available. Located in the historic town of Kinsale with restaurants, pubs, cafés, art and craft shops. Activities nearby: golfing, fishing, sailing, walking, historical sites.

A luxury boutique style hotel situated in the heart of Kinsale. Recently refurbished, each room is individually furnished with exquisite furniture, the ultimate in luxury pocket sprung beds, plasma TVs and finer touches to make each room unique. The Blue Haven is famous for its fine cuisine and service excellence, superb dining experience in our luxurious restaurant 'Blu', our charming bar 'The Fishmarket' or our stylish café 'Café Blue'.

This Georgian period townhouse is situated close to the yacht club marina and within easy walking distance of restaurants and town centre amenities. It offers quality accommodation in a maritime ambience. The tranquil lounge on the 1st floor overlooks the harbour. The WHEELCHAIR ACCESSIBLE GROUND FLOOR ROOMS (1 twin / 1 single, sharing accessible shower / toilet) are also very convenient for the elderly. TV, direct dial phone, tea/coffee making facilities, hairdryer in all rooms.

Bookable on www.irelandhotels.com | *Bookable on www.irelandhotels.com*

B&B from €70.00 to €120.00 | **Room Rate from €160.00 to €220.00** | **B&B from €33.00 to €46.00**

Jack Walsh
General Manager

Activities:

Member of:

Ciarán Fitzgerald
Proprietor

Activities:

Member of:

Berny & Capt. Rudi
Teichmann
Co-Owners

Member of:

Special Offer: *Weekend Specials from €185.00 pps (2 Nights B&B & 1 Dinner)*

73 73

17 17

6 4

Closed 08 - 27 January	Open All Year	Open All Year

B&B Rates are per Person Sharing per Night incl. Breakfast.
or **Room Rates** are per Room per Night - See also Page 8

Cotters Quayside House

Pier Road,
Kinsale,
Co. Cork
Tel: 021-477 2188 Fax: 021-477 2664
Email: quaysidehouse@eircom.net
Web: www.euroka.com/quayside

GUESTHOUSE ★★★ MAP 2 H 2

A family-run guesthouse ideally located in a picturesque setting overlooking Kinsale Harbour adjacent to town centre, yachting marina and all amenities. All bedrooms are en suite with direct dial telephone, TV and tea/coffee making facilities. Kinsale's famous gourmet restaurants are all within walking distance and Kinsale Golf Club is just a five minute drive. Sea angling trips can be arranged.

B&B from €32.50 to €50.00

Mary Cotter

Member of:
IRISH HOTELS FEDERATION

🖶 📞 ☎🖵C❄☂♨♪♪🏃
6 6

Open All Year

Friar's Lodge

Friar's Street,
Kinsale,
Co. Cork
Tel: 021-477 7384 Fax: 021-477 4363
Email: mtierney@indigo.ie
Web: www.friars-lodge.com

GUESTHOUSE ★★★★ MAP 2 H 2

Welcome, Friar's Lodge is situated in the heart of beautiful award-winning, historical Kinsale. An ideal base for exploring the wonders of West Cork. All the rooms are luxurious, offering our guest every facility. A short stroll to the world famous restaurants and lively bars. Golfers welcomed, tee times can be arranged and we have a golf club drying room. Secure off street car park. RAC ◆◆◆◆◆, AA ◆◆◆◆.

Bookable on www.irelandhotels.com

B&B from €40.00 to €70.00

*Maureen Tierney
Owner*

🖶 📞 ☎🖵🔲TC♪P↑S♀✉ Inet WiFi
🐕
18 18

Closed 23 - 27 December

Jim Edwards

Market Quay,
Kinsale,
Co. Cork
Tel: 021-477 2541 Fax: 021-477 3228
Email: info@jimedwardskinsale.com
Web: www.jimedwardskinsale.com

GUESTHOUSE ★★ MAP 2 H 2

Family-run since 1971, Jim Edwards has a tradition of a warm, friendly welcome. All rooms are en suite and tastefully decorated with TV, telephone, tea/coffee making facilities. The guesthouse boasts an excellent seafood restaurant (fully licensed) which is a member of Kinsale Good Food Circle. The bar with its nautical theme throughout serves bar food all day. Situated in the heart of the town means easy access to all the lively bars and entertainment. Local amenities include golf, deep sea angling, sailing, horse riding.

B&B from €35.00 to €45.00

Jim Edwards

Special Offer: *Midweek Specials from €105.00 pps (3 Nights B&B)*

🖶 📞 ☎🖵CCM♪🖵⛽🏇
7 7

Open All Year

B&B Rates are per Person Sharing per Night incl. Breakfast.
or **Room Rates** are per Room per Night - See also Page 8

South West 61

Kinsale

Kilcaw House	Old Bank House	Tierney's Guest House
Kinsale, Situated On R600, Co. Cork	11 Pearse Street, Next To Post Office, Kinsale, Co. Cork	Main Street, Kinsale, Co. Cork
Tel: 021-477 4155 Fax: 021-477 4755	Tel: 021-477 4075 Fax: 021-477 4296	Tel: 021-477 2205 Fax: 021-477 4363
Email: info@kilcawhouse.com	Email: oldbank@indigo.ie	Email: info@tierneys-kinsale.com
Web: www.kilcawhouse.com	Web: www.oldbankhousekinsale.com	Web: www.tierneys-kinsale.com

GUESTHOUSE ★★★ MAP 2 H 2 | **GUESTHOUSE ★★★★ MAP 2 H 2** | **GUESTHOUSE ★★ MAP 2 H 2**

A family-run guesthouse, just 1km from Kinsale Town centre, with safe off the road parking and beautifully landscaped gardens. The guesthouse is built with a traditional flair yet is modern and luxurious. The bedrooms are spacious, furnished in antique pine, en suite with TV, phone and tea/coffee making facilities. Just a 20 minute drive from Cork Airport and ferry. An ideal base for touring Blarney, Cobh, West Cork and Old Head of Kinsale. We welcome you to experience the warmth and hospitality of our home.

The Old Bank House is a Georgian residence of great character and charm providing luxurious accommodation in the historic harbour town of Kinsale. Each bedroom has super king or twin beds, antique furniture and original art, whilst bathrooms are beautifully appointed with tub and shower, top quality toiletries and Egyptian cotton towels and bathrobes. Gourmet breakfast by award-winning Master Chef Michael Riese. Golf friendly and tee times arranged. Voted one of the "Top 100 Places to Stay in Ireland" every year since 1993. RAC ◆◆◆◆◆, AA ◆◆◆◆◆.

Tierney's Guesthouse is a well established guesthouse situated in the heart of award-winning Kinsale. We offer TV, hairdryer, tea/coffee in each room, all of which are en suite. Browse in our craft outlet and from Spring 2006 enjoy our courtyard conservatory café. A warm welcome is guaranteed and we will be only too happy to direct you to the many activities available and places to visit in Kinsale.

Member of Hidden Ireland

Bookable on www.irelandhotels.com

B&B from €30.00 to €45.00	B&B from €85.00 to €122.50	B&B from €30.00 to €45.00

Henry & Christina Mitchell Owners

Michael & Marie Riese Proprietors

Activities: ✓

Jeanette McCarthy Owner

Member of: IRISH HOTELS FEDERATION (all three)

7 7 | 17 17 | 9 9

Open All Year	Closed 01 - 28 December	Closed 23 - 26 December

B&B Rates are per Person Sharing per Night incl. Breakfast. or **Room Rates** are per Room per Night - See also Page 8

Trident Hotel

World's End,
Kinsale,
Co. Cork
Tel: 021-477 9300 Fax: 021-477 4173
Email: info@tridenthotel.com
Web: www.tridenthotel.com

HOTEL U MAP 2 H 2

The Trident enjoys an idyllic location on the water's edge in historic Kinsale with unrivalled views and award-winning cuisine. Extensively redeveloped in 2005, it now offers all of the facilities and services of a 4**** standard hotel including a choice of executive bedrooms & luxury suites. The Savannah Waterfront Restaurant is a member of Kinsale's Good Food Circle and holds an AA Rosette and 2 RAC Dining Awards. Enjoy scenic walks, explore Kinsale or just relax and enjoy the views.

Bookable on www.irelandhotels.com

B&B from €50.00 to €130.00

Hal McElroy
Managing Director

Activities:

Member of:

Special Offer: Weekend Specials from €120.00 pps
(2 Nights B&B & 1 Dinner)

75 75

Closed 24 - 26 December

White House

Pearse St. & The Glen,
Kinsale,
Co. Cork
Tel: 021-477 2125 Fax: 021-477 2045
Email: whitehse@indigo.ie
Web: www.whitehouse-kinsale.ie

GUESTHOUSE ★★★ MAP 2 H 2

The White House epitomises Kinsale hospitality with 3*** accommodation, Le Restaurant D'Antibes and a thoroughly modern bar and bistro where all the old values of guest satisfaction, comfort and value for money prevail. We have welcomed both visitors and locals since the 1850s and from its earliest days it has enjoyed a reputation for fine food, drinks of good cheer and indulgent service. Today we pride ourselves on enhancing that tradition. A member of Kinsale's Good Food Circle, West Cork Fuschia branding and Féile Bia Charter.

Member of Premier Guesthouses

B&B from €47.50 to €80.00

Michael & Rose Frawley
Proprietors

Activities:

Member of:

10 10

Closed 24 - 25 December

Castle Hotel & Leisure Centre

Main Street,
Macroom,
Co. Cork
Tel: 026-41074 Fax: 026-41505
Email: castlehotel@eircom.net
Web: www.castlehotel.ie

HOTEL ★★★ MAP 2 F 3

Nestled between Blarney and Killarney, Macroom is the ideal base to explore the scenic south west. Our extensive €5 million development features superior bedrooms and suites, "B's" award-winning restaurant (AA Rosette 92 - 05), "Dan Buckleys" bar (Black & White Munster hotel bar of the year), and 'The Ardilaun' conference and banqueting suite. Relax in our luxurious leisure centre or spoil yourself with a pamper treatment. Reduced green fees on Macroom's 18 hole golf course.

Bookable on www.irelandhotels.com
Member of Irish Country Hotels

B&B from €70.00 to €85.00

Don & Gerard Buckley
Proprietors

Member of:

Special Offer: Weekend Specials from €165.00 pps
(2 Nights B&B & 1 Dinner)

60 60

Closed 24 - 28 December

B&B Rates are per Person Sharing per Night incl. Breakfast.
or Room Rates are per Room per Night - See also Page 8

South West 63

Coolcower House

Coolcower,
Macroom,
Co. Cork
Tel: 026-41695 Fax: 026-42119
Email: coolcowerhouse@eircom.net

GUESTHOUSE ★★ MAP 2 F 3

Coolcower House is a large country residence on picturesque grounds. The house is ideally located within easy driving distance of all the tourist attractions in the Cork-Kerry region including Killarney, Kenmare, Kinsale, Blarney and Bantry. Located on the river's edge for coarse fishing and boating. Also outdoor tennis court. The restaurant offers the best of home produce on its à la carte and dinner menus. Fully licensed bar. TVs and tea/coffee making facilities, also direct dial telephones and hairdryers in all bedrooms.

B&B from €38.00 to €45.00

Evelyn Casey

Activities:

🐦

Member of:
IRISH HOTELS FEDERATION

Special Offer: Midweek Specials from €100.00 pps
(3 Nights B&B)

12 12

Closed 07 December - 07 March

Lee Valley Hotel

The North Square,
Macroom,
Co. Cork
Tel: 026-41082 Fax: 026-42148
Email: leevalleyhotel@eircom.net
Web: www.leevalleyhotel.com

HOTEL ★★ MAP 2 F 3

The Lee Valley Hotel (formerly The Victoria) is a newly refurbished boutique hotel situated in the heart of Macroom town. The ground floor which was extensively modernised now boasts a bistro, a luxurious bar, beer garden and reception. Live music on Thursdays and Sundays as well as late bar facilities at the weekend makes the Lee Valley Hotel ideal for a group or party destination. Recently upgraded rooms can be sought at excellent rates, with all mod cons available. Local attractions include angling, rock climbing, forest park, golf, pitch & putt and water sports.

B&B from €35.00 to €55.00

Robert McCarthy
Proprietor

Activities:

🐦🐦

Special Offer: Midweek Specials from €99.00 pps
(3 Nights B&B)

14 14

Closed 24 - 26 December

Hibernian Hotel and Leisure Centre

Main Street,
Mallow,
Co. Cork
Tel: 022-21588 Fax: 022-22632
Email: info@hibernianhotelmallow.com
Web: www.hibernianhotelmallow.com

HOTEL ★★★ MAP 2 G 4

The Hibernian Hotel and Leisure Centre is located in the centre of Mallow, at the heart of the Munster region within easy access of Cork, Limerick, Blarney and Killarney. The hotel boasts full leisure facilities including swimming pool, steam room, sauna, jacuzzi and gym. Conference rooms with Wi Fi, lively pub with evening entertainment and all day Coffee Dock. Spacious en suite rooms feature courtesy tray, iron, sattelite TV, phone and hairdryer.

Bookable on www.irelandhotels.com

B&B from €50.00 to €80.00

Shane McShortall
General Manager

Activities:

🐦🐦

Member of:
IRISH HOTELS FEDERATION

Special Offer: Weekend Specials from €100.00 pps
(2 Nights B&B & 1 Dinner)

54 54

Closed 25 December

Springfort Hall Hotel

Mallow,
Co. Cork

Tel: 022-21278 Fax: 022-21557
Email: stay@springfort-hall.com
Web: www.springfort-hall.com

HOTEL ★★★ MAP 2 G 4

Springfort Hall 18th century Georgian manor house, owned by the Walsh Family. Highly recommended restaurant, fully licensed bar, bedrooms en suite, colour TV and direct outside dial. 6km from Mallow off the Limerick Road, N20. Ideal for touring the South West, Blarney, Killarney, Ring of Kerry. Local amenities, 18-hole golf course, horse riding, angling on River Blackwater. Gulliver Central Reservations.

Bookable on www.irelandhotels.com

B&B from €65.00 to €85.00

*Walsh Family
Proprietors*

Activities:

Member of:

Special Offer: Midweek Specials from €145.00 pps
(3 Nights B&B)

49 49

Closed 24 - 26 December

B&B Rates are per Person Sharing per Night incl. Breakfast.
or Room Rates are per Room per Night - See also Page 8

John Jameson & Son's supreme selection from the Midleton Distillery, County Cork

AGED TO PERFECTION
AND BOTTLED IN THE YEAR
— 2001 —

JAMESON
IRISH WHISKEY

The Old Midleton Distillery, Co. Cork

GUIDED TOURS
10.00 a.m. – 6.00 p.m.
(last tour at 5.00 p.m.)
Open all year round, 7 days:
(Except Good Friday, Dec 25th, 26th, 27th & Jan 1st)

Also at the Distillery

The 'Malt House' Restaurant serving hot & cold lunches, gourmet salads & sandwiches, homemade bread & cakes and the most memorable Irish Coffee.

Jameson Gift & Whiskey Shop.

International Whiskey Delivery Service:
callsave: 1850 22 0002 or
faxsave: 1850 330003 or
email: gift.deliveries@idl.ie

The Old Midleton Distillery, Distillery Walk, Midleton, Co. Cork
Tel: 00 353 21 4613594
Fax: 00 353 21 4613642
www.whiskeytours.ie

Discover for yourself how Jameson became the world's favourite Irish Whiskey!

Co. Cork

Midleton / Mitchelstown

Barnabrow Country House	Midleton Park Hotel & Spa	Fir Grove Hotel

Barnabrow Country House

Cloyne,
Midleton,
East Cork
Tel: 021-465 2534 Fax: 021-465 2534
Email: barnabrow@eircom.net
Web: www.barnabrowhouse.ie

GUESTHOUSE ★★★ MAP 313

17th century family-run country house set in 35 acres of parkland adjacent to the historic village of Cloyne (580 AD). The house has been extensively refurbished to offer a perfect blend of old world charm & new world comfort. Trinity Rooms, our new restaurant, provides a unique venue for that special celebration. This is the perfect setting to relax and soak up an atmosphere of peaceful unhurried living with log fires and candlelit dinners. Nearby: Ballymaloe & Stephen Pearse Pottery.

B&B from €60.00 to €85.00

Geraldine O'Brien
Proprietor

Member of:

19 19

Closed 24 - 28 December

Midleton Park Hotel & Spa

Old Cork Road,
Midleton,
Co. Cork
Tel: 021-463 5100 Fax: 021-463 5101
Email: resv@midletonpark.com
Web: www.midletonpark.com

HOTEL U MAP 313

The Midleton Park Hotel & Spa of 4 star standard is ideal for business or pleasure. Located 20 minutes drive east of Cork City in the bustling town of Midleton. The hotel boasts luxurious guest rooms and award-winning leisure facilities. Our wellness centre and spa specialises in alternative therapies and treatments designed to revitalise body and mind. Local attractions include Old Midleton Distillery, Fota Wildlife Park and Queenstown Story. Tailored golf packages available on request.

Bookable on www.irelandhotels.com

B&B from €65.00 to €85.00

Clodagh O'Donovan
Deputy General Manager

Member of:

*Special Offer: Weekend Specials from €140.00 pps
(2 Nights B&B & 1 Dinner)*

79 79

Closed 24 - 26 December

Fir Grove Hotel

Cahir Hill,
Mitchelstown,
Co. Cork
Tel: 025-24111 Fax: 025-84541
Email: info@firgrovehotel.com
Web: www.firgrovehotel.com

HOTEL ★★ MAP 315

The Fir Grove Hotel is a modern newly renovated hotel, set in its own grounds in the shadow of the Galtee Mountains. Situated on the N8, main Cork/Dublin route, we are the ideal base for touring Munster. Our Mulberry Restaurant and Gradoge Bar serve good local food at affordable prices. All bedrooms are en suite with multi channel TV. Local facilities include golf, fishing, hill walks, pony-trekking and Mitchelstown Caves.

B&B from €40.00 to €60.00

Brenda & Pat Tangney
Proprietors

Member of:

14 14

Closed 24 - 26 December

B&B Rates are per Person Sharing per Night incl. Breakfast.
or **Room Rates** are per Room per Night - See also Page 8

Celtic Ross Hotel Conference & Leisure Centre

Rosscarbery,
West Cork

Tel: 023-48722 Fax: 023-48723
Email: info@celticrosshotel.com
Web: www.celticrosshotel.com

HOTEL ★★★ MAP 2 F 1

West Cork is an area of outstanding beauty; the Celtic Ross Hotel nestled in Rosscarbery Bay, is at the heart of this charming and historical region - the ideal base for touring West Cork and the Islands. Superior 3 star hotel with 66 well appointed rooms, many with sea views. Druids Restaurant offers table d'hôte and à la carte menu, our Kingfisher bar and lounge offers high quality meals all day. Conference and banqueting facilities for up to 250 people. Leisure centre: 15m heated pool, bubble pool, baby pool, steam room, sauna and gym. Beauty and massage therapies in our Holistic Suite!

Bookable on www.irelandhotels.com
Member of Select Hotels

B&B from €65.00 to €110.00

Peter McDermott
Managing Director

Activities:

Member of:

Special Offer: Weekend Specials from €135.00 pps
(2 Nights B&B & 1 Dinner)

66 66

Closed 02 - 23 January

Corthna-Lodge Guesthouse

Airhill,
Schull,
Co. Cork

Tel: 028-28517 Fax: 028-28032
Email: info@corthna-lodge.net
Web: www.corthna-lodge.net

GUESTHOUSE ★★★ MAP 1 D 1

Charming high standard guesthouse in a quiet setting, within walking distance of the lovely Schull Village and harbour. It is an ideal base for all activities such as walking, sailing, golfing, horse trekking, whale watching etc. Boat trips to Sherkin Island and Cape Clear. Our large garden, with an outdoor hot tub, is the ideal place to relax. All our nicely decorated bedrooms are en suite with TV, phone and hairdryer. Free use of our gym, petanque field and putting green, as well as our BBQ and picnic area . We take Mastercard, Visa and Laser Cards.

B&B from €40.00 to €65.00

Andrea & Martin Mueller
Owners

Member of:

7 7

Closed 01 October - 15 April

B&B Rates are per Person Sharing per Night incl. Breakfast.
or Room Rates are per Room per Night - See also Page 8

Co. Cork

Shanagarry / Skibbereen

Ballymaloe House

Shanagarry,
Midleton,
Co. Cork
Tel: 021-465 2531 Fax: 021-465 2021
Email: res@ballymaloe.ie
Web: www.ballymaloe.ie

GUESTHOUSE ★★★★ MAP 3 J 3

A large country house on a 400 acre farm near the coast, owned and run by the Allen family. Home and locally grown produce is served in the award-winning restaurant. Small golf course, tennis court, outdoor pool, woodlands, gardens and pleasant walks are on the premises, also a craft and kitchen shop. The Ballymaloe Cookery School is nearby. Sea and river fishing can be arranged. Approx. 6 miles south of the N25 highway. Turn off outside Midleton or at Castlemartyr. Two miles beyond Cloyne on the Ballycotton Road. See map no 3. Also closed 12 - 19 January.

Member of Ireland's Blue Book

B&B from €105.00 to €150.00

Myrtle Allen
Proprietor

Activities:

Member of:

33 33

Closed 23 - 26 December

Garryvoe Hotel

Ballycotton Bay,
Shanagarry,
Co. Cork
Tel: 021-464 6718 Fax: 021-464 6824
Email: res@garryvoehotel.com
Web: www.garryvoehotel.com

HOTEL ★★ MAP 3 J 3

The coastal location of Garryvoe Hotel directly overlooking 5 km of one of Ireland's finest beaches, is an ideal holiday destination. The hotel provides the holidaymakers with a warm and friendly feeling which will be long remembered. This beautiful area of Cork has an abundance of sporting and leisure pursuits. Combined with the above and only 30 minutes drive from Cork City, Garryvoe Hotel has added 38 new bedrooms to compliment the spectacular views from the hotel.

Bookable on www.irelandhotels.com
Member of Irish Country Hotels

B&B from €75.00 to €85.00

Stephen Belton
General Manager

Member of:

Special Offer: *Weekend Specials from €145.00 pps (2 Nights B&B & 1 Dinner)*

55 55

Closed 24 - 25 December

West Cork Hotel

Ilen Street,
Skibbereen,
Co. Cork
Tel: 028-21277 Fax: 028-22333
Email: info@westcorkhotel.com
Web: www.westcorkhotel.com

HOTEL ★★★ MAP 2 E 1

The West Cork Hotel offers one of the warmest welcomes you will find in Ireland, and combines old-fashioned courtesy with the comfort of tastefully decorated and well-equipped accommodation. Guests can enjoy the friendly bar atmosphere or dine in the elegant restaurant. However long your stay, the West Cork Hotel is the perfect base from which to discover and explore the glorious surroundings and activities available in West Cork.

B&B from €52.00 to €80.00

David Harney
General Manager

Activities:

Member of:

Special Offer: *Weekend Specials from €115.50 pps (2 Nights B&B & 1 Dinner)*

30 30

Closed 22 - 28 December

B&B Rates are per Person Sharing per Night incl. Breakfast. or Room Rates are per Room per Night - See also Page 8

Aherne's Townhouse & Seafood Restaurant

163 North Main Street,
Youghal,
Co. Cork
Tel: 024-92424 Fax: 024-93633
Email: ahernes@eircom.net
Web: www.ahernes.com

GUESTHOUSE ★★★★ MAP 3 J 3

Open turf fires and the warmest of welcomes await you in this family-run guesthouse in the historic walled port of Youghal. Our rooms exude comfort and luxury, stylishly furnished with antiques and paintings. Our restaurant and bar food menus specialise in the freshest of locally landed seafood. Youghal is on the N25, 35 minutes from Cork Airport and is a golfer's paradise. There are 18 golf courses within 1 hour's drive. Find us in Ireland's Blue Book and other leading guides. Old Head of Kinsale 50 minutes drive.

Bookable on www.irelandhotels.com
Member of Ireland's Blue Book

B&B from €80.00 to €115.00

The Fitzgibbon Family

Activities:

Member of:
IRISH HOTELS FEDERATION

🖅 🐾 ☎️🖥️🅃🄲🧵CM🎵🄿🅂📠🆒🐕
13 13

Closed 23 - 29 December

Quality Hotel and Leisure Centre Youghal

Redbarn,
Youghal,
Co. Cork
Tel: 024-93050 Fax: 024-20699
Email: info@qualityhotelyoughal.com
Web: www.qualityhotelyoughal.com

HOTEL N MAP 3 J 3

Commanding the perfect location on the beach at Redbarn, among the many blue flag beaches around Youghal, with breathtaking views of the Atlantic Ocean. Facilities include Club Vitae leisure centre with 4 treatment and therapy rooms, 2 outdoor floodlit pitches, childrens' playground, Lannigans Restaurant and Bar with superb sea views. The resort offers a range of different room types including double en suite, family rooms and apartments with special family facilities. Demand is high for our sea view apartments where a supplement applies.

Bookable on www.irelandhotels.com
Member of Quality Hotels

B&B from €39.00 to €99.00

*Allen McEnery
General Manager*

Activities:

Member of:
IRISH HOTELS FEDERATION

Special Offer: Weekend Specials from €109.00 pps
(2 Nights B&B & 1 Dinner)

🖅 🐾 ☎️🖥️🅃/🄰🧵🄲CMCS✳️🆒
24 24
🖥️🍺🎵🎵🄿🅂🆒🖥️ inet 🐾

Closed 20 - 26 December

Skibbereen Heritage Centre

The Great Famine Commemoration Exhibition uses today's multimedia to bring this period of Irish history to life.

Lough Hyne Visitor Centre reveals the unique nature of Ireland's first Marine Nature Reserve.

GENEALOGY INFORMATION

All situated in a beautifully restored historic riverside building with features on the Old Gasworks and its history

Open: 10am to 6pm, with last admission at 5.15pm 7 day opening during high season (mid May to Mid September)

Tuesday to Saturday February to mid May and mid September to the end of November.

Winter opening by appointment

Old Gas Works Building, Upper Bridge Street, Skibbereen, West Cork.

Telephone: 028 40900
info@skibbheritage.com
www.skibbheritage.com

B&B Rates are per Person Sharing per Night incl. Breakfast.
or **Room Rates** are per Room per Night - See also Page 8

Co. Cork - Co. Kerry
Youghal / Ballinskelligs / Ballybunion

Walter Raleigh Hotel

O'Brien Place,
Youghal,
Co. Cork
Tel: 024-92011 Fax: 024-93560
Email: walterraleighhotel@eircom.net
Web: www.walterraleighhotel.com

HOTEL ★★★ MAP 3 J 3

Breathtaking sea views, a warm welcome and an ideal location for tourists and golfers alike await you at the Walter Raleigh Hotel. Combining luxury with a taste of country living, a sea-front location beside a beautiful green park, spectacular sea views, close to golf and Youghal's pristine blue flag beach, coastline and countryside. We guarantee you a comfortable and pleasant stay at the Walter Raleigh Hotel. Golf packages a speciality.

B&B from €45.00 to €75.00

Eoin Daly
General Manager

Activities:

Member of:

Special Offer: Weekend Specials from €120.00 pps
(2 Nights B&B & 1 Dinner)

40 40

Closed 24 - 25 December

Ballinskelligs Inn

Ballinskelligs,
Co. Kerry
Tel: 066-947 9104 Fax: 066-947 9418
Email: ballinskelligsinn@eircom.net
Web: www.ballinskelligsinn.com

GUESTHOUSE P MAP 1 B 3

The Ballinskelligs Inn has hosted visitors for over 100 years. Located on one of Ireland's premier Blue Flag beaches, awaken to the sound of gentle surf rolling along the beautiful sandy beach at the end of the gardens. Stroll to the castle or perhaps further to the 12th century abbey. Breathtaking scenery will allow you to relax, have a drink & eat at your leisure. Meals served 12 to 9:30pm Mon - Sun. Parties, weddings catered for. Beach is only 1 minute walk from hotel and we have fishing boats to rent. Horse riding & trips to the Skelligs can be arranged. So many places to go and see.

Bookable on www.irelandhotels.com

B&B from €35.00 to €45.00

Charlie McGowan
Manager

Special Offer: Stay 5 Nights and 6th is Free

14 14

Open All Year

19th Lodge (The)

Golf Links Road,
Ballybunion,
Co. Kerry
Tel: 068-27592 Fax: 068-27830
Email: the19thlodge@eircom.net
Web: www.the19thlodgeballybunion.com

GUESTHOUSE ★★★★ MAP 5 D 6

The 19th Lodge is a golfer's paradise. Aptly named for its enviable location directly opposite Ballybunion's famous links. Good five iron to first tee. Guaranteed tee times on Ballybunion old course are available for residents of our golf lodge. Magnificent air-conditioned bedrooms overlooking the links with stunning views. Enjoy your breakfast while you watch others tee off. Golf storage and drying room and green fee concessions for our valued guests.

B&B from €60.00 to €100.00

Mary & James Beasley
Owners

Member of:

12 12

Closed 18 December - 02 January

B&B Rates are per Person Sharing per Night incl. Breakfast. or **Room Rates** are per Room per Night - See also Page 8

Cashen Course House

Golf Links,
Ballybunion,
Co. Kerry
Tel: 068-27351 Fax: 068-28934
Email: golfstay@eircom.net
Web: www.playballybunion.com

GUESTHOUSE ★★★★ MAP 5 D 6

Welcome to our luxury guesthouse overlooking Ballybunion's famous golf courses with panoramic views of golf links, Cashen River & countryside. After a day's golf, relax in our magnificent rooms & enjoy a jacuzzi bath in one of our luxurious bathrooms. Air-con, DD phone, computer access, trouser press. Small groups welcome for conference/golfing breaks. Beside Clubhouse. Private parking for buses & cars. Concession green fees October to June incl. Golf packages for Ballybunion Old Course & Cashen Course. Drying room. AA ◆◆◆◆◆.

B&B from €50.00 to €90.00

Deirdre O'Brien
Owner / Manager

Activities:
✓

Member of:
IRISH HOTELS FEDERATION

🏠🦮 ☎️📠🆃©🚗CM❄️🕓✓JPSY♨️ Inet
9 9 🐕

Closed 01 November - 01 March

Eagle Lodge

Ballybunion,
Co. Kerry

Tel: 068-27224

GUESTHOUSE U MAP 5 D 6

Owner managed, delightful guesthouse situated in town centre. All bedrooms with bathrooms and central heating throughout. A beautiful lounge and private car park for guests. Local amenities include two championship golf courses, sea fishing, tennis, pitch and putt, swimming and boating. Extra value reduced green fees at Ballybunion Golf Club. Cliff walks and surfing also available.

B&B from €35.00 to €60.00

Mildred Gleasure

Member of:
IRISH HOTELS FEDERATION

🏠🦮 ☎️📠🆃©CMJPS
8 8

Open All Year

Harty Costello Town House

Main Street,
Ballybunion,
Co. Kerry
Tel: 068-27129 Fax: 068-27489
Email: hartycostello@eircom.net
Web: www.hartycostello.com

GUESTHOUSE ★★★★ MAP 5 D 6

Four star townhouse with traditional bar and seafood restaurant, in the centre of Ballybunion just a short walk from the beach. The en suite bedrooms are spacious and have been refurbished in a refreshing modern style with satellite TV and direct dial phone. The townhouse has an informal atmosphere and is a charming base from which to enjoy links golf and the beauty of Kerry. Local amenities, two championship golf links, cliff walks, hot seaweed baths, fishing, four golden beaches, bird watching & pony trekking. Tee times available for Old Course & Cashen.

Bookable on www.irelandhotels.com
Member of Ballybunion Marketing Group

B&B from €60.00 to €95.00

Davnet & Jackie Hourigan
Owners

Activities:
✓

Member of:
IRISH HOTELS FEDERATION

Special Offer: Weekend Specials from €130.00 pps
(2 Nights B&B & 1 Dinner)

🏠🦮 ☎️📠🆃U✓J🆂♨️ 🔤♨️
8 8

Closed 30 October - 01 April

B&B Rates are per Person Sharing per Night incl. Breakfast.
or **Room Rates** are per Room per Night - See also Page 8

Marine Links Hotel

Sandhill Road,
Ballybunion,
Co. Kerry
Tel: 068-27139 Fax: 068-27666
Email: info@marinelinkshotel.com
Web: www.marinelinkshotel.com

HOTEL ★★ MAP 5 D 6

Overlooking the mouth of the River Shannon and the Atlantic Ocean, a warm welcome awaits you at the Marine Links Hotel from the Nagle Family and all the staff. Our hotel is committed to providing excellent food and good service and we have been awarded the RAC Merit Award for hospitality for the past number of years.

B&B from €40.00 to €75.00

Derek Nagle
Proprietor / General Manager

Member of:

11 11

Closed 31 October - 01 April

Teach de Broc

Link Road,
Ballybunion,
Co. Kerry
Tel: 068-27581 Fax: 068-27919
Email: teachdebroc@eircom.net
Web: www.ballybuniongolf.com

GUESTHOUSE ★★★★ MAP 5 D 6

Tea to tee in 2 minutes is a reality when you stay at the 4**** accommodation offered at Teach de Broc. Awarded Guesthouse / Country house of the Year 2005 by the Irish Golf Tour Operators Association. With its enviable location directly opposite the entrance gates to Ballybunion Golf Club, you can enjoy the personal attention that is synonymous with this golfer's haven. Tee times are available through Teach de Broc which is an ideal base for golfers with ease of access to Lahinch, Doonbeg and Tralee. Visit our website at www.ballybuniongolf.com

Bookable on www.irelandhotels.com
Member of Ballybunion Marketing Group

B&B from €60.00 to €100.00

Seamus & Aoife Brock
Owners

Member of:

14 14

Closed 15 December - 15 March

Derrynane Hotel

Caherdaniel,
Ring Of Kerry,
Co. Kerry
Tel: 066-947 5136 Fax: 066-947 5160
Email: info@derrynane.com
Web: www.derrynane.com

HOTEL ★★★ MAP 1 C 2

Amidst the most spectacular scenery in Ireland, halfway round the famous Ring of Kerry (on the N70) lies the Derrynane Hotel. 70 en suite bedrooms. Facilities: 15m outdoor heated pool, steam room, sauna, gym, luxurious seaweed bath suite, childrens' games room, tennis court & gardens. We are surrounded by beautiful beaches, hills, lovely walks & Derrynane House & National Park. Deep sea angling, lake fishing, golf, horse riding, seasports, boat trips to Skelligs Rock all within short distance. Hotel's own walking guide with maps to the area. Georgina Campbell Family Hotel of the Year 2005.

Bookable on www.irelandhotels.com

B&B from €75.00 to €95.00

Mary O'Connor
Manager / Director

Activities:

Member of:

Special Offer: *Special Offers Available*

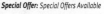
70 70

Closed 02 October - 12 April

B&B Rates are per Person Sharing per Night incl. Breakfast.
or **Room Rates** are per Room per Night - See also Page 8

Scarriff Inn	Ring Of Kerry Hotel	Ard-Na-Sidhe

Scarriff Inn
Caherdaniel,
Co. Kerry

Tel: 066-947 5132 Fax: 066-947 5425
Email: scarriff1@aol.com
Web: www.caherdaniel.net

Ring Of Kerry Hotel
Valentia Road,
Cahersiveen,
Co. Kerry

Tel: 066-947 2543 Fax: 066-947 2893
Email: ringhotel@eircom.net
Web: www.ringofkerryhotel.ie

Ard-Na-Sidhe
Caragh Lake,
Killorglin,
Co. Kerry

Tel: 066-976 9105 Fax: 066-976 9282
Email: sales@kih.liebherr.com
Web: www.killarneyhotels.ie

GUESTHOUSE ★★ MAP 1 C 3 | **HOTEL U MAP 1 B 3** | **HOTEL ★★★★ MAP 1 D 4**

This family-run guesthouse overlooks the best view in Ireland, with majestic views of Derrynane, Kenmare and Bantry Bay, situated halfway round the Ring of Kerry. All our rooms have sea views. Dine in our seafood restaurant and enjoy outstanding cuisine as recommended by Sir Andrew Lloyd Webber or relax in our Vista Bar and enjoy scenery and ambience. The area is varied in activities with, the Kerry Way and several beautiful beaches within walking distance. Day trips to the Skellig Rocks.

This is a small family-run hotel located on the coast, close to Blue Flag beaches. Bar, restaurant, health & beauty salon and comfortable rooms, some with a jacuzzi. We offer regular live music, board games and information on local heritage. Enjoy the friendly atmosphere, excellent cuisine and discover beautiful South Kerry. Bíodh sos, suaimhneas agus spóirt agat. Fáilte roimh gach éinne.

18 bedroom 4**** de luxe Victorian mansion delightfully located in its own park on Caragh Lake. Tastefully furnished with antiques and open fireplaces. Luxurious lounges and restaurant. Free boating, fishing and facilities of sister hotels - Hotel Europe and Hotel Dunloe Castle - available to guests. 10 major golf courses nearby. Special green fees. Central Reservations Tel: 064-71350 Fax: 064-37900.

Bookable on www.irelandhotels.com
Member of Killarney Hotels Ltd

Bookable on www.irelandhotels.com

B&B from €40.00 to €55.00 | **B&B from €35.00 to €70.00** | **B&B from €75.00 to €105.00**

 Katie O'Carroll Proprietor — Member of: IRISH HOTELS FEDERATION

 Marian O'Sullivan Manager — Member of: IRISH HOTELS FEDERATION
Special Offer: Special Offers Available

 Adrian O'Sullivan — Activities:
Special Offer: Weekend Specials from €205.00 pps (2 Nights B&B & 1 Dinner)

6 6 | 23 23 | 18 18

Closed 01 November - 01 April | **Open All Year** | **Closed 03 October - 01 May**

Co. Kerry
Caragh Lake / Castlegregory

Carrig Country House

Caragh Lake,
Killorglin,
Co. Kerry
Tel: 066-976 9100 Fax: 066-976 9166
Email: info@carrighouse.com
Web: www.carrighouse.com

GUESTHOUSE ★★★★ MAP 1 D 4

Charming Victorian Manor on acres of woodlands & gardens (935 plant species) running down to the lake shore. Furnished in period style with antique furniture. Central to 12 superb golf courses, fishing, shooting, hill walking or just lazing by the fireside with a good book. Critically acclaimed restaurant (open to non residents). Ideal for touring the Ring of Kerry, Dingle & Killarney. Recommended by Bridgestone Guide, 100 Best Places to Stay in Ireland 2005, Georgina Campbell's Jameson Guide, AA "Country House of the Year" Ireland 2004.

Bookable on www.irelandhotels.com
Member of Private Ireland

B&B from €70.00 to €135.00

Frank & Mary Slattery
Hosts / Proprietors

Activities:

Member of:

16 16

Closed 01 December - 01 March

Crutch's Hillville House Hotel

Conor Pass Road, Castlegregory,
Dingle Peninsula,
Co. Kerry
Tel: 066-713 8118 Fax: 066-713 8159
Email: macshome@iol.ie
Web: www.dinglehotel.com

HOTEL ★★ MAP 1 C 5

Step back in time at this delightful country house hotel overlooking Brandon Bay on the scenic Dingle Peninsula. Bedrooms are tastefully decorated, a number offering seaviews, 4 poster beds, all with spacious bathrooms. We offer a friendly country house atmosphere with a cosy bar & open fires. The restaurant offers traditional home cooking using local fresh produce & has an established reputation for fine foods & wine. Located 4km west of Stadbally Village on the Conor Pass Road. Local activities: golf, walks, sea & river fishing, surf & dive schools, pony trekking, bird watching & island tours.

Bookable on www.irelandhotels.com
Member of Irish Country Hotels

B&B from €45.00 to €85.00

Ron & Sandra
Proprietors

Special Offer: 3 Nights Dinner, B&B from €225.00 pps

19 19
inet

Open All Year

Harbour House & Leisure Centre

Scraggane Pier,
Castlegregory,
Co. Kerry
Tel: 066-713 9292 Fax: 066-713 9557
Email: stay@iol.ie
Web: www.maharees.ie

GUESTHOUSE N MAP 1 C 5

The family-run Harbour House is superbly located on the tip of the Maharees Peninsula and has its own indoor heated swimming pool, sauna and gym. Its Islands Restaurant has panoramic views of the breathtaking scenery of the Maharees Islands and offers an excellent range of locally caught seafood, prime steak, meat and vegetarian dishes. If you want tranquillity, serenity, charm and true Irish hospitality, this is the place for you. Local amenities include golf, walking, scuba diving, windsurfing, surfing, fishing, horse riding, cycling etc.

Bookable on www.irelandhotels.com

B&B from €35.00 to €45.00

Pat & Ronnie Fitzgibbon

Member of:

15 15
alc inet

Closed 15 December - 03 January

B&B Rates are per Person Sharing per Night incl. Breakfast. or **Room Rates** are per Room per Night - See also Page 8

Co. Kerry

Cloghane / Dingle (An Daingean)

O'Connor's Guesthouse

Cloghane,
Dingle Peninsula,
Co. Kerry
Tel: 066-713 8113 Fax: 066-713 8270
Email: oconnorsguesthouse@eircom.net
Web: www.cloghane.com

GUESTHOUSE ★★ MAP 1 B 5

A long established, spacious country home with spectacular views of sea and mountains, overlooking Brandon Bay and within easy reach of Dingle on the Dingle Way. Private car park, guest lounge, open fire, home cooked meals, pub and a warm welcome are just some of the things awaiting our guests.

B&B from €30.00 to €50.00

Micheal & Elizabeth O'Dowd
Owners

Member of:

Special Offer: Week Partial Board from €350.00 pps
(7 Nights B&B & 7 Dinners)

Closed 01 November - 28 February

Alpine House

Mail Road,
Dingle,
Co. Kerry
Tel: 066-915 1250 Fax: 066-915 1966
Email: alpinedingle@eircom.net
Web: www.alpineguesthouse.com

GUESTHOUSE ★★★ MAP 1 B 4

Superb guesthouse run by the O'Shea Family. AA ♦♦♦♦ and RAC ♦♦♦♦ highly acclaimed. Elegant en suite bedrooms with TV, direct dial phone, hairdryers, central heating and tea/coffee facilities. Spacious dining room with choice of breakfast. Delightful guest lounge. 2 minutes walk to town centre, restaurants, harbour and bus stop. Local amenities include Slea Head Drive and Blasket Islands. Also pony trekking, angling and boat trips to Fungi the dolphin. Non-smoking premises.

B&B from €35.00 to €48.00

Paul O'Shea
Proprietor

Member of:

Open All Year

An Bothar Guesthouse, Restaurant & Bar

Cuas, Ballydavid,
Dingle Peninsula, Tralee,
Co Kerry
Tel: 066-915 5342
Email: botharpub@eircom.net
Web: www.botharpub.com

GUESTHOUSE ★★★ MAP 1 B 5

An Bothar Guesthouse, Restaurant and Bar is a family-run guesthouse and pub situated at the foot of Mount Brandon just 7 miles from Dingle. An ideal base for a walking holiday close to beaches fishing and golf. In the heart of the Gaeltacht, Gaelic is the first language of the house. À la carte menu and bar food available during season, March to September. Meals arranged by request out of season. Home-baking and local produce on menu.

B&B from €40.00 to €55.00

Maurice Walsh
Owner

Member of:

Special Offer: Midweek Specials from €120.00 pps
(3 Nights B&B)

Closed 24 - 25 December

<u>B&B Rates</u> are per Person Sharing per Night incl. Breakfast.
or <u>Room Rates</u> are per Room per Night - See also Page 8

Dingle (An Daingean)

An Portán	Bambury's Guest House	Barr na Sraide Inn

An Portán

Dunquin,
Co. Kerry

Tel: 066-915 6212
Email: donn@eircom.net
Web: www.anportan.com

Bambury's Guest House

Mail Road,
Dingle,
Co. Kerry

Tel: 066-915 1244 Fax: 066-915 1786
Email: info@bamburysguesthouse.com
Web: www.bamburysguesthouse.com

Barr na Sraide Inn

Upper Main Street,
Dingle,
Co. Kerry

Tel: 066-915 1331 Fax: 066-915 1446
Email: barrnasraide@eircom.net
Web: www.barrnasraide.com

GUESTHOUSE N MAP 1 B 4

Located in Dún Chaoin, the most westerly village in Ireland, opposite Blasket Islands. 15 - 20 minute drive from An Daingean / Dingle. Blasket ferry 1km, 18 hole golf links 4 km, horse riding 4.5 km, shore angling. Award-winning restaurant fully licensed, small conference room, 14 bedrooms each with separate entrance in secluded setting. Private car park.

GUESTHOUSE ★★★ MAP 1 B 4

AA Selected ♦♦♦♦, new house, excellent location, 2 minutes walk to town centre. Offering peaceful accommodation in spacious, double, twin or triple rooms all en suite with direct dial telephone and satellite TV. Attractive guest lounge to relax in. Private car parking, choice of breakfast in spacious dining room. Local attractions, Dingle Peninsula, horse riding, angling and golf on local 18 hole golf links. Reduced green fees can be arranged. Listed in all leading guides.

GUESTHOUSE ★★★ MAP 1 B 4

Family-run guesthouse and bar. Located in the town centre. The Barr na Sraide Inn has been recently refurbished to a very high standard. An extensive menu awaits our guests for breakfast. End each day with a relaxing drink in our comfortable bar amongst the locals. Private enclosed car park. Ideal base for your stay in the South West. Golf, fishing, sailing, cycling, horse riding and trips to Fungi the dolphin available nearby.

Bookable on www.irelandhotels.com

B&B from €35.00 to €35.00

Rónán O'Donnchadha

B&B from €35.00 to €60.00

Bernie Bambury
Proprietor

Member of:
IRISH HOTELS FEDERATION

B&B from €35.00 to €60.00

Patricia Geaney

Member of:
IRISH HOTELS FEDERATION

Special Offer: *Weekend Specials from €90.00 pps*
(2 Nights B&B & 1 Dinner)

🛏🏠 ☎️🖥️📺CM🅿️🅿️Ⓢ📶♨🐕
14 14

🛏🏠 ☎️🖥️🛏🅿️
12 12

🛏🏠 ☎️🖥️Ⓒ🗑🅿️🛏♨
22 22

Closed 01 October - 01 April	Open All Year	Closed 18 - 26 December

B&B Rates are per Person Sharing per Night incl. Breakfast.
or <u>Room Rates</u> are per Room per Night - See also Page 8

Boland's Guesthouse

Upper Main Street,
Dingle,
Co. Kerry
Tel: 066-915 1426
Email: bolanddingle@eircom.net
Web: www.ireland.com

GUESTHOUSE ★★ MAP 1 B 4

Boland's Guesthouse is situated at the top of Main Street overlooking Dingle Bay. Minutes walk to restaurants, pubs, entertainment, fishing, golfing, horse riding, hill walking and trips to Fungi the dolphin. Our guest rooms are bright and spacious with modern amenities, some with views of Dingle Bay. Full breakfast is served in our conservatory dining room. You can relax in our guest lounge overlooking Dingle Bay.

Bookable on www.irelandhotels.com

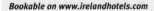

B&B from €30.00 to €50.00

Breda Boland
Owner

🛏 🐾 ☎ ▯ Ⓣ Ⓒ ↺ ⋃ ♪ 🏇
8   8

Closed 20 - 31 December

Castlewood House

The Wood,
Dingle,
Co. Kerry
Tel: 066-915 2788
Email: castlewoodhouse@eircom.net
Web: www.castlewooddingle.com

GUESTHOUSE P MAP 1 B 4

At Castlewood House a warm welcome awaits you. Luxurious new guesthouse located on the shores of Dingle Bay offering de luxe and superior rooms. All rooms are spacious and individually styled to a very high standard. Facilities include en suite bathrooms, pressure showers, TV, DD phone, internet access and hospitality tray. Elevator access. Speciality breakfast served in our dining room with its collection of Irish art, or relax in our drawing room with spectacular views of Dingle Bay.

B&B from €49.00 to €90.00

Helen Woods Heaton & Brian Heaton

Member of:

IRISH
HOTELS
FEDERATION

🛏 🐾 ☎ ▯ ▤ Ⓣ Ⓒ ❋ ⋃ ♪ Ⓟ 🏇 Inet
12   12

Closed 10 January - 14 February

Coastline Guesthouse

The Wood,
Dingle,
Co. Kerry
Tel: 066-915 2494 Fax: 066-915 2493
Email: coastlinedingle@eircom.net
Web: www.coastlinedingle.com

GUESTHOUSE ★★★ MAP 1 B 4

Beautiful new seafront guesthouse on the water's edge of Dingle Bay. All rooms are en suite with direct dial phone, TV, hairdryer, tea/coffee facilities and all have panoramic views of the harbour. Ground floor rooms available. Enjoy our excellent breakfast. Relax in our guest lounge and watch the local fishing fleet return with their catch. Private car park. Restful garden. 5 minute walk to town centre. Ideal base to enjoy all Dingle has to offer - excellent restaurants and pubs.

B&B from €35.00 to €47.00

Vivienne O'Shea
Proprietor

Member of:
IRISH
HOTELS
FEDERATION

🛏 🐾 ☎ ▯ Ⓣ ❋ ♪ Ⓟ Ⓢ ▤
7   7

Closed 18 November - 10 February

<u>B&B Rates</u> are per Person Sharing per Night incl. Breakfast.
or <u>Room Rates</u> are per Room per Night - See also Page 8

Dingle (An Daingean)

Dingle Bay Hotel	Dingle Benners Hotel	Dingle Skellig Hotel & Peninsula Spa

Dingle Bay Hotel

Strand Street,
Dingle,
Co. Kerry

Tel: 066-915 1231 Fax: 066-915 2740
Email: info@dinglebayhotel.com
Web: www.dinglebayhotel.com

HOTEL N MAP 1 B 4

Newly built luxury hotel, perfectly situated by the pier/marina in the heart of Dingle Town. The family owned hotel has been designed to the highest standards, from its stylish bar to its tastefully furnished bedrooms. Paudie's Bar and Long's Restaurant offer exceptional food and outstanding service. Seafood a speciality. The hotel offers regular live entertainment. Guests receive discounts at the nearby Harmony Health Club and Dingle Golf Links.

B&B from €50.00 to €110.00

Kathleen Sheehy
General Manager

Member of:
IRISH HOTELS FEDERATION

Special Offer: Midweek Specials from €99.00 pps (3 Nights B&B)

25 25

inet

Closed 18 - 26 December

Dingle Benners Hotel

Main Street,
Dingle,
Co. Kerry

Tel: 066-915 1638 Fax: 066-915 1412
Email: info@dinglebenners.com
Web: www.dinglebenners.com

HOTEL U MAP 1 B 4

Located in the heart of Dingle Town, the hotel is favoured for its old world charm and style. Luxuriously appointed bedrooms provide an intimate cosy atmosphere complemented by authentic Irish antique furnishings. Mrs. Benner's Bar & Lounges will captivate you on arrival, have a warm friendly welcome and will fill you with a sense of yesteryear. Special weekend and midweek packages available.

Bookable on www.irelandhotels.com
Member of Manor House Hotels

B&B from €61.00 to €105.00

Muireann Nic Giolla Ruaidh
General Manager

Activities:

Member of:
IRISH HOTELS FEDERATION

Special Offer: Midweek Specials from €132.00 pps (3 Nights B&B)

52 52

Closed 24 - 26 December

Dingle Skellig Hotel & Peninsula Spa

Dingle,
Co. Kerry

Tel: 066-915 0200 Fax: 066-915 1501
Email: reservations@dingleskellig.com
Web: www.dingleskellig.com

HOTEL ★★★★ MAP 1 B 4

Renowned hotel situated on the beautiful harbour of Dingle Bay. Luxurious leisure club & pool. Fungi Kids Club & Crèche on weekends & holidays. Excellent cuisine in our Coastguard Restaurant. Established conference & banqueting centre with stunning views for up to 250 people. New Peninsula Spa features Yon-Ka face & body treatments, hydrotherapy, wraps, hot stone massage, holistic & sports massage, tanning & beauty. Relaxation suite, outdoor hot tub with stunning views, sauna and steam room. Voted Yonka's Destination Spa of the Year 2005.

Bookable on www.irelandhotels.com

B&B from €70.00 to €120.00

Graham Fitzgerald
General Manager

Activities:

Member of:
IRISH HOTELS FEDERATION

Special Offer: Weekend Specials from €155.00 pps (2 Nights B&B & 1 Dinner)

110 110

Closed 19 - 27 December

B&B Rates are per Person Sharing per Night incl. Breakfast. or **Room Rates** are per Room per Night - See also Page 8

Doyles Seafood Bar & Town House

John Street,
Dingle,
Co. Kerry
Tel: 066-915 1174 Fax: 066-915 1816
Email: cdoyles@iol.ie
Web: www.doylesofdingle.com

GUESTHOUSE ★★★★ MAP 1 B 4

The Town House has some of the most delightful rooms in Dingle. All 8 spacious rooms with full bathrooms have recently been refurbished in a most comfortable style. Satellite TV, phone, trouser press/iron, tea/coffee facilities. The world renowned restaurant has an old range & súgán chairs. Natural stone & wood combination gives Doyles a cosy country atmosphere. The menu consists only of fresh food and is chosen on a daily basis from the fish landed on Dingle boats. AA◆◆◆◆, RAC◆◆◆◆, Les Routiers "Restaurant of the Year" 2002.

Member of Blue Book

B&B from €45.00 to €75.00

John Cluskey
Host

Member of:
IRISH HOTELS FEDERATION

🛏🔥 ☎🖥©CMU🍴🐕🗑
8   8

Closed 15 November - 14 February

Emlagh House

Dingle,
Co. Kerry
Tel: 066-915 2345 Fax: 066-915 2369
Email: info@emlaghhouse.com
Web: www.emlaghhouse.com

GUESTHOUSE ★★★★ MAP 1 B 4

The Kavanagh family look forward to welcoming you to their country house. Individually designed, de luxe oversized guest rooms with your comfort in mind from waffle bathrobes to air-conditioning to CD players. Home baking every morning. A stroll from restaurants. Relax in our drawing room and admire the sea views. Award-winning Emlagh House, featured in all the best guides… more than just a place to stay.
AA Guesthouse of the Year 2005.

Bookable on www.irelandhotels.com

B&B from €90.00 to €150.00

Grainne & Marion Kavanagh

Member of:
IRISH HOTELS FEDERATION

🛏🔥 ☎🖥📶✻J🅿🖥 WiFi🐴
10 10

Closed 01 November - 15 March

Gorman's Clifftop House and Restaurant

Glaise Bheag, Ballydavid,
Dingle Peninsula, Tralee,
Co. Kerry
Tel: 066-915 5162 Fax: 066-915 5003
Email: info@gormans-clifftophouse.com
Web: www.gormans-clifftophouse.com

GUESTHOUSE ★★★★ MAP 1 B 5

A welcoming cliff-top refuge on the western edge of the Dingle Peninsula. All rooms pay homage to the landscape, offering breathtaking views of the ocean and mountains. Our emphasis is on comfort, mini suites boasting king sized beds and jacuzzi baths. Downstairs guests can gather around the fire to read or chat, dine handsomely in our fully licensed restaurant. AA ◆◆◆◆◆ Premier Select. Les Routiers "Hidden Gem Ireland" 2001. Georgina Campbell 'Guesthouse of the Year' 2002 (Jameson Guide). Les Routiers 'Hotel of the Year 2001'.

B&B from €50.00 to €75.00

Vincent & Sile O'Gormain
Proprietors

Member of:
IRISH HOTELS FEDERATION

Special Offer: *Weekend Specials from €155.00 pps*
(2 Nights B&B & 1 Dinner)

🛏🔥 ☎🖥T©✻U J🅿🖥 WiFi
9   9

Closed 24 - 26 December

<u>**B&B Rates**</u> are per Person Sharing per Night incl. Breakfast.
or <u>Room Rates</u> are per Room per Night - See also Page 8

Dingle (An Daingean)

Greenmount House

Upper John Street,
Dingle,
Co. Kerry
Tel: 066-915 1414 Fax: 066-915 1974
Email: greenmounthouse@eircom.net
Web: www.greenmount-house.com

GUESTHOUSE ★★★★ MAP 1 B 4

Greenmount House is the proud recipient of the 1997 RAC Guesthouse of the Year for Ireland. A charming 4**** country house yet centrally located. Spacious lounges to relax in and take advantage of its magnificent scenic location overlooking Dingle Town & Harbour. Each bedroom has private bathroom, TV/ radio & direct dial phone. Award-winning buffet breakfasts served in conservatory with commanding views of Dingle. Luxurious, peaceful retreat. Recognised by all leading guides.

B&B from €50.00 to €75.00

*John & Mary Curran
Owners*

Member of:
IRISH HOTELS FEDERATION

9 9

Closed 10 - 27 December

Heaton's Guesthouse

The Wood,
Dingle,
Co. Kerry
Tel: 066-915 2288 Fax: 066-915 2324
Email: heatons@iol.ie
Web: www.heatonsdingle.com

GUESTHOUSE ★★★★ MAP 1 B 4

Superb 4**** family-run guesthouse situated on the shore of Dingle Bay with spectacular views, 5 minutes walk from the town. All rooms are en suite (pressure shower and bath), with TV, DD phone and tea/coffee welcome tray. Breakfast is our speciality. Luxury junior suites and de luxe rooms recently opened (rates available on request). Local amenities include golf, sailing, fishing, surfing, cycling, walking, horse riding and the renowned gourmet restaurants. Awarded Guesthouse of the Year for Ireland 2002 - Les Routiers.

Bookable on www.irelandhotels.com
Member of Les Routiers

B&B from €44.00 to €67.00

*Nuala & Cameron Heaton
Proprietors*

Member of:
IRISH HOTELS FEDERATION

16 16

Closed 02 January - 04 February

Hillgrove Inn

Spa Road,
Dingle,
Co. Kerry
Tel: 066-915 1131 Fax: 066-915 1272
Email: hillgrovedingle@eircom.net
Web: www.hillgroveinn.com

GUESTHOUSE N MAP 1 B 4

The Hillgrove is family owned and managed. Located 5 minutes walk from Dingle's main street. Our rooms are all en suite, with DD phone, TV and tea/coffee making facilities. Our private lounge is the ideal place to relax with full bar facilities available. The Hillgrove offers a perfect combination of professional service with cheerful and helpful staff. We will ensure that your stay is the highlight of your visit to our beautiful town.

Bookable on www.irelandhotels.com

B&B from €40.00 to €65.00

Sandra Kennedy

Member of:
IRISH HOTELS FEDERATION

Special Offer: Midweek Specials from €100.00 pps (3 Nights B&B)

12 12

Closed 01 October - 01 May

B&B Rates are per Person Sharing per Night incl. Breakfast. or Room Rates are per Room per Night - See also Page 8

Mainstay Guesthouse (The)

Dykegate Street,
Dingle,
Co. Kerry
Tel: 066-915 1598 Fax: 066-915 2376
Email: info@mainstaydingle.com
Web: www.mainstaydingle.com

GUESTHOUSE U MAP 1 B 4

Located on a quiet street in the heart of Dingle this is a charming guesthouse of great character. All rooms are en suite with satellite TV, in-room coffee and tea, hairdryer and direct telephone. Breakfast here is an indulgence, served in the well appointed open hearth dining room. The landscaped garden and cozy lounge provide a restful retreat after a day's adventure in Kerry.

Bookable on www.irelandhotels.com

B&B from €35.00 to €55.00

*Ruth & Gus Cero
Proprietors*

Member of:
IRISH HOTELS FEDERATION

🛏️ 🐾 ☎️ 🖥️ 🅲 CM❄️ 🍴 ald 🚲
14 14

Open All Year

Milltown House

Dingle,
Co. Kerry
Tel: 066-915 1372 Fax: 066-915 1095
Email: info@milltownhousedingle.com
Web: www.milltownhousedingle.com

GUESTHOUSE ★★★★ MAP 1 B 4

Award-winning family-run Milltown House is ideally located overlooking Dingle Bay and Town from our private gardens. All rooms which retain the character of the 130 year old house are en suite, have tea/coffee making facilities, direct dial phone, TV, trouser press, hairdryer and safety deposit box. The house was home to Robert Mitchum during the making of David Lean's epic movie "Ryan's Daughter". Assistance in planning your day. One of the most scenic and tranquil locations in the town area, less than 15 minutes walk or 2 minutes drive!

Bookable on www.irelandhotels.com

B&B from €55.00 to €75.00

Tara Kerry

Member of:
IRISH HOTELS FEDERATION

🛏️ 🐾 ☎️ 🖥️ T U 🍴 P 🐾 🐎
10 10

Closed 30 October - 27 April

Old Pier, Restaurant and Guesthouse

An Fheothanach,
Ballydavid, Dingle,
Co. Kerry
Tel: 066-915 5242
Email: info@oldpier.com
Web: www.oldpier.com

GUESTHOUSE ★★★ MAP 1 B 4

Situated in the heart of the West Kerry Gaeltacht on the Dingle Peninsula overlooking beautiful Smerwick Harbour and the Atlantic Ocean. This family-run establishment offers 3★★★ accommodation with beautiful sea and mountain vistas. The Old Pier Restaurant offers a broad range of locally caught seafood, prime steak and meat dishes. Adjacent activities include 18 hole golf course, deep sea angling, mountain walking and archaeology sites. A warm welcome awaits you.

B&B from €35.00 to €50.00

Padraig & Jacqui O'Connor

Member of:
IRISH HOTELS FEDERATION

Special Offer: Special Offers Are Available

🛏️ 🐾 🖥️ 🅲 CM❄️ U 🍴 P 🍴 S 🅲 ald 🐾 🐎
6 6

Open All Year

<u>B&B Rates</u> are per Person Sharing per Night incl. Breakfast.
or <u>Room Rates</u> are per Room per Night - See also Page 8

Co. Kerry

Dingle (An Daingean) / Glenbeigh

Pax House	Smerwick Harbour Hotel	Towers Hotel
Upper John Street, Dingle, Co. Kerry	Ballyferriter, Dingle, Co. Kerry	Glenbeigh, Co. Kerry

Pax House
Upper John Street,
Dingle,
Co. Kerry
Tel: 066-915 1518 Fax: 066-915 2461
Email: paxhouse@iol.ie
Web: www.pax-house.com

GUESTHOUSE ★★★★ MAP 1 B 4

Superb 4**** AA 5♦♦♦♦♦ family-run guesthouse. Voted one of the top ten places to stay in Ireland. Pax House has undeniably one of the most spectacular views in the peninsula. All rooms including suites (rates on request) are beautifully appointed & include a fridge & safe. Enjoy our award-winning breakfast. We offer guests charm, tranquillity & unequalled hospitality. Sit on the balcony & watch the activity in the bay & a sighting of "Fungi" the dolphin. Golf nearby with reduced fees & tee times arranged. Pax House is 1km from Dingle Town.

Member of Premier Guesthouses

B&B from €50.00 to €70.00

Ron & Joan Brosnan Wright Owners

Member of:

12 12

Closed 01 November - 01 April

Smerwick Harbour Hotel
Ballyferriter,
Dingle,
Co. Kerry
Tel: 066-915 6470 Fax: 066-915 6473
Email: info@smerwickhotel.com
Web: www.smerwickhotel.com

HOTEL ★★★ MAP 1 B 5

Smerwick Harbour Hotel & Seafood Restaurant, with its old world bar, is located a short distance from Dingle Town. Our local 18 hole golf course is on your doorstep, 4km away, with reduced green fees for guests. All rooms en suite (family rooms also). Spacious lounge. Enjoy excellent cuisine in our seafood restaurant, specialising in local seafood and char grilled steaks. Quality bar food also available. Old world ambience, as featured on our website. The best sandy beaches in Ireland nearby. Suitable for Disabled. Groups & weddings catered for.

B&B from €40.00 to €80.00

Fionnbar Walsh Manager

Activities:

Member of:

Special Offer: Weekend Specials from €99.00 pps (2 Nights B&B & 1 Dinner)

32 32

Closed 01 November - 01 April

Towers Hotel
Glenbeigh,
Co. Kerry
Tel: 066-976 8212 Fax: 066-976 8260
Email: towershotel@eircom.net
Web: www.towershotel.com

HOTEL ★★★ MAP 1 C 4

The family-run Towers Hotel, on The Ring of Kerry, is an ideal place to relax and enjoy the splendours of Kerry. The hotel is a short distance from sandy beaches and dramatic mountains. Paradise for golfers, walkers, fishermen and anyone interested in the Kerry landscape. The Towers internationally known restaurant is renowned for its excellent seafood and distinguished atmosphere. Its traditional pub provides a chance to mingle with the people of Glenbeigh in a real Kerry atmosphere. 30 minutes drive from Kerry Airport.

Bookable on www.irelandhotels.com
Member of Irish Country Hotels

B&B from €50.00 to €65.00

Dolores Sweeney Proprietor

Activities:

Special Offer: Golf Group Rate from €80.00 pps Dinner, B&B

28 28

Closed 01October - 31 March

B&B Rates are per Person Sharing per Night incl. Breakfast. or **Room Rates** are per Room per Night - See also Page 8

Ashberry Lodge

Sneem Road,
N70, Kenmare,
Co. Kerry
Tel: 064-42720
Email: ashberry@iolfree.ie
Web: www.ashberrylodge.com

GUESTHOUSE ★★★ MAP 1 D 3

Welcome to the Murphy's 3*** guesthouse, offering superb scenery, hospitality, spacious accommodation and an extensive breakfast menu with only a 5-7 minute walk to Kenmare town centre using the Kerry Way shortcut. All bedrooms are en suite with views of the Kerry Mountains. Conveniently located on the beautiful Ring of Kerry which makes it an ideal homebase to tour the Ring of Beara, Ring of Kerry, Killarney, Gap of Dunloe & Glengarriff. It is situated between two fine 18 hole golf courses. Enjoy the peace of the country with the convenience of the town!

Bookable on www.irelandhotels.com

B&B from €30.00 to €40.00

Francie & Regina Murphy

Member of:
IRISH HOTELS FEDERATION

8 8

Closed 24 - 26 December

Brass Lantern

Old Railway Road,
Kenmare,
Co. Kerry
Tel: 064-42600 Fax: 064-41311
Email: info@brasslanternkenmare.com
Web: www.brasslanternkenmare.com

GUESTHOUSE ★★★ MAP 1 D 3

Award-winning guesthouse in Kenmare town near Holy Cross Church. All bedrooms and guest rooms are bright, large, spacious and tastefully furnished with everything the guest requires. A private, free car park is located at the rear of the house. Ground floor rooms perfect for anyone who has difficulty with stairs. Great hospitality and a good breakfast guaranteed! Ask about special offers.

B&B from €29.00 to €49.00

*Siobhan Jones
Manager*

Special Offer: Midweek Specials from €99.00 pps (3 Nights B&B)

6 6

Closed 02 January - 10 March

B&B Rates are per Person Sharing per Night incl. Breakfast. or Room Rates are per Room per Night - See also Page 8

Kenmare

Brook Lane Hotel	Davitts	Lansdowne Arms Hotel
Kenmare, Co. Kerry	Henry Street, Kenmare, Co. Kerry	Main Street, Kenmare, Co. Kerry
Tel: 064-42077 Fax: 064-40869	Tel: 064-42741 Fax: 064-42756	Tel: 064-41368 Fax: 064-41114
Email: info@brooklanehotel.com	Email: davittskenmare@eircom.net	Email: info@lansdownearms.com
Web: www.brooklanehotel.com	Web: www.davitts-kenmare.com	Web: www.lansdownearms.com

HOTEL N MAP 1 D 3	GUESTHOUSE ★★★ MAP 1 D 3	HOTEL ★★★ MAP 1 D 3
The Brook Lane is like no other place you've stayed in. A boutique hotel, it's small, quirky and full of little surprises. A place where design is contemporary, hospitality is instinctive and atmosphere is easygoing. Great big beds to dive into, soft fluffy pillows to get lost in and heated floors to keep your toes warm. Food is our passion - we serve up a range of classic favourites with a modern twist. Come and visit our hideaway, just a short walk from the pretty town of Kenmare.	If you are looking for luxury accommodation in the heart of Kenmare, then Davitt's is the guesthouse for you. Bar/bistro, restaurant downstairs serving excellent food throughout the year. Family-run premises that offers everything for a perfect holiday under one roof. All our luxury bedrooms are en suite with satellite TV, DD phones (pc compatible) and hairdryers. The rooms are situated at the back of the building guaranteeing a restful night in spacious, beautifully decorated rooms.	Built in the 1790s and situated at the top of Kenmare Town. The Lansdowne Arms Hotel, now owned by the Quill family, has undergone extensive refurbishment throughout. Enjoy a relaxed atmosphere in front of the open fires and the hospitality from the warm and friendly staff. All of the 26 rooms and bathrooms have been redecorated and finished to a very high standard with king sized beds, safes, hairdryers, tea/coffee facility, telephone, TV and ironing presses. Private parking.

B&B from €65.00 to €95.00	B&B from €38.00 to €50.00	B&B from €45.00 to €75.00

Dermot & Una Brennan Proprietors

Activities: 🏌️

Donal & Mary Cremin Proprietors

Julie O'Sullivan Manager

Activities: 🏌️🎣

Member of:

IRISH HOTELS FEDERATION

20 20 ... Inet WiFi

11 11 ... Inet

26 26 ...

Closed 24 - 26 December	Closed 24 - 27 December	Closed 24 - 25 December

B&B Rates are per Person Sharing per Night incl. Breakfast. or Room Rates are per Room per Night - See also Page 8

Lodge (The)

Killowen Road,
Kenmare,
Co. Kerry
Tel: 064-41512 Fax: 064-42724
Email: thelodgekenmare@eircom.net
Web: www.thelodgekenmare.com

GUESTHOUSE ★★★★ MAP 1 D 3

Purpose built luxury guesthouse situated opposite Kenmare's 18 hole golf course. Within 3 minutes walk of some of the finest restaurants & pubs in Ireland. All rooms are elegantly furnished with king beds & en suite bathrooms. All rooms are extremely well appointed with DD telephone, TV, safes, controllable central heating, iron, tea/coffee facilities. The Lodge is renowned for its vast home cooked breakfast & freshly baked breads. 4 of the rooms are at ground level, 1 of which is especially equipped for wheelchair use.

B&B from €45.00 to €55.00

Rosemarie Quill
Proprietor

🛏️🦮 ☎️🖥️TC❄️🚶♨️🅿️🍴
10 10

O'Donnabhain's

Henry Street,
Kenmare,
Co. Kerry
Tel: 064-42106 Fax: 064-42321
Email: info@odonnabhain-kenmare.com
Web: www.odonnabhain-kenmare.com

GUESTHOUSE ★★★ MAP 1 D 3

Conveniently located in the centre of Kenmare Town, providing affordable accommodation with lashings of charm. Spacious en suite rooms (direct dial phone, TV-6 channels). Some with king size beds, finished with the comfort of the guests in mind. Rooms are located away from the bar, so as to ensure no sleepless nights - quietness in the centre of town. Ideal base to discover the South's attractions. Private car park.

Bookable on www.irelandhotels.com

B&B from €38.00 to €52.00

Jeremiah Foley
Owner

Activities:
:/

Member of:
IRISH HOTELS FEDERATION

Special Offer: Stay 7 Nights and Pay Only for 6 Nights

🛏️🦮 ☎️🖥️TU🚶🎵🅿️🍴🆔♿📶 inet
10 10

B&B Rates are per Person Sharing per Night incl. Breakfast.
or **Room Rates** are per Room per Night - See also Page 8

Kenmare

Park Hotel Kenmare	Sea Shore Farm	Sheen Falls Lodge

Park Hotel Kenmare

Kenmare,
Co. Kerry

Tel: 064-41200 Fax: 064-41402
Email: info@parkkenmare.com
Web: www.parkkenmare.com

HOTEL ★★★★★ MAP 1 D 3

Since 1897 travellers have enjoyed the gracious elegance of the Park Hotel Kenmare. In a heavenly location overlooking Kenmare Bay the hotel is renowned for its attentive service & international standards. In the De luxe Destination Spa SAMAS guests can indulge in the ethos of a true spa to rejuvenate the body, mind & spirit. A host of classes & activities encompass the wonderful location of this special corner of Ireland. 18 Hole golf course, tennis, 12 acres of gardens & 40 acre National Park adjoin the grounds. Enjoy Ireland in one of its most magnificent locations.

Bookable on www.irelandhotels.com
Member of Ireland's Blue Book

B&B from €166.00 to €228.00

Francis Brennan
Proprietor

Activities:

Member of:
IRISH HOTELS FEDERATION

Special Offer: Lifestyle Programmes from €550.00 per person

47 47

Closed 04 January - 11 February

Sea Shore Farm

Tubrid,
Kenmare,
Co. Kerry

Tel: 064-41270 Fax: 064-41270
Email: seashore@eircom.net
Web: www.seashorehouse.net

GUESTHOUSE ★★★ MAP 1 D 3

Our setting on the Bay is uniquely peaceful and private yet only 1 mile from town. Our farm extends to the shore affording unspoilt field walks in natural habitat with plentiful bird/wildlife. Large en suite rooms with panoramic seascapes, king beds, phone, tea facilities, etc. AA ◆◆◆◆ Selected, Recommended Guide du Routard, Los Angeles Times. Sign posted 300m from Kenmare by Esso Station - junction N71/N70 Killarney/Ring of Kerry Sneem Road.

Member of Friendly Homes of Ireland

B&B from €50.00 to €65.00

Mary Patricia O'Sullivan
Proprietor

Member of:
IRISH HOTELS FEDERATION

6 6

Closed 01 November - 01 March

Sheen Falls Lodge

Kenmare,
Co. Kerry

Tel: 064-41600 Fax: 064-41386
Email: info@sheenfallslodge.ie
Web: www.sheenfallslodge.ie

HOTEL ★★★★★ MAP 1 D 3

Uniquely set on the shores of Kenmare Bay & Sheen River, only 2km from the Heritage Town of Kenmare, located on a 300-acre woodland estate. Our signature restaurant La Cascade, offers a distinctive fine dining experience overlooking the Sheen Waterfalls. We also offer casual dining in Oscar's Bar & Bistro situated on the riverside. Choose from an extensive array of Estate activities from salmon fishing to horse riding, or unwind with luxurious treatments in our Health Spa. Dedicated staff uphold the most outstanding service to make your stay as unforgettable & unique as Ireland itself.

Bookable on www.irelandhotels.com
Member of Relais et Châteaux

Room Rate from €280.00 to €425.00

Adriaan Bartels
General Manager

Activities:

Member of:
IRISH HOTELS FEDERATION

Special Offer: Weekend Specials from €320.00 pps
(2 Nights B&B & 1 Dinner)

66 66

Closed 03 January - 04 February

B&B Rates are per Person Sharing per Night incl. Breakfast. or **Room Rates** are per Room per Night - See also Page 8

Virginia's Guesthouse

36 Henry Street,
Kenmare,
Co Kerry
Tel: 064-41021 Fax: 064-42415
Email: virginias@eircom.net
Web: www.virginias-kenmare.com

GUESTHOUSE ★★★ MAP 1 D 3

Welcome to Virginia's 3*** (AA ◆◆◆◆) family-run guesthouse in the heart of Kenmare, minutes from the pubs and shops, and a short stroll to the tranquil seashore of Kenmare Bay. Guest rooms are bright, spacious and beautifully appointed with power showers, 40 channel digital TV and extremely comfortable beds. Excellent breakfast features home-baked breads and a superb 3-course menu. Enjoy dinner at Mulcahy's award-winning restaurant on the ground floor. Virginia's is recommended by "The Good Hotel Guide" and "Alistair Sawday's Special Places to Stay".

B&B from €40.00 to €60.00

Neil & Noreen Harrington

Member of:
IRISH HOTELS FEDERATION

Special Offer: Midweek Specials from €110.00 pps
(3 Nights B&B)

8 8 📞🛏📺🧺🅿️

Closed 10 - 20 February

19th Green (The)

Lackabane,
Fossa, Killarney,
Co. Kerry
Tel: 064-32868 Fax: 064-32637
Email: 19thgreen@eircom.net
Web: www.19thgreen-bb.com

GUESTHOUSE ★★★ MAP 2 E 4

Family-run guesthouse 3km from Killarney Town. Ring of Kerry Road; adjacent to Killarney's 3 x 18 hole championship courses. Ideal for golfers playing Killarney, Beaufort, Dooks, Waterville, Tralee or Ballybunion. All tee times arranged. Tours arranged: Gap of Dunloe, Ring of Kerry and Dingle Peninsula. All rooms en suite with direct dial phone and TV, tea/coffee facilities in guest rooms. Full à la carte restaurant also offering value menu. Groups of up to 35 catered for in accommodation and restaurant.

Bookable on www.irelandhotels.com

B&B from €35.00 to €60.00

John & Freda Sheehan
Proprietors

Activities:
🏌

Member of:
IRISH HOTELS FEDERATION

Special Offer: Weekend Specials from €105.00 pps
(2 Nights B&B & 1 Dinner)

13 13 📞🛏📺🅒CM🅙🅟🅢🅨alc🐾

Open All Year

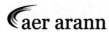

B&B Rates are per Person Sharing per Night incl. Breakfast.
or **Room Rates** are per Room per Night - See also Page 8

Co. Kerry

Killarney

Abbey Lodge	Aghadoe Heights Hotel & Spa	Aisling House

Muckross Road,
Killarney,
Co. Kerry
Tel: 064-34193 Fax: 064-35877
Email: abbeylodgekly@eircom.net
Web: www.abbey-lodge.com

Lakes of Killarney,
Killarney,
Co. Kerry
Tel: 064-31766 Fax: 064-31345
Email: info@aghadoeheights.com
Web: www.aghadoeheights.com

Countess Road,
Killarney,
Co. Kerry
Tel: 064-31112 Fax: 064-30079
Email: aislinghouse@eircom.net

GUESTHOUSE ★★★★ MAP 2 E 4 | **HOTEL ★★★★★ MAP 2 E 4** | **GUESTHOUSE ★★★ MAP 2 E 4**

A genuine Irish welcome awaits you at Abbey Lodge. Our guesthouse is family-run and boasts 15 luxurious en suite rooms with TV, direct dial phone, power showers and central heating. We are conveniently located on the Muckross Road (N71) a mere three minute walk to the town centre. The house is tastefully decorated throughout and features many interesting antiques and art. With 30 years in the business - anywhere else is a compromise.

Located in Ireland's most spectacular natural setting. Aghadoe Heights Hotel & Spa is the premier destination Spa resort in Ireland. Consistently recognised for its service, guest rooms, suites & penthouse. Aghadoe is one of only 4 hotels in Ireland to have achieved five Red Stars from the Automobile Association. We invite you to visit with us and be inspired by the breathtaking views, spellbound by the myth and legend, soothed by our Aveda Spa and enchanted by our people. www.thespakillarney.com

Aisling House located in peaceful surroundings just 800 metres off Muckross Road and 8 minutes walk from the centre of Killarney. All bedrooms are en suite, with TV and central heating. Tea/coffee facilities available to guests at all times. There is private car parking and a garden for guests. Aisling House is well within walking distance of Killarney National Park, Ross Castle and Muckross House. Tours of the Ring of Kerry/Dingle may be arranged. Nearby facilities include golf, horse riding, angling.

Bookable on www.irelandhotels.com
Member of Premier Guesthouses

Bookable on www.irelandhotels.com
Member of Preferred Hotels and Resorts Worldwide

B&B from €40.00 to €70.00 | *B&B from €100.00 to €250.00* | *B&B from €32.00 to €35.00*

Muireann King
Host

Member of:

Special Offer: Stay Friday & Saturday & receive Sunday night at half price

Pat & Marie Chawke
General Managers

Activities:

Member of:

Patrick O'Donoghue / Patricia O'Donoghue
Owner / Manager

Member of:

| 15 15 | 75 75 | 10 10 |

| Closed 20 - 28 December | Closed 30 December - 01 March | Closed 30 November - 01 February |

B&B Rates are per Person Sharing per Night incl. Breakfast. or <u>Room Rates</u> are per Room per Night - See also Page 8

Arbutus Hotel

College Street,
Killarney,
Co. Kerry
Tel: 064-31037 Fax: 064-34033
Email: stay@arbutuskillarney.com
Web: www.arbutuskillarney.com

HOTEL ★★★ MAP 2 E 4

The Arbutus Hotel and the Buckley family - at the heart of Killarney hospitality since 1926. Generations of visitors have enjoyed their personal introduction to the many attractions of the area whilst enjoying the warmth of a townhouse hotel where loving attention to detail is evident in home-cooked food, the original Buckley's Bar and the marvellous Celtic Deco design throughout. A truly special hotel.

Bookable on www.irelandhotels.com

B&B from €65.00 to €95.00

*Sean Buckley
Proprietor*

Activities:
✓

Member of:
IRISH HOTELS FEDERATION

🏨 🛏 ☎ ⌨ ⚕ 🆃 🅲 CM♫🕹📠🔤 ⚿
35 35

Open All Year

Ashville Guesthouse

Rock Road,
Killarney,
Co. Kerry
Tel: 064-36405 Fax: 064-36778
Email: info@ashvillekillarney.com
Web: www.ashvillekillarney.com

GUESTHOUSE ★★★ MAP 2 E 4

Ashville is a spacious family-run guesthouse, 2 mins walk from town centre, on main Tralee Road (N22). Private car park. Comfortably furnished en suite rooms include DD telephone, multi channel TV, hairdryer. Sample our varied breakfast menu. Convenient to Killarney National Park, pony trekking, golf & fishing. Ideal touring base for Ring of Kerry, Dingle & Beara. Declan & Elma assure you of a warm welcome at Ashville. Awarded AA ◆◆◆◆, RAC ◆◆◆◆ & Sparkling Diamond Award 2002 & Hospitality Award 2004. Ground floor rooms available.

Bookable on www.irelandhotels.com
Member of Premier Guesthouses

B&B from €35.00 to €55.00

*Declan & Elma Walsh
Proprietors*

Activities:
✓

Member of:
IRISH HOTELS FEDERATION

🏨 🛏 ☎ 🆃 🅲 ♻ ✈ 🅿 🆂 ⚿
12 12

Closed 01 December - 31 January

B&B Rates are per Person Sharing per Night incl. Breakfast.
or **Room Rates** are per Room per Night - See also Page 8

Brehon (The)

Muckross Road,
Killarney,
Co. Kerry
Tel: 064-30700 Fax: 064-30701
Email: info@thebrehon.com
Web: www.thebrehon.com

HOTEL N MAP 2 E 4

The Brehon & The Angsana Spa, where luxury meets style, is located adjacent to Killarney National Park. 125 de luxe rooms & suites designed with exceptional grace and elegance with superb views of the surrounding natural beauty. Each room is well appointed with individual temperature control, internet access and spacious marble bathrooms. The Brehon is home to Europe's first Angsana Spa, a holistic and spiritual spa experience all the way from Thailand.

Bookable on www.irelandhotels.com
Member of Luxury Lifestyle Hotels & Resorts

B&B from €70.00 to €290.00

Seán O'Driscoll
General Manager

Activities:
:／🍷♨

*Special Offer: Weekend Specials from €199.00 pps
(2 Nights B&B & 1 Dinner)*

125 125

Open all Year

Brook Lodge Hotel

High Street,
Killarney,
Co. Kerry
Tel: 064-31800 Fax: 064-35001
Email: brooklodgekillarney@eircom.net
Web: www.brooklodgekillarney.com

HOTEL ★★★ MAP 2 E 4

De luxe family-run hotel in Killarney town centre off the street with private parking and landscaped gardens. Four star standard accommodation, large bedrooms & junior suites include tea/coffee facilities, hairdryer, iron & ironing board, TV, elevator, wheelchair friendly. Free internet access available. Our hotel has justifiably earned an outstanding reputation for its friendly personal service and relaxed atmosphere, excellent cuisine in Brooks Restaurant or a nightcap in the residents' bar. RAC 3*** hotel and Sparkling Diamond Award.

B&B from €50.00 to €110.00

Joan Counihan
Owner

Member of:
IRISH
HOTELS
FEDERATION

*Special Offer: Weekend Specials from €150.00 pps
(2 Nights B&B & 1 Dinner)*

24 24

Closed 01 November - 06 April

Cahernane House Hotel

Muckross Road,
Killarney,
Co. Kerry
Tel: 064-31895 Fax: 064-34340
Email: reservations@cahernane.com
Web: www.cahernane.com

HOTEL ★★★★ MAP 2 E 4

Formerly the residence of the Herbert family, Earls of Pembroke, Cahernane House dates back to the 17th century. Cahernane House Hotel is situated on its own parklands on the edge of Killarney's National Park, an area of outstanding natural beauty with its untamed landscape of mountains, lakes and woodland walks and is only 10 minutes walk from Killarney Town. All of the 38 bedrooms are beautifully appointed, many with antique furniture, jacuzzis and private balconies. No pets allowed.

Bookable on www.irelandhotels.com
Member of Manor House Hotels

B&B from €80.00 to €140.00

Jimmy Browne
Proprietor

Member of:
IRISH
HOTELS
FEDERATION

38 38

Closed 23 December - 05 January

B&B Rates are per Person Sharing per Night incl. Breakfast.
or **Room Rates** are per Room per Night - See also Page 8

Castlelodge Guesthouse

Muckross Road,
Killarney,
Co. Kerry
Tel: 064-31545 Fax: 064-32325
Email: castlelodge@eircom.net

GUESTHOUSE U MAP 2 E 4

Conveniently located, just two minutes walk from Killarney Town centre. Open all year round excluding Christmas, our guesthouse offers very friendly staff, a homely atmosphere and easy access to all the major attractions and magnificent scenery in Killarney. Good restaurants and live music will be recommended, come and see the sights, hear the music and taste the atmosphere.

B&B from €40.00 to €55.00

*Aoife O'Shea &
Michelle Corcoran
Hosts*

🍽️🛏️ ☎️🗒️🆃🅲❄️🅄🅹🅿️📠
25 25

Closed 24 - 26 December

Castlerosse Hotel, Golf & Leisure Club

Lower Lake,
Killarney,
Co. Kerry
Tel: 064-31144 Fax: 064-31031
Email: res@castlerosse.ie
Web: www.castlerosse.com

HOTEL ★★★ MAP 2 E 4

The location of the Castlerosse Hotel can claim to be one of the most scenic spots in all of Ireland. Just 2km from the town, it is flanked by Killarney Golf and Fishing Club on one side and the National Park on the other. It commands majestic views of Killarney's Lower Lake and the Magillicuddys, Ireland's highest mountains. The Castlerosse Hotel comprises 121 recently refurbished bedrooms each with en suite bathroom, TV and tea/coffee making facility. Leisure facilities include 9 hole golf course, leisure centre with 20m swimming pool and 2 floodlit tennis courts. Special offers online at www.castlerosse.com.

Bookable on www.irelandhotels.com

B&B from €45.00 to €85.00

*Danny Bowe
General Manager*

Activities:
⛷️🏌️

Member of:
IRISH HOTELS FEDERATION

*Special Offer: Midweek Specials from €165.00 pps
(3 Nights B&B & 2 Dinners)*

🍽️🛏️ ☎️🗒️🆃🅲➡️CM❄️🏊🅂🏖️🍴🐕🐎🅄
121 121 🎵🎹🅿️🆂🔒♿🐕

Closed 02 November - 12 March

<u>B&B Rates</u> are per Person Sharing per Night incl. Breakfast.
or <u>Room Rates</u> are per Room per Night - See also Page 8

Killarney

Crystal Springs	Darby O'Gills Country House Hotel	Dromhall Hotel

Crystal Springs

Ballycasheen (Off N22),
Killarney,
Co. Kerry
Tel: 064-33272 Fax: 064-35518
Email: crystalsprings@eircom.net
Web: http://homepage.eircom.net/~doors/

GUESTHOUSE N MAP 2 E 4

Located on the banks of the peaceful River Flesk offering fishing on location. Just off N22/Cork Road, only a short walk to town centre, where many traditional pubs and fine restaurants can be found. Close to lakes, National Park, Ring of Kerry and I.N.E.C. Spacious en suite rooms, AA ♦♦♦♦ award. TV, tea/coffee facilities, hairdryers, DD phones, trouser press and refrigerators. Extensive menus including vegetarian and home specialities. Ample safe parking.

B&B from €35.00 to €45.00

Eileen & Tim Brosnan

Member of:
IRISH HOTELS FEDERATION

7   7

Closed 20 - 29 December

Darby O'Gills Country House Hotel

Lissivigeen,
Mallow Road, Killarney,
Co. Kerry
Tel: 064-34168 Fax: 064-36794
Email: darbyogill@eircom.net
Web: www.darbyogillskillarney.com

HOTEL ★★★ MAP 2 E 4

Darby O'Gills Country House Hotel is a charming family-run hotel located in a quiet rural setting just on the edge of Killarney Town. We are positioned ideally for touring the wonders of Kerry & Cork, playing golf, fishing, hill walking or relaxing. Killarney Town centre is only a five minute drive. We are a family friendly hotel & personal attention is guaranteed. Open all year with excellent rates offering great value. Special breaks away & childrens' combined rates make our hotel unique. Entertainment every weekend & nightly during the summer.

Bookable on www.irelandhotels.com
Member of Countrywide Hotels - MinOtel Ireland

B&B from €45.00 to €80.00

Pat & Joan Gill & Family

Member of:
IRISH HOTELS FEDERATION

Special Offer: *Midweek Specials from €135.00 pps*
(3 Nights B&B)

29   29

Open All Year

Dromhall Hotel

Muckross Road,
Killarney,
Co. Kerry
Tel: 064-39300 Fax: 064-39301
Email: info@dromhall.com
Web: www.dromhall.com

HOTEL ★★★★ MAP 2 E 4

Killarney's famous mountain scenes provide a magnificent backdrop for the Dromhall Hotel. Located 5 minutes walk from town, the hotel offers the comfort and service one associates with a first class hotel while retaining the friendliness and welcome of a family-run hotel. From the moment you enter the elegant marbled lobby the scene is set for a special experience. Banquet and conference facilities for up to 300. Award-winning Kaynes Bistro. Full leisure centre. Offers the ultimate in relaxation.

Bookable on www.irelandhotels.com

B&B from €55.00 to €125.00

Bernadette Randles
Managing Director

Activities:

Member of:
IRISH HOTELS FEDERATION

Special Offer: *Weekend Specials from €139.00 pps*
(2 Nights B&B & 1 Dinner)

70   70

Closed 23 - 27 December

B&B Rates are per Person Sharing per Night incl. Breakfast. or **Room Rates** are per Room per Night - See also Page 8

Earls Court House

Woodlawn Junction,
Muckross Road, Killarney,
Co. Kerry
Tel: 064-34009 Fax: 064-34366
Email: info@killarney-earlscourt.ie
Web: www.killarney-earlscourt.ie

GUESTHOUSE ★★★★ MAP 2 E 4

Our family-run 4 star residence is 5 minutes walk to town centre. National winner of "Ireland's Best Breakfast Award 2003" & Jameson's "Guesthouse of the Year for Ireland" 2004. Your stay here will be the highlight of your Irish visit. Experience traditional country house charm, open fires and home baking. Breakfast is special - a feast offering tempting choices. Spacious bedrooms are graced with antiques, soft furnishings, king beds, full bathrooms and four poster suites. Wheelchair friendly, tea facilities, elevator & private parking.

Bookable on www.irelandhotels.com

B&B from €58.00 to €70.00

Emer & Ray Moynihan Owners

Activities:
✓

Member of:
IRISH HOTELS FEDERATION

Special Offer: Midweek Specials from €170.00 pps (3 Nights B&B)

24 24

Closed 14 November - 01 February

Eviston House Hotel

New Street,
Killarney,
Co. Kerry
Tel: 064-31640 Fax: 064-33685
Email: evishtl@eircom.net
Web: www.killarney-hotel.com

HOTEL ★★★ MAP 2 E 4

Our charming hotel is located in the town centre, yet only minutes from Killarney's famous beauty spots and championship golf. Our luxurious bedrooms have all the facilities to ensure your peace and comfort. Enjoy candlelit dinner in the Colleen Bawn Restaurant or dine in our famous pub, 'The Danny Mann', while enjoying lively traditional Irish music. Health conscious guests will appreciate our new exercise suite, sauna, hot tub and sunbed. We also offer parking and free email and internet access exclusively for our guests. A warm welcome is just the beginning!

Bookable on www.irelandhotels.com
Member of Best Western Hotels

B&B from €39.00 to €79.00

Edward Eviston Proprietor

Activities:
✓

Member of:
IRISH HOTELS FEDERATION

75 75

Open All Year

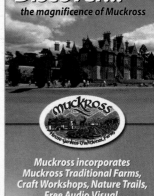

B&B Rates are per Person Sharing per Night incl. Breakfast.
or **Room Rates** are per Room per Night - See also Page 8

Killarney

Failte Hotel	Fairview Guesthouse	Foley's Townhouse

College Street,
Killarney,
Co. Kerry
Tel: 064-33404 Fax: 064-36599
Email: failtehotel@eircom.net

Michael Collins Place,
College Street, Killarney,
Co. Kerry
Tel: 064-34164 Fax: 064-71777
Email: info@fairviewkillarney.com
Web: www.fairviewkillarney.com

23 High Street,
Killarney,
Co. Kerry
Tel: 064-31217 Fax: 064-34683
Email: info@foleystownhouse.com
Web: www.foleystownhouse.com

HOTEL ★★ MAP 2 E 4 | **GUESTHOUSE ★★★★ MAP 2 E 4** | **GUESTHOUSE ★★★★ MAP 2 E 4**

The Failte Hotel, furnished to a very high standard, is owned and managed by the O'Callaghan family. It is internationally known for its high standard of cuisine. Paudie supervises the award-winning bar. It is situated in the town centre, adjacent to railway station, new factory outlet, shopping complex. Also close by are many local cabarets & night clubs. Local amenities include golfing, fishing, walking.

Superbly located in the heart of Killarney Town, yet out of noise's way, Fairview is a luxurious boutique style guesthouse that is unique in quality, location, service and elegance. Parking, spacious rooms with optional jacuzzi suites, all modern anemities including lift & wheelchair facilities. A de luxe base from which to tour, golf or socialise. Privately owned and managed. Awards include AA and RAC ◆◆◆◆◆, Sparkling Diamond & Warm Welcome Award, Killarney Best New Development & Guesthouse Awards & the prestigious Little Gem Awards. New restaurant & additional executive de luxe rooms opening Spring 2006.

Originally a 19th C Coaching Inn, this old house has hosted generations of travellers. Newly refurbished, this is a 4**** family-run town centre guesthouse. Luxury bedrooms are individually designed for comfort with every modern amenity, including lift, wheelchair access & 2 de luxe suites. Downstairs is our award-winning seafood & steak restaurant. Chef / Owner Carol provides meals from fresh local produce. Choose from approx 300 wines. Personal supervision. Private parking. Awarded AA ◆◆◆◆◆, RAC Highly Acclaimed.

Bookable on www.irelandhotels.com

Bookable on www.irelandhotels.com
Member of Premier Guesthouses

B&B from €45.00 to €75.00 | *B&B from €39.50 to €69.50* | *B&B from €59.00 to €75.00*

Dermot & Eileen O'Callaghan
Proprietors

Activities:
✓

Member of:
IRISH HOTELS FEDERATION

James & Shelley O' Neill
Proprietors

Activities:
✓

Member of:
IRISH HOTELS FEDERATION

Carol Hartnett
Proprietor

Activities:
✓

Member of:
IRISH HOTELS FEDERATION

14 14 | 18 18 inet WiFi | 28 28 inet

Closed 23 - 26 December	Closed 24 - 25 December	Closed 01 December - 31 January

B&B Rates are per Person Sharing per Night incl. Breakfast.
or **Room Rates** are per Room per Night - See also Page 8

Friars Glen	Fuchsia House	Gleann Fia Country House

Mangerton Road, Muckross, Killarney, Co. Kerry	Muckross Road, Killarney, Co. Kerry	Old Deerpark, Killarney, Co. Kerry
Tel: 064-37500 Fax: 064-37388	Tel: 064-33743 Fax: 064-36588	Tel: 064-35035 Fax: 064-35000
Email: fullerj@indigo.ie	Email: fuchsiahouse@eircom.net	Email: info@gleannfia.com
Web: www.friarsglen.ie	Web: www.fuchsiahouse.com	Web: www.gleannfia.com

GUESTHOUSE ★★★★ MAP 2 E 4 | **GUESTHOUSE ★★★★ MAP 2 E 4** | **GUESTHOUSE ★★★ MAP 2 E 4**

This 4**** guesthouse, built in a traditional style, offers a haven of peace and tranquillity. Set in its own 28 acres of wood and pastureland and located in the heart of Killarney National Park. Reception rooms have a rustic feel, with a warm and friendly atmosphere, finished in stone and wood with open fires and antiques. Bedrooms & bathrooms are finished to the highest standards. The dining room, patio & garden have a terrific mountain view. An ideal base in the South West. Highly recommended by Michelin.

We invite you to enjoy the affordable luxury of Fuchsia House which is set well back from Muckross Road in mature leafy gardens. Only 7 minutes walk from Killarney Town centre. Purpose built to combine the amenities of a modern 4**** guesthouse with the elegance of an earlier age. We offer spacious rooms with orthopaedic beds, dressed in crisp cotton and linen, DD phone, private bath with power shower. Spacious lounges and conservatory. Irish and Vegetarian menus. Recognized by all leading guidebooks.

Gleann Fia Country House, open year round, is located 2km from Killarney Town. Situated on 5 acres of gardens, river & woodland walks. Our location is perfect for touring scenic sights of Kerry, playing golf on world renowned ch'ship parklands & links courses, fishing & hill walking. All bedrooms are tastefully decorated, some furnished with antiques & all rooms have pleasant views of the surrounding countryside. Breakfast is hot & cold buffet with fresh juices, breads, yogurts, cheese platters. Safe & secure parking. A professional & friendly home style service.

Bookable on www.irelandhotels.com
Member of Premier Collection

B&B from €45.00 to €65.00 | *B&B from €45.00 to €70.00* | *B&B from €35.00 to €70.00*

Mary Fuller
Proprietor

Member of:
IRISH HOTELS FEDERATION

Mary Treacy
Owner

Activities: ✓

Member of:
IRISH HOTELS FEDERATION

Bridget & Conor O'Connell
Proprietors / Managers

Activities: ✓

Member of:
IRISH HOTELS FEDERATION

Special Offer: Midweek Specials from €120.00 pps (3 Nights B&B)

Special Offer: Special Offers Available

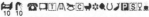

🏠🔥 ☎️🖥️TC❄️🅿️♿ 10 10 | 🏠🔥 ☎️🖥️T🅰️🔥🐕❄️♿☂️🅿️S♿ 10 10 | 🏠🔥 ☎️🖥️TC❄️🅿️🐾🅿️🔥S♿ Inet WiFi 🐕 19 19

Closed 30 November - 01 March	Open All Year	Open All Year

B&B Rates are per Person Sharing per Night incl. Breakfast.
or **Room Rates** are per Room per Night - See also Page 8

South West 95

Killarney

Glena Guesthouse	Gleneagle Hotel	Heights Hotel - Killarney (The)

Glena Guesthouse

Muckross Road,
Killarney,
Co. Kerry
Tel: 064-32705 Fax: 064-35611
Email: glena@iol.ie
Web: www.glenahouse.com

GUESTHOUSE ★★★ MAP 2 E 4

Glena House - Killarney's award-winning 3 star guesthouse, AA ◆◆◆◆, RAC ◆◆◆◆, Sparkling Diamond Award 2003/2004, Failte Ireland approved. It's the simple things that make it a great place to stay - great location 5 minutes from town centre, evening meals available during season, orthopaedic beds to rest in, a shower/bath en suite to invigorate, tea/coffee when you want, homebaking & preserves, healthy options breakfast, a bowl of ice, dispense bar service & a host and staff eager to make your stay happy & memorable. Parking on site. Access to internet.

Bookable on www.irelandhotels.com

B&B from €35.00 to €50.00

Kayan Culloty Rice
Manager

Member of:

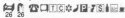

*Special Offer: Weekend Specials from €129.00 pps
3 Nights (Fri, Sat & Sun) & 1 Dinner*

🛏️🐾 ☎️🍽️📺📞✈️🚲⛵️
26 26

Open All Year

Gleneagle Hotel

Killarney,
Co. Kerry

Tel: 064-36000 Fax: 064-32646
Email: info@gleneaglehotel.com
Web: www.gleneaglehotel.com

HOTEL ★★★ MAP 2 E 4

Ireland's leading leisure and conference/convention hotel, adjacent to Killarney's National Park with beautifully furnished rooms. Ireland's National Events Centre is ideally suited for conventions, conferences, exhibitions, sporting events, concerts and theatrical productions. Our award-winning chefs will delight you in both our restaurants. We have a great line-up of entertainment all year round. Relax and unwind using our indoor/outdoor leisure facilities.

Bookable on www.irelandhotels.com
Member of Gleneagle Group

B&B from €50.00 to €140.00

O'Donoghue Family
Proprietors

Activities:
🏊⛳️

Member of:

🛏️🐾 ☎️🍽️📺📞✈️🚲⛵️C♦CMCS❄️🎿🏊
246 246
🏌️⛵️⛷️♪📺📶

Open All Year

Heights Hotel - Killarney (The)

Cork Road,
Killarney,
Co. Kerry
Tel: 064-31158 Fax: 064-35198
Email: info@killarneyheights.ie
Web: www.killarneyheights.ie

HOTEL ★★★ MAP 2 E 4

Situated 1km from Killarney Town Centre on the Cork Road, this beautiful 70 bedroomed hotel overlooks the majestic Torc & Mangerton Mountains. Open fires, olde world flagstone floors and pitch pine furnishings create a unique nostalgic atmosphere in the bars, restaurants and bistro. The hotel is easily accessed by mainline rail or by flying into Kerry Airport, just 14km away. The Heights Hotel, Killarney is the perfect venue for the perfect holiday, to begin your tour of our beautiful scenic countryside.

Bookable on www.irelandhotels.com

B&B from €45.00 to €86.50

Kieran O'Driscoll
General Manager

Member of:

*Special Offer: Weekend Specials from €89.00 pps
(2 Nights B&B & 1 Dinner)*

🛏️🐾 ☎️🍽️📺📞✈️🚲⛵️♦CM❄️🚲♪📺📶
70 70
🔌♿️🐕

Closed 24 - 25 December

B&B Rates are per Person Sharing per Night incl. Breakfast.
or **Room Rates** are per Room per Night - See also Page 8

Holiday Inn Killarney

Muckross Road,
Killarney,
Co. Kerry
Tel: 064-33000 Fax: 064-33001
Email: reservations@holidayinnkillarney.com
Web: www.holidayinnkillarney.com

HOTEL ★★★ MAP 2 E 4

Holiday Inn Killarney enjoys a quiet but central location close to Killarney Town centre. Its 100 spacious en suite guest rooms including 24 suites, are tastefully decorated to the highest standards. Our fully equipped Leisure Centre is the perfect place to relax and unwind. Our Library Point Restaurant serves the finest of local cuisine while Saddlers Pub serves food daily and has a live entertainment programme. A haven for all seasons!

B&B from €65.00 to €115.00

Ivan Tuohy
General Manager

Member of:

Special Offer: Weekend Specials from €129.00 pps
(2 Nights B&B & 1 Dinner)

100 100 🛏️🍴☎️🖥️📺🅃🛗♿️📶CMCS❄️🅿️
🛁⛵🎵PS🔟🆓 inet 🐾

Closed 24 - 25 December

Hotel Dunloe Castle

Killarney,
Co. Kerry

Tel: 064-44111 Fax: 064-44583
Email: sales@kih.liebherr.com
Web: www.killarneyhotels.ie

HOTEL ★★★★★ MAP 2 E 4

5 star resort hotel overlooking the famous Gap of Dunloe. 98 spacious bedrooms including suites, all of which are refurbished and all with balconys overlooking Gap of Dunloe or surrounding parkland. Historical park & botanic gardens with ruins of castle. Elegant décor with many valuable antiques. Luxurious lounges, cocktail bar, gourmet restaurant. Extensive leisure facilities: pool, sauna, gym, riding, putting green, tennis, jogging track. 10 ch'ship courses nearby. Sister hotels: Ard-na-Sidhe & Hotel Europe. Spa opening Summer 2006.
Central Res: Tel: 064-71350, Fax: 064-37900.

Bookable on www.irelandhotels.com
Member of Killarney Hotels Ltd

B&B from €92.00 to €105.00

Hilary O'Mara
Manager

Activities:
⛳🏊🎾

Special Offer: Midweek Specials from €255.00 pps
(3 Nights B&B)

98 98 🛏️🍴☎️🖥️📺🅃🛗♿️📶CM❄️🅿️🐾
🛁⛵🎵P🐾🐕🆓 inet WiFi

Closed 04 October - 01 May

Hotel Europe

Killarney,
Co. Kerry

Tel: 064-71300 Fax: 064-37900
Email: sales@kih.liebherr.com
Web: www.killarneyhotels.ie

HOTEL ★★★★★ MAP 2 E 4

5 Star resort hotel, internationally known for its spectacular location on the Lakes of Killarney. 205 spacious bedrooms and suites, all of which have been refurbished, many with balconies overlooking lake or golf course. Elegant lounges, cocktail bar, Panorama Restaurant. Boutique. Health/fitness centre, 25m indoor pool, sauna, gym. Tennis, horse riding, fishing, boating, cycling. 10 championship golf courses nearby. Sister hotels: Hotel Dunloe Castle and Ard-na-Sidhe. Contact us at central reservations: Tel 064 71350.

Bookable on www.irelandhotels.com
Member of Killarney Hotels Ltd

B&B from €90.00 to €97.00

Michael W. Brennan

Activities:
⛳🏊🎾

Member of:

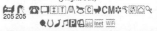

Special Offer: Midweek Specials from €255.00 pps
(3 Nights B&B)

205 205 🛏️🍴☎️🖥️📺🅃🛗♿️📶CM❄️🅿️🐾
🛁⛵🎵P🅿️🔟🆓 inet WiFi

Closed 31 October - 17 March

B&B Rates are per Person Sharing per Night incl. Breakfast.
or **Room Rates** are per Room per Night - See also Page 8

Killarney

Husseys Townhouse & Bar	International Best Western Hotel	Inveraray Farm Guesthouse

43 High Street,
Killarney,
Co. Kerry
Tel: 064-37454 Fax: 064-33144
Email: geraldine@husseystownhouse.com
Web: www.husseystownhouse.com

Killarney,
Co. Kerry
Tel: 064-31816 Fax: 064-31837
Email: inter@iol.ie
Web: www.killarneyinternational.com

Beaufort,
Killarney,
Co. Kerry
Tel: 064-44224 Fax: 064-44775
Email: inver@indigo.ie
Web: www.inver-aray.com

GUESTHOUSE ★★★ MAP 2 E 4 | **HOTEL ★★★ MAP 2 E 4** | **GUESTHOUSE ★★ MAP 2 E 4**

Centrally located, within walking distance of Killarney National Park, the principal shopping areas and the best restaurants in town. This family owned house offers peaceful accommodation in tastefully decorated rooms, equipped to a high standard. Enjoy a choice of breakfast in our delightful dining room, relax in our comfortable guest lounge or cosy friendly bar. For walkers, cyclists, golfers or touring Kerry, this is the discerning traveller's perfect choice. Private parking.

A warm welcome awaits you at the International Hotel. This town centre hotel has been welcoming guests since 1906 and in preparation for its 100th Anniversary, has undergone a carefully planned refurbishment. 90 luxurious bedrooms, 10 with jacuzzi en suite & 3 junior suites all individually decorated and furnished to exceed your expectations. Excellent cuisine served daily in our award-winning Hannigan's Bar & Restaurant. Overall winner of Killarney Looking Good and Best Hotel Award. Opening Spring '06 - 3 Dimensional Golf Simulator allowing you to play world-famous courses.

Bookable on www.irelandhotels.com
Member of Best Western Hotels

A luxury farm guesthouse in a quiet sylvan setting. Views of Killarney Lakes, Mountains and Gap of Dunloe. 9km west of Killarney, 1km off N72, left over Laune Bridge at Shop. Free private trout and salmon fishing on River Laune. A walkers' paradise, angling, walking and golfer groups catered for. Tours arranged. Tea room, playroom, playground and pony for children. Singing pubs, horse riding locally. Home-baking, seafood and dinner a speciality with good, wholesome home cooking. Recommended Le Guide du Routard 2005 and Michelin 2005.

Bookable on www.irelandhotels.com

B&B from €35.00 to €45.00 | **B&B from €50.00 to €120.00** | **B&B from €30.00 to €35.00**

 | |

Geraldine O'Leary
Owner

Terence Mulcahy
General Manager

Eileen & Noel Spillane
Proprietors

Activities:

Member of: | Member of: | Member of:

IRISH HOTELS FEDERATION | IRISH HOTELS FEDERATION | IRISH HOTELS FEDERATION

Special Offer: Midweek Specials from €99.00 pps (3 Nights B&B) | **Special Offer:** Weekend Specials from €139.00 pps (2 Nights B&B & 1 Dinner) | **Special Offer:** Midweek Specials from €85.00 pps (3 Nights B&B)

Closed 25 October - 14 April | **Closed 23 - 26 December** | **Closed 30 November - 20 February**

B&B Rates are per Person Sharing per Night incl. Breakfast. or **Room Rates** are per Room per Night - See also Page 8

Kathleens Country House

Madams Height, Tralee Road,
Killarney,
Co. Kerry
Tel: 064-32810 Fax: 064-32340
Email: info@kathleens.net
Web: www.kathleens.net

GUESTHOUSE ★★★★ MAP 2 E 4

Attentiveness, friendliness, traditional hospitality make Kathleens special. Awarded RAC "Small Hotel of the Year for Ireland", AA ◆◆◆◆◆. A tranquil oasis on 3 acres of mature gardens, one mile to town. Award-winning Breakfast menu. Guest library. Spacious elegant bedrooms with private bathroom, orthopaedic beds, tea/coffee facilities, hairdryer and telephone. Original paintings adorn every wall. RAC ◆◆◆◆◆. Ideal base for Golfing or Touring. Singles welcome. Non smoking. Easy to get to! Hard to leave!

Bookable on www.irelandhotels.com

B&B from €50.00 to €70.00

Kathleen O'Regan Sheppard
Proprietor

Activities:
✓

Member of:
IRISH HOTELS FEDERATION

Special Offer: *Midweek Specials from €140.00 pps (3 Nights B&B) Mar/Apr/Oct 2006*

17 17

Closed 01 November - 14 March

Killarney Avenue Hotel

Town Centre,
Killarney,
Co. Kerry
Tel: 064-32522 Fax: 064-33707
Email: kavenue@odonoghue-ring-hotels.com
Web: www.odonoghue-ring-hotels.com

HOTEL ★★★★ MAP 2 E 4

This boutique 4**** hotel has an idyllic setting in the heart of Killarney. Well appointed air-conditioned guest rooms provide guests with every care and comfort. Druids Restaurant provides a perfect blend of local and classical cuisine. The Kenmare Rooms is a distinctly different hotel bar. Guests are welcome to use the leisure facilities of our sister hotel (Killarney Towers Hotel), 100m away. Underground garage parking available. Close to shopping, vistor attractions and Kerry's premier golf courses.

Bookable on www.irelandhotels.com

B&B from €65.00 to €95.00

Denis McCarthy
General Manager

Activities:
✓ 🦢

Member of:
IRISH HOTELS FEDERATION

Special Offer: *Weekend Specials from €149.00 pps (2 Nights B&B & 1 Dinner)*

66 66

Closed 01 November - 14 March

Killarney Great Southern Hotel

Killarney,
Co. Kerry

Tel: 064-38000 Fax: 064-31642
Email: res@killarney-gsh.com
Web: www.greatsouthernhotels.com

HOTEL ★★★★ MAP 2 E 4

The Great Southern Hotel Killarney combines old world charm and modern elegance. Originally built in 1854 this Victorian hotel was extensively renovated in 2002. Facilities include Garden Room Restaurant, Peppers à la carte restaurant, Innisfallen Spa with swimming pool, steam room, monsoon shower, hydrotherapy bath, beauty treatments. Conference facilities for 800. Bookable worldwide through UTELL Intl or Central Reservations Tel: 01-214 4800.

Bookable on www.irelandhotels.com

Room Rate from €89.00 to €270.00

Conor Hennigan
General Manager

Activities:
🍽 🌡

Member of:
IRISH HOTELS FEDERATION

Special Offer: *Weekend Specials from €199.00 pps (2 Nights B&B & 1 Dinner)*

172 172

Open All Year

B&B Rates are per Person Sharing per Night incl. Breakfast.
or **Room Rates** are per Room per Night - See also Page 8

Killarney

Killarney Lodge

Countess Road,
Killarney,
Co. Kerry
Tel: 064-36499 Fax: 064-31070
Email: klylodge@iol.ie
Web: www.killarneylodge.net

GUESTHOUSE ★★★★ MAP 2 E 4

Welcome to Killarney Lodge, a purpose built four star guesthouse set in private walled-in gardens, yet only 2 minutes walk from Killarney Town centre. The Lodge provides private parking, spacious en suite air-conditioned bedrooms with all modern amenities. Guests can avail of internet access at the Lodge. Enjoy an extensive breakfast menu, relax in comfortable lounges with open fires where traditional home baking is served. The Lodge has justifiably earned an outstanding reputation for quality of service, relaxed atmosphere and friendliness.

B&B from €50.00 to €70.00

Catherine Treacy
Owner

Activities:

Member of:

16 16

Closed 15 November - 01 February

Killarney Oaks

Muckross Road,
Killarney,
Co. Kerry
Tel: 064-37600 Fax: 064-37619
Email: info@killarneyoaks.com
Web: www.killarneyoaks.com

HOTEL ★★★ MAP 2 E 4

Set in the picturesque area of Killarney, 69 de luxe & superior bedrooms, offering every modern amenity and comfort. Set on the edge of Killarney National Park and convenient to Killarney town centre. Enjoy the Acorn Bar & Restaurant, with live music during the season. Our restaurant offers superb local and international dishes, warm and friendly atmosphere. Activities can be arranged for guests. Local amenities include golf, angling, horse riding, sandy beaches and hill walking. Resident car park.

Bookable on www.irelandhotels.com

B&B from €50.00 to €100.00

Eamon Courtney
Proprietor

Member of:

Special Offer: Weekend Specials from €100.00 pps
(2 Nights B&B & 1 Dinner)

69 69

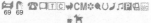

Closed 01 December - 01 February

Killarney Park Hotel

Town Centre,
Killarney,
Co. Kerry
Tel: 064-35555 Fax: 064-35266
Email: info@killarneyparkhotel.ie
Web: www.killarneyparkhotel.ie

HOTEL ★★★★★ MAP 2 E 4

Superbly located in the heart of Killarney Town on its own grounds, this family owned hotel is renowned as a place of elegance laced with warmth and hospitality. The hotel offers 68 beautifully appointed guest rooms and suites complemented by a luxurious full service spa. Other hotel features include a 20m swimming pool, outdoor hot-tub, jacuzzi, library, drawing room, billiards room, games room, golf locker and drying room. Conference facilities for up to 150 delegates. A warm welcome awaits you.

Bookable on www.irelandhotels.com
Member of Leading Small Hotels of the World.

B&B from €132.50 to €217.50

Niamh O'Shea
General Manager

Activities:

Member of:

68 68

Closed 24 - 27 December

B&B Rates are per Person Sharing per Night incl. Breakfast.
or Room Rates are per Room per Night - See also Page 8

Killarney Plaza Hotel & Spa

Town Centre,
Killarney,
Co. Kerry
Tel: 064-21111 Fax: 064-21190
Email: info@killarneyplaza.com
Web: www.killarneyplaza.com

HOTEL U MAP 2 E 4

The Killarney Plaza successfully blends gracious hospitality, quality service and amenities in such a way that guests using the hotel for business or pleasure feel at ease. This elegant hotel enjoys a wonderful location in Killarney. The leisure area and Molton Brown Spa allow guests to unwind and relax in luxurious surroundings. All bedrooms and suites are luxuriously furnished and air-conditioned. The Killarney Plaza is a "must see, must stay" rendezvous.

Bookable on www.irelandhotels.com
Member of Utell

B&B from €85.00 to €150.00

Michael O'Donoghue
Managing Director

Activities:

Member of:

Special Offer: *Weekend Specials from €179.00 pps (2 Nights B&B & 1 Dinner)*

198 198

Closed 01 January - 01 February

Killarney Royal

College Street,
Killarney,
Co. Kerry
Tel: 064-31853 Fax: 064-34001
Email: royalhot@iol.ie
Web: www.killarneyroyal.ie

HOTEL U MAP 2 E 4

Privately owned by the Scally family & located in the heart of Killarney, the Killarney Royal is the perfect base for walking, golfing, & touring the South West of Ireland. Air-conditioned throughout, this 4 star standard boutique property boasts 24 de luxe rooms and also has 5 junior suites tastefully designed by the proprietor Mrs. Scally, who modestly uses a country classical design at the Killarney Royal Hotel. "Overall, outstanding service with a positive attitude. I would recommend it to anyone looking for a small hotel with charm & loads of hospitality" - Peter Zummo.

Bookable on www.irelandhotels.com

B&B from €75.00 to €160.00

Noreen Cronin & Gillian O'Dea
Senior Assistant Managers

Activities:

Member of:

29 29

Closed 23 - 26 December

Killarney Valley Hotel & Suites

Fossa,
Killarney,
Co. Kerry
Tel: 064-23600 Fax: 064-23601
Email: killarneyvalley@eircom.net
Web: www.killarneyvalley.com

HOTEL P MAP 2 E 4

The new Killarney Valley Hotel and Suites is located 3 miles outside of Killarney on the gateway to the Ring of Kerry. This suite hotel comprises 64 en suite bedrooms, which can also be converted into 1 or 2 bedroom suites, a restaurant on the first floor with spectacular views of the Killarney lakes and mountains and the charming Village Bar, which serves an extensive bar food menu.

Member of Gleneagle Group

B&B from €50.00 to €90.00

O'Donoghue Family

Activities:

64 64

Closed 31 October - 01 March

B&B Rates are per Person Sharing per Night incl. Breakfast.
or Room Rates are per Room per Night - See also Page 8

South West 101

Killarney

Killeen House Hotel	Kingfisher Lodge Guesthouse	Lake Hotel

Killeen House Hotel

Aghadoe,
Lakes Of Killarney,
Co. Kerry
Tel: 064-31711 Fax: 064-31811
Email: charming@indigo.ie
Web: www.killeenhousehotel.com

HOTEL ★★★ MAP 2 E 4

The Killeen House is truly a charming little hotel. With only 23 rooms, 8 of them de luxe, it is the ideal base for touring 'God's own country', the magical Kingdom of Kerry. With our DIY Golf Pub and Rozzers elegant dining room you are assured of a memorable experience. Go on, do the smart thing and call us now! We look forward to extending the 'hostility of the house' to you!

Bookable on www.irelandhotels.com

B&B from €70.00 to €120.00

Geraldine & Michael Rosney
Owners

Member of:

IRISH HOTELS FEDERATION

Special Offer: Any 3 Nights Dinner, B&B from €345.00 pps

23 23

Closed 01 November - 10 April

Kingfisher Lodge Guesthouse

Lewis Road,
Killarney,
Co. Kerry
Tel: 064-37131 Fax: 064-39871
Email: kingfisherguesthouse@eircom.net
Web: www.kingfisherkillarney.com

GUESTHOUSE ★★★ MAP 2 E 4

Kingfisher Lodge, an award-winning family-run luxury 3*** Fáilte Ireland, AA ◆◆◆◆ registered guesthouse. Quietly located yet just 4 minutes walk from town centre pubs, restaurants, entertainment and shopping. Beautifully decorated spacious bedrooms with TV, phone, hairdryer, tea/coffee, internet access available. Guest lounge with satellite TV, books, magazines. Varied breakfast menu. Private parking, large gardens. Tackle, drying rooms, tours, golfing, walking, angling arranged with Donal, a qualified guide. Non-smoking house.

Bookable on www.irelandhotels.com
Member of Insight Web Marketing

B&B from €30.00 to €55.00

Ann & Donal Carroll
Proprietors

Activities:

Member of:

IRISH HOTELS FEDERATION

10 10

Closed 12 December - 10 February

Lake Hotel

On Lake Shore,
Muckross Road, Killarney,
Co. Kerry
Tel: 064-31035 Fax: 064-31902
Email: info@lakehotel.com
Web: www.lakehotel.com

HOTEL ★★★ MAP 2 E 4

The most beautiful location in Ireland. Set on Killarney's lake shore. Open log fires, double height ceilings, relaxed & friendly atmosphere. Woodland view standard rooms, superior lakeside rooms with jacuzzi, balcony & some four poster beds. 40 new de luxe superior lakeside rooms in 2006 (10 with jacuzzi by window in room!). "Spa Sensations" with hot tub on the lakeshore, sauna, steam room, gym and treatment rooms. Residents' library. Bookable on www.lakehotel.com

Bookable on www.irelandhotels.com

B&B from €50.00 to €150.00

Niall Huggard
General Manager

Activities:

Member of:

IRISH HOTELS FEDERATION

Special Offer: 2 Nights B&B and 1 Dinner from €113.00 pps

70 70

Closed 10 - 26 December

B&B Rates are per Person Sharing per Night incl. Breakfast. or Room Rates are per Room per Night - See also Page 8

Lime Court

Muckross Road,
Killarney,
Co. Kerry
Tel: 064-34547 Fax: 064-35611
Email: limecrt@iol.ie
Web: www.hoztel.com

GUESTHOUSE ★★★ MAP 2 E 4

Lime Court has the perfect location for those wishing to completely unwind. Just 5 minutes walk from Killarney Town centre, easy on street parking, on the main Ring of Kerry route and Muckross Road. Located beside 4 excellent pubs offering traditional Irish music and good food. Lime Court is also ideally located to take advantage of the INEC, which is 5 minutes walk away. If you would care to walk for another 5 minutes, you are in the heart of Killarney National Park, with the ripples from the world famous Lakes of Killarney breaking at your feet. Lime Court offers a truly serene environment. Access to internet.

B&B from €30.00 to €40.00

Kayan Culloty Rice
Manager

Special Offer: Midweek Specials from €70.00 pps (3 Nights B&B)

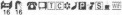
16 16

Open All Year

Loch Lein Country House

Golf Course Road,
Fossa, Killarney,
Co. Kerry
Tel: 064-31260 Fax: 064-36151
Email: stay@lochlein.com
Web: www.lochlein.com

HOTEL U MAP 2 E 4

A secluded Country House with magnificent uninterrupted views over Killarney's famous Lower Lake and the MacGillicuddy Reeks. The hotel's emphasis is on friendly personal service and high standards of food and accommodation. Spacious non-smoking bedrooms have many thoughtful touches to enhance a comfortable and relaxing stay. Ideally located on the Ring of Kerry/Dingle roads, near the Gap of Dunloe. Nearby four golf courses, fishing and horse riding. May we welcome you.

Bookable on www.irelandhotels.com
Member of Les Routiers

B&B from €55.00 to €100.00

Paul & Annette Corridan
Hosts

Member of:

25 25

Closed 05 November - 16 March

McSweeney Arms Hotel

College Street,
Killarney,
Co. Kerry
Tel: 064-31211 Fax: 064-34553
Email: sales@mcsweeneyarms.com
Web: www.mcsweeneyarms.com

HOTEL ★★★ MAP 2 E 4

McSweeney Arms Hotel is a superior 3 star hotel, situated in Killarney Town centre, an ideal base for golfing, touring and shopping. It boasts 26 beautifully appointed bedrooms with private bathroom, TV and direct dial phone. Tony's Sandtrap Bar & Restaurant, where we boast our own lobster tank, specialises in fresh seafood and traditional Irish cuisine. Both the bar and the restaurant host a relaxed friendly atmosphere.

Bookable on www.irelandhotels.com

B&B from €55.00 to €90.00

Tony McSweeney
Proprietor

Activities:

Member of:

26 26

Closed 01 December - 31 January

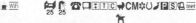

B&B Rates are per Person Sharing per Night incl. Breakfast.
or Room Rates are per Room per Night - See also Page 8

Co. Kerry

Killarney

Muckross Park Hotel

Lakes Of Killarney,
Muckross Village, Killarney,
Co. Kerry
Tel: 064-31938 Fax: 064-31965
Email: info@muckrosspark.com
Web: www.muckrosspark.com

HOTEL ★★★★ MAP 2 E 4

A 70 bedroom de luxe Victorian Hotel set in the heart of Killarney National Park with easy access to the top championship golf courses in Kerry and Cork. Conference Centre, 4 breakaway meeting rooms, mediaeval Atrium Banquet & Reception Hall and Abbey Suite. Two restaurants, GB Shaw's and the Blue Pool. Home to the famous Molly Darcy's Traditional Irish Pub & Restaurant. Winner of Pub of the Year for 9 consecutive years. Launching in 2006, a 10 treatment roomed International Wellbeing Spa.

Bookable on www.irelandhotels.com

B&B from €100.00 to €160.00

*Jackie Lavin
Proprietor*

Activities:
✽✔♪🎾

Member of:
IRISH HOTELS FEDERATION

🛏️🐾 ☎🖥️📋🇹🇨🚗CM✽🅿️🐕⛵♪🎵🏴
🆂🅿️🆑ac🚭Inet WiFi🎄

Open All Year

Murphys of Killarney

College Street,
Killarney,
Co. Kerry
Tel: 064-31294 Fax: 064-31294
Email: info@murphysofkillarney.com
Web: www.murphysofkillarney.com

GUESTHOUSE ★★★ MAP 2 E 4

Murphy's of Killarney: a town centre family-run guesthouse with all rooms newly refurbished, adjacent to bus & rail stations. Incorporating Lord Kenmare's renowned restaurant, Murphy's Traditional Irish Bar, where you can enjoy live Irish music and the more contemporary Squires Bar. Sean, Maire & the staff will make sure that your visit to "Murphy's" is enjoyable & memorable. Amenities include: golf, fishing, horse riding, scenic walks and shopping. Local tours arranged. "Murphy's - a sense of Tradition".

B&B from €40.00 to €55.00

*Maire & Sean Murphy
Proprietors*

🛏️🐾 ☎🖥️📋🇹🇨🚗CM🅿️♪🎵🅿️📺⛷️⛰️
20 20

Closed 19 - 26 December

Old Weir Lodge

Muckross Road,
Killarney,
Co. Kerry
Tel: 064-35593 Fax: 064-35583
Email: oldweirlodge@eircom.net
Web: www.oldweirlodge.com

GUESTHOUSE ★★★★ MAP 2 E 4

A magnificent, luxurious, family-run 4* (AA ♦♦♦♦♦) guesthouse 5 minutes walk from town, on main road, towards National Park. Set in 3/4 acre landscaped gardens. 30 large bedrooms, some with king sized beds, bath, power showers, orthopaedic beds, telephone, multi-channel TV, tea/coffee facilities, ice and hairdryers. 2 lounges, fresh flowers, private parking, home baking, traditional, vegetarian, coeliac breakfasts. Friendly staff, ground floor bedrooms and elevator, drying room. Local advice offered, all tours arranged.

Bookable on www.irelandhotels.com

B&B from €40.00 to €65.00

*Maureen & Dermot O'Donoghue
Proprietors*

Activities:
✽✔

Member of:
IRISH HOTELS FEDERATION

🛏️🐾 ☎🖥️📋🇹🇨🚗CM⛵🅿️📺⛷️
30 30

Closed 23 - 26 December

104   *South West*

B&B Rates are per Person Sharing per Night incl. Breakfast. or **Room Rates** are per Room per Night - See also Page 8

Quality Resort Killarney

Cork Road,
Killarney,
Co. Kerry
Tel: 064-26200 Fax: 064-32438
Email: reservations@qualityhotelkillarney.com
Web: www.qualityhotelkillarney.com

HOTEL ★★★ MAP 2 E 4

The Quality Resort Killarney: Quality accommodation to suit everyone, luxury guest rooms, holiday homes, family apartments & suites in Ireland's favourite holiday destination. A real guest welcome in a fun, friendly atmosphere. A wealth of dining facilities and entertainment. The holiday the whole family can agree on.

Bookable on www.irelandhotels.com
Member of Quality Hotels

B&B from €39.00 to €119.00

Patrick Dillon
General Manager

Member of:

Special Offer: Weekend Specials from €109.00 pps
(2 Nights B&B & 1 Dinner)

291 291

Closed 23 - 26 December

Randles Court Clarion Hotel

Muckross Road,
Killarney,
Co. Kerry
Tel: 064-35333 Fax: 064-35206
Email: info@randlescourt.com
Web: www.randlescourt.com

HOTEL ★★★★ MAP 2 E 4

This AA/RAC 4**** hotel is one of Killarney's gems. Family owned and run, this de luxe hotel offers all the elegance and charm of a country house. Dating back to 1906, the hotel has been tastefully restored with beautiful furniture and open fires. Checker's Restaurant is truly a unique dining experience. The leisure club offers the ultimate in relaxation with its own treatment rooms. The fully automated conference suite is ideal for all events. The perfect setting for a special wedding day. Also closed 23 - 27 December.

Bookable on www.irelandhotels.com

B&B from €70.00 to €150.00

Tom Randles
General Manager

Activities:
:/⏐

Member of:

Special Offer: Weekend Specials from €159.00 pps
(2 Nights B&B & 1 Dinner)

50 50

Closed 01 January - 28 February

Rivermere

Muckross Road,
Killarney,
Co. Kerry
Tel: 064-37933 Fax: 064-37944
Email: info@killarney-rivermere.com
Web: www.killarney-rivermere.com

GUESTHOUSE ★★★★ MAP 2 E 4

Rivermere is a custom built, family-run 4**** guesthouse within walking distance of Lakes and National Park and only 7 minutes walk from town centre. All rooms are spacious with TV, radio, direct dial phone, orthopaedic beds, bath, power showers, hairdryer. Rivermere is in a delightful setting and combines luxury with charm, elegance and serenity, walkers' and golfers' paradise. Drying room available. Private parking. Choose from our delicious breakfast menu. A warm welcome awaits you.

B&B from €40.00 to €65.00

Hannah & Andrew Kissane
Proprietors

Activities:
:/

Member of:

8   8

Closed 04 November - 10 March

B&B Rates are per Person Sharing per Night incl. Breakfast.
or **Room Rates** are per Room per Night - See also Page 8

Killarney

Riverside Hotel	Ross (The)	Scotts Gardens Hotel
Muckross Road, Killarney, Co. Kerry Tel: 064-39200 Fax: 064-39202 Email: stay@riversidehotelkillarney.com Web: www.riversidehotelkillarney.com	Kenmare Place, Killarney, Co. Kerry Tel: 064-31855 Fax: 064-31139 Email: info@theross.ie Web: www.theross.ie	Killarney, Co. Kerry Tel: 064-31060 Fax: 064-36656 Email: scottskill@eircom.net Web: www.gleneagle-hotel.com

UNDER REFURBISHMENT - REOPENING JUNE 2006

UNDER REFURBISHMENT - RE-OPENING JULY 2006

HOTEL U MAP 2 E 4 | **HOTEL R MAP 2 E 4** | **HOTEL R MAP 2 E 4**

On the Muckross Road, the main road to Killarney National Park & Lakes and just 5 mins from town centre. The hotel offers 69 well appointed bedrooms with many overlooking the famous Flesk River against the back drop of the beautiful MacGillycuddy Reeks. Excellent cuisine is prepared by our award-winning chef in the Bacchus Restaurant. Combined with our fine wines and attentive service you can be assured of a wonderful dining experience. While staying at the Riverside, indulge in the pleasure of a health or beauty treatment in our new Rejuvenation Suite.

The Ross, an exciting new boutique hotel which will be re-opening in early Summer 2006. Located in the heart of Killarney Town, with 32 luxurious bedrooms and a stylish bar and restaurant, the Ross will offer a unique experience. As always, a warm welcome awaits you.

Town centre hotel with car parking facilities. 52 bedrooms, re-furbished to 3*** standard with DD phone, satellite TV, hairdryer, tea/coffee facilities. Re-opening July 2006 with 22 two bedroomed suites and 23 de luxe bedrooms. Exciting new restaurant and bar facilities. Tours, cruises, golf, fishing arranged. Entertainment nightly July, August, September and weekends throughout rest of year.

Bookable on www.irelandhotels.com
Member of Irish Court Hotels

Member of The Gleneagle Group

B&B from €45.00 to €125.00 | *B&B from €85.00 to €110.00* | *B&B from €50.00 to €95.00*

Una Young
General Manager

Member of:

Special Offer: Weekend Specials from €109.00 pps (2 Nights B&B & 1 Dinner)

69 69

Padraig & Janet Treacy
Proprietors

Activities:

Member of:

32 32

Maurice Eoin O'Donoghue
Proprietor

Member of:

52 52

Closed 24 - 26 December	Closed 01 January - 31 May	Closed 01 January - 30 June

B&B Rates are per Person Sharing per Night incl. Breakfast. or **Room Rates** are per Room per Night - See also Page 8

Tuscar Lodge	Victoria House Hotel	Wayside House
Golf Course Road, Fossa, Killarney, Co. Kerry	Muckross Road, Killarney, Co. Kerry	Muckross Road, Killarney, Co. Kerry
Tel: 064-31978 Fax: 064-31978 Email: tuscarlodge@eircom.net	Tel: 064-35430 Fax: 064-35439 Email: info@victoriahousehotel.com Web: www.victoriahousehotel.com	Tel: 064-20630 Email: info@guesthousekillarney.com Web: www.guesthousekillarney.com

GUESTHOUSE P MAP 2 E 4 | **HOTEL ★★★ MAP 2 E 4** | **GUESTHOUSE U MAP 2 E 4**

Tuscar Lodge

Tuscar Lodge is a family-run guesthouse. The proprietress Mrs Fitzgerald and her family always ensure that the guests have an enjoyable stay. Situated in scenic surroundings overlooking Loch Lein, with a magnificent view of the Magillycuddy Reeks. With its own car park, it is very central for touring the beauty spots of West Cork and Kerry. Pony trekking, boating, fishing and mountain climbing all nearby. Walking distance to Killarney's three championship golf courses.

Victoria House Hotel

Set at the gateway to Killarney's National Park, this charming and cosy boutique hotel, family owned, and managed, offers the ambience of a country house, with first class personal and friendly staff. Our 35 bedrooms offer comfort and luxury, and are decorated and maintained to an exceptionally high standard. Frequent live music and traditional sessions in "The Ivy Room Bar" add to the ambience of this unique hotel. Private parking available.

Bookable on www.irelandhotels.com

Wayside House

Family-run, 10 bedroom guesthouse within walking distance of both Killarney town and National Park. All bedrooms are on ground floor and are wheelchair accessible.

B&B from €30.00 to €45.00	*B&B from €50.00 to €90.00*	*B&B from €30.00 to €55.00*

Eileen Fitzgerald Proprietor

Activities:

John Courtney Proprietor

Member of:

HOTELS
FEDERATION

Mary O'Sullivan & John Quinn Proprietors

Member of:

HOTELS
FEDERATION

Special Offer: Midweek Specials from €85.00 pps (3 Nights B&B)

5 5	35 35	10 10

Closed 30 October - 01 March	**Closed 01 December - 01 February**	**Open All Year**

B&B Rates are per Person Sharing per Night incl. Breakfast.
or Room Rates are per Room per Night - See also Page 8

Woodlawn House

Woodlawn Road,
Killarney,
Co. Kerry
Tel: 064-37844 Fax: 064-36116
Email: woodlawn@ie-post.com
Web: www.woodlawn-house.com

GUESTHOUSE ★★★ MAP 2 E 4

Old style charm and hospitality. Family-run. Relaxed atmosphere. All modern conveniences. Ideally located 5 minutes walk from town centre. Near leisure centre, lakes and golf courses. Tours arranged. Private parking. Decorated with natural pine wood. Orthopaedic beds dressed in white cotton and linen. Irish and vegetarian menus. Our wholesome breakfasts include freshly squeezed orange juice, homemade preserves and bread. Early bird breakfast also available. A warm welcome assured.

Member of Kerry - Insight

B&B from €45.00 to €60.00

James & Anne Wrenn

Member of:
IRISH HOTELS FEDERATION

Special Offer: Midweek Specials from €112.00 pps
(3 Nights B&B)

🏨🍴 ☎❏🆃©❄✳♨🅹🅿🆂📶
10 10

Closed 23 - 30 December

Bianconi

Killorglin,
Ring Of Kerry,
Co. Kerry
Tel: 066-976 1146 Fax: 066-976 1950
Email: info@bianconi.ie
Web: www.bianconi.ie

GUESTHOUSE ★★★ MAP 1 D 4

Family-run inn on The Ring of Kerry. Gateway to Dingle Peninsula, Killarney 18km. On the road to Glencar - famous for its scenery, lakes, hill walking and mountain climbing. Famous for its table. High standard of food in bar. Table d'hôte and à la carte available. 50 minutes to Waterville, Tralee & Ballybunion golf courses. 15 minutes to Dooks & Beaufort courses. 5 minutes to Killorglin course. 15 mins to Killarney course. Private access to Caragh Lake. Own boat. Mentioned by many guides.

B&B from €50.00 to €60.00

Ray Sheehy
Owner

Activities:
∴✓

Member of:
IRISH HOTELS FEDERATION

🏨🍴 ☎❏🆃©CMU✓♫🆂🆀🔤📶
15 15

Closed 24 - 29 December

Grove Lodge Riverside Guesthouse

Killarney Road,
Killorglin,
Co. Kerry
Tel: 066-976 1157 Fax: 066-976 2330
Email: info@grovelodge.com
Web: www.grovelodge.com

GUESTHOUSE ★★★ MAP 1 D 4

Peace and tranquillity. Relax in luxury riverside accommodation, with spacious de luxe bedrooms and stroll through our mature gardens and riverside walks. Delia prepares an extensive gourmet breakfast menu, home baking from local fresh produce. We are a short walk to Killorglin town centre which has many fine restaurants and lively Irish pubs. We are centrally located to all of Kerry's tourist anemities and attractions. We are highly acclaimed where the majority of our business is repeated and referrals from satisfied customers.

Member of Premier Guesthouses

B&B from €45.00 to €60.00

Fergus & Delia Foley
Owners & Managers

Activities:
∴✓

🏨🍴 ☎❏🆃©❄✳♨🅹🅿📶
10 10

Closed 01 - 31 December

B&B Rates are per Person Sharing per Night incl. Breakfast. or Room Rates are per Room per Night - See also Page 8

Westfield House	Moorings (The)	Parknasilla Great Southern Hotel

Killorglin, Co. Kerry	Portmagee, Co. Kerry	Sneem, Co. Kerry

Westfield House
Tel: 066-976 1909 Fax: 066-976 1996
Email: westhse@iol.ie
Web: www.westfieldhse.com

Moorings (The)
Tel: 066-947 7108 Fax: 066-947 7220
Email: moorings@iol.ie
Web: www.moorings.ie

Parknasilla Great Southern Hotel
Tel: 064-45122 Fax: 064-45323
Email: res@parknasilla-gsh.com
Web: www.greatsouthernhotels.com

GUESTHOUSE ★★★ MAP 1 D 4 | **GUESTHOUSE ★★★ MAP 1 B 3** | **HOTEL ★★★★ MAP 1 C 3**

Westfield House is a family-run guesthouse. All rooms are bright & spacious en suite, orthopaedic beds, direct dial telephone, TV, tea/coffee maker. Extra large family room available. We are situated on the Ring of Kerry in a quiet peaceful location only 5 minutes walk from town with panoramic views of McGillycuddy Reeks. There are five 18 hole golf courses within 20 minutes drive. Recognised stop for many weary cyclists. Ideal location for the hill walker and climber.

The Moorings is a family owned guesthouse & restaurant overlooking the picturesque fishing port in Portmagee. Excellent cuisine, specialising in locally caught seafood. Adjacent to the Moorings is the Bridge Bar, also run by the family, where you can enjoy a wonderful night of music, song & dance. The Moorings is central to all local amenities including angling, diving, watersports, 18 hole golf course etc. Trips to Skellig Michael can be arranged. RAC ♦♦♦♦, BIM Seafood Award 2004.

Acknowledged as one of Ireland's finest hotels, Parknasilla is a 19th century house set in 300 acres of grounds. A classically individual hotel with 83 bedrooms equipped with every modern amenity. Leisure facilities include indoor heated swimming pool, sauna, steam room, jacuzzi, hydrotherapy baths, outdoor hot tub, clay pigeon shooting, horse riding, archery, private 12 hole golf course - special green fees for guests, and guided walks. UTELL International or Central Reservations Tel: 01-214 4800.

Bookable on www.irelandhotels.com

Bookable on www.irelandhotels.com

B&B from €37.50 to €40.00 | *B&B from €40.00 to €60.00* | *Room Rate from €150.00 to €270.00*

Marie & Leonard Clifford Proprietors

Patricia & Gerard Kennedy Proprietors

Activities:

Andrew Rees General Manager

Activities:

Member of:
IRISH HOTELS FEDERATION

Member of:
IRISH HOTELS FEDERATION

Member of:
IRISH HOTELS FEDERATION

Special Offer: Midweek Specials from €100.00 pps (3 Nights B&B)

Special Offer: Weekend Specials from €199.00 pps (2 Nights B&B & 1 Dinner)

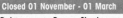
10 10

14 14

83 83

Closed 01 November - 01 March	Closed 01 November - 01 March	Open All Year

B&B Rates are per Person Sharing per Night incl. Breakfast.
or **Room Rates** are per Room per Night - See also Page 8

Co. Kerry
Tahilla / Tarbert / Tralee

Tahilla Cove Country House	Kirby's Lanterns Hotel	Abbey Gate Hotel

Tahilla Cove Country House

Tahilla,
Near Sneem,
Co. Kerry
Tel: 064-45204 Fax: 064-45104
Email: tahillacove@eircom.net
Web: www.tahillacove.com

GUESTHOUSE ★★★ MAP 1 D 3

Travel writers have described this family-run, fully licensed seashore guesthouse as the most idyllic spot in Ireland - the haunt of Irish/British dignitaries. Located on The Ring of Kerry seashore. 14 acre estate boasts mature gardens & private pier. Ideal place for a relaxing holiday/touring centre. Each room has en suite facilities, phone, TV, radio, hairdryer, iron and tea/coffee facilities. Log fires, superb views, home cooking. Take Sneem Road from Kenmare (N70).

B&B from €60.00 to €70.00

James / Deirdre /Chas Waterhouse Owners

Member of:

Special Offer: *7 Nights B&B & 5 Dinners from €570.00 pps*

9 9

Closed 15 October - 01 April

Kirby's Lanterns Hotel

Glin / Tarbert Coast Road,
Tarbert,
Co. Kerry
Tel: 068-36210 Fax: 068-36553
Email: reservations@thelanternshotel.ie
Web: www.thelanternshotel.ie

HOTEL N MAP 5 E 7

The Kirby family of Kirby's Brogue Inn Tralee are the new owners of Kirby's Lanterns Hotel. Overlooking the majestic Shannon Estuary, Kirby's Lanterns Hotel is an ideal tourist base for Kerry, Limerick and Clare. Central to world famous golf courses at Ballybunion, Tralee, Killarney, Adare, Doonbeg & Lahinch. Enjoy a stay at Kirby's Lanterns Hotel. Superb accommodation, great food & friendly service. Food served from 6.30a.m. to 10.00p.m. daily. Music sessions every weekend. Call to Kirby's Lanterns Hotel where a warm Kirby welcome awaits you. Special mid-week and weekend breaks available year round.

Bookable on www.irelandhotels.com

B&B from €50.00 to €75.00

Marie Kirby Manager

Member of:

22 22

Closed 25 December

Abbey Gate Hotel

Maine Street,
Tralee,
Co. Kerry
Tel: 066-712 9888 Fax: 066-712 9821
Email: info@abbeygate-hotel.com
Web: www.abbeygate-hotel.com

HOTEL ★★★ MAP 1 D 5

Welcome, the Abbey Gate Hotel is located in the heart of Tralee. All 100 rooms are spacious with full facilities. The Old Market Place Pub is Tralee's liveliest venue with great pub grub served all day and casual dining in our Bistro at night. Or try our fabulous Toscana Ristorante Italiano for the best in authentic Italian cuisine. The Abbey Gate Hotel is your gateway to the delights of Kerry.

Bookable on www.irelandhotels.com

B&B from €65.00 to €99.95

Kieran Murphy General Manager

Activities:

Member of:

Special Offer: *Weekend Specials from €99.00 pps (2 Nights B&B & 1 Dinner)*

100 100

Closed 24 - 26 December

B&B Rates are per Person Sharing per Night incl. Breakfast. or <u>Room Rates</u> are per Room per Night - See also Page 8

Ballygarry House Hotel

Killarney Road,
Tralee,
Co. Kerry
Tel: 066-712 3322 Fax: 066-712 7630
Email: info@ballygarryhouse.com
Web: www.ballygarryhouse.com

HOTEL ★★★★ MAP 1 D 5

Set on 4 acres of mature themed gardens, Ballygarry House is a newly refurbished country manor with all the treasures associated with times past. Traditional design & contemporary twists lend itself to that 'home away from home' air of wellbeing. With 61 luxurious guest rooms, 1 master suite & 5 junior suites, Library, Drawing room, residents' lounge, renowned award-winning restaurant, old world bar & numerous landscaped walkways. This with our 'Nádúr Spa' makes Ballygarry House a haven for relaxation. 1.5km from Tralee & 6km from Kerry Airport, an ideal location for golfing or touring.

Bookable on www.irelandhotels.com

B&B from €80.00 to €125.00

Padraig McGillicuddy
General Manager

Activities:

Member of:
IRISH HOTELS FEDERATION

Special Offer: Any 2 Nights B&B and 1 Dinner from €159.00 - €199.00 pps

61 61

Closed 23 - 26 December

Ballyroe Heights Hotel

Ballyroe,
Tralee,
Co. Kerry
Tel: 066-712 6796 Fax: 066-712 5066
Email: info@ballyroe.com
Web: www.ballyroe.com

HOTEL ★★★ MAP 1 D 5

A modern luxurious hotel set in six and a half acres of woodland and sloping gardens. Tralee's leading Wedding and Conference venue is just 3km from Tralee Town. Enjoy breathtaking views of The Sliabh Mish Mountains and Tralee Bay from our Bar and Restaurant. All en suite bedrooms have TV, tea/coffee making facilities and hairdryer. Completion of 42 bedroomed extension Summer 2006.

Bookable on www.irelandhotels.com

B&B from €62.00 to €100.00

Mark Sullivan
General Manager

Activities:

Member of:
IRISH HOTELS FEDERATION

Special Offer: Midweek Specials from €145.00 pps (3 Nights B&B)

25 25

Open All Year

B&B Rates are per Person Sharing per Night incl. Breakfast.
or Room Rates are per Room per Night - See also Page 8

Co. Kerry

Tralee

Ballyseede Castle Hotel

Ballyseede,
Tralee,
Co. Kerry
Tel: 066-712 5799 Fax: 066-712 5287
Email: ballyseede@eircom.net
Web: www.ballyseedecastle.com

HOTEL U   MAP 1 D 5

Ballyseede Castle Hotel is a wonderful, intimate 15th century castle set on 35 acres of parkland and garden. The castle has a tradition of excellent cuisine and lovely public areas for morning tea or afternoon coffee. The castle is ideally located for touring Kerry, Cork and Clare. It is a sister hotel of Cabra Castle. Also closed from 02 January to 15 March.

Bookable on www.irelandhotels.com

B&B from €65.00 to €125.00

Marnie Corscadden
General Manager

Member of:

Special Offer: Weekend Specials from €185.00 pps (2 Nights B&B & 1 Dinner)

12 12

Closed 24 - 26 December

Brandon Hotel Conference and Leisure Centre

Princes Street,
Tralee,
Co. Kerry
Tel: 066-712 3333 Fax: 066-712 5019
Email: sales@brandonhotel.ie
Web: www.brandonhotel.ie

HOTEL ★★★   MAP 1 D 5

Renowned, privately owned premises ideally located in the heart of Tralee Town, close to shopping and visitor attractions. The hotel offers a range of accommodation - standard rooms, de luxe rooms and suites, with a choice of bars and restaurants. It is also equipped with full leisure centre incorporating swimming pool, sauna, steam room, jacuzzi, gymnasium and beauty treatment rooms, as well as extensive conference and banqueting facilities. Private Parking available. Tralee is accessible by mainline rail and air with Kerry Airport just 10 miles away.

Bookable on www.irelandhotels.com

B&B from €55.00 to €120.00

Shay Livingstone
General Manager

Activities:

Member of:

Special Offer: Weekend Specials from €109.00 pps (2 Nights B&B & 1 Dinner)

183 183

Closed 23 - 29 December

Brandon Inn

James Street,
Tralee,
Co. Kerry
Tel: 066-712 9666 Fax: 066-712 5019
Email: sales@brandonhotel.ie
Web: www.brandonhotel.ie

HOTEL U   MAP 1 D 5

The concept - quality at a fixed price. Located in Tralee Town centre. Bright, modern and spacious rooms, each en suite with tea/coffee making facilities. The room only price remains fixed whether the room is occupied by 1, 2 or 3 adults or 2 adults and 2 children. Guests at The Brandon Inn have full use of facilities at our sister hotel, Brandon Hotel, which is located a stone throw away. Private parking available for guests.

Room Rate from €79.00 to €99.00

Shay Livingstone
General Manager

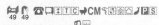

49 49

Closed 01 December - 29 January

B&B Rates are per Person Sharing per Night incl. Breakfast. or **Room Rates** are per Room per Night - See also Page 8

Brook Manor Lodge

Fenit Road,
Tralee,
Co. Kerry
Tel: 066-712 0406 Fax: 066-712 7552
Email: brookmanor@eircom.net
Web: www.brookmanorlodge.com

GUESTHOUSE ★★★★ MAP 1 D 5

A warm welcome awaits you at our new 4**** luxurious, family-run lodge. Only minutes drive from Tralee, golden beaches and Arnold Palmer designed golf course. 30 minutes from Killarney. 40 minutes from Ballybunion. The Lodge is situated in acres of meadowlands and surrounded by a babbling brook. All our rooms are en suite with full facilities. Brook Manor Lodge is the ideal place for the perfect holiday.

B&B from €45.00 to €70.00

Margaret & Vincent O'Sullivan
Owners

Member of:

🛏️ 👤 ☎️ ⛑️ 🅣 🅒 ❄️ 🐾 🅿️ 🆂
8   8

Open All Year

Glenduff House

Kielduff,
Tralee,
Co. Kerry
Tel: 066-713 7105 Fax: 066-713 7099
Email: glenduffhouse@eircom.net
Web: www.glenduff-house.com

GUESTHOUSE ★★★ MAP 1 D 5

Enter the old world charm of the 19th century in our family-run period house set on 6 acres with mature gardens. Refurbished to give the comforts of the modern day, yet keeping its original character with antiques & paintings. Personal attention assured. Relax & enjoy a drink in our friendly bar. Also self catering cottages in the courtyard. Ideally situated for golf and sports amenities. From Tralee take route to racecourse off N21 at Joe Keohane Roundabout. Continue for 4.5 miles and turn right at large sign on right.

Bookable on www.irelandhotels.com
Member of Premier Guesthouses

B&B from €38.00 to €58.00

George & Carmel Ferreira
Owners

Member of:

5   5

Closed 18 December - 06 January

Grand Hotel

Denny Street,
Tralee,
Co. Kerry
Tel: 066-712 1499 Fax: 066-712 2877
Email: info@grandhoteltralee.com
Web: www.grandhoteltralee.com

HOTEL ★★★ MAP 1 D 5

The Grand Hotel is a 3*** hotel situated in Tralee Town centre. Established in 1928, its open fires, ornate ceilings and mahogany furnishings offer guests old world charm in comfortable surroundings. All our rooms are equipped with direct dial telephone, computer point, satellite TV and tea/coffee welcoming trays. Residents can avail of reduced rates to the fabulous Aqua Dome Waterworld complex. Family rooms are available at discounted rates. Limited parking available.

Bookable on www.irelandhotels.com

B&B from €55.00 to €75.00

Dick Boyle
General Manager

Activities:

🏊 🎾

Member of:

🛏️ 👤 ☎️ ⛑️ 🅣 🅒 🐾 CM ⛱️ 🗑️ ♪ 🆂 🈁 📶 Inet
44   44

Special Offer: Weekend Specials from €135.00 pps
(2 Nights B&B & 1 Dinner)

Closed 24 - 27 December

B&B Rates are per Person Sharing per Night incl. Breakfast.
or Room Rates are per Room per Night - See also Page 8

Tralee

Manor West Hotel, Spa & Leisure Club

Manorwest,
Tralee,
Co. Kerry
Tel: 066-719 4500 Fax: 066-719 4545
Email: info@manorwesthotel.ie
Web: www.manorwesthotel.ie

HOTEL P MAP 1 D 5

Tralee's latest edition with 77 bedrooms, including top floor suites. The Manor West Hotel is designed with the discerning 4 star client in mind. Situated on the main Limerick / Killarney road, just over a mile from the town centre, we provide all the facilities you would associate with a contemporary de luxe hotel. A visit to the Harmony Spa & Leisure Club is a must.

Bookable on www.irelandhotels.com
Member of Select Hotels of Ireland

B&B from €60.00 to €120.00

Jim Feeney
General Manager

Activities:

Member of:
HOTELS FEDERATION

Special Offer: Midweek Specials from €99.00 pps
(2 Nights B&B & 1 Dinner)

77 77

Closed 25 - 26 December

Meadowlands Hotel

Oakpark,
Tralee,
Co. Kerry
Tel: 066-718 0444 Fax: 066-718 0964
Email: medlands@iol.ie
Web: www.meadowlands-hotel.com

HOTEL ★★★★ MAP 1 D 5

A charming and intimate hotel, set in a tranquil corner of Tralee, on its own beautiful landscaped gardens. This luxurious hotel comprises 58 superbly appointed rooms, including suites. Our award-winning restaurant specialises in the freshest of locally caught seafood and shellfish cuisine. State of the art conference centre. Ideal base for golfing enthusiasts and touring the Dingle Peninsula, The Ring of Kerry. Experience an experience.

Bookable on www.irelandhotels.com

B&B from €70.00 to €180.00

Padraig & Peigi O' Mathuna
Owners

Activities:

Member of:
HOTELS FEDERATION

Special Offer: Weekend Specials from €150.00 pps
(2 Nights B&B & 1 Dinner)

58 58

Closed 24 - 26 December

Oakley House

Ballymullen,
Tralee,
Co. Kerry
Tel: 066-712 1727 Fax: 066-712 1727
Email: info@oakleyguesthouse.com
Web: www.oakleyguesthouse.com

GUESTHOUSE ★★ MAP 1 D 5

Spacious period house with old world charm and character. Situated on road to Dingle, Killorglin and Ring of Kerry. On N70 Road, turn right at Ballymullen Roundabout, right at next junction, situated on left. Situated on the outskirts of Tralee Town. Overlooking Slieve Mish Mountains. Ideal touring base. 8 minutes walk from town centre, National Folk Theatre, Mediaeval Experience. 10 minutes walk from Aqua Dome. Private car park. Convenient to beaches, angling, golf, horse riding and pony trekking. A céad míle fáilte awaits you.

B&B from €32.00 to €35.00

Michael & Philomena Bennis
Proprietors

Member of:
HOTELS FEDERATION

Special Offer: Midweek Specials from €90.00 pps
(3 Nights B&B)

7 7

Closed 01 - 31 December

B&B Rates are per Person Sharing per Night incl. Breakfast.
or **Room Rates** are per Room per Night - See also Page 8

Tralee Townhouse	Bay View Hotel	Brookhaven Country House

High Street, Tralee, Co. Kerry	Waterville, Co. Kerry	New Line Road, Waterville, Co. Kerry
Tel: 066-718 1111 Fax: 066-718 1112	Tel: 066-947 4122 Fax: 066-947 4504	Tel: 066-947 4431 Fax: 066-947 4724
Email: traleetownhouse@eircom.net	Email: info@bayviewhotelwaterville.com	Email: brookhaven@esatclear.ie
Web: www.traleetownhouse.com	Web: www.bayviewhotelwaterville.com	Web: www.watervilleguesthouse.com

GUESTHOUSE ★★★ MAP 1 D 5	HOTEL CR MAP 1 B 3	GUESTHOUSE ★★★★ MAP 1 B 3

Tralee Townhouse

Centrally located beside all of Tralee's visitor attractions; - Siamsa Tire, Aqua Dome, Geraldine Experience, Kerry County Museum, Blennerville Windmill, Steam Train and the new Tralee Marina. Local amenities include - for the golf enthusiast, the world renowned Tralee & Ballybunion Golf Courses are only a few miles away. 2 excellent 9 hole courses are within 1 mile of the town centre. Fishing, horse riding, hill walking, sports centre with indoor pool, etc. 3*** AA.

Bay View Hotel

The Bay View Hotel has old world charm with beautiful spacious bedrooms with front rooms facing the Atlantic. On the Ring of Kerry in the middle of the village of Waterville the hotel is an ideal location for exploring the peninsula with its breathtaking scenery and archaeological sites. Make sure you visit the Sceilig Rock.

Brookhaven Country House

New purpose built, family-run 4**** country house, overlooking the Atlantic Ocean, and the Waterville Golf Course. Luxury spacious en suite rooms, with all modern facilities, e.g. golf, fishing, (lake and sea) beaches, surfing, horse riding, walking Kerry Way, cycling, Skellig Islands and gourmet restaurants. Private parking and drying room available for golfers, anglers and walkers. On Ring of Kerry route, surrounded by colourful gardens. AA & RAC ♦♦♦♦, plus repeated Sparkling Diamond Accolades.

Bookable on www.irelandhotels.com
Member of Premier Collection Marketing Group

Bookable on www.irelandhotels.com

B&B from €29.50 to €49.00	B&B from €35.00 to €45.00	B&B from €40.00 to €60.00

Eleanor Collins
Manager

Michael O'Shea
Manager

Mary Clifford
Proprietor

Activities:

Member of:
IRISH HOTELS FEDERATION

Member of:
IRISH HOTELS FEDERATION

Member of:
IRISH HOTELS FEDERATION

19 19

58 58

5 5

Closed 24 - 28 December	Closed 01 November - 01 March	Closed 01 January - 01 March

B&B Rates are per Person Sharing per Night incl. Breakfast. or Room Rates are per Room per Night - See also Page 8

South West 115

Co. Kerry

Waterville

Butler Arms Hotel

Waterville,
Co. Kerry

Tel: 066-947 4144 Fax: 066-947 4520
Email: reservations@butlerarms.com
Web: www.butlerarms.com

HOTEL ★★★★ MAP 1 B 3

This charming hotel, on the scenic Ring of Kerry, has been run by 4 generations of the Huggard Family. Tastefully furnished bedrooms, many with magnificent seaviews, cosy lounges, award-winning restaurant specializing in local seafood and the Fishermens Bar with its cosmopolitan ambience. Only 1 mile from Waterville's Championship Golf Links. Renowned salmon and seatrout fishing, sandy beaches, horse riding, hill walking.

Bookable on www.irelandhotels.com
Member of Manor House Hotels

B&B from €90.00 to €150.00

Mary & Peter Huggard Proprietors

Activities:

Member of:

Special Offer: Weekend Specials from €160.00 pps (2 Nights B&B & 1 Dinner)

40 40

Closed 31 October - 08 April

Lakelands Farm Guesthouse

Lake Road,
Waterville,
Co. Kerry

Tel: 066-947 4303 Fax: 066-947 4678
Email: lakelands@eircom.net
Web: www.lakelandshouse.com

GUESTHOUSE ★★★ MAP 1 B 3

Luxury family-run guesthouse in unique location set on Europe's best salmon and sea trout lake. Spectaculor views from all windows. Spacious en suite bedrooms, some with balcony or jacuzzi. Two lounges on ground and first floor. Proprietor is a professional guide with own boats and motors available. Trips to Church Island and free practice golf on site. Activities nearby: horse riding, surfing, walking Kerry Way, trips to Skellig Island. All arranged. Close to Waterville (2 golf courses).

Bookable on www.irelandhotels.com

B&B from €35.00 to €45.00

Anne & Frank Donnelly Proprietors

Activities:

Member of:

12 12

Closed 24 - 26 December

Smugglers Inn

Cliff Road,
Waterville,
Co. Kerry

Tel: 066-947 4330 Fax: 066-947 4422
Email: info@the-smugglers-inn.com
Web: www.the-smugglers-inn.com

GUESTHOUSE ★★★ MAP 1 B 3

The Smugglers Inn, family-run, was an 180 year old farmhouse restored by the Hunt Family in 1980. Since then it has become renowned world-wide for its warm welcome and super restaurant. Situated in a quiet location on a 2km sandy beach, adjacent to Waterville Golf Links, a haven for golfing, fishing, surfing, scuba diving, walking. Comfortable guest bedrooms many with sea views. Panoramic views from our conservatory restaurant. Chef/Proprietor Henry Hunt. Fully licenced bar serving bar food. It has been said "if our fish was any fresher it would have to be cooked underwater".

B&B from €40.00 to €65.00

Henry & Lucille Hunt Proprietors

Activities:

Special Offer: 3 Nights Dinner, B&B from €240.00 pps

14 14

Closed 31 October - 15 March

116 *South West*

B&B Rates are per Person Sharing per Night incl. Breakfast. or Room Rates are per Room per Night - See also Page 8

Waterville Lodge Hotel

Waterville,
Co. Kerry

Tel: 066-947 4436 Fax: 066-947 4502
Email: info@watervillelodge.com
Web: www.watervillelodge.com

HOTEL ** MAP 1 B 3

The Waterville Lodge Hotel is located in Main Street, Waterville, Co. Kerry on the world famous Ring of Kerry. The hotel is overlooking spectacular scenery (beach), only a few minutes drive from the world famous Waterville Golf Course and close to Caherciveen. A natural centre for outdoor pursuits, including golf, watersports, cycling, walking, horse riding and the very best fishing for salmon and trout.

B&B from €35.00 to €50.00

James Hillis
Proprietor

Activities:

Special Offer: Weekend Specials from €90.00 pps
(2 Nights B&B & 1 Dinner)

Closed 24 - 26 December

One source...
Endless possibilities

irelandhotels.com
Official Website of the Irish Hotels Federation

IRISH
HOTELS
FEDERATION

B&B Rates are per Person Sharing per Night incl. Breakfast.
or Room Rates are per Room per Night - See also Page 8

Map of Shannon Region

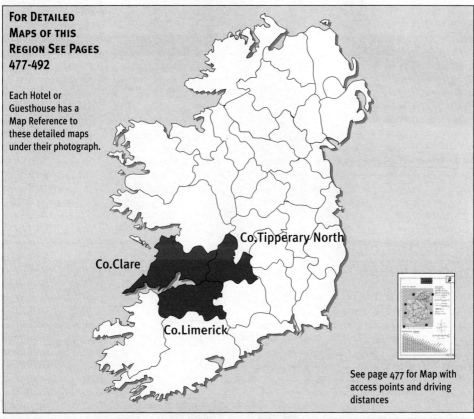

FOR DETAILED MAPS OF THIS REGION SEE PAGES 477-492

Each Hotel or Guesthouse has a Map Reference to these detailed maps under their photograph.

Co.Tipperary North

Co.Clare

Co.Limerick

See page 477 for Map with access points and driving distances

Locations listing

irelandhotels.com
Official Website of the Irish Hotels Federation

INCLUDES DETAILED MAPS & GREAT VALUE SPECIAL OFFERS.

Shannon Region
Romantic and Exciting

IRELAND'S SHANNON REGION

Your holiday in the Shannon Region can be as active or as placid as you choose. Whichever you choose, you are guaranteed relaxation and enjoyment. All the ingredients are there: the towering cliffs and golden beaches of Clare; the enigmatic rockscapes of the Burren; the gentle beauty of the rolling Slieve Bloom Mountains in South Offaly; Tipperary's fertile pastures and the woodland estates in the heart of County Limerick. And, of course, the mighty Shannon River, which has bestowed its riches on the surrounding countryside and glories in its beauty.

This is one of the few remaining places on earth where clean, unpolluted air is taken for granted. You have the space to breathe, to refresh your spirit a universe away from frenetic and crowded cities.

There is a sense of timelessness aided by the many physical reminders of Ireland's turbulent past. Castles, forts and ancient churches, spanning centuries of history, abound, many have been lovingly restored.

At the famous Bunratty Castle, visitors can slip back in time and take part in a 15th century mediaeval banquet of romance and merriment. The Bunratty Folk Park, in the castle grounds, accurately recreates Irish village life at the turn of the century.

Sporting facilities, in contrast, are very much up to date. Imagine golfing in a magnificent, scenic setting or fishing some of the most productive and versatile fishing waters in Europe. Take to the saddle on horse-back and the countryside is yours. If boating is your pleasure, the possibilities are, literally, limitless.

There are many elements to a really memorable holiday and the Shannon Region can provide them all. One of the most important is the feeling of being really welcome, of being valued. This intangible but very real feature of a Shannon holiday will be immediately evident in the sense of fun which you will encounter and an eagerness to treat you as an honoured guest.

In Ireland, enjoyment is an art form. Go to one of the many festivals in the Shannon Region and you will experience the art at its best. Entertainment, spontaneous or organised, is everywhere, so too is good food and good company.

For further information contact:

Tourist Information Office, Arthur's Quay, Limerick. Tel: 061 317522. Fax: 061 317939. Visit our website: www.ShannonRegionTourism.ie

GUINNESS **Calendar of Events** **GUINNESS**

July
Willie Clancy Summer School, Milltown Malbay, Co Clare.

Event details correct at time of going to press.
enjoy Guinness sensibly.

Co. Clare

Ballyvaughan

Ballyvaughan Lodge	Cappabhaile House	Drumcreehy House

Ballyvaughan Lodge

Ballyvaughan,
Co. Clare

Tel: 065-707 7292 Fax: 065-707 7287
Email: ballyvau@iol.ie
Web: www.ballyvaughanlodge.com

GUESTHOUSE ★★★ MAP 6 F 10

Located in the heart of Ballyvaughan, a small fishing village overlooking Galway Bay. A custom built modern guesthouse, dedicated to the comfort and relaxation of our guests. Each room is en suite having TV, direct dial phone, tea/coffee making facilities, etc. Allow us to plan your carefree days in the most unspoilt natural environment imaginable, The Burren, including Neolithic caves, sea fishing, hill walking, cycling, Cliffs of Moher and the Aran Islands.

B&B from €32.50 to €40.00

Pauline Burke
Owner

Member of:
IRISH HOTELS FEDERATION

11 11

Closed 25 - 26 December

Cappabhaile House

Ballyvaughan,
Co. Clare

Tel: 065-707 7260
Email: cappabhaile@oceanfree.net
Web: www.cappabhaile.com

GUESTHOUSE ★★★ MAP 6 F 9

Relax, enjoy the peace & quiet, luxury & comfort and a warm family welcome at Cappabhaile House, a 4 ◆◆◆◆ AA establishment. All rooms are very generously sized with private bathrooms. We have fantastic scenic views of the Burren Mountains, Newtown Castle & Ailwee Cave. Also a private car park, games room & the Burren Gallery, are FREE to our guests. We are a short walk to the Burren Way/ Nature Trail and various pubs/ restaurants and we will provide plenty of information on the area. Perfect base for touring The Burren, Aran Islands, Cliffs of Moher, Galway and Connemara.

Bookable on www.irelandhotels.com

B&B from €33.00 to €46.00

Conor & Margaret Fahy
Proprietors

Member of:
IRISH HOTELS FEDERATION

*Special Offer: Midweek Specials from €90.00 pps
(3 Nights B&B)*

8 8

Closed 30 November - 01 March

Drumcreehy House

Ballyvaughan,
Co. Clare

Tel: 065-707 7377 Fax: 065-707 7379
Email: info@drumcreehyhouse.com
Web: www.drumcreehyhouse.com

GUESTHOUSE ★★★ MAP 6 F 10

Delightful country style house overlooking Galway Bay and the surrounding Burren landscape. Open fires, antique furnishings plus a friendly and personal service by conscientious hosts Armin and Bernadette who help to make your stay both enjoyable and memorable. Tastefully decorated rooms, all en suite and equipped with TV and direct dial phone. Extensive breakfast menu and simple country style cooking in a relaxed and homely atmosphere. AA ◆◆◆◆◆.

B&B from €35.00 to €50.00

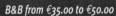

A & B Moloney-Grefkes
Proprietors

Member of:
IRISH HOTELS FEDERATION

10 10

Open All Year

B&B Rates are per Person Sharing per Night incl. Breakfast.
or Room Rates are per Room per Night - See also Page 8

Gregans Castle Hotel

The Burren,
Ballyvaughan,
Co. Clare
Tel: 065-707 7005 Fax: 065-707 7111
Email: stay@gregans.ie
Web: www.gregans.ie

HOTEL ★★★★ MAP 6 F 10

Family-run 4****, luxurious retreat. Set amidst the rugged, unspoilt beauty of the Burren hills. Overlooking Galway Bay. Extensive gardens, gracious country house comforts and blazing turf fires. Restaurant with fresh, organic local produce. Elegantly decorated bedrooms. Swimming, hill walking, horse riding, day trips to Aran Islands. Cliffs of Moher. Golf at Lahinch, Gort and Doonbeg. Situated halfway between Kerry and Connemara. One hour from both Shannon and Galway airports. Book online at www.gregans.ie.

Bookable on www.irelandhotels.com
Member of Ireland's Blue Book

B&B from €85.00 to €105.00

Simon Haden
Managing Director

Member of:
IRISH HOTELS FEDERATION

Special Offer: Weekend Specials from €99.50 pps
(2 Nights B&B & 1 Dinner)

🛏 🐕 ☎ Ⓣ Ⓒ 🍴 CM ✳ ♨ ♫ Ⓟ ⓐⓘⓒ WiFi
21 21

Closed 23 October - 06 April

Hyland's Burren Hotel

Ballyvaughan,
Co. Clare

Tel: 065-707 7037 Fax: 065-707 7131
Email: hylandsburren@eircom.net
Web: www.hylandsburren.com

HOTEL ★★★ MAP 6 F 10

Hyland's Burren Hotel is a charming hotel, dating back to the 18th century and now tastefully modernised. It is located in the picturesque village of Ballyvaughan, nestling in the unique Burren landscape of County Clare. Experience bygone charm with the best of modern facilities, open turf fires, informal bars and restaurants specialising in the finest local seafood. An ideal base for golfing and walking enthusiasts and truly an artist's haven. Also closed during November.

Bookable on www.irelandhotels.com
Member of Irish Country Hotels

B&B from €50.00 to €75.00

Dorothy Costello
Manager

Member of:
IRISH HOTELS FEDERATION

Special Offer: Weekend Specials from €129.00 pps
(2 Nights B&B & 1 Dinner)

🛏 🐕 ☎ Ⓣ Ⓒ 🍴 CM ✳ ♨ ♫ Ⓟ ♿ Ⓢ ⓐ

ⓐ 🐕
29 29

Closed 05 - 30 January

B&B Rates are per Person Sharing per Night incl. Breakfast.
or Room Rates are per Room per Night - See also Page 8

Explore
Ireland's
Heritage

Ardfert Cathedral, Co. Kerry

Portumna Castle, Co. Galway

Roscrea Heritage, Tipperary

with a

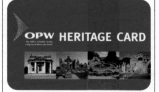
OPW HERITAGE CARD

To find out more:
Tel: (01) 647 6587
heritagecard@opw.ie

Check opening times at:

www.heritageireland.ie

Rusheen Lodge

Ballyvaughan,
Co. Clare

Tel: 065-707 7092 Fax: 065-707 7152
Email: rusheen@iol.ie
Web: www.rusheenlodge.com

GUESTHOUSE ★★★★   MAP 6 F 10

Rusheen Lodge is a 4****, AA ♦♦♦♦♦, RAC ♦♦♦♦♦ luxury guesthouse nestling in the Burren Mountains, providing elegant tastefully designed en suite bedrooms, suites, dining room and resident's lounge, ensuring a comfortable and relaxing stay. Previous winner Jameson Guide and RAC Guesthouse of the Year. RAC Sparkling Diamond and Warm Welcome Award. Ideally located for touring the Shannon region, Aran Islands and Connemara. Non-smoking.

Bookable on www.irelandhotels.com

B&B from €38.00 to €48.00

*Karen McGann
Proprietor*

Member of:
IRISH HOTELS FEDERATION

Special Offer: Midweek Specials from €102.60 pps
(3 Nights B&B)

🛏🐾 ☎🖥📺TC🌤🔆∪♪🅿🇸📶🐕
9 9

Closed 18 November - 02 February

Bunratty Castle Hotel

Bunratty,
Co. Clare

Tel: 061-478700 Fax: 061-364891
Email: info@bunrattycastlehotel.com
Web: www.bunrattycastlehotel.com

HOTEL ★★★   MAP 6 G 7

The new Bunratty Castle Hotel is a 3*** Georgian hotel. Situated 8km from Shannon Airport, in the centre of Bunratty Village overlooking the historic Bunratty Castle and just across the road from Ireland's oldest pub, Durty Nellies. The rooms have been tastefully decorated in the traditional style. All rooms have air-conditioning, satellite TV and have every modern comfort. Relax in Kathleens Pub and Restaurant and enjoy great food. We welcome you to experience the warmth and hospitality here.

Bookable on www.irelandhotels.com

B&B from €55.00 to €95.00

*Deirdre Welch
General Manager*

Activities:
🎣

Member of:
IRISH HOTELS FEDERATION

🛏🐾 ☎🖥📺TC🌤CM🅀∪♪🅿📺
abc 📺 Inet WiFi 🐕
78 78

Closed 24 - 25 December

Bunratty Grove

Castle Road (Low Road),
Bunratty,
Co. Clare

Tel: 061-369579 Fax: 061-369561
Email: bunrattygrove@eircom.net
Web: http://homepage.eircom.net/~bunrattygrove

GUESTHOUSE ★★★   MAP 6 G 7

Bunratty Grove is a purpose built luxurious guesthouse. This guesthouse is located within 3 minutes drive of Bunratty Castle and Folk Park and is 10 minutes from Shannon Airport. Fishing, golfing, historical interests within a short distance. Ideally located for tourists arriving or departing Shannon Airport. Bookings for Bunratty and Knappogue Banquets taken on request. All rooms en suite with multi-channel TV, hairdryer, tea/coffee facilities and direct dial phone.

B&B from €30.00 to €50.00

*Joe & Maura Brodie
Proprietors*

🛏🐾 ☎🖥TC🌤🔆∪♪🅿🇸📶
9 9

Open All Year

B&B Rates are per Person Sharing per Night incl. Breakfast. or **Room Rates** are per Room per Night - See also Page 8

Bunratty Manor Hotel

Bunratty,
Co. Clare

Tel: 061-707984 Fax: 061-360588
Email: bunrattymanor@eircom.net
Web: www.bunrattymanor.net

HOTEL ★★★ MAP 6 G 7

Bunratty Manor is a "home from home" style relaxed intimate family-run hotel renowned for friendliness and hospitality. Just two minutes walk from the mediaeval banquets of Bunratty Castle and Folk Park, it serves as an ideal touring base for the Cliffs of Moher, The Burren and numerous championship golf courses. Our intimate restaurant has a delicately selective menu with locally sourced seafood and meats. It is very popular locally so booking is strongly advised. All rooms have been tastefully redecorated. Come and enjoy the unequalled warmth of Bunratty Manor.

B&B from €59.00 to €69.00

Fiona & Noel Wallace Owners

Activities:

Member of:

14 14

Closed 22 December - 07 January

Bunratty Woods Country House

Low Road,
Bunratty,
Co. Clare
Tel: 061-369689 Fax: 061-369454
Email: bunratty@iol.ie
Web: www.bunrattywoods.com

GUESTHOUSE ★★★ MAP 6 G 7

Bunratty Woods is wonderful 'old world' style guesthouse, all rooms en suite. TV, telephone, hairdryer. At Bunratty Castle turn sharp left on to LOW ROAD, we are the 5th house on left side. 5 miles to Shannon Airport and half a mile to Bunratty Castle/Folk Park, Duty Free shops, pubs and restaurants. Breakfast menu: Our pancakes are famous!! Recommended by Frommer, Michelin, Don McClelland and Fodor Guide Books. Closed mid November to mid March but available for telephone, fax, email bookings for 2006.

B&B from €35.00 to €50.00

Maureen & Paddy O'Donovan Owners

14 14

Closed 10 November - 15 March

THE BURREN Centre

Discover the unique magic of

the Burren Region in 'A Walk Through Time' at the New Burren Centre. The new visitor centre in the historic village of Kilfenora boosts a fantastic new exhibition, audio visual film theatre, local craft shop and tea room.

Opening Times:
Mid March to May
10am to 5pm,
June, July & August
9:30am to 6pm,
September to October
10am to 5pm,
Last Admission 30 min before closing.

Explore the flora, fauna, archaeology and natural history of the Burren in the all new Burren Centre.

Services: Tourist Information Point, Free parking, Beside Kilfenora High Crosses, all Burren reference Maps & Guides available in new craft shop.

Burren Centre, Kilfenora, Co. Clare.
Tel: 065-7088030
Fax: 065-7088102
e-mail: info@theburrencentre.ie
website: www.theburrencentre.ie

B&B Rates are per Person Sharing per Night incl. Breakfast.
or Room Rates are per Room per Night - See also Page 8

Co. Clare

Doolin

Aran View House Hotel & Restaurant

Coast Road,
Doolin,
Co. Clare
Tel: 065-707 4061 Fax: 065-707 4540
Email: bookings@aranview.com
Web: www.aranview.com

HOTEL ★★★ MAP 5 E 9

A Georgian house built in 1736, it has a unique position commanding panoramic views of the Aran Islands, the Burren region and the Cliffs of Moher. Situated on 100 acres of farmland, Aran View echoes spaciousness, comfort and atmosphere in its restaurant and bar. Menus are based on the best of local produce, fish being a speciality. All rooms with private bathroom, colour TV and direct dial phone. Visitors are assured of a warm and embracing welcome at the Aran View House Hotel.

B&B from €50.00 to €80.00

*Theresa & John Linnane
Proprietors*

Activities:
:✓/

Member of:
IRISH HOTELS FEDERATION

🐾🦆 ☎️📺🆃🅲⇄CM✿♻️🅟🐾🅐ℹ️
19 19

Closed 31 October - 14 April

Ballinalacken Castle Country House & Restaurant

Coast Road,
Doolin,
Co. Clare
Tel: 065-707 4025 Fax: 065-707 4025
Email: ballinalackencastle@eircom.net
Web: www.ballinalackencastle.com

HOTEL ★★★ MAP 5 E 9

A romantic peaceful oasis steeped in history and ambience offering the most spectacular views of the Cliffs of Moher, Aran Islands, Atlantic Ocean & Connemara Hills. Built in 1840 as the home of Lord O'Brien. Family members radiate a warm friendly welcome. Peat and log fires add to the cosy atmosphere. Ideal base for exploring Clare. Recommended by Egon Ronay, Michelin, Fodor, Frommer, Charming Hotels of Ireland, New York Times, Washington Post & London Times.

B&B from €50.00 to €88.00

*Mary & Denis O'Callaghan
Proprietors*

Activities:
:✓/

Member of:
IRISH HOTELS FEDERATION

🐾🦆 ☎️📺🆃🅲⇄🅟🐾🅐ℹ️
12 12

Closed 31 October - 22 April

Ballyvara House

Ballyvara,
Doolin,
Co. Clare
Tel: 065-707 4467 Fax: 065-707 4868
Email: bvara@iol.ie
Web: www.ballyvarahouse.com

GUESTHOUSE N MAP 5 E 9

Luxury accommodation and exceptional service await you at Ballyvara House. Renovated to 4 star standards with nothing spared regarding guests' comfort: all the spacious rooms have at least a queen-size bed with our luxurious suites boasting king-size sleigh beds. Every bath is either a jacuzzi or spa bath. Relax and unwind in our lounge bar which serves wine and beer or courtyard garden over a glass of fine wine after a day of exploring the Aran Islands, Burren or Cliffs of Moher. AA ◆◆◆◆◆ and Super Supper Award.

B&B from €35.00 to €75.00

*John & Rebecca Flanagan
Hosts*

Member of:
IRISH HOTELS FEDERATION

Special Offer: *Weekend Specials from €109.00 pps
(2 Nights B&B & 1 Dinner)*

🐾🦆 ☎️📺🆃🅲⇄CM✿♻️🅟🅟🅢🆈🅐🔷
11 11
Inet 🐕

Closed 01 November - 01 March

B&B Rates are per Person Sharing per Night incl. Breakfast.
or **Room Rates** are per Room per Night - See also Page 8

Cullinan's Seafood Restaurant & Guesthouse	Doonmacfelim House	O'Connors Farmhouse

Cullinan's Seafood Restaurant & Guesthouse

Doolin,
Co. Clare

Tel: 065-707 4183 Fax: 065-707 4239
Email: cullinans@eircom.net
Web: www.cullinansdoolin.com

Doonmacfelim House

Doolin,
Co. Clare

Tel: 065-707 4503 Fax: 065-707 4129
Email: doonmacfelim@iol.ie
Web: www.doonmacfelim.com

O'Connors Farmhouse

Doolin,
Co. Clare

Tel: 065-707 4314 Fax: 065-707 4498
Email: joan@oconnorsdoolin.com
Web: www.oconnorsdoolin.com

GUESTHOUSE ★★★ MAP 5 E 9

Unique setting overlooking the Aille river, centrally located in the heart of Doolin. Our elegant bedrooms all have spacious bathrooms with power showers, tea/coffee making facilities, telephones & hairdryers. Private car parking. Imaginative menus are carefully chosen by the chef/owner, specialising in locally caught seafood. Accredited Best Restaurant Award 2004. Highly recommended by Michelin, Fodors, Bridgestone, Geogina Campbell. RAC ◆◆◆, AA ◆◆◆ and RAC Dining Award 2004.

GUESTHOUSE ★★★ MAP 5 E 9

Doonmacfelim House is a 3*** guesthouse, situated on our farm in the village of Doolin, famous for traditional Irish music. Excellent location for visiting Cliffs of Moher, boat to Aran Islands, visiting prehistoric ruins. Its geology, flora, caves, archaeology and history set it apart as a place of mystery and beauty. All rooms en suite, with hairdryers, direct dial telephone. Shannon Airport & Killimer Car Ferry 70km. Hard tennis court, rackets supplied.

GUESTHOUSE N MAP 5 E 9

Spacious modern guesthouse situated in the heart of Doolin, within 5 minutes stroll from pubs, shops and restaurants. Home-baking, breakfast menu and laundry facilities. We offer a high standard of accommodation in comfortable spacious bedrooms. All rooms are en suite with direct dial telephones, television, tea/coffee facilities and hairdryers. Recommended by travel writers. Tourism award winners. A warm Irish welcome awaits you. Group rates available on request.

Member of Irish Farmhouse Holidays

B&B from €30.00 to €45.00

*James & Carol Cullinan
Owners*

Member of:

B&B from €30.00 to €38.00

*Majella & Frank Moloney
Owners*

B&B from €35.00 to €40.00

*Jaon & Pat O'Connor
Owners*

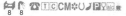

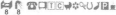

Closed 23 - 26 December	Closed 22 - 28 December	Closed 01 December - 31 January

B&B Rates are per Person Sharing per Night incl. Breakfast.
or **Room Rates** are per Room per Night - See also Page 8

Ennis

Ardilaun Guesthouse

Galway Road,
Ennis,
Co. Clare
Tel: 065-682 2311 Fax: 065-684 3989
Email: purcells.ennis@eircom.net
Web: www.ardilaun.com

GUESTHOUSE ★★★ MAP 6 F 8

Ardilaun is a modern, architect designed 3*** guesthouse overlooking the River Fergus and Ballyallia Lake amenity area. Most rooms enjoy panoramic views of the river and all are superbly decorated with en suite, phone, TV, hairdryer, tea/coffee facilities. Our gym, sauna & fishing facilities also overlook the river and are available to guests only. Ardilaun is just 2 mins drive to the new Ennis swimming pool. Situated 20 mins drive from Shannon Airport on N18. Ideal touring base for Clare, Limerick & Galway. Recently received certificate of Merit Award 2002.

Bookable on www.irelandhotels.com

B&B from €37.50 to €45.00

*Anne Purcell
Proprietress*

Activities:

10 10

Closed 24 - 27 December

Ashford Court Boutique Hotel

Old Mill Road,
Ennis,
Co. Clare
Tel: 065-689 4444 Fax: 065-689 4455
Email: info@ashfordcourt.ie
Web: www.ashfordcourt.ie

HOTEL P MAP 6 F 8

The Ashford Court Hotel is a new boutique style hotel, conveniently located within walking distance of Ennis town centre. Each of the individually decorated rooms is en suite with power shower, satellite TV, DD phone, computer/internet access, ironing facilities and hairdryer. Kingsize beds & crisp white linens offer the ultimate in luxury, comfort & style. Juliano's Restaurant led by Chef Lachini offers authentic Italian cuisine & specialises in local seafood & certified Irish Angus Beef. Ideally situated within minutes of Shannon Airport, the Burren, Cliffs of Moher, Bunratty Castle, Ailwee Caves, Dunbeg & Lahinch Golf Courses.

B&B from €40.00 to €90.00

*Corinne Mannion
Proprietor*

Member of:
IRISH HOTELS FEDERATION

*Special Offer: Weekend Specials from €115.00 pps
(2 Nights B&B & 1 Dinner)*

27 27

WiFi

Closed 24 - 29 December

Auburn Lodge Hotel

Galway Road,
Ennis,
Co. Clare
Tel: 065-682 1247 Fax: 065-682 1232
Email: stay@irishcourthotels.com
Web: www.irishcourthotels.com

HOTEL ★★★ MAP 6 F 8

Located in the historic town of Ennis, the 95 bedroom Auburn Lodge Hotel is the ideal base for the Golf or Fishing Holiday. Convenient to Lahinch, Shannon, Dromoland, Woodstock and Ennis. It offers a wide choice of rolling parkland or links courses - with golf to suit everyone. Within a few miles drive are the Cliffs of Moher, Scenic Burren, Ailwee Caves and Bunratty Castle and Folk Park. Enjoy nightly traditional music in Tailor Quigleys Pub and re-live the day's golf. Shannon International Airport 15km. Leisure Centre opening late 2006.

Bookable on www.irelandhotels.com
Member of Irish Court Hotels

B&B from €35.00 to €115.00

*Angela Lyne
Proprietor*

Activities:

Member of:
IRISH HOTELS FEDERATION

*Special Offer: Weekend Specials from €99.00 pps
(2 Nights B&B & 1 Dinner)*

95 95

Inet

Closed 25 December

B&B Rates are per Person Sharing per Night incl. Breakfast.
or Room Rates are per Room per Night - See also Page 8

Banner Lodge

Market Street,
Ennis,
Co. Clare
Tel: 065-682 4224 Fax: 065-682 1670
Email: bannerlodge_ennis@eircom.net
Web: www.bannerlodge.com

GUESTHOUSE ★★ MAP 6 F 8

Located in the heart of Ennis Town within easy reach of shops and restaurants. 10 miles from Shannon International Airport and within 30 minutes drive of all county tourist attractions. Downstairs Henry J's Bar provides nightly entertainment. All bedrooms are en suite with TV, phone and tea/coffee facilities. Local attractions include the Aran Islands, The Burren, Cliffs of Moher and Bunratty Castle.

B&B from €35.00 to €35.00

Noel Carr

8 8 ☎📺🎵🍴🅿📶

Closed 23 December - 07 January

Cill Eoin House

Kildysert Cross,
Clare Road, Ennis,
Co. Clare
Tel: 065-684 1668 Fax: 065-684 1669
Email: cilleoin@iol.ie
Web: www.euroka.com/cilleoin

GUESTHOUSE ★★★ MAP 6 F 8

Cill Eoin, named after the nearby 13th century abbey, is a 3*** guesthouse on the main tourist route to the west coast of Clare, with its unparallelled beauty in the scenery of the desolate Burren and the majestic vistas that are the Cliffs of Moher. Golf, with a links and three courses nearby, is abundantly available. Horse riding, fishing and many other pastimes are well provided for in the area. Call and see us soon, you will feel at home.

Bookable on www.irelandhotels.com

B&B from €35.00 to €40.00

Bridget & Pat Glynn Lucey

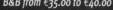

Member of:

HOTELS
FEDERATION

Special Offer: *Midweek Specials from €90.00 pps
(3 Nights B&B)*

14 14 ☎📺📶✳💧🅿📶🍴🅿🏷

Closed 24 - 27 December

Fountain Court

Lahinch Road,
Ennis,
Co. Clare
Tel: 065-682 9845 Fax: 065-684 5030
Email: kyran@fountain-court.com
Web: www.fountain-court.com

GUESTHOUSE ★★★ MAP 6 F 8

Peaceful rural setting yet only 4 minutes drive to Ennis. Superb bedrooms with king sized beds, TV, tea making facilities, Hi Fi, bath and power shower. Family-run with delicious breakfasts. Beautiful reception rooms and the personal service of the owners make Fountain Court the ideal base to tour The Burren National Park, Cliffs of Moher and Bunratty Castle and Folk Park. Golf, fishing and horse riding all within easy reach. Shannon Airport 15km. Fax & Internet access from all rooms. Mini-bars in all rooms. AA ◆◆◆◆ - Red Diamond Award.

Member of Premier Guesthouses

B&B from €35.00 to €50.00

Kyran & Breed Carr

Member of:
IRISH
HOTELS
FEDERATION

12 12 ☎📺📶✳💧🅿📶🍴🅿📶🏷

Closed 01 December - 07 March

B&B Rates are per Person Sharing per Night incl. Breakfast.
or **Room Rates** are per Room per Night - See also Page 8

Shannon 127

Magowna House Hotel

Inch,
Ennis,
Co. Clare
Tel: 065-683 9009 Fax: 065-683 9258
Email: info@magowna.com
Web: www.magowna.com

HOTEL ★★★ MAP 6 F 8

We are a beautifully located, family managed, country house hotel with extensive gardens and lovely views. Ideal for an active or purely relaxing break. Close to excellent golf courses, angling and walks. (Mid-Clare Way 1.5km). Shannon Airport, Cliffs of Moher, The Burren, Doolin, Bunratty Castle, Killimer Car Ferry to Kerry within easy reach. Function/Conference room (capacity 200). Enjoy hospitality, comfort, good food and a genuine welcome in the heart of County Clare.

Member of Irish Family Hotels

B&B from €50.00 to €56.00

Gay Murphy
Proprietor

Activities:
✓

Member of:
IRISH HOTELS FEDERATION

Special Offer: Weekend Specials from €130.00 pps
(2 Nights B&B & 1 Dinner)

10 10 ☎□▥▣ⓣⒸ CM☀♂♪-♀S🖱⊞ 🐕

Closed 24 - 26 December

Old Ground Hotel

O'Connell Street,
Ennis,
Co. Clare
Tel: 065-682 8127 Fax: 065-682 8112
Email: reservations@oldgroundhotel.ie
Web: www.flynnhotels.com

HOTEL ★★★ MAP 6 F 8

Ivy clad manor house dates to the 18th century. The hotel offers 83 de luxe rooms and luxurious new rooms with king beds and spacious suites. Our elegant formal dining room is renowned for excellent cuisine. Visit our recently opened Town Hall Café. The hotel is located in the heart of Ennis, 20 minutes drive from Shannon Airport, close to the Cliffs of Moher, The Burren, Bunratty Castle and many superb challenging golf courses, such as Doonbeg and Lahinch. GDS Access LE. Online reservations at www.flynnhotels.com

Bookable on www.irelandhotels.com
Member of Flynn Hotels

B&B from €52.50 to €75.00

Allen Flynn, Managing Dir
Mary Gleeson, Gen Manager

Activities:
✓

Member of:
IRISH HOTELS FEDERATION

Special Offer: Weekend Specials from €115.00 pps
(2 Nights B&B & 1 Dinner)

83 83 ☎□▥▣ⓣⒸ ♥CM☀♂♪S🖱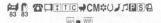

Closed 24 - 25 December

Temple Gate Hotel

The Square,
Ennis,
Co. Clare
Tel: 065-682 3300 Fax: 065-682 3322
Email: info@templegatehotel.com
Web: www.templegatehotel.com

HOTEL ★★★ MAP 6 F 8

This charming town house hotel, family owned and managed is truly a haven in the heart of Ennis. Built on the site of 19th century. convent, it offers a unique combination of historical beauty & exceptional service. Preachers Pub features live music & an acclaimed bar menu. JM's bistro - awarded the prestigious AA Rosette for 9 consecutive years. The great hall - Conference, Wedding & Banqueting suite, a unique venue. Near Shannon Intl. Airport, Bunratty, Cliffs of Moher and Lahinch & Doonbeg golf courses. Awarded Ireland's Best Service Excellence Award 2004.

Bookable on www.irelandhotels.com

B&B from €72.50 to €89.00

Paul Madden
Managing Director

Activities:
✓⊤

Member of:

IRISH HOTELS FEDERATION

Special Offer: Weekend Specials from €129.00 pps
(2 Nights B&B & 1 Dinner)

70 70 ☎□▥▣ⓣⒸ♥CM☀♂♪S⊞

Closed 24 - 27 December

B&B Rates are per Person Sharing per Night incl. Breakfast. or Room Rates are per Room per Night - See also Page 8

Westbrook House

Galway Road,
Ennis,
Co. Clare
Tel: 065-684 0173 Fax: 065-686 7777
Email: westbrook.ennis@eircom.net
Web: www.westbrookhouse.net

GUESTHOUSE ★★★ MAP 6 F 8

Westbrook House is a recently built luxury guesthouse in Ennis. All rooms are fitted to exceptionally high standards. Within walking distance of the centre of historic Ennis, with its friendly traditional pubs and fantastic shopping. Ideal base for golfing holidays, special discounts with local golf courses. A short drive to the majestic Cliffs of Moher, The Burren or Bunratty Castle and Folk Park. Only 15 minutes from Shannon Airport.

B&B from €35.00 to €45.00

*Sheelagh & Domhnall Lynch
Proprietors*

Member of:
IRISH HOTELS FEDERATION

🏠 🐾 ☎ 🖥 T C ✳ ♨ U J P S Y 🖶 Inet 🐕
10 10

Closed 23 - 26 December

Falls Hotel Spa & Leisure Centre

Ennistymon, Near Lahinch,
Co. Clare
Tel: 065-707 1004 Fax: 065-707 1367
Email: sales@fallshotel.ie
Web: www.fallshotel.ie

HOTEL ★★★ MAP 5 E 9

The Falls Hotel is conveniently located for touring The Burren, The Cliffs of Moher and for the golfer The Championship Lahinch Golf Course is a mere 3 km, with Doonbeg only a 20 minutes drive. The hotel itself is surrounded by 50 acres of woodland and riverside walks. The Falls Hotel exudes warmth & atmosphere - the Georgian manor entrance, 140 spacious bedrooms, fully equipped Spa & Leisure Centre - with 20 metre pool, gym, sauna, treatment rooms - Bar, Bistro, Restaurant & Conference and Banqueting facilities for 350 people.

Bookable on www.irelandhotels.com

B&B from €60.00 to €75.00

*James O'Brien
General Manager*

Activities:
⛳ 🎣 ♨

Member of:
IRISH HOTELS FEDERATION

🏠 🐾 ☎ 🖥 ± T 🌊 C ✎ CM ✳ 🎯 👁 📷 🔍
♨ U J 🎵 P S 🛗 ✳ 🐾
140 140

Open All Year

Grovemount House

Lahinch Road,
Ennistymon,
Co. Clare
Tel: 065-707 1431 Fax: 065-707 1823
Email: grovmnt@eircom.net
Web: www.grovemount.com

GUESTHOUSE ★★★ MAP 5 E 9

Grovemount House is a family-run guesthouse situated on the outskirts of Ennistymon Town. From here you can access with ease the renowned Cliffs of Moher and the spectacular and unique Burren. Just 5 minutes drive away is Lahinch championship golf links and Blue Flag Beach. Whatever is your pleasure: fishing, golfing, sightseeing, horse riding or the best traditional music, enjoy and then return to luxurious tranquillity in Grovemount House.

Bookable on www.irelandhotels.com
Member of Premier Guesthouses

B&B from €32.00 to €40.00

*Sheila Linnane
Owner*

Activities:
⛳ 🎵

Member of:
IRISH HOTELS FEDERATION

*Special Offer: Midweek Specials from €90.00 pps
(3 Nights B&B)*

🏠 🐾 ☎ 🖥 T 🖥 ✎ CM ✳ J P S
7 7

Closed 01 November - 30 April

B&B Rates are per Person Sharing per Night incl. Breakfast.
or Room Rates are per Room per Night - See also Page 8

Co. Clare

Kilkee

Halpin's Townhouse Hotel

Erin Street,
Kilkee,
Co. Clare
Tel: 065-905 6032 Fax: 065-905 6317
Email: halpinshotel@iol.ie
Web: www.halpinsprivatehotels.com

HOTEL ★★★ MAP 5 D 7

Highly acclaimed 3*** town house hotel. Combination of old world charm, fine food, vintage wines & modern comforts - overlooking old Victorian Kilkee, near Shannon Airport & Killimer car ferry. Ideal base for touring - Cliffs of Moher, Bunratty, The Burren & Loop drive. Nearby golf courses - Lahinch, Doonbeg & Ballybunion. Accolades- RAC, AA, Times, Best Loved Hotels, Johansens. Sister property of Aberdeen Lodge and Merrion Hall.
USA toll free 1800 617 3178.
Global free phone +800 12838155.
Direct Dial 353 65 905 6032.

Bookable on www.irelandhotels.com
Member of Best Loved Hotels of the World

B&B from €40.00 to €65.00

Pat Halpin
Proprietor

Activities:
✓

Member of:
IRISH HOTELS FEDERATION

🛏🦮☎□TC꒿CM✳♒J P S🎱ab📺
12 12

Closed 15 November - 15 March

Kilkee Bay Hotel

Kilrush Road,
Kilkee,
Co. Clare
Tel: 065-906 0060 Fax: 065-906 0062
Email: info@kilkee-bay.com
Web: www.kilkee-bay.com

HOTEL ★★★ MAP 5 D 7

A superb location - 3 minutes walk from Kilkee's renowned Blue Flag beach and town centre. This modern hotel has 41 spacious en suite bedrooms with direct dial phone, tea/coffee facilities and TV. On site tennis court, bar and bistro. The perfect base for touring the Cliffs of Moher, Burren and Ailwee Caves. Shannon Airport/Limerick City within an hour's drive. Luxury spa and leisure centre opening 2006.

B&B from €40.00 to €65.00

Michael Connolly
General Manager

Activities:
✓ 🎣 ⛳

Member of:
IRISH HOTELS FEDERATION

*Special Offer: Weekend Specials from €109.00 pps
(2 Nights B&B & 1 Dinner)*

🛏🦮☎□Ⓣ꒿♒☐CM✳🎰🐾
41 41
♫🎵P S🎱ab🍴

Closed 26 October - 11 March

Strand Guest House

The Strand Line,
Kilkee,
Co. Clare
Tel: 065-905 6177 Fax: 065-905 6177
Email: thestrandkilkee@eircom.net
Web: www.clareguesthouse.com

GUESTHOUSE ★★★ MAP 5 O 7

Situated on the seafront in Kilkee, one of the most westerly seaside resorts in Europe. Kilkee is built around a 1.5km beach, considered one of the best and safest bathing places in the west with breathtaking coastal walks. The Strand makes an ideal touring base - visit The Burren, Cliffs of Moher, Ailwee Caves. For golf enthusiasts there is a local 18 hole course, Kilrush 13km, Doonbeg 13km, Lahinch 42km or Ballybunion 40km (via car ferry). Restaurant fully licenced, specialises in local seafood.

Bookable on www.irelandhotels.com

B&B from €35.00 to €55.00

Johnny & Caroline Redmond

Member of:
IRISH HOTELS FEDERATION

Special Offer: Midweek Specials Available

🛏🦮☎□TC꒿J🎱ab
6 6

Open All Year

B&B Rates are per Person Sharing per Night incl. Breakfast.
or Room Rates are per Room per Night - See also Page 8

Thomond Guesthouse & Kilkee Thalassotherapy Centre

Grattan Street,
Kilkee,
Co. Clare
Tel: 065-905 6742 Fax: 065-905 6762
Email: info@kilkeethalasso.com
Web: www.kilkeethalasso.com

GUESTHOUSE ★★★ MAP 5 D 7

Thomond Guesthouse is a magnificent premises with 5 en suite rooms coupled with Kilkee Thalassotherapy Centre, offering natural seaweed baths, algae body wraps, beauty salon and other thalassotherapy treatments. Non-smoking. Children over 16 welcome. Ideal for those looking for a totally unique and relaxing break. Situated in beautiful Kilkee with golfing, scuba diving, deep sea angling, dolphin watching, swimming, pony trekking & spectacular cliff walks, nearby. Private car parking. Winner Best Day Spa 2004 - Irish Beauty Industry.

B&B from €35.00 to €45.00

Eileen Mulcahy
Proprietor

Activities:

Special Offer: 2 Nights B&B and 6 Treatments from €300.00 pps

5   5

Closed 20 December - 10 January

Lakeside Hotel & Leisure Centre

Killaloe,
Co. Clare

Tel: 061-376122 Fax: 061-376431
Email: lakesidehotelkilaloe@eircom.net
Web: www.lakeside-killaloe.com

HOTEL ★★★ MAP 6 H 8

On the banks of the River Shannon, overlooking Lough Derg, the Lakeside is the ideal base for touring Counties Clare, Limerick and Tipperary. Enjoy our fabulous indoor leisure centre with its 40 metre water-slide, swimming pools, sauna and steam rooms, jacuzzi, gym, snooker and creche rooms. Our 3*** hotel has 46 en suite bedrooms. Fully licensed restaurant and conference facilities available.

B&B from €55.00 to €75.00

Christopher Byrnes
General Manager

Member of:

IRISH
HOTELS
FEDERATION

46   46

Closed 23 - 26 December

Lantern House

Ogonnelloe,
Killaloe,
Co. Clare
Tel: 061-923034 Fax: 061-923139
Email: phil@lanternhouse.com
Web: www.lanternhouse.com

GUESTHOUSE ★★★ MAP 6 H 8

Ideally situated overlooking Lough Derg in a beautiful part of East Clare, 6 miles north of historic Killaloe and 45 minutes drive from Shannon Airport. Our en suite rooms are non-smoking, have semi-orthopaedic beds, direct dial phone, TV and radio. Residents' lounge, homely atmosphere and safe car parking. Enjoy the wonderful views from our fully licenced restaurant. Owner chef. Local activities include golf, watersports, fishing, pony trekking and walking.

B&B from €39.00 to €45.00

Elizabeth Coppen /
Philip Hogan
Owners

6   6

Closed 01 November - 01 March

B&B Rates are per Person Sharing per Night incl. Breakfast.
or Room Rates are per Room per Night - See also Page 8

Shannon   131

Central Guesthouse

46 Henry Street,
Kilrush,
Co. Clare
Tel: 065-905 1332 Fax: 065-905 1332
Email: centralguesthouse@eircom.net
Web: www.westclare.com

GUESTHOUSE ★★★ MAP 5 E 7

Family-run attractive Georgian town house on N67 route (Kilrush-Heritage Town). Close to Shannon Airport - Killimer / Tarbert Car Ferry - Cliffs of Moher - The Burren and Loop Head Drive. Major golf courses nearby - Kilrush, Kilkee, Doonbeg, Lahinch and Ballybunion. Attractive woodlands with walled gardens and walks. Marina within walking distance, boat trips to Scattery Island. Also, dolphin watching on River Shannon. Close to all restaurants and amenities.

Member of Premier Guesthouses

B&B from €45.00 to €50.00

Mary & Sean Cotter
Proprietors

Member of:

Closed 23 - 26 December

Atlantic Hotel

Main Street,
Lahinch,
Co. Clare
Tel: 065-708 1049 Fax: 065-708 1029
Email: info@atlantichotel.ie
Web: www.atlantichotel.ie

HOTEL ★★★ MAP 5 E 9

The Atlantic Hotel is a family-run hotel where comfort and friendliness are our priority. The intimate dining room offers the very best in local seafood. All rooms are en suite and have direct dial phone, TV, hairdryer and tea/coffee making facilities. 51km from Shannon Airport, 5 minutes from the famous Lahinch championship golf courses, Cliffs of Moher and The Burren. Recently refurbished and upgraded, this charming little hotel has much to offer our special guests. A warm welcome awaits you.

B&B from €55.00 to €65.00

Alan Logue
Managing Director

Member of:

Open All Year

Dough Mor Lodge

Station Road,
Lahinch,
Co. Clare
Tel: 065-708 2063 Fax: 065-707 1384
Email: dough@gofree.indigo.ie
Web: www.doughmorlodge.com

GUESTHOUSE ★★★ MAP 5 E 9

Purpose-built family-run guesthouse with residents' lounge and dining room. Private car parking and large garden. You can see Lahinch's famous golf links from the house. Tee times can be booked and arranged for guests. This is an ideal location for golfing, touring The Burren or visiting the Cliffs of Moher. The beach is within 5 minutes walk. Lahinch Sea World has a fine heated indoor swimming pool. The ideal place to unwind and enjoy your holiday.

Bookable on www.irelandhotels.com
Member of Premier Collection

B&B from €45.00 to €60.00

Jim Foley

Activities:

Member of:

Special Offer: Midweek Specials from €125.00 pps (3 Nights B&B)

Closed 31 October - 31 March

B&B Rates are per Person Sharing per Night incl. Breakfast. or Room Rates are per Room per Night - See also Page 8

Greenbrier Inn Guesthouse

Lahinch,
Co. Clare

Tel: 065-708 1242 Fax: 065-708 1247
Email: gbrier@indigo.ie
Web: www.greenbrierinn.com

GUESTHOUSE ★★★ MAP 5 E 9

Luxurious 3*** guesthouse, overlooking Lahinch Golf Links and the Atlantic Ocean. Situated 300 yards from Lahinch Village with its excellent restaurants, pubs and shops. All rooms are en suite with antique style pine furnishings, pressurised showers, orthopaedic beds, DD phones, multi-channel TV, tea/coffee making facilities. An excellent base from which to visit the Cliffs of Moher, play the famous Lahinch Golf Links or the spectacular Greg Norman designed Doonbeg Golf Links 18 miles away. "Come and enjoy our home while away from your own".

Member of Premier Guesthouses of Ireland

B&B from €35.00 to €85.00

*Margaret & Victor Mulcahy
Proprietors*

Activities:

Member of:
IRISH HOTELS FEDERATION

14 14

Closed 20 November - 07 March

Lahinch Golf & Leisure Hotel

Lahinch,
Co. Clare

Tel: 065-708 1100 Fax: 065-708 1228
Email: info@lahinchgolfhotel.com
Web: www.lahinchgolfhotel.com

HOTEL U MAP 5 E 9

Situated on the former site of the Aberdeen Arms, this property has undergone an extensive renovation, which has transformed the hotel into a luxurious property in the heart of Lahinch. Relax and de-stress in our leisure centre or avail of our many treatments in the Lahinch Golf & Leisure Club. Enjoy an intimate dining experience in our Dunes Restaurant or relax in the cosy atmosphere of the Aberdeen Bar. Only 5 mins from Lahinch Golf Course, the hotel is an ideal base for the discerning golfer. The Blue Flag Beach at Lahinch is only a stroll away. The perfect base for touring The Burren and West Clare.

B&B from €55.00 to €85.00

*John O' Meara
General Manager*

Activities:

*Special Offer: Weekend Specials from €155.00 pps
(2 Nights B&B & 1 Dinner)*

144 144

Open All Year

B&B Rates are per Person Sharing per Night incl. Breakfast.
or Room Rates are per Room per Night - See also Page 8

Moy House

Lahinch,
Co. Clare

Tel: 065-708 2800 Fax: 065-708 2500
Email: moyhouse@eircom.net
Web: www.moyhouse.com

GUESTHOUSE ★★★★ MAP 5 E 9

Moy House prevails over the breathtaking seascape of Lahinch Bay, set on 15 acres of ground, adorned by mature woodland and a picturesque river. Major restoration has transformed this 18th century country house in keeping with present day expectations of superior standards, yet preserving its unique character style and period ambience. Personal attention and relaxation of a sanctuary, yet minutes away from the many amenities available, are the hallmarks that distinguish us.

Member of Ireland's Blue Book

B&B from €105.00 to €125.00

Brid O'Meara
General Manager

Member of:
IRISH HOTELS FEDERATION

9 9

Open All Year

Sancta Maria Hotel

Lahinch,
Co. Clare

Tel: 065-708 1041 Fax: 065-708 1529
Email: sanctamaria01@eircom.net
Web: www.sancta-maria.ie

HOTEL ★★ MAP 5 E 9

The McInerney Family have welcomed holiday makers to the Sancta Maria for over 50 years. Many of the attractive bedrooms overlook the famous Lahinch Golf Links and golden beach, which are within 100 metres of the hotel. Our restaurant specialises in fresh produce and special emphasis is placed on local seafoods and home-baking. The Sancta Maria is the ideal base for touring The Burren or visiting the Cliffs of Moher and Aran Islands.

Bookable on www.irelandhotels.com

B&B from €42.00 to €52.00

Thomas McInerney
Proprietor

Activities:

Member of:
IRISH HOTELS FEDERATION

Special Offer: Midweek Specials from €120.00 pps (3 Nights B&B)

24 24

Closed 01 November - 01 March

Shamrock Inn Hotel

Main Street,
Lahinch,
Co. Clare

Tel: 065-708 1700 Fax: 065-708 1029
Email: info@shamrockinn.ie
Web: www.shamrockinn.ie

HOTEL ★★ MAP 5 E 9

Situated right in the heart of charming Lahinch. All tastefully decorated rooms have direct dial phone, TV, hairdryer and tea/coffee making facilities. Our restaurant is renowned for its warm and intimate atmosphere offering a choice of excellent cuisine, catering for all tastes. Delicious home-cooked bar food is served daily and by night the bar comes to life with the sound of music. Whatever your interest, golf, fishing or horse riding, we can arrange it for you.

B&B from €55.00 to €65.00

Alan Logue
Managing Director

Member of:
IRISH HOTELS FEDERATION

10 10

Open All Year

B&B Rates are per Person Sharing per Night incl. Breakfast. or Room Rates are per Room per Night - See also Page 8

Vaughan Lodge
The Lodge At Lahinch

Ennistymon Road,
Lahinch,
Co Clare
Tel: 065-7081111 Fax: 065-7081011
Email: info@vaughanlodge.ie
Web: www.vaughanlodge.ie

HOTEL P MAP 5 E 9

New purpose built designer country house hotel situated on the edge of the village overlooking the links. Bedrooms are spacious and include power showers. Fourth generation hoteliers specialising in traditional hospitality and fine food. This hotel is one of a select group of intimate hotels offering an international standard of design and ambience while retaining the lovely atmosphere of a traditional owner-run lodge. A relaxing, charming retreat.

B&B from €70.00 to €125.00

Maria & Michael Vaughan
Owners / Managers

Member of:
IRISH HOTELS FEDERATION

Special Offer: Midweek Specials from €180.00 pps
(3 Nights B&B)

22 22

Closed 22 December - 01 March

Logue's Liscannor Hotel

Liscannor,
Co. Clare
Tel: 065-708 6000 Fax: 065-708 1713
Email: info@loguesliscannorhotel.com
Web: www.loguesliscannorhotel.com

HOTEL ★★★ MAP 5 E 9

Nestling between the Cliffs of Moher and The Burren overlooking the Atlantic Ocean the newly re-developed Logue's Liscannor Hotel offers superb accommodation and cuisine. 55km from Shannon Airport, 5 minutes from the world-famous Lahinch Golf Course, the Cliffs of Moher and The Burren makes it the ideal base for touring or relaxation. All rooms are en suite with DD phone, TV, hairdryer and tea/coffee making facilities. Our newly decorated banqueting suite combined with our ideal setting makes the hotel the perfect location for your wedding day. Let us make your dream a reality.

Bookable on www.irelandhotels.com

B&B from €55.00 to €70.00

Derek Logue
Proprietor

Special Offer: Weekend Specials from €115.00 pps
(2 Nights B&B & 1 Dinner)

50 50

Open All Year

B&B Rates are per Person Sharing per Night incl. Breakfast. or Room Rates are per Room per Night - See also Page 8

Lisdoonvarna

Kincora House and Gallery Restaurant

Lisdoonvarna,
Co. Clare

Tel: 065-707 4300 Fax: 065-707 4490
Email: kincorahotel@eircom.net
Web: www.kincora-hotel.com

GUESTHOUSE ★★★ MAP 5 E 9

Award-winning country inn, where the Drennan family offers a warm welcome to our guests. A landmark building since 1860, the house exudes charm, character and a lovely ambience. Comfortable en suite bedrooms all with lovely views. Enjoy fine food and fine art in our Gallery Restaurant which is set in beautiful gardens. Relax in our old atmospheric pub with turf fires. Ideal base for The Burren, the Cliffs of Moher, Lahinch Golf Course, Shannon Airport 1 hour. AA ♦♦♦♦ RAC ♦♦♦♦. National Garden Awards. Irish Inn of the Year 1998, 2001 & 2003.

Bookable on www.irelandhotels.com
Member of Signpost Premier Hotels

B&B from €35.00 to €65.00

Doreen & Diarmuid Drennan Proprietors

Member of:

14 14

Closed 31 October - 15 March

Lisdoon Lodge

Kilfenora Road,
Lisdoonvarna,
Co. Clare

Tel: 065-707 5849 Fax: 065-707 5849
Email: lisdoonlodge@eircom.net
Web: www.lisdoonlodge.com

GUESTHOUSE N MAP 5 E 9

Situated 5 minutes walk from Spa Wells on Kilfenora Road. De luxe bedrooms, some ground floor, TV, DD phones, hairdryers, tea/coffee facility. Friendly & welcoming atmosphere. Extensive breakfast menu, sauna, Indian head massage, reiki crystal therapy extra. Burren & sea walks, pub craic, golf, pitch & putt, Cliffs of Moher, Doolin, Aran Islands, Aillwee Caves, Lahinch all within 10 minutes drive. 1 hour from Shannon. Private parking, package holidays - relaxation. All welcome. Céad Míle Fáilte.

Bookable on www.irelandhotels.com

B&B from €30.00 to €40.00

Oliver Connolly & Bernadette Keyes

Member of:

Special Offer: *Midweek Specials from €89.00 pps (3 Nights B&B)*

8 8

Open All Year

Lynchs Hotel

The Square,
Lisdoonvarna,
Co. Clare

Tel: 065-707 4010 Fax: 065-707 4611
Email: lynchshotel@eircom.net
Web: www.lynchsoflisdoonvarna.ie

HOTEL ★ MAP 5 E 9

Situated in the centre of Lisdoonvarna, Lynch's offers the best of value. This family-run premises is ideal for summer family holidays or off season weekend getaways. 12 rooms en suite with all the necessities, comfortable lounge bar with open fires, Victorian style dining hall for evening meals and a café veranda with views of the village from all corners. Heated, seated and covered outdoor terrace with the best of live music at weekends.

B&B from €25.00 to €65.00

Niall Byrne Manager

Special Offer: *Weekend Specials from €70.00 pps (2 Nights B&B & 1 Dinner)*

12 12

Closed 15 January - 15 February

B&B Rates are per Person Sharing per Night incl. Breakfast. or Room Rates are per Room per Night - See also Page 8

Rathbaun Hotel

Lisdoonvarna,
Co. Clare

Tel: 065-707 4009 Fax: 065-707 4009
Email: rathbaunhotel@eircom.net
Web: www.rathbaunhotel.com

HOTEL ★★ MAP 5 E 9

Rathbaun Hotel is on the main street of Lisdoonvarna. We are renowned for our live music. Quality accommodation, excellent homemade food with genuinely friendly and personal service. A happy, welcoming atmosphere and brilliant value for money are the hallmarks of our hotel. We offer maps and helpful information to all our guests on the Burren. Céad míle fáilte.

Bookable on www.irelandhotels.com
Member of Countrywide Hotels - MinOtel Ireland

B&B from €30.00 to €50.00

John Connolly

Member of:
IRISH HOTELS FEDERATION

Special Offer: 3 Nights Special B&B from €90.00 pps

12 12

Closed 10 October - 01 April

Sheedy's Country House Hotel

Lisdoonvarna,
Co. Clare

Tel: 065-707 4026 Fax: 065-707 4555
Email: info@sheedys.com
Web: www.sheedys.com

HOTEL ★★★ MAP 5 E 9

Set among herb and vegetable gardens, Sheedy's is described in the Campbell Guide as "One of the West of Ireland's Best Loved Small Hotels". Rooms are individually decorated with power showers, luxury bathrooms and music centres. The Sheedy house dates back to the mid 1700s, the oldest in the village. 5 minutes drive from Doolin. Cliffs of Moher and the Burren region are close by. John's cooking has been awarded 2 rosettes from AA and Best Breakfast in Munster 2004. Less than 1 hour from Shannon.

Bookable on www.irelandhotels.com
Member of Manor House Hotels

B&B from €60.00 to €90.00

John & Martina Sheedy

Member of:
IRISH HOTELS FEDERATION

Special Offer: Weekend Specials from €139.00 pps
(2 Nights B&B & 1 Dinner)

11 11

Closed 01 October - 15 March

B&B Rates are per Person Sharing per Night incl. Breakfast.
or Room Rates are per Room per Night - See also Page 8

Aran Islands Cruise
and Angling

Liscannor, Co. Clare

Visit the Islands and view the cliffs

Visit all of the three of the Aran Islands and view the spectacular Cliffs of Moher on the way with the only cruise of its kind which enables you to do it all in one day, giving ample time on each island for sightseeing, laze on the beach, or stroll around and commune with the magic that is Aran.

These Islands are extremely picturesque and the inhabitants retain the old Irish way of life. There are numerous archaeological and historical sites to be visited on the Islands. Mini bus and pony and trap tours available. Bicycles for hire. There are restaurants and pubs on all the islands, most with traditional music sessions.

Sunset cruises to the cliffs of Moher.

Deep sea fishing for groups and individuals

Available for charter.

O Callaghan Angling,
The Pier, Liscannor, Co. Clare.
Tel: 065-6821374
Mobile: 086-2673704 /
BOOKINGS
086-1527755
Email:
mocallaghan.ennis@eircom.net
Web: www.ocallaghanangling.com

M.V." True Light."
42ft Interceptor, Built 2002,
2 x 300 H.P. Engines,
Passenger Licence
for 38 Passengers.

Co. Clare

Milltown Malbay

Admiralty Lodge

Spanish Point,
Miltown Malbay,
Co. Clare
Tel: 065-708 5007 Fax: 065-708 5030
Email: info@admiralty.ie
Web: www.admiralty.ie

GUESTHOUSE N MAP 5 E 8

A truly charming country lodge in a romantic setting located on the west coast of Co. Clare. Developed to a 4**** specification, all superior rooms are individually designed with king sized French style 4 poster beds, Italian marble en suites, air-conditioning, Bose Surround System & LCD flat screen televisions. Winner of the Georgina Campbell 'Newcomer of the Year' award 2005. Our luxurious "Piano Room" restaurant offers modern, contemporary cuisine where flavour & taste are paramount & presentation is key. Enjoy the tranquillity of this peaceful part of Ireland. Helipad on site.

Bookable on www.irelandhotels.com

B&B from €75.00 to €100.00

Pat O'Malley
Proprietor

Special Offer: Weekend Specials from €180.00 pps
(2 Nights B&B & 1 Dinner)

12 12

Closed 01 January - 09 March

Bellbridge House Hotel

Spanish Point,
Milltown Malbay,
Co. Clare
Tel: 065-708 4038 Fax: 065-708 4830
Email: info@bellbridgehotelclare.com
Web: www.bellbridgehotelclare.com

HOTEL ★★★ MAP 5 E 8

Situated on the West Clare coastline, this hotel offers excellent accommodation and cuisine. Adjacent to Spanish Point Golf Course, sandy beaches, horse riding, fishing, tennis and water sports. Ideal base for touring the Burren, Cliffs of Moher, Ailwee Caves, Bunratty Castle and Folk Park. A hotel with friendly and efficient staff whose aim is to make your stay enjoyable and memorable. All rooms have hairdryer, tea/coffee making facilities, DD phone and colour TV. World famous Lahinch and Doonbeg Golf Courses are within a 10 minutes drive. Where memories are made and nothing is overlooked but the sea.

Bookable on www.irelandhotels.com
Member of Select Hotels of Ireland

B&B from €55.00 to €75.00

Derek Logue
Proprietor

Activities:
✓

Member of:
IRISH HOTELS FEDERATION

Special Offer: Weekend Specials from €115.00 pps
(2 Nights B&B & 1 Dinner)

59 59

Open All Year

Burkes Armada Hotel

Spanish Point,
Milltown Malbay,
Co. Clare
Tel: 065-708 4110 Fax: 065-708 4632
Email: info@burkesarmadahotel.com
Web: www.burkesarmadahotel.com

HOTEL ★★★ MAP 5 E 8

The re-developed Burkes Armada Hotel commands a superb ocean-front setting in the beautiful seaside resort of Spanish Point. All rooms are furnished to a very high standard with suites and superior rooms available. The Cape Restaurant offers exceptional cuisine under the attention of an award-winning culinary team, in contemporary modern surroundings with private bar area. The hotel also offers a private garden area, fitness room and reading room. Holiday packages available. Also extensive conference and banqueting facilities.

Bookable on www.irelandhotels.com
Member of Irish Country Hotels

B&B from €50.00 to €85.00

John J.Burke
General Manager

Member of:
IRISH HOTELS FEDERATION

Special Offer: Midweek Specials from €99.00 pps
(3 Nights B&B)

61 61

Closed 25 December

B&B Rates are per Person Sharing per Night incl. Breakfast. or Room Rates are per Room per Night - See also Page 8

Mountshannon Hotel

Mountshannon,
Co. Clare

Tel: 061-927162 Fax: 061-927272
Email: info@mountshannon-hotel.ie

HOTEL ★★ MAP 6 H 9

The Mountshannon Hotel, situated in the rural and peaceful village of Mountshannon, offers you first class accommodation in friendly surroundings. All bedrooms are en suite with direct dial phone, TV, tea/coffee making facilities and hairdryer. Our continental style restaurant, which is known for excellent and reasonably priced cuisine, overlooks our garden and Lough Derg. Private car park. 4 mins walk from Mountshannon Harbour. Fishing, pony trekking and golf are available. Large function room catering for weddings & parties.

Member of The Independents Hotel Association

B&B from €40.00 to €45.00

Pauline & Michael Madden
Director / Owner

Activities:

Member of:

16 16

Closed 24 - 26 December

Dromoland Castle

Newmarket-on-Fergus,
Co. Clare

Tel: 061-368144 Fax: 061-363355
Email: sales@dromoland.ie
Web: www.dromoland.ie

HOTEL ★★★★★ MAP 6 G 8

Located 13km from Shannon Airport. Stately halls, elegant public areas and beautifully furnished guest rooms are steeped in a timeless atmosphere that is unique to Dromoland. The international reputation for excellence is reflected in the award-winning cuisine in the castle's Earl of Thomond & Fig Tree Restaurant in the Dromoland Golf & Country Club. A completely renovated 18-hole championship golf course, fishing, horse riding, clay shooting, health and beauty clinic and much more.

Member of Preferred Hotels & Resorts WW

Room Rate from €225.00 to €509.00

Mark Nolan
General Manager

Member of:

Special Offer: *Weekend Specials from €410.00 pps*
(2 Nights B&B & 1 Dinner)

100 100

Open All Year

Golf View

Latoon, Quin Road,
Newmarket-on-Fergus,
Co. Clare

Tel: 061-368095 Fax: 065-682 8624
Email: mhogangolfviewbandb@eircom.net
Web: www.golf-view.com

GUESTHOUSE ★★★ MAP 6 G 8

New purpose built family-run 3*** guesthouse, overlooking Dromoland Castle and Clare Inn Golf Course, one hundred metres off N18 on Quin Road at the entrance to the Clare Inn Hotel. Non-smoking en suite rooms on the ground floor with phone, multi-channel TV and hairdryers. Local tourist attractions include Bunratty and Knappogue Castles, many 18 hole golf courses and horse riding schools. Castle banquets can be arranged. Shannon Airport 10 minutes. Private car park.

B&B from €40.00 to €50.00

Maureen Hogan
Proprietor

Member of:

6 6

Closed 20 - 28 December

B&B Rates are per Person Sharing per Night incl. Breakfast.
or **Room Rates** are per Room per Night - See also Page 8

Co. Clare - Co. Limerick

Newmarket-on-Fergus / Shannon Airport / Adare

Hunters Lodge	Great Southern Hotel	Adare Manor Hotel & Golf Resort

Hunters Lodge

The Square,
Newmarket-on-Fergus,
Co. Clare
Tel: 061-368577 Fax: 061-368057
Email: hunterslodge@eircom.net

Great Southern Hotel

Shannon Airport,
Shannon,
Co. Clare
Tel: 061-471122 Fax: 061-471982
Email: res@shannon-gsh.com
Web: www.greatsouthernhotels.com

Adare Manor Hotel & Golf Resort

Adare,
Co. Limerick

Tel: 061-396566 Fax: 061-396124
Email: reservations@adaremanor.com
Web: www.adaremanor.com

GUESTHOUSE ★★★ MAP 6 G 8

HOTEL ★★★ MAP 6 G 7

HOTEL ★★★★★ MAP 6 G 7

Ideally situated for visitors arriving or departing from Shannon Airport (12km). We offer 6 comfortable bedrooms en suite with telephone and TV. Our olde worlde pub and restaurant specialises in good quality fresh food served in a relaxed atmosphere with a friendly and efficient service. Local tourist attractions include Bunratty Folk Park, castle banquets and many 18 hole golf courses. Ideal stopover for touring Co. Clare or commencing your trip to the West of Ireland.

Shannon Great Southern is a hotel with exceptional style and comfort within walking distance of the terminal building at Shannon Airport. All 115 rooms are en suite with direct dial phone, TV, tea/coffee making facilities, hairdryer and trouser press. Leisure facilities include a gym and steam room. Bookable worldwide through UTELL International or central reservations Telephone Number: 01-214 4800.

Located 20 miles from Shannon Airport. Adare Manor Hotel & Golf Resort, set on the banks of the River Maigue, boasts splendour in its luxuriously finished rooms. The Oak Room Restaurant provides haute cuisine laced with Irish charm. Indoor heated pool, fitness room, spa. Outdoor pursuits include fishing, laser shooting, horse riding, and the Robert Trent Jones Senior championship golf course. An ideal venue for a romantic getaway or group event.

Bookable on www.irelandhotels.com

Bookable on www.irelandhotels.com
Member of Leading Small Hotels of the World

B&B from €40.00 to €45.00

Room Rate from €89.00 to €160.00

Room Rate from €284.00 to €414.50

*Robert & Kathleen Healy
Proprietors*

*Louise O'Hara
General Manager*

Activities:

Member of:
IRISH HOTELS FEDERATION

*Anita Carey
General Manager*

Activities:

Member of:
IRISH HOTELS FEDERATION

Special Offer: Inclusive Packages Available Subject to Availability

6 6

115 115
Inet WiFi

63 63
WiFi

Open All Year

Closed 24 - 26 December

Open All Year

B&B Rates are per Person Sharing per Night incl. Breakfast.
or **Room Rates** are per Room per Night - See also Page 8

Carrabawn House

Killarney Road (N21),
Adare,
Co. Limerick

Tel: 061-396067 Fax: 061-396925
Email: bridget@carrabawnhouseadare.com
Web: www.carrabawnhouseadare.com

GUESTHOUSE ★★★ MAP 6 G 7

Only 20 miles from Shannon Airport, beside Adare Manor Golf Resort. This superior quality guest accommodation is a must for the weary traveller. We take pride in caring for you as though you were a member of our family. Tastefully decorated, Carrabawn House is ideally located within a few minutes walk of the village centre. Set among award-winning gardens, a delight in all seasons, your stay is assured of being memorable indeed. Many of our guests return from year to year, such is our friendly service. So come stay a while and "be our guest". First prize winners "Garden Award" 2003 and 2004.

Member of Premier Guesthouses

B&B from €35.00 to €45.00

Bridget Lohan
Proprietor

Activities:
✓

Member of:

Special Offer: Midweek Specials from €90.00 pps
(3 Nights B&B)

🐾 🐕 🐎 📺 T ☀ 🔌 J P S 🛏 Inet
8 8

Closed 24 - 26 December

Dunraven Arms Hotel

Adare,
Co. Limerick

Tel: 061-396633 Fax: 061-396541
Email: reservations@dunravenhotel.com
Web: www.dunravenhotel.com

HOTEL ★★★★ MAP 6 G 7

Established in 1792 a 4**** old world hotel surrounded by ornate thatched cottages, in Ireland's prettiest village. Each bedroom, including 24 suites, is beautifully appointed with antique furniture, dressing room and bathroom en suite. Award-winning restaurant, AA Three Red Rosettes. Leisure centre comprised of a 17m pool, steam room, gymnasium and massage and beauty therapy rooms. Equestrian and golf holidays a speciality. 30 minutes from Shannon Airport. Hotel of the Year 2004 - Georgina Campbell Jameson Guide.

Bookable on www.irelandhotels.com
Member of Small Luxury Hotels of the World

Room Rate from €135.00 to €200.00

Louis Murphy
Proprietor

Member of:

Special Offer: Weekend Specials from €150.00 pps
(2 Nights B&B & 1 Dinner)

🐾 🐕 🐎 📺 T C 🅿 CM ☀ 🖨 🔓 💻 J
♫ P 🔓 Inet WiFi 🐕 🐎

Open All Year

B&B Rates are per Person Sharing per Night incl. Breakfast.
or **Room Rates** are per Room per Night - See also Page 8

Co. Limerick

Adare / Castleconnell / Limerick City

Fitzgeralds Woodlands House Hotel, Health and Leisure Spa

Knockanes,
Adare,
Co. Limerick
Tel: 061-605100 Fax: 061-396073
Email: reservations@woodlands-hotel.ie
Web: www.woodlands-hotel.ie

HOTEL ★★★ MAP 6 G 7

Luxurious 94 bedroom hotel located in the splendour of Adare, on its own grounds of 44 acres, the gateway to the scenic south west. Superior and executive suites available boasting whirlpool baths. Brennan Room Restaurant, Timmy Mac's Traditional Bar and Bistro, music sessions on selected dates. Reva's Hair, Beauty & Relaxation Spa boasting Balneotherapy spa baths & Stone Therapy massage. State of the art Health & Leisure Spa. Golf & health spa breaks a speciality. Excellent Wedding and Conference Facilities.

Bookable on www.irelandhotels.com
Member of Irish Country Hotels

B&B from €50.00 to €150.00

Dick, Mary & David Fitzgerald Hosts

Activities:

Member of:

Special Offer: Midweek Specials from €120.00 pps (3 Nights B&B)

94 94

Closed 24 - 25 December

Castle Oaks House Hotel & Country Club

Castleconnell,
Co. Limerick

Tel: 061-377666 Fax: 061-377717
Email: info@castleoaks.ie
Web: www.castleoaks.ie

HOTEL ★★★ MAP 6 H 7

Experience our casual country elegance. Located 7 minutes from Limerick City, just off the new Limerick by-pass. The Castle Oaks House Hotel and Leisure Club is situated on 26 acres of mature gardens. The hotel boasts 20 lavishly appointed bedrooms and 22 (2 bedroomed) suites with individual private lounges, 19 4**** self-catering homes and new day spa. Extensive conference and banqueting facilities. Award-winning Acorn Restaurant. Fishing on site. Golf, equestrian facilities nearby. Shannon Airport 40 minutes away.

Bookable on www.irelandhotels.com
Member of Great Fishing Houses of Ireland

B&B from €59.00 to €120.00

*Tom Walsh
General Manager / Proprietor*

Member of:

64 64

Closed 24 - 26 December

Castletroy Park Hotel

Dublin Road,
Limerick

Tel: 061-335566 Fax: 061-331117
Email: sales@castletroy-park.ie
Web: www.castletroy-park.ie

HOTEL ★★★★ MAP 6 H 7

Limerick's finest 4 star hotel offering the ultimate in comfort & luxury. The Castletroy Park Hotel, stands on 14 acres of beautifully landscaped gardens overlooking the Clare Hills & is a short stroll from the River Shannon & the entrance to the 500 acres of Plassey Park, home to University of Limerick. This elegant hotel offers the McLaughlin's award-winning restaurant, the Merry Pedlar Irish Pub & Bistro with a superb fitness & leisure centre. The 101 rooms & 6 suites are equipped to the highest standards offering high-speed broadband Internet access.

Bookable on www.irelandhotels.com

B&B from €80.00 to €130.00

*Brian Harrington
General Manager*

Activities:

Member of:

Special Offer: Weekend Specials from €199.00 pps (2 Nights B&B & 1 Dinner)

107 107

Closed 24 - 26 December

B&B Rates are per Person Sharing per Night incl. Breakfast.
or Room Rates are per Room per Night - See also Page 8

Clarion Hotel Limerick

Steamboat Quay,
Limerick

Tel: 061-444100 Fax: 061-444101
Email: info@clarionhotellimerick.com
Web: www.clarionhotellimerick.com

HOTEL ★★★★ MAP 6 H 7

Irelands tallest hotel, boasts spectacular riverside location with magnificent views of the River Shannon. All bedrooms & suites are finished to an excellent standard. The Sinergie Restaurant offers the ultimate dining experience, from its waterfront location, while Kudos Bar specialises in Malaysian food. Health & Leisure club includes swimming pool, gym, sauna, steam room & jacuzzi. Within 10 mins of hotel there are 20 dining options, the Hunt Museum, King Johns Castle, Bunratty Castle & Folk Park, Limerick Racecourse & a wide variety of golf courses. The hotel is 20 mins from Shannon International Airport.

Bookable on www.irelandhotels.com
Member of Choice Hotels Ireland

B&B from €65.00 to €140.00

*Sean Lally
Managing Partner*

Activities:

Member of:

93 93

Closed 24 - 26 December

Clifton House Guest House

Ennis Road,
Limerick

Tel: 061-451166 Fax: 061-451224
Email: cliftonhouse@eircom.net

GUESTHOUSE ★★★ MAP 6 H 7

Set in 1 acre of landscaped gardens. All sixteen rooms en suite, with multi-channel TV, trouser press, hairdryers, direct dial telephone. Complimentary tea/coffee available in our spacious TV lounge. We are situated on the main Limerick/ Shannon Road. Within 15 minutes walk of city centre. 22 space car park. AA listed. Friendly welcome awaits you.

Member of Premier Guesthouses

B&B from €40.00 to €45.00

*Michael & Mary Powell
Proprietors*

Member of:

16 16

Closed 19 December - 05 January

Greenhills Hotel Conference/Leisure

Ennis Road,
Limerick

Tel: 061-453033 Fax: 061-453307
Email: info@greenhillsgroup.com
Web: www.greenhillsgroup.com

HOTEL ★★★ MAP 6 H 7

The newly refurbished Greenhills Hotel, set in 3.5 acres of tended gardens offers a superb base to explore the attractions of the South West. 5 minutes from Limerick City and 15 minutes from Shannon Airport. Enjoy "Bryan's" Bar and "Hughs on the Greene" Restaurant. Relax in our award-winning Leisure Centre, which includes an 18m pool. State of the art conference and banqueting facilities catering for up to 400. Lots of local attractions and amenities. Newly added is Rachael's Beauty Rooms, offering a range of various pamper treatments.

Room Rate from €75.00 to €90.00

*Daphne Greene
General Manager*

Activities:

Member of:

Special Offer: Weekend Specials from €130.00 pps
(2 Nights B&B & 1 Dinner)

59 59

Closed 24 - 26 December

B&B Rates are per Person Sharing per Night incl. Breakfast.
or **Room Rates** are per Room per Night - See also Page 8

Co. Limerick

Limerick City

Jurys Inn Limerick

Lower Mallow Street,
Limerick

Tel: 061-207000 Fax: 061-400966
Email: jurysinnlimerick@jurysdoyle.com
Web: www.jurysinns.com

HOTEL ★★★ MAP 6 H 7

Set in the heart of the city along the banks of the Shannon and just a two minute stroll from the shopping and cultural centre of Limerick. This very welcoming Inn provides an excellent base from which to explore many scenic delights in Limerick City, Co. Limerick and Co. Clare.

Bookable on www.irelandhotels.com
Member of Jurys Doyle Hotel Group

Room Rate from €59.00 to €89.00

Aileen Phelan
General Manager

Member of:

151 151

Closed 23 - 28 December

Kilmurry Lodge Hotel

Castletroy,
Limerick

Tel: 061-331133 Fax: 061-330011
Email: info@kilmurrylodge.com
Web: www.kilmurrylodge.com

HOTEL ★★★ MAP 6 H 7

This newly refurbished hotel set among four acres of landscaped gardens is perfectly located adjacent to the University of Limerick on the Dublin road (N7), whilst still only minutes from the thriving city centre. The business and conference services (1 - 300 people) exceed the highest of expectations and the hotel's "Olde World" character and charm is complemented by the latest in technology including free broadband access in all guest bedrooms.

Bookable on www.irelandhotels.com

B&B from €49.00 to €70.00

Siobhan Hoare
Proprietor

Activities:

Member of:

100 100

Closed 24 - 27 December

Old Quarter Lodge

Denmark Street,
Limerick

Tel: 061-315320 Fax: 061-316995
Email: lodge@oldquarter.ie
Web: www.oldquarter.ie

GUESTHOUSE ★★★ MAP 6 H 7

Old Quarter Lodge, formerly known as Cruises House. Newly refurbished, luxurious en suite rooms, situated in the heart of Limerick City centre, convenient to our finest shops & tourist attractions. All rooms en suite with DD telephone, hairdryer, tea/coffee making facilities, satellite TV. Additional facilities include room service, selection of suites, conference rooms, guest lounge, wireless internet access, fax/photocopying & bureau de change. Old Quarter Bar & Cafe also located within the building. A warm & friendly welcome awaits you. AA ♦♦♦ recognition.

Bookable on www.irelandhotels.com

B&B from €40.00 to €50.00

Carole Kelly
Lodge Manager

Activities:

Member of:

26 26

Closed 24 December - 02 January

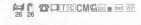

B&B Rates are per Person Sharing per Night incl. Breakfast.
or Room Rates are per Room per Night - See also Page 8

Pery's Hotel

Glentworth Street,
Limerick

Tel: 061-413822 Fax: 061-413073
Email: info@perys.ie
Web: www.perys.ie

HOTEL ★★★ MAP 6 H 7

An historic city centre boutique hotel, Pery's is located right in the heart of georgian Limerick. Following a complete refurbishment, Pery's now offers a striking yet warm, stylish and intimate ambience. Elegant evening dining in Tait's Restaurant, or choose from our delicous yet informal bar menu. Railway station, shopping, theatres, museums, restaurants, bars & nightclubs all within minutes. Gym, sauna & private car park. Shannon Airport 20 minutes drive.

Bookable on www.irelandhotels.com
Member of Best Western

B&B from €50.00 to €80.00

Barry Deane
General Manager

Member of:

62 62

Closed 25 - 26 December

Radisson SAS Hotel

Ennis Road,
Limerick

Tel: 061-456200 Fax: 061-327418
Email: sales.limerick@radissonsas.com
Web: www.limerick.radissonsas.com

HOTEL ★★★★ MAP 6 H 7

The Radisson SAS Hotel, Limerick is strategically located on the Ennis Road (N18) just 5 minutes drive from Limerick City and 15 minutes from Shannon Airport. Set in landscaped gardens, the hotel boasts 154 de luxe bedrooms including luxurious suites. Dine in our award-winning restaurant or relax with a drink in our pub. Healthstyles Leisure Club offer a swimming pool, sauna, steam room, gymnasium, solarium and beauty salon. Outdoor tennis courts, childrens' playground and complimentary parking. Just 5 minutes from Bunratty Castle. Destination Spa to open Autumn 2006.

Bookable on www.irelandhotels.com
Member of Rezidor SAS Hotels & Resorts

B&B from €99.00 to €150.00

Stephen Hanley
General Manager

Member of:

154 154

Special Offer: Weekend Specials from €140.00 pps
(2 Nights B&B & 1 Dinner)

Open All Year

Railway Hotel

Parnell Street,
Limerick

Tel: 061-413653 Fax: 061-419762
Email: sales@railwayhotel.ie
Web: www.railwayhotel.ie

HOTEL ★★ MAP 6 H 7

Family-run hotel, owned and managed by the McEnery/Collins Family, this hotel offers Irish hospitality at its best. Personal attention is a way of life, along with an attractive lounge/bar, comfortable en suite accommodation and good home cooked food, one can't ask for more. Ideally situated, opposite rail/bus station, convenient to city centre, it is the perfect stop for the tourist and business person alike. All major credit cards accepted.

B&B from €35.00 to €48.00

Pat & Michele Mcenery
Owners / Managers

Member of:

30 25

Closed 24 - 26 December

B&B Rates are per Person Sharing per Night incl. Breakfast.
or Room Rates are per Room per Night - See also Page 8

Sarsfield Bridge Hotel

Sarsfield Bridge,
Limerick City

Tel: 061-317179 Fax: 061-317182
Email: info@tsbh.ie
Web: www.tsbh.ie

HOTEL N MAP 6 H 7

The Sarsfield Bridge Hotel located in the heart of Limerick City beside the River Shannon. Ease of access for sightseeing, shopping, sports events or business makes our hotel the perfect city centre location. All 55 en suite bedrooms are bright, comfortable and relaxing. On the ground floor, our very attractive Pier One Bar & Restaurant overlooking the Shannon offers excellent cuisine. 20 minutes from Shannon Airport. GDS Access Code UI.

Bookable on www.irelandhotels.com

B&B from €55.00 to €60.00

Daragh O'Neill
Proprietor

Member of:
IRISH HOTELS FEDERATION

Special Offer: *Weekend Specials from €135.00 pps*
(2 Nights B&B & 1 Dinner)

55 55

Open All Year

Woodfield House Hotel

Ennis Road,
Limerick

Tel: 061-453022 Fax: 061-326755
Email: woodfieldhotel@eircom.net
Web: www.woodfieldhousehotel.com

HOTEL ★★★ MAP 6 H 7

Woodfield House Hotel ideally located within strolling distance of Limerick City Centre, Georgian streets, lovely quays, along the Shannon and King John's Castle, St. Mary's Cathedral and the Hunt Museum. Complete your evening in our Bistro where fine cuisine and attentive service create a special dining experience. Our Lansdowne Bar offers a welcoming retreat for both locals and visitors alike. We are also ideally located within walking distance of Thomond Rugby Park for all the rugby buffs.

Member of MinOtel Ireland Hotel Group

B&B from €55.00 to €75.00

Ken & Majella Masterson
Proprietors

Activities:

26 26

WiFi

Closed 24 - 26 December

Courtenay Lodge Hotel

Newcastle West,
Co. Limerick

Tel: 069-62244 Fax: 069-77184
Email: res@courtenaylodge.iol.ie
Web: www.courtenaylodgehotel.com

HOTEL ★★★ MAP 2 F 6

A warm welcome awaits you at the Courtenay Lodge Hotel situated on the main Limerick to Killarney Road and only 15 minutes from the picturesque village of Adare. The newly-built, tastefully decorated, en suite rooms complete with TV, direct dial phone, power showers, trouser press, tea/coffee facilities, etc. ensure a level of comfort second to none. The ideal base for touring the Shannon and South West regions and the perfect location for golfers to enjoy some of the most renowned courses.

Bookable on www.irelandhotels.com

B&B from €45.00 to €80.00

Declan O'Grady
General Manager

Activities:

Member of:
IRISH HOTELS FEDERATION

Special Offer: *Weekend Specials from €95.00 pps*
(2 Nights B&B & 1 Dinner)

39 39

Closed 25 December

B&B Rates are per Person Sharing per Night incl. Breakfast.
or Room Rates are per Room per Night - See also Page 8

Sunville Country House & Restaurant

Sunville,
Pallasgreen,
Co. Limerick
Tel: 061-384822 Fax: 061-384823
Email: amgarvey@eircom.net
Web: www.sunvillehouse.com

GUESTHOUSE N MAP 6 H 7

Elegant Georgian country house, set on 7 acres of gardens, walks & woodland, outside the village of Pallasgreen (N24, 11 miles from Tipperary & 14 miles from Limerick) in the heart of The Golden Vale. Built in 1826, with an original walled kitchen garden & stone courtyard with its old Belltower. Beautifully & sensitively refurbished with features & antiques, once home to relatives of the Duke of Wellington. It now plays host to guests who relax in its splendour & dine on organic produce. Ideal base for corporate events, accommodation & touring. 4 golf courses, horse riding, boating, fishing & team building weekends.

Bookable on www.irelandhotels.com

B&B from €58.00 to €168.00

Gerry & Anne Garvey

Member of:

Special Offer: Weekend Specials from €149.00 pps (2 Nights B&B & 1 Dinner)

6 6

Closed 16 February - 01 March

Rathkeale House Hotel

Rathkeale,
Co. Limerick

Tel: 069-63333 Fax: 069-63300
Email: info@rathkealehousehotel.com
Web: www.rathkealehousehotel.com

HOTEL ★★★ MAP 6 G 6

Rathkeale House Hotel, located just off the N21 Limerick to Killarney route and 4 miles west of Ireland's prettiest village, Adare. 26 superior en suite rooms, O'Deas Bistro open each evening 6-9.30pm. Chestnut Tree Bar where carvery lunch is available each day. Conference & banqueting facilities for 300 guests. Golf packages a speciality. Local courses, Adare, Adare Manor, Newcastle West (Ardagh), Charleville. Spacious gardens for your relaxation. A warm welcome awaits you.

Bookable on www.irelandhotels.com

B&B from €55.00 to €75.00

*Gerry O'Connor
General Manager*

Activities:

Member of:

26 26

Closed 25 December

Abbey Court Hotel and Trinity Leisure Club

Dublin Road,
Nenagh,
Co. Tipperary
Tel: 067-41111 Fax: 067-41022
Email: info@abbeycourt.ie
Web: www.abbeycourt.ie

HOTEL ★★★ MAP 6 I 8

Situated in the historic town of Nenagh, the Abbey Court is the ideal gateway to Lough Derg. Just off the Dublin to Limerick Road (N7). Set on its own award-winning landscaped gardens the hotel presents 82 tastefully decorated superior Bedrooms, exclusive Conference & Banqueting facilities, Cloisters Restaurant, Abbots Bar, coupled with a 20m Indoor Pool, Techno Gym, Rugrats Kiddies Club, Crèche, Hair Salon, a Spa & Beauty Centre with Balneotherapy Unit. A genuine Céad Míle Fáilte awaits, whether you are on business or taking that long promised & well deserved break.

B&B from €55.00 to €95.00

*Pat Galvin
General Manager*

Activities:

Member of:

82 82

Closed 24 - 27 December

B&B Rates are per Person Sharing per Night incl. Breakfast. or Room Rates are per Room per Night - See also Page 8

Co. Tipperary North

Roscrea

Grant's Hotel

Castle Street,
Roscrea,
Co. Tipperary
Tel: 0505-23300 Fax: 0505-23209
Email: grantshotel@eircom.net
Web: www.grantshotel.com

HOTEL ★★★ MAP 7 J 9

Located on the main link roads between Dublin or Rosslare and the West. Grant's Hotel is opposite the castle in the heart of the Heritage Town of Roscrea. The hotel features 25 en suite bedrooms pleasantly furnished in warm-toned colours. Lunch and evening meals served in Kitty's Tavern daily. The award-winning Lemon Tree Restaurant is the ideal place to relax after a day's golfing, fishing or exploring Ely O'Carroll country. Special golf, pitch'n'putt, fishing, hill walking and Canadian canoeing packages available.

B&B from €39.00 to €55.00

Charlie Horan
General Manager

Activities:

Member of:

Special Offer: Weekend Specials from €59.00 pps (2 Nights B&B & 1 Dinner)
25 25

Closed 25 December

Racket Hall Country House Golf & Conference Hotel

Dublin Road,
Roscrea,
Co. Tipperary
Tel: 0505-21748 Fax: 0505-23701
Email: racketh@iol.ie
Web: www.rackethallhotel.com

HOTEL U MAP 7 J 9

Located on the main N7 just outside the Heritage Town of Roscrea and set in the heart of the monastic Midlands beneath the Slieve Bloom Mountains, this charming family-run olde world residence boasts 40 new luxurious guest rooms. The ideal location for the avid golfer, hill walking, fishing enthusiast or history buff. An extremely convenient stopping off point from Dublin to Limerick, Shannon, Clare or Kerry. Award-winning Lily Bridges Steakhouse Bar and Willow Tree Restaurant. Fully wheelchair accessible.

B&B from €49.00 to €99.00

Eamonn Cunningham
General Manager

Activities:

Member of:

Special Offer: Weekend Specials from €129.00 pps (2 Nights B&B & 1 Dinner)
40 40

Open All Year

Tower Guesthouse, Bar & Restaurant

Church Street,
Roscrea,
Co. Tipperary
Tel: 0505-21774 Fax: 0505-22425
Email: info@thetower.ie

GUESTHOUSE ★★★ MAP 7 J 9

Tucked away on the side of the road beside a mediaeval Round Tower this is a wonderful combination of a guesthouse, restaurant & bar. Situated in the centre of the town, with ample car parking, this is an ideal touring base with golfing, hill walking, horse riding and fishing all within close proximity. The en suite bedrooms are beautifully appointed and tastefully decorated. Overall this establishment has everything for lovers of good food, quality accommodation and classical bars.

B&B from €35.00 to €50.00

Bridie & Gerard Coughlan
Proprietors

Member of:

10 10

Closed 25 - 29 December

B&B Rates are per Person Sharing per Night incl. Breakfast. or Room Rates are per Room per Night - See also Page 8

Templemore Arms Hotel

Main Street,
Templemore,
Co. Tipperary
Tel: 0504-31423 Fax: 0504-31343
Email: info@templemorearmshotel.com
Web: www.templemorearmshotel.com

HOTEL ★★ MAP 7 J 8

The Templemore Arms Hotel is located in the shadow of one of Ireland's most prominent landmarks, The Devil's Bit, in the centre of the town of Templemore. Recently rebuilt to match the demands of the most discerning guests, it boasts lounge bars, carvery, restaurant, banqueting suite and conference room, providing first class service. Visit the Templemore Arms Hotel and experience an enjoyable getaway.

B&B from €50.00 to €80.00

Dan Ward

Activities:

Member of:
IRISH HOTELS FEDERATION

15 15

Closed 25 December

Anner Hotel & Leisure Centre

Dublin Road,
Thurles,
Co. Tipperary
Tel: 0504-21799 Fax: 0504-22111
Email: info@annerhotel.ie
Web: www.annerhotel.ie

HOTEL ★★★ MAP 7 J 7

The Anner Hotel located on the outskirts of Thurles, 5 minutes walk from the town centre with beautiful landscaped gardens. We offer our guests a warm welcome, excellent food and a friendly service in comfortable surroundings. Superb leisure facilities boasts 18m pool, kiddies pool, jacuzzi, sauna and gym. Close to Holy Cross Abbey and The Rock of Cashel. Ideal base for touring, golf, walking, leisure breaks, conference and meetings.

B&B from €60.00 to €90.00

*Catherine Harrington
Manager*

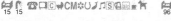

Activities:

96 96

Special Offer: Weekend Specials from €110.00 pps
(2 Nights B&B & 1 Dinner)

Closed 25 - 26 December

B&B Rates are per Person Sharing per Night incl. Breakfast.
or Room Rates are per Room per Night - See also Page 8

Map of West Region

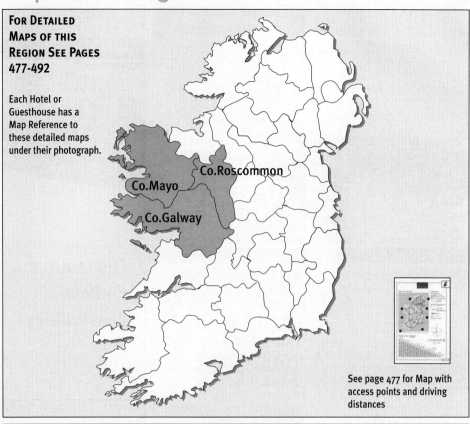

FOR DETAILED MAPS OF THIS REGION SEE PAGES 477-492

Each Hotel or Guesthouse has a Map Reference to these detailed maps under their photograph.

Co.Roscommon

Co.Mayo

Co.Galway

See page 477 for Map with access points and driving distances

Locations listing

Galway, Mayo & Roscommon

There is a special quality about these three counties in the West of Ireland which is unique in Europe. The welcome is heart-warming, the quality of life, people and landscapes are all there for the visitor to enjoy. The spectacularly beautiful countryside, the coast that has been etched by the Atlantic, the rambling hills and mountains and the enchanting lakes and bays that mirror that special light from the clear skies over the countryside. Each county has its own special attractions and is rich in all that is best in Irish folklore, music and song. There is something here for everyone. You will not be disappointed.

Major Attractions

Galway City has a host of attractions on offer, including Galway Irish Crystal Heritage Centre, Lynch's Castle, the Spanish Arch, Nora Barnacle House and the Taibhdhearc – Ireland's only Irish-speaking theatre. In Co. Galway you have Thoor Ballylee, the home of the poet W.B. Yeats, and Coole Park Visitor Centre, former home of Lady Gregory, both located just north of Gort. The Battle of Aughrim Interpretative Centre near Ballinasloe gives a fascinating account of one of the most decisive battles in European history. Other major attractions include Dartfield Ireland's Horse Museum near Loughrea, Aughnanure Castle in Oughterard, Dan O'Hara's Pre-Famine Farm near Clifden, Leenane Cultural Centre, Kylemore Abbey in Letterfrack, Connemara, Glengowla Mines near Oughterard and Ionad Arann, Aran's Heritage Centre on Inishmore. Amongst the attractions worth a visit in Co. Mayo are the Ceide Fields in Ballycastle, Foxford Woollen Mills, The National Museum of Ireland –

Country Life, Knock Shrine & Folk Museum, Ballintubber Abbey & the Westport Visitor Centre. Clew Bay Heritage Centre, Ballintubber Abbey & Westport House Country Park, Hennigan's Heritage Farm, Killasser, Kiltimagh Museum, Old Railway Station-Kiltimagh, Mayo Abbey, Michael Davitt Museum-Straide, Mayo North Family Heritage Centre-Ballina, Partry House, The Quiet Man Cottage Museum-Cong, Achill Folklife Centre-Achill Island, Croagh Patrick Visitor Centre-Westport, Eachleim Heritage Centre, Belmullet. Roscommon can boast the County Heritage & Genealogical centre in Strokestown, Strokestown Park House, Gardens & Famine Museum, Clonalis House-Castlerea, Douglas Hyde Interpretative Centre in Porthard, King House and Boyle Abbey in Boyle and the magnificent Lough

Key Forest Park. For information and accommodation bookings in Counties Galway, Mayo and Roscommon contact:
www.irelandwest.ie

Ireland West Tourism,
Aras Fáilte, Forster Street,
Galway
Tel: 00353 91 537700
Fax: 00353 91 537733
Email: info@irelandwest.ie

Tourist Information Office,
James Street, Westport,
Co. Mayo
Tel: 00353 98 25711
Fax: 00353 98 26709
Email: westport@irelandwest.ie

Tourist Information Office,
(Seasonal)
Boyle, Co. Roscommon.
Tel: 00353 71 966 2145

Calendar of Events

June
Guinness Castlebar Blues Festival, Castlebar, Co. Mayo.

July
Ballina Arts Festival, Ballina , Co. Mayo.
Galway Arts Festival, Galway City.

July / August
Guinness Galway Racing Festival, Galway City.

September
Guinness Clarenbridge Oyster Festival, Clarenbridge, Co. Galway.
Guinness Galway International Oyster Festival, Galway City.

September / October
Ballinasloe International Horse Fair & Festival, Ballinasloe, Co. Galway.

Event details correct at time of going to press.
enjoy Guinness sensibly.

Aran Islands

Aran Islands Hotel - Ostan Arann

Kilronan,
Inis Mor, Aran Islands,
Co. Galway
Tel: 099-61104 Fax: 099-61225
Email: info@aranislandshotel.com
Web: www.aranislandshotel.com

HOTEL P MAP 5 D 10

Enjoy the serenity & beauty of Inis Mor at Ostan Arann, The Aran Islands Hotel. All bedrooms are spacious & beautifully appointed with all the usual facilities. Unwind & enjoy a pint of stout or Irish coffee, and the best of craic & entertainment in the hotel's traditional bar. Our restaurant offers the best of fresh local produce, showcasing the extraordinary quality & variety of the area's seafood and organically grown vegetables.

Bookable on www.irelandhotels.com

B&B from €45.00 to €90.00

*Fionnuala Hernon
Assistant Manager*

*Special Offer: Weekend Specials from €119.00 pps
(2 Nights B&B & 1 Dinner)*

20 20

Closed 20 - 29 December

Ard Einne Guesthouse

Inismor,
Aran Islands,
Co. Galway
Tel: 099-61126 Fax: 099-61388
Email: ardeinne@eircom.net
Web: www.ardeinne.com

GUESTHOUSE ★★★ MAP 5 D 10

Ard Einne provides high quality standards & comfortable accommodation. Our dining room is renowned for its home-made cuisine. Located in a picturesque & unspoilt area of unrivalled beauty with spectacular views from all bedroom windows of Clare & Galway coastlines. The ideal getaway for a unique relaxing break, Ard Einne's cosy atmosphere will guarantee a therapeutic stay. Here you can experience the real pace of island life. It is a perfect base for cyclists, walkers, botanists, bird-watching & pilgrimages. Close to cliffs, monastic monuments & historical sites. Situated beside airport, 2km from pier.

Bookable on www.irelandhotels.com

B&B from €36.00 to €45.00

*Clodagh Ni Ghoill
Manager*

Member of:
IRISH HOTELS FEDERATION

14 14

Closed 01 December - 01 February

Kilmurvey House

Kilronan,
Inismor, Aran Islands,
Co. Galway
Tel: 099-61218 Fax: 099-61397
Email: kilmurveyhouse@eircom.net
Web: www.kilmurveyhouse.com

GUESTHOUSE ★★★ MAP 5 D 10

Kilmurvey House is a 150 year old country house once the home of "The Ferocious O'Flahertys" constructed within an early ecclesiastical site. We are situated at the foot of Dun Aonghus and beside Dun Aonghus Visitor Centre. Just 3 minutes walk from a Blue Flag beach we are an ideal location for cyclists, botanists, archaeologists and walkers and those who just want to relax. Group rates available. Free access to Dun Aonghus National Monument available to our guests. Recommended by several travel guides.

B&B from €40.00 to €55.00

*Treasa Joyce
Proprietor*

Activities:

Member of:
IRISH HOTELS FEDERATION

12 12

Closed 30 October - 01 April

<u>B&B Rates</u> are per Person Sharing per Night incl. Breakfast.
or <u>Room Rates</u> are per Room per Night - See also Page 8

Pier House Guesthouse

Lower Kilronan,
Aran Islands,
Co. Galway
Tel: 099-61417 Fax: 099-61122
Email: pierh@iol.ie
Web: www.pierhousearan.com

GUESTHOUSE ★★★ MAP 5 D 10

Pier House is perfectly located less than 100m from Kilronan Village, within walking distance of sandy beaches, pubs and historical remains. This modern house is finished to a very high standard and has many extra facilities, TV, tea/coffee facilities in bedrooms and a restaurant on the premises. The bedrooms are well appointed and have perfect sea and landscape views. If it is comfort and old fashioned warmth and hospitality you expect, then Pier House is the perfect location to enjoy it.

B&B from €45.00 to €60.00

Maura Joyce
Proprietor

Member of:
IRISH HOTELS FEDERATION

🛏🛏 12 12

Closed 01 November - 01 March

Tigh Fitz

Killeany, Kilronan,
Inishmore, Aran Islands,
Co. Galway
Tel: 099-61213 Fax: 099-61386
Email: penny@tighfitz.com
Web: www.tighfitz.com

GUESTHOUSE ★★★ MAP 5 D 10

Tigh Fitz, a family-run guesthouse, bar and lounge is in Killeany, Inishmore. Offering luxurious accommodation in this unspoilt area of the Aran Isles. Tigh Fitz is unique in its situation, in its spaciousness and proximity to beaches and areas of archaeological and historical remains. In this area are the tall Cliffs of Aran and the magnificent pre-historic forts. Tigh Fitz is 1.6km from the island capital Kilronan and close to the Aer Arann airstrip.

B&B from €40.00 to €60.00

Penny Fitzpatrick
Proprietor

Member of:
IRISH HOTELS FEDERATION

11 11

Closed 01 - 28 December

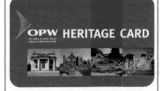
B&B Rates are per Person Sharing per Night incl. Breakfast.
or Room Rates are per Room per Night - See also Page 8

Castlegate Hotel	Ballynahinch Castle Hotel	Carna Bay Hotel

Castlegate Hotel

Northgate Street,
Athenry,
Co. Galway
Tel: 091-845111 Fax: 091-845154
Email: info@castlegatehotel.com
Web: www.castlegatehotel.com

HOTEL ★★ MAP 6 G 10

Small family-run hotel situated in the heart of mediaeval Athenry, a heritage status town, with 14 well appointed comfortable en suite bedrooms with TV. 15 minutes from Galway City in close proximity to the train station. Hot food served daily 9.30am to 9.30pm. Live traditional music four nights a week.

B&B from €40.00 to €60.00

*Andrew Kelly
Proprietor*

Member of:

14 14

Closed 31 October - 01 March

Ballynahinch Castle Hotel

Recess,
Connemara,
Co. Galway
Tel: 095-31006 Fax: 095-31085
Email: bhinch@iol.ie
Web: www.ballynahinch-castle.com

HOTEL ★★★★ MAP 5 D 11

Once home to the O'Flaherty Chieftains, pirate queen Grace O'Malley, Humanity Dick Martin & Maharajah Ranjitsinji, Ballynahinch is now a 4**** hotel. With casual country elegance, overlooking both river & mountains, offering an unpretentious service & an ideal centre from which to tour the West. Log fires & a friendly fisherman's pub complement a restaurant offering the best in fresh game, fish & produce. Voted in the Top 20 Hotels in the World by Fodor's, Ballynahinch is the jewel in Connemara's crown. RAC 2 Rosettes Dining Award and Food & Wine Magazine Hotel Restaurant of the Year.

Bookable on www.irelandhotels.com
Member of Great Fishing Houses of Ireland

B&B from €105.00 to €132.00

*Patrick O'Flaherty
General Manager*

Activities:

Member of:

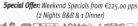

Special Offer: *Weekend Specials from €225.00 pps
(2 Nights B&B & 1 Dinner)*

40 40

Closed Christmas Week & February

Carna Bay Hotel

Carna,
Connemara,
Co. Galway
Tel: 095-32255 Fax: 095-32530
Email: carnabay@iol.ie
Web: www.carnabay.com

HOTEL ★★★ MAP 9 D 11

Are you looking for somewhere special? Allow us to plan your carefree days in the most magical scenery in Ireland. Connemara, unique landscape, flora and fauna, unspoilt beaches, mountain ranges. Beautiful Western Way walking routes. Our kitchen offers the finest fresh Irish produce. Locally: St. McDara's Island, Connemara National Park, Kylemore Abbey, Aran and Inisbofin Ferry 40 minutes drive.

Bookable on www.irelandhotels.com
Member of Irish Country Hotels

B&B from €45.00 to €75.00

*Michael & Sheamus Cloherty
Proprietors*

Member of:

26 26

Closed 23 -27 December

B&B Rates are per Person Sharing per Night incl. Breakfast. or **Room Rates** are per Room per Night - See also Page 8

Hotel Carraroe

Carraroe,
Co. Galway

Tel: 091-595116 Fax: 091-595187
Email: hotelcarraroe@eircom.net
Web: www.hotelcarraroe.com

HOTEL U MAP 5 D 10

The Hotel Carraroe is a 25 bedroomed en suite family-run hotel situated in the heart of the Connemara Gaeltacht. The village of Carraroe itself is renowned for its traditional values and music. Daily boat trips to the Aran Islands are from nearby Rossaveal Harbour. Our local friendly staff will provide information on where to fish, play golf, horse ride or tour beautiful Connemara. Enjoy our new Irish Themed Bar.

B&B from €30.00 to €100.00

Seosamh O Loideain

Member of:

IRISH HOTELS FEDERATION

Special Offer: Weekend Specials from €95.00 pps
(2 Nights B&B & 1 Dinner)

25 25

Open All Year

Cashel House Hotel

Cashel,
Connemara,
Co. Galway

Tel: 095-31001 Fax: 095-31077
Email: info@cashel-house-hotel.com
Web: www.cashel-house-hotel.com

HOTEL ★★★★ MAP 5 D 11

Elegance in a wilderness on the shores of the Atlantic. It is set amidst the most beautiful gardens in Ireland. Enjoy long walks, cycling and fishing. Later, relax in front of a peat fire in this elegant residence appointed with antique furniture and period paintings. Most guest rooms look onto the gardens and some onto the sea. Dine on bounty from the sea and garden - enjoy vintage wine.

Bookable on www.irelandhotels.com
Member of Relais et Châteaux

B&B from €96.00 to €141.00

McEvilly Family
Proprietors

Activities:

Member of:

IRISH HOTELS FEDERATION

Special Offer: Weekend Specials from €203.00 pps
(2 Nights B&B & 1 Dinner)

32 32   Inet

Closed 05 January - 05 February

B&B Rates are per Person Sharing per Night incl. Breakfast.
or **Room Rates** are per Room per Night - See also Page 8

Co. Galway

Cashel Bay / Claregalway / Clifden

Zetland Country House Hotel

Cashel Bay,
Connemara,
Co. Galway
Tel: 095-31111 Fax: 095-31117
Email: zetland@iol.ie
Web: www.zetland.com

HOTEL ★★★★ MAP 5 D 11

Overlooking Cashel Bay this 19th century manor house is renowned for its peace and commanding views. The bedrooms and superb seafood restaurant overlook the gardens and Cashel Bay. Facilities include tennis court and billiard room and there are many activities, hill walking and golf in the surrounding area. Good Hotel Guide recommended, AA Courtesy of Care Award and Gilbeys Gold Medal Winner. 4**** Manor House Hotel.

Bookable on www.irelandhotels.com
Member of Manor House Hotels

B&B from €95.00 to €115.00

Ruaidhri Prendergast
Proprietor

Member of:
IRISH HOTELS FEDERATION

Special Offer: Weekend Specials from €205.00 pps (2 Nights B&B & 1 Dinner)

20 20

Open All Year

Claregalway Hotel

Claregalway,
Co. Galway
Tel: 091-738300 Fax: 091-738311
Email: stay@claregalwayhotel.ie
Web: www.claregalwayhotel.ie

HOTEL P MAP 6 11 G

The Claregalway Hotel is superbly located on the edge of Galway City on the Junction of N17 & N18 routes. With the best of contemporary design throughout the hotel, professional and friendly staff and the latest facilities at your fingertips, the Claregalway Hotel has the right ingredients to make your stay a memorable occasion.

Bookable on www.irelandhotels.com

B&B from €59.00 to €130.00

Paul Gill
Proprietor

Member of:
IRISH HOTELS FEDERATION

48 48

Closed 23 - 27 December

Abbeyglen Castle Hotel

Sky Road,
Clifden,
Co. Galway
Tel: 095-22832 Fax: 095-21797
Email: info@abbeyglen.ie
Web: www.abbeyglen.ie

HOTEL ★★★★ MAP 9 C 12

Abbeyglen Castle Hotel was built in 1832 in the heart of Connemara by John D'Arcy of Clifden Castle. It is romantically set in beautiful gardens with waterfalls and streams, has a panoramic view of Clifden and the bay with a backdrop of the Twelve Bens. Abbeyglen provides a long list of indoor/outdoor facilities, cuisine of international fame, unique qualities of peace, serenity and ambience. Complimentary afternoon tea a speciality. AA 1 rosette for good food and service. Reservations from USA 011 353 95 22832, from Europe 00 353 95 22832.

Bookable on www.irelandhotels.com
Member of Manor House Hotels

B&B from €92.00 to €113.00

Brian / Paul Hughes
Manager / Proprietor

Member of:
IRISH HOTELS FEDERATION

45 45

Closed 08 January - 03 February

B&B Rates are per Person Sharing per Night incl. Breakfast.
or Room Rates are per Room per Night - See also Page 8

Alcock and Brown Hotel

Clifden,
Connemara,
Co. Galway
Tel: 095-21206 Fax: 095-21842
Email: alcockandbrown@eircom.net
Web: www.alcockandbrown-hotel.com

HOTEL ★★★ MAP 9 C 12

Alcock and Brown Hotel is family owned and operated. Situated in the centre of Clifden Village, featuring Brownes Restaurant with AA Rosette and 2 RAC ribbons for food and service. Ideal base for touring Connemara. Pursuits to be enjoyed are pony trekking, golfing on Connemara championship links course. Sea angling, guided heritage walks and mountain climbing. Numerous sandy beaches nearby.

Bookable on www.irelandhotels.com

B&B from €55.00 to €79.00

Deirdre Keogh
Manager

Activities:

Member of:
IRISH HOTELS FEDERATION

19 19

Closed 22 - 27 December

Ardagh Hotel & Restaurant

Ballyconneely Road,
Clifden,
Co. Galway
Tel: 095-21384 Fax: 095-21314
Email: ardaghhotel@eircom.net
Web: www.ardaghhotel.com

HOTEL ★★★ MAP 9 C 12

A quiet family-run 3*** hotel, 2km from Clifden on Ardbear Bay, AA and RAC recommended. Bedrooms individually decorated with television, telephone and tea/coffee facilities. Award-winning restaurant, 2 AA rosettes & 3 dining seals by RAC. Specialises in lobsters, salmon, oysters and Connemara lamb with homegrown vegetables and a wide selection of wines. Local amenities: golf, fishing and beaches. Reservations by post, phone, fax, email and website. Superior suites with bay view available.

Bookable on www.irelandhotels.com
Member of Irish Country Hotels

B&B from €75.00 to €90.00

Stephane & Monique Bauvet
Proprietor / Manager / Chef

Activities:

Special Offer: Weekend Specials from €135.00 pps
(2 Nights B&B & 1 Dinner)

17 17

Closed 31 October - 14 April

Kylemore Abbey & Garden

Neo-Gothic Castle and Church

Abbey Exhibition Rooms
(Under Restoration)
Neo-Gothic Church
(Under Restoration)
"Cathedral in miniature"
•Lake Walk • Video • Craft Shop
• Pottery Studio • Restaurant

A 'Great Garden of Ireland'

**6-Acre Victorian
Walled Garden**
(Under Restoration)
**featuring Formal Flower
& Kitchen Garden**
• Woodland Walk •
Exhibition • Museum

Opening Times:

Abbey, Craft Shop & Restaurant
Mar - Nov: 9.30am - 5.30pm
Nov - Mar: 10.30am - 4.00pm
(except Christmas week & Good Friday)

Garden
Easter - October: 10.30am - 4.30pm

Kylemore Abbey & Garden,
Kylemore, Connemara,
Co. Galway, Ireland

Tel: +353 95 41146
Fax: +353 95 41440
Email: info@kylemoreabbey.ie
www.kylemoreabbey.com

B&B Rates are per Person Sharing per Night incl. Breakfast.
or Room Rates are per Room per Night - See also Page 8

Clifden

Ben View House

Bridge Street,
Clifden, Connemara,
Co. Galway
Tel: 095-21256 Fax: 095-21226
Email: benviewhouse@ireland.com
Web: www.benviewhouse.com

GUESTHOUSE ★★ MAP 9 C 12

Dating from 1848 Benview has been owned and managed by our family since 1926. See our history on website. Recommended by Frommer and Le Petit Fute Guides. RAC ♦♦♦ and AA ♦♦♦ approved. Enjoy all the modern comforts of this elegant guesthouse, surrounded by antiques and old world atmosphere. Walking distance to all amenities, harbour and seaside. Free on-street parking. Lock-up garage available for motorcycles and bicycles. Your hostess Eileen wishes everyone a safe and pleasant journey.

B&B from €30.00 to €40.00

Eileen Morris
Proprietor

Activities:
✓ ⁄ 🦢

Member of:

HOTELS

Special Offer: Midweek Specials from €90.00 pps (3 Nights B&B)

🛏🔥 ☎T C U S ⬇
9   9

Closed 24 - 26 December

Benbaun House

Lydons,
Westport Road, Clifden,
Co. Galway
Tel: 095-21462 Fax: 095-21462
Email: benbaunhouse@eircom.net
Web: www.benbaunhouse.com

GUESTHOUSE ★★★ MAP 9 C 12

We invite you to enjoy the affordable luxury of Benbaun, set well back from the road in mature, leafy gardens, 2 minutes walk from Clifden Town centre. Newly refurbished to a very high standard. We offer a variety of en suite rooms with TV, DD phone, hairdryers and a hospitality trolley in the study. Breakfast is special, a feast offering tempting choices. Whether you're sightseeing, fishing, rambling or golfing Benbaun House is where you'll find a home away from home.

B&B from €30.00 to €40.00

Dr Brendan Lydon
Proprietor

Member of:

HOTELS

🛏🔥 ☎T A C CM❋U J P S ⬇ inet
12 12

Closed 20 September - 15 May

Buttermilk Lodge

Westport Road,
Clifden,
Co. Galway
Tel: 095-21951 Fax: 095-21953
Email: buttermilklodge@eircom.net
Web: www.buttermilklodge.com

GUESTHOUSE ★★★ MAP 9 C 12

A warm friendly home from home, 400m from Clifden Town centre. Spacious bedrooms each with multi-channel TV, DD phone, personal toiletries, hairdryer, ironing facilities and private bath/shower room. Your warm welcome includes tea/coffee and home baking by the turf fire where there is always a cuppa available. Our breakfast options, tasteful décor, interesting cow collection, stunning mountain views, friendly Connemara Ponies and many extra touches ensure return visits. Irish Tourist Board 3***, RAC ♦♦♦♦♦, AA ♦♦♦♦.

Bookable on www.irelandhotels.com

B&B from €35.00 to €50.00

Cathriona & Patrick O'Toole
Proprietors / Hosts

Member of:

HOTELS

Special Offer: Midweek Specials from €95.00 pps (3 Nights B&B)

🛏🔥 ☎T C ❋U J P S inet 🐴
11 11

Closed 02 January - 01 March

B&B Rates are per Person Sharing per Night incl. Breakfast.
or **Room Rates** are per Room per Night - See also Page 8

Byrne Mal Dua House

Galway Road,
Clifden, Connemara,
Co. Galway
Tel: 095-21171 Fax: 095-21739
Email: info@maldua.com
Web: www.maldua.com

GUESTHOUSE ★★★★ MAP 9 C 12

Award-winning 4**** Byrne Mal Dua House offers luxury in a relaxed friendly atmosphere. Spacious rooms have all facilities for your comfort. Relax in our landscaped gardens. Perfect base to enjoy the beauty of Connemara. RAC Little Gem Award 2005, Les Routiers Award 2001, RAC ◆◆◆◆◆ AA ◆◆◆◆, Karen Brown's Guide, Michele Erdvig. Internet access. Use of nearby leisure centre. USA Toll Free: 1 866 891 9420 & UK Free Phone: 0800 904 7532.

Bookable on www.irelandhotels.com
Member of Premier Collection

B&B from €45.00 to €85.00

The Byrne Family

Member of:

Special Offer: Midweek Specials from €119.00 pps
(3 Nights B&B)

14 14

Closed 22 - 26 December

Clifden Station House Hotel

Clifden,
Connemara,
Co. Galway
Tel: 095-21699 Fax: 095-21667
Email: info@clifdenstationhouse.com
Web: www.clifdenstationhouse.com

HOTEL ★★★ MAP 9 C 12

Anyone who loves shopping, wining and dining will feel instantly at home at the Clifden Station House. Here on your break, to get away from it all, you can do all those things you love to but in a relaxed contemporary environment. In the courtyard surrounding the hotel are a wonderful selection of speciality shops, hair salon, body and skincare clinic, full leisure facilities, self catering apartments and museum.

Bookable on www.irelandhotels.com
Member of Sweeney Hotels

B&B from €55.00 to €119.00

Daniel Loosley
General Manager

Activities:

Member of:

78 78

Closed 24 - 25 December

Connemara Country Lodge

Westport Road,
Clifden,
Co. Galway
Tel: 095-22122 Fax: 095-21122
Email: connemara@unison.ie
Web: www.bedandbreakfastgalway.com

GUESTHOUSE U MAP 9 C 12

Delightful Georgian home with spacious bedrooms, 2 minutes walk from Clifden, on extensive grounds with large private car park. All bedrooms are en suite with TV, tea/coffee making facilities, telephones and hairdryers. Why not join Mary for an evening of traditional Irish music and song in her large lounge - a truly unique experience - as Mary is a well known performer. Her home and ballad singing have been recorded for broadcasting on American TV. French and German spoken by Mary. Home-baking a speciality.

B&B from €25.00 to €45.00

Mary Corbett
Proprietress

Activities:

Special Offer: Group Discounts Available on Request

10 10

Open All Year

B&B Rates are per Person Sharing per Night incl. Breakfast.
or Room Rates are per Room per Night - See also Page 8

West 159

Dun Ri Guesthouse

Hulk Street,
Clifden,
Co. Galway
Tel: 095-21625 Fax: 095-21635
Email: dunri@anu.ie
Web: www.connemara.net/dun-ri

GUESTHOUSE ★★★ MAP 9 C 12

Centrally located and purpose built, on a quiet street in the heart of picturesque Clifden. Dun Ri offers private parking and the spacious rooms have private bathrooms (many with bath tubs), DD phone and TVs. Our attractive lounge is the ideal place to relax over a coffee/tea after a day of exploring Connemara. Our guesthouse is just 1 minute's walk from the town centre, Clifden's excellent restaurants, traditional pubs and a short pleasant drive to beaches, golf and many more attractions. Secure motorcycle parking.

B&B from €30.00 to €40.00

Michael King
Proprietor

Activities: ✓

Member of: IRISH HOTELS FEDERATION

Special Offer: Midweek Specials from €85.00 pps (3 Nights B&B)

13 13

Closed 20 - 28 December

Foyles Hotel

Clifden,
Connemara,
Co. Galway
Tel: 095-21801 Fax: 095-21458
Email: info@foyleshotel.com
Web: www.foyleshotel.com

HOTEL U MAP 9 C 12

One of Connemara's longest established hotels, trading since 1836 and owned by the Foyles for nearly a century. The hotel is situated in the centre of Clifden and is an ideal central point for exploring Connemara. The hotel's old world elegance and atmosphere have been gracefully retained through recent renovations, each room being individually decorated and furnished with charm and warmth. The Foyles and their staff offer you a warm welcome and will be happy to assist you in enjoying the area.

Bookable on www.irelandhotels.com

B&B from €45.00 to €65.00

Eddie Foyle
Proprietor

Member of: IRISH HOTELS FEDERATION

26 26

Closed 24 December - 14 February

Joyces Waterloo House

Galway Road,
Clifden, Connemara,
Co. Galway
Tel: 095-21688 Fax: 095-22044
Email: pkp@joyces-waterloo.com
Web: www.joyces-waterloo.com

GUESTHOUSE ★★★ MAP 9 C 12

Luxury lodge in a beautiful wooded river valley. Clifden 15 min walk. 6' King or 5' Queen Bedrooms, most with 21" TV, VCRs, each with tea/coffee, hairdryer, phone/radio, & expected luxuries. Bathrooms have power showers/complimentary toiletries. Peaceful, relaxed home, emphasis on Connemara hospitality, trademark for past decade. Guest lounge with open fire, board/card games, large TV & small library. Superb outdoor hot tub (elevated site under oak trees), fantastic after a day's exploring. Our candlelit dinners and breakfasts are superb. Private parking, bike hire.

Bookable on www.irelandhotels.com
Member of Premier Collection

B&B from €38.00 to €57.00

Patricia & P.K. Joyce
Hosts

Member of: IRISH HOTELS FEDERATION

Special Offer: Midweek Specials from €89.00 pps (3 Nights B&B)

8 8

Closed 23 - 27 December

B&B Rates are per Person Sharing per Night incl. Breakfast. or **Room Rates** are per Room per Night - See also Page 8

Quay House (The)	Rock Glen Country House Hotel	Fairhill House Hotel

Quay House (The)

Beach Road,
Clifden,
Co. Galway
Tel: 095-21369 Fax: 095-21608
Email: thequay@iol.ie
Web: www.thequayhouse.com

GUESTHOUSE ★★★★ MAP 9 C 12

The Quay House is Clifden's oldest building, c.1820. It now comprises 14 individually furnished rooms, some with balconies and working fireplaces, and has a wonderful collection of Georgian furniture and family portraits. It's just 7 minutes walk into town. Fishing, golf, pony-trekking, etc. are all nearby. Owned by Julia and Paddy Foyle whose family have been innkeepers in Connemara since 1917. Staying at the Quay House is a completely different experience. Outright winner of "Cesar" Award for Ireland 2003.

Member of Hidden Ireland

B&B from €70.00 to €85.00

Paddy & Julia Foyle
Owners

Member of:
IRISH HOTELS FEDERATION

🛏 🅟 ☎ ⛱ Ⓣ Ⓒ ⚒ CM❄⛵♨ 🅿 🆂 🍽
14 14

Closed 01 November - 14 March

Rock Glen Country House Hotel

Clifden,
Connemara,
Co. Galway
Tel: 095-21035 Fax: 095-21737
Email: rockglen@iol.ie
Web: www.rockglenhotel.com

HOTEL ★★★★ MAP 9 C 12

A delightful 4**** country house hotel. Spectacular views, tasteful décor & open fires. The restaurant is well known for its excellent cuisine. The quiet bedrooms offer all facilities for your comfort. A short drive to Connemara's 27 hole golf links, horse riding, trekking, fishing & hill walking. Clifden has many art galleries & shops where you can buy local handcrafts, tweeds, linens & gifts. Visit Kylemore Abbey, the Victorian Gardens & National Park. National AA Courtesy and Care Award winners 2000.

Bookable on www.irelandhotels.com
Member of Manor House Hotels

B&B from €75.00 to €110.00

Peadar Nevin
Host

Activities:
☑️

Member of:
IRISH HOTELS FEDERATION

🛏 🅟 ☎ ⛱ Ⓣ Ⓒ CM❄☎♨ 🅿 🍽
27 27

Special Offer: *Weekend Specials from €179.00 pps*
(2 Nights B&B & 1 Dinner) Subject to Availability

Closed 05 January - 05 March

Fairhill House Hotel

Clonbur (An Fháirche),
Co. Galway
Tel: 094-954 6176 Fax: 094-954 6176
Email: fairhillhouse@eircom.net
Web: www.fairhillhouse.com

HOTEL N MAP 9 E 12

Established in 1830, Fairhill House Hotel is a beautifully refurbished hotel located in one of the most scenic parts of the west of Ireland. RAC 3***. In the village of Clonbur, nestled between the magical lakes of Lough Mask and Lough Corrib, Fairhill House Hotel will give you an opportunity to explore the west from a luxurious, comfortable, friendly hotel. Fairhill House Hotel has been in the Lynch family for three generations. Very famous for its seafood menu, old world bar, open fires, traditional music entertainment, free fishing, hill walking and friendly atmosphere. You could meet anybody in Clonbur!

B&B from €45.00 to €65.00

Edward Lynch
Proprietor

Activities:
☑️ 🏹 ⛵

Member of:
IRISH HOTELS FEDERATION

🛏 🅟 ☎ ⛱ Ⓣ Ⓒ ❄☎♨ 🅿 🍽
20 20
inet 🐕

Open All Yaer

B&B Rates are per Person Sharing per Night incl. Breakfast.
or **Room Rates** are per Room per Night - See also Page 8

St. Clerans Manor House

Craughwell,
Co. Galway

Tel: 091-846555 Fax: 091-846600
Email: stclerans@iol.ie
Web: www.stclerans.com

GUESTHOUSE ★★★★ MAP 6 G 10

St. Clerans is a truly magical 18th century manor house. The ambience here is wonderfully warm and relaxing and a very warm welcome awaits all who visit and experience the hospitality and home comfort that is "St. Clerans". Set in 45 acres of pure peace and tranquillity and described by its former owner, film director John Huston, as "one of the most beautiful houses in all of Ireland".

B&B from €162.50 to €262.50

Ken Bergin
General Manager

Activities:
✓

Member of:
IRISH HOTELS FEDERATION

Special Offer: Exclusive House Rental Available

12   12

Open All Year

Connemara Coast Hotel

Furbo,
Co. Galway

Tel: 091-592108 Fax: 091-592065
Email: reservations@connemaracoasthotel.com
Web: www.sinnotthotels.com

HOTEL ★★★★ MAP 6 F 10

Perched on the shores of Galway Bay, just ten minutes from the city this is the ideal base for your precious leisure time. View unspoilt sea and landscapes of the Aran Islands and the Clare Hills from the comfort of our Canadian hot tub. Luxurious public areas, spacious bedrooms, superb meeting facilities, an award-winning leisure centre and bar. Extensive grounds sweep down to the shore and ample free car parking provides a unique setting to relax and enjoy Galway City and County at its best.

Bookable on www.irelandhotels.com
Member of Sinnott Hotels Ireland

B&B from €70.00 to €150.00

Karl Reinhardt

Activities:
⚑

Member of:
IRISH HOTELS FEDERATION

Special Offer: Weekend Specials from €165.00 pps
(2 Nights B&B & 1 Dinner)

113 113

Open All Year

Abbey House

113 Upper Newcastle,
Galway

Tel: 091-524394 Fax: 091-528217
Email: abbeyhouse@eircom.net
Web: www.abbeyhousegalway.com

GUESTHOUSE ★★ MAP 6 F 10

Family-run guesthouse located on the N59 leading to Connemara. Convenient to city centre. Rooms are en suite with cable TV and direct dial phones. Private car parking. Close to golf, fishing, tennis, swimming pool, horse riding, seaside and city centre. Excellent location for touring Connemara, Aran Islands and The Burren. A warm welcome awaits you from the Darby family.

Bookable on www.irelandhotels.com

B&B from €30.00 to €50.00

John Darby

Member of:
IRISH HOTELS FEDERATION

10   10

Closed 14 - 28 December

B&B Rates are per Person Sharing per Night incl. Breakfast.
or Room Rates are per Room per Night - See also Page 8

Adare Guest House

9 Father Griffin Place,
Galway

Tel: 091-582638 Fax: 091-583963
Email: adare@iol.ie
Web: www.adarebedandbreakfast.com

GUESTHOUSE ★★★ MAP 6 F 10

Adare Guesthouse is a family managed guesthouse, within 5 minutes of city centre (train/bus). Refurbished with old time pine furniture & floors, you can enjoy your multi-choice breakfast in our dining room overlooking our beautiful patio area. All bedrooms have en suite, direct dial phones, cable TV & hairdryers. Tea/coffee & ironing facilities are available. 2 new suites built to a high standard with baths, direct dial fax phone, trouser press/iron, tea/coffee, cable TV/radio. Safe facilities available.

B&B from €40.00 to €55.00

Padraic & Grainne Conroy
Proprietors

Activities: ✓

Member of:
HOTELS FEDERATION

Special Offer: Midweek Specials from €99.00 pps
(3 Nights B&B) October - March

11 11

Closed 21 - 27 December

Anno Santo Hotel

Threadneedle Road,
Salthill,
Galway

Tel: 091-523011 Fax: 091-522110
Email: info@annosantosalthill.com
Web: www.annosantosalthill.com

HOTEL ★★ MAP 6 F 10

Small family-run hotel located in quiet residential area. Galway's major tennis/badminton and squash club lies opposite the hotel. The golf club is also close by (1km), while Galway City and beaches are within easy reach. We are also on a main bus route. All rooms are en suite, with TV, complimentary tea/coffee and direct dial telephone. Your hosts, the Vaughan family, provide high class service in comfortable bedrooms at budget prices.

Bookable on www.irelandhotels.com

Room Rate from €55.00 to €145.00

Gerard & Joanna Vaughan
Proprietors

Activities: ✓

Member of:
HOTELS FEDERATION

Special Offer: Midweek Specials from €135.00 pps
(3 Nights B&B)

14 14

Closed 20 December - 20 January

B&B Rates are per Person Sharing per Night incl. Breakfast.
or Room Rates are per Room per Night - See also Page 8

Co. Galway

Galway City

Ardawn House

31 College Road,
Galway

Tel: 091-568833 Fax: 091-563454
Email: ardawn@iol.ie
Web: www.galway.net/pages/ardawn-house/

GUESTHOUSE ★★★ MAP 6 F 10

Ardawn House is a luxurious haven for the discerning visitor to Galway. Located within five minutes walking of city centre, train & bus. Antiques, fresh flowers, silver and china help to make our multi choice home-cooked breakfast famous. All bedrooms have en suite, direct dial phones, cable TV & hairdryers. Tea/coffee & ironing facilities are also available. Highly recommended in Guide du Routard, AA and many other guide books.

B&B from €45.00 to €75.00

Mike & Breda Guilfoyle
Proprietors

Member of:

8 8 🛏️👤☎️🖥️T✏️P🅿️S

Closed 22 - 26 December

Ardilaun House Hotel, Conference Centre & Leisure Club

Taylor's Hill,
Galway

Tel: 091-521433 Fax: 091-521546
Email: info@ardilaunhousehotel.ie
Web: www.ardilaunhousehotel.ie

HOTEL ★★★ MAP 6 F 10

Ardilaun is a family-owned 89 bedroomed 4**** hotel on charming grounds. All rooms en suite with DD phone & TV, trouser press, tea and coffee making facilities, hairdryer. In May '06 the redevelopment programme, to include 32 bedrooms, 4 Garden Suites and extension to bar and restaurant will be completed. Wired & wireless internet connections. White Flag awarded Leisure Club & Beauty Salon. Banqueting facilities for up to 300 guests.

Bookable on www.irelandhotels.com
Member of Select Hotels of Ireland

B&B from €85.00 to €125.00

John Ryan
Managing Director

Activities:

🎣

Member of:

Special Offer: Weekend Specials from €160.00 pps
(2 Nights B&B & 1 Dinner)

89 89 🛏️👤☎️🖥️T🅲♥CM❄️🍴🐟🏊‍♀️♨️🚶‍♂️U
J P 🎣 S 🅰️ 📺 Inet WiFi 🎿🐴

Closed 23 - 28 December

Ashford Manor

No 7 College Road,
Galway City

Tel: 091-563941 Fax: 091-563941
Email: info@ashfordaccommodation.com
Web: www.ashfordaccommodation.com

GUESTHOUSE ★★★ MAP 6 F 10

City Centre - Facilities include relaxing wine bar and evening menu. Beside train and bus station - 5 mins drive to Galway Airport, 1 hour and 15 mins to Shannon Airport, 1 hour to Knock Airport. All en suite rooms with TV, phone, tea and coffee making facilities. Car parking - credit cards accepted. Featured in holiday programme "Bon Voyage". Tours organised of Connemara, Aran Islands, Burren and the Cliffs of Moher. Golfing trips arranged. Groups welcome. Fishing available.

B&B from €30.00 to €70.00

Corinne Mannion
Proprietor

Member of:

5 5 🛏️👤☎️🖥️T🅲♥CM✏️P🅿️S🆈🅱️💻

Closed 24 - 30 December

B&B Rates are per Person Sharing per Night incl. Breakfast.
or **Room Rates** are per Room per Night - See also Page 8

Atlantic View Guesthouse

4 Ocean Wave,
Dr. Colohan Road,
Galway
Tel: 091-582109 Fax: 091-528566
Email: atlanticbandb@hotmail.com
Web: www.atlanticbandb.com

GUESTHOUSE ★★★ MAP 6 F 10

Atlantic View House is a luxurious haven overlooking Galway Bay with a large sun balcony. Some of our rooms have stunning views of the sea, with balconies. The house overlooks the beach with spectacular views of the Aran Islands and the Burren Mountains. We are only a short walk from the mediaeval City of Galway and the seaside resort of Salthill. Our rooms are luxuriously decorated with direct dial phone, satellite TV, trouser press, hairdryer, hospitality tray and clock-radio. Mobile: 086 - 8524579.

B&B from €27.50 to €99.00

Jennifer Treacy
Proprietor

Member of:

5   5

Closed 23 - 28 December

Best Western Flannery's Hotel

Dublin Road,
Galway
Tel: 091-755111 Fax: 091-753078
Email: flanneryshotel@eircom.net
Web: www.flanneryshotel.net

HOTEL ★★★ MAP 6 F 10

Flannerys Hotel is long established in Galway as an hotel offering comfort and style within relaxed surroundings. A welcome choice for the business traveller or leisure guest. We take pride in ensuring that a special emphasis is placed on guest comfort enhanced by a genuinely caring and efficient service. Recently refurbished, the interior features tasteful décor, excellent restaurant and relaxing bar offering all-day food service. Sample a selection of 136 rooms and suites. Member of Best Western.

Bookable on www.irelandhotels.com
Member of Best Western Hotels

B&B from €35.00 to €125.00

Mary Flannery
Proprietor

Activities:

Member of:

Special Offer: Midweek Specials from €120.00 pps
(3 Nights B&B)

136 136

Inet

Closed 22 - 29 December

Brennans Yard Hotel

Lower Merchants Road,
Galway
Tel: 091-568166 Fax: 091-568262
Email: info@brennansyardhotel.com
Web: www.brennansyardhotel.com

UNDER REFURBISHMENT - RE-OPENING APRIL 2006

HOTEL R MAP 6 F 10

Ideally situated in Galway City centre, this luxurious boutique hotel will offer an ambience of warmth and Irish hospitality. All bedrooms including superior rooms and suites are individually designed and equipped with luxuriously appointed bathrooms, laptop safe and flat screen TV. Free broadband internet available throughout the hotel. The hotel's spacious ground floor bar and restaurant with an open plan kitchen specialises in modern international cuisine.

Bookable on www.irelandhotels.com

Room Rate from €210.00 to €220.00

Pierce Connell
General Manager

Member of:

41   41

WiFi

Closed 01 January - 15 April

B&B Rates are per Person Sharing per Night incl. Breakfast.
or Room Rates are per Room per Night - See also Page 8

West 165

Galway City

Corrib Great Southern Hotel

Renmore,
Galway

Tel: 091-755281 Fax: 091-751390
Email: res@corrib-gsh.com
Web: www.greatsouthernhotels.com

HOTEL ★★★★ MAP 6 F 10

This 4**** hotel overlooks Galway Bay. It has 175 well appointed guest rooms. Leisure facilities include indoor heated swimming pool, steam room, jacuzzi, gym. Evening entertainment and childrens' play centre during summer months. Currach Restaurant and O'Malley's Bar. Convention centre accommodates up to 750 delegates. Bookable through central reservations 01-214 4800 or UTELL International.

Bookable on www.irelandhotels.com

Room Rate from €79.00 to €250.00

Cian O' Broin
General Manager

Activities:

Member of:

Special Offer: Weekend Specials from €169.00 pps
(2 Nights B&B & 1 Dinner)

175 175

Closed 24 - 26 December

Corrib Haven

107 Upper Newcastle,
Galway

Tel: 091-524171 Fax: 091-582414
Email: corribhaven@eircom.net

GUESTHOUSE ★★★ MAP 6 F 10

Corrib Haven's motto is quality hospitality for discerning people. AA Selected ◆◆◆◆. It is purpose built, located in Galway City on the N59 leading to Connemara. All rooms en suite, power showers, posture sprung beds, cable TV, DD phones. Tea/coffee facility, breakfast menu, private parking. Convenient to city centre, good restaurants, nightly entertainment. Ideal for touring Connemara, Aran Islands. Smooth professionalism with personal warmth to our visitors. Non-smoking. 20 mins drive from Galway Airport. Close to NUI Galway & hospital. Bus No.4 to city centre.

Bookable on www.irelandhotels.com
Member of Premier Guesthouses

B&B from €25.00 to €60.00

Tom & Angela Hillary
Proprietors

Special Offer: Midweek Specials from €75.00 pps
(3 Nights B&B)

9 9

Closed 10 December - 10 January

Courtyard By Marriott

Headford Point,
Headford Road,
Galway City

Tel: 091-513200 Fax: 091-513201
Email: galway.reservations@courtyard.com
Web: www.galwaycourtyard.com

HOTEL N MAP 6 F 10

Located at Headford Point within walking distance of Eyre Square & Shop St, the first Courtyard by Marriott in the West of Ireland is the ideal base to explore Galway City & its surrounds. Our 90 guest rooms will be spacious & comfortable featuring high speed internet access, air-conditioning, pay per view movies, built in mini fridge & safe. The Olive Tree Bistro features popular Irish cuisine with a contemporary & Mediterannean influence. Additional facilities include the Point Bar, a fitness suite, business centre & complimentary car park for residents. Our state of the art meeting suites can cater for 10 - 120 delegates.

Room Rate from €140.00 to €180.00

Cian Landers
General Manager

Activities:

Member of:

90 90

Open All Year

B&B Rates are per Person Sharing per Night incl. Breakfast. or Room Rates are per Room per Night - See also Page 8

Days Hotel Galway	Eyre Square Hotel	Fairgreen Hotel

Days Hotel Galway

Dublin Road,
Galway City East,
Galway
Tel: 1890-776655 Fax: 091-753187
Email: info@dayshotelgalway.com
Web: www.dayshotelgalway.com

HOTEL **R** MAP 6 F 10

Following a €30 million refurbishment, the former Galway Ryan Hotel now boasts 311 spectacular guest rooms and suites. Situated just 2km from Galway City, the hotel has retained its renowned friendly service and welcoming atmosphere. Superb leisure centre with 20m pool, toddlers' pool, sauna, steam room, jacuzzi and gym. Kids Club operates at weekends and during school holidays. Reuben's Restaurant and Bar Solo open daily. Meeting rooms available for up to 40 delegates. Free parking. Hotel Direct Line: 091 381200.

Bookable on www.irelandhotels.com
Member of Days Hotels Ireland

B&B from €39.00 to €129.00

Siobhan Burke
General Manager

Activities:

Member of:

Special Offer: From €159.00 pps
(3 Nights B&B and 2 Dinners)

311 311

Open All Year

Eyre Square Hotel

Forster Street,
Off Eyre Square,
Galway
Tel: 091-569633 Fax: 091-569641
Email: eyresquarehotel@eircom.net
Web: www.byrne-hotels-ireland.com

HOTEL ★★★ MAP 6 F 10

The Eyre Square Hotel is situated right in the heart of Galway adjacent to both bus and rail stations. The Eyre Square Hotel caters for both the tourist and business person offering a very high standard of accommodation. Rooms en suite with direct dial phone, satellite TV and tea/coffee making facilities. Enjoy excellent cuisine in our Red's Bistro or visit the lively Red Square Pub. A warm and friendly welcome awaits you at the Eyre Square Hotel.

Member of Byrne Hotel Group

B&B from €50.00 to €150.00

Michelle O'Brien
General Manager

Member of:
HOTELS

Special Offer: Midweek Specials from €89.00 pps
(2 Nights B&B and 1 Dinner)

52 52

Closed 24 - 26 December

Fairgreen Hotel

Fairgreen Road,
Lough Atalia,
Galway
Tel: 091-513100 Fax: 091-864444
Email: info@fairgreenhotel.com
Web: www.fairgreenhotel.com

HOTEL **N** MAP 6 F 10

The Fairgreen Hotel is situated in the heart of Galway's energetic city. Only a 2 minute walk from Eyre Square, this outstanding hotel has rooms to suit every taste. The Fairgreen Hotel offers you an oasis of tranquillity to take time, relax and unwind. The hotel also boasts free access to the leisure facilities of the award-winning Spirit One Spa and free overnight car parking.

Bookable on www.irelandhotels.com
Member of Mercer Accommodtion Group

Room Rate from €55.00 to €125.00

Fabiola Heredia
Duty Manager

Member of:

44 44

Closed 23 - 29 December

B&B Rates are per Person Sharing per Night incl. Breakfast.
or **Room Rates** are per Room per Night - See also Page 8

Galway City

Forster Court Hotel

Forster Street,
Galway City

Tel: 091-564111 Fax: 091-539839
Email: sales@forstercourthotel.com
Web: www.forstercourthotel.com

HOTEL ★★★ MAP 6 F 10

This new hotel is excellently located in Galway City centre and is easily accessed by all major approach roads. The hotel is impeccably finished incorporating every comfort for our guests. It comprises 48 stylish en suite guest rooms, all designed to cater for your every need. Enjoy dining in the intimacy of Elwood's Restaurant or why not relax in our extensive Morgans Bar. The Forster Court Hotel gives you Freedom of the City.

Bookable on www.irelandhotels.com
Member of Select Hotels of Ireland

B&B from €45.00 to €80.00

Padraic Whelan & James Montague Proprietors

Activities:
✓

Member of:
IRISH HOTELS FEDERATION

Special Offer: *Weekend Specials from €130.00 pps (2 Nights B&B & 1 Dinner)*

48 48

Inet WiFi

Open All Year

G (The)

Wellpark,
Galway

Tel: 091-865200 Fax: 091-865203
Email: reservetheg@monogramhotels.ie
Web: www.monogramhotels.ie

HOTEL P MAP 6 F 10

The exuberant spirit of Galway is captured in The G, built to 5***** standards, located just minutes from Eyre Square with views over Lough Atalia. The design-conscious G Hotel boasts a strikingly contemporary exterior, with design director Philip Treacy ensuring that G is for glamour in each of the 98 guest bedrooms, with ultra-modern facilities & luxurious comforts, & in the intimate lounge & bar areas. The hotel's restaurant, Santini at the G, offers a luxury dining experience. Its event & conference suites are bright and open spaces. A luxury ESPA urban spa & impeccable standards of service complete the G experience.

Member of Small Luxury Hotels of the World

B&B from €185.00 to €225.00

Michéal Cunningham General Manager

Activities:
♟

Member of:
IRISH HOTELS FEDERATION

98 98

alc Inet WiFi 🐕

Open All Year

Galway Bay Hotel, Conference & Leisure Centre

The Promenade,
Salthill,
Galway

Tel: 091-520520 Fax: 091-520530
Email: info@galwaybayhotel.net
Web: www.galwaybayhotel.net

HOTEL ★★★★ MAP 6 F 10

This AA**** hotel situated on Galway City's seafront at the Promenade, Salthill, has all the advantages of a city location while being situated on a beautiful beach overlooking the famous Galway Bay. All bedrooms are designed for maximum guest comfort. The hotel has a fully equipped leisure centre and swimming pool. Enjoy dining in the Lobster Pot Restaurant which offers modern style cuisine with strong emphasis on fresh fish and lobster from the lobster tank.

Bookable on www.irelandhotels.com

B&B from €80.00 to €150.00

Dan Murphy General Manager

Activities:
✓ ♟ 🎾

Member of:
IRISH HOTELS FEDERATION

Special Offer: *Midweek Specials from €120.00 pps (2 Nights B&B & 1 Dinner)*

153 153

Open All Year

B&B Rates are per Person Sharing per Night incl. Breakfast. or <u>Room Rates</u> are per Room per Night - See also Page 8

Glenlo Abbey Hotel	Great Southern Hotel	Harbour Hotel

Bushypark,
Galway

Tel: 091-526666 Fax: 091-527800
Email: info@glenloabbey.ie
Web: www.glenlo.com

HOTEL ★★★★ MAP 6 F 10

Glenlo Abbey Hotel - an 18th century country estate, is located on a 138 acre lakeside golf course just 4km from Galway City. A Fáilte Ireland rated 5***** hotel, Glenlo Abbey is one of the most entertaining properties in the West of Ireland. All 46 rooms are de luxe standard. There is a choice for dining including the Pullman Restaurant aboard the Orient Express. Golf, fishing, lake boating all on-site with a spa being developed in the near future. Galway City 5 mins drive. Choice of suites available - enquire with reservations.

Bookable on www.irelandhotels.com
Member of Small Luxury Hotels

Room Rate from €155.00 to €315.00

John & Peggy Bourke
Proprietors

Activities:

Member of:

Special Offer: Midweek Specials from €300.00 pps
(3 Nights B&B and 2 Dinners)

46 46

Open All Year

Eyre Square,
Galway

Tel: 091-564041 Fax: 091-566704
Email: res@galway-gsh.com
Web: www.greatsouthernhotels.com

HOTEL ★★★ MAP 6 F 10

Originally built in 1845, this Victorian hotel was extensively renovated in 2003. Overlooking Eyre Square, the Great Southern is a stylish combination of old world features and modern luxuries. Its 99 guest rooms offer a range of executive rooms, junior and senior suites. The award-winning Oyster Room Restaurant has an extensive menu. The Square Spa & Health Club has a wide range of fitness equipment, outdoor Canadian hot tub and beauty treatments. Bookable through UTELL International or Central Reservations Tel: 01-214 4800.

Bookable on www.irelandhotels.com

Room Rate from €89.00 to €270.00

Richard Collins
General Manager

Activities:

Member of:

Special Offer: Weekend Specials from €199.00 pps
(2 Nights B&B & 1 Dinner)

99 99

Closed 24 - 26 December

New Dock Road,
Galway

Tel: 091-569466 Fax: 091-569455
Email: stay@harbour.ie
Web: www.harbour.ie

HOTEL U MAP 6 F 10

The Harbour is located in the city centre adjacent to the waterfront area. This contemporary style hotel offers 96 spacious rooms, a chic bar and restaurant along with "state of the art" meeting rooms to cater for up to 100 people. The Harbour also boasts Haven Health & Beauty, an exclusive leisure suite, which includes a gym, steam room, jacuzzi and treatment rooms. The Harbour prides itself on its outstanding levels of service and quality in refreshingly unique surroundings.

Bookable on www.irelandhotels.com

B&B from €59.00 to €180.00

Sinead O'Reilly
General Manager

Activities:

Member of:

Special Offer: Midweek Specials from €149.00 pps
(3 Nights B&B)

96 96

Closed 22 - 28 December

B&B Rates are per Person Sharing per Night incl. Breakfast.
or **Room Rates** are per Room per Night - See also Page 8

Co. Galway

Galway City

Hotel Spanish Arch	Imperial Hotel	Inishmore Guesthouse
Quay Street, Galway	Eyre Square, Galway	109 Fr. Griffin Road, Lower Salthill, Galway
Tel: 091-569600 Fax: 091-569191 Email: info@spanisharchhotel.ie Web: www.spanisharchhotel.ie	Tel: 091-563033 Fax: 091-568410 Email: imperialhtl@hotmail.com Web: www.imperialhotelgalway.ie	Tel: 091-582639 Fax: 091-589311 Email: inishmorehouse@eircom.net Web: www.galwaybaygolfholidays.com

HOTEL **U** MAP 6 F 10 | HOTEL ★★★ MAP 6 F 10 | GUESTHOUSE ★★★ MAP 6 F 10

Situated in Galway City centre. 20 superbly appointed en suite bedrooms with bath & shower, direct dial telephone, TV, hairdryer, tea & coffee making facilities. Ideally located for shopping, theatres, art galleries, museums, pubs, restaurants and clubs. Bar food served daily in the Spanish Arch Bar and an à la carte menu is available in the evening. Live entertainment weekly including Trad and Jazz sessions. Our team of friendly, professional staff will do everything to make your stay a relaxing and enjoyable one.

A bustling hotel in the centre of Galway City with modern comfortable 3 star bedrooms. Located in the main shopping area surrounded by a large choice of restaurants, pubs and quality shops. Five minutes walk from the new Galway Theatre, main bus and rail terminals. Beside main taxi rank with multi storey parking nearby. Full service hotel with friendly and informative staff. No service charge. RAC 3 ***.

A charming family residence with secure carpark within 5 minutes walk of city and beach. All rooms contain direct dial phone, multi-channel TV and hairdryers. Tea/coffee and ironing facilities available. German spoken. An ideal base for touring the Aran Islands, Burren and Connemara. All day tours can be organised. Golf holidays, sea angling trips and coarse or game fishing arranged. Recommended by many leading travel guides. Specialise in Golf Package Holidays.

Bookable on www.irelandhotels.com

B&B from €45.00 to €130.00 | *B&B from €55.00 to €105.00* | *B&B from €30.00 to €60.00*

 Aidan & Martina McIntyre, General Manager
 John Kelleher, General Manager
 Marie & Peter, Proprietors

Special Offer: Midweek Specials from €140.00 pps (3 Nights B&B)

Closed 25 - 26 December | Closed 24 - 27 December | Closed 23 December - 07 January

170 West

B&B Rates are per Person Sharing per Night incl. Breakfast. or **Room Rates** are per Room per Night - See also Page 8

Jurys Inn Galway

Quay Street,
Galway

Tel: 091-566444 Fax: 091-568415
Email: jurysinngalway@jurysdoyle.com
Web: www.jurysinns.com

HOTEL ★★★ MAP 6 F 10

Jurys Inn Galway is located beside the historic Spanish Arch, overlooking Galway Bay. Just a few minutes walk through twisting mediaeval streets to the buzz of Galway's commercial and shopping districts. Convenient also to main access routes to the haunting landscape of Connemara and the Atlantic Coast. There couldn't be a better location!

Bookable on www.irelandhotels.com
Member of Jurys Doyle Hotel Group

Room Rate from €64.00 to €260.00

Fergal Somers
General Manager

Member of:
IRISH HOTELS FEDERATION

130 130

Closed 24 - 26 December

Knockrea Guest House

55 Lower Salthill,
Galway

Tel: 091-520145 Fax: 091-529985
Email: knockrea@eircom.net
Web: www.knockrea.com

GUESTHOUSE ★★★ MAP 6 F 10

A 3*** family-run guesthouse established 1956. Refurbished to a high standard with pine floors throughout. Car park at rear. 1km from city centre on bus route. 300 metres from Salthill Promenade. Restaurants, theatres, golf, tennis, horse riding close by. Perfect base for touring Connemara, Burren and Aran Islands. Within walking distance of Spanish Arch and Quay Street. Irish pub music entertainment available locally. All rooms en suite, with TV and direct dial phone, tea making facilities, hairdryer. Frommers Guide recommended. Established in 1956, celebrating 50 years in business.

Bookable on www.irelandhotels.com

B&B from €30.00 to €45.00

Eileen Storan
Proprietor

Member of:
IRISH HOTELS FEDERATION

6 6

Closed 23 - 26 December

Marian Lodge Guesthouse

Knocknacarra Road,
Salthill Upper,
Galway

Tel: 091-521678 Fax: 091-528103
Email: celine@iol.ie
Web: www.marian-lodge.com

GUESTHOUSE ★★★ MAP 6 F 10

AA ◆◆◆◆ "A home from home". Family-run. Period furniture. Adjacent to promenade/beach in Salthill Upr. Private parking. Daily tours arranged Connemara/Burren/Aran Islands. City bus route. Home baking. Bedrooms en suite, cable TV, DD phone, clock radio, orthopaedic beds, hairdryers, tea/coffee facilities. Iron, trouser press available. Large family rooms. Children welcome. Convenient to nightly entertainment, Leisureland, Aquarium, tennis, windsurfing, fishing, horse riding, bird sanctuary. Beside golf course, driving range, hair salon, restaurant, pubs & shops.

Member of Premier Guesthouses of Ireland

B&B from €35.00 to €55.00

Celine Molloy

Member of:
IRISH HOTELS FEDERATION

Special Offer: Midweek Specials from €102.00 pps (3 Nights B&B)

6 6

Closed 23 - 28 December

B&B Rates are per Person Sharing per Night incl. Breakfast.
or **Room Rates** are per Room per Night - See also Page 8

Menlo Park Hotel and Conference Centre	Ocean Crest House	O'Connors Warwick Hotel
Terryland, Headford Road, Galway	No 6 Ocean Wave, Seapoint Promenade, Salthill, Galway	Salthill, Galway
Tel: 091-761122 Fax: 091-761222	Tel: 091-589028 Fax: 091-529399	Tel: 091-522740 Fax: 091-521815
Email: menlopkh@iol.ie	Email: oceanbb@iol.ie	Email: info@thewarwick.com
Web: www.menloparkhotel.com	Web: www.oceanbb.com	Web: www.thewarwick.com

HOTEL ★★★ MAP 6 F 10	GUESTHOUSE ★★★ MAP 6 F 10	HOTEL U MAP 6 F 10

Situated near Galway's City centre the Menlo Park offers the best of modern facilities with old fashioned hospitality. All rooms have TV/satellite, welcome tray, power showers, ironing centres, rich colour schemes. Executive rooms also feature king beds, sofas, work desks. Contemporary chic but casual restaurant; MP's Bar and Lounge. Bar food/carvery all day. Entertainment, traditional and folk at weekends. Easy access, free parking. WiFi access.

We chose this site and built this guesthouse to provide what our guests love, a taste of subtropical elegance, overlooking Galway Bay and beaches with panoramic views of The Burren Mountains. We are walking distance from the bustling mediaeval city of Galway and across the road we have the Promenade. Our bedrooms are beautifully appointed with multi channel TV, en suite facilities, phone, trouser press, hairdryers, hospitality tray and armchairs.

O'Connors Warwick Hotel is a modern family-run hotel in the heart of Salthill, across the road from the famous Salthill Prom. Our beautifully appointed rooms feature tea/coffee making facilities, safes, TV and free WiFi. A popular entertainment venue with live music and nightclub and Beo! Bar serving an excellent bar menu. The award-winning Butler Brasserie is open all day, serving a full à la carte menu.

Bookable on www.irelandhotels.com

B&B from €50.00 to €125.00	B&B from €35.00 to €55.00	B&B from €45.00 to €70.00
David Keane General Manager	*Sharon McEvaddy Manager*	*Sandra Butler & Dermot O'Connor Proprietors*

Member of:

Special Offer: 3 Night Midweek Specials from €25.00 pps per Night, Oct - Apr

Special Offer: Weekend Specials from €130.00 pps (2 Nights B&B & 1 Dinner)

64 64	9 9	32 32

Closed 24 - 26 December	Closed 24 - 28 December	Closed 22 - 30 December

B&B Rates are per Person Sharing per Night incl. Breakfast. or **Room Rates** are per Room per Night - See also Page 8

Park House Hotel & Park Room Restaurant

Forster Street,
Eyre Square,
Galway
Tel: 091-564924 Fax: 091-569219
Email: parkhousehotel@eircom.net
Web: www.parkhousehotel.ie

HOTEL ★★★★ MAP 6 F 10

Superb and convenient location in the heart of Galway City centre, Park House Hotel is an oasis of luxury and hospitality. Air-conditioning and broadband access are standard in all bedrooms. Secure private car park on hotel grounds. Galway Chamber of Commerce Business of the Year Award 2005 for "Customer Care/Service". AA & RAC Rosettes for Fine Foods. Failte Ireland, AA, RAC 4**** hotel.

B&B from €49.50 to €175.00

Eamon Doyle & Kitty Carr
Proprietors

Member of:
IRISH HOTELS FEDERATION

84 84

Closed 24 - 26 December

Radisson SAS Hotel & Spa Galway

Lough Atalia Road,
Galway

Tel: 091-538300 Fax: 091-538380
Email: sales.galway@radissonsas.com
Web: www.radissonhotelgalway.com

HOTEL ★★★★ MAP 6 F 10

Located overlooking Lough Atalia, the Radisson SAS Hotel & Spa Galway is a few steps away from Eyre Square and the main bus and railway stations. Restaurant Marinas specialises in seafood and international cuisine. The Atrium Bar & Lounge serves a selection of light meals. Ireland's most exclusive Spa 'Spirit One Spa' offers many unique heat, steam & relaxation facilities. LEVEL 5, the panoramic club floor, guarantees privacy with secure members-only access in addition to individual terraces, club lounge, business centre & more spacious & luxurious rooms.

Bookable on www.irelandhotels.com
Member of Radisson SAS Hotels & Resorts

B&B from €75.00 to €150.00

Tom Flanagan
General Manager

Activities:

Member of:
IRISH HOTELS FEDERATION

217 217

Open All Year

Rockbarton Park Hotel

5-7 Rockbarton Park,
Salthill,
Galway
Tel: 091-522 018 Fax: 091-527 692
Email: info@rockbartonparkhotel.com
Web: www.rockbartonparkhotel.com

HOTEL ★★ MAP 6 F 10

Small family-run hotel located in quiet residential area, but only 2 min walk from the Prom, beaches and downtown Salthill. Golf club is also close by (1km). All rooms are en suite with TV, complimentary tea/coffee and direct dial telephone. The hotel boasts one of Galway's finest Seafood Restaurants, serving the highest quality contemporary Irish & International Cuisine. The Chef / proprietor is an internationally renowned certified Master Chef who has worked in some of the best hotels around the world.

B&B from €45.00 to €50.00

Ciaran & Tamara Gantly
Proprietors

Activities:

Member of:
IRISH HOTELS FEDERATION

Special Offer: Weekend Specials from €115.00 pps
(2 Nights B&B & 1 Dinner)

11 11

Open All Year

B&B Rates are per Person Sharing per Night incl. Breakfast.
or Room Rates are per Room per Night - See also Page 8

Salthill Court Hotel

The Promenade,
Salthill,
Galway
Tel: 091-522711 Fax: 091-521855
Email: salthillhotel@eircom.net
Web: www.byrne-hotels-ireland.com

HOTEL ★★★ MAP 6 F 10

A Byrne Hotel, 50m from Salthill's sandy beach. All rooms en suite, direct dial phone, tea making facilities, hairdryer. Excellent cuisine and service. Live entertainment nightly with a choice of live bands or trad on the Prom, which is a contemporary Irish show featuring an electrifying mix of music, song and dance. 100m from Leisureland and indoor swimming pool. Overlooking Galway Bay with a large car park. Less than 2 miles from the mediaeval City of Galway.

Member of Byrne Hotel Group

B&B from €80.00 to €115.00

*Pauline Griffin
Manager*

Activities:

Member of:
IRISH HOTELS FEDERATION

*Special Offer: Weekend Specials from €210.00 pps
(2 Nights B&B & 1 Dinner)*

75 75   Inet WiFi

Closed 23 - 26 December

Skeffington Arms Hotel

Eyre Square,
Galway
Tel: 091-563173 Fax: 091-561679
Email: reception@skeffington.ie
Web: www.skeffington.ie

HOTEL ★★★ MAP 6 F 10

The Skeffington Arms Hotel has been caring for guests for over 100 years. Overlooking Eyre Square, within walking distance of rail and bus terminals, it enjoys an enviable position in the heart of Galway. This privately owned hotel is justifiably proud of its new bars and à la carte menu which is very popular with both locals and guests alike. The bedrooms, which are newly refurbished, have multi-channel TV, tea/coffee making facilities, direct dial phone and bath/shower en suite. Ironing and iron board facilities.

B&B from €50.00 to €130.00

*Kerry Seward
Reservations Manager*

Member of:
IRISH HOTELS FEDERATION

23 23

Closed 25 - 26 December

Sunrise Lodge

3 Ocean Wave,
Dr. Colohan Road, Salthill,
Galway
Tel: 091-527275 Fax: 091-583130
Email: sunrisegalway@eircom.net
Web: www.galway.net/pages/sunrise

GUESTHOUSE N MAP 6 F 10

Sunrise Lodge, a purpose built guesthouse (1996). All rooms are en suite with tea/coffee makers, DD phone, cable TV, hairdryer. Located overlooking Galway Bay just 5 minutes taxi ride from Galway City centre. Beautiful, unique views of Galway Bay, the Burren & Aran Islands. We are Ideally located to tour these areas. Also Connemara and Cliffs of Moher are 1 hours drive. We are 57 miles/92km north of Shannon Airport. A warm welcome awaits you at Sunrise Lodge for a relaxing break. On parle Français…

Bookable on www.irelandhotels.com

B&B from €35.00 to €70.00

Peadar & Joan Cunningham

Member of:
IRISH HOTELS FEDERATION

6 6

Closed 23 - 28 December

B&B Rates are per Person Sharing per Night incl. Breakfast.
or <u>Room Rates</u> are per Room per Night - See also Page 8

Victoria Hotel

Victoria Place,
Eyre Square,
Galway
Tel: 091-567433 Fax: 091-565880
Email: victoriahotel@eircom.net
Web: www.byrne-hotels-ireland.com

HOTEL ★★★ MAP 6 F 10

The Victoria Hotel is centrally located just 100 yards off Eyre Square, within walking distance of all shops, theatres, pubs and cinemas. Each of the 57 spacious en suite rooms is beautifully appointed with direct dial phone, TV, tea/coffee making facilities and hairdryer. The hotel restaurant serving à la carte dinner along with a lively bar serving lunches will all add up to make your stay at the Victoria as enjoyable as possible. The Victoria is your enclave in the city, dedicated to pleasing you.

Bookable on www.irelandhotels.com
Member of Byrne Hotel Group

B&B from €45.00 to €100.00

Elizabeth McIntyre
Front Office Manager

Activities:

Member of:

57 57

Closed 24 - 26 December

Wards Hotel

Lower Salthill,
Galway
Tel: 091-581508 Fax: 091-520353

Web: www.wardshotel.com

HOTEL ★ MAP 6 F 10

Wards comfortable family-run hotel is located 5 minutes from Galway's City centre and a short stroll from Salthill. All our rooms are en suite with hairdryer and multi channel TV. Secure car park. Renowned for its friendly service and convenient location - this provides an excellent base for business or pleasure.

B&B from €45.00 to €55.00

Anthony Finnerty
Host

Member of:

12 12

Closed 19 December - 02 January

Waterfront Hotel

Salthill,
Galway
Tel: 091-588100 Fax: 091-588107
Email: info@waterfront.ie
Web: www.waterfront.ie

HOTEL U MAP 6 F 10

Our superbly located hotel sits on the shores of Galway Bay in the delightful suburb of Salthill, just 5 minutes from Galway's vibrant city centre. Each of our spacious 64 en suite rooms offers a dazzling, panoramic ocean view, and is amply furnished with a large lounge or kitchenette. Adjacent to the hotel is the famous Kitty O'Shea's Bar and Restaurant. Family rooms and free, secure car parking. Reservations: Call Save 1850 588 488.

B&B from €45.00 to €95.00

Cathy Melia
General Manager

Member of:

64 64

Closed 01 - 29 December

B&B Rates are per Person Sharing per Night incl. Breakfast.
or **Room Rates** are per Room per Night - See also Page 8

Co. Galway

Galway City

West Winds

5 Ocean Wave,
Salthill,
Galway
Tel: 091-520223 Fax: 091-520223
Email: westwinds@eircom.net
Web: www.westwindsgalway.com

GUESTHOUSE ★★ MAP 6 F 10

West Winds is a charming family-managed guesthouse overlooking Galway Bay, 10 minutes walk from Galway City, an ideal base for all travellers wishing to explore The Burren, Connemara and the Aran Islands. We are situated at the city end of Salthill Promenade, with restaurants, nightly entertainment and all other amenities 5-10 minutes walk. All rooms have en suite bathrooms with power shower, hairdryer, cable TV, tea/coffee making facilities. Our hospitality awaits!

B&B from €30.00 to €50.00

Rita & Patrick Joyce
Proprietors

8 8

Closed 01 November - 27 April

Westwood House Hotel

Dangan,
Upper Newcastle,
Galway
Tel: 091-521442 Fax: 091-521400
Email: resmanager@westwoodhousehotel.com
Web: www.westwoodhousehotel.com

HOTEL ★★★★ MAP 6 F 10

The 4**** Westwood House Hotel stands amidst a rural landscape of greenery combining a mellow taste of the countryside with the city's cutting edge. Air-conditioned throughout, the hotel features 58 superbly appointed bedrooms, the Meridian Restaurant, split level bar, conference and banqueting facilities and complimentary private car parking. Winner of CIE National Award of Excellence 2003/4.

Bookable on www.irelandhotels.com

B&B from €80.00 to €150.00

Declan Curtis
General Manager

Activities:

Member of:
HOTELS FEDERATION

58 58

Special Offer: Midweek Specials from €139.00 pps (2 Nights B&B & 1 Dinner)

Closed 24 - 26 December

White House

2 Ocean Wave,
Seapoint Promenade, Salthill,
Galway
Tel: 091-529399 Fax: 091-529399
Email: whitehouseadsi@eircom.net
Web: www.oceanbb.com

GUESTHOUSE ★★★ MAP 6 F 10

New and beautiful purpose built guesthouse in Galway's finest location, overlooking Galway Bay and the Burren Mountains. Minutes walk to Galway's mediaeval city and Salthill's new hotel, the Galway Bay. Large bedrooms with armchairs and tables, iron and board, multi-channel TV, hospitality tray and hairdryer.

B&B from €35.00 to €55.00

Sharon McEvaddy
Manager

9 9

Special Offer: Midweek Specials from €25.00 pps per night(3 Nights B&B) October - April

Closed 24 - 28 December

176 *West*

B&B Rates are per Person Sharing per Night incl. Breakfast. or Room Rates are per Room per Night - See also Page 8

Lady Gregory Hotel

Ennis Road,
Gort,
Co. Galway
Tel: 091-632333 Fax: 091-632332
Email: sales@ladygregoryhotel.ie
Web: www.ladygregoryhotel.ie

HOTEL ★★★ MAP 6 G 9

Situated in the West of Ireland near Coole Park, home of Lady Gregory in the town of Gort, with its many historic and local attractions. A warm friendly welcome awaits you as you enter the architectural splendour of the Lady Gregory Hotel. 48 beautifully appointed rooms, Copper Beech Restaurant, lively Jack B Yeats Bar and magnificent Gregory Suite. Relax in our Kiltartan Reading Room. Discounted green fees available from reception for Gort Golf Course, located less than 1 hour from Shannon Airport.
www.ladygregoryhotel.ie

B&B from €65.00 to €95.00

Leonard Murphy
General Manager

Activities:

Member of:
HOTELS

48 48

Closed 24 - 27 December

Sullivan's Royal Hotel

The Square,
Gort,
Co. Galway
Tel: 091-631257 Fax: 091-631916
Email: jsullinsauc@eircom.net

HOTEL ★★ MAP 6 G 9

Sullivan's Hotel is family-run hotel with 12 newly refurbished (2004) en suite bedrooms situated on the main road between Galway City (25 mins) and Shannon Airport (40 mins). Dining Pub of the Year winner 2000 - 2005 for service, quality and value. Additional phone number: 091-631401.

B&B from €30.00 to €50.00

Johnny & Annie Sullivan
Proprietors

Member of:
HOTELS

Special Offer: Group Discounts Available

12 12

Open All Year

Day's Inishbofin House Hotel

Inishbofin,
Connemara,
Co. Galway
Tel: 095-45809 Fax: 095-45803
Email: info@inishbofinhouse.com
Web: www.inishbofinhouse.com

HOTEL P MAP 9 C 12

Inishbofin lies 6 miles off the Galway coast and is one of Ireland's most thriving and beautiful islands. A 30 minute ferry journey from the north Connemara village of Cleggan. Inishbofin is a physical gem and a favourite haven among botanists, geologists and environmentalists due to its huge diversity of natural life. Day's Inishbofin House is a new de luxe hotel (the first on an Irish island) with a marine spa which commands exquisite views of the beautiful harbour. Built on the site of the old Day's Hotel, this family owned hotel offers a warm welcome, friendly and efficient service and excellent food, particularly seafood!

B&B from €70.00 to €120.00

Tony Conneely

Activities:

Member of:
HOTELS

34 34

Open All Year

B&B Rates are per Person Sharing per Night incl. Breakfast.
or **Room Rates** are per Room per Night - See also Page 8

Doonmore Hotel

Inishbofin Island,
Co. Galway

Tel: 095-45804 Fax: 095-45804
Email: info@doonmorehotel.com
Web: www.doonmorehotel.com

HOTEL ★★ MAP 9 C 12

Uniquely situated on a beautiful and historic island, commanding magnificent views of the surrounding sea and islands. Inishbofin, a haven for artists, fishermen, bird watchers, nature lovers or those who just wish to escape from the hectic pace of life. Fine sandy beaches. Sea trips and boat angling can be arranged. Facilities for divers. Excellent shore fishing. Doonmore Hotel is owned and managed by the Murray family, unpretentious but friendly and comfortable.

Merriman Inn & Restaurant

Main Street,
Kinvara,
Co. Galway

Tel: 091-638222 Fax: 091-637686
Email: merrimanhotel@eircom.net
Web: www.merrimanhotel.com

HOTEL ★★★ MAP 6 G 10

Old style country warmth permeates this charming, rustic 32 bedroom inn, situated in the picturesque village, Kinvara. On our doorstep are, The Burren, Galway Bay and the Hills of Connemara, while across the harbour nestles Dunguaire Castle providing mediaeval banquets. Under the unique thatched roof of the hotel, named after the poet, Brian Merriman, sample the savoury delights of the "Quilty Room" Restaurant, or the quaintly named contemporary bar, "M'Asal Beag Dubh". Welcome.

Leenane Hotel

Leenane,
Connemara,
Co. Galway

Tel: 095-42249 Fax: 095-42376
Email: info@leenanehotel.com
Web: www.leenanehotel.com

HOTEL ★★★ MAP 9 D 12

On the shores of Killary Harbour, Ireland's only Fjord, lies Ireland's oldest Coaching Inn. The Leenane Hotel, recently refurbished to the highest of standards, boasts the most spectacular views in Ireland. Being a family-run hotel, we understand the appreciation for traditional home-cooking. Fresh seafood from the harbour and vegetables and herbs from the hotel garden are brought in every day. The hotel's position makes it without doubt the best base for exploring Connemara, the most romantic and unspoiled region of Ireland.

Bookable on www.irelandhotels.com

B&B from €40.00 to €60.00

Aileen Murray
Manager

Activities:

Special Offer: *Weekend Specials from €140.00 pps
(2 Nights B&B & 1 Dinner)*

19 19

🐴

Closed 30 September - 07 April

B&B from €50.00 to €75.00

Terence Egan
Manager

Member of:

Special Offer: *Weekend Specials from €115.00 pps
(2 Nights B&B & 1 Dinner)*

32 32

Closed 23 - 28 December

B&B from €49.00 to €80.00

Conor Foyle
Manager

Special Offer: *Week Partial Board from €399.00 pps
(7 Nights B&B & 7 Dinners)*

29 29

Closed 01 November - 23 March

B&B Rates are per Person Sharing per Night incl. Breakfast.
or **Room Rates** are per Room per Night - See also Page 8

Portfinn Lodge

Leenane,
Co. Galway

Tel: 095-42265 Fax: 095-42315
Email: rorydaly@anu.ie
Web: www.portfinn.com

GUESTHOUSE ★★ MAP 9 D 12

Portfinn Lodge is a family-run guesthouse offering 8 comfortable en suite rooms including double and triple bedrooms, a guest lounge and a restaurant which has an international reputation for its fresh seafood. Rory and Brid Daly will be delighted to make you feel welcome. An ideal centre from which beaches, walking, angling, watersports etc. are within easy reach. When in Connemara, stay at Portfinn. Member of Premier Guesthouses.

Member of Premier Guesthouses of Ireland

B&B from €35.00 to €45.00

Brid & Rory Daly
Owners

Member of:

8 8

Closed 01 November - 31 March

Rosleague Manor Hotel

Letterfrack,
Connemara,
Co. Galway

Tel: 095-41101 Fax: 095-41168
Email: info@rosleague.com
Web: www.rosleague.com

HOTEL ★★★★ MAP 9 C 12

Rosleague is a Regency manor now run as a first class country house hotel by Mark Foyle and Eddie Foyle. It lies 7 miles north west of Clifden on the coast overlooking a sheltered bay and surrounded by the Connemara Mountains, beside the National Park. It is renowned for its superb cuisine personally supervised by the owners with all the amenities expected by today's discerning guest.
Recommended by Good Hotel Guide, Bridgestone 100 Best, Karen Brown, Georgina Campbell, Alastair Sawday's and many more. Also a member of Ireland's Blue Book.

Bookable on www.irelandhotels.com
Member of I.C.H.R.A. (Blue Book)

B&B from €75.00 to €110.00

Eddie Foyle / Mark Foyle
Owner / Manager

Activities:

Member of:

Special Offer: Midweek Specials from €269.00 pps
(3 Nights B&B & 2 Dinners)

20 20

Closed 17 November - 14 March

Meadow Court Hotel

Clostoken,
Loughrea,
Co. Galway

Tel: 091-841051 Fax: 091-842406
Email: meadowcourthotel@eircom.net
Web: www.meadowcourthotel.com

HOTEL ★★★ MAP 6 H 10

Newly extended and refurbished the Meadow Court Hotel's en suite rooms have full facilities, multi channel TV & hairdryer, iron on request. Superb dining is on offer in our award-winning restaurant renowned for its outstanding cuisine. Enjoy after dinner drinks in our Derby Bar. Situated on the main Galway Dublin Road, 2 miles from Loughrea, 18 miles from Galway, convenient to all local 18-hole golf courses, angling, horse riding, water sports. Banqueting & conference facilities. Carpark.

B&B from €50.00 to €100.00

Tom & David Corbett
Directors

Activities:

Member of:

21 21

Closed 25 - 26 December

B&B Rates are per Person Sharing per Night incl. Breakfast.
or **Room Rates** are per Room per Night - See also Page 8

O'Deas Hotel	Peacockes Hotel & Complex	Oranmore Lodge Hotel, Conference & Leisure Centre

O'Deas Hotel

Bride Street,
Loughrea,
Co. Galway
Tel: 091-841611 Fax: 091-842635
Email: odeashotel@eircom.net
Web: www.odeashotel.com

Peacockes Hotel & Complex

Maam Cross,
Connemara,
Co. Galway
Tel: 091-552306 Fax: 091-552216
Email: peacockes@eircom.net
Web: www.peacockeshotel.com

Oranmore Lodge Hotel, Conference & Leisure Centre

Oranmore,
Co. Galway
Tel: 091-794400 Fax: 091-790227
Email: orlodge@eircom.net
Web: www.oranmorelodge.com

HOTEL ★★★ MAP 6 H 10

HOTEL ★★★ MAP 6 F 10

HOTEL U MAP 6 G 10

O'Deas Hotel is a family hotel, a Georgian town house hotel of character, with open fires and within walking distance of Loughrea's game fishing lake. It is an ideal touring base situated on the N6 (exactly halfway between Clonmacnoise, 35 miles to the east and the Cliffs of Moher, 35 miles to the west). The start of the Burren country is just 12 miles away. Galway City 20 miles.

Newly built, nestling between the lakes and mountains at the crossroads to Connemara. Peacockes Hotel is the ideal base for hill walking, cycling, golfing, fishing, horse riding or watersports. After a day's travel, relax with a drink by the open turf fire in the Bogdale Bar or enjoy a sumptuous meal in our Quiet Man Restaurant. Visit our 20m high viewing tower, extensive craft shop and replica Quiet Man cottage.

This manor house hotel 5 minutes from Galway City, 3 Kms from Galway Airport. Located in the picturesque village of Oranmore, which overlooks Galway Bay. Rooms consisting of 2 queen size beds and luxury executive suites, swimming pool, sauna, steam room, jacuzzi, gym. New conference rooms with a.c., plasma screens and up-to-date communications technology. Your host and the friendly staff look forward to welcoming you.

Member of Countrywide Hotels - MinOtel Ireland

Bookable on www.irelandhotels.com

Bookable on www.irelandhotels.com

B&B from €65.00 to €65.00

B&B from €55.00 to €95.00

B&B from €45.00 to €150.00

Mary O'Neill
Proprietor / Manager

Eimear Killian
General Manager

Brian J. O'Higgins
Managing Director

Activities:
Member of:

Activities:
Member of:

Activities:
Member of:

Special Offer: Weekend Specials from €120.00 pps (2 Nights B&B & 1 Dinner)

Special Offer: Weekend Specials from €99.00 pps (2 Nights B&B & 1 Dinner)

32 32

25 25

68 68

Closed 24 - 26 December

Closed 23 - 26 December

Closed 22 - 27 December

B&B Rates are per Person Sharing per Night incl. Breakfast. or **Room Rates** are per Room per Night - See also Page 8

Quality Hotel and Leisure Centre Galway

Oranmore,
Co. Galway

Tel: 091-792244 Fax: 091-792246
Email: res@qualityhotelgalway.com
Web: www.qualityhotelgalway.com

HOTEL ★★★ MAP 6 F 10

Superior 3* hotel on the N6 to Galway, adjacent to Oranmore, just 10 mins drive from Galway City. 113 spacious rooms, crisp white duvets, t/c facilities, hairdryer, satellite TV, trousers press & en suite bath/shower. Lannigans Restaurant - international dining in a friendly, relaxed atmosphere. Q Bar & Café - regular entertainment & all day menu. Superb leisure centre: 20m pool, jacuzzi, gym, steam room, sauna, solarium, QHealth & Beauty Salon. Family rooms for 5. Playroom every weekend year round, bank hols, midterms, all July/Aug. Beside cinema, bowling, laser quest, pool & arcade.

Bookable on www.irelandhotels.com
Member of Quality Hotels

Room Rate from €79.00 to €199.00

Dermot Comerford
General Manager

Member of:

Special Offer: *Weekend Specials from €99.00 pps (2 Nights B&B & 1 Dinner)*

113 113

Closed 24 - 26 December

Boat Inn (The)

The Square,
Oughterard,
Co. Galway

Tel: 091-552196 Fax: 091-552694
Email: info@theboatinn.com
Web: www.theboatinn.com

GUESTHOUSE ★★★ MAP 5 E 11

3*** guesthouse in the heart of Oughterard, just 25 minutes from Galway. 5 minutes to Lough Corrib and redesigned 18 hole golf course. Ideal base to explore Connemara. The Boat Bar and Restaurant offer an imaginative choice of food, drink and wine. Enjoy the continental feel of our terrace and rear gardens. Live music in the bar. All bedrooms en suite with TV, radio, phone and tea & coffee making facilities.

B&B from €35.00 to €40.00

Joe Walsh & Annette Wrafter
Proprietors

Special Offer: *Midweek Specials from €95.00 pps (3 Nights B&B)*

10 10

Closed 25 December

Carrown Tober House

Arvarna,
Oughterard,
Co. Galway

Tel: 091-552166 Fax: 091-866 8981
Email: info@carrowntober.com
Web: www.carrowntober.com

GUESTHOUSE P MAP 5 E 11

Carrown Tober House, situated just off the N59 and within walking distance of Oughterard. Family-run guesthouse with all rooms en suite, with TVs and direct dial telephones. Within easy access of the Connemara Mountains and the famous Lough Corrib. Choice of 4 championship golf courses and numerous fishing lakes.

B&B from €30.00 to €35.00

McDonnell Family

Activities:

7 7

Open All Year

B&B Rates are per Person Sharing per Night incl. Breakfast.
or **Room Rates** are per Room per Night - See also Page 8

Oughterard

| Connemara Gateway Hotel | Corrib House Hotel | Corrib Wave Guest House |

Connemara Gateway Hotel

Oughterard,
Co. Galway

Tel: 091-552328 Fax: 091-552332
Email: gateway@iol.ie
Web: www.connemaragateway.com

HOTEL ★★★ MAP 5 E 11

You will find this hotel located just 16 miles outside Galway City in the picturesque location of Oughterard known as "The Gateway to Connemara". Surrounded by well maintained mature grounds, you will be able to relax in front of the welcoming turf fire in the pine panelled lobby. With entertainment in O'Nuallains Bar, attractive restaurant menus, indoor heated swimming pool & sauna plus a new gymnasium, this is an ideal place to enjoy true Irish hospitality. All rooms are en suite & enjoy views overlooking the gardens. Conference facilities for corporate events.

Bookable on www.irelandhotels.com

B&B from €50.00 to €125.00

*Michelle & Denis Doherty
Managers*

Activities:

Member of:
HOTELS
FEDERATION

Special Offer: *Weekend Specials from €99.00 pps
(2 Nights B&B & 1 Dinner)*

62 62

Closed 21 - 27 December

Corrib House Hotel

Bridge Street,
Oughterard,
Co. Galway

Tel: 091-552329 Fax: 091-552522
Email: info@corribhotel.com
Web: www.corribhotel.com

HOTEL P MAP 5 E 11

Family-run hotel offering good food and quality service. Ideally situated for golf, angling, walking, cycling or just to relax. Music every weekend. Bar food served all day. Situated beside Owen Riff River, with close proximity to Lough Corrib, the angler's paradise.

B&B from €35.00 to €45.00

*Rory Clancy
Manager*

Member of:
HOTELS
FEDERATION

Special Offer: *Weekend Specials from €100.00 pps
(2 Nights B&B & 1 Dinner)*

18 18

Closed 25 December

Corrib Wave Guest House

Portacarron,
Oughterard, Connemara,
Co. Galway

Tel: 091-552147 Fax: 091-552736
Email: cwh@gofree.indigo.ie
Web: www.corribwave.com

GUESTHOUSE ★★★ MAP 5 E 11

Panoramic lakeside guesthouse - the home of Michael & Maria Healy. As our guests, you are assured of a warm welcome to a family home with every comfort and Irish hospitality, superb home-cooking, excellent wines, beautiful en suite bedrooms (all with double and single beds), TVs, hairdryers. Spectacular views, turf fire, peace and tranquillity. Angling specialists, boats, engines. Boatmen for hire. Wild brown trout, salmon, pike, lakeside walks. 18 hole golf 1km. Colour brochure on request. For more information contact us direct.

B&B from €35.00 to €40.00

*Maria & Michael Healy
Proprietors*

Activities:

Member of:
HOTELS
FEDERATION

Special Offer: *3 Day Special €145.00 - €160.00 pps
(3 B&B and 2 Dinners)*

10 10

Closed 01 December - 01 February

B&B Rates are per Person Sharing per Night incl. Breakfast.
or **Room Rates** are per Room per Night - See also Page 8

Currarevagh House	Mountain View Guest House	Ross Lake House Hotel
Oughterard, Connemara, Co. Galway Tel: 091-552312 Fax: 091-552731 Email: mail@currarevagh.com Web: www.currarevagh.com	Aughnanure, Oughterard, Co. Galway Tel: 091-550306 Fax: 091-550133 Email: tricia.oconnor@eircom.net	Rosscahill, Oughterard, Co. Galway Tel: 091-550109 Fax: 091-550184 Email: rosslake@iol.ie Web: www.rosslakehotel.com

GUESTHOUSE ★★★★ MAP 5 E 11	GUESTHOUSE ★★★ MAP 5 E 11	HOTEL ★★★ MAP 5 E 11

A charming country mansion, built in 1842, romantically situated beside Lough Corrib in 60 ha. of private woodlands. The relaxing atmosphere & classically simple menus receive much international praise. Own fishing, boats, tennis court, with golf & riding locally. Recommendations: Egon Ronay, Guide Michelin, Footprint Guide, Lonely Planet, Karen Brown's Irish Country Inns, Good Food Guide, Good Hotel Guide & many other international hotel & food guides. They suggest that you stay at least 3 nights to absorb the atmosphere & gently explore Connemara.

Bookable on www.irelandhotels.com
Member of Ireland's Blue Book

Situated just off the N59, 24kms from Galway City and within 2-4 km of Oughterard, with the Connemara mountains in the distance and Lough Corrib nearby. Leisure activities include; golf at the renowned Oughterard Golf Club, established walks along scenic routes, boating or fishing on Lough Corrib. All bedrooms en suite, with TV, direct dial phones, tea/coffee making facilities and hairdryers.

Ross Lake House is a wonderful Georgian house set in the magnificent wilderness of Connemara. Six acres of mature gardens surround the house creating an air of peace and tranquillity. Hosts Henry and Elaine Reid have beautifully restored this manor house to its former glory. A high quality Irish menu is prepared daily featuring a tempting variety of fresh produce from nearby Connemara hills, streams and lakes as well as fish straight from the Atlantic.

Bookable on www.irelandhotels.com

B&B from €77.00 to €115.00	B&B from €30.00 to €35.00	B&B from €75.00 to €100.00

Harry & June Hodgson
Proprietors

Richard & Patricia O'Connor
Proprietors

Activities:

Elaine & Henry Reid
Proprietors

Member of:
HOTELS FEDERATION

Member of:
HOTELS FEDERATION

Member of:
HOTELS FEDERATION

Special Offer: 3 - 6 Days Half Board from €125.00 pps per day
15 15

Special Offer: Midweek Specials from €85.00 pps (3 Nights B&B)
10 10

Special Offer: Midweek Specials from €325.00 pps (3 Nights B&B and 3 Dinners)
13 13

Closed 20 October - 01 April	Closed 23 - 28 December	Closed 01 November - 14 March

B&B Rates are per Person Sharing per Night incl. Breakfast.
or **Room Rates** are per Room per Night - See also Page 8

Shannon Oaks Hotel & Country Club

Portumna,
Co. Galway

Tel: 090-974 1777 Fax: 090-974 1357
Email: sales@shannonoaks.ie
Web: www.shannonoaks.ie

HOTEL ★★★ MAP 6 I 9

Shannon Oaks Hotel & Country Club lies adjacent to the 17th century Portumna Castle and estate, by the shores of Lough Derg. All our rooms have satellite television, DD phone and an en suite bathroom. A distinguished menu of classic and fusion Irish dishes are available each evening. Our leisure centre, with its indoor heated swimming pool, sauna, steam room and gymnasium provides the stress free atmosphere in which to relax and unwind.

Bookable on www.irelandhotels.com
Member of Irish Country Hotels

B&B from €90.00 to €105.00

John Pardy
Proprietor

Activities:

Member of:

Special Offer: *Weekend Specials from €170.00 pps (2 Nights B&B & 1 Dinner)*

63 63

Open All Year

Lough Inagh Lodge

Recess,
Connemara,
Co. Galway

Tel: 095-34706 Fax: 095-34708
Email: inagh@iol.ie
Web: www.loughinaghlodgehotel.ie

HOTEL ★★★★ MAP 5 D 11

Lough Inagh Lodge was built in 1880. It offers all the comforts of an elegant modern hotel in an old world atmosphere, open log fires in the library and oak panelled bar symbolises the warmth of Inagh hospitality. The lodge is surrounded by famous beauty spots including the Twelve Bens Mountain Range and the Connemara National Park. Kylemore Abbey is also nearby. Ideal base for hill walking, cycling and fishing.

Bookable on www.irelandhotels.com
Member of Manor House Hotels

B&B from €92.00 to €113.00

Maire O'Connor
Proprietor

Activities:

Member of:

Special Offer: *Weekend Specials from €202.00 pps (2 Nights B&B & 1 Dinner)*

13 13

Closed 11 December - 16 March

Maol Reidh Lodge

Tullycross,
Renvyle,
Co. Galway

Tel: 095-43844 Fax: 095-43784
Email: maolreidhhotel@eircom.net
Web: www.maolreidhhotel.com

HOTEL N MAP 9 C 12

Situated in the delightful village of Tullycross, Renvyle the new Maol Reidh Lodge offers guests a high standard of luxury. We are close to Connemara National Park and Kylemore Abbey. For the active guest, we are nestled in the Twelve Bens and Maamturk Mountains, and only a few minutes drive from Scuba-Dive West and Oceans Alive sealife centre. A perfect place to enjoy the natural paradise of Connemara.

Bookable on www.irelandhotels.com

B&B from €55.00 to €85.00

Jack & Monica Lydon
Proprietors

Special Offer: *Weekend Specials from €130.00 pps (2 Nights B&B & 1 Dinner)*

12 12

inet

Closed 30 October - 01 March

B&B Rates are per Person Sharing per Night incl. Breakfast.
or **Room Rates** are per Room per Night - See also Page 8

Renvyle House Hotel

Renvyle,
Connemara,
Co. Galway
Tel: 095-43511 Fax: 095-43515
Email: info@renvyle.com
Web: www.renvyle.com

HOTEL ★★★ MAP 9 C 12

Historic coastal hotel set amid the magical beauty of sea, lake and mountains, the keynotes are warmth and comfort with award-winning fine fare. Turf fires and cosy lounges make you relax and feel at home. Golf, tennis, horse riding, swimming pool, snooker, boating, fishing are the facilities to name but a few. Wonderful walking and cycling routes throughout an area that hosts a vast National Park. Additional facilities include claypigeon shooting.

Bookable on www.irelandhotels.com

B&B from €30.00 to €115.00

Zoe Coyle
Sales & Marketing Manager

Member of:
IRISH HOTELS FEDERATION

Special Offer: Midweek Specials from €75.00 pps
(3 Nights B&B)

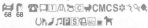
68 68

Closed 08 January - 12 February

Eldons Hotel

Roundstone,
Connemara,
Co. Galway
Tel: 095-35933 Fax: 095-35722
Email: eldonshotel@eircom.net
Web: www.eldonshotel.com

HOTEL ★★ MAP 9 C 11

Situated in the village of Roundstone, has a view of the harbour and Twelve Bens mountain range. We are a newly built, family-run hotel, offering all bedrooms with private bathrooms, colour TV and D.D. phones. Locally; 18 hole golf course and sea angling. Our Beola Restaurant has been operating successfully for many years and is renowned for its fine food, with lobster being its speciality. Credit cards taken. New annexe consisting of 6 superior rooms with a lift.

B&B from €40.00 to €65.00

Ann & Noleen Conneely
Owner / Chef

Activities:

Member of:
IRISH HOTELS FEDERATION

19 19

Closed 02 November - 14 March

Roundstone House Hotel

Roundstone,
Connemara,
Co. Galway
Tel: 095-35864 Fax: 095-35944
Email: vaughanshotel@eircom.net
Web: www.irishcountryhotels.com

HOTEL ★★ MAP 9 C 11

Roundstone House Hotel is a family hotel situated in the picturesque village of Roundstone. Roundstone is a fascinating place for a holiday offering a wide range of interests for the holidaymakers. Many outdoor activities are available locally including sea angling, watersports, hill walking, pony trekking and a championship 18 hole golf course nearby. Come to beautiful Roundstone for a holiday to remember.

Bookable on www.irelandhotels.com
Member of Irish Country Hotels

B&B from €50.00 to €55.00

Maureen Vaughan
Proprietor

Member of:
IRISH HOTELS FEDERATION

13 13

Closed 01 November - 06 April

B&B Rates are per Person Sharing per Night incl. Breakfast.
or **Room Rates** are per Room per Night - See also Page 8

Spiddal

An Cruiscin Lan Hotel	Park Lodge Hotel	Tigh Chualain

An Cruiscin Lan Hotel

Spiddal,
Co. Galway

Tel: 091-553148 Fax: 091-553712
Email: info@cruiscinlanhotel.com
Web: www.cruiscinlanhotel.com

HOTEL ★★ MAP 5 E 10

An Cruiscin Lan Hotel is located in the heart of Irish speaking Spiddal Village at the gateway to the Gaeltacht, Connemara and the Aran Islands. All rooms are en suite with a colour TV and direct dial telephone. The hotel offers a snug bar, lounge bar, dining conservatory and beer garden with spectacular views of Galway Bay. Our restaurant is renowned locally for quality, value and a commitment to service. Our meeting room is suitable for up to 20 delegates.

B&B from €40.00 to €80.00

John Foye

Member of:
IRISH HOTELS FEDERATION

14 14

Closed 25 December

Park Lodge Hotel

Park,
Spiddal,
Co. Galway

Tel: 091-553159 Fax: 091-553494
Email: parklodgehotel@eircom.net
Web: www.parklodgehotelandrentacottage.com

HOTEL U MAP 5 E 10

The Park Lodge Hotel is owned and run by the Foyle Family. It is situated on the coast road from Galway to Connemara, 16km west of Galway City and just east of Spiddal Village. Most of the 23 bedrooms have a view of Galway Bay. There are also seven detached cottages on the grounds, each self-catering and fully equipped for 5 persons. Cottages open all year.

B&B from €50.00 to €70.00

*Jane Marie Foyle
Manager*

Member of:
IRISH HOTELS FEDERATION

23 23

Closed 01 October - 31 May

Tigh Chualain

Kilroe East,
Spiddal,
Co. Galway

Tel: 091-553609 Fax: 091-553049
Email: tighchualain@eircom.net

GUESTHOUSE ★★★ MAP 5 E 10

Tigh Chualain is a charming, family-run 3*** guesthouse, 16km west of Galway City and 2km west of Spiddal Village, en route to the Aran Islands' Ferry. Overlooking Galway Bay, with a nearby Blue Flag beach, it is in the heart of the Connemara Gaeltacht. An obvious starting point for exploring the rugged beauty of Connemara with its manifold attractions. All bedrooms are en suite with direct dial telephone and colour TV.

B&B from €30.00 to €40.00

*Nora & Colm Folan
Proprietors*

*Special Offer: Midweek Specials from €85.00 pps
(3 Nights B&B)*

9 9

Closed 31 October - 31 March

B&B Rates are per Person Sharing per Night incl. Breakfast.
or **Room Rates** are per Room per Night - See also Page 8

Achill Cliff House Hotel	Grays Guest House	McDowell's Hotel & Activity Centre
Keel, Achill Island, Co. Mayo Tel: 098-43400 Fax: 098-43007 Email: info@achillcliff.com Web: www.achillcliff.com	Dugort, Achill Island, Co. Mayo Tel: 098-43244	Slievemore Road, Dugort, Achill, Co. Mayo Tel: 098-43148 Email: mcdowellshotel@eircom.net Web: www.achill-leisure.ie

HOTEL ★★★ MAP 9 C 14	GUESTHOUSE ★★★ MAP 9 C 14	HOTEL ★★ MAP 9 C 14
New family-run smoke free hotel in a superb location. Keel Beach, ideal for walking is only 2 minutes away. The hotel commanding magnificent views offers excellent home-made food, comfortable accommodation and good value. Fine wines and an extensive breakfast menu are available. All facilities are nearby, fishing, horse riding, golf, walking, painting, photography. The Deserted Village and House of Prayer. There is no nightclub. Check out our website for last minute special offers. RAC Dining Award 2005.	Vi McDowell welcomes you to Grays where you are assured of a restful holiday, with good food, comfort and personal attention. Turf fires and electric blankets. Late dinner is served at 7pm. There are three lounges, colour TV, table tennis room and croquet lawn and swings in an enclosed garden. Art gallery for use of artists staying in guesthouse.	Family-run hotel, nestled at the base of the Slievemore Mountain, offering a warm welcome and a friendly service. Cuisine is the best of home-cooked local fresh produce - à la carte, bar food, seafood, childrens' choice. Our restaurant overlooks the majestic Minaun Heights. Relax in our cosy turf fire bar. Adventure and leisure activity facilities.

Bookable on www.irelandhotels.com

B&B from €40.00 to €70.00	B&B from €40.00 to €55.00	B&B from €50.00 to €60.00

Teresa McNamara Proprietor

Activities:

Member of:

Special Offer: Weekend Specials from €109.00 pps (2 Nights B&B & 1 Dinner)

10 10   Inet

| Closed 23 -27 December |

Vi McDowell Owner / Manager

15 15

| Closed 24 - 26 December |

Richard & Tina O'Hara Proprietors

Member of:

10 9

| Closed 01 November - 01 March |

B&B Rates are per Person Sharing per Night incl. Breakfast.
or **Room Rates** are per Room per Night - See also Page 8

Ostan Oilean Acla

Achill Sound,
Co. Mayo

Tel: 098-45138 Fax: 098-45198
Email: reservations@achillislandhotel.com
Web: www.achillislandhotel.com

HOTEL U MAP 9 C 14

Enjoy the panoramic views of Achill Island from our new luxury hotel situated at the gateway to Achill Island. In our elegant Seafood Restaurant choose from a wide range of local produce. Relax and enjoy a drink in our friendly traditional bar. Convenient to 5 Blue Flag beaches, the highest cliffs in Europe, golf courses, pitch and putt course, outdoor activities. A warm friendly welcome awaits you at Ostan Oilean Acla.

B&B from €45.00 to €80.00

Michael & Una McLoughlin
Proprietors

Activities:
✓ ♪ ✈

Member of:
IRISH HOTELS FEDERATION

26 26

Open All Year

Belleek Castle

Belleek,
Ballina,
Co. Mayo

Tel: 096-22400 Fax: 096-71750
Email: belleekcastlehotel@eircom.net
Web: www.belleekcastle.com

HOTEL U MAP 10 F 15

Historic, romantic, set in 1000 acres of woodland on banks of River Moy - wine/dine till midnight - Gourmet organic food enthusiasts welcomed - 'Perchance to Dream' in a four poster. For your added pleasure: tour of 16th century castle armoury, giant fossil exhibits, Spanish Armada Bar, dramatic artefacts and timbers salvaged from Galleons wrecked off the Irish West Coast 1588. Sporting: international surfing, golf, fishing, tennis, riding, ten stables in castle.

B&B from €70.00 to €120.00

Marshall & Jacqueline Doran

15 15

Closed 09 January - 25 March

Downhill House Hotel

Ballina,
Co. Mayo

Tel: 096-21033 Fax: 096-21338
Email: info@downhillhotel.ie
Web: www.downhillhotel.ie

HOTEL ★★★ MAP 10 F 15

3*** Downhill House Hotel, privately owned country house a short walk from shops, bars & restaurants of Ballina Town, offering a perfect blend of olde world charm & new world comfort. This stylish hotel is set in mature tranquil gardens, offering excellent cuisine with superb facilities on-site. Eagles Leisure Club holder of White Flag incorporates 2 swimming pools, steam room, sauna, jaccuzi & floodlit tennis courts. Conference centre, piano bar (national & international entertainment). 18 hole golf courses nearby. River, lake & deep sea fishing.

Bookable on www.irelandhotels.com
Member of D'Arcy Marketing

B&B from €81.00 to €97.50

Rachael Moylett

Activities:
✓ ♪ ✈

Member of:
IRISH HOTELS FEDERATION

Special Offer: Weekend Specials from €176.50 pps
(2 Nights B&B & 1 Dinner)

60 60

Closed 22 - 27 December

B&B Rates are per Person Sharing per Night incl. Breakfast. or <u>Room Rates</u> are per Room per Night - See also Page 8

Downhill Inn

Sligo Road,
Ballina,
Co. Mayo
Tel: 096-73444 Fax: 096-73411
Email: info@downhillinn.ie
Web: www.downhillinn.com

HOTEL ★★★ MAP 10 F 15

A family-run 3*** hotel, located 1 mile outside Ballina Town on the main Sligo Road (N59). Contemporary in its design with 45 well-appointed triple rooms. All rooms are en suite with multi-channel TV, hairdryer, tea/coffee facilities and DD phone. The region offers superb fishing on the River Moy, Lough Conn and Killala Bay. An excellent selection of golf courses: Enniscrone, Ballina, Carne, to mention but a few. Enjoy a drink at the bar or a meal in our Terrace Restaurant. Rest assured!

Bookable on www.irelandhotels.com
Member of Holiday Ireland Hotels

B&B from €45.00 to €75.00

John Raftery / Nicola Moylett
Proprietors

Member of:
HOTELS

Special Offer: Weekend Specials from €100.00 pps
(2 Nights B&B & 1 Dinner)

45 45

Inet

Closed 21- 26 December

JJ Gannons
Bar, Restaurant & Hotel

Main Street,
Ballinrobe (Lake District),
Co. Mayo
Tel: 094-954 1008 Fax: 094-952 0018
Email: info@jjgannons.com
Web: www.jjgannons.com

HOTEL N MAP 9 F 12

Built in 1838, Niki & Jay Gannon restored the building (3rd generation) in 2004. At Gannons, guests enjoy much more than the luxurious accommodation with large bedrooms boasting stunning balcony views and super-king size beds. The "Red" Fine Dining Restaurant is a haven of urban serenity. The bar food signature dishes with wonderful wines and champagne available by the glass prove a rare treat. Fishing, golfing, fly-tying, guided walks, guided cycle routes, "tune-in" mind, body & soul weekends and cookery course packages available.

B&B from €60.00 to €75.00

Niki & Jay Gannon
Proprietors

Activities:
✓ ♪ ⚼

Special Offer: Midweek Specials from €180.00 pps
(3 Nights B&B & 2 Dinners)

11 11

Inet WiFi

Open All Year

Stella Maris
Country House Hotel

Ballycastle,
Co. Mayo

Tel: 096-43322 Fax: 096-43965
Email: Info@StellaMarisIreland.com
Web: www.StellaMarisIreland.com

HOTEL U MAP 9 E 16

Stella Maris was built in 1853 as a coastguard fortress and later became a convent overlooking Bunatrahir Bay. Strategically located between the world-renowned golf links of Enniscrone and Carne/Belmullet, and close to Nick Faldo's Bartra Island. Sea and freshwater fishing outside the door. Stella Maris features high quality linens, antique furnishings, its own gardens for produce, fine dining, an inviting bar/lounge, and mesmerizing conservatory facing the Atlantic Ocean. Recommended by most major tour guides. Member of Ireland's Blue Book.

Bookable on www.irelandhotels.com
Member of Ireland's Blue Book

B&B from €92.50 to €117.50

Frances Kelly / Terence McSweeney
Proprietors

Activities:
✓ ♪

Member of:

HOTELS

Special Offer: Specials upon request

12 12

Inet WiFi

Closed 03 October - 12 April

B&B Rates are per Person Sharing per Night incl. Breakfast.
or Room Rates are per Room per Night - See also Page 8

West 189

Sea Rod Inn	**Western Strands Hotel**	**Kennys Guest House**
Doohoma, Belmullet, Ballina, Co. Mayo Tel: 097-86767 Fax: 097-86809 Email: info@thesearodinn.ie Web: www.thesearodinn.ie	Main Street, Belmullet, Co. Mayo Tel: 097-81096 Fax: 097-81096	Lucan Street, Castlebar, Co. Mayo Tel: 094-902 3091 Email: kennys@castlebar.ie Web: www.castlebar.ie/stay/kennys

GUESTHOUSE ★★ MAP 10 F 15	HOTEL ★ MAP 9 C 16	GUESTHOUSE ★★★ MAP 9 E 14

Located on the southern shore of Doohoma Peninsula, The Sea Rod Inn is a fully licensed premises with a beautifully decorated bar and lounge, and nine magnificent bedrooms all of which are en suite with TV and central heating. Tea/coffee making facilities are all available in a separate sitting room, exclusive to guests, where you can enjoy panoramic views of Achill Island and the Atlantic Ocean. Our in-house entertainment during the summer months ensures that parents with young families can have a carefree holiday with no childcare worries.

A small, family-run hotel situated in the centre of Belmullet Town. Easy access to safe, sandy beaches, some with Blue Flag awards. Local amenities include deep sea angling and fresh water fishing, 5 minutes drive to Carne Golf Links, rated No. 5 golf links course in Ireland. Close to U.I.S.C.E, a water sports centre with sailing and surfing, near Aughrim Heritage Centre (archaeology, local history and folklore centre). There are 10 en suite bedrooms with TV and telephone. Also closed Good Friday.

Castlebar's only 3 star family-run guesthouse offers luxury and comfort. Decorated and furnished to a very high standard. All rooms are en suite with TV, DD telephone and hairdryer. Relax in the residents lounge with complimentary tea/coffee or avail of the numerous facilities nearby e.g. organised walks, fishing, bowling, swimming, golf, fine restaurants and entertainment. Location: town centre. Private car park. Mobile: 087 984 0759.

Member of North & West Coast Links Ireland

Bookable on www.irelandhotels.com

B&B from €30.00 to €40.00	B&B from €32.50 to €32.50	B&B from €35.00 to €45.00

Michael & Bernadette Barrett

Emer O'Toole
Proprietor

Activities:

Susanna & Raymond Kenny

Member of:
IRISH HOTELS FEDERATION

Member of:
IRISH HOTELS FEDERATION

Special Offer: *Week Partial Board from €300.00 pps (7 Nights B&B & 7 Dinners)*

Special Offer: *€30 per person for a group of 8 or more for B&B*

9 9

10 10

8 8

Open All Year	Closed 23 - 27 December	Open All Year

B&B Rates are per Person Sharing per Night incl. Breakfast. or **Room Rates** are per Room per Night - See also Page 8

TF Royal Hotel & Theatre

Old Westport Road,
Castlebar,
Co. Mayo
Tel: 094-902 3111 Fax: 094-902 3111
Email: info@tfroyalhotel.com
Web: www.tfroyalhotel.com

HOTEL ★★★ MAP 9 E 14

The TF Royal Hotel & Theatre is a luxury boutique 3*** family hotel adjacent to Castlebar Town centre. Renovation & refurbishment has provided luxurious bedrooms decorated to an excellent standard with air con, security safe, ISDN lines, TV, VCR, trouser press, hairdryer. Executive/master suites & connecting family rooms. Modern conference & theatre facility. Café Bar & Bistro. Tamarind Seed Restaurant. Dedicated business centre. Adjacent to Institute of Technology, Mayo General Hospital, Harlequin Shopping Centre and main shopping.

Bookable on www.irelandhotels.com
Member of Countrywide Hotels - MinOtel Ireland

B&B from €65.00 to €85.00

Pat & Mary Jennings
Proprietors

Activities:
✓/🎭

Member of:
IRISH HOTELS FEDERATION

🛏🦽 ☎🖥️T©✉CM♪♫P🅿S🄳🆎Inet
27 27
WiFi

Closed 24 - 26 December

Riverside Guesthouse & Restaurant

Church Street,
Charlestown,
Co. Mayo
Tel: 094-925 4200 Fax: 094-925 4207
Email: riversiderestaurant@eircom.net
Web: www.riversiderest.com

GUESTHOUSE ★★ MAP 10 G 14

Situated on the intersection of N17 & N5 primary routes. 10 minutes to Knock International Airport, 20 minutes to Knock Shrine. Ideal base for touring Mayo, Sligo, Roscommon and Galway. A charming family-run guesthouse with all rooms en suite and with TV. Modern Irish food served and prepared in our Olde World restaurant by award-winning chef/owner Anthony Kelly and his wife Anne. Special restaurant licence to serve all alcohol to diners. A warm Irish welcome awaits you.

B&B from €35.00 to €40.00

Anthony & Anne Kelly
Proprietors

Member of:
IRISH HOTELS FEDERATION

🛏🦽 🖥️T©CMP🅿🄳🆎
10 8

Closed 24 - 27 December

Ashford Castle

Cong,
Co. Mayo

Tel: 094-954 6003 Fax: 094-954 6260
Email: ashford@ashford.ie
Web: www.ashford.ie

HOTEL ★★★★★ MAP 9 E 12

13th century castle located 40 minutes from Galway. Once the estate of Lord Ardilaun and the Guinness Family. Ashford opened as a luxury hotel in 1939. 83 guest rooms are of the highest standards with incredible lake or river views. We offer 9 hole golf and tennis which is complimentary to residents. Our activities include clay pigeon shooting, archery, fishing and Ireland's only school of falconry. Our Health and Beauty features jacuzzi, steam room, sauna, gym and treatment rooms. Various suites and state rooms available, enquire with reservations@ashford.ie

Bookable on www.irelandhotels.com
Member of The Leading Small Hotels of the World

Room Rate from €225.00 to €546.00

Niall Rochford
General Manager

Activities:
✓/🎣🎭

Member of:
IRISH HOTELS FEDERATION

Special Offer: Available Upon Request

🛏🦽 ☎🖥️T♪CM✻🅭🄫🔍🍷♪♫P
83 83
🄳🆎Inet WiFi

Open All Year

B&B Rates are per Person Sharing per Night incl. Breakfast.
or **Room Rates** are per Room per Night - See also Page 8

West 191

Cong

Lydons Lodge Hotel

Cong,
Co. Mayo

Tel: 094-954 6053 Fax: 094-954 6523
Email: lydonslodge@eircom.net
Web: www.lydonslodgefreeservers.com

HOTEL ★★ MAP 9 E 12

Lydons Lodge combines the most modern amenities with old world charm. Located in Cong, village of 'Quiet Man' film fame it offers salmon, pike and famous Lough Corrib wild brown trout fishing. Boats, engines and boatmen can be arranged. Choice of 3 local golf clubs, horse riding and tennis. Minutes' walk from Ashford Castle and gardens. Hill walks and mountain climbing with spectacular lake views, an archaeological and geological paradise. Traditional music and bar food.

B&B from €35.00 to €55.00

Frank & Carmel Lydon
Owners

Member of:

11 11

Closed 05 November - 01 February

Michaeleen's Manor

Lisloughrey,
Quay Road,
Cong, Co. Mayo

Tel: 094-954 6089 Fax: 094-954 6448
Email: info@quietman-cong.com
Web: www.quietman-cong.com

GUESTHOUSE ★★★ MAP 9 E 12

Guesthouse themed on Quiet Man Film in the heart of Quiet Man Country. Promising a unique experience for all Quiet Man enthusiasts with TV, DVD, hot tub, sauna, tennis court. Located only 1/2 mile from Lough Corrib which is a fisherman's paradise. Historical sites, monuments, forest walks, hill climbing. One of the most central guesthouses for touring Connemara, Galway, Westport, Achill Island, The Aran Islands. Also mini-golf and golf academy. Cong once seen is never forgotten.

B&B from €30.00 to €45.00

Margaret Collins
Owner / Manager

Member of:

11 11

Open All Year

Ryan's Hotel

Main Street,
Cong,
Co. Mayo

Tel: 094-954 6243 Fax: 094-954 6634
Email: info@ryanshotelcong.ie
Web: www.ryanshotelcong.ie

HOTEL ★★ MAP 9 E 12

Under new ownership, the hotel boasts personal attention to our customers. All rooms are large and en suite, tea/coffee making facilities in each room. Situated in the centre of Connemara, an ideal base to explore the scenic West of Ireland. Great fishing on both Lough Corrib and Lough Mask. Great golf courses and mini golf nearby and loads of activities, ie horse riding, canoeing, wood walks and cycling.

B&B from €35.00 to €60.00

Denis Lenihan & Michael Crowe
Owners

Activities:

Special Offer: *2 Nights B&B, 1 Scenic Boat Ride and 1 Dinner from €110.00 pps*

12 12

Closed 23 - 25 December

B&B Rates are per Person Sharing per Night incl. Breakfast.
or **Room Rates** are per Room per Night - See also Page 8

Teach Iorrais

Geesala,
Ballina,
Co. Mayo
Tel: 097-86888 Fax: 097-86855
Email: teachlor@iol.ie
Web: www.teachiorrais.com

HOTEL ★★★ MAP 10 F 15

Situated in an area of unrivalled beauty, Teach Iorrais is an exclusive and luxurious hotel in Co. Mayo. The hotel boasts 31 exquisite en suite bedrooms which are decorated to the highest standard and offer awe-inspiring views of the surrounding Neiphinn Mountains and the Atlantic Ocean. Award-winning An Neiphinn Restaurant offers the best of fine dining in a relaxing and intimate environment. Our themed bar, Bear Synge, is one of the Irish Pubs of Distinction. Carne Links Golf Course located 15 minutes drive from hotel.

B&B from €46.00 to €55.00

Patricia Gaughan
Manager

Activities:

31 31

Open All Year

Belmont Hotel

Knock,
Co. Mayo
Tel: 094-938 8122 Fax: 094-938 8532
Email: reception@belmonthotel.ie
Web: www.belmonthotel.ie

HOTEL ★★★ MAP 10 G 13

A haven of hospitality nestled at the rear entrance to Knock Shrine off N17. The hotel radiates old country warmth from the moment you arrive. RAC 3***, Failte Ireland 3*** and AA 3*** status. Daily carvery and sumptuous bar food menu complement our award-winning Bialann Restaurant. Our specially developed Natural Health Therapy packages are very professional and attractive. Tastefully furnished bedrooms with facilities.

Bookable on www.irelandhotels.com

B&B from €50.00 to €70.00

Della Boland
Manager

Activities:

Member of:

Special Offer: Pamper Packages from €195.00 pps
(2 Nights B&B & 1 Dinner & 2 Therapies Of Your Choice)

63 63

Open all year

Knock House Hotel

Ballyhaunis Road,
Knock,
Co. Mayo
Tel: 094-938 8088 Fax: 094-938 8044
Email: info@knockhousehotel.ie
Web: www.knockhousehotel.ie

HOTEL ★★★ MAP 10 G 13

Located in over 100 acres of parkland and nestling behind the Basilica, this 6 year old hotel is a gem! With 68 comfortable bedrooms, of which 6 are designed for wheelchair users, every need is catered for. The superb Four Seasons Restaurant - open all day - and the glazed reception and lounge areas, surrounded by local limestone, overlook countryside. This well run, tranquil hotel will be hard to leave.

Bookable on www.irelandhotels.com

B&B from €53.00 to €73.00

Brian Crowley
General Manager

Activities:

Member of:

68 68

Open All Year

B&B Rates are per Person Sharing per Night incl. Breakfast.
or Room Rates are per Room per Night - See also Page 8

Park Inn Mulranny

Mulranny,
Westport,
Co. Mayo
Tel: 098-36000 Fax: 098-36899
Email: info.mulranny@rezidorparkinn.com
Web: www.mulranny.parkinn.ie

HOTEL **P** MAP 9 D 14

A stunning hotel on a unique site, overlooking Clew Bay on 42 acres of woodland. Alll rooms have spectacular sea or woodland views. Its original character and charm has been retained, with the elegant Nephin Restaurant, lively Waterfront Bar and relaxing lounge. Extensive conference facilities are available. Complimentary use of leisure facilities for all our guests. Excellent midweek breaks available. For further details on this unique hotel, call 098-36000.

Member of Rezidor SAS

B&B from €75.00 to €99.00

Stephen O'Connor
General Manager

Activities:

Member of:
HOTELS

Special Offer: Midweek Specials from €150.00 pps (3 Nights B&B)

61 61

Closed 24 - 26 December

Healys Restaurant & Country House Hotel

Pontoon,
Foxford,
Co. Mayo
Tel: 094-925 6443 Fax: 094-925 6572
Email: info@healyspontoon.com
Web: www.healyspontoon.com

HOTEL **U** MAP 9 F 14

Boutique style hotel with dining room, restaurant & bar all serving award-winning food from 8.00-21.30 with over 100 wines to choose from. AA Rosette for cuisine 5 consecutive years; Georgina Campbell Guide; Trout & Salmon Magazine; Dining Pub of the Year for 4 years; Feile Bia; Mayo Magazine; Hooked on the Moy; Ireland West & many more. Golfing & fishing arranged locally. On the shores of Loughs Conn & Cullen for trout & salmon, 5 mins to Rr. Moy: world renowned for salmon fishing. 30 mins from Enniscrone Golf Links & Westport GC in the heart of Mayo's best golf & fishing region. Single supplement €20.

B&B from €45.00 to €45.00

John Dever & Josette Maurer
Proprietors

Activities:

Member of:
HOTELS

14 14

Closed 25 December

Pontoon Bridge Hotel

Pontoon,
Foxford,
Co. Mayo
Tel: 094-925 6120 Fax: 094-925 6688
Email: relax@pontoonbridge.com
Web: www.pontoonbridge.com

HOTEL ★★★ MAP 10 F 14

Family managed hotel on the shores of Lough Conn & Cullin in the centre of Mayo. Famous trout & salmon fishing - Rr. Moy, golf, horse riding, scenery, central for touring. Twin Lakes Restaurant boasts the best food in Mayo. Geary's Waterfront Bar & Bistro with seasonal live music. Two panoramic restaurants on water's edge. Tennis court, sandy beaches, archery school locally, conference facilities. Families welcome. School of fly fishing, landscape painting & cookery. Friendly welcome. Hot tub, sauna, treatment rooms & small gym. Wonderful lake-view suites. Member of Select Hotels. See you soon in Pontoon!

Member of Great Fishing Houses of Ireland

B&B from €75.00 to €110.00

Breeta Geary
General Manager

Activities:

Member of:
HOTELS

Special Offer: Midweek Specials from €180.00 pps (2 Nights B&B & 2 Dinners)

58 58

Closed 24 - 26 December

B&B Rates are per Person Sharing per Night incl. Breakfast. or **Room Rates** are per Room per Night - See also Page 8

Ardmore Country House Hotel and Restaurant

The Quay,
Westport,
Co. Mayo
Tel: 098-25994 Fax: 098-27795
Email: ardmorehotel@eircom.net
Web: www.ardmorecountryhouse.com

HOTEL ★★★★ MAP 9 E 13

Ardmore Country House and Restaurant is a small luxurious 4**** hotel, owned and managed by Pat and Noreen Hoban and family, offering warm hospitality. Ardmore House is idyllically situated overlooking Clew Bay with breathtaking sunsets, in the shadow of Croagh Patrick. The restaurant offers the best of local produce, including fresh fish from Clew Bay, organic vegetables and herbs from local producers and a selection of Irish farmhouse cheeses. All bedrooms are non-smoking.

B&B from €85.00 to €125.00

Noreen & Pat Hoban

Member of:
HOTELS FEDERATION

Special Offer: *Weekend Specials from €220.00 pps (2 Nights B&B & 1 Dinner)*

13 13

Closed 01 January - 15 March

Atlantic Coast Hotel

The Quay,
Westport,
Co. Mayo
Tel: 098-29000 Fax: 098-29111
Email: reservations@atlanticcoasthotel.com
Web: www.atlanticcoasthotel.com

HOTEL ★★★ MAP 9 E 13

Established as one of Westport's finest & most popular hotels, on the waterfront at Westport Quay overlooking Clew Bay. Superb contemporary cuisine in our unique top floor award-winning restaurant, The Blue Wave. The Atlantic Club features pool, gym, sauna, steam room & massage, including seaweed hydrotherapy bath treatments. Elysium, Health and Beauty Spa offers an extensive range of treatments and therapies. Championship golf, angling, scenic walks, islands & Blue Flag beaches nearby. Callsave: 1850 229 000.

Bookable on www.irelandhotels.com
Member of Carlton Hotel Group

B&B from €70.00 to €135.00

Lynda Foley
General Manager

Activities:

Member of:
HOTELS FEDERATION

Special Offer: *Weekend Specials from €175.00 pps (2 Nights B&B & 1 Dinner)*

85 85

Closed 23 - 27 December

Augusta Lodge

Golf Links Road,
Westport,
Co. Mayo
Tel: 098-28900 Fax: 098-28995
Email: info@augustalodge.ie
Web: www.augustalodge.ie

GUESTHOUSE ★★★ MAP 9 E 13

Augusta Lodge is a purpose built 3*** guesthouse situated just 5 minutes walk from the town centre of Westport. A warm and friendly welcome awaits you in this family-run guesthouse and Liz and Dave will ensure that your stay is a memorable one. A golfer's haven with tee times and green fees arranged at Westport and adjacent courses. Putting green on-site for guests' use. Listed in all leading guides.

Bookable on www.irelandhotels.com

B&B from €35.00 to €50.00

Liz O'Regan

Activities:

Member of:
HOTELS FEDERATION

Special Offer: *Midweek Specials from €100.00 pps (3 Nights B&B)*

10 10

Closed 23 - 27 December

B&B Rates are per Person Sharing per Night incl. Breakfast.
or Room Rates are per Room per Night - See also Page 8

Boffin Lodge

The Quay,
Westport,
Co. Mayo
Tel: 098-26092 Fax: 098-28690
Email: pa@achh.iol.ie
Web: www.boffinlodge.com

GUESTHOUSE N MAP 9 E 13

Boffin Lodge was purpose built in 1999. It is located very close to the fashionable quay area of Westport where many of the town's best hotels, restaurants and pubs are located. Boffin Lodge has many special features such as a four poster room, a bedroom with a steam room and another with a jacuzzi bath. Our breakfast menu is extensive and can be seen on www.boffinlodge.com. We look forward to meeting you.

B&B from €35.00 to €45.00

Patrick Aylward
Proprietor

Member of:

10   10

Open All Year

Castlecourt Hotel Conference and Leisure Centre

Castlebar Street,
Westport,
Co. Mayo
Tel: 098-55088 Fax: 098-28622
Email: info@castlecourthotel.ie
Web: www.castlecourthotel.ie

HOTEL ★★★ MAP 9 E 13

This stunning family hotel is now one of the largest leisure hotels in the West of Ireland. It offers guests indoor heated swimming pool, spa jacuzzi, sauna, steam room, children's pool, hairdressing salon, beautician and health suites for aromatherapy and massage. Additional choice of restaurants and bars in adjoining Westport Plaza Hotel, opening Spring 2006. A short stay with us and you will soon see why we are so famously known for our warm and welcoming atmosphere!!

Bookable on www.irelandhotels.com

B&B from €39.00 to €105.00

Anne Corcoran / Joseph Corcoran
Managers

Activities:

Member of:

Special Offer: *Weekend Specials from €129.00 pps (2 Nights B&B & 1 Dinner)*

140 140

Closed 24 - 26 December

Clew Bay Hotel

James Street,
Westport,
Co. Mayo
Tel: 098-28088 Fax: 098-25783
Email: info@clewbayhotel.com
Web: www.clewbayhotel.com

HOTEL ★★★ MAP 9 E 13

Our newly refurbished hotel is located in the heart of Westport town. This family-run hotel offers a warm welcome to all our guests. Renowned for good food whether you choose to dine in our bistro or Riverside Restaurant. Our popular new bar features music regularly. Guests can enjoy free access to Westport Leisure Park. The hotel is ideally located for exploring the stunning sites of the West.

Bookable on www.irelandhotels.com
Member of Irish Country Hotels

B&B from €45.00 to €100.00

Maria Ruddy & Darren Madden
Proprietors

Member of:

Special Offer: *Weekend Specials from €125.00 pps (2 Nights B&B & 1 Dinner)*

28   28

Closed 22 - 28 December

B&B Rates are per Person Sharing per Night incl. Breakfast.
or **Room Rates** are per Room per Night - See also Page 8

Hotel Westport, Leisure, Spa, Conference

Newport Road,
Westport,
Co. Mayo
Tel: 098-25122 Fax: 098-26739
Email: reservations@hotelwestport.ie
Web: www.hotelwestport.ie

HOTEL ★★★ MAP 9 E 13

Award-winning, RAC 4 star hotel in the heart of Westport. A reputation for friendly, professional service & excellent food. Westport's Premier White Flag Leisure Centre and new Ocean Spirit Spa for pampering. A variety of theme & leisure holidays to enjoy as part of your precious relaxation & leisure time: golf, golden holidays & murder mystery intrigue. Family holidays with childrens' 'Panda Club' a daily activity programme with the 'Fun Fellows', seasonal. One of Ireland's best loved hotels! LoCall reservations (ROI): 1850 536373 (NI/UK): 0870 8765432.

Bookable on www.irelandhotels.com

B&B from €90.00 to €130.00

Gerry Walshe
General Manager

Activities:

Member of:

Special Offer: Weekend Specials from €165.00 pps
(2 Nights B&B & 1 Dinner)

129 129

Open All Year

Knockranny House Hotel & Spa

Westport,
Co. Mayo
Tel: 098-28600 Fax: 098-28611
Email: info@khh.ie
Web: www.khh.ie

HOTEL ★★★★ MAP 9 E 13

Beautifully appointed in secluded gardens overlooking Westport and Clew Bay, this Victorian style hotel offers sheer luxury in opulent surroundings. Log fires and friendly service combine to provide a wonderfully warm and tranquil atmosphere. The new destination spa, Spa Salveo, includes a vitality pool, thermal suite, fitness suite, 12 treatment rooms, serail, mud chamber, hammam massage, dry floatation and various relaxation areas. The thermal suite consists of a brine inhalation room, aroma grotto, herbal sauna, scented steam room and monsoon shower.

Bookable on www.irelandhotels.com
Member of Manor House Hotels

B&B from €105.00 to €130.00

Geraldine & Adrian Noonan
Proprietors

Activities:

Member of:

Special Offer: Weekend Specials from €170.00 pps
(2 Nights B&B & 1 Dinner)

54 54

Closed 22 - 27 December

Knockranny Lodge

Knockranny,
Westport,
Co. Mayo
Tel: 098-28595 Fax: 098-28805
Email: info@knockrannylodge.ie
Web: www.knockrannylodge.ie

GUESTHOUSE ★★★★ MAP 9 E 13

Perched on an elevated position overlooking the town of Westport, Croagh Patrick and the island-studded waters of Clew Bay, Knockranny Lodge is Mayo's only 4 star guesthouse. All rooms are designed to a luxury hotel standard with pressure jet shower, TV, trouser press and hairdryer. De luxe rooms available. We are the only guesthouse or bed and breakfast in the area to offer free use of Westport's award-winning leisure centre, the C-Club Leisure Centre located in the Castlecourt Hotel. Discounted rates for dinner in two sister hotels.

Bookable on www.irelandhotels.com

B&B from €40.00 to €65.00

Mary McDermott

Special Offer: Midweek Specials from €99.00 pps
(3 Nights B&B)

16 16

Closed 01 December - 30 January

B&B Rates are per Person Sharing per Night incl. Breakfast.
or **Room Rates** are per Room per Night - See also Page 8

Olde Railway Hotel

The Mall,
Westport,
Co. Mayo
Tel: 098-25166 Fax: 098-25090
Email: railway@anu.ie
Web: www.theolderailwayhotel.com

HOTEL ★★★ MAP 9 E 13

1780 Coaching Inn, full of charm and character. Beautifully situated alongside the tree lined 'Carrowbeg River', in the heart of picturesque Westport. Renowned for traditional country fare and fine wines served in our 'Bistro on the Mall'. Awarded AA Rosette. Residents lounge and library. Private car park and garden. Complimentary use of hotel bicycles and fishing rods, complimentary 24 hr tea and coffee service to bedroom. Standard and superior accommodation. Recommended in all leading guides.

B&B from €49.00 to €90.00

Karl Rosenkranz
Proprietor

Activities:

Member of:
IRISH HOTELS FEDERATION

Special Offer: Weekend Specials from €135.90 pps (2 Nights B&B & 1 Dinner)

15 15

Open All Year

Quay West

Quay Road,
Westport,
Co. Mayo
Tel: 098-27863 Fax: 098-28379
Email: quaywest@eircom.net
Web: www.quaywestport.com

GUESTHOUSE ★★ MAP 9 E 13

Quay West is a purpose built house situated 10 minutes walk from town and 5 minutes from the harbour and directly opposite Westport Woods Hotel, where guests can enjoy the superb leisure facilities at discounted rates. Rooms are en suite with power showers, orthopaedic beds and TV. Lounge for guest comfort with tea/coffee facilities. Perfect base for touring beautiful Mayo, Connemara and relaxing in some of Westport's famous pubs and restaurants.

B&B from €30.00 to €38.00

David Kelly
Proprietor

6 6

Closed 24 - 27 December

Westport Inn Hotel

Town Centre,
Mill Street, Westport,
Co. Mayo
Tel: 098-29200 Fax: 098-29250
Email: info@westportinn.ie
Web: www.westportinn.ie

HOTEL ★★ MAP 9 E 13

The Westport Inn is a boutique hotel ideally situated in the heart of Westport where the visitor can immerse themselves in all of the amenities that the town has to offer. The hotel boasts beautifully appointed bedrooms, a charming lounge, quality restaurant, a lively bar and the avant garde Oscar's entertainment venue. The Westport Inn prides itself on high customer service standards, quality accommodation, fine food and entertainment. Relax, unwind and enjoy a warm and friendly atmosphere at this charming hotel.

Bookable on www.irelandhotels.com

B&B from €55.00 to €95.00

Catherine O'Grady-Powers
General Manager

Member of:
IRISH HOTELS FEDERATION

Special Offer: 3 Nights B&B & 1 Dinner from €159.00 pps

34 34

Closed 24 - 27 December

B&B Rates are per Person Sharing per Night incl. Breakfast. or **Room Rates** are per Room per Night - See also Page 8

Westport Plaza Hotel

Castlebar Street,
Westport,
Co. Mayo
Tel: 098-51166 Fax: 098-51133
Email: info@westportplazahotel.ie
Web: www.westportplazahotel.ie

UNDER CONSTRUCTION - OPENING APRIL 2006

HOTEL P MAP 9 E 13

Opening Spring 2006 & located in the centre of Westport, the luxurious 4**** standard Westport Plaza Hotel comprises 83 de luxe rooms, including executive & superior suites. With king size beds and air-conditioning as standard & a selection of rooms with balconies overlooking the hotel courtyard, the Westport Plaza Hotel is a haven of contemporary luxury. As the sister hotel of the adjoining Castlecourt Hotel, guests can avail of the Castlecourt C Club leisure facilities, entertainment, a selection of bars and restaurants within the Castlecourt & the Plaza, as well as a spectacular new spa facility opening in 2006.

B&B from €59.00 to €125.00

Anne Corcoran, Joseph Corcoran

Activities:

Special Offer: Weekend Specials from €149.00 pps
(2 Nights B&B & 1 Dinner)

83 83

Closed 24 - 26 December

Westport Woods Hotel & Spa

Quay Road,
Westport,
Co. Mayo
Tel: 098-25811 Fax: 098-26212
Email: info@westportwoodshotel.com
Web: www.westportwoodshotel.com

HOTEL ★★★ MAP 9 E 13

The ambience that greets you as you enter the spacious foyer of the Westport Woods Hotel & Spa is a combination of activity and relaxation. You'll see people getting ready to go hill walking, surfing, horse riding or families off to a nearby Blue Flag beach. Your holiday can be as eventful as you wish, with our Get! Together! co-ordinators who organise a diverse range of activities. Enjoy unforgettable family holidays with our Go! Kids! Club.

Bookable on www.irelandhotels.com
Member of Brian McEniff Hotels

B&B from €65.00 to €149.00

Michael Lennon & Joanne McEniff
Management Team

Activities:

Member of:
IRISH HOTELS FEDERATION

Special Offer: Weekend Specials from €139.00 pps
(2 Nights B&B & 1 Dinner)

111 111

Open All Year

Wyatt Hotel

The Octagon,
Westport,
Co. Mayo
Tel: 098-25027 Fax: 098-26316
Email: info@wyatthotel.com
Web: www.wyatthotel.com

HOTEL ★★★ MAP 9 E 13

The award-winning Wyatt Hotel is a stunning boutique style hotel, commanding one of the finest locations in the heart of Westport. The Wyatt is renowned for its friendly efficient service, superb cuisine and relaxing ambience. Croagh Patrick, Westport Leisure Park, Blue Flag beaches, golf, islands, scenic drives, lively bars and restaurants, whether for business or leisure, The Wyatt Hotel is your perfect Westport base. FREEPHONE 1800 205270.

Bookable on www.irelandhotels.com
Member of Select Hotels of Ireland

B&B from €35.00 to €120.00

Chris McGauley
General Manager

Activities:

Member of:

IRISH HOTELS FEDERATION

Special Offer: Available Upon Request

52 52

Closed 24 - 26 December

B&B Rates are per Person Sharing per Night incl. Breakfast.
or **Room Rates** are per Room per Night - See also Page 8

West 199

Whitehouse Hotel

Ballinlough,
Co. Roscommon

Tel: 094-964 0112 Fax: 094-964 0993
Email: thewhitehousehotel@eircom.net
Web: www.white-house-hotel.com

HOTEL U MAP 10 H 13

Located on the Roscommon Mayo border stands the all-new luxurious Whitehouse Hotel. Enjoy our lunchtime carvery in the bar whilst our Blue Room Restaurant offers the finest in contemporary and traditional cuisine. Frequent live music and traditional sessions throughout the year add to the ambience of this unique hotel. The hotel is just a short drive from Lough O'Flynn and within 6 miles of Ballyhaunis and Castlerea Golf Clubs.

Bookable on www.irelandhotels.com

B&B from €55.00 to €69.50

Olivia Mc Dermott
General Manager

Activities:

Member of:
IRISH HOTELS FEDERATION

Special Offer: Weekend Specials from €109.00 pps
(2 Nights B&B & 1 Dinner)

19 19

Closed 25 December

Royal Hotel

Bridge Street,
Boyle,
Co. Roscommon

Tel: 071-966 2016 Fax: 071-966 4949

HOTEL ★★ MAP 10 I 14

Royal Hotel is over 250 years old, located in the centre of Boyle Town, close to the famous Lough Key Forest Park. Under the new ownership of Shirley Regan and Cathy Doherty, it consists of 16 en suite bedrooms. Coffee Shop open daily 8am - 6pm serving hot/cold food including carvery lunch. Dining room open nightly at 6pm. Private car park.

B&B from €48.00 to €55.00

Shirley Regan

Member of:
IRISH HOTELS FEDERATION

16 16

Closed 23 - 27 December

Abbey Hotel, Conference and Leisure Centre

Galway Road,
Roscommon Town

Tel: 090-662 6240 Fax: 090-662 6021
Email: info@abbeyhotel.ie
Web: www.abbeyhotel.ie

HOTEL ★★★ MAP 10 I 12

Charming 18th century manor house hotel, set idyllically on private grounds. Following an extensive development programme the Abbey is the perfect choice for business or pleasure. Facilities include 50 spacious bedrooms decorated to an exceptional standard, a fabulous leisure club with a 20m pool, dedicated conference rooms catering for groups large and small, while the "Terrace" Restaurant and Bar have been transformed building on their long established reputation.

Bookable on www.irelandhotels.com
Member of Irish Country Hotels

B&B from €60.00 to €100.00

Tom Grealy
Operations Manager

Activities:

Member of:
IRISH HOTELS FEDERATION

Special Offer: Please Phone Reservations For Special Offers

50 50

Closed 24 - 26 December

B&B Rates are per Person Sharing per Night incl. Breakfast.
or <u>Room Rates</u> are per Room per Night - See also Page 8

Gleesons Townhouse & Restaurant

Market Square,
Roscommon Town,
Co. Roscommon
Tel: 090-662 6954 Fax: 090-662 7425
Email: info@gleesonstownhouse.com
Web: www.gleesonstownhouse.com

GUESTHOUSE ★★★ MAP 10 | 12

The location is ideal – in the centre of Roscommon, overlooking the town's historic square. If you are seeking comfort, value for money & superb home-cooking & baking, this is the place. Eamonn & Mary Gleeson have lovingly restored their listed 19th century townhouse to a very high standard. The combination of well appointed rooms, suites, café, fully licensed restaurant, private car park, meeting rooms, complimentary broadband access mixed in with the Gleeson's charming hospitality creates a relaxed buzz. Member of AA, RAC, Les Routiers, Premier Guesthouses of Ireland.

Bookable on www.irelandhotels.com
Member of Les Routiers

B&B from €55.00 to €90.00

Mary & Eamonn Gleeson
Proprietors

Activities:

Member of:

Special Offer: Weekend Specials from €135.00 pps
(2 Nights B&B & 1 Dinner)

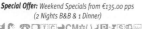
19 19

Closed 25 - 26 December

O'Gara's Royal Hotel

Castle Street,
Roscommon Town
Tel: 090-662 6317 Fax: 090-662 6225
Email: royalhotelros@eircom.net
Web: www.ogarasroyalhotel.com

HOTEL ★★ MAP 10 | 12

O'Gara's Royal Hotel family-run, situated on the Dublin to Castlebar/Westport route. 19 bedrooms en suite, radio, direct dial phone, TV, video, hairdryer. Comfortable modern dining room with good food and friendly service. Coffee dock/carvery. Spacious lounge bar with pleasant surroundings. Private car park. A warm welcome awaits you. 3 new conference rooms are available, catering for up to 500 people, fully equipped with the latest facilities. Golfing holidays a speciality with a number of top golf courses locally.

Bookable on www.irelandhotels.com

B&B from €40.00 to €65.00

Aileen & Larry O'Gara
Proprietors

Activities:

Member of:

19 19

Closed 25 December & Good Friday

Percy French Hotel (The)

Bridge Street,
Strokestown,
Co. Roscommon
Tel: 071-963 3300 Fax: 071-963 3856
Email: percyfrenchhotel@eircom.net
Web: www.percyfrenchhotel.com

HOTEL ★★ MAP 10 | 13

A superbly appointed family-run hotel, with warm and comfortable fully equipped en suite rooms. Excellent home-cooked food served all day. Carvery lunch served from 12 - 2:30 in our bright, modern carvery restaurant. Full bar menu serves from 2:30 until 9:00pm in our traditional Irish bar. You will receive a warm welcome from pleasant, professional staff catering to your every need. Ample car parking to the rear. The famous Strokestown Park House and Gardens with its Famine Museum are a short walk from the hotel. Golf, angling and horse riding are also available in the locality.

B&B from €45.00 to €55.00

Aine & Paul McNally

Member of:

Special Offer: Weekend Specials from €110.00 pps
(2 Nights B&B & 1 Dinner)

11 11

Open All Year

B&B Rates are per Person Sharing per Night incl. Breakfast.
or Room Rates are per Room per Night - See also Page 8

Map of North West Region

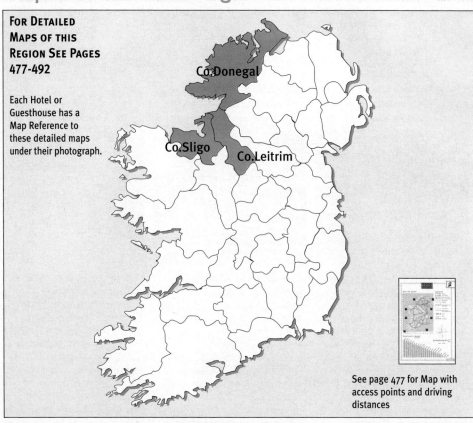

FOR DETAILED MAPS OF THIS REGION SEE PAGES 477-492

Each Hotel or Guesthouse has a Map Reference to these detailed maps under their photograph.

Co.Donegal

Co.Sligo

Co.Leitrim

See page 477 for Map with access points and driving distances

Locations listing

irelandhotels.com
Official Website of the Irish Hotels Federation

INCLUDES DETAILED MAPS & GREAT VALUE SPECIAL OFFERS.

North West
Atlantic and Lakelands

Ireland's North West spans a huge variety of landscape, from the rolling drumlins and tranquil lakes of counties Cavan and Monaghan in the east, to the lovely valleys of Leitrim and Sligo and the dramatic wild landscape of Co. Donegal in the west. Three of the counties, Donegal, Leitrim and Sligo bathe their feet in the restless Atlantic and the Shannon Erne Waterway connects the other great water courses in the region, the Shannon and the Erne Rivers.

Festivals and Events

The North West offers many unexplored peaceful spots, but lively action too. Festivals and events from James Morrison Traditional Festival, Riverstown, Co. Sligo to Patrick Kavanagh writers weekend in Inniskeen, Co. Monaghan and Belturbet Festival of Erne in Co. Cavan to the Donegal International Walking Festival, Co. Donegal, An Tostal, Co. Leitrim and the exciting Rory Gallagher tribute festival in Ballyshannon, Co. Donegal. Many other festivals occur throughout the year, visit www.irelandnorthwest.ie/whats_on

Major Attractions

Two major attractions are Yeat's Grave at Drumcliffe Church and the Visitor Centre at Carrowmore near Sligo, one of the largest and most important megalithic site in Europe. Not to be missed in Co.

Donegal are the Lakeside Museum at Dunlewy, Fr. McDyer Folk village and Museum Glencolumbkille, Glenveagh National Park, Donegal Castle, the Vintage Car Museum in Buncrana and Donegal Parian China and Celtic Weave in Ballyshannon.

In Co. Cavan, visit the Cavan Crystal and Cavan County Museum and explore Swan Island Visitor Farm and Moon River Cruises on the Shannon in Co. Leitrim. In Co. Monaghan, visit the Patrick Kavanagh Centre in Inniskeen, also worth a visit are Ireland's only motor sport activity centre at Rally School Ireland in Scotstown or for that 'something different', Irish Quads in Iniskeen, Co. Monaghan, and also the award-winning Monaghan County Museum. Near Sligo Town, follow the sculpture trail through Hazelwood Forest, pamper yourself at the seaweed baths in Strandhill/Enniscrone or bring yourself back in time at the Sligo

folk Park Riverstown, Co. Sligo. Alternatively, discover our culture in the lively traditional music sessions that are held in pubs throughout the region.

For further information and assistance in planning your holiday and making accommodation reservations please contact:-

North West Tourism Authority, Temple Street, Sligo.
Tel: 071 916 1201
Fax: 071 916 0360
Email:
info@irelandnorthwest.ie
Web: www.irelandnorthwest.ie

OR

North West Tourism, Neil T Blaney Road, Letterkenny, Co. Donegal.
Tel: 074 912 1160
Fax: 074 912 5180

GUINNESS. **Calendar of Events** GUINNESS.

July
Buncrana Festival, Buncrana, Co. Donegal.

July / August
Ballyshannon Traditional and Folk Music Festival, Co. Donegal.

August
Fleadh Cheoil na hEireann, Letterkenny, Co. Donegal.

Event details correct at time of going to press.
enjoy Guinness sensibly.

Nesbitt Arms Hotel	Woodhill House	Arranmore House Hotel

Nesbitt Arms Hotel

Main Street,
Ardara,
Co. Donegal
Tel: 074-954 1103 Fax: 074-954 1895
Email: info@nesbittarms.com
Web: www.nesbittarms.com

Woodhill House

Ardara,
Co. Donegal
Tel: 074-954 1112 Fax: 074-954 1516
Email: yates@iol.ie
Web: www.woodhillhouse.com

Arranmore House Hotel

Arranmore Island,
Co. Donegal
Tel: 074-952 0918 Fax: 074-952 0981
Email: arranmorehousehotel@eircom.net
Web: www.arranmorehousehotel.ie

HOTEL U MAP 13 H 18

GUESTHOUSE ★★★ MAP 13 H 18

HOTEL P MAP 13 H 20

Family-run hotel. Built in 1838, refurbished 2004, in Heritage Town of Ardara, famed for tweeds, hand knits, unspoilt sandy beaches. Ideal base for touring Donegal. 50 modern en suite bedrooms, new function room, elevator. Excellent food. Choice of Weavens Bar / Bistro or Restaurant. Live music in bar. Locally, golf, fishing, horse riding, hill walking, cycling, boating. We have 3 bedrooms specially adapted for wheelchair users.

An historic country house, the site dates back to the 17th century. The house is set in its own grounds, overlooking the Donegal Highlands. There is a quality restaurant, with fully licensed bar and occasional music. The area is famous for its Donegal tweeds and woollen goods. Also offers salmon and trout fishing, pony trekking, golf, boating, cycling, bathing beaches, many archaeological sites, Sheskinmore Wildlife Reserve, Glenveagh National Park, Slieve League and some of the most unspoilt scenery in Europe.

Superbly appointed new hotel overlooking the beach with panoramic views and only 20 minutes from Burtonport by the frequently running daily car ferry. The hotel has already established a reputation for excellent food sourced locally and served by friendly staff. With a magnificent tradition for both game and sea fishing, the island is a magnet for those interested in culture, archaeology, walking, snorkelling and diving and its unique wild life. Each bedroom has broadbank internet access and TV/video. Wirefree internet access planned for early 2006.

B&B from €45.00 to €55.00

B&B from €48.00 to €75.00

B&B from €40.00 to €60.00

*Paul & Marie Gallagher
Proprietor / Manager*

*Nancy & John Yates
Owners*

Peter Williams

Activities:

Member of:

Member of:

Special Offer: *Weekend Specials from €120.00 pps
(2 Nights B&B & 1 Dinner)*

50 50   WiFi

Special Offer: *Weekend Specials from €129.00 pps
(2 Nights B&B & 1 Dinner)*

9 9

Special Offer: *2 Nights B&B & 1 Evening Meal
from €120.00 pps*

20 20

Closed 25 December	Closed 20 - 27 December	Open All Year

B&B Rates are per Person Sharing per Night incl. Breakfast.
or <u>Room Rates</u> are per Room per Night - See also Page 8

B&B Rates are per Person Sharing per Night incl. Breakfast. or Room Rates are per Room per Night - See also Page 8

Villa Rose Hotel

Main Street,
Ballybofey,
Co. Donegal
Tel: 074-913 2266 Fax: 074-913 0666
Email: info@villarose.net
Web: www.villarose.net

HOTEL ★★★ MAP 13 J 19

As Donegal is one of the most welcoming and entertaining counties in Ireland, the Villa Rose Hotel offers quality and service second to none. The hotel is convenient to all the major shopping centres including McElhinney's Department Store, Golf Courses, Theatre, Salmon Fishing and Walking Trails. Come and visit Donegal's best kept secret.

B&B from €45.00 to €60.00

Thomas Gallen
Proprietor

Member of:
IRISH HOTELS FEDERATION

Special Offer: *Midweek Specials from €120.00 pps (2 Nights B&B and 1 Dinner, Stay 3rd Night Free)*

16 16   ⊞ □ ■ T C ⟲ C M ⟲ ♪ P S 🔊 📶 ⚡
Inet

Closed 24 - 26 December

Doherty's Pollan Beach Hotel

Shore Road,
Ballyliffin,
Co. Donegal
Tel: 074-937 8840 Fax: 074-937 8844
Email: pollanbeachhotel@eircom.net
Web: www.pollanbeachhotel.com

HOTEL ★★★ MAP 14 K 21

Doherty's Pollan Beach Hotel is situated 100 yds from sandy beach with childrens' playground. All bedrooms are en suite, equipped with modern facilities. Most bedrooms have sea views. Spacious dining room and bar overlooking the beach and Atlantic Ocean. The hotel overlooks the two 18 hole golf courses in Ballyliffin, the Classic Old Links and the New Glashedy Links. Ideal for: golf, fishing, cycling and walking. 40 minutes drive from City of Derry Airport, 2 hours drive from Belfast International. Perfect retreat for short break. 3*** Hotel.

Bookable on www.irelandhotels.com
Member of Leisure Breaks International

B&B from €45.00 to €65.00

Kathleen & Vincent Doherty
Proprietors

Special Offer: *Midweek Specials from €99.00 pps (2 Nights B&B and 1 Dinner)*

21 21   ⊞ □ ■ 🛏 C ⟲ C M ❄ ♪ ♫ P S 🔊 📶
⚡ Inet 🐾

Open All Year

Dorrians Imperial Hotel

Main Street,
Ballyshannon,
Co. Donegal
Tel: 071-985 1147 Fax: 071-985 1001
Email: info@dorriansimperialhotel.com
Web: www.dorriansimperialhotel.com

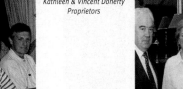

HOTEL ★★★ MAP 13 I 17

Town centre family-run hotel (built 1781). All rooms en suite, TV, telephone, tea/coffee facilities. Private car park. Open fire. Hotel recently renovated, embracing old and new décor, elevator. Ideally suited for touring North West and North East Ireland and ideally located for golfing, fishing & beaches. Sligo 45km, Belfast 202km, Dublin 216km.

Bookable on www.irelandhotels.com

B&B from €55.00 to €85.00

Ben & Mary Dorrian
Proprietors

Activities:
✓ ♪ 🐾

Special Offer: *Weekend Specials from €155.00 pps (2 Nights B&B & 1 Dinner)*

47 47   ⊞ □ ■ T C C M ♪ ♫ P 🔊 📶 ⚡ 🐎

Closed 22 - 29 December

B&B Rates are per Person Sharing per Night incl. Breakfast.
or **Room Rates** are per Room per Night - See also Page 8

Ostan Radharc Na Mara / Sea View Hotel

Bunbeg,
Co. Donegal

Tel: 074-953 1159 Fax: 074-953 2238
Email: info@seaviewhotel.ie
Web: www.visitgweedore.com

HOTEL ★★ MAP 13 I 20

In an area where nature remains untouched, the air is rich and pure, ensuring a heavy appetite. In the Seaview Hotel, guests are treated to wonderful food. The à la carte menu always includes a seasonal selection of fresh, local seafood dishes, with salmon, trout, lobster and oysters a speciality.

B&B from €60.00 to €80.00

James Boyle
General Manager

Member of:

Special Offer: Weekend Specials from €140.00 pps (2 Nights B&B & 1 Dinner)

36 36

Closed 23 - 28 December

Harbour Inn Hotel (The)

Derry Road,
Buncrana,
Co. Donegal

Tel: 074-932 1810 Fax: 074-932 1842
Email: theharbourinn@eircom.net
Web: www.harbourinnhotel.com

HOTEL P MAP 14 K 20

The Harbour Inn Hotel is set against the beautiful hillside looking down over Lough Swilly. The accommodation comprises thirty spacious and luxurious bedrooms, all en suite with TV, tea/coffee making facilities, hairdyer and personal safe. We boast an excellent seventy-seater restaurant serving lunch and evening meals daily. Directions: As you enter Buncrana, Lisfannon Beach and the North West Golf Club are on the left. Top filling station is on the right and we are the next building on the right.

B&B from €45.00 to €55.00

Kathleen & Hugh Doherty

Member of:

29 29

Closed Christmas & New Year

B&B Rates are per Person Sharing per Night incl. Breakfast.
or **Room Rates** are per Room per Night - See also Page 8

Co. Donegal

Buncrana / Bundoran

Inishowen Gateway Hotel	Grand Central Hotel	Great Northern Hotel

Railway Road,
Buncrana, Inishowen,
Co. Donegal
Tel: 074-936 1144 Fax: 074-936 2278
Email: info@inishowengateway.com
Web: www.inishowengateway.com

Main Street,
Bundoran,
Co. Donegal
Tel: 071-984 2722 Fax: 071-984 2656
Email: info@grandcentralbundoran.com
Web: www.grandcentralbundoran.com

Bundoran,
Co. Donegal

Tel: 071-984 1204 Fax: 071-984 1114
Email: reservations@greatnorthernhotel.com
Web: www.greatnorthernhotel.com

HOTEL ★★★ MAP 14 K 20

HOTEL ★★★ MAP 13 I 17

HOTEL ★★★★ MAP 13 I 17

This elegant three star hotel has 79 bedrooms and is situated on the sandy shores of Lough Swilly, on the Inishowen Peninsula of North Donegal. The Gateway offers superb leisure facilities including the luxurious Gateway Health & Fitness Club and brand new health and beauty spa, Seagrass Wellbeing Centre. The hotel's excellent Peninsula Restaurant serves the finest local produce overlooking sea, sand and golf courses.

The Grand Central Hotel in Bundoran is the unique place to be. We are located in the heart of the town. We are recognised as the best value for money 3*** family hotel in Donegal. Our 62 bedrooms provide the ultimate in comfort and luxury for the discerning travellers. 50m from Blue Flag Beach. Sea view rooms. Feile Bia Restaurant approved. Lively bar with nightly entertainment. Golfing, surfing, horse riding, angling, hill walking packages available. WiFi —— free broadband access.

Great Northern Hotel, Conference & Leisure Centre Bundoran. The hotel is situated in the middle of an 18 hole championship golf course overlooking Donegal Bay. 4**** hotel with 96 bedrooms with top leisure facilities for all the family. This hotel has all en suite bedrooms, a restaurant, grill room, lounge, ballroom and syndicate rooms. Leisure centre with swimming pool, gymnasium, private jacuzzi, sauna, steam room, beauty salon and hairdressing salon. We now offer a new state of the art conference centre.

Bookable on www.irelandhotels.com

Bookable on www.irelandhotels.com

Bookable on www.irelandhotels.com
Member of Brian McEniff Hotels

B&B from €50.00 to €65.00	B&B from €45.00 to €75.00	B&B from €100.00 to €120.00

Patrick Doherty
Proprietor

Francois De Dietrich
Group General Manager

Philip McGlynn
General Manager

Activities:
✓ 💧

Activities:
✓ 🏌

Member of:

Member of:

Member of:

Special Offer: Weekend Specials from €120.00 pps
(2 Nights B&B & 1 Dinner)

79 79

62 62

96 96

Closed 24 - 26 December	Open All Year	Closed 19 - 26 December

B&B Rates are per Person Sharing per Night incl. Breakfast.
or <u>Room Rates</u> are per Room per Night - See also Page 8

McGrorys of Culdaff

Culdaff,
Inishowen,
Co. Donegal
Tel: 074-937 9104 Fax: 074-937 9235
Email: info@mcgrorys.ie
Web: www.mcgrorys.ie

GUESTHOUSE ★★★ MAP 14 L 21

This contemporary and stylish premises located on scenic Inishowen Peninsula is an ideal base for touring the North and North West within easy distance from the City of Derry, Foyle Ferry and Ballyliffin. Our award-winning restaurant serves excellent seafood, steaks and house specialities. Famous Macs Backroom Bar features such acts as Altan, Tommy Emmanuel, Frankie Gavin, Ritchie Havens and more. Traditional sessions regularly in Front Bar.

B&B from €55.00 to €85.00

John & Neil McGrory / Anne Doherty

Activities:

Member of:

IRISH HOTELS FEDERATION

Special Offer: Midweek Specials from €135.00 pps
(3 Nights B&B)

17 17

Inet

Closed 23 - 27 December

Ard Na Breátha

Drumrooske Middle,
Donegal Town
Tel: 074-972 2288 Fax: 074-974 0720
Email: info@ardnabreatha.com
Web: www.ardnabreatha.com

GUESTHOUSE ★★★ MAP 13 I 18

Ard na Breatha Restaurant & Guesthouse is located 1.5km from Donegal Town just off the road to lovely Lough Eske. You will be assured of a warm welcome in our cosy lounge, complete with open hearth, which has magnificent views of the Bluestack Mountains. Our en suite bedrooms (all with bath) have tea/coffee facilities, TV, phone and hairdryer. Our fully licensed restaurant specialises in modern Irish cuisine with an emphasis on local seafood and an extensive wine list.

Bookable on www.irelandhotels.com

B&B from €35.00 to €50.00

Theresa Morrow Proprietor

Member of:

IRISH HOTELS FEDERATION

Special Offer: Weekend Specials from €109.00 pps
(2 Nights B&B & 1 Dinner)

6 6

Inet

Closed 12 January - 12 February

B&B Rates are per Person Sharing per Night incl. Breakfast.
or **Room Rates** are per Room per Night - See also Page 8

Co. Donegal
Donegal Town

Donegal Manor	Harvey's Point Country Hotel	Mill Park Hotel, Conference Centre & Leisure Club

Donegal Manor

Letterkenny Road,
Donegal Town,
Co. Donegal
Tel: 074-972 5222 Fax: 074-972 5688
Email: info@donegalmanor.com
Web: www.donegalmanor.com

GUESTHOUSE N MAP 13 | 18

If you like a little bit of fuss, good food and the warmth of an open turf / log fire, Donegal Manor is the place for you. Donegal's newest guesthouse is family managed with all rooms designed to a luxury hotel standard with power shower and bath, TV, telephone, hairdryer and refreshment tray. Residents can enjoy a buffet breakfast, snacks and light suppers, served in Nana Murphy's Tea Room. Free laundry facilities available for guests staying 2 or more nights. Ideal location for touring the North West or Northern Ireland. A warm welcome awaits.

Member of Premier Guesthouse

B&B from €35.00 to €60.00

Sian Breslin
Proprietor

Member of: IRISH HOTELS FEDERATION

Special Offer: Midweek Specials from €105.00 pps (3 Nights B&B)

9 9

Closed 23 - 26 December

Harvey's Point Country Hotel

Lough Eske,
Donegal Town,
Co. Donegal
Tel: 074-972 2208 Fax: 074-972 2352
Email: info@harveyspoint.com
Web: www.harveyspoint.com

HOTEL ★★★ MAP 13 | 18

Hidden in the hills of Donegal, Harvey's Point will meet and exceed your expectations of the very best in accommodation to international standards, fine dining cuisine and traditional hospitality. This exclusive hotel is situated on the shores of Lough Eske, 6km from Donegal Town. Michelin and Good Hotel Guide listed, AA 2 Rosette and RAC 2 Dining Awards. During Winter (November to March), hotel closed Sunday, Monday & Tuesday nights. Open Christmas and New Year. Owned and managed by the Swiss Family Gysling since 1989.

Bookable on www.irelandhotels.com

B&B from €99.00 to €185.00

Deirdre McGlone & Marc Gysling
Proprietors

Member of: IRISH HOTELS FEDERATION

Special Offer: Weekend Specials from €199.00 pps (2 Nights B&B & 1 Dinner)

60 60

WiFi

Open All Year

Mill Park Hotel, Conference Centre & Leisure Club

The Mullins,
Donegal Town,
Co. Donegal
Tel: 074-972 2880 Fax: 074-972 2640
Email: info@millparkhotel.com
Web: www.millparkhotel.com

HOTEL ★★★ MAP 13 | 18

A warm welcome awaits you at the Mill Park Hotel. A few minutes from Donegal Town, the hotel is a perfect base for touring the North West and its many attractions. The hotel has 100 luxurious bedrooms, a fully equipped Leisure Centre and Wellness Centre. The heart of the hotel is the unique styled Granary, along with a choice of 2 restaurants, café bar and Lounge. An excellent choice.

Bookable on www.irelandhotels.com
Member of Irish Country Hotels

B&B from €45.00 to €90.00

Tony McDermott

Activities:

Member of: IRISH HOTELS FEDERATION

Special Offer: Weekend Specials from €139.00 pps (2 Nights B&B & 1 Dinner)

100 100

Closed 23 - 27 December

---

210 *North West*

B&B Rates are per Person Sharing per Night incl. Breakfast. or Room Rates are per Room per Night - See also Page 8

| **Ostan Na Tra (Beach Hotel)** | **Rosapenna Hotel and Golf Links** | **Arnolds Hotel** |

Downings,
Letterkenny,
Co. Donegal
Tel: 074-915 5303 Fax: 074-915 5907
Email: beachhoteldonegal@eircom.net

Downings,
Co. Donegal
Tel: 074-915 5301 Fax: 074-915 5128
Email: rosapenna@eircom.net
Web: www.rosapenna.ie

Dunfanaghy,
Co. Donegal
Tel: 074-913 6208 Fax: 074-913 6352
Email: enquiries@arnoldshotel.com
Web: www.arnoldshotel.com

HOTEL ★ MAP 13 J 21

HOTEL ★★★★ MAP 13 J 21

HOTEL ★★★ MAP 13 J 21

The Beach Hotel is family-run, situated on the breathtaking Atlantic Drive, having safe Downings Beach at the back door. In the heart of Rosguill, golf enthusiasts can avail of the Rosapenna Golf Courses (36 holes) and St. Patrick's Carrigart. Ideally placed for angling, diving and walking, within easy driving distance of Glenveagh National Park, Glebe Gallery, Horn Head and Letterkenny. Sea trips to Tory Island, and diving for wrecks and shark fishing easily arranged.

Situated in North West Donegal on the shore of Sheephaven Bay, The Rosapenna Hotel offers four star comfort and a quiet, relaxing atmosphere. Rosapennna has superb golfing facilities with two 18 hole links courses to choose from, the Old Tom Morris Course and the Sandy Hill Links. A golf pavilion overlooking the course opened in 2005. Rosapenna...a place to remember...and return to.

Established in 1922 the hotel has been in the Arnold Family for three generations. Situated at the entrance to the village and overlooking Horn Head and Sheephaven Bay, we are an ideal base for touring North Donegal, Glenveagh National Park and Gardens close by. Enjoy one of the many activities organised by the hotel, horse riding from the hotel stables, golf on the local golf courses, fishing, walking, painting tuition, photography weekends and creative writing.

Bookable on www.irelandhotels.com
Member of Irish Country Hotels

B&B from €40.00 to €45.00

B&B from €85.00 to €95.00

B&B from €59.00 to €79.00

Charlie & Mairead McClafferty

Hilary & Frank Casey

Arnold Family Proprietors

Activities:

Activities:

Activities:

Member of:

Member of:

Member of:

HOTELS

HOTELS

HOTELS

Special Offer: Midweek Specials from €100.00 pps (3 Nights B&B)

Special Offer: 3 Nights Dinner, B&B and 3 Green Fees Old Tom Morris Course from €375.00 pps

Special Offer: Midweek Specials from €153.00 pps (2 Nights B&B & 1 Dinner)

20 20

53 53

30 30

Closed 01 January - 28 Feburary

Closed 30 October - 17 March

Closed 01 November - 06 April

B&B Rates are per Person Sharing per Night incl. Breakfast.
or **Room Rates** are per Room per Night - See also Page 8

Ostan Na Rosann	Highlands Hotel	Bay View Hotel & Leisure Centre

Ostan Na Rosann

Mill Road,
Dungloe,
Co. Donegal
Tel: 074-952 2444 Fax: 074-952 2400
Email: info@ostannarosann.com
Web: www.ostannarosann.com

HOTEL ★★★ MAP 13 I 19

The Ostan na Rosann is a family-run hotel in the heart of the Gaeltacht/Rosses, overlooking the spectacular Dungloe Bay. The hotel is warm, welcoming and is known for its friendly atmosphere. Our facilities include a leisure centre, childrens' play area, patio areas, restaurant, lounge bar and beautician. All our bedrooms are en suite, have tea & coffee making facilities, hairdryer, television, direct dial telephone and internet access.

B&B from €40.00 to €69.00

Niamh Gallagher
General Manager

Member of:

IRISH HOTELS FEDERATION

Special Offer: Midweek Specials from €129.00 pps
(3 Nights B&B)

48   48

Open All Year

Highlands Hotel

Glenties,
Co. Donegal
Tel: 074-955 1111 Fax: 074-955 1564
Email: highlandhotel@eircom.net
Web: www.thehighlandshotel.com

HOTEL ★★ MAP 13 I 19

The Highlands Hotel is renowned for its warm and friendly atmosphere and good food. An attractive family-run hotel ideally situated depending on what pastime you prefer, whether it be fishing, golfing, horse riding or relaxing on the beautiful sandy beach of Narin. Famous for its excellent cuisine the hotel offers a wide-ranging choice of à la carte menus. Special rates for families and golfing weekends are our speciality.

B&B from €50.00 to €60.00

Johnny, Christine & Sinead Boyle

Activities:

Member of:

IRISH HOTELS FEDERATION

Special Offer: Weekend Specials from €115.00 pps
(2 Nights B&B & 1 Dinner)

25   25

Closed 24 - 28 December

Bay View Hotel & Leisure Centre

Main Street,
Killybegs,
Co. Donegal
Tel: 074-973 1950 Fax: 074-973 1856
Email: info@bayviewhotel.ie
Web: www.bayviewhotel.ie

HOTEL ★★★ MAP 13 H 18

One of Donegal's newest hotels, overlooking the splendour of Donegal Bay. We offer 40 en suite bedrooms with satellite TV, hairdryer, trouser press, tea/coffee makers, DD phone. Theme bar and carvery, seafood restaurant. Fully equipped leisure centre, indoor swimming pool. Deep sea angling, fresh water fishing, golf, hill walking. Scenic boat trips. An ideal touring base. Wheelchair accessible rooms. Lift.

B&B from €55.00 to €80.00

Seamus Caldwell
General Manager

Activities:

Member of:

IRISH HOTELS FEDERATION

Special Offer: Weekend Specials from €130.00 pps
(2 Nights B&B & 1 Dinner)

40   40

Closed 25 - 27 December

B&B Rates are per Person Sharing per Night incl. Breakfast.
or **Room Rates** are per Room per Night - See also Page 8

Tara Hotel	Moorland Guesthouse	Castle Grove Country House Hotel
Main Street, Killybegs, Co. Donegal Tel: 074-974 1700 Fax: 074-974 1710 Email: info@tarahotel.ie Web: www.tarahotel.ie	Laghey, R.232, Donegal Town, Co. Donegal Tel: 074-973 4319 Fax: 074-973 4319 Email: moorland@eircom.net Web: www.moorland-guesthouse.com	Ballymaleel, Letterkenny, Co. Donegal Tel: 074-915 1118 Fax: 074-915 1384 Email: reservations@castlegrove.com Web: www.castlegrove.com

HOTEL N MAP 13 H 18 | **GUESTHOUSE ★★★ MAP 13 I 18** | **HOTEL ★★★★ MAP 13 J 19**

Newly opened in Sept 2004, luxury hotel built to 3 star standards in the centre of Killybegs, overlooking Killybegs Harbour. All of the 31 en suite bedrooms are beautifully appointed, with all modern facilities. Centrally located near all amenities and popular with many golfers, anglers and walkers. Our hotel is the perfect base for exploring South West Donegal and Slieve League (Europe's highest sea cliffs). Killybegs is fast becoming the gourmet capital of the North West and our panoramic Turntable Restaurant is no exception. We look forward to your visit. Special offers available online at www.tarahotel.ie

Have a break from the hustle and bustle. A guesthouse with family character, situated in a wild, high moor/hill landscape. We offer good cuisine. Available on the premises: Treatment with reflexology, body massage, cosmetics salon and sauna. Lounge with open fire and TV. Special relaxing and riding weeks. Arrangements made for golf and fishing. Excellent 18-hole golf links not far away. Ideal place for relaxation. Very quiet and remote. German spoken.

Castle Grove is a 17th century country house set on its own rolling estate overlooking Lough Swilly. Its bedrooms are spacious and with all modern facilities. Downstairs in both drawing room and library you find a perfect blend of old and new. The dining room offers excellent cuisine, much of its produce from the Walled Garden. To the discerning guest Castle Grove has to be visited to be appreciated. While here you can fish, golf, or simply enjoy the locality. This House may be exclusively booked for family or business functions.

Bookable on www.irelandhotels.com | *Bookable on www.irelandhotels.com*

B&B from €60.00 to €90.00 | **B&B from €32.00 to €45.00** | **B&B from €70.00 to €95.00**

*Johnny, Paul &
Breege McGuinness
Owners* | *Rosemarie & Walter Schaffner
Proprietors* | *Raymond & Mary T. Sweeney
Owners*

Activities:

Member of:

Member of:

Special Offer: Midweek Specials from €105.00 pps (3 Nights B&B)

31 31 inet

8 8

Special Offer: Midweek Specials from €185.00 pps (3 Nights B&B)

15 15

Open All Year | **Open All Year** | **Closed 23 - 29 December**

B&B Rates are per Person Sharing per Night incl. Breakfast.
or **Room Rates** are per Room per Night - See also Page 8

Co. Donegal

Letterkenny

Clanree Hotel Conference & Leisure Centre

Derry Road,
Letterkenny,
Co. Donegal
Tel: 074-912 4369 Fax: 074-912 5389
Email: info@clanreehotel.com
Web: www.clanreehotel.com

HOTEL ★★★ MAP 13 J 19

Conveniently located on the outskirts of Letterkenny town centre, the Clanree Hotel offers luxury accommodation in an elegant setting. Full health and fitness club with gym, pool and beauty salon. Aileach Restaurant renowned for excellent à la carte, carvery and early bird menu. Tara Bar offering bar food and entertainment. Close by you'll find Glenveigh National Park, Grianan of Aileach, Inishowen and Derry City as well as Blue Flag beaches, golf courses, hills and lakes. Check www.clanreehotel.com for cheapest rates, events and special offers.

Bookable on www.irelandhotels.com

B&B from €70.00 to €90.00

Michael Naughton
General Manager

Activities:

Member of:
IRISH HOTELS FEDERATION

Special Offer: *Midweek Specials from €220.00 pps (3 Nights B&B and 2 Dinner)*

121 121

Closed 23 - 27 December

Downings Bay Hotel

Downings,
Letterkenny,
Co. Donegal
Tel: 074-915 5586 Fax: 074-915 4716
Email: info@downingsbayhotel.com
Web: www.downingsbayhotel.com

HOTEL N MAP 13 J 19

Situated on Sheephaven Bay and the picturesque Atlantic Drive. Newly built to 3*** standards. Spacious bedrooms, many of them interconnecting, are luxuriously finished. The Sheephaven Suite available for 20-350 people. JC's Bar and The Haven dining room serve locally sourced fresh food daily. Secrets Beauty Salon for those who wish to pamper themselves. Local activities include golf, fishing, horse riding & water activities. Within driving distance of Glenveagh National Park.

Bookable on www.irelandhotels.com

B&B from €40.00 to €75.00

Eileen Rock
Manager

Activities:

Member of:
IRISH HOTELS FEDERATION

Special Offer: *Weekend Specials from €130.00 pps (2 Nights B&B & 1 Dinner)*

40 40

Closed 25 December

Gleneany House

Port Road,
Letterkenny,
Co. Donegal
Tel: 074-912 6088 Fax: 074-912 6090
Email: gleneanyhouse@eircom.net
Web: www.gleneany.com

GUESTHOUSE ★★★ MAP 13 J 19

Gleneany House, located in the town centre, opposite bus station in the heart of Letterkenny, offers both corporate and leisure clientèle an excellent level of personal and friendly service. Renowned for its consistency in excellent cuisine, food is served all day. Our 19 en suite bedrooms have satellite TV and direct dial telephone. Our lounge bar is the ideal place for a quiet relaxing drink. An ideal base for touring beautiful Donegal, private car parking available. A warm welcome awaits all at the Gleneany House. So when next in town, call and experience for yourself our hospitality.

B&B from €49.00 to €75.00

Paul Kelly

Special Offer: *Weekend Specials from €125.00 pps (2 Nights B&B & 1 Dinner)*

19 19

Closed 22 - 28 December

---

214 *North West*

B&B Rates are per Person Sharing per Night incl. Breakfast. or Room Rates are per Room per Night - See also Page 8

Radisson SAS Hotel

The Loop Road,
Letterkenny,
Co. Donegal
Tel: 074-919 4444 Fax: 074-919 4455
Email: info.letterkenny@radissonsas.com
Web: www.radissonsas.com

HOTEL N MAP 13 J 19

The new Radisson SAS Hotel Letterkenny, is located just five minutes walk from the town centre with 114 bedrooms designed in a contemporary Irish style, featuring all the facilities one would expect from a four star standard de luxe hotel; such as cable and pay TV, fast internet connections with broadband, minibar, direct dial phones with voicemail, trouser press and 24hr room service. The hotel also boasts state of the art conference and banqueting facilities and full leisure centre including 17m pool.

Bookable on www.irelandhotels.com
Member of Radisson SAS Hotels & Resorts

B&B from €64.50 to €79.50

Ray Hingston
General Manager

Activities:

Member of:

Special Offer: Weekend Specials from €139.00 pps
(2 Nights B&B & 1 Dinner)

114 114

Open All Year

Ramada Encore - Letterkenny

Lower Main Street,
Letterkenny,
Co. Donegal
Tel: 074-912 3100 Fax: 074-912 3100
Email: info@encoreletterkenny.com
Web: www.encoreletterkenny.com

UNDER CONSTRUCTION - OPENING AUGUST 2006

HOTEL P MAP 13 J 19

Situated on Letterkenny's Lower Main Street the Ramada Encore brand is a new concept in hotels offering sophisticated high style at affordable prices. All 81 bedrooms will offer modern facilities along with FREE unlimited broadband internet access and in-room movies. The emphasis is on quality and service while offering value for money. A great location from which to explore all Letterkenny and Donegal has to offer. Adapted rooms and access for guests with special requirements.

Member of Ramada International

B&B from €35.00 to €55.00

Brian & Christine Gallagher
Proprietors

Activities:

Special Offer: Weekend Specials from €115.00 pps
(2 Nights B&B & 1 Dinner)

81 81

Open All Year

Shandon Hotel Spa and Wellness

Marble Hill Strand,
Co. Donegal

Tel: 074-913 6137 Fax: 074-913 6430
Email: shandonhotel@eircom.net
Web: www.shandonhotel.com

HOTEL U MAP 13 J 19

Shandon Hotel Spa and Wellness boasts a spa that has been specifically designed to offer a host of luxurious treatments for the ultimate relaxing and de-stressing holiday. It is a hidden gem waiting to be discovered with delicious home-cooked food, children's play centre, 9 hole par three golf course, all weather floodlit tennis court, Marble Hill beach and the awe-inspiring Sheephaven Bay. Come and experience our warm welcome.

B&B from €80.00 to €150.00

Dermot & Catherine McGlade

Activities:

Member of:

50 50

Closed 6 November - 15 March

B&B Rates are per Person Sharing per Night incl. Breakfast.
or **Room Rates** are per Room per Night - See also Page 8

Silver Tassie Hotel	Malin Hotel	Milford Inn Hotel

Silver Tassie Hotel

Ramelton Road,
Letterkenny,
Co. Donegal
Tel: 074-912 5619 Fax: 074-912 4473
Email: info@silvertassiehotel.ie
Web: www.silvertassiehotel.ie

HOTEL ★★★ MAP 13 J 19

Nestled in the beautiful hills of Donegal overlooking Lough Swilly this charming family-run hotel combines old world charm with modern comfort and elegance. Luxurious en suite bedrooms (standard, superior or family) equipped with all modern facilities offer unrivalled comfort and luxury with an old country house feel. Renowned for excellent food and friendly service. Relax by the open fires or enjoy afternoon tea in the magnificent glass fronted foyer. Only 5 minutes drive from the bustling town of Letterkenny. Ideal base for touring the stunning North West.

Bookable on www.irelandhotels.com
Member of Blaney Group

B&B from €45.00 to €90.00

Rose & Ciaran Blaney

Activities:
✓ ♪ 🎿

Member of:
IRISH HOTELS FEDERATION

Special Offer: *Weekend Specials from €99.00 pps (2 Nights B&B & 1 Dinner)*

36 36

Closed 25 December

Malin Hotel

Malin Town,
Inishowen,
Co. Donegal
Tel: 074-937 0606 Fax: 074-937 0770
Email: malinhotel@eircom.net
Web: www.malinhotel.ie

HOTEL ★★ MAP 14 L 21

The Malin Hotel is situated on one of the most beautiful village greens in Ireland. It offers quality accommodation, excellent gourmet food menu and a tranquil setting for a relaxing getaway. The hotel is under new management and has an extensive events and entertainments programme to suit all tastes. You will receive a warm Irish welcome, with cordial and pleasant staff catering to your every need. Special offer excludes July & August and Bank Holiday Weekends.

B&B from €45.00 to €65.00

Jacqueline Byrne Manager

Activities:
✓ ♪ 🎿 💧

Member of:
IRISH HOTELS FEDERATION

Special Offer: *Midweek & Weekend Specials from €99.00 pps*

14 14

Open all Year

Milford Inn Hotel

Milford,
Co. Donegal
Tel: 074-915 3313 Fax: 074-915 3388
Email: info@milfordinnhotel.ie
Web: www.milfordinnhotel.ie

HOTEL ★★★ MAP 13 J 20

Situated 10 miles from Letterkenny between the town of Milford and the Heritage Town of Ramelton, this luxurious family-run hotel is ideally located for the visitor to explore Donegal's rugged Atlantic Coast. Relax in comfort and style in a choice of standard or superior rooms all offering the highest standard. Renowned for its consistency in serving quality food with carvery lunches daily and food served all day. Pamper yourself in the Zone Hair & Beauty Salon which has been awarded a five star accolade as a member of the Good Salon Guide.

Bookable on www.irelandhotels.com
Member of Blaney Group

B&B from €35.00 to €80.00

Mandy & Neil Blaney

Activities:
✓ ♪ 🎿

Member of:
IRISH HOTELS FEDERATION

Special Offer: *Weekend Specials from €79.00 pps (2 Nights B&B & 1 Dinner)*

33 33

inet

Closed 25 - 27 December

B&B Rates are per Person Sharing per Night incl. Breakfast.
or **Room Rates** are per Room per Night - See also Page 8

Carlton Redcastle Hotel & Thalasso Spa	Lake House Hotel	Portsalon Golf Hotel

**Redcastle,
Moville,
Co. Donegal**
Tel: 074-938 5555 Fax: 074-938 2214
Email: info@carltonredcastle.ie
Web: www.carltonredcastle.ie

**Narin,
Portnoo,
Co. Donegal**
Tel: 074-954 5123 Fax: 074-954 5444
Email: lakehouse@iol.ie
Web: www.lakehousehotel.ie

**Drum,
Portsalon, Letterkenny,
Co. Donegal**
Tel: 074-915 9806 Fax: 074-915 9854
Email: info@portsalongolfhotel.com
Web: www.portsalongolfhotel.com

HOTEL CR MAP 14 L 21

HOTEL ★★★ MAP 13 H 19

HOTEL ★★ MAP 13 K 21

Nestled along the banks of Lough Foyle, on the stunning Inishowen Peninsula, this newly opened hotel is an ideal base for a leisure break. Discover one of the most beautiful regions in the country, with world-class golf courses, ancient monuments & magnificent Blue Flag beaches. 93 luxury rooms & suites - all with spectacular sea or golf course views; Thalasso Spa Centre - a wide selection of invigorating sea therapy treatments available; gym; fine dining Waters Edge Restaurant; Snug Captain's Bar; extensive banqueting suite with panoramic sea views; business suites; 9 hole parkland golf course.

Member of Carlton Group

A country house hotel overlooking Narin golf course, minutes away from the Blue Flag Beach at Narin. 14 en suite luxury bedrooms decorated with a feeling of elegance and spaciousness, with television, DD telephone, hairdryer and complimentary tea/coffee making facilities. Family rooms available. The hotel boasts dining experiences from fine dining in the award-winning restaurant to a grill/bar menu in the lounge. Conference and Banqueting facilities also available. Please note the hotel is also closed 19 - 27 December.

Located beside the quiet fairways of Portsalon Championship Golf Course and host of the Irish Ladies Close June 2005. The hotel is just a short walk from the stunning Portsalon beach. The area is a haven of tranquil beauty and serenity amid Donegal's legendary landscape.

B&B from €55.00 to €95.00

B&B from €45.00 to €80.00

B&B from €35.00 to €70.00

*Jason Foody
General Manager*

Activities:

Member of:
IRISH HOTELS FEDERATION

*Frank Barber
Managing Director*

Member of:
IRISH HOTELS FEDERATION

William Moore

Activities:

Member of:
IRISH HOTELS FEDERATION

Special Offer: *Weekend Specials from €145.00 pps
(2 Nights B&B & 1 Dinner)*

93 93

14 14

Special Offer: *2 B&B & 18 Holes of Golf
(Sun-Thurs) from €110.00 pps*

22 22

Closed 23 - 27 December	Closed 03 January - 31 January	Closed 07 November - 01 March

B&B Rates are per Person Sharing per Night incl. Breakfast.
or **Room Rates** are per Room per Night - See also Page 8

Fort Royal Hotel

Rathmullan,
Co. Donegal

Tel: 074-915 8100 Fax: 074-915 8103
Email: fortroyal@eircom.net
Web: www.fortroyalhotel.com

HOTEL ★★★ MAP 14 K 20

One of the most beautifully situated hotels in Ireland with 7 hectares of lovely grounds and gardens, beside Lough Swilly include a sandy beach, hard tennis court, par 3 golf course. Especially friendly welcome accounts for the large number of regular visitors from all parts of the world to this peaceful unspoilt part of Donegal. Member of Manor House Hotels, Irish Tourist Board and AA***. GDS Access Code: UI Toll Free 1-800-44-UTELL.

Bookable on www.irelandhotels.com
Member of Manor House Hotels

B&B from €82.00 to €101.00

*Tim & Tina Fletcher
Proprietor / Manager*

Activities:
✓

Member of:
IRISH HOTELS FEDERATION

*Special Offer: Weekend Specials from €190.00 pps
(2 Nights B&B & 1 Dinner)*

15 15

Closed 01 November - 31 March

Rathmullan House

Lough Swilly,
Rathmullan,
Co. Donegal

Tel: 074-915 8188 Fax: 074-915 8200
Email: info@rathmullanhouse.com
Web: www.rathmullanhouse.com

HOTEL ★★★★ MAP 14 K 20

Unique seaside setting with a 3 mile beach 100 yards from the front door. Award-winning restaurant offering seasonal table d'hôte menu. Supporters of 'Slow Food' movement and organic produce. 32 bedrooms with their own distinctive style from garden view superior rooms to spacious family rooms. Indoor heated pool, 2 outdoor tennis courts and resident masseuse. State of the art conference facility hosts up to 80 delegates.

Member of Ireland's Blue Book

B&B from €93.50 to €121.00

*Wheeler Family
Hosts*

Member of:
IRISH HOTELS FEDERATION

32 32

Closed 18 to 27 December

Sandhouse Hotel

Rossnowlagh,
Co. Donegal

Tel: 071-985 1777 Fax: 071-985 2100
Email: info@sandhouse.ie
Web: www.sandhouse.ie

HOTEL ★★★★ MAP 13 I 17

A delightful seaside setting overlooking the Atlantic Ocean on Donegal Bay. This 4* luxury hotel, a transformed mid 19th century fishing lodge, is an oasis of comfort and relaxation on a 2 mile golden sandy beach. It combines elegant accommodation, open log fires, a marine spa and an award-winning restaurant. A splendid location to explore the spectacular Donegal landscapes. Nearby 3 championship golf links courses. Described as one of Ireland's west coast treasures. Dublin 3hrs, Shannon 4hrs.

Bookable on www.irelandhotels.com
Member of Manor House Hotels

B&B from €85.00 to €130.00

*Paul Diver
Manager*

Activities:
✓ ⚐ 💧

Member of:
IRISH HOTELS FEDERATION

*Special Offer: Weekend Specials from €199.00 pps
(2 Nights B&B & 1 Dinner)*

55 55

Closed 01 December - 01 February

B&B Rates are per Person Sharing per Night incl. Breakfast.
or **Room Rates** are per Room per Night - See also Page 8

Commercial & Tourist Hotel

Ballinamore,
Co. Leitrim

Tel: 071-964 4675 Fax: 071-964 4679
Email: commercialhotel@oceanfree.net
Web: www.hotelcommercial.com

HOTEL ★★ MAP 11 J 15

Ideally situated in the centre of the greenest & most uncluttered part of Ireland in the heart of lovely Leitrim. Completely re-built to 3 star de luxe standard. Large comfortable rooms with queen size beds all en suite. Private car parking & elevator along with excellent cuisine & personal service. Local amenities include river cruising on the Shannon - Erne Waterway, scenic drives, hill walking & golfing. Fishing in the area is an absolute must. Special rates for golfers & commercial travellers. The Commericial Hotel is your ideal base for breathtaking tours or business. Dublin/Belfast 2 hrs, Shannon 3 hrs.

Bookable on www.irelandhotels.com

B&B from €50.00 to €70.00

Karen Walsh
Manageress

Special Offer: *Weekend Specials from €130.00 pps*
(2 Nights B&B & 1 Dinner)

28 28

Closed 25 December

Glenview Guesthouse

Aughoo,
Ballinamore,
Co. Leitrim

Tel: 071-964 4157 Fax: 071-964 4814
Email: glenvhse@iol.ie
Web: www.glenview-house.com

GUESTHOUSE ★★ MAP 11 J 15

Glenview House, 2 miles south of Ballinamore is a holiday haven, 500m from the Shannon-Erne Waterway. Exclusive fully licensed restaurant with extensive wine list. Enjoy Riverbus boat trips, country drives, horse riding, animal farm, golf and hill walking locally. Glenview has its own tennis court, games room, folk museum and play area for children. Self-catering houses within grounds, two of which are wheelchair friendly.

B&B from €40.00 to €45.00

Teresa Kennedy

6 6

Closed 23 - 28 December

Riversdale Farm Guesthouse

Ballinamore,
Co. Leitrim

Tel: 071-964 4122 Fax: 071-964 4813
Email: riversdaleguesthouse@eircom.net
Web: www.riversdale.biz

GUESTHOUSE ★★★ MAP 11 J 15

Riversdale is an impressive residence beautifully situated in parkland overlooking the Shannon-Erne Waterway. Spacious rooms and lounges mean a comfortable and peaceful ambience. We have our own heated indoor pool, squash court, sauna and fitness suite for when the weather is unkind - or hot! Local golf, horse riding, walking, riverbus, boat trips and scenic drives. Wide choice of interesting day trips. Brochure available - special family suites.

B&B from €40.00 to €48.00

The Thomas Family
Owners

Member of:

IRISH HOTELS FEDERATION

Special Offer: *Midweek Specials from €99.00 pps*
(3 Nights B&B)

13 13

Closed 15 November - 31 January

B&B Rates are per Person Sharing per Night incl. Breakfast.
or **Room Rates** are per Room per Night - See also Page 8

Co. Leitrim

Carrick-on-Shannon / Leitrim Village

Aisleigh Guest House	Bush Hotel	Leitrim Marina Hotel

Dublin Road,
Carrick-On-Shannon,
Co. Leitrim
Tel: 071-962 0313 Fax: 071-962 0675
Email: aisleigh@eircom.net
Web: www.aisleighguesthouse.com

Carrick-on-Shannon,
Co. Leitrim

Tel: 071-967 1000 Fax: 071-962 1180
Email: info@bushhotel.com
Web: www.bushhotel.com

Leitrim Village,
Co. Leitrim

Tel: 071-962 2262
Email: info@leitrimmarina.ie
Web: www.leitrimmarina.ie

GUESTHOUSE ★★★ MAP 10 | 14

HOTEL ★★★ MAP 10 | 14

HOTEL ★★★ MAP 10 | 14

A warm welcome awaits you at our family-run guesthouse situated 1km from the centre of the picturesque town of Carrick-on-Shannon, Ireland's best kept secret. Facilities include en suite bedrooms with TV, direct dial telephones (fax also available) games room and sauna. Local genealogy a speciality. Nearby there is golfing, swimming, tennis, squash, cruising, fishing (tackle & bait supplies) horse riding, walking, cycling, etc.

An hotel of ambience, style and comfort, The Bush Hotel (one of Ireland's oldest) has just completed a major refurbishment and extension whilst still retaining its olde world charm and character. Centrally located in the town centre, the hotel has 50 modern bedrooms with all facilities, theme bars, coffee shop and restaurant. New state of the art business and banqueting centre. Attractions: Arigna Mining Museum, Strokestown House, King House, etc.

Opening in November 2005 this hotel and apartment complex with its nautical theme offers the perfect location for golfers, fishermen, sporting enthusiasts or just exploring the Leitrim and surrounding landscapes. It has 10 luxuriously furnished bedrooms, beautiful restaurant with panoramic views over the marina, river and distant hills. The comfortable bar and terrace help create a wonderfully relaxing atmosphere. The hotel offers a childrens' play area, putting green and day boats and ribs for hire (March to October).

Bookable on www.irelandhotels.com

Bookable on www.irelandhotels.com

B&B from €40.00 to €50.00

B&B from €59.50 to €79.50

B&B from €40.00 to €50.00

Sean & Charlotte Fearon Owners

Member of:

Joseph Dolan Managing Director

Activities:

Member of:

Dave Pearce Proprietor

Activities:

Special Offer: Midweek Specials from €129.00 pps (2 Nights B&B & 1 Dinner)

Special Offer: Weekend Specials from €99.50 pps (2 Nights B&B & 1 Dinner)

10 10

50 50

10 10

Open All Year	Closed 24 - 27 December	Open All Year

220 *North West*

B&B Rates are per Person Sharing per Night incl. Breakfast.
or Room Rates are per Room per Night - See also Page 8

Glebe House

Ballinamore Road,
Mohill,
Co. Leitrim
Tel: 071-963 1086 Fax: 071-963 1886
Email: glebe@iol.ie
Web: www.glebehouse.com

GUESTHOUSE ★★★ MAP 11 J 14

At the end of a sweeping driveway this lovely Georgian former Rectory dating to 1823, is set on 50 acres of mature trees and farmland and has been carefully restored by the Maloney family. Enjoy the tranquillity of this unspoilt part of Ireland. Ideal touring base. Assistance given with genealogy. 2/3 bedroom suite available which is suitable for groups or families. Internet/computer for visitor use. Discount on bookings if more than one night.

Bookable on www.irelandhotels.com

B&B from €40.00 to €50.00

Laura Maloney
Manager

Member of:

IRISH
HOTELS
FEDERATION

Special Offer: Midweek Specials from €115.00 pps
(3 Nights B&B)

🏠🏠 ☎🖥TC❄CM✿♨♫P🅂♿🐾
8 8

Open All Year

Shannon Key West Hotel

The River Edge,
Rooskey,
Co. Leitrim
Tel: 071-963 8800 Fax: 071-963 8811
Email: info@shannonkeywest.com
Web: www.shannonkeywest.com

HOTEL ★★★ MAP 11 J 13

Situated on N4 Dublin Sligo route. Rooskey is an elegant marina village nestling between Carrick-On-Shannon & Longford Town. Dromod Train Station only 2km from hotel. This beautiful 39 bedroom hotel with Greek, Georgian & modern architecture offers panoramic views of the Rr. Shannon from both bedrooms & roof gardens. Excellent cuisine & personal service. Facilities: gym, steam room, jacuzzi, sunbed and outdoor tennis/basketball. In-house beauty salon and golf courses nearby. Rooskey is a stress free comfort zone. Online booking www.shannonkeywest.com

Bookable on www.irelandhotels.com
Member of Best Western Hotels

B&B from €62.50 to €80.00

Anne Marie Frisby
General Manager

Activities:
✔️🛁♨

Member of:

IRISH
HOTELS
FEDERATION

Special Offer: Midweek Specials from €89.00 pps
(2 Nights B&B & 1 Dinner)

🏠🏠 ☎🖥TC❄CM🍽♨♫P🅂
39 39

♿ 🐾 WiFi

Closed 24 - 26 December

Kingsfort Country House

Ballintogher,
Co. Sligo
Tel: 071-911 5111 Fax: 071-911 5979
Email: info@kingsfortcountryhouse.com
Web: www.kingsfortcountryhouse.com

GUESTHOUSE P MAP 10 H 15

Located in the quaint and scenic village of Ballintogher, Kingsfort Country House is a peaceful and relaxing haven 15 minutes from the town of Sligo. This recently refurbished 18th century house is your ideal base for visiting the North West of Ireland. All of our rooms are to the highest standards and all requirements are catered for. Close to 5 golf courses, fishing spots and lovely walks

B&B from €40.00 to €80.00

Corine Ledanois
Proprietor

Activities:
✔️

Member of:

IRISH
HOTELS
FEDERATION

Special Offer: Weekend Specials from €99.00 pps
(2 Nights B&B & 1 Dinner)

🏠🏠 ☎TC❄CM♫P🅂♿
8 5

Open All Year

B&B Rates are per Person Sharing per Night incl. Breakfast.
or **Room Rates** are per Room per Night - See also Page 8

Markree Castle	Yeats County Inn Hotel	Beach Hotel and Leisure Club
Collooney, Co. Sligo	Curry, Co. Sligo	The Harbour, Mullaghmore, Co. Sligo
Tel: 071-916 7800 Fax: 071-916 7840	Tel: 094-925 5050 Fax: 094-925 5053	Tel: 071-916 6103 Fax: 071-916 6448
Email: markree@iol.ie	Email: info@yeatscountyinn.com	Email: beachhot@iol.ie
Web: www.markreecastle.ie	Web: www.yeatscountyinn.com	Web: www.beachhotelmullaghmore.com

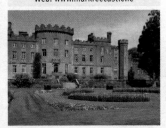  

HOTEL P MAP 10 H 15	HOTEL ★★ MAP 10 G 14	HOTEL ★★ MAP 13 H 17

A spectacular castle set in lovely gardens and large estate, in the same ownership for over 350 years. Markree Castle offers a relaxing, friendly and quiet place to stay. Wonderful wood and plaster work complements the friendly service and the restaurant enjoys a reputation of excellence throughout Ireland.

A warm welcome awaits you at this family-run hotel, a comfortable and relaxing venue, situated on the N17 between Charlestown and Tubbercurry. All our spacious bedrooms are en suite with tea and coffee making facilities, hairdryer and direct dial telephone. We provide free car parking facilities, and we are ideally based for fishing, golfing and touring the west of Ireland. Situated just 8 miles from Knock Airport and 25 miles from Sligo Airport, with access to major bus routes just outside our door. Relax and unwind at The Yeats County Inn.

Overlooking the beach in the picturesque fishing village of marvellous Mullaghmore. Leisure club with 15m swimming pool, jacuzzi, steam room, sauna, gym, sunbed, excellent restaurant and trendy bars all on site. Golf, fishing, horse riding, scuba diving, watersports and boat trips locally. Murder Mysteries. Family friendly. Romantic location.

B&B from €80.00 to €116.00	*B&B from €30.00 to €40.00*	*B&B from €45.00 to €90.00*
Mary & Charles Cooper	*Sven Anders* / *Manager*	*Paddy Donnelly* / *Manager*

Member of:

Member of:

Special Offer: *Weekend Specials from €115.00 pps (2 Nights B&B & 1 Dinner)*

28 28	10 10	28 28

Closed 24 - 27 December	Open All Year	Open All Year

B&B Rates are per Person Sharing per Night incl. Breakfast. or <u>Room Rates</u> are per Room per Night - See also Page 8

Pier Head Hotel, Spa and Leisure Centre

Mullaghmore,
Co. Sligo

Tel: 071-916 6171 Fax: 071-916 6473
Email: pierhead@eircom.net
Web: www.pierheadhotel.ie

HOTEL U MAP 13 H 17

With its unique setting in the picturesque seaside village of Mullaghmore, the Pier Head Hotel has been owned by the McHugh family for almost 100 years. 40 en suite rooms, many with balconies or access to roof garden with stunning views of Mullaghmore Harbour and Donegal Bay. Facilities include swimming pool, seaweed baths, steam showers, sauna, gym and outdoor hot tub. The hotel offers luxurious accommodation and excellent facilities and makes it the ideal venue for your stay in the North West.

B&B from €50.00 to €95.00

John McHugh

Member of:

IRISH HOTELS FEDERATION

Special Offer: *Weekend Deals, Midweek Specials & Activity Programs Available*

40 40 ☎ 🖥 📺 C M ⚑ 🍽 🅿 📶 U ♪ 🎹
🕭 🔥 🆒

Open All Year

Yeats Country Hotel, Spa & Leisure Club

Rosses Point,
Co. Sligo

Tel: 071-917 7211 Fax: 071-917 7203
Email: info@yeatscountryhotel.com
Web: www.yeatscountryhotel.com

HOTEL ★★★ MAP 10 H 16

A family-run, 3*** hotel. All rooms en suite, cable TV, direct dial phone, tea/coffee facilities, hairdryer. Within 3km of sandy beaches and Sligo's 18 hole championship golf courses at concession rates. Amenities include de luxe leisure club with 18m swimming pool, sauna, jacuzzi, steam room and hi-tech gymnasium. Also available tennis, basketball. Supervised creche and indoor play areas during the months of July and August, and Bank Holiday Weekends. Local activities: golf, yachting, fishing, scenic drives.

Bookable on www.irelandhotels.com
Member of McEniff Hotels

B&B from €65.00 to €105.00

Fiona McEniff
Managing Director

Activities:
🚲 🎾 💧

Member of:

IRISH HOTELS FEDERATION

Special Offer: *Weekend Specials from €149.00 pps (2 Nights B&B & 1 Dinner)*

98 98 ☎ 🖥 📺 T A ⚑ 🍽 C M C S ⚑ 🍽 📶
♨ U ♪ 🎹 🅿 🕭 🆒 🐕 🐾 ✝

Closed 05 - 22 January

B&B Rates are per Person Sharing per Night incl. Breakfast.
or **Room Rates** are per Room per Night - See also Page 8

Sligo Town

Clarion Hotel Sligo	Innisfree Hotel	Lisadorn

Clarion Hotel Sligo

Clarion Road,
Sligo

Tel: 071-911 9000 Fax: 071-911 9001
Email: info@clarionhotelsligo.com
Web: www.clarionhotelsligo.com

HOTEL P MAP 10 H 16

White Egyptian linen, fluffy white towels, cable TV and free broadband are all standard in each of the 167 bedrooms and suites. Our conference centre offers small suites perfect for private dining or board meetings, the ballroom for conferences or weddings. Our Sinergie Restaurant serves beautifully presented modern European flavours. Kudos Bar offers Asian food freshly prepared from wok stations. Sanovitae offers pool, treatment rooms, sauna, gym, aerobics room, & childrens' club.

Member of Clarion Group

Room Rate from €99.00 to €290.00

Jason Sleator
Sales & Marketing Manager

Activities:

Member of:

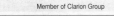

Special Offer: Weekend Specials from €149.00 pps (2 Nights B&B & 1 Dinner)

167 167

Open All Year

Innisfree Hotel

High Street,
Sligo Town

Tel: 071-914 2014 Fax: 071-914 5745
Email: innisfreehotelsligo@eircom.net

HOTEL ★★ MAP 10 H 16

Located in the heart of Sligo Town this comfortable hotel has a special, friendly atmosphere. All rooms are en suite with TV, direct dial phone and tea making facilities. Excellent food served all day or visit the lively Ark Bar with its seafaring theme. Convenient to theatre and shops. Explore W.B. Yeats' breathtaking countryside, the Lake Isle of Innisfree, Glencar, and Sligo's renowned golf courses and seaside resorts. Specialising in commercial traveller rates and golf holidays.

B&B from €50.00 to €65.00

Denis Deery
Owner

Member of:

19 19

Closed 24 - 26 December

Lisadorn

Donegal Road,
Sligo Town

Tel: 071-914 3417 Fax: 071-914 6418
Email: cjoconnor@eircom.net
Web: http://homepage.eircom.net/~lisadorn/

GUESTHOUSE ★★★ MAP 10 H 16

Sligo Town's first and only 3*** guesthouse situated on the N15 within 5 minutes of town centre. Ideal base for North bound traffic. All rooms en suite, remote control colour TVs, direct dial telephones, fax, hairdryers and hospitality tray. Beside pitch & putt and 10 minutes to Rosses Point. 2006 Madness - Bed & Breakfast €25 per person sharing all year round except June, July, August, September, Saturday nights and major holidays.

B&B from €25.00 to €35.00

Marian O'Connor
Proprietor

6 6

Closed 15 November - 17 March

B&B Rates are per Person Sharing per Night incl. Breakfast.
or Room Rates are per Room per Night - See also Page 8

Radisson SAS Hotel Sligo

Ballincar,
Rosses Point,
Sligo
Tel: 071-914 0008 Fax: 071-914 0005
Email: info.sligo@radissonsas.com
Web: www.sligo.radissonsas.com

HOTEL R MAP 10 H 16

Located in beautiful Rosses Point with stunning views of Sligo Bay and surroundings. 132 luxurious bedrooms. Dine in the 'Classiebawn Restaurant' serving local and international cuisine. Benwiskin Bar offers a varied menu. Magnificent leisure facilities include 18m swimming pool, steam room, sauna, jacuzzi and outdoor Canadian hot tub. The hotel's Spa and Wellness centre is a haven of relaxation incorporating exquisite treatment rooms and a relaxation suite. Within easy reach of some of the best golf courses in Ireland.

Bookable on www.irelandhotels.com
Member of Rezidor SAS

B&B from €65.00 to €100.00

Eoin Little
General Manager

Member of:

132 132

Open All Year

Sligo City Hotel

Quay Street,
Sligo
Tel: 071-914 4000 Fax: 071-914 6888
Email: info@sligocityhotel.com
Web: www.sligocityhotel.com

HOTEL ★★★ MAP 10 H 16

The Sligo City Hotel is located in the heart of Sligo Town, with immediate access to Sligo's new shopping centre and a host of lively bars on its doorstep. All 58 bedrooms are en suite with cable TV and direct dial phone, fast internet connections with broadband and tea/coffee making facilities. The Sligo City Hotel offers a warm welcome to all our guests and prides itself on delivering service excellence. Specialising in room only rates, commercial traveller rates and golfing holidays.

Room Rate from €55.00 to €129.00

Edel McPartland
General Manager

Activities:

Member of:

Special Offer: Weekend Specials from €125.00 pps
(2 Nights B&B & 1 Dinner)

58 58

Closed 24 - 28 December

Sligo Park Hotel & Leisure Centre

Pearse Road,
Sligo
Tel: 071-919 0400 Fax: 071-916 9556
Email: sligo@leehotels.com
Web: www.leehotels.com

HOTEL ★★★ MAP 10 H 16

Situated one mile south of Sligo on the Dublin side, the Sligo Park Hotel is set on seven acres of gardens. A 3*** hotel with 138 new bedrooms, the hotel has one of the finest leisure centres in the country. In the heart of Yeats country, the Sligo Park is surrounded by some of the most scenic countryside in Ireland ranging from the majestic Benbulben to the gentle waters of Lough Gill. For that special break, the Sligo Park has all the facilities for your enjoyment.

Bookable on www.irelandhotels.com
Member of Lee Hotels

B&B from €55.00 to €120.00

Gerard Moore
General Manager

Activities:

Member of:

138 138

Open All Year

B&B Rates are per Person Sharing per Night incl. Breakfast.
or Room Rates are per Room per Night - See also Page 8

Co. Sligo

Sligo Town / Strandhill / Tubbercurry

Sligo Southern Hotel & Leisure Centre	Ocean View Hotel	Cawley's
Strandhill Road, Sligo Town	Strandhill, Co. Sligo	Emmet Street, Tubbercurry, Co. Sligo
Tel: 071-916 2101 Fax: 071-916 0328	Tel: 071-916 8115 Fax: 071-916 8009	Tel: 071-918 5025 Fax: 071-918 5963
Email: reservations@sligosouthernhotel.com	Email: oceanviewhotel@eircom.net	Email: cawleysguesthouse@eircom.net
Web: www.sligosouthernhotel.com		

HOTEL ★★★ MAP 10 H 16 | HOTEL ★★★ MAP 10 H 16 | GUESTHOUSE ★★ MAP 10 G 15

The Sligo Southern Hotel is situated in the heart of Sligo Town, adjacent to the railway and bus stations. The Sligo Southern Hotel blends old world intimacy with every modern convenience. All 99 rooms are en suite, cable TV, phone, hairdryers, tea/coffee making facilities. Indoor swimming pool, gym, jacuzzi, sauna and steam room. Entertainment most nights in high season. Reservations Tel: 1850 520052 or Free phone NI & UK 0800 783 9024.

Bookable on www.irelandhotels.com
Member of Brian McEniff Hotels

Visit the Ocean View Hotel beside the Atlantic Ocean and discover the charms of the North West of Ireland. An owner managed small hotel with modern comforts and excellent home-cooked food. Strandhill prides itself on sandy beaches, golf courses, hidden glens, seaweed baths, horse riding, surfing, pubs & restaurants, the oldest tombs in Europe all at the foot of the picturesque Knocknarea Mountain. Strandhill is only 10 minutes scenic drive from Sligo Town. Free secure parking on grounds.

Cawley's is a large 3 storey family-run guesthouse with full bar license. We offer high standards in accommodation with tastefully decorated rooms. Our home cooking and personal service make this premises your home for the duration of your stay. Private parking, landscaped gardens, easily accessed by air, rail and bus. Local amenities include fishing, 9 hole golf course and horse riding. Seaside resorts close by. Major credit cards accepted. For further information please contact a member of the Cawley family on 071-918 5025.

B&B from €60.00 to €99.00 | **B&B from €55.00 to €75.00** | **B&B from €27.50 to €37.50**

 Kevin McGlynn General Manager

Activities:

Member of:

Jean Burke & Shay Burke Proprietors

Member of:

Teresa Cawley / Pierre Krebs

Member of:

Special Offer: *Weekend Specials from €125.00 pps (2 Nights B&B & 1 Dinner)*

99 99

Special Offer: *3 Nights B&B from €32.50 pps per night (excluding July - September)*

12 12

17 10

Closed 24 - 26 December	Closed 01 December - 12 March	Closed 23 - 27 December

226 **North West**

B&B Rates are per Person Sharing per Night incl. Breakfast.
or **Room Rates** are per Room per Night - See also Page 8

Map of North Region

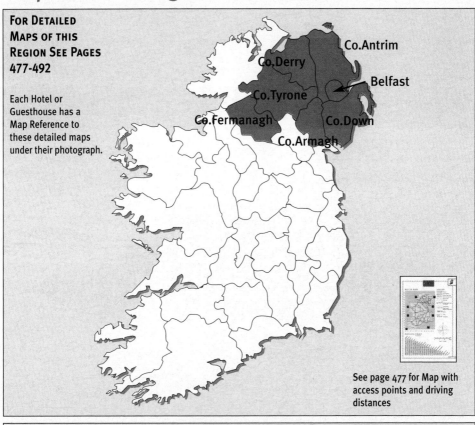

FOR DETAILED MAPS OF THIS REGION SEE PAGES 477-492

Each Hotel or Guesthouse has a Map Reference to these detailed maps under their photograph.

Co.Antrim
Co.Derry
Belfast
Co.Tyrone
Co.Fermanagh
Co.Down
Co.Armagh

See page 477 for Map with access points and driving distances

Locations listing

irelandhotels.com
Official Website of the Irish Hotels Federation

IRISH HOTELS FEDERATION

INCLUDES DETAILED MAPS & GREAT VALUE SPECIAL OFFERS.

northern ireland

Immerse yourself in its beauty, feel the warmth of its people.

The Apartment - Belfast

Bushmills Distillery - Co. Antrim

Talking on Derry's Walls - Co. Derry

Mourne Mountains - Co. Down

Where can you catch glimpses of the life of Ireland's patron saint, Patrick; from the site of his first church to the spires and lush countryside he loved looking over; from his 'sweet hill' to his final resting place?

Where are the myth and mystery of the legendary Cuchulainn, St Columba and Finn McCool as much alive today as they were 3,000 years ago?

Where can you sample the delights of the world's oldest distillery, visit the famous Giant's Causeway World Heritage Site and play golf on one of the world's top 15 golf courses?

The Giant's Causeway - Co. Antrim

Traditional Music - Belfast

Dunluce Castle - Co. Antrim

Belleek Pottery - Co. Fermanagh

St. Patrick's Trian, Co. Armagh

Ulster American Folk Park - Co. Tyrone

Golf at Royal Portrush - Co. Antrim

Where can you taste what life was like in the new and old worlds in the 18th and 19th centuries during the potato famine and the great emigration or visit the ancestral homes of numerous American presidents and Davy Crockett?

Where can you watch the renowned craftsmen of Belleek Pottery and Tyrone Crystal at work, roam in some of the most spectacularly wild and unspoiled countryside in Ireland and join in the traditional music and dancing of hundreds of festivals?

Where? Northern Ireland. A land where time stands still and memories never fade. A land of spectacular coastline and breathtaking countryside. A potent mix of heritage and culture and the home of that most famous of Irish traits, a welcome and craic that's second to none.

To find out more about visiting Northern Ireland visit
www.discovernorthernireland.com or call us on **+44 (0) 28 9024 6609**

Co. Antrim
Ballintoy / Bushmills

Fullerton Arms

22-24 Main Street,
Ballintoy,
Co. Antrim BT54 6LX
Tel: 028-2076 9613 Fax: 028-2076 9613
Email: info@fullertonarms.co.uk
Web: www.fullertonarms.co.uk

GUESTHOUSE ★★★ MAP 15 O 21

The Fullerton Arms is a family-run guesthouse, bar and restaurant. It is situated amongst some of the most spectacular scenery in the North of Ireland. The proprietors Anne and Lyle Taggart pride themselves on their high standard of customer service and attention to detail, which ensures every guest has an enjoyable stay.

B&B from £25.00 to £75.00

Anne Taggart
Proprietor

Member of:

11 11

Open All Year

Bayview Hotel

2 Bayhead Road,
Portballintrae,
Bushmills, BT57 8RZ
Tel: 028-2073 4100 Fax: 028-2073 4330
Email: info@bayviewhotelni.com
Web: www.bayviewhotelni.com

HOTEL ★★★ MAP 14 N 21

Opened 2001, the Bayview Hotel is situated in the heart of the picturesque village of Portballintrae, one mile from Bushmills. Overlooking the Atlantic Ocean and close to the Giant's Causeway and Old Bushmills Distillery, with 25 luxurious bedrooms, standard, superior, premier, interlinking and ambulant disabled rooms available. Excellent conference facilities, Porthole Restaurant and Bar. Lift and private car park. This small luxury hotel is the ideal destination for conferencing, golfing, business, incentive travel and leisure.

Bookable on www.irelandhotels.com
Member of North Coast Hotels Ltd.

B&B from £40.00 to £70.00

Mary O'Neill
Group Marketing Manager

Activities:

Member of:

Special Offer: Weekend Specials from £99.00 pps
(2 Nights B&B)

25 25
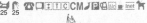

Open All Year

Bushmills Inn Hotel

9 Dunluce Road,
Bushmills,
Co. Antrim BT57 8QG
Tel: 028-2073 3000 Fax: 028-2073 2048
Email: mail@bushmillsinn.com
Web: www.bushmillsinn.com

HOTEL ★★★ MAP 14 N 21

A "living museum of Ulster Hospitality". In the village that is home to the world's oldest distillery between the Giant's Causeway and Royal Portrush Golf Club, this multi award-winning hotel, on the banks of the River Bush, with turf fires, oil lamps, nooks, crannies and even a secret room presents an extensive range of intriguing bedrooms, an atmospheric restaurant (new Irish cuisine), a turf-fired old kitchen and a Victorian bar still lit by gas light - you're welcome.

Bookable on www.irelandhotels.com
Member of Ireland's Blue Book

B&B from £69.00 to £79.00

Stella Minogue &
Alan Dunlop
Managers

Activities:

Member of:

Special Offer: Weekend Specials from £128.00 pps
(2 Nights B&B & 1 Dinner)

32 32

Open All Year

B&B Rates are per Person Sharing per Night incl. Breakfast.
or Room Rates are per Room per Night - See also Page 8

Causeway Hotel

40 Causeway Road,
Bushmills,
Co. Antrim BT57 8SU
Tel: 028-2073 1226 Fax: 028-2073 2552
Email: reception@giants-causeway-hotel.com
Web: www.giants-causeway-hotel.com

HOTEL ★★ MAP 14 N 21

Situated on the North Antrim Coast at the entrance to the world famous Giant's Causeway. This old family hotel established in 1836 has been tastefully renovated and restored to provide modern facilities while retaining its old grandeur and charm. The 28 centrally heated bedrooms have TV, tea/coffee making facilities and bathrooms en suite.

B&B from £35.00 to £40.00

Johanna Armstrong
Manager

Member of:

Special Offer: 2 Nights Dinner, B&B from £85.00 pps

28 28

Open All Year

Londonderry Arms Hotel

Glens Of Antrim, 20 Harbour Road,
Carnlough,
Co. Antrim BT44 0EU
Tel: 028-2888 5255 Fax: 028-2888 5263
Email: lda@glensofantrim.com
Web: www.glensofantrim.com

HOTEL ★★★ MAP 15 P 20

This beautiful Georgian hotel was built in 1847. Once owned by Sir Winston Churchill, it is now owned and managed by Mr. Frank O'Neill. With its open log fires, private lounges and award-winning restaurant, this premier hotel in the Glens of Antrim is the perfect place to stay and discover the north eastern part of Ireland. Member of Irish Country Hotels. Ideal for incentive travel, close to the Giant's Causeway. Suits tour parties and conferences.

Bookable on www.irelandhotels.com
Member of Irish Country Hotels

B&B from £40.00 to £55.00

Frank O'Neill
Proprietor

Activities:

Special Offer: Weekend Specials from £85.00 pps
(2 Nights B&B & 1 Dinner)

35 35

Closed 24 - 26 December

Clarion Hotel

75 Belfast Road,
Carrickfergus,
Co. Antrim BT38 8PH
Tel: 028-9336 4556 Fax: 028-9335 1620
Email: info@clarioncarrick.com
Web: www.clarioncarrick.com

HOTEL ★★★ MAP 15 P 18

Mediterranean style hotel situated 15 minutes from Belfast City centre at the gateway to the Causeway Coastal Route. The hotel boasts 68 de luxe bedrooms, including 4 suites with panoramic views of Belfast Lough. Each room offers king-size bed, multi-channel TV with in-house movie channels, Gameboy systems, DD telephone, executive desk with internet connection, trouser press, hairdryer & complimentary tea/coffee making facilities. Variety of dining from the grill bar menu in Bar 75 to fine dining in the intimate surroundings of the Red Pepper Restaurant. Entertainment Friday and Saturday nights.

Member of Choice Hotels Europe

B&B from £40.00 to £45.00

Nina Kelly
Sales & Marketing Manager

Member of:

Special Offer: Weekend Specials from £85.00 pps
(2 Nights B&B & 1 Dinner)

68 68

Inet WiFi

Closed 24 - 26 December

B&B Rates are per Person Sharing per Night incl. Breakfast.
or **Room Rates** are per Room per Night - See also Page 8

Dobbins Inn Hotel

6/8 High Street,
Carrickfergus,
Co. Antrim BT38 7AF
Tel: 028-9335 1905 Fax: 028-9335 1905
Email: info@dobbinsinnhotel.co.uk
Web: www.dobbinsinnhotel.co.uk

HOTEL ★★ MAP 15 P 18

A family-run hotel, built in the 15th Century and with its own ghost 'Maud', the hotel has 15 en suite bedrooms with tea/coffee facilities, colour TV, telephone and trouser press. Meals are available all day in the Paul Jones Lounge or the de Courcy Restaurant. The hotel has regular evening entertainment including a quiz night, live music & karaoke nights. Situated close to Carrickfergus Castle and well located for a pleasant drive to the Giant's Causeway or a day's shopping in Belfast.

B&B from £38.00 to £48.00

Derek & Maureen Fallis
Hosts

Member of:

Special Offer: Weekend Specials from £69.00 pps
(2 Nights B&B & 1 Dinner)

15 15

Closed 25 - 26 December

Aaranmore Lodge

14 Coleraine Road,
Portrush,
Co. Antrim BT56 8EA
Tel: 028-7082 4640 Fax: 028-7082 4640
Email: aaranmore@talk21.com
Web: www.accommodation-northernireland.com

GUESTHOUSE ★★ MAP 14 N 21

Aaranmore Lodge, Portrush, offers superior accommodation in its spacious refurbished guest rooms. Situated on the A29 from Coleraine, close to the A2, it offers off-street parking and is the ideal choice for exploring the renowned Causeway Coast. Just minutes from Royal Portrush Golf Course, and with seven superb courses close by, Aaranmore attracts a world-wide golfing clientèle. Pubs, restaurants and entertainment within walking distance. Internet facilities.

B&B from £25.00 to £30.00

J & F Duggan

Member of:

4 4

Closed 20 - 30 December

Comfort Hotel Portrush

73 Main Street,
Portrush,
Co. Antrim BT56 8BN
Tel: 028-7082 6100 Fax: 028-7082 6160
Email: info@comforthotelportrush.com
Web: www.comforthotelportrush.com

HOTEL ★★★ MAP 14 N 21

Hotel of the Year 2004/5 (Northern Ireland Tourism Awards) - the award-winning 3*** Comfort Hotel Portrush opened 2001, situated overlooking the Atlantic Ocean in the centre of Portrush. 50 en suite bedrooms with interlinking and ambulant disabled rooms and lift. Ideal base for golfing, walking, cycling, angling, sightseeing, families, tour parties and conferences. Golf at Royal Portrush, Portstewart, Castlerock, Ballycastle and Galgorm Castle Golf Courses. Sister hotel "Bayview Hotel Portballintrae, Bushmills".

Bookable on www.irelandhotels.com
Member of Choice Hotels Europe

B&B from £35.00 to £55.00

Ann Donaghy
Group General Manager

Activities:

Member of:

Special Offer: Winter Rate Specials from £55.00 pps
(2 Nights B&B)

50 50

Open All Year

B&B Rates are per Person Sharing per Night incl. Breakfast.
or **Room Rates** are per Room per Night - See also Page 8

Ballymac	Templeton Hotel	Armagh City Hotel

Ballymac

7a Rock Road,
Stoneyford,
Co. Antrim BT28 3SU
Tel: 028-9264 8313 Fax: 028-9264 8312
Email: info@ballymachotel.co.uk
Web: www.ballymac.com

HOTEL ★★ MAP 15 O 18

The Ballymac Hotel set amid tranquil surroundings. Spectacularly reincarnated, the contemporarily designed 15 en suite bedrooms with excellent facilities including DD phones, modem facilities, hairdryers, TVs and hospitality trays. Our Grill Bar/Lounge and à la carte restaurant feature outstanding cuisine along with an extensive wine list. The Ballymac also boasts well-equipped function suites suitable for weddings, parties, trade shows and conferences. Extensive private parking is available in our grounds.

B&B from £50.00 to £60.00

Cathy Muldoon
General Manager

Activities:

Member of:

15 15

Closed 25 December

Templeton Hotel

882 Antrim Rd, Templepatrick,
Ballyclare,
Co. Antrim BT39 0AH
Tel: 028-9443 2984 Fax: 028-9443 3406
Email: reception@templetonhotel.com
Web: www.templetonhotel.com

HOTEL ★★★ MAP 15 O 18

This privately owned hotel, 5 minutes from Belfast International Airport, 20 minutes from Belfast City centre and Belfast and Larne Ports, offers total quality for all tastes. With the choice of Raffles à la carte restaurant, the Upton Grill Room and the spacious lounge bar, you are guaranteed an enjoyable dining experience. Sam's Bar hosts a pub quiz every Monday evening and offers a late bar at weekends. Our 24 en suite bedrooms, including executive suites, are ideal for a relaxing and comfortable stay.

B&B from £40.00 to £55.00

Alison McCombe / Claire Kerr
General Manager /
Marketing Manager

24 24

Closed 25 - 26 December

Armagh City Hotel

2 Friary Road,
Armagh BT60 4FR,
Co. Armagh
Tel: 028-3751 8888 Fax: 028-3751 2777
Email: info@armaghcityhotel.com
Web: www.mooneyhotelgroup.com

HOTEL ★★★ MAP 14 N 16

Located only 45 minutes from Belfast & 90 minutes from Dublin, in the heart of the ecclesiastic capital of Ireland, the hotel is surrounded by beautiful orchard country, the historic Palace Demesne & the County Armagh Golf Club. Guests can enjoy 99 luxurious en suite bedrooms, delicious modern Irish cuisine in the Friary Restaurant as well as a state of the art health & leisure club. The Armagh City Hotel is officially Northern Ireland's largest hotel conference facility & can accommodate up to 1200 delegates. Friendly & professional service. Free car parking. Families welcome.

Bookable on www.irelandhotels.com

B&B from £39.50 to £75.00

Zoe Millar
General Manager

Activities:

Member of:

99 99

Closed 24 - 26 December

B&B Rates are per Person Sharing per Night incl. Breakfast.
or **Room Rates** are per Room per Night - See also Page 8

Charlemont Arms Hotel	Ashburn Hotel	Days Hotel, Belfast

Charlemont Arms Hotel

57-65 English Street,
Armagh City,
Co. Armagh BT61 7LB
Tel: 028-3752 2028 Fax: 028-3752 6979
Email: info@charlemontarmshotel.com
Web: www.charlemontarmshotel.com

HOTEL ★★ MAP 14 N 16

A family-run hotel set in the city centre, offering the best of both worlds, traditional and modern. Convenient to shops, 18 hole golf course, leisure centre and all major tourist attractions including the 2 Cathedrals and other places of interest. 30 en suite bedrooms including one for the disabled, a 60 seat restaurant, 80 seat lounge bar, Turner's theme bar and Basement Bistro/Winebar that offers a unique dining experience for Armagh.

Ashburn Hotel

81 William Street,
Lurgan,
Co. Armagh BT66 6JB
Tel: 028-3832 5711 Fax: 028-3834 7194
Email: info@theashburnhotel.com
Web: www.theashburnhotel.com

HOTEL ★★ MAP 15 O 17

Owned and managed by the McConaghy Family, the Ashburn Hotel is friendly and efficient. Conveniently situated with easy access to the motorway (M1), rail network and town centre. An ideal base for angling or golfing trips - 5 miles from the River Bann and 1 mile from local golf course. All bedrooms are en suite with colour TV, direct dial telephone and hospitality tray. Entertainment each weekend in our popular nightclub.

Days Hotel, Belfast

40 Hope Street,
Belfast,
Co. Antrim
Tel: 028-9024 2494 Fax: 028-9024 2495
Email: mail@dayshotelbelfast.co.uk
Web: www.dayshotelbelfast.co.uk

HOTEL ★★★ MAP 15 P 18

Days Hotel Belfast offers great value for money in a prime city centre location. Many of the city's shops, restaurants, attractions and nightlife are right on your doorstep. The hotel is also ideally located for all transport links. Facilities include hotel bar, restaurant, 2 meeting rooms and 300 on-site car parking spaces. Parking is free for residents.

Member of Andras House

B&B from £37.50 to £40.00	B&B from £28.00 to £34.00	Room Rate from £65.00 to £95.00

The Forster Family

Member of:

30 30

John F. McConaghy

Member of:

12 12

Lee Madden
General Manager

Member of:

244 244

Closed 25 - 26 December	Closed 24 - 26 December	Open All Year

B&B Rates are per Person Sharing per Night incl. Breakfast.
or **Room Rates** are per Room per Night - See also Page 8

Dukes Hotel

65/67 University Street,
Belfast BT7 1HL

Tel: 028-9023 6666 Fax: 028-9023 7177
Email: info@dukes-hotel-belfast.co.uk
Web: www.welcome-group.co.uk

HOTEL U MAP 15 P 18

A bright new modern hotel constructed in one of Belfast's more distinguished Victorian buildings. Located beside Queen's University, Ulster Museum and the Botanic Gardens, the hotel is less than 1 mile from the city centre. Golf courses only minutes away. 12 en suite bedrooms with TV, hairdryers and direct dial telephones. A sauna is also available. There is a popular bar for the smart set and a beer garden. The Glassroom Restaurant serves local cuisine. A friendly and welcome service is guaranteed.

B&B from £35.00 to £45.00

San Wong
Managing Director

Member of:

Special Offer: *Weekend Specials from £79.00 pps*
(2 Nights B&B & 1 Dinner)

12 12

Closed 25 - 28 December

Dunadry Hotel and Country Club

2 Islandreagh Drive,
Dunadry,
Co. Antrim BT41 2HA

Tel: 028-9443 4343 Fax: 028-9443 3389
Email: info@dunadry.com
Web: www.mooneyhotelgroup.com

HOTEL ★★★★ MAP 15 O 18

One of Northern Ireland's best loved hotels, the Dunadry offers every guest the ultimate in elegance, charm & warm hospitality. Delightful food awaits you in the Mill Race Bistro & the Linen Mill Restaurants, as well as the comfort of 83 luxurious en suite bedrooms. Indulge yourself at the Country Club & take a tour round the extensive gardens. Cycling & fishing available on site; country walking, golf & horse riding closeby. Conference facilities for up to 400 delegates. Free car parking. Families welcome. Located 15 mins from Belfast City & 40 mins from the North Coast.

Bookable on www.irelandhotels.com

B&B from £45.00 to £80.00

Cate McConville
General Manager

Activities:

Member of:

83 83

Closed 24 - 26 December

B&B Rates are per Person Sharing per Night incl. Breakfast.
or Room Rates are per Room per Night - See also Page 8

Belfast City

Express By Holiday Inn	Hastings Europa Hotel	Jurys Inn Belfast
106a University Street, Belfast, Co Antrim BT7 1HP	Great Victoria Street, Belfast BT2 7AP	Fisherwick Place, Great Victoria St, Belfast BT2 7AP
Tel: 028-9031 1909 Fax: 028-9031 1910	Tel: 028-9027 1066 Fax: 028-9032 7800	Tel: 028-9053 3500 Fax: 028-9053 3511
Email: mail@exhi-belfast.com	Email: res@eur.hastingshotels.com	Email: jurysinnbelfast@jurysdoyle.com
Web: www.exhi-belfast.com	Web: www.hastingshotels.com	Web: www.jurysinns.com

HOTEL ★★★ MAP 15 P 18 | **HOTEL ★★★★ MAP 15 P 18** | **HOTEL ★★★ MAP 15 P 18**

Express By Holiday Inn

Express By Holiday Inn is a modern 3*** hotel situated in Belfast's vibrant Queen's Quarter. The 114 en suite bedrooms offer power showers, satellite TV and radio, movies, hairdryer and tea & coffee making facilities. Our restaurant boasts an enticing international cuisine and our bar is the perfect place to relax and absorb the hotel's easy-going atmosphere. Our experienced staff are always at hand to ensure your stay with us exceeds your every expectation.

Hastings Europa Hotel

The Europa Hotel is superbly located in the heart of Belfast, convenient to the business and commerical districts. The hotel is a 10 minute drive from all major motorways, ferry & air terminals, with a rail link next door. The Europa has a total of 240 bedrooms including 56 executive bedrooms. Each bedroom is exquisitely appointed and traditonally furnished offering guests the ultimate in comfort & style.

Jurys Inn Belfast

Located in the centre of Belfast, adjacent to the Opera House, the City Hall and the city's main commercial district. Just two minutes walk away are the prime shopping areas of Donegall Place and the Castlecourt Centre, while the city's golden mile, with its myriad lively bars and restaurants, is also within walking distance. The hotel is 15 minutes walk away from the Odyssey Arena and all 190 bedrooms have been recently refurbished.

Bookable on www.irelandhotels.com
Member of Hastings hotels Group

Bookable on www.irelandhotels.com
Member of Jurys Doyle Hotel Group

B&B from £32.50 to £39.50	B&B from £60.00 to £110.00	Room Rate from £63.00 to £109.00

Lee Madden
General Manager

James McGinn
General Manager

Margaret Nagle
General Manager

Member of:

Member of:

Member of:

Special Offer: Weekend Specials from £99.00 pps
(2 Nights B&B & 1 Dinner)

114 114 | 240 240 | 190 190

Open All Year	Closed 24 - 26 December	Closed 24 - 26 December

B&B Rates are per Person Sharing per Night incl. Breakfast. or Room Rates are per Room per Night - See also Page 8

La Mon Hotel & Country Club

41 Gransha Road,
Castlereagh,
Belfast BT23 5RF
Tel: 028-9044 8631 Fax: 028-9044 8026
Email: info@lamon.co.uk
Web: www.lamon.co.uk

HOTEL ★★★★ MAP 15 P 18

This modern 4 star hotel offers 88 en suite bedrooms, excellent banqueting & conference facilities in a tranquil setting just 8 miles south east of Belfast City centre. Guests will enjoy the superb luxury leisure facilities including 15 metre swimming pool, childrens' pool, sauna, jacuzzi, steam room, gymnasium, hair studio & beauty salon. A wide range of dining options is also available with table d'hôte and à la carte menus in the Shakespeare Restaurant. Casual dining with a cosmopolitan flavour is also available in our lively bistro. An ideal venue for business or leisure.

Bookable on www.irelandhotels.com

B&B from £47.50 to £62.50

Francis Brady
Managing Director

Activities:

🍸

Member of:
NIHF

Special Offer: Weekend Specials from £139.00 pps (2 Nights B&B & 1 Dinner)

88 88

Closed 24 - 26 December

Malone Lodge Hotel & Apartments

60 Eglantine Avenue,
Malone Road,
Belfast BT9 6DY
Tel: 028-9038 8000 Fax: 028-9038 8088
Email: info@malonelodgehotel.com
Web: www.malonelodgehotel.com

HOTEL ★★★★ MAP 15 P 18

In the leafy suburbs of the university area of South Belfast, discover one of Northern Ireland's finest 4★★★★ hotels. The centre piece of a beautiful Victorian terrace, the Malone Lodge Hotel offers you an oasis of calm and quiet elegance. The hotel offers luxury en suite accommodation, an award-winning restaurant, bar with big screen, conference & banqueting facilities and a fitness suite & sauna.

Bookable on www.irelandhotels.com
Member of Select Hotels of Ireland

B&B from £50.00 to £75.00

Brian & Mary Macklin

Activities:

:/🍸

Member of:
NIHF

Special Offer: Weekend Specials from £85.00 pps (2 Nights B&B & 1 Dinner)

51 51

Open All Year

Park Avenue Hotel

158 Holywood Road,
Belfast BT4 1PB
Tel: 028-9065 6520 Fax: 028-9047 1417
Email: frontdesk@parkavenuehotel.co.uk
Web: www.parkavenuehotel.co.uk

HOTEL ★★★ MAP 15 P 18

The Park Avenue Hotel is nearest to Belfast City Airport & situated a few mins from city centre. Close to Odyssey Arena, Belfast's Waterfront Hall & the Titanic Quarter. Excellent road, rail & air links. A cinema complex & an array of shops are steps away. All 56 rooms are modern, bright, spacious & provide full en suite facilities. Each room is equipped with satellite TV, direct dial phone & wireless broadband. Free on site car parking. Griffin Restaurant & Gelston's Corner Bar, both serve food daily. We can cater for conferences & events for up to 600 people. Winners NIHF Reception of the Year 2005.

Bookable on www.irelandhotels.com
Member of The Independents

B&B from £35.00 to £47.50

Mandy Martin
Director

Activities:

🍸

Member of:
NIHF

Special Offer: Weekend Specials from £75.00 pps (2 Nights B&B & 1 Dinner)

56 56

Closed 25 December

B&B Rates are per Person Sharing per Night incl. Breakfast.
or Room Rates are per Room per Night - See also Page 8

North 237

Wellington Park Hotel	Brown Trout Golf & Country Inn	Beech Hill Country House Hotel

Wellington Park Hotel

21 Malone Road,
Belfast BT9 6RU

Tel: 028-9038 1111 Fax: 028-9066 5410
Email: info@wellingtonparkhotel.com
Web: www.mooneyhotelgroup.com

HOTEL ★★★★ MAP 15 P 18

Located in the fashionable Malone Road area, this family owned and managed hotel is a Belfast institution. The hotel offers guests the ultimate experience in hospitality & modern comfort with 75 bedrooms. Guests can unwind & relax on the overstuffed sofas of the Arts Café or sample the finest local cuisine in the Piper Bistro. Attractions such as museums, theatres, public gardens & golf clubs are close by. Large conference facilities. Free parking for residents. Families welcome. Only 5 mins from city centre & 10 mins from Belfast City Airport.

Bookable on www.irelandhotels.com
Member of Best Western Hotels

B&B from £45.00 to £80.00

Malachy Toner
General Manager

Activities:

Member of:

🐴🛶 ☎🖥🚭📺🅣🅒 ⚓CM♫PS🅿👶♿ ⚓
75 75
inet WiFi 👤

Closed 24 - 26 December

Brown Trout Golf & Country Inn

209 Agivey Road,
Aghadowey, Coleraine,
Co. Derry BT51 4AD

Tel: 028-7086 8209 Fax: 028-7086 8878
Email: bill@browntroutinn.com
Web: www.browntroutinn.com

HOTEL ★★★ MAP 14 N 20

The Brown Trout Golf and Country Inn nestles near the River Bann only 12.8km from the picturesque Causeway Coast. This old inn with 15 rooms, and four 5 star cottages, is Northern Ireland's first golf hotel. Gerry, Jane or Joanna will happily organise golf, horse riding and fishing packages with professional tuition if required or you can just enjoy a relaxing break and the craic with the locals. The warm hospitality and 'Taste of Ulster' restaurant will make your stay enjoyable.

Bookable on www.irelandhotels.com
Member of Irish Country Hotels

B&B from £35.00 to £45.00

Jane O'Hara
Owner

Member of:

Special Offer: Weekend Specials from £75.00 pps
(2 Nights B&B & 1 Dinner)

🐴🛶 ☎🖥🚭📺🅣🅐🅒 ⚓CM♫🌂👶♿♫🎵
15 15
🅿🚲🐕🅰🄰🅰 inet WiFi 🌂👤

Open All Year

Beech Hill Country House Hotel

32 Ardmore Road,
Derry BT47 3QP

Tel: 028-7134 9279 Fax: 028-7134 5366
Email: info@beech-hill.com
Web: www.beech-hill.com

HOTEL ★★★★ MAP 14 L 20

Beech Hill is a privately owned country house hotel, 2 miles from Londonderry. It retains the elegance of country living & has been restored to create a hotel of charm, character & style. Its ambience is complemented by the surrounding grounds, planted with a myriad trees, including beech. Superb cuisine using local produce and homemade specialties. NITB Highly Commended Marketing Excellence Award 2004 & Flavour of Northern Ireland 2005. Sauna, steam room, jacuzzi & gym available. Relaxation weekends, aromatherapy, reiki, massage & beauty therapies. Booking advisable.

Bookable on www.irelandhotels.com
Member of Manor House Hotels

B&B from £45.00 to £55.00

Seamus Donnelly
Proprietor

Member of:

Special Offer: Weekend Specials from £99.00 pps
(2 Nights B&B & 1 Dinner)

🐴🛶 ☎🖥🚭📺🅣🅒 ⚓CM♫🌂🎣⚓♿🅟
27 27

🅢🅰🄰🅰 inet 👤

Closed 24 - 26 December

B&B Rates are per Person Sharing per Night incl. Breakfast.
or **Room Rates** are per Room per Night - See also Page 8

Best Western White Horse Hotel

68 Clooney Road,
Derry BT47 3PA

Tel: 028-7186 0606 Fax: 028-7186 0371
Email: info@whitehorsehotel.biz
Web: www.whitehorsehotel.biz

HOTEL ★★★ MAP 14 L 20

A luxury family-run hotel with 57 bedrooms including 16 executive rooms and leisure complex. The hotel is ideal for pleasure and business with 4 conference suites. The leisure complex consists of 22m swimming pool, childrens' pool, sauna, steam room, jacuzzi, aerobics studio and state of the art gymnasium. Only 10 minutes from the historic city of Londonderry and on the main route to the Giant's Causeway. Award-winning restaurant and bar, very keen room rates. AA selected. Horse riding, golf and fishing close by. Children welcome.

Bookable on www.irelandhotels.com
Member of Best Western

B&B from £35.00 to £65.00

Issam Horshi
Proprietor

Member of:

Special Offer: *Weekend Specials from £80.00 pps*
(2 Nights B&B & 1 Dinner)

57 57

Open All Year

City Hotel

Queens Quay,
Derry BT48 7AS

Tel: 028-7136 5800 Fax: 028-7136 5801
Email: res@derry-gsh.com
Web: www.greatsouthernhotels.com

HOTEL ★★★★ MAP 14 L 20

The City Hotel is a stylish modern 4 star hotel in the heart of the city centre. Ideally located on Queen's Quay, it has magnificent views of the River Foyle and the Guildhall. Leisure facilities include indoor swimming pool, jacuzzi, steam room and gym. Thompson's on the River, the hotel's restaurant, is one of Derry's finest. The hotel has conference facilities for up to 450 delegates. A Great Southern Hotel. Bookable through UTELL International or central reservations in Dublin at tel: 01-214 4800.

Bookable on www.irelandhotels.com

Room Rate from £50.00 to £120.00

Colin Ahern
General Manager

Activities:

Member of:

Special Offer: *Weekend Specials from £80.00 pps*
(2 Nights B&B & 1 Dinner)

145 145

Closed 24 - 26 December

Tower Hotel Derry

Off The Diamond,
Derry City

Tel: 028-7137 1000 Fax: 028-7137 1234
Email: reservations@thd.ie
Web: www.towerhotelderry.com

HOTEL ★★★★ MAP 14 L 20

The only hotel located inside Derry's historic city walls, the Tower is a truly stylish hotel in a city becoming more & more popular as a base from which to explore the spectacular Northern Coast. Spacious & comfortable guest rooms come well equipped & guests can relax & unwind in the leisure suite complex with sauna & steam room. The Bistro at the Tower has been awarded an AA Rosette & a passion for good food is evident. The stylish Lime Tree Bar regularly hosts true music, a fitting tribute to a city renowned for its musical tradition. Special offers available on www.towerhotelgroup.com

Bookable on www.irelandhotels.com
Member of Tower Hotel Group

B&B from £35.00 to £60.00

Collette Ferguson
General Manager

Activities:

Member of:

Special Offer: *Weekend Specials from £89.00 pps*
(2 Nights B&B & 1 Dinner)

93 93

Closed 24 - 26 December

B&B Rates are per Person Sharing per Night incl. Breakfast.
or **Room Rates** are per Room per Night - See also Page 8

Waterfoot Hotel & Country Club

Caw Roundabout,
14 Clooney Road,
Derry BT47 6TB
Tel: 028-7134 5500 Fax: 028-7131 1006
Email: info@thewaterfoothotel.co.uk
Web: www.thewaterfoothotel.co.uk

HOTEL ★★★ MAP 14 L 20

A superbly appointed family-run hotel including indoor leisure centre guaranteeing a luxurious and restful stay. Located on the banks of the River Foyle and only a 5 minute drive to city centre. The hotel restaurant is renowned for its excellent cuisine and this reputation for fine food and drink has been an integral part of the Waterfoot philosophy. Midweek and weekend breaks available throughout the year.

Bookable on www.irelandhotels.com
Member of Holiday Ireland Hotels

B&B from £25.00 to £40.00

*Johanne Ferguson
General Manager*

Member of:

48 48

Closed 25 - 27 December

Radisson SAS Roe Park Resort

Roe Park,
Limavady,
Co. Londonderry BT49 9LB
Tel: 028-7772 2222 Fax: 028-7772 2313
Email: reservations@radissonroepark.com
Web: www.radissonroepark.com

HOTEL ★★★★ MAP· 14 M 20

One of the North Coast's only 4 **** de luxe resorts. Old and new combine to create a world class resort and featuring 118 bedrooms and suites, indoor heated pool, unrivalled leisure spa with extensive range of treatments, an excellent 18 hole parkland golf course, driving range and indoor golf academy. The award-winning Greens Restaurant serves classic fare with Irish flair and the Coach House Brasserie has a relaxed charm.

Bookable on www.irelandhotels.com
Member of Radisson SAS Hotels & Resorts

B&B from £52.50 to £59.50

John O' Carroll

Activities:

Member of:

Special Offer: *Weekend Specials from £119.00 pps
(2 Nights B&B & 1 Dinner)*

118 118

Open All Year

Cairn Bay Lodge

The Cairn, 278 Seacliff Road,
Bangor,
Co. Down BT20 5HS
Tel: 028-9146 7636 Fax: 028-9145 7728
Email: info@cairnbaylodge.com
Web: www.cairnbaylodge.com

GUESTHOUSE ★★★ MAP 15 Q 18

Award-winning guesthouse set in extensive gardens directly overlooking Ballyholme Bay. Bangor Business Award -"Best Tourist Accommodation" - 3rd year in succession. The lodge is family-run, offering the highest standards of food, accommodation and service in luxurious surroundings. An oasis of calm yet only 5 minutes walk from Bangor Town centre and marina. 50m from Ballyholme Yacht Club, 5 golf courses within 5 miles, in-house Guinot appointed beauty salon. Off street parking.

Member of Kingdoms of Down

B&B from £35.00 to £40.00

*Chris & Jenny Mullen
Proprietors*

Member of:

3 3

Open all year

B&B Rates are per Person Sharing per Night incl. Breakfast. or **Room Rates** are per Room per Night - See also Page 8

Clandeboye Lodge Hotel

10 Estate Road,
Bangor,
Co. Down BT19 1UR
Tel: 028-9185 2500 Fax: 028-9185 2772
Email: info@clandeboyelodge.co.uk
Web: www.clandeboyelodge.com

HOTEL ★★★ MAP 15 Q 18

Recognised as one of the very best AA hotels in Northern Ireland, the Clandeboye Lodge offers unparalleled elegance, gracious hospitality and exacting service standards. With its tranquil location adjacent to Blackwood Golf & only 15 mins from Belfast City centre, air & sea port, the hotel offers 43 recently refurbished executive & standard bedrooms with dining options in a fantastic award-winning restaurant or the lobby bar. Fitness suite with the latest design technogym, mini office with hi-tech communications equipment & free, unlimited WiFi internet access from all guest rooms, hotel lounge & conference centre.

Member of Belfast Visitor & Convention Bureau

B&B from £42.50 to £57.50

Pim Dalm
Proprietor

Activities:

Member of:

Special Offer: Weekend Specials from £85.00 pps
(2 Nights B&B & 1 Dinner)

43 43

Closed 24 - 27 December

Royal Hotel

26/28 Quay Street,
Bangor,
Co. Down BT20 5ED
Tel: 028-9127 1866 Fax: 028-9146 7810
Email: royalhotelbangor@aol.com
Web: www.royalhotelbangor.com

HOTEL ★★ MAP 15 Q 18

Overlooking Bangor Marina this family-run hotel is probably the best known landmark on Bangor's seafront. All rooms en suite include 7 executive suites. Satellite TV, direct dial phone, courtesy tray and hairdryer are all standard throughout. Renowned for our food, Café Royal servery for lunch, Quays Restaurant for evening dining. Weddings our speciality, also conferences and functions. 15 minutes from Belfast City Airport. Direct rail link from Dublin and Derry.

B&B from £30.00 to £40.00

Paul Donegan
Proprietor

Activities:

Member of:

Special Offer: Weekend Specials from £59.00 pps
(2 Nights B&B & 1 Dinner)

50 50

Closed 25 - 26 December

Shelleven House

61 Princetown Road,
Bangor BT20 3TA,
Co. Down
Tel: 028-9127 1777 Fax: 028-9127 1777
Email: shellevenhouse@aol.com
Web: www.shellevenhouse.com

GUESTHOUSE ★★★ MAP 15 Q 18

Victorian townhouse with great charm, providing luxurious accommodation in a warm, relaxing atmosphere. Situated in a quiet conservation area of Bangor, close to the Marina, the Promenade and the town centre, Shelleven is set back from the road with gardens and private parking to the front. 11 en suite rooms, some with sea views. Train/bus station 5 minutes away, with direct link to Dublin service and to Belfast City Airport. Several golf courses nearby.

Member of Kingdoms of Down

B&B from £30.00 to £32.50

Mary Weston

Member of:

11   11

Open All Year

B&B Rates are per Person Sharing per Night incl. Breakfast.
or Room Rates are per Room per Night - See also Page 8

Co. Down

Castlewellan / Newcastle / Newry

King's Inn	Burrendale Hotel and Country Club	Canal Court Hotel

King's Inn

28/34 Lower Square,
Castlewellan,
Co. Down BT31 9DW
Tel: 028-437 78247
Email: info@kingscastlewellan.com
Web: www.kingscastlewellan.com

GUESTHOUSE ★   MAP 12 P 16

In the old market town of Castlewellan, the King's Inn is ideally situated to take advantage of the Mournes, the seaside town of Newcastle and all the amenities of South Down. Royal County Down is only 5 minutes away as are the forest parks and the beaches of Dundrum Bay. The Inn is renowned for excellent bar food, friendly atmosphere and also boasts a superb à la carte restaurant. World's biggest maze close by.

Burrendale Hotel and Country Club

51 Castlewellan Road,
Newcastle,
Co. Down BT33 0JY
Tel: 028-4372 2599 Fax: 028-4372 2328
Email: reservations@burrendale.com
Web: www.burrendale.com

HOTEL ★★★   MAP 12 P 16

At the foot of the Mournes, the Burrendale is the ideal location for your family, golfing holiday or short break. The hotel comprises a Country Club, Beauty Salon, à la carte Vine Restaurant, bistro style Cottage Kitchen Restaurant, Cottage Bar and excellent banqueting / conference facilities. In close proximity are 15 golf courses including Royal County Down, golden beaches, nature walks, forest parks and pony trekking. Superb hospitality awaits you.

Canal Court Hotel

Merchants Quay,
Newry,
Co. Down BT35 8HF
Tel: 028-3025 1234 Fax: 028-3025 1177
Email: manager@canalcourthotel.com
Web: www.canalcourthotel.com

HOTEL ★★★★   MAP 12 O 15

This fabulous 4 star hotel is located in the heart of Newry City. The perfect location for a special break. With 112 beautiful bedrooms and suites and an extensive leisure complex it is the ideal location to relax and unwind. Enjoy the shopping opportunities or visit the wealth of visitor and tourist attractions this city has to offer.

Bookable on www.irelandhotels.com

B&B from £30.00 to £50.00

*John & Fionnuala King
Proprietors*

Member of:
NIHF

🔢 7 7   ▢▢T▢C▢CMU♪♫P▢▢☆

B&B from £55.00 to £65.00

*Denis Orr
General Manager*

Activities:
🏊/🏌

Member of:
NIHF

Special Offer: Weekend Specials from £115.00 pps
(2 Nights B&B & 1 Dinner)

🔢 69 69   ☎▢▢☆T▢☜◻▢CM☼☆▢▢▢☆
♪P S▢▢▢☆ WiFi 🏃🚶

B&B from £65.00 to £80.00

*Michelle Barrett
General Manager*

Activities:
🏌

Member of:
NIHF

Special Offer: Weekend Specials from £109.00 pps
(2 Nights B&B & 1 Dinner)

🔢 112 112   ☎▢▢☆T▢CM☆☆▢▢▢U♪♫P
▢▢☆☆ 🏃🚶

Open All Year	Open All Year	Closed 25 December

B&B Rates are per Person Sharing per Night incl. Breakfast. or <u>Room Rates</u> are per Room per Night - See also Page 8

Narrows (The)	Portaferry Hotel	Customs House Country Inn

Narrows (The)

8 Shore Road,
Portaferry,
Co. Down BT22 1JY
Tel: 028-4272 8148 Fax: 028-4272 8105
Email: info@narrows.co.uk
Web: www.narrows.co.uk

GUESTHOUSE ★★★ MAP 15 Q 17

Since it opened in 1996, The Narrows has taken the Northern Ireland hospitality industry by storm. With numerous awards and reviews for its architecture, cuisine, accommodation, accessibility, conference facilities and wedding receptions, you will see why our guests keep coming back. Our 13 en suite rooms, restaurant and conference room all have stunning views of Strangford Lough. British Airways Tourism Award for Best Catering in Northern Ireland. Residents' bar and walled garden for your relaxation.

Member of Kingdoms of Down

B&B from £45.00 to £45.00

Gillian & Ian Killen
Proprietors

Member of:
NIHF

🛏🛎 ☎📞🖨📺🅣©CM☀♨✆🅟🅒🆔⛵ inet
13 13   🏇👩‍🦽

Closed 25 December

Portaferry Hotel

10 The Strand,
Portaferry,
Co. Down BT22 1PE
Tel: 028-4272 8231 Fax: 028-4272 8999
Email: info@portaferryhotel.com
Web: www.portaferryhotel.com

HOTEL ★★★ MAP 15 Q 17

Loughside hotel in spectacular setting. Award-winning cuisine and fine wines. Explore or simply relax and do nothing; just peace and tranquillity. BA Tourism Endeavour Award, RAC Restaurant of the Year Award, AA Rosette, Taste of Ulster, Good Hotel Guide. 29 miles from Belfast.

Member of Northern Ireland's Best Kept Secrets

B&B from £45.00 to £55.00

Shane & Lynne Braniff
Proprietors

Member of:
NIHF

Special Offer: Midweek Specials from £99.00 pps
(2 Nights B&B and 1 Dinner)

🛏🛎 ☎📞🖨📺🅣©✆CM✆🅟🅒🆔
14 14

Closed 23 - 26 December

Customs House Country Inn

25 - 27 Main Street,
Belcoo,
Co. Fermanagh
Tel: 028-6638 6285 Fax: 028-6638 6936
Email: info@customshouseinn.com
Web: www.customshouseinn.com

GUESTHOUSE ★★★★ MAP 11 J 16

Situated in the award-winning village of Belcoo, overlooking Lough McNean, is The Customs House Country Inn. A visit to the Customs House will not disappoint with luxurious accommodation, cuisine that excels and service that emphasises the personal atmosphere of this family-run inn. Marble Arch Caves, Belleek Pottery and Florencecourt House are close by. Ideal for golfing, walking, cycling and fishing. AA◆◆◆◆, RAC◆◆◆◆ and RAC Dining Award plus RAC Warm Welcome Award.

Bookable on www.irelandhotels.com

B&B from £30.00 to £40.00

John Roche
General Manager

Member of:
NIHF

Special Offer: Weekend Specials from £69.00 pps
(2 Nights B&B & 1 Dinner)

🛏🛎 ☎📞🖨📺🅣©CM♪🎵🅟🅢🆔
9 9

Closed 24 - 26 December

B&B Rates are per Person Sharing per Night incl. Breakfast.
or **Room Rates** are per Room per Night - See also Page 8

Co. Fermanagh

Belleek / Enniskillen / Irvinestown

Hotel Carlton	Killyhevlin Hotel	Mahons Hotel

Hotel Carlton

2 Main Street,
Belleek,
Co. Fermanagh BT93 3FX
Tel: 028-6865 8282 Fax: 028-6865 9005
Email: reception@hotelcarlton.co.uk
Web: www.hotelcarlton.co.uk

HOTEL ★★ MAP 13 I 17

Nestling on the shores of the River Erne at the heart of the Irish lake district in the picturesque village of Belleek. The Hotel Carlton, on the footsteps of the world famous Belleek Pottery, is ideally suited for those wishing to experience the perfect break. The Hotel Carlton boasts 35 luxurious well appointed bedrooms, some with views of the River Erne. "We offer nothing less than perfection". Facilities available for persons with special mobility requirements.

Bookable on www.irelandhotels.com
Member of Countrywide Hotels

B&B from £45.00 to £45.00

Angela & Sheamus Rooney

Member of:

Special Offer: Weekend Specials from £90.00 pps (2 Nights B&B & 1 Dinner)

35 35

Closed 24 - 25 December

Killyhevlin Hotel

Killyhevlin,
Enniskillen,
Co. Fermanagh BT74 6RW
Tel: 028-6632 3481 Fax: 028-6632 4726
Email: info@killyhevlin.com
Web: www.killyhevlin.com

HOTEL ★★★★ MAP 11 K 16

Killyhevlin Hotel and chalets are situated on the shores of scenic Lough Erne yet only 1km from the historic town of Enniskillen. All 70 spacious bedrooms and suites have been finished to an exceptional standard, broadband connection in each. Silks Restaurant and the Boathouse Grill offer a wide variety of menus daily. The fabulous new Health Club and Elemis Spa are complete with pool, gym, outdoor hot tub and four treatment Suites.

Bookable on www.irelandhotels.com
Member of Irish Country Hotels

B&B from £50.00 to £80.00

Rodney J. Watson Managing Director

Member of:

Special Offer: Midweek Specials from £99.00 pps (2 Nights B&B and 1 Dinner)

70 70

Closed 24 - 26 December

Mahons Hotel

Enniskillen Road,
Irvinestown,
Co. Fermanagh BT94 1GS
Tel: 028-6862 1656 Fax: 028-6862 8344
Email: info@mahonshotel.co.uk
Web: www.mahonshotel.co.uk

HOTEL U MAP 13 K 17

Situated in the heart of the Fermanagh Lakeland. Ideal for visiting all major tourist attractions: Belleek Pottery 20 mins, Marble Arch Caves 30 mins, Necarne Equestrian Centre 5 mins, Lough Erne 5 mins, Donegal 20 mins. All rooms en suite, TV, tea making facilities. Bushmills Bar of the Year winner, entertainment at weekends, private car park. Family-run from 1883. Visit us in our second century. Cycling, horse riding, tennis & golf all available. Hotel has under gone a major renovation for 2006 season and is awaiting re-grading by the tourist board. Bedrooms have modem access and DVD.

B&B from £35.00 to £45.00

Joe Mahon Manager

Member of:

Special Offer: Midweek Specials from £75.00 pps (3 Nights B&B)

18 18

Closed 24 - 25 December

B&B Rates are per Person Sharing per Night incl. Breakfast. or Room Rates are per Room per Night - See also Page 8

Tullylagan Country House Hotel

40b Tullylagan Road,
Cookstown,
Co. Tyrone BT80 8UP
Tel: 028-8676 5100 Fax: 028-8676 1715
Email: reservations@tullylagan.fsnet.co.uk
Web: www.tullylagan.co.uk

HOTEL ★★ MAP 14 M 18

This 19th century style manor is set in 30 acres of mature grounds and plantation, situated in the heart of Mid-Ulster. The rural setting lends itself to being the ideal place for a relaxing meal, short breaks, venue for a wedding or a business conference. This family-run hotel offers 15 en suite country style bedrooms. The hotel restaurant with its warm & relaxed atmosphere, offers high quality food and friendly service in gracious surroundings. A welcome addition to the estate is our newly opened wine bar. Certainly worth a visit!

Member of The Good Food Circle

B&B from £34.95 to £34.95

Adrian & Paul Martin
Proprietors

Member of:

Special Offer: Midweek Specials from £75.00 pps (2 Nights B&B & 1 Dinner)

15 15

Closed 24 - 26 December

Silverbirch Hotel

5 Gortin Road,
Omagh,
Co. Tyrone BT79 7DH
Tel: 028-8224 2520 Fax: 028-8224 9061
Email: info@silverbirchhotel.com
Web: www.silverbirchhotel.com

HOTEL ★★★ MAP 14 L 18

The hotel is situated on the outskirts of Omagh on the B48 leading to the Gortin Glens, Sperrins and the Ulster American Folk Park. Set in its own spacious and mature grounds, the hotel now has 46 new en suite bedrooms to 3*** standard. Other facilities include Buttery Grill open all day, newly refurbished dining room, function suite for 250 guests for weddings, dinners or conferences. Award-winning leisure centre 300 metres away.

B&B from £41.00 to £49.50

Allan Duncan
Manager

Member of:

Special Offer: Weekend Specials from £81.00 pps (2 Nights B&B & 1 Dinner)

46 46

Closed 25 December

<u>B&B Rates</u> are per Person Sharing per Night incl. Breakfast.
or <u>Room Rates</u> are per Room per Night - See also Page 8

Map of East Coast Region

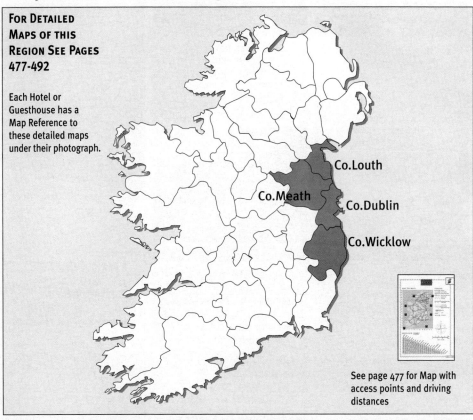

FOR DETAILED MAPS OF THIS REGION SEE PAGES 477-492

Each Hotel or Guesthouse has a Map Reference to these detailed maps under their photograph.

Co.Louth

Co.Meath

Co.Dublin

Co.Wicklow

See page 477 for Map with access points and driving distances

Locations listing

INCLUDES DETAILED MAPS & GREAT VALUE SPECIAL OFFERS.

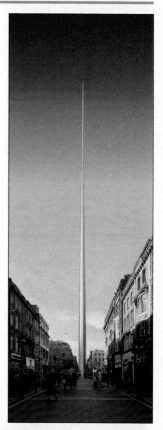

DUBL!N™

Welcome to Dublin, one of Europe's oldest capitals, with a charming mix of mediaeval, Georgian and modern architecture and a wealth of history and culture. There has never been a better time to visit!

Dublin has undergone major changes in recent times, but the new Dublin didn't replace the old, it just added to the mix. The legendary friendliness is still there. You can still find a quiet pub to while away a relaxing afternoon, stroll the classic Georgian streets, wander along the canals, or experience the refreshing peacefulness of Trinity College smack in the centre of the city. Dublin is a compact city, as sophisticated and stylish as our European neighbours, yet still intimate as a village and friendly as a pub.

Dublin offers spectacular scenery, a relaxed pace of life and a distinct cultural character, but the real appeal of Dublin is her people. Their courtesy, wit and hospitality will captivate you and draw you back year after year. Céad Míle Fáilte is not an empty slogan in Dublin, but is on the lips of everyone you will meet on your stay.

Dublin has something to suit everyone. The best way to see Dublin is to pick up a **"Dublin Pass"** giving you free entry to over 30 of Dublin's top attractions, free transfer with Aircoach from Dublin Airport to the city, and 25 Special Offers at restaurants, shops and transport, so saving you time and money! Buy online at www.dublinpass.com or pick up at one of the 5 tourist offices in Dublin. Other exciting events throughout the year include; March - St Patrick's Festival, June - The Docklands Maritime Festival, July - Celebration of Shaw's 150th Anniversary, August - Fáilte Ireland Horse Show.

Enjoy your stay!
www.visitdublin.com

Calendar of Events

April/May
Bray Jazz Festival, Bray, Co. Wicklow.

July
Carlsberg Arklow Seabreeze, Arklow, Co. Wicklow .

August
Wicklow Regatta, Wicklow Town.

September
Guinness All Ireland Final, Championship Final, Croke Park, Dublin.
Baileys Champion Stakes, Leopardstown, Dublin.

Event details correct at time of going to press.
enjoy Guinness sensibly.

Bracken Court Hotel

Bridge Street,
Balbriggan,
Co. Dublin
Tel: 01-841 3333 Fax: 01-841 5118
Email: info@brackencourt.ie
Web: www.brackencourt.ie

HOTEL ★★★ MAP 12 O 12

The Bracken Court Hotel is conveniently located in the seaside town of Balbriggan, 35 minutes north of Dublin City and 15 minutes from Dublin Airport making it an ideal location for access to the city, airport and as a gateway to the north. The 68 bedroom hotel provides luxurious surroundings where comfort and a wide range of facilities combine to satisfy the needs of both business and leisure guest. Ireland's Best Service Excellence Award 2002 & 2003.

Bookable on www.irelandhotels.com
Member of The Moriarty Group

B&B from €39.00 to €149.00

Luke Moriarty
Owner

Activities:
:/🍴

Member of:
IRISH HOTELS FEDERATION

Special Offer: Weekend Specials from €109.00 pps
(2 Nights B&B & 1 Dinner)

68 68 🖨 Inet

Open All Year

Radisson SAS St Helen's Hotel

Stillorgan Road,
Co. Dublin
Tel: 01-218 6000 Fax: 01-218 6010
Email: info.dublin@radissonsas.com
Web: www.radissonsas.com

HOTEL ★★★★★ MAP 8 O 11

Conveniently located just 3 miles from the city centre on the N11, the hotel has established itself as one of the finest hotels in the Irish capital. Facilities include 151 en suite rooms, 25 of which are suites. 11 conference rooms with natural daylight. A fitness centre, snooker room, ample free parking. The hotel is serviced by AirCoach. Dining options include our authentic Italian restaurant talavera, the Orangerie Bar and Ballroom Lounge. Free broadband to all residents.

Bookable on www.irelandhotels.com
Member of Radisson SAS Hotels & Resorts

Room Rate from €155.00 to €350.00

Neil Lane
General Manager

Activities:

Member of:

151 151  Inet WiFi

Open All Year

Stillorgan Park Hotel

Stillorgan Road,
Blackrock,
Co. Dublin
Tel: 01-288 1621 Fax: 01-283 1610
Email: sales@stillorganpark.com
Web: www.stillorganpark.com

HOTEL ★★★ MAP 8 O 11

Dublin's premier city hotel, located only 3 miles from St. Stephen's Green, easily accessible from M50 motorway and all main city arteries. Boasting 165 en suite, contemporary bedrooms, fully air-conditioned. Purpose built conference area catering for 2-600 delegates, traditional Irish bar with AA Rosette winning restaurant, Whitepebble Spa and guest gym. Complimentary shuttle service available, Aircoach airport transfer also available. Free 300 car parking spaces. AA★★★★ and RAC★★★★.

Bookable on www.irelandhotels.com
Member of Talbot Hotel Group

B&B from €60.00 to €110.00

Pat Kenny
General Manager

Activities:

Member of:

Special Offer: Weekend Specials from €135.00 pps
(2 Nights B&B & 1 Dinner)

165 165 🖨 Inet WiFi

Closed 25 - 26 December

B&B Rates are per Person Sharing per Night incl. Breakfast.
or **Room Rates** are per Room per Night - See also Page 8

Airport View

Cold Winters,
Blakes Cross,
Co. Dublin
Tel: 01-843 8756 Fax: 01-807 1949
Email: gerrybutterly@hotmail.com
Web: www.airportviewguesthouse.com

GUESTHOUSE ★★★ MAP 8 O 11

Newly built luxurious guesthouse 7 minutes from Dublin Airport on a 7 acre site, incorporates 4 poster bedroom with jacuzzi bath, DVD, TV, tea/coffee, fax and computer outlet facilities and large rooms. TV lounge, snooker room. Large car park, conference rooms. Winter's Restaurant with its excellent reputation for superb cuisine (fish and fillets speciality dishes). Conveniently located on R129 50yds off old main Dublin-Belfast road, now called R132. It has all the features of a luxury hotel. Airport View will become a hotel in 2006.

B&B from €49.50 to €55.00

Gerard Butterly / Annemarie Beggs
Proprietor
Activities:
🏌

Special Offer: *Weekend Specials from €125.00 pps (2 Nights B&B & 1 Dinner)*

🏠🍴 ☎📠🏧💳CM✳♨♫🅿️🅂🔒
10 10

🆔 📶 Inet

Closed 24 - 26 December

Waterside Hotel

Donabate,
Co. Dublin
Tel: 01-843 6153 Fax: 01-843 6111
Email: info@thewatersidehotel.com
Web: www.thewatersidehotel.com

HOTEL ★★★ MAP 12 O 12

The Waterside Hotel is situated on the beach in Donabate. Located just 10 minutes away from Dublin Airport and 11 miles from the city centre. The hotel is adorned by no less than 6 golf courses. The clubhouse bar combines comfort, atmosphere and breathtaking views of Howth and Lambay Island. There is an extensive bar menu available up to 6pm. Links Restaurant provides an Early Bird menu up to 7.30pm. Live music is provided in the bar during the summer months.

Bookable on www.irelandhotels.com

B&B from €50.00 to €120.00

Paula Baldwin
Proprietor
Activities:
☑🏌

Member of:
IRISH HOTELS FEDERATION

Special Offer: *Weekend Specials from €120.00 pps (2 Nights B&B & 1 Dinner)*

🏠📶 ☎📠🏧CM✳♨♫🅿️🅂🔒🆔
19 19   🐕

Closed 25 December

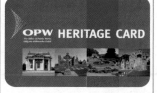
B&B Rates are per Person Sharing per Night incl. Breakfast.
or Room Rates are per Room per Night - See also Page 8

Airport Manor	Bewley's Hotel Dublin Airport	Carlton Dublin Airport Hotel

Airport Manor

Naul Road,
Knocksedan, Swords,
Co. Dublin
Tel: 01-840 1818 Fax: 01-870 0010
Email: info@airportmanor.com
Web: www.airportmanor.com

Bewley's Hotel Dublin Airport

Malahide Road,
Nr. Dublin Airport,
Dublin 17
Tel: 01-871 1000 Fax: 01-871 1001
Email: dub@bewleyshotels.com
Web: www.bewleyshotels.com

Carlton Dublin Airport Hotel

Old Airport Road,
Cloghran,
Co. Dublin
Tel: 01-866 7500

Web: www.carlton.ie

UNDER CONSTRUCTION - OPENING APRIL 2006

UNDER CONSTRUCTION - OPENING APRIL 2006

GUESTHOUSE ★★★★ MAP 12 O 12

HOTEL P MAP 12 O 12

HOTEL P MAP 12 O 11

Airport Manor combines the warmth of an Irish welcome with the luxury of private and convenient accommodation. The perfect location to enjoy the peace and tranquillity of the countryside, yet only 5 minutes from Dublin Airport, 20 minutes from city centre and easily accessible from all major routes. Whether you are arriving or departing from Dublin Airport, Airport Manor is the ideal overnight accommodation.

Welcome to a comfortable new hotel, ideally located near the airport just off the M1/M50 interchange. Offering 467 contemporary soundproofed rooms and built with the latest technology, all rooms offer high-speed internet. Our Brasserie and Lounge offer a wide range of dining options throughout the day, and meetings are well catered for, with 17 highly specified executive boardrooms. Real-time online reservations and availability at www.bewleyshotels.com

Situated on the perimeter of Dublin Airport this modern designed property is built to 4**** standards and will open in April 2006. Just 5 minutes from the airport terminal, the hotel comprises of 100 rooms, 24 conference and banqueting suites for up to 450 delegates and the Carlton Signature Rooftop Restaurant. Complimentary free car parking and airport courtesy coach are also available to our customers. If convenience and proximity to Dublin Airport is a requirement then the Carlton Dublin Airport Hotel is an ideal choice.

Bookable on www.irelandhotels.com

Member of Carlton Hotel Group

B&B from €50.00 to €85.00

Room Rate from €89.00 to €89.00

Room Rate from €110.00 to €280.00

Michelle Lynch
Manager

Member of:
IRISH HOTELS FEDERATION

The Team at
Bewley's Hotel Dublin Airport

John Varley
Director of Operations

Activities:

17 17

467 467

100 100

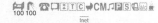

Closed 24 December - 02 January

Closed 24 - 26 December

Closed 24 - 27 December

B&B Rates are per Person Sharing per Night incl. Breakfast. or **Room Rates** are per Room per Night - See also Page 8

Clarion Hotel Dublin Airport

Dublin Airport,
Co. Dublin

Tel: 01-808 0500 Fax: 01-844 6002
Email: reservations@clarionhoteldublinairport.com
Web: www.clarionhoteldublinairport.com

HOTEL ★★★★ MAP 12 O 11

Modern 4**** hotel on the airport complex offering standard and executive accommodation. All rooms are air-conditioned and offer tea/coffee making facilities, mini-bar, trouser press, hairdryer, TV and pay movies. 24hr courtesy coach to/from airport. Superb choice of dining options including The Bistro Restaurant, Sampans Oriental Restaurant, Café Express Lounge and 24hr room service. Residents have complimentary access to ALSAA Leisure Centre, swimming pool, gym & sauna.

Member of Choice International Hotels

Room Rate from €120.00 to €250.00

Janet Richardson
General Manager

Activities:

Member of:

247 247

Closed 24 - 25 December

Crowne Plaza, Dublin Airport

Northwood Park,
Santry Demesne,
(Nr Dublin Airport), Dublin 9
Tel: 01-862 8888 Fax: 01-862 8800
Email: info@crowneplazadublin.ie
Web: www.cpdublin-airport.com

HOTEL ★★★★ MAP 8 O 11

A luxurious haven set in a mature and tranquil parkland, located 5 minutes from Dublin Airport and 15 minutes from the city centre. The hotel boasts 204 superb 4**** standard unique guest rooms and suites, with exceptional facilities for both business and leisure. There are 12 state of the art conference rooms along with a coffee lounge, restaurant and bar. Complimentary car parking and airport courtesy coach are also available. A new 1,000 seater conference and event centre will be available from summer 2006.

Bookable on www.irelandhotels.com
Member of Intercontinental Hotel Group

Room Rate from €110.00 to €390.00

Mary Buckley
General Manager

Activities:

Member of:

204 204

Closed 24 - 25 December

Glenmore House

Airport Road,
Nevinstown, Swords,
Co. Dublin
Tel: 01-840 3610 Fax: 01-840 4148
Email: rebeccagibney@eircom.net
Web: www.glenmorehouse.com

GUESTHOUSE ★★★ MAP 12 O 12

Ideally situated just 1km from Dublin Airport and 20 minutes from the city centre, on the main airport/city bus routes, Glenmore House is a spacious family-run guesthouse set in 2 acres of gardens, lawns and private secure carparks. All rooms are beautifully decorated with bathroom, phone, TV, tea/coffee facilities and hairdryer. The warmest of welcomes at a very reasonable cost for business and leisure alike. Pick up service available from the airport at certain times of day.

B&B from €45.00 to €69.50

Rebecca Gibney
Proprietor

Member of:

Special Offer: Weekend Specials from €127.50 pps
(2 Nights B&B & 1 Dinner)

30 30

Closed 24 - 25 December

<u>B&B Rates</u> are per Person Sharing per Night incl. Breakfast.
or <u>Room Rates</u> are per Room per Night - See also Page 8

Co. Dublin

Dublin Airport / Dublin City

Great Southern Hotel	Hilton Dublin Airport	Abberley Court Hotel
Dublin Airport, Co. Dublin	Northern Cross, Near Dublin Airport, Malahide Road, Dublin 17	Belgard Road, Tallaght, Dublin 24
Tel: 01-844 6000 Fax: 01-844 6001	Tel: 01-866 1800 Fax: 01-866 1866	Tel: 01-459 6000 Fax: 01-462 1000
Email: res@dubairport-gsh.com	Email: dublin.airport@hilton.com	Email: abberley@iol.ie
Web: www.greatsouthernhotels.com	Web: www.hilton.co.uk/dublinairport	Web: www.abberley.ie

HOTEL ★★★★ MAP 12 O 11   **HOTEL P MAP 12 O 12**   **HOTEL ★★★ MAP 8 O 11**

Situated within the airport complex, just two minutes from the main terminal, the Great Southern Hotel provides a tranquil haven for the busy traveller. The guest rooms have every convenience and allow guests unwind in stylish surroundings. The hotel has a wide range of conference rooms. Bookable worldwide through Utell International or Central Reservations on 01-214 4800.

A brand new Hilton Hotel, 5 minutes from Dublin Airport near where the M50 and M1 meet, making this one of the most accessible hotels in Ireland, whether you are travelling from the North, South or West of Ireland or flying into Dublin Airport. A hotel designed to provide a fantastic destination for people on business or pleasure, conferencing or attending a meeting, celebrating or preparing to fly.

This hotel is situated in the town centre of Tallaght, being only 5 minutes from the M50 motorway. The hotel is easily accessible from Dublin Airport, Dublin City Centre and Dublin Ferry Port. The hotel is within minutes walking distance of hundreds of shops, super-stores, cinemas, restaurants, pubs and nightclubs.The facilities include 40 en suite rooms, Kilcawleys contemporary style lounge, The Library traditional style lounge, The Leaf Chinese Restaurant and private car parking. Only 2 minute walk from LUAS (Dublin light rail) stop.

Bookable on www.irelandhotels.com   *Bookable on www.irelandhotels.com*
Member of Hilton Hotels

Bookable on www.irelandhotels.com

Room Rate from €99.00 to €270.00   **Room Rate from €120.00 to €320.00**   **B&B from €35.00 to €72.00**

Fergal O'Connell
General Manager

Friedrich Schaefer
Area General Manager Ireland

Karen Garry & Mairead Slye

Activities:

Activities:

Member of:

Member of:

Special Offer: Weekend Specials from €129.50 pps
(2 Nights B&B & 1 Dinner)

Special Offer: Weekend Specials from €89.00 pps
(2 Nights B&B & 1 Dinner)

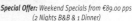
229 229

166 166

40 40

Closed 24 - 26 December	**Open All Year**	**Closed 24 - 27 December**

B&B Rates are per Person Sharing per Night incl. Breakfast. or Room Rates are per Room per Night - See also Page 8

Abbey Hotel

52 Middle Abbey Street,
Dublin 1

Tel: 01-872 8188 Fax: 01-872 8585
Email: reservations@abbey-hotel.com
Web: www.abbey-hotel.com

HOTEL ★★ MAP 8 O 11

Small, intimate hotel in the heart of
Dublin city centre. It is close to all main
shopping areas and night life. The
stylish rooms are decorated to a high
standard. The hotel offers a full à la
carte menu daily to 9pm. Only minutes
walk from O'Connell Street and Temple
Bar. Facilities include TV, telephone, car
park, bar, restaurant, entertainment and
lift. 21 rooms all en suite.

Bookable on www.irelandhotels.com

B&B from €45.00 to €125.00

Sheila O'Riordan
General Manager

Member of:

I R I S H
HOTELS
FEDERATION

🛏🚶 ☎🖥📺🅣©CM♫🅟🅢📶 aid 🐾 Inet
21 21   🐕

Closed 24 - 26 December

B&B Rates are per Person Sharing per Night incl. Breakfast.
or Room Rates are per Room per Night - See also Page 8

Sightseeing tours
Dublin

Dublin Bus Tours ☘

CityTour ☘
Hop on-Hop off

The complete tour lasts 1 hour 15 minutes, but your 24 hour ticket
will allow you to hop on and off, as often as you wish. Most of the city's
major attractions can be reached on the tour and buses operate frequently
throughout the day. There are 21 stops conveniently located and all display
the distinctive green and cream open-top bus sign. To enhance your
enjoyment we have arranged discounts for you at a selection of the most
popular attractions en route. Tour operates daily.

TICKET VALID 24 HOURS **24**

North Coast + Castle ☘

The Tour takes in Dublin's northern coastline, before visiting the stately
Malahide Castle, and then crossing the summit of Howth Head with
panoramic views of Dublin Bay. Tour operates daily.
Admission to Malahide Castle is included.

South Coast + Gardens ☘

Passing through Dun Laoghaire, and Bray the tour climbs into the beautiful
Wicklow Mountains and the enchanting old-world village of Enniskerry to
Powerscourt Estate in its spectacular mountain setting. Tour operates daily.
Admission to Powercourt is included.

Buy your ticket at
59 Upr. O'Connell Street, Dublin 1.
Tel. 8734222 9am to 7pm Mon - Sat

Dublin Bus ☘
www.dublinbus.ie

Co. Dublin
Dublin City

Abbott Lodge

87/88 Lower Gardiner Street,
Dublin 1

Tel: 01-836 5548 Fax: 01-836 5549
Email: abbottlodge@eircom.net
Web: www.abbottlodge.com

GUESTHOUSE P MAP 8 O 11

Abbott Lodge is a warm and friendly-run, refurbished Georgian guesthouse situated in the heart of Dublin city. Located on the main bus route from Dublin Airport and close to all major tourist attractions, Temple Bar, shopping areas and nightlife. An excellent base for touring our wonderful city. All 29 guest rooms have en suite bathrooms, TV and tea/coffee making facilities. Our helpful staff at reception, which is open 24 hours, will be glad to help with tours, restaurant and theatre reservations. You can book online at www.abbottlodge.com.

B&B from €30.00 to €55.00

Patrick Healy
Reservations

29 29 🛏️🚭🅿️©️

Closed 23 - 28 December

Aberdeen Lodge

53 Park Avenue,
Off Ailesbury Road, Ballsbridge,
Dublin 4

Tel: 01-283 8155 Fax: 01-283 7877
Email: aberdeen@iol.ie
Web: www.halpinsprivatehotels.com

GUESTHOUSE ★★★★ MAP 8 O 11

Award-winning, 4****, a luxurious combination of Edwardian grace, fine food, modern comforts, all that one expects of a private hotel, aircon suites with jacuzzi, executive facilities, landscaped gardens and guest car park. Close to city centre, airport and car ferry terminals by DART or bus. Accolades - RAC, AA, Best Loved Hotels, Green Book, Johansens. Sister property of Merrion Hall, Blakes and Halpins Hotel.
USA toll free 1800 617 3178.
Global free phone +800 1283 8155.
Direct Dial 353 1 283 8155.

Bookable on www.irelandhotels.com
Member of Bridgestone 100 Best Places to Stay

B&B from €59.00 to €99.00

Pat Halpin
Proprietor

Activities:

✓

Member of:
IRISH HOTELS FEDERATION

20 20 🛏️🚭📞🖥️T C CM❄️📷 J P S 🔒📺
Inet WiFi

Open All Year

Abrae Court

9 Zion Road,
Rathgar,
Dublin 6

Tel: 01-492 2242 Fax: 01-492 3944
Email: abrae@eircom.net
Web: www.longfields.ie/abrae

GUESTHOUSE ★★★ MAP 8 O 11

Built in 1864, family-run, 3*** Victorian guesthouse is located in the prestigious residential area of Rathgar, just ten minutes from the heart of Dublin City. Guest rooms are furnished with en suite bathroom, colour TV, direct dial phone and coffee/tea making facilities. Laundry service and a lock up car park are available. Bus routes, a good selection of restaurants, pubs, tourist attractions and various sports. We are "Kosher Friendly".

Bookable on www.irelandhotels.com

B&B from €49.50 to €54.00

Alina Ignat
Manageress

Member of:
IRISH HOTELS FEDERATION

Special Offer: Midweek Specials from €135.00 pps (3 Nights B&B)

18 18 🛏️🚭📞T C U P S 📺

Open All Year

B&B Rates are per Person Sharing per Night incl. Breakfast. or **Room Rates** are per Room per Night - See also Page 8

Adams Trinity Hotel

28 Dame Street,
Dublin 2

Tel: 01-670 7100 Fax: 01-670 7101
Email: reservations@adamstrinityhotel.com
Web: www.adamstrinityhoteldublin.com

HOTEL ★★★ MAP 8 O 11

What better location in Dublin than the Adams Trinity Hotel? Located mid-way between Dublin Castle, Grafton Street and Trinity College; it faces the vibrant Temple Bar area. Traditional style bedrooms are finished to an exceptionally luxurious standard. The hotel features the Mercantile Bar and Restaurant, O'Brien's Traditional Bar and café style Brokers Bar. The Adams Trinity Hotel offers all guests that same personal attention and warmth, it has that little something special. Special rates apply from Sunday - Thursday.

B&B from €60.00 to €127.00

Fran Ryder / Peter Hanahoe
Proprietors

Member of:
IRISH
HOTELS
FEDERATION

Special Offer: *Weekend Specials from €149.00 pps*
(2 Nights B&B & 1 Dinner)
28 28

Closed 24 - 27 December

JAMESON
IRISH WHISKEY

The Old Jameson Distillery, Dublin

Discover for yourself how Jameson became the world's favourite Irish Whiskey!

Guided tours:
9.30 a.m. – 6.00 p.m.
(last tour at 5.30 p.m.)
Open 7 days

Also at the Distillery

"The Still Room Restaurant":
Serving light lunches and the most memorable of Irish Coffees!

"1780" Public Bar
The perfect spot to enjoy an afternoon or evening of easy relaxation with friends.
(Lunch served 12.00 p.m. – 2.30 p.m.)

Jameson Gift & Whiskey Shop

The Old Jameson Distillery,
Bow Street,
Smithfield,
Dublin 7
E: reservations@ojd.ie
www.jamesondistillery.ie

Uncover the secret to Jameson's smoothness!

B&B Rates are per Person Sharing per Night incl. Breakfast.
or **Room Rates** are per Room per Night - See also Page 8

Dublin City

Aishling House

19/20 St. Lawrence Road,
Clontarf,
Dublin 3
Tel: 01-833 9097 Fax: 01-833 8400
Email: info@aishlinghouse.com
Web: www.aishlinghouse.com

GUESTHOUSE ★★★ MAP 8 O 11

Elegant listed family-run Victorian residence, situated in Clontarf, north Dublin's most exclusive suburb. Ideally located only minutes drive from Point Theatre, city centre and Dublin Port, yet only 15 minutes from airport. Numerous golf courses nearby and short walk to leisure complex. Tranquil elegant lounge, half acre grounds, child's play area, car park, fax facilities. We offer superb luxury accommodation at affordable prices. A treasure of outstanding quality.

Bookable on www.irelandhotels.com

B&B from €40.00 to €55.00

Frances & Robert English
Owners

Member of:
IRISH HOTELS FEDERATION

Special Offer: Midweek Specials from €135.00 pps
(3 Nights B&B)

🛏 🛱 ☎ 🖵 T ⬟ © C M ❖ 🅙 P 🔲
9   9

Closed 21 December - 06 January

Alexander Hotel O'Callaghan

At Merrion Square,
Dublin 2
Tel: 01-607 3700 Fax: 01-661 5663
Email: info@ocallaghanhotels.com
Web: www.ocallaghanhotels.com

HOTEL ★★★★ MAP 8 O 11

Contemporary spacious de luxe hotel, ideally located in Dublin City centre beside Merrion Square within minutes walk of Trinity College and the main business and shopping districts. A strong E-business hotel, the O'Callaghan Alexander is fully installed with wired and wireless broadband. 102 air-conditioned bedrooms, gymnasium, state of the art conference facilities, parking and newly refurbished Caravaggio's Restaurant and Winner's Bar. USA toll free reservations 1800 569 9983 or on line at www.ocallaghanhotels.com

Bookable on www.irelandhotels.com
Member of O'Callaghan Hotels

B&B from €87.50 to €189.00

Declan Fitzgerald
General Manager

Activities:

Member of:
IRISH HOTELS FEDERATION

🛏 🛱 ☎ 🖵 ⬟ T ↝ C M 🔆 P 🔲 🆎 inet WiFi
102 102

Closed 24 - 30 December

An Glen Guesthouse

84 Lower Gardiner Street,
Dublin 1
Tel: 01-855 1374 Fax: 01-855 2506
Email: theglen@eircom.net
Web: www.theglenguesthouse.com

GUESTHOUSE ★★ MAP 8 O 11

The Glen is a beautifully restored and maintained guesthouse. Located in the heart of Dublin City, adjacent to shops, theatres, cinemas, galleries, museums and Dublin's famous night spots. Close to bus and train stations en route to airport. Rooms en suite, TV, direct dial phones, tea and coffee facilities in all rooms.

Bookable on www.irelandhotels.com

B&B from €23.00 to €52.00

John Murray
Manager

Member of:
IRISH HOTELS FEDERATION

🛏 🛱 ☎ 🖵 T © C 🥄 📺 🔲
15 15

Open All Year

B&B Rates are per Person Sharing per Night incl. Breakfast. or **Room Rates** are per Room per Night - See also Page 8

This should cover it Madam!

... accepted by over 30 of Dublin's top visitor attractions!

The Dublin Pass, giving you the best value from the very best of Dublin, with free entry to over 30 of Dublin's top visitor attractions, 25 special offers, free 84-page guidebook, airport transfer to the city centre and much more. Check out our website for full range of the savings available.

www.dublinpass.ie

The Dublin Pass is available on-line or from Dublin Tourism's tourist information offices.

B&B Rates are per Person Sharing per Night incl. Breakfast.
or Room Rates are per Room per Night - See also Page 8

Dublin & East Coast   257

Anglesea Town House

63 Anglesea Road,
Ballsbridge,
Dublin 4
Tel: 01-668 3877 Fax: 01-668 3461

GUESTHOUSE ★★★★ MAP 8 0 11

This is a world-renowned guesthouse of national breakfast award fame. It has been featured on TV in both Ireland and the UK and has won entry in British, Irish, European and American travel guides and journals. It is a fine Edwardian residence of 7 en suite rooms with phone and TV, offering quiet elegance to discerning guests who wish to combine country-style charm with convenience to town. A warm welcome awaits you from your hostess Helen Kirrane and her family.

B&B from €65.00 to €70.00

Helen Kirrane
Owner

🏨 🐾 ☎ 🖥 🇹🇨 ♦ ❄ 🅿
7 7

Closed 22 December - 06 January

Ardagh House

No.1 Highfield Road,
Rathgar,
Dublin 6
Tel: 01-497 7068 Fax: 01-497 3991
Email: enquiries@ardagh-house.ie
Web: www.ardagh-house.ie

GUESTHOUSE ★★★ MAP 8 0 11

Having been recently totally refurbished, Ardagh House is conveniently situated in a premier residential area. This imposing turn of the century premises contains many of the gracious and spacious features of a fine detached residence of that era and yet incorporating modern creature comforts. Within easy distance of the city centre, RDS, etc. This fine property stands on approximately 1/2 acre with ample off street car parking and good gardens.

Bookable on www.irelandhotels.com

B&B from €40.00 to €70.00

Willie & Mary Doyle
Proprietors

Member of:

🏨 🐾 ☎ 🖥 🇹🇨 ♦ 🚗 🅿
19 19

Closed 23 December - 03 Janunary

Ardmore Hotel

Tolka Valley,
Dublin 11

Tel: 01-864 8300 Fax: 01-864 8311
Email: reservations@ardmore-hotel.com
Web: www.ardmore-hotel.com

HOTEL P MAP 8 0 11

The Ardmore Hotel is a new, purpose built hotel situated 10 minutes from both Dublin Airport and Dublin City centre. This contemporary styled hotel offers 96 superbly appointed rooms which include iron and ironing board, tea and coffee facilities, flat screen cable television, DD telephone and high speed internet access. We also provide excellent conference facilities including state of the art audiovisual equipment. Secure private parking is also available. A spacious bar and international restaurant makes this the perfect hotel for both business and pleasure..

Member of Cara Hotels

Room Rate from €69.00 to €199.00

Patrick Lernihan
General Manager

🏨 🐾 ☎ 🖥 🇹🇨 🚗 CM ♫ 🅿 📶 alc 🔌 Inet
96 96   WiFi 🐕

Closed 24 - 27 December

B&B Rates are per Person Sharing per Night incl. Breakfast. or **Room Rates** are per Room per Night - See also Page 8

Ariel House

50 - 54 Lansdowne Road,
Ballsbridge,
Dublin 4
Tel: 01-668 5512 Fax: 01-668 5845
Email: reservations@ariel-house.net
Web: www.ariel-house.net

GUESTHOUSE ★★★★ MAP 8 O 11

In the heart of Dublin's embassy belt, just a stone's throw from the city centre lies Ariel House. Ideally located for a visit to Dublin, Ariel House boasts 37 magnificent bedrooms and a true Victorian drawing room. Return to a life in the 1850s and make Ariel House your stylish residence in Ballsbridge.

Bookable on www.irelandhotels.com

B&B from €29.50 to €90.00

Deirdre McDonald
Manager

*Special Offer: Weekend Specials from €99.00 pps
(2 Nights B&B & 1 Dinner)*

37 37 ⌂ ♨ ☎ ⛶ Ⓣ Ⓒ ✦❄Ⓟ Ⓨ 🖩 inet

Closed 23 - 28 December

Arlington Hotel

23/25 Bachelors Walk,
O'Connell Bridge,
Dublin 1
Tel: 01-804 9100 Fax: 01-804 9152
Email: info@arlington.ie
Web: www.arlington.ie

HOTEL ★★★ MAP 8 O 11

The most central hotel in Dublin, overlooking the River Liffey at O'Connell Bridge. Dublin's top attractions and shopping districts on your doorstep. 116 en suite bedrooms, free underground parking, meeting room. Magnificent mediaeval Knightsbridge Bar with live Irish music and dancing 7 nights a week all year round (free admission). Carvery lunch and à la carte bar menu available, candle-lit Knights Bistro. Perfect base for business or pleasure.

Bookable on www.irelandhotels.com

B&B from €65.00 to €120.00

Pat Geoghegan
Operations Manager

Member of:

*Special Offer: Midweek Specials from €160.00 pps
(3 Nights B&B)*

116 116 ⌂ ♨ ☎ ⛶ Ⓣ Ⓒ ⒸⓂ 🎜 Ⓟ Ⓢ 🜨 🖩

Closed 24 - 26 December

B&B Rates are per Person Sharing per Night incl. Breakfast.
or **Room Rates** are per Room per Night - See also Page 8

Dublin City

Ashling Hotel	Aston Hotel	Beacon Hotel

Ashling Hotel

Parkgate Street,
Dublin 8

Tel: 01-677 2324 Fax: 01-679 3783
Email: info@ashlinghotel.ie
Web: www.ashlinghotel.ie

HOTEL ★★★ MAP 8 O 11

A spacious hotel in a superb location, the Ashling provides excellent access to Dublin City centre and the rest of Ireland. Modern en suite bedrooms, conference/meeting rooms, free car/coach parking. 20 minutes walk to city centre/Temple Bar, or by bus, taxi or Dublin's new tram system, the LUAS. Adjacent to intercity rail station Heuston, Guinness Brewery, Phoenix Park and more. Easy access to the M50 motorway and all major routes. Direct "Airlink" bus from Dublin Airport to Heuston Station.

Bookable on www.irelandhotels.com
Member of Best Western Hotels

B&B from €54.00 to €130.00

Alan Moody
General Manager

Activities:

Member of:

Special Offer: Midweek Specials from €147.00 pps (3 Nights B&B)

150 150

Closed 23 - 26 December

Aston Hotel

7/9 Aston Quay,
Dublin 2

Tel: 01-677 9300 Fax: 01-677 9007
Email: stay@aston-hotel.com
Web: www.aston-hotel.com

HOTEL U MAP 8 O 11

A warm welcome awaits you at the Aston Hotel, located in Temple Bar and overlooking the River Liffey. Friendly staff and pleasant surroundings will make your stay a memorable one. All our 27 rooms are en suite and offer every guest comfort including direct dial phone, colour TV, hairdryer and tea/coffee making facilities. A leisurely stroll from the Aston brings you to all Dublin's top attractions and amenities and makes it an ideal base for exploring the capital.

Bookable on www.irelandhotels.com

Room Rate from €70.00 to €240.00

Ann Walsh
Manager

Member of:

27 27

Closed 24 - 26 December

Beacon Hotel

Beacon Court,
Sandyford,
Dublin 18

Tel: 01-291 5000 Fax: 01-291 5005
Email: reservations@thebeacon.com
Web: www.thebeacon.com

HOTEL N MAP 8 O 11

The Beacon is an exciting mix of all that is special about a Design Hotel. Cool clean lines, white interior spaces, magnificent glass chandeliers, specially commissioned art pieces and a four poster design bed in the lobby. Situated on the corner of the M50 and the link road to Dundrum, it is only a short walk from the LUAS. The Beacon includes 5 meeting rooms, a contemporary bar "Crystal Bar" and an Asian Pacific restaurant "My Thai".

Member of Fitzpatricks

Room Rate from €120.00 to €220.00

Sandra Doyle
General Manager

Member of:

82 82

Closed 24 - 26 December

B&B Rates are per Person Sharing per Night incl. Breakfast. or **Room Rates** are per Room per Night - See also Page 8

Belgrave House

8-9 Belgrave Square,
Rathmines,
Dublin 6
Tel: 01-496 3760 Fax: 01-497 9243
Email: info@belgraveguesthouse.com
Web: www.belgraveguesthouse.com

GUESTHOUSE P MAP 8 O 11

Luxury, elegance and style are the
distinguishing qualities of this recently
renovated guesthouse. Enjoy the peace
and tranquillity of overlooking a mature
square and our extensive garden to the
rear. Belgrave House provides the
perfect retreat for business and
pleasure. Situated a 5 minute tram ride
from city centre, we are convenient to
the Point, RDS and Lansdowne Road.

B&B from €40.00 to €100.00

*Paul & Mary O'Reilly
Proprietors*

*Special Offer: Midweek Specials from €50.00 pps
(3 Nights B&B)*

14 14

Closed 22 December - 02 January

Beresford Hall

2 Beresford Place,
Dublin 1
Tel: 01-801 4500 Fax: 01-801 4501
Email: stay@beresfordhall.ie
Web: www.beresfordhall.ie

GUESTHOUSE ★★★★ MAP 8 O 11

Beresford Hall is a city centre, Gandon
designed, listed Georgian townhouse
overlooking the historic Customs
House, adjacent to the financial
services centre and close to the Point
Depot, Temple Bar, shopping districts
and cultural attractions. Enjoy both the
elegance and charm of this
authentically restored townhouse with
splendidly decorated spacious rooms.
We offer a friendly and premier guest
service to ensure a memorable
experience.

B&B from €60.00 to €80.00

*Collette Scheer
Manager*

Member of:

HOTELS
FEDERATION

16 16

Closed 23 December - 03 January

CUSTOM HOUSE
Visitor Centre

An exhibition on the
history of the building
which is over 200 years old
and has been heavily
involved in the social and
political history of the city.

Custom House Quay,
Dublin 1
Telephone: 01 8882538

OPEN
MID-MARCH TO OCTOBER
Monday to Friday
10am to 12.30pm.
Saturday Sunday and Bank
Holidays 2pm – 5pm.

NOVEMBER TO MID-MARCH
Wednesday to Friday
10am to 12.30pm.
Sunday 2pm to 5pm.

PRICE
**Individual €1.00,
Family €3.00,
Groups €0.50 each,
Students Free.**

B&B Rates are per Person Sharing per Night incl. Breakfast.
or Room Rates are per Room per Night - See also Page 8

Dublin City

Berkeley Court (The)

Lansdowne Road,
Ballsbridge,
Dublin 4
Tel: 01-665 3200 Fax: 01-661 7238
Email: berkeleycourt@jurysdoyle.com
Web: www.jurysdoyle.com

HOTEL ★★★★★ MAP 8 O 11

The Berkeley Court is a premium hotel, offering discreet and personal service in intimate and warm surroundings. Part of the fabric of life, business and success in the locality, contemporary Ireland comes here for the Berkeley Court's brand of personal service and discreet but active networking, business, entertainment and meeting facilities. Set on its own grounds, behind a stand of fine trees, in the prestigious Georgian location of Ballsbridge, the city centre is a leisurely short walk or a 5 minute drive away.

Bookable on www.irelandhotels.com
Member of Jurys Doyle Hotel Group

B&B from €102.00 to €266.00

Geraldine Dolan
General Manager

Member of:

188 188

Inet

Open All Year

Best Western Academy Hotel

Findlater Place,
Off O'Connell Street,
Dublin 1
Tel: 01-878 0666 Fax: 01-878 0600
Email: stay@academyhotel.ie
Web: www.academyhotel.ie

HOTEL ★★★ MAP 8 O 11

The natural choice for the discerning visitor to Dublin, we offer the ultimate in comfort and convenience. Located off the city's main thoroughfare, O'Connell Street, only a short stroll from the very best of international shopping, galleries, theatres and the cosmopolitan area of Temple Bar. Our beautifully appointed en suite, air-conditioned rooms represent the perfect retreat after a demanding meeting or a hectic day of shopping or sightseeing. Bar, restaurant, conference facilities, and free wireless internet access.

Bookable on www.irelandhotels.com
Member of Best Western Hotels

B&B from €49.00 to €89.00

Peter Collins
Manager

Activities:

Member of:

Special Offer: Midweek Specials from €149.00 pps
(3 Nights B&B)

98 98

Closed 24 - 27 December

Bewley's Hotel Ballsbridge

Merrion Road,
Ballsbridge,
Dublin 4
Tel: 01-668 1111 Fax: 01-668 1999
Email: bb@BewleysHotels.com
Web: www.BewleysHotels.com

HOTEL ★★★ MAP 8 O 11

Bewley's Hotel, Ballsbridge is situated next to the RDS and minutes away from the attractions of the city centre. Accommodating you in style with 304 de luxe bedrooms and 9 well-equipped meeting rooms. Award-winning O'Connell's Restaurant offers a wide range of wonderful dining options. Bewley's Hotel provides a setting that is contemporary, relaxed and informal, at a fixed room rate - Every Room Every Night. The hotel is serviced by Aircoach. Real time on line reservations and availability at www.BewleysHotels.com

Room Rate from €99.00 to €99.00

Carol Burke
General Manager

Member of:

304 304

WiFi

Closed 24 - 26 December

B&B Rates are per Person Sharing per Night incl. Breakfast. or **Room Rates** are per Room per Night - See also Page 8

Bewley's Hotel Leopardstown

Central Park,
Leopardstown Road,
Leopardstown, Dublin 18
Tel: 01-293 5000 Fax: 01-293 5099
Email: Leop@bewleyshotels.com
Web: www.bewleyshotels.com

HOTEL ★★★ MAP 8 O 11

A contemporary, relaxed and informal hotel, located just off the M50 and N11 and close to several corporate and business parks. Leopardstown racecourse and the LUAS tram station are a short walk away, while Aircoach links the hotel with the airport. Our Brasserie and Lounge allow a choice of flexible dining options throughout the day. Free high speed internet is provided in all rooms. Real-time online reservations and availability at www.bewleyshotels.com

Bewley's Hotel Newlands Cross

Newlands Cross,
Naas Road (N7),
Dublin 22
Tel: 01-464 0140 Fax: 01-464 0900
Email: res@bewleyshotels.com
Web: www.bewleyshotels.com

HOTEL ★★★ MAP 8 O 11

A unique blend of quality, value and flexibility for independent discerning guests. Located just off the N7, minutes from the M50, Dublin Airport and the city centre. Our large spacious family size rooms are fully equipped with all modern amenities. The Brasserie offers you a range of dining options, from traditional Irish breakfast to full table service à la carte. Real time on line reservations and availability at www.bewleyshotels.com

Room Rate from €89.00 to €89.00

Clio O'Gara
Brand Manager

Room Rate from €89.00 to €89.00

Jennie Hussey
General Manager

Member of:

352 352

258 258

Closed 24 - 25 December

Closed 24 - 26 December

B&B Rates are per Person Sharing per Night incl. Breakfast.
or Room Rates are per Room per Night - See also Page 8

DUBLIN'S CITY HALL
The Story *of the* Capital

Multi-media exhibition tracing the history of Dublin. A story of change, highlighting major events that have influenced the growth of the city and civic governance over the past 1,000 years, creating the Dublin we know today.

Admission Times
Monday/Saturday 10am to 5.15pm. Sunday 2.00pm to 5.00pm

Further Information
City Hall Exhibition, City Hall, Dame Street, Dublin 2.
Tel +353 1 222 2204
Fax +353 1 222 2620
Email cityhall@dublincity.ie
www.dublincity.ie

Dublin City Council
Comhairle Cathrach Bhaile Átha Cliath

Blooms Hotel	Brooks Hotel	Burlington (The)

| 6 Anglesea Street,
Temple Bar,
Dublin 2

Tel: 01·671 5622 Fax: 01·671 5997
Email: info@blooms.ie
Web: www.blooms.ie | Drury Street,
Dublin 2

Tel: 01·670 4000 Fax: 01·670 4455
Email: reservations@brookshotel.ie
Web: www.sinnotthotels.com | Upper Leeson Street,
Dublin 4

Tel: 01·660 5222 Fax: 01·660 8496
Email: burlington@jurysdoyle.com
Web: www.jurysdoyle.com |

HOTEL ★★★ MAP 8 O 11 | **HOTEL ★★★★ MAP 8 O 11** | **HOTEL ★★★★ MAP 8 O 11**

Blooms Hotel is situated at the centre of Dublin's cultural and artistic heart - Temple Bar. The hotel itself is only a few minutes stroll from Grafton Street's shopping and most of the city's best sights. And for those who want to set the town alight, Blooms is on the doorstep of Dublin's most famous nightlife - not least of which is its own nightclub, Club M. Blooms Hotel is a perfect choice for everyone looking to experience Temple Bar and Dublin's city centre.

Located in the fashionable heart of Dublin City, three minutes stroll from Grafton St, Temple Bar, Dublin Castle and Trinity College. Brooks is a designer/boutique hotel with high standards throughout, appealing to the discerning international traveller. Superbly appointed air-conditioned accommodation with wireless internet access. Jasmine Bar, residents' drawing room, Francesca's Restaurant and executive meeting facilities, a fitness suite with sauna and screening room coupled with secure car-parking opposite makes this the ideal base for the sophisticated traveller.

The Burlington is a Dublin institution, always at the heart of the action and central to the whole whirl of Dublin life. Its lively bars and restaurants and friendly open charm conspire to create an atmosphere that is hard to forget. Dublin City's largest conference hotel, it is centrally located - just a 5 minute stroll to the city centre.

Bookable on www.irelandhotels.com | Member of Sinnott Hotels | *Bookable on www.irelandhotels.com*
Member of Jurys Doyle Hotel Group

B&B from €50.00 to €100.00	B&B from €85.00 to €160.00	Room Rate from €126.00 to €356.00

Barry O'Sullivan
General Manager

Anne McKiernan
General Manager

Activities:

John Clifton
General Manager

Member of:

Member of:

Member of:

Special Offer: Midweek Specials from €240.00 pps
(3 Nights B&B)

86 86 | 98 98 | 500 500

Closed 24 - 26 December	Open All Year	Open All Year

B&B Rates are per Person Sharing per Night incl. Breakfast.
or <u>Room Rates</u> are per Room per Night - See also Page 8

Buswells Hotel

23/27 Molesworth Street,
Dublin 2

Tel: 01-614 6500 Fax: 01-676 2090
Email: buswells@quinn-hotels.com
Web: www.quinnhotels.com

HOTEL ★★★ MAP 8 O 11

Ideally located in the centre of Dublin City, we are minutes walk from St. Stephen's Green, Trinity College and the fashionable Grafton Street. Refurbished throughout in 2005, our 67 classic bedrooms allow you to relax and unwind after a long day in the busy city centre. WiFi access available in all bedrooms and public areas. Secure overnight car parking available in Dawson car park to all our guests from 5.30pm to 9.30am.

Bookable on www.irelandhotels.com
Member of Quinn Hotels

B&B from €60.00 to €120.00

Paul Gallagher
General Manager

Activities:

Member of:

67 67

Butlers Town House

44 Lansdowne Road,
Ballsbridge,
Dublin 4

Tel: 01-667 4022 Fax: 01-667 3960
Email: info@butlers-hotel.com
Web: www.butlers-hotel.com

GUESTHOUSE ★★★★ MAP 8 O 11

An oasis of country tranquillity in the heart of Dublin, Butlers Town House is an experience as opposed to a visit. Opened in March 1997, fully restored to reflect its former glory, but with all modern comforts from air-conditioning to modem points. Butlers Town House is renowned for its elegance and premier guest service. Private secure car park available. 5 Diamond RAC rated.

Bookable on www.irelandhotels.com
Member of Manor House Hotels

B&B from €65.00 to €90.00

Suzanne Cole
General Manager

Member of:

20 20

Camden Court Hotel

Camden Street,
Dublin 2

Tel: 01-475 9666 Fax: 01-475 9677
Email: sales@camdencourthotel.com
Web: www.camdencourthotel.com

HOTEL ★★★ MAP 8 O 11

The Camden Court Hotel is situated in the heart of Dublin within a 5 minute walk of Grafton Street, adjacent to the LUAS line on Harcourt Street. The hotel comprises 246 well-appointed bedrooms all en suite with hairdryer, direct dial phone, colour TV, trouser press and tea/coffee making facilities. We also provide excellent conference facilities, restaurant and themed bar. Our state of the art leisure centre consists of a 16m swimming pool, sauna, steam room, jacuzzi and a fully equipped gym. Complimentary secure carparking on site.

Member of Cara Hotels

B&B from €49.50 to €145.00

Darren Darwin
General Manager

Activities:

Member of:

246 246

Co. Dublin
Dublin City

Cassidys Hotel	**Castle Hotel**	**Castleknock Hotel and Country Club**

Cassidys Hotel

Cavendish Row,
Upper O'Connell St.,
Dublin 1
Tel: 01-878 0555 Fax: 01-878 0687
Email: stay@cassidyshotel.com
Web: www.cassidyshotel.com

HOTEL ★★★ MAP 8 O 11

A little gem in the heart of the city. Cassidys is a modern 88 bedroomed townhouse hotel located opposite the famous Gate Theatre in the city centre. Cassidys is a short walk from numerous museums, theatres, bars, shopping districts and I.F.S.C. The warm and welcoming atmosphere of Groomes Bar lends a traditional air to Cassidys and fine dining is assured in the stylish surroundings of Restaurant 6. Limited parking for guests. Conference facilities available.

Bookable on www.irelandhotels.com
Member of Platinum Hotels

B&B from €54.00 to €130.00

Martin Cassidy
General Manager

Member of:

Special Offer: Midweek Specials from €125.00 pps (2 Nights B&B & 1 Dinner)

88 88

Closed 24 - 26 December

Castle Hotel

2-4 Gardiner Row,
Dublin 1
Tel: 01-874 6949 Fax: 01-872 7674
Email: info@castle-hotel.ie
Web: www.castle-hotel.ie

HOTEL ★★ MAP 8 O 11

Elegant Georgian hotel close to Dublin's main shopping district, renowned for its friendly service. One of Dublin's oldest hotels. Authentically restored, the décor and furnishings offer modern comfort combined with olde world features: crystal chandeliers, antique mirrors, marble fireplaces and period staircases. The individually decorated rooms offer private bathroom, TV, direct dial phone, hairdryers and beverage making facilities. The hotel has an intimate resident's bar and private parking.

Bookable on www.irelandhotels.com
Member of Castle Hotel Group

B&B from €49.50 to €85.00

Yvonne Evans
Manageress

Member of:

Special Offer: Midweek Specials from €140.00 pps (3 Nights B&B)
38 38

Closed 24 - 27 December

Castleknock Hotel and Country Club

Porterstown Road,
Castleknock,
Dublin 15
Tel: 01-640 6300 Fax: 01-640 6303
Email: reservations@chcc.ie
Web: www.towerhotelgroup.com

HOTEL N MAP 8 O 11

Built to an exceptionally high 4**** standard, this modern & stylish hotel has a premier location just outside Castleknock Village with stunning views of an 18 hole golf course & the surrounding countryside. Ideal for business & leisure guests. 9km from Dublin City, 13km from Dublin Airport & within easy access of the M50 motorway. Extensive conference facilities, magnificent leisure, health & beauty facilities, 2 bars & 2 restaurants including a fine dining restaurant. Ample parking. RAC **** approved. Special offers available online - www.towerhotelgroup.com

Bookable on www.irelandhotels.com
Member of Tower Hotel Group

B&B from €75.00 to €160.00

John Caffrey
General Manager

Activities:

Member of:

Special Offer: Weekend Specials from €189.00 pps (2 Nights B&B & 1 Dinner)
144 144

Closed 24 - 26 December

B&B Rates are per Person Sharing per Night incl. Breakfast. or Room Rates are per Room per Night - See also Page 8

Celtic Lodge Guesthouse

81/82 Talbot Street,
Dublin 1

Tel: 01-878 8732 Fax: 01-878 8698
Email: celticguesthouse@eircom.net
Web: www.celticaccommodation.net

GUESTHOUSE ★ MAP 8 O 11

This gracious Victorian residence is in the heart of the city centre adjacent to the bus and train stations and 15 minutes from the airport. A stroll from our door is the vibrant Temple Bar district with its numerous pubs, restaurants and clubs. Trinity College, Christchurch Cathedral, Dublin Castle and a number of theatres are within a stone's throw. All rooms en suite and finished to a very high standard with cable TV & tea/coffee making facilities. Next door a traditional bar with Irish music seven nights a week, free.

Bookable on www.irelandhotels.com

B&B from €35.00 to €55.00

Caroline Kearns
Reservations Manager

Special Offer: Available Upon Request

🏨 🍴 □ T C ☕
29 29

Closed 22 - 27 December

Central Hotel

1-5 Exchequer Street,
Dublin 2

Tel: 01-679 7302 Fax: 01-679 7303
Email: reservations@centralhotel.ie
Web: www.centralhotel.ie

HOTEL ★★★ MAP 8 O 11

City centre location. Award-winning Library Bar, Exchequer Bar and dining room. Temple Bar, Dublin's Left Bank, one block away. Trinity College, Grafton Street and Christchurch Cathedral are 5 minutes from the hotel. Rooms en suite include DD phones, voicemail, hairdryers, tea/coffee making facilities, multi-channel TV. 8 private meeting rooms. Secure parking available nearby.

Bookable on www.irelandhotels.com
Member of Best Western Hotels

B&B from €70.00 to €135.00

Heath Hayward
General Manager

Member of:
IRISH
HOTELS
FEDERATION

🏨 🍴 ☎ □ ☀ T C ♨ C M S 🔒 a/c inet WiFi
70 70

Closed 24 - 27 December

B&B Rates are per Person Sharing per Night incl. Breakfast.
or **Room Rates** are per Room per Night - See also Page 8

Dublin City

Charleville Lodge

268-272 North Circular Road,
Phibsborough,
Dublin 7
Tel: 01-838 6633 Fax: 01-838 5854
Email: info@charlevillelodge.ie
Web: www.charlevillelodge.ie

GUESTHOUSE ★★★ MAP 8 0 11

Charleville Lodge, (former home of Lord Charleville), is a Victorian property located 10 minutes walk from the city centre, Trinity College, Temple Bar and en route to Dublin Airport and car ferry. Modernised to offer all the facilities normally associated with a larger hotel, while retaining the family-run atmosphere. There is a free car park, tea/coffee facility and broadband internet access. Rated ♦♦♦♦ by AA and RAC, we are holders of the Sparkling Diamond Award. Let us make your arrangements with local golf clubs.

Bookable on www.irelandhotels.com
Member of Premier Collection

B&B from €30.00 to €90.00

Val & Anne Stenson
Owners

Activities:
:✓

Member of:
IRISH HOTELS FEDERATION

Special Offer: *Midweek Specials from €85.00 pps*
(3 Nights B&B)

🛏🛗 ☎🖥📺🆃🅲❄🅿🆂
30 30

Closed 20 - 26 December

Chief O'Neill's Hotel

Smithfield Village,
Dublin 7
Tel: 01-817 3838 Fax: 01-817 3839
Email: reservations@chiefoneills.com
Web: www.chiefoneills.com

HOTEL **U** MAP 8 0 11

Situated in the "New Smithfield" and only a tram ride away from Dublin's vibrant shopping areas, Chief O'Neill's provides the perfect location for holiday and business visitors alike. With contemporary design, each of the 73 en suite bedrooms is equipped with a CD/hi-fi player, cable TV, direct dial phone and tea/coffee facilities. One can also enjoy the spectacular views of Dublin from Chief O'Neill's "Chimney Viewing Tower".

Bookable on www.irelandhotels.com

Room Rate from €79.00 to €250.00

Pat Hevey
General Manager

Activities:
🍴

Member of:
IRISH HOTELS FEDERATION

Special Offer: *Midweek Specials from €148.50 pps*
(3 Nights B&B)

🛏🛗 ☎🖥📺🆃🅲📶CM♫🅿📧🔤📶 inet
73 73

Closed 24 - 26 December

Clara House

23 Leinster Road,
Rathmines,
Dublin 6
Tel: 01-497 5904 Fax: 01-497 5580
Email: clarahouse@eircom.net
Web: www.clarahouse.com

GUESTHOUSE ★★★ MAP 8 0 11

Clara House is a beautifully maintained listed Georgian house with many original features skillfully combined with modern day comforts. Each bedroom has en suite bathroom, remote control colour TV, direct dial telephone, radio/alarm clock, tea/coffee making facilities, hairdryer and trouser press. Clara House is a mile from downtown Dublin with bus stops for Ballsbridge/RDS and city centre 200 metres away. Secure parking at rear of house.

Bookable on www.irelandhotels.com

B&B from €45.00 to €70.00

Dave Pearce
Proprietor

Member of:
IRISH HOTELS FEDERATION

Special Offer: *Midweek Specials from €120.00 pps*
(3 Nights B&B)

🛏🛗 ☎🖥📺🆃🅲🅿📶 inet WiFi
13 13

Closed 24 - 26 December

<u>B&B Rates</u> are per Person Sharing per Night incl. Breakfast. or <u>Room Rates</u> are per Room per Night - See also Page 8

Clarence (The)	Clarion Hotel Dublin IFSC	Clarion Hotel Dublin Liffey Valley

Clarence (The)

6-8 Wellington Quay,
Dublin 2

Tel: 01-407 0800 Fax: 01-407 0820
Email: reservations@theclarence.ie
Web: www.theclarence.ie

HOTEL U MAP 8 O 11

Located on the River Liffey, in the heart of the city, The Clarence was built in 1852 and was transformed into a boutique hotel in 1996. Owned by Bono and The Edge of the rock group U2, The Clarence has 49 individually designed bedrooms and suites. A massage and treatment room, fitness room and valet parking are all available. The renowned Tea Room Restaurant and Octagon Bar, famous for its cocktails, are located here.

Bookable on www.irelandhotels.com
Member of Leading Small Hotels of the World

Room Rate from €340.00 to €370.00

Oliver Sevestre
Hotel Manager

Activities:

Member of:

49 49

Closed 24 - 27 December

Clarion Hotel Dublin IFSC

Excise Walk,
International Financial Services Centre,
Dublin 1

Tel: 01-433 8800 Fax: 01-433 8801
Email: info@clarionhotelifsc.com
Web: www.clarionhotelifsc.com

HOTEL ★★★★ MAP 8 O 11

4**** centrally located hotel with full leisure facilities including an 18m indoor swimming pool, sauna, steam room and jacuzzi. Bedrooms with every modern convenience you would expect from a contemporary 4**** hotel. Enjoy a choice of dining experiences from Sinergie restaurant to Kudos bar.

Bookable on www.irelandhotels.com
Member of Choice Hotels Ireland

Room Rate from €100.00 to €152.50

Dermot De Loughry
General Manager

Member of:

163 163

Open all year

Clarion Hotel Dublin Liffey Valley

Liffey Valley,
Dublin 22

Tel: 01-625 8000 Fax: 01-625 8001
Email: info@clarionhotelliffeyvalley.com
Web: www.clarionhotelliffeyvalley.com

HOTEL N MAP 8 O 11

This stylish new hotel is conveniently located on the N4 beside the Liffey Valley Shopping Centre (85 shops), close to the M50, and just 6 miles from the city centre. Spacious and comfortable guest bedrooms with Sinergie Restaurant (Irish cuisine with Mediterranean influences), Kudos Bar with Asian Wok Station, 24 hour room service and SanoVitae Health & Fitness Club, make this a hotel you will want to re-visit. Conference facilities for up to 400 people, ample car parking.

Member of Clarion Hotels

B&B from €54.50 to €140.00

Eamon Daly
General Manager

Activities:

Member of:

Special Offer: Weekend Specials from €129.00 pps (2 Nights B&B & 1 Dinner)

284 284

Closed 24 - 26 December

B&B Rates are per Person Sharing per Night incl. Breakfast.
or Room Rates are per Room per Night - See also Page 8

Co. Dublin

Dublin City

Clifden Guesthouse

32 Gardiner Place,
Dublin 1

Tel: 01-874 6364 Fax: 01-874 6122
Email: info@clifdenhouse.com
Web: www.clifdenhouse.com

GUESTHOUSE ★★★ MAP 8 O 11

A refurbished city centre Georgian home. Our private car park provides security for guests' cars, even after check-out. All rooms are non-smoking and have shower, WC, WHB, TV, direct dial phone and tea-making facilities. We cater for single, twin, double, triple and family occupancies. Convenient to airport, ferryports, Bus Aras (bus station) and DART. We are only 5 minutes walk from O'Connell Street. AA approved.

Bookable on www.irelandhotels.com
Member of Premier Collection

B&B from €35.00 to €110.00

Jack & Mary Lalor

Member of:
IRISH HOTELS FEDERATION

Special Offer: Midweek Specials from €95.00 pps (3 Nights B&B)

15 15

Closed 21 - 27 December

Clontarf Castle Hotel

Castle Avenue,
Clontarf,
Dublin 3

Tel: 01-833 2321 Fax: 01-833 0418
Email: info@clontarfcastle.ie
Web: www.clontarfcastle.ie

HOTEL ★★★★ MAP 8 O 11

A magnificent historic castle, dating back to 1172, is today a luxurious 4**** de luxe 111 room hotel. Ideally located only 10 minutes from the city centre and 15 minutes from Dublin Airport, complimentary car parking also available. Superb bedrooms, equipped with all the modern facilities, featuring wireless broadband access. Templar's Bistro specialising in modern international cuisine, 2 unique bars and state of the art conference and banqueting facilities.

Bookable on www.irelandhotels.com

B&B from €65.00 to €200.00

Dermot Hennessy
General Manager

Activities:

Member of:
IRISH HOTELS FEDERATION

111 111

Closed 24 - 25 December

Comfort Inn Parnell Square

Great Denmark Street,
Off Parnell Square,
Dublin 1

Tel: 01-873 7700 Fax: 01-873 7777
Email: info@comfortinndublin.com
Web: www.comfortinndublin.com

HOTEL U MAP 8 O 11

The Comfort Inn Parnell Square, is situated in the heart of Dublin, in a unique blend of Georgian excellence and modern amenities. A perfect base from which to explore shops, theatres, museums and restaurants. Comfort and style are an integral part of this hotel, where the business individual or families are well catered for. Our spacious 92 en suite rooms are tastefully decorated to the highest standard with DD phone, multi-channel TV, hairdryer & tea/coffee facilities. Both family and disabled rooms are available. Complimentary broadband, internet available in guest rooms.

Bookable on www.irelandhotels.com
Member of Choice Hotels

Room Rate from €79.00 to €229.00

Denise Batt
General Manager

Member of:
IRISH HOTELS FEDERATION

92 92

Closed 22 - 29 December

B&B Rates are per Person Sharing per Night incl. Breakfast. or **Room Rates** are per Room per Night - See also Page 8

Comfort Inn Smithfield

Smithfield,
Dublin 7

Tel: 021-490 8278 Fax: 021-427 1489
Email: info@choicehotelsireland.ie
Web: www.comfortinnireland.com

UNDER CONSTRUCTION - OPENING MARCH 2006

HOTEL P MAP 8 O 11

The Comfort Inn Smithfield is a purpose built contemporary inn, which is superbly located behind the Four Courts on the new Smithfield Plaza. The Comfort Inn is within a short walk of the main shopping, entertainment, sightseeing and business districts of the city. On its doorstep is one of the main LUAS light rail stations giving easy access to the airport and main bus and rail stations. Up to the minute technology including free broadband in all bedrooms as standard. Adapted rooms for guests with special needs.

Member of Choice Hotels Ireland

Room Rate from €79.00 to €229.00

Mark Long
General Manager

92 92

Closed 22 - 29 December

Conrad Dublin

Earlsfort Terrace,
Dublin 2

Tel: 01-602 8900 Fax: 01-676 5424
Email: dublininfo@conradhotels.com
Web: www.ConradHotels.com

HOTEL ★★★★ MAP 8 O 11

Conrad Dublin completed its refurbishment in 2005. Located in the heart of Dublin's city centre, only a few minutes walk from Grafton Street. 192 de luxe guest rooms including 16 suites with CD player, ergonomic work stations, broadband internet, multi-channel television, air-conditioning, turndown service, bathrobes, slippers and hairdryer. The hotel offers a choice of two bars, a restaurant, 24 hour room service, a state of the art fitness centre, fully equipped business centre, extensive conference and meeting facilities.

Bookable on www.irelandhotels.com

Room Rate from €200.00 to €420.00

Laurens Zieren
General Manager

Activities:

Member of:

192 192

Open All Year

Davenport Hotel O'Callaghan

At Merrion Square,
Dublin 2

Tel: 01-607 3500 Fax: 01-661 5663
Email: info@ocallaghanhotels.com
Web: www.ocallaghanhotels.com

HOTEL ★★★★ MAP 8 O 11

The O'Callaghan Davenport is an elegant landmark Dublin hotel with a historic facade dating to 1863. Ideally located in the city centre beside Merrion Square within minutes walk of Trinity College and the main shopping and business districts. Fully installed with wired and wireless broadband, the O'Callaghan Davenport has excellent conference facilities. 115 air-conditioned de luxe bedrooms, discreet club like bar, fine dining restaurant, parking and gymnasium facilities. USA Toll Free Reservations 1800 569 9983 and on line at www.ocallaghanhotels.com

Member of O'Callaghan Hotels

B&B from €87.50 to €189.00

John Clesham
General Manager

Activities:

Member of:

115 115

Open All Year

B&B Rates are per Person Sharing per Night incl. Breakfast.
or Room Rates are per Room per Night - See also Page 8

Days Hotel Rathmines

Lower Rathmines Road,
Dublin 6

Tel: 1890-776 655 Fax: 01-406 6200
Email: reservations@dayshotelrathmines.com
Web: www.dayshotelrathmines.com

HOTEL ★★★ MAP 8 O 11

Situated just fifteen minutes walk from the city centre, in the bustling area of Rathmines. Days Hotel comprises 66 rooms, including a selection of luxurious suites with living room and small fitted kitchen. All rooms offer CD player, trouser press, tea/coffee station and safe. The spectacular Tram Co. Bar, Restaurant and Club, offers complimentary admission to residents. Secure underground car parking available free of charge. The ultimate shopping experience, Dundrum Town Centre is located ten minutes drive away. Hotel direct line: (01) 406 6100.

Bookable on www.irelandhotels.com
Member of Days Hotels Ireland

Room Rate from €79.00 to €199.00

Ciara Sweeney
General Manager

Member of:

Special Offer: Room Rate from €79.00

66 66
WiFi

Open All Year

Days Inn Talbot Street

95-98 Talbot Street,
Dublin 1

Tel: 1890-776 655 Fax: 01-874 9672
Email: info@daysinntalbot.com
Web: www.daysinntalbot.com

GUESTHOUSE ★★★ MAP 8 O 11

Talbot Street boasts the perfect location, just 2 minutes walk from O'Connell Street. In the surrounding area, you will find many shops, restaurants, pubs, theatres and nightclubs. Temple Bar and Trinity College are just a short stroll away. All rooms are en suite, with colourful modern décor. Full Irish breakfast available every morning. Hotel direct line (01) 874 9202.

Bookable on www.irelandhotels.com
Member of Days Hotels Ireland

Room Rate from €79.00 to €220.00

Michael Keane
General Manager

Member of:

Special Offer: Room Rate from €79.00

60 60

Closed 24 - 28 December

Dergvale Hotel

4 Gardiner Place,
Dublin 1

Tel: 01-874 4753 Fax: 01-874 8276
Email: dergvale@indigo.ie
Web: www.dergvalehotel.com

HOTEL ★★ MAP 8 O 11

The Dergvale Hotel is located within walking distance of all principal shopping areas, cinemas, museums, Trinity College, Dublin Castle and airport bus. Most bedrooms with showers en suite, colour TV and direct dial telephone. Fully licensed. A courteous and efficient staff are on hand to make your stay an enjoyable one. The hotel is under the personal supervision of Gerard and Nancy Nolan.

Bookable on www.irelandhotels.com

B&B from €38.00 to €65.00

Gerard Nolan
Owner

Member of:

Special Offer: Midweek Specials from €110.00 pps
(3 Nights B&B)

20 17

Closed 24 December - 07 January

B&B Rates are per Person Sharing per Night incl. Breakfast.
or Room Rates are per Room per Night - See also Page 8

Donnybrook Lodge

131 Stillorgan Road,
Donnybrook,
Dublin 4
Tel: 01-283 7333 Fax: 01-260 4770
Email: info@donnybrooklodge.com
Web: www.donnybrooklodge.com

GUESTHOUSE ★★★ MAP 8 O 11

Relax in comfortable surroundings in the heart of Dublin's most exclusive area. Ideally situated close to city centre, ferryports and adjacent to RDS, Lansdowne, UCD and RTE. A short stroll from a host of restaurants and entertainment. Recently refurbished, our well-appointed rooms feature en suite bathrooms, direct dial phone and TV. Private parking available. Enjoy a leisurely breakfast in our elegant dining room, overlooking gardens. A relaxed atmosphere and warm welcome awaits you.

B&B from €40.00 to €75.00

Pat Butler

Member of:

HOTELS FEDERATION

🏠 🦮 ☎️ 📺 T C ✳️ P 🅿️
7   7

Open All Year

Drury Court Hotel

28-30 Lower Stephen Street,
Dublin 2
Tel: 01-475 1988 Fax: 01-478 5730
Email: druryct@indigo.ie
Web: www.drurycourthotel.com

HOTEL ★★★ MAP 8 O 11

Located in the heart of Dublin, beside Stephen's Green and Grafton Street. Convenient to the hotel are theatres, galleries, museums, Trinity College and Temple Bar. The hotel comprises 42 luxurious bedrooms all en suite with direct dial phone, computer lines, multi-channel TV/Radio and tea/coffee facilities. There is also the Bia Bar, a lively bar serving sumptuous food all day. The hotel is adjacent to secure public parking, just perfect for the leisure or business visitor.

Bookable on www.irelandhotels.com
Member of MinOtel Ireland Hotel Group

B&B from €60.00 to €155.00

Paul Hand
General Manager

Member of:

HOTELS FEDERATION

🏠 🦮 ☎️ 📺 T C 🚭 CM 🍴 S 🅰️ 🔇 Inet
42 42

Closed 23 - 27 December

Dublin Skylon Hotel

Upper Drumcondra Road,
Dublin 9
Tel: 01-837 9121 Fax: 01-837 2778
Email: andrew_hyland@skylon.org
Web: www.skylonhotel.com

HOTEL ★★★ MAP 8 O 11

A smart hotel on the northern approach, ten minutes from the airport and five from the city centre. Dublin Skylon Hotel has just the right blend of style and informality to make your stay special. Its restaurant and bar are welcoming and just as popular in the neighbourhood as with guests.

Bookable on www.irelandhotels.com
Member of Brian McEniff Hotels

Room Rate from €69.00 to €359.00

Brian McEniff / Andrew
Hyland
Proprietor / General Manager

Activities:

🍸

Member of:

HOTELS FEDERATION

Special Offer: B&B from €44.50 pps per night (Sun - Thurs)

🏠 🦮 ☎️ 📺 T C 🚭 CM 🍴 P S 🅰️ 🔇 🔌
88 88
Inet WiFi 🐾

Closed 24 - 26 December

B&B Rates are per Person Sharing per Night incl. Breakfast.
or **Room Rates** are per Room per Night - See also Page 8

Dublin & East Coast   273

Egan's Guesthouse	Ferryview House	Fitzsimons Hotel
7/9 Iona Park, Glasnevin, Dublin 9 Tel: 01-830 3611 Fax: 01-830 3312 Email: info@eganshouse.com Web: www.eganshouse.com	96 Clontarf Road, Clontarf, Dublin 3 Tel: 01-833 5893 Fax: 01-853 2141 Email: ferryview@oceanfree.net Web: www.ferryviewhouse.com	21-22 Wellington Quay, Temple Bar, Dublin 2 Tel: 01-677 9315 Fax: 01-677 9387 Email: info@fitzsimonshotel.com Web: www.fitzsimonshotel.com

GUESTHOUSE ★★★ MAP 8 O 11   **GUESTHOUSE ★★★ MAP 8 O 11**   **HOTEL ★★ MAP 8 O 11**

Egan's House is an elegant terrace of Edwardian houses in a quiet area but only 1.7km from Dublin's city centre. All 23 guest rooms are en suite with television, telephone, hairdryer, electronic safe, ironing centre, power shower and tea/coffee facility. Free car parking. Dublin Airport is just 10 minutes by taxi and the car ferry is also close by, as is Croke Park, the Point Depot, RDS and championship golf courses. Broadband internet access available.

Ferryview House is located in the exclusive coastal suburb of Clontarf, 2.5 miles from the city centre on a regular bus route. The totally refurbished family-run guesthouse is also selected ◆◆◆◆ with the Automobile Association. The house is close to Dublin Port, the Point Theatre, East Point Business Park (2km) and Dublin Airport is 15 minutes away. Local facilities include restaurants, coastal walks, Clontarf Rugby Club, tennis and 3 golf clubs.

Fitzsimons Hotel a boutique hotel situated on the banks of the River Liffey in the heart of Temple Bar. Its location offers the visitor, doorstep access to this vibrant, exciting locale and all it has to offer, theatres, galleries, bars, restaurants, live music venues and alternative shops. Fitzsimons offers visitors a great place to socialise now with 4 floors of entertainment including our new open air Roof Terrace with bar, bars on all floors, restaurant and nightclub, seven nights a week.

Bookable on www.irelandhotels.com
Member of Premier Guesthouses

Bookable on www.irelandhotels.com

B&B from €29.99 to €79.99	*B&B from €35.00 to €55.00*	*B&B from €40.00 to €100.00*

Pat & Monica Finn Proprietors

Activities:
⚬/

Member of:
IRISH HOTELS FEDERATION

Special Offer: Midweek Specials from €79.99 pps (3 Nights B&B)

Margaret Allister

Member of:
IRISH HOTELS FEDERATION

Georgia Howard Reservations

Member of:
IRISH HOTELS FEDERATION

Closed 22 - 27 December	**Closed 21 December - 01 January**	**Closed 24 - 26 December**

B&B Rates are per Person Sharing per Night incl. Breakfast. or Room Rates are per Room per Night - See also Page 8

Fitzwilliam Hotel

St. Stephen's Green,
Dublin 2

Tel: 01-478 7000 Fax: 01-478 7878
Email: enq@fitzwilliamhotel.com
Web: www.fitzwilliamhotel.com

HOTEL ★★★★★ MAP 8 O 11

A modern, Conran designed classic uniquely positioned on St. Stephen's Green, paces away from Grafton Street, Ireland's premiere shopping location. Understated luxury, a fresh approach & impeccable service make it the perfect hotel for business & pleasure. Dine in the highly acclaimed 2 Michelin star Thornton's Restaurant or the fashionable Citron. Recent additions include complimentary broadband & air-conditioning in all bedrooms. WiFi in all public areas. State of the art digital media in meeting rooms, Beauty & Hair Salon. Dublin's newest & most stylish penthouse. 2000 sq feet of ultimate luxury.

Bookable on www.irelandhotels.com
Member of Summit Hotels & Resorts

Room Rate from €200.00 to €460.00

John Kavanagh
General Manager

Activities:
🍴 💧

Member of:
IRISH HOTELS FEDERATION

🛏️ 🐾 ☎️ 🖥️ 🅣 🅒 ♨️CM📶PS🔲🎿 ♨️
139 139
Inet WiFi

Open All Year

Fitzwilliam Townhouse

41 Upper Fitzwilliam Street,
Dublin 2

Tel: 01-662 5155 Fax: 01-676 7488
Email: fitzwilliamguesthouse@eircom.net
Web: www.fitzwilliamguesthouse.ie

GUESTHOUSE ★★★ MAP 8 O 11

Centrally located in the heart of elegant Georgian Dublin, minutes walk from St. Stephen's Green, National Concert Hall and Galleries. Enjoy the charm of this spacious townhouse. Rooms with en suite facilities, colour TV, direct dial telephone, clock/radios and hairdryers. Overnight car parking available. Excellent restaurants nearby. Our friendly staff will ensure your stay is a relaxed and memorable one.

B&B from €50.00 to €70.00

Caragh Whelan
Manager

Member of:
IRISH HOTELS FEDERATION

🛏️ 🐾 ☎️ 🖥️ 🅣 🅒 🅢 🔲 🐕
13 13

Closed 23 December - 03 January

Fleet Street Hotel (The)

19/20 Fleet Street,
Temple Bar,
Dublin 2

Tel: 01-670 8122 Fax: 01-670 8103
Email: principalhotel@eircom.net
Web: www.principalhotel.com

HOTEL ★★★ MAP 8 O 11

The Fleet Street Hotel is ideally located in the Temple Bar area of the city. We offer the finest traditions of quality and service. We are ideally based for both business and leisure, walking distance from Trinity College, Grafton Street and all the local bars and restaurants. All rooms are en suite with tea and coffee facilities, direct dial telephone, hairdryer and trouser press. T.V. in all bedrooms.

B&B from €50.00 to €110.00

Fergal Byrne
General Manager

Member of:
IRISH HOTELS FEDERATION

🛏️ 🐾 ☎️ 🖥️ 🅣 🅒 CM🔲🎿 ♨️
71 71

Closed 24 - 27 December

B&B Rates are per Person Sharing per Night incl. Breakfast.
or **Room Rates** are per Room per Night - See also Page 8

Dublin & East Coast 275

Four Seasons Hotel Dublin	George Frederic Handel Hotel	Glenogra House

Four Seasons Hotel Dublin

Simmonscourt Road,
Dublin 4

Tel: 01-665 4000 Fax: 01-665 4099
Email: reservations.dublin@fourseasons.com
Web: www.fourseasons.com/dublin

HOTEL ★★★★★ MAP 8 O 11

The charm of Irish tradition & hospitality combine to provide the stage for Four Seasons Hotel, Dublin. The hotel offers a location of cosmopolitan convenience in the prestigious embassy & residential district, bringing together exceptional guest rooms and suites with the finest facilities for business & leisure. Reflective of Dublin's architectural heritage, the hotel is just minutes from the cultural & entertainment options of the city centre. The hotel features 18,000 sq ft of meeting and banqueting space, fine dining in Seasons Restaurant, Ice Bar and an 11,000 sq ft full service spa. Luxurious suites available up to €2,400 per night.

Room Rate from €255.00 to €680.00

John Brennan
General Manager

Activities:

Member of:

259 259

Open All Year

George Frederic Handel Hotel

16-18 Fishamble Street,
Christchurch, Temple Bar,
Dublin 8

Tel: 01-670 9400 Fax: 01-670 9410
Email: info@handelshotel.com
Web: www.handelshotel.com

HOTEL U MAP 8 O 11

Our secret is out! Centrally located, while situated in the heart of Dublin's vibrant Temple Bar area, the George Frederic Handel Hotel is also within easy walking distance of the city's main tourist attractions and financial districts. We offer a high standard of accommodation combined with a warm Irish welcome - all at a great price. Live online booking system at www.handelshotel.com

Room Rate from €75.00 to €210.00

Jonathan Hynes
Operations Manager

Member of:

40 40

Closed 24 - 27 December

Glenogra House

64 Merrion Road,
Ballsbridge,
Dublin 4

Tel: 01-668 3661 Fax: 01-668 3698
Email: info@glenogra.com
Web: www.glenogra.com

GUESTHOUSE ★★★★ MAP 8 O 11

Glenogra is a beautiful Edwardian guesthouse situated in Ballsbridge, 10 minutes from Dublin city centre. Opposite the RDS and Four Seasons Hotel, Glenogra is close to amenities including Sandymount DART station, bus routes, the Air Coach, car ferries, embassies and a range of excellent restaurants and traditional bars. Rated 4**** accommodation by Fáilte Ireland and ◆◆◆◆◆ by RAC and AA. Glenogra is a non-smoking guesthouse. Free car park.

Bookable on www.irelandhotels.com
Member of Premier Guesthouses

B&B from €54.50 to €62.50

Joseph Donohoe
Manager

Member of:

13 13

Closed 20 - 31 December

B&B Rates are per Person Sharing per Night incl. Breakfast. or **Room Rates** are per Room per Night - See also Page 8

Grafton Capital Hotel

Stephens Street Lower,
Dublin 2

Tel: 01-648 1100 Fax: 01-648 1122
Email: info@graftoncapitalhotel.com
Web: www.capital-hotels.com

HOTEL ★★★ MAP 8 O 11

Arrive and feel immediately "at home" in The Grafton Capital. Located in the very heart of Dublin City centre, fashion, culture, entertainment and fun are a stones throw away. Experience an Irish welcome at its best as we guarantee our best efforts to make your stay a pleasant and memorable one. Trinity College, Grafton Street, Temple Bar are all within easy walking distance. Residents enjoy complimentary admission to a variety of popular nightclubs. Popular Break for the Border Bar, Restaurant and Club, adjacent.

Bookable on www.irelandhotels.com
Member of Capital Hotel Group

B&B from €60.00 to €120.00

Frances Dempsey
General Manager

Member of:

Special Offer: Midweek Specials from €139.00 pps (3 Nights B&B)

75 75

Closed 24 - 26 December

Grand Canal Hotel

Grand Canal Street,
Dublin 4

Tel: 01-646 1000 Fax: 01-646 1001
Email: sales@grandcanalhotel.com
Web: www.grandcanalhotel.com

HOTEL ★★★ MAP 8 O 11

Located in fashionable Ballsbridge, the hotel is convenient to Dublin's main attractions - National Art Gallery, Trinity College, the RDS and Lansdowne Road stadium. Ten minutes from the city centre it is easily accessed by train, DART, airport and city buses. Kitty O'Sheas original pub is an integral part of this modern hotel which boasts private parking, five meeting and conference rooms and all bedrooms have high speed internet access.

Bookable on www.irelandhotels.com
Member of Cara Hotels

Room Rate from €99.00 to €215.00

Martin Mangan
General Manager

Activities:

Member of:

Special Offer: Weekend Specials from €150.00 pps (2 Nights B&B & 1 Dinner)

142 142

Closed 23 - 28 December

Gresham (The)

23 Upper O'Connell Street,
Dublin 1

Tel: 01-874 6881 Fax: 01-878 7175
Email: info@thegresham.com
Web: www.gresham-hotels.com

HOTEL ★★★★ MAP 8 O 11

The Gresham, a landmark building in Dublin City centre, is a 4**** hotel that has undergone a dramatic transformation. Relax over afternoon tea in our airy lobby, or enjoy an excellent dining experience in our award-winning Restaurant '23'. 289 bedrooms including the executive Lavery Wing. Penthouse suites with views over the city individually re-designed in a range of superb styles. Car parking (charge applies). AA and RAC approved.

Bookable on www.irelandhotels.com
Member of Gresham Hotel Group

B&B from €100.00 to €250.00

Paul McCracken
Operations Director

Activities:

Member of:

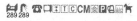
289 289

Open All Year

B&B Rates are per Person Sharing per Night incl. Breakfast.
or **Room Rates** are per Room per Night - See also Page 8

Harcourt Hotel	Harding Hotel	Harrington Hall

Harcourt Hotel

60 Harcourt Street,
Dublin 2

Tel: 01-478 3677 Fax: 01-478 1557
Email: reservations@harcourthotel.ie
Web: www.harcourthotel.ie

HOTEL ★★★ MAP 8 O 11

The Harcourt Hotel's Georgian exterior conceals its contemporary interior. The boutique style hotel is famous for once being home to George Bernard Shaw. Facilities include a convivial Bar D-Two, a landscaped year-round beer garden (heated), restaurant "Little Caesers" & a nightclub from Wed - Sat (usually). It is best described as a lively hotel (some rooms can suffer from noise, particularly at the weekends). Local secure car parking available at under €5 per night. The hotel is located off the South West corner of St. Stephen's Green. It is one LUAS (tram) stop away from Grafton Street. The LUAS also services the new Dundrum Town Centre.

B&B from €44.00 to €140.00

Danielle McGill
Operations Manager

Member of:
IRISH HOTELS FEDERATION

Special Offer: From Sun - Thur - Jan, Feb, Oct, Nov, Dec €69.00 Room Only Rate inc VAT for 1, 2, 3 or 4 persons

51 51

Closed 24 - 26 December

Harding Hotel

Copper Alley,
Fishamble Street,
Dublin 2

Tel: 01-679 6500 Fax: 01-679 6504
Email: info@hardinghotel.ie
Web: www.hardinghotel.ie

HOTEL ★★ MAP 8 O 11

The Harding Hotel is a stylish city centre hotel located within Dublin's Temple Bar. All 53 en suite rooms have television, direct dial telephone, hairdryer, tea/coffee making facilities and wireless internet access. Relax and enjoy a drink in Darkey Kelly's Bar or a wonderful meal in the new Copper Alley Bistro. Groups and individuals welcome.

Room Rate from €64.00 to €131.00

Aine Hickey
Manager

Member of:
IRISH HOTELS FEDERATION

53 53

Closed 23 - 26 December

Harrington Hall

70 Harcourt Street,
Dublin 2

Tel: 01-475 3497 Fax: 01-475 4544
Email: harringtonhall@eircom.net
Web: www.harringtonhall.com

GUESTHOUSE ★★★★ MAP 8 O 11

Harrington Hall with its secure private parking in the heart of Georgian Dublin, provides the perfect location for holiday and business visitors alike to enjoy the surrounding galleries, museums, cathedrals, theatres, fashionable shopping streets, restaurants and pubs. All rooms are equipped to today's exacting standards with en suite, direct dial phone, hospitality tray, trouser press and multi channel TV, access to fax facilities, e-mail and internet. All floors are serviced by elevator. AA ♦♦♦♦♦ and RAC ♦♦♦♦♦.

Bookable on www.irelandhotels.com

B&B from €70.00 to €145.00

Henry King
Proprietor

Member of:
IRISH HOTELS FEDERATION

Special Offer: Midweek Specials from €195.00 pps (3 Nights B&B)

28 28

Open All Year

B&B Rates are per Person Sharing per Night incl. Breakfast.
or **Room Rates** are per Room per Night - See also Page 8

Herbert Park Hotel

Ballsbridge,
Dublin 4

Tel: 01-667 2200 Fax: 01-667 2595
Email: reservations@herbertparkhotel.ie
Web: www.herbertparkhotel.ie

HOTEL ★★★★ MAP 8 O 11

The award-winning Herbert Park Hotel is located in Ballsbridge, five minutes from the city centre with spectacular views over 48 acres of Herbert Park. Bedrooms are comfortably appointed with modern features including broadband, air-conditioning, mini-bar, safe, interactive television with playstation and pay per view movies. Facilities include the Pavilion Restaurant overlooking Herbert Park, Exhibition Bar, cardiovascular gym, meeting rooms and complimentary car parking for residents. Herbert Park Hotel is adjacent to the RDS and Lansdowne Road Stadium.

Member of Supranational Hotels

B&B from €67.50 to €156.50

Ewan Plenderleith
Director / General Manager

Activities:

Member of:

153 153

Open All Year

Holiday Inn Dublin City Centre

98-107 Pearse Street,
Dublin 2

Tel: 01-670 3666 Fax: 01-670 3636
Email: info@holidayinndublin.ie
Web: www.holidayinndublincitycentre.ie

HOTEL ★★★ MAP 8 O 11

Located in heart of the city centre with Dublin's main tourist attractions and principal shopping areas within walking distance of the IFSC, Point Depot, RDS, Lansdowne Road and Temple Bar. Featuring 101 en suite bedrooms, car parking, resident's gym and business centre. Conference facilities for up to 400. Our Green Bistro & Bar offers a full menu throughout the day helped along by one of the finest pints of Guinness in Dublin. Whether here for business or pleasure the Holiday Inn Dublin City Centre is the ideal location.

Member of Intercontinental Hotels Group

B&B from €52.00 to €150.00

Trevor Smith
General Manager

Activities:

Member of:

101 101

Open All Year

Hotel Isaacs

Store Street,
Dublin 1

Tel: 01-813 4700 Fax: 01-836 5390
Email: hotel@isaacs.ie
Web: www.hotelisaacs.com

HOTEL ★★★ MAP 8 O 11

Situated in the heart of Dublin City, Hotel Isaacs, a converted wine warehouse, is the perfect location for any visitor to Dublin. Only a short walk to the IFSC, Temple Bar, Point Depot, Croke Park, O'Connell Bridge and Busaras, this location cannot be beaten. All rooms are en suite with telephone, TV, tea/coffee, garment press, safe and hairdryer. Other facilities include Le Monde Café Bar and Il Vignardo Italian Restaurant.

Bookable on www.irelandhotels.com

Room Rate from €50.00 to €230.00

Justin Lowry
General Manager

Activities:

Member of:

90 90

Closed 24 - 27 December

B&B Rates are per Person Sharing per Night incl. Breakfast.
or **Room Rates** are per Room per Night - See also Page 8

Co. Dublin

Dublin City

Hotel St. George

7 Parnell Square,
Dublin 1

Tel: 01-874 5611 Fax: 01-874 5582
Email: info@hotel-st-george.ie
Web: www.hotel-st-george.ie

HOTEL U MAP 8 O 11

The historical Hotel St. George is located on Parnell Square at the top of O'Connell Street, Dublin's principal thoroughfare. Within walking distance of the Abbey and the Gate Theatre, Municipal Art Gallery, Dublin's Writers Museum, principal shopping district and other major tourist attractions. Each bedroom is en suite, individually decorated with every modern comfort, including direct dial phone, colour TV and tea/coffee making facilities. Private car park and residents bar.

Bookable on www.irelandhotels.com
Member of Castle Hotel Group

B&B from €50.00 to €99.00

*Jim Staunton
Proprietor*

Member of:
IRISH HOTELS FEDERATION

Special Offer: Midweek Specials from €165.00 pps (3 Nights B&B)
53 53

Closed 24 - 27 December

IMI Residence

Sandyford Road,
Dublin 16

Tel: 01-207 5900 Fax: 01-207 5962
Email: reservations@imires.ie
Web: www.imi.ie/res

HOTEL P MAP 8 O 11

Newly opened in January 2004, the IMI Residence offers tranquil surroundings with easy access into Dublin City. Located within walking distance of the new Dundrum Town Centre, the LUAS and a 5 minute drive to the M50 motorway. Recently awarded 'Best Commercial Building' 2005 by the Royal Institute of Architects in Ireland.

Bookable on www.irelandhotels.com
Member of Prem Group

Room Rate from €69.00 to €150.00

*Mark Williams
General Manager*

Activities:

Member of:
IRISH HOTELS FEDERATION

50 50
Inet WiFi

Closed 24 December - 01 January

Inishowen Guest House

199 South Circular Road,
Dublin 8

Tel: 01-453 6272 Fax: 01-454 4564
Email: terry@inishowen-guesthouse.com
Web: www.inishowen-guesthouse.com

GUESTHOUSE ★★ MAP 8 O 11

Inishowen Guesthouse, providing comfort and service of a very high standard. Cable TV and secure car park. 10 minutes from city centre. Close to Temple Bar and traditional pubs, excellent restaurants, discos and clubs. Excellent base for exploring Dublin's famed attractions. (Guiness Brewery, Trinity College, Dublin Castle, St. Patrick's Cathedral, Christchurch Cathedral, Kilmainham Museum) buses 19, 121 and 122. We look forward to hosting you and according you a warm welcome.

B&B from €38.00 to €50.00

Terry McCabe

8 4

Closed 20 December - 01 January

B&B Rates are per Person Sharing per Night incl. Breakfast. or Room Rates are per Room per Night - See also Page 8

119 - B+B (handwritten)

Jackson Court Hotel

29/30 Harcourt Street,
Dublin 2

Tel: 01-475 8777 Fax: 01-475 8793
Email: info@jackson-court.ie
Web: www.jackson-court.ie

HOTEL ★★ MAP 8 0 11

Minutes walk from Grafton Street, St. Stephen's Green and most of Dublin's historic landmarks. All rooms en suite with cable TV, direct dial telephone and tea and coffee making facilities. Hairdryers, irons and safe available at reception free of charge. Rates include full Irish breakfast, service and taxes and admission to Dublin's hottest night spot, Copper Face Jacks, open 7 nights a week. We look forward to welcoming you.

Bookable on www.irelandhotels.com

B&B from €30.00 to €75.00

*Paula Jackson
Proprietor*

Member of:
IRISH HOTELS FEDERATION

25 25

Closed 24 - 28 December

Jurys Ballsbridge Hotel

Pembroke Road,
Ballsbridge,
Dublin 4

Tel: 01-660 5000 Fax: 01-660 5540
Email: ballsbridge@jurysdoyle.com
Web: www.jurysdoyle.com

HOTEL ★★★★ MAP 8 0 11

One of Dublin's top international business hotels, Jurys Ballsbridge is renowned for its genial charm. Luxury accommodation, excellent restaurants and bars, a superb leisure centre and all the charms of the capital close at hand.

Towers (The)

14900 (handwritten)

Lansdowne Road, Dublin 4
Tel: 01-660 5000 Fax: 01-660 5540
Email: towers@jurysdoyle.com

5 star superior hotel adjacent to Jurys Ballsbridge Hotel.

Bookable on www.irelandhotels.com
Member of Jurys Doyle Hotel Group

Room Rate from €115.00 to €423.00

*Richard Bourke
General Manager*

Member of:
IRISH HOTELS FEDERATION

404 404

Open All Year

Jurys Croke Park Hotel

Jones's Road,
Dublin 3

Tel: 01-871 4444 Fax: 01-871 4400
Email: crokepark@jurysdoyle.com
Web: www.jurysdoyle.com

HOTEL P MAP 8 0 11

Located a short distance from the city centre and within easy reach of Dublin's main retail and entertainment areas as well as business districts and the airport, the new Jurys Croke Park Hotel is the perfect base for business or leisure trips. The hotel will bridge the gap between home and work by providing spacious, luxurious bedrooms and bathrooms with up to date entertainment systems, an excellent restaurant and bar serving fresh, healthy food and meeting rooms with state-of-the-art technology.

Bookable on www.irelandhotels.com

Room Rate from €104.00 to €295.00

Edward Stephenson

232 232

Closed 25 December

Dublin City

Jurys Inn Christchurch	Jurys Inn Custom House	Jurys Inn Parnell Street

Jurys Inn Christchurch

Christchurch Place,
Dublin 8

Tel: 01-454 0000 Fax: 01-454 0012
Email: jurysinnchristchurch@jurysdoyle.com
Web: www.jurysinns.com

HOTEL ★★★ MAP 8 O 11

Located in Dublin's oldest quarter in the heart of the city just opposite the historical Christchurch Cathedral, Jurys Inn Christchurch is within easy strolling distance of Temple Bar, St. Patrick's Cathedral, Trinity College and fashionable Grafton Street.

Bookable on www.irelandhotels.com
Member of Jurys Doyle Hotel Group

Room Rate from €89.00 to €254.00

Stephen Hanna
General Manager

Member of:

HOTELS

Special Offer: B&B Midweek Rate from €114.00
(Sun - Thurs)

182 182

Closed 24 - 26 December

Jurys Inn Custom House

Custom House Quay,
Dublin 1

Tel: 01-607 5000 Fax: 01-829 0400
Email: jurysinncustomhouse@jurysdoyle.com
Web: www.jurysinns.com

HOTEL ★★★ MAP 8 O 11

Jurys Inn Custom House is centrally and attractively located along the River Liffey in the International Financial Services Centre. Within easy walking distance are all of the city's main shopping districts and cultural attractions. Innfusion Restaurant - open for breakfast, lunch and dinner. The Inntro Bar is perfect for a quick lunch or drink and Il Barista serves gourmet coffee to go and fresh pastries.

Bookable on www.irelandhotels.com
Member of Jurys Doyle Hotel Group

Room Rate from €89.00 to €254.00

Anna O'Dell
General Manager

Member of:

HOTELS

239 239

Closed 24 - 26 December

Jurys Inn Parnell Street

Parnell Street,
Dublin 1

Tel: 01-878 4900 Fax: 01-878 4999
Email: jurysinnparnellst@jurysdoyle.com
Web: www.jurysinns.com

HOTEL ★★★ MAP 8 O 11

Jurys Inn Parnell Street is ideally located in the heart of Dublin's City Centre, within a 2 minute walk from the main shopping, business and entertainment districts and within easy walking distance of Temple Bar and Trinity College.

Bookable on www.irelandhotels.com
Member of Jurys Doyle Hotel Group

Room Rate from €89.00 to €254.00

Bobby Fitzpatrick
General Manager

Member of:

HOTELS

253 253

Closed 24 - 26 December

B&B Rates are per Person Sharing per Night incl. Breakfast. or **Room Rates** are per Room per Night - See also Page 8

Jurys Montrose Hotel	Kellys Hotel	Kilronan Guesthouse

Jurys Montrose Hotel

Stillorgan Road,
Dublin 4

Tel: 01-269 3311 Fax: 01-269 3376
Email: montrose@jurysdoyle.com
Web: www.jurysdoyle.com

HOTEL ★★★ MAP 8 O 11

A delightful, traditional fully serviced 3*** hotel on Dublin's southside, overlooking the impressive grounds of University College Dublin and close to RTE TV studios & 10mins drive from the city centre on the N11. The hotel is serviced by aircoach from Dublin Airport, departing every 15min. Bedrooms are modern & comfortable with broadband facilities. The hotel has a fully serviced business centre & 8 well appointed, air-conditioned meeting rooms. This hotel offers exceptional value for money.

Bookable on www.irelandhotels.com
Member of Jurys Doyle Hotel Group

Room Rate from €99.00 to €220.00

Jerry Russell
General Manager

Member of:
HOTELS

178 178

Open All Year

Kellys Hotel

South Great Georges Street,
Dublin 2

Tel: 01-677 9277 Fax: 01-671 3216
Email: kellyhtl@iol.ie
Web: www.kellyshtl.com

HOTEL U MAP 8 O 11

Situated in the heart of Dublin beside fashionable Grafton Street. A few minutes walk to Trinity College. Temple Bar and many of Dublin's famous pubs and restaurants are on our doorstep. Places of historical, cultural and literary interest are close by. Kelly's is a family-run budget hotel of unbeatable value for a city centre location. There is no service charge and our prices include breakfast. Frommers recommended. Parking available in adjacent public multi-storey carpark (for fee). Renovated in 2002.

Bookable on www.irelandhotels.com

B&B from €50.00 to €67.50

Gerard Lynam
Proprietor

Member of:
HOTELS

24 24

Closed 20 - 26 December

Kilronan Guesthouse

70 Adelaide Road,
Dublin 2

Tel: 01-475 5266 Fax: 01-478 2841
Email: info@dublinn.com
Web: www.dublinn.com

GUESTHOUSE ★★★ MAP 8 O 11

This exclusive AA RAC ◆◆◆◆ recommended Georgian house is in a secluded setting, within walking distance of St. Stephen's Green, Trinity College, National Concert Hall, Dublin Castle, St. Patrick's and Christchurch Cathedrals and most of Dublin's historic landmarks. Well appointed bedrooms with private shower, direct dial phone, TV, hairdryers, tea/coffee facilities and quality orthopaedic beds. Commended by New York Times, Beth Byrant, Michelin Guide, Fodors, Frommer & Karen Browns.

Bookable on www.irelandhotels.com
Member of Premier Guesthouses

B&B from €45.00 to €85.00

Rose & Terry Masterson
Owners

Member of:
HOTELS

12 12

Open All Year

B&B Rates are per Person Sharing per Night incl. Breakfast.
or **Room Rates** are per Room per Night - See also Page 8

La Stampa Hotel

35/36 Dawson Street,
Dublin 2

Tel: 01-677 4444 Fax: 01-677 4411
Email: hotel@lastampa.ie
Web: www.lastampa.ie

HOTEL P MAP 8 O 11

Situated in the heart of Dublin and centrally located within easy reach of its main shopping, dining, nightspots and heritage areas, La Stampa is a perfect combination of beautifully designed interiors, exquisite surroundings with a renowned reputation for top class food and luxury accommodation.

Room Rate from €200.00 to €275.00

Michael Donald
Resident Manager

Member of:

27 27

Closed 25 - 27 December

Lansdowne Hotel

27-29 Pembroke Road,
Ballsbridge,
Dublin 4

Tel: 01-668 2522 Fax: 01-668 5585
Email: reception@lansdownehotel.ie
Web: www.lansdownehotel.ie

HOTEL ★★★ MAP 8 O 11

The Lansdowne Hotel is a boutique 3*** hotel set in the prestigious suburb of Ballsbridge. Minutes walk from Dublin City, Royal Dublin Society (RDS) and Lansdowne Road Rugby Stadium. Relax in our Den Bar where fine food is served daily or dine in Druids Restaurant which serves the finest local produce. Each bedroom is luxuriously appointed with multi-channel TVs, tea/coffee making facilities and en suite bathrooms. Private car parking for guests.

Bookable on www.irelandhotels.com
Member of Countrywide Hotels - MinOtel Ireland

B&B from €45.00 to €80.00

George Hook
General Manager

Activities:

Member of:

Special Offer: Weekend Specials from €125.00 pps
(2 Nights B&B & 1 Dinner)

40 40

Closed 24 - 27 December

Leeson Inn Downtown

24 Lower Leeson Street,
Dublin 2

Tel: 01-662 2002 Fax: 01-662 1567
Email: info@leesoninndowntown.com
Web: www.leesoninndowntown.com

GUESTHOUSE N MAP 8 O 11

Located on the fashionable southside of the city centre on the Leeson Street side of St. Stephen's Green. Five minutes from Grafton Street the capital's premier shopping street. Major attractions such as the National Concert Hall, National Gallery, National Museum, Oireachtas (Parliament), National Gallery, Trinity College, many government buildings and an abundance of restaurants, theatres, night clubs and bars are all within easy walking distance.

Bookable on www.irelandhotels.com
Member of Utell

B&B from €45.00 to €110.00

Majella Mcguane
General Manager

Member of:

24 24

Closed 22 - 29 December

B&B Rates are per Person Sharing per Night incl. Breakfast.
or Room Rates are per Room per Night - See also Page 8

Longfields Hotel

9/10 Fitzwilliam Street Lower,
Dublin 2

Tel: 01-676 1367 Fax: 01-676 1542
Email: info@longfields.ie
Web: www.longfields.ie

HOTEL ★★★ MAP 8 O 11

Longfield's, a charming and intimate hotel in the heart of Ireland's capital where, with its award-winning No. 10 Restaurant, one can relax in opulence reminiscent of times past. Avid followers of good food guides and well known accommodation publications will have noted numerous accolades bestowed upon this renowned residence. Its central location and its impeccable service make it a must for discerning travellers.

Bookable on www.irelandhotels.com
Member of Manor House Hotels

B&B from €75.00 to €125.00

Kalvi Rutz
General Manager

Member of:

Special Offer: *Midweek Specials from €67.50 pps per night (Min Stay 3 Nights B&B)*

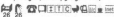
26   26

Open All Year

Lynam's Hotel

63/64 O'Connell Street,
Dublin 1

Tel: 01-888 0886 Fax: 01-888 0890
Email: lynamshtl@eircom.net
Web: www.lynams-hotel.com

HOTEL U MAP 12 O 11

A boutique style 42 bedroomed hotel located on O'Connell Street, close to the GPO and all of Dublin's many attractions. Decorated with elegance and individuality. All rooms are en suite, have direct dial phones and data port. 2 comfortable lounges are provided for guest use and our restaurant offers modern Italian style cuisine. Lynam's has a superb city centre location at great value.

Room Rate from €85.00 to €195.00

Conor O'Donovan
Group Sales & Marketing Manager

Member of:

Special Offer: *Midweek Specials from €129.00 pps (3 Nights B&B)*

42   42

Open All Year

Lynch Green Isle Hotel Spa & Suites

Newlands Cross,
Dublin 22

Tel: 01-459 3406 Fax: 01-459 2178
Email: cro@lynchotels.com
Web: www.lynchotels.com

HOTEL ★★★ MAP 8 O 11

The newly re-modelled Lynch Green Isle Hotel offers easy access off the N7 from Kerry, Cork and Limerick to the M50 and all of Dublin, with the LUAS 5 minutes distant. 240 bedrooms and suites; Sorrel's à la carte restaurant; Rosie O'Grady's pub; café bar; multi-storey car park with 400 spaces; convention facilities for 500 delegates inc. 40 new syndicate rooms; spa/gym/pool opening Autumn 2005. Free Wi-Fi access. City West Business Campus, Liffey Valley and Blanchardstown shopping centres nearby.

Member of Lynch Hotels Group

Room Rate from €99.00 to €159.00

Jim Flynn
General Manager

Activities:

Member of:

240 240

Open All Year

B&B Rates are per Person Sharing per Night incl. Breakfast.
or Room Rates are per Room per Night - See also Page 8

Dublin & East Coast   285

Lyndon Guesthouse	Maple Hotel	Maples House Hotel

Lyndon Guesthouse

26 Gardiner Place,
Dublin 1

Tel: 01-878 6950 Fax: 01-878 7420
Email: lyndonh@gofree.indigo.ie
Web: www.lyndonhouse.net

GUESTHOUSE ★★ MAP 8 O 11

Lyndon House is an extremely popular, beautifully restored Georgian guesthouse incorporating modern design. It is excellently located in the heart of Dublin's city centre off Parnell Square at the top of O'Connell Street and is on 41/41c airport bus route. It is family-run, so emphasis is on good value, warm atmosphere and friendly service. All rooms with bathroom en suite, TV, internal telephone and hospitality tray. Highly Acclaimed AA ♦♦.

B&B from €40.00 to €100.00

Colm & Magella Hilliard

Member of:

Open All Year

Maple Hotel

75 Lower Gardiner Street,
Dublin 1

Tel: 01-874 0225 Fax: 01-874 5239
Email: info@maplehotel.com
Web: www.maplehotel.com

HOTEL ★★ MAP 8 O 11

The Maple Hotel is situated in the heart of the city, just off O'Connell Street beside all theatres, cinemas, galleries, museums, main railway and central bus station, with a direct link to Dublin Airport. The hotel is owned and run by the Sharkey family who have been welcoming guests here for over 40 years. All luxurious bedrooms en suite with colour TV, direct dial phones, hairdryer and tea/coffee facilities. Private car parking. As stated in 'Time Out', "if you're after the charm and comfort of the chintz and doily school of hospitality then you've hit the jackpot here".

B&B from €40.00 to €80.00

The Sharkey Family

Member of:

Closed 16 December - 13 January

Maples House Hotel

Iona Road,
Glasnevin,
Dublin 9

Tel: 01-830 4227 Fax: 01-830 3874
Email: info@mapleshotel.com
Web: www.mapleshotel.com

HOTEL ★★ MAP 8 O 11

The friendly and welcoming Maples House Hotel is a beautifully newly refurbished 20th century Edwardian building situated north of the city centre just 15 minutes from Temple Bar. Croke Park is just 1 mile while international football/rugby grounds, concert venues, airport and golf courses are easily accessible. Our 22 bedrooms are of high quality as is our restaurant, bar, lounge and function room. We also cater for conferences, weddings, funerals and banquets.

B&B from €50.00 to €65.00

Ann O'Hanlon &
Avril McCarthy
Proprietors

Activities:

Member of:

Special Offer: Midweek Specials from €135.00 pps
(3 Nights B&B)

Closed 24 - 27 December

B&B Rates are per Person Sharing per Night incl. Breakfast.
or **Room Rates** are per Room per Night - See also Page 8

Marian Guest House

21 Upper Gardiner Street,
Dublin 1

Tel: 01-874 4129
Email: enquiries@marianguesthouse.ie
Web: www.marianguesthouse.ie

GUESTHOUSE ★ MAP 8 O 11

The Marian Guesthouse is owned and run by the McElroy family. It is just off Mountjoy Square and five minutes walk from city centre and all principal shopping areas, cinemas, theatres, museums. Well appointed bedrooms some of which are en suite. Tea and coffee making facilities available and use of private car park.

B&B from €25.00 to €45.00

McElroy Family
Owners

Member of:
IRISH HOTELS FEDERATION

🛏️ 🛎️ 🖵 C ✿ P
6 5

Open All Year

Mercer Hotel

Mercer Street Lower,
Dublin 2

Tel: 01-478 2179 Fax: 01-478 0328
Email: info@mercerhotel.ie
Web: www.mercerhotel.ie

HOTEL ★★★ MAP 8 O 11

The Mercer Hotel is a luxurious, boutique style hotel located in the vibrant heart of Dublin city. The hotel offers a modern yet relaxed atmosphere; all rooms are beautifully appointed and fully equipped with all you need for a great stay including TV, CD player, internet access, a fridge and complimentary mineral water. After a busy day you can indulge in Cusack's Bar & Restaurant with a variety of innovative menus to suit all tastes.

Bookable on www.irelandhotels.com
Member of Mercer Accommodation Group

B&B from €55.00 to €125.00

Catherine McGrath
General Manager

Member of:
IRISH HOTELS FEDERATION

🛏️ 🛎️ ☎ 🖵 ⚡ T C ↻ C M P 📶 inet
41 41

Closed 22 - 29 December

Merrion Hall

54 Merrion Road,
Ballsbridge,
Dublin 4
Tel: 01-668 1426 Fax: 01-668 4280
Email: merrionhall@iol.ie
Web: www.halpinsprivatehotels.com

GUESTHOUSE ★★★★ MAP 8 O 11

The 4**** award-winning manor house offers an elegant combination of Edwardian grace, fine food & modern comforts, all one expects of a private hotel, aircon suites, executive facilities, spa, 4-poster beds, private car park & gardens. Adjacent to RDS & Four Seasons Hotel, close to city centre, airport & car ferry terminals by DART or bus. Accolades: AA ♦♦♦♦♦, JDB Hotels, RAC Property of Year, Times, Johansens. Sister property of adjoining Blakes, Aberdeen Lodge & Halpins Hotel, Co. Clare. Spa opening Spring 2006.
USA toll free 1800 617 3178.
Global free phone +800 128 38155.

Bookable on www.irelandhotels.com
Member of Manor House Hotels

B&B from €79.00 to €119.00

Pat Halpin
Proprietor

Activities:
✈️ 🏥 💧

Member of:
IRISH HOTELS FEDERATION

🛏️ 🛎️ ☎ 🖵 ⚡ T C C M ✿ 🕙 J P S 📶
30 30
inet WiFi

Open All Year

B&B Rates are per Person Sharing per Night incl. Breakfast.
or Room Rates are per Room per Night - See also Page 8

Dublin & East Coast 287

Co. Dublin

Dublin City

Merrion Hotel	Mespil Hotel	Mont Clare Hotel O'Callaghan

Merrion Hotel

Upper Merrion Street,
Dublin 2

Tel: 01-603 0600 Fax: 01-603 0700
Email: info@merrionhotel.com
Web: www.merrionhotel.com

HOTEL ★★★★★ MAP 8 O 11

Dublin's most stylish 5***** hotel, located in the city centre opposite Government Buildings and created from four restored Georgian Townhouses. Many of the 143 bedrooms and suites overlook 18th century gardens including the luxurious Penthouse. Bars include The Cellar Bar and intimate cocktail bar, No. 23. The Cellar Restaurant serves traditional Irish cuisine, while Restaurant Patrick Guilbaud offers formal dining. Other features include an 18m pool, spa and private underground car park.

Bookable on www.irelandhotels.com
Member of Leading Hotels of the World

Room Rate from €370.00 to €470.00

Peter MacCann
General Manager

Member of:

143 143

inet 🐕

Open All Year

Mespil Hotel

Mespil Road,
Dublin 4

Tel: 01-488 4600 Fax: 01-667 1244
Email: mespil@leehotels.com
Web: www.leehotels.com

HOTEL ★★★ MAP 8 O 11

The Mespil boasts an ideal city centre location overlooking the banks of the Grand Canal and just 15 minutes walk to St. Stephen's Green and many major attractions including museums, theatres and shopping areas. All 255 en suite guest bedrooms are bright, spacious and tastefully furnished. Relax and unwind in our Terrace Bar or enjoy some tantalising dishes from the Glaze Restaurant. Wireless Internet service (Wi-Fi) now available. A warm and friendly welcome awaits you at the Mespil Hotel.

Bookable on www.irelandhotels.com
Member of Lee Hotels

Room Rate from €108.00 to €195.00

Martin Holohan
General Manager

Member of:

***Special Offer:** Room Only Specials from €99.00*

255 255

🐕

Closed 24 - 27 December

Mont Clare Hotel O'Callaghan

Merrion Square,
Dublin 2

Tel: 01-607 3800 Fax: 01-661 5663
Email: info@ocallaghanhotels.com
Web: www.ocallaghanhotels.com

HOTEL ★★★ MAP 8 O 11

A traditional Dublin hotel, the O'Callaghan Mont Clare is centrally located on Dublin's Merrion Square, just a few minutes walk to all major attractions including Trinity College, museums, theatres, business and shopping areas. 74 newly refurbished bedrooms with air-conditioning, a charming lounge bar, Goldsmith's Restaurant, conference facilities and parking. Reservations via UTELL International Worldwide. USA Toll Free Reservations 1800 5699983 and online at www.ocallaghanhotels.com

Bookable on www.irelandhotels.com
Member of O'Callaghan Hotels

B&B from €67.50 to €112.00

Karen Donegan
General Manager

Activities:

Member of:

74 74

Closed from 24 - 27 December

B&B Rates are per Person Sharing per Night incl. Breakfast.
or Room Rates are per Room per Night - See also Page 8

Morgan Hotel

10 Fleet Street,
Temple Bar,
Dublin 2
Tel: 01-643 7000 Fax: 01-643 7060
Email: reservations@themorgan.com
Web: www.themorgan.com

HOTEL **U** MAP 8 O 11

The Morgan is a boutique contemporary hotel offering a lifestyles elegance, with modern chic décor, located in the heart of Dublin's Temple Bar. The Morgan offers a cool modern interior that contrasts from the dynamic street life in the area and provides the ultimate in comfort and luxury for the discerning traveller. All bedrooms including de luxe rooms and suites are individually designed and are equipped with TV/video, mini Hi-Fi, mini bar and bathrobes. High speed internet available in all rooms. Online bookings, www.themorgan.com

Bookable on www.irelandhotels.com

Room Rate from €126.00 to €252.00

Alva Kenny
General Manager

Activities:

Member of:

Special Offer: Midweek Specials from €210.00 pps (3 Nights B&B)

66 66

Closed 24 - 27 December

Morrison (The)

Lower Ormond Quay,
Dublin 1
Tel: 01-887 2400 Fax: 01-878 3185
Email: info@morrisonhotel.ie
Web: www.morrisonhotel.ie

HOTEL ★★★★ MAP 8 O 11

One of the most sophisticated hotels in Dublin, the Morrison is in the heart of the city overlooking the River Liffey. The 128 superior rooms, 9 suites & the uniquely designed penthouse are decorated in a style combining the use of natural Irish materials. Features include Halo Restaurant which offers Irish organic home from home-cooking, the well established Café Bar and 7 flexible meeting and event venues catering from 8-230 delegates. The latest edition to the Morrison is our wellbeing spa offering Turkish baths and holistic relaxation treatments.

Bookable on www.irelandhotels.com
Member of Sterling Hotels & Resorts

B&B from €220.00 to €320.00

Andrew O'Neill
General Manager

Activities:

Member of:

138 138

WiFi

Closed 24 - 27 December

Mount Herbert Hotel

Herbert Road,
Lansdowne Road, Ballsbridge,
Dublin 4
Tel: 01-668 4321 Fax: 01-660 7077
Email: info@mountherberthotel.ie
Web: www.mountherberthotel.ie

HOTEL **U** MAP 8 O 11

A rare gem of a hotel located in Dublin city's fashionable Ballsbridge. Beside Lansdowne Road Stadium and RDS. Easy access to the city centre and airport by train or bus. Guests can enjoy all of the hotel's modern facilities, including 172 bedrooms, the Tritonville Bar & Terrace, brasserie, conference and business centre and complimentary car park. Its outstanding value has made it one of Dublin's most popular hotels for many years.

Bookable on www.irelandhotels.com

B&B from €39.50 to €99.50

Conor Doyle
General Manager

Activities:

Member of:

Special Offer: Midweek Specials from €105.00 pps (3 Nights B&B)

172 172

WiFi

Closed 23 - 29 December

B&B Rates are per Person Sharing per Night incl. Breakfast.
or **Room Rates** are per Room per Night - See also Page 8

Co. Dublin

Dublin City

Number 31	O'Sheas Hotel	Othello House
31 Leeson Close, Dublin 2	19 Talbot Street, Dublin 1	74 Lower Gardiner Street, Dublin 1
Tel: 01-676 5011 Fax: 01-676 2929 Email: number31@iol.ie Web: www.number31.ie	Tel: 01-836 5670 Fax: 01-836 5214 Email: osheashotel@eircom.net Web: www.osheashotel.com	Tel: 01-855 4271 Fax: 01-855 7460 Email: othello1@eircom.net Web: www.othelloguesthouse.com

GUESTHOUSE ★★★★ MAP 8 O 11 | **HOTEL U MAP 8 O 11** | **GUESTHOUSE ★★ MAP 8 O 11**

An award-winning guesthouse right in the heart of Georgian Dublin. The former home of Ireland's leading architect Sam Stephenson just a few minutes walk from St. Stephen's Green and galleries. An oasis of tranquillity and greenery, where guests are encouraged to come back and relax and feel at home at any time of the day. Vast breakfasts in the dining room or in a sunny plant filled conservatory. Recommended by the Good Hotel Guide, Egon Ronay, Bridgestone 100 Best Places, Fodors.

Member of Hidden Ireland

O'Sheas Hotel - renowned the world over for its close association with Irish music, song & dance - it's this that provides the theme for the hotel, with its typical Irish pub and restaurant serving the best in Irish cuisine with a healthy sprinkling of international dishes. O'Sheas Hotel has 34 recently refurbished en suite bedrooms, the hotel also has function and conference room facilities for up to 180 people and provides live entertainment seven nights. We look forward to welcoming you.

Othello is 150m from Abbey Theatre, 200m from Dublin's main O'Connell Street, 50m from central bus station. Number 41 bus direct from Dublin Airport stops outside door. 150m to Connolly Railway Station, 1 mile to ferry terminal, 800m to Point Theatre. Lock up secure car park. All rooms en suite with TV, telephone, tea/coffee making facilities. Trinity College, National Museum, National Library all within walking distance.

Room Rate from €100.00 to €240.00 | *B&B from €60.00 to €60.00* | *B&B from €45.00 to €60.00*

 Deirdre & Noel Comer Proprietors

 John McCormack Manager

John Galloway Manager

Member of: IRISH HOTELS FEDERATION | Member of: IRISH HOTELS FEDERATION

18 18 | 34 34 | 22 22

Open All Year | **Closed 24 - 25 December** | **Closed 23 - 27 December**

B&B Rates are per Person Sharing per Night incl. Breakfast. or Room Rates are per Room per Night - See also Page 8

Palmerstown Lodge

Palmerstown Village,
Dublin 20

Tel: 01-623 5494 Fax: 01-623 6214
Email: info@palmerstownlodge.com
Web: www.palmerstownlodge.com

GUESTHOUSE ★★★ MAP 8 O 11

Prime location adjacent to all amenities and facilities this superb purpose-built property adjoins the N4/M50 motorway. Minutes from the city centre and a mere 12 minutes drive to the airport we offer all the features and standards of a hotel. Each elegant en suite bedroom has individual temperature control, ambient lighting, automated door locking system, phone, TV, etc. Separate tea/coffee and iron/trouser press facilities. Private car park. Golf packages available.

B&B from €50.00 to €80.00

Gerry O'Connor
Owner

Member of:

19 19

Open All Year

Paramount Hotel

Parliament Street & Essex Gate,
Temple Bar,
Dublin 2

Tel: 01-417 9900 Fax: 01-417 9904
Email: sales@paramounthotel.ie
Web: www.paramounthotel.ie

HOTEL ★★★ MAP 8 O 11

Set in Temple Bar's quieter west end, Paramount Hotel is one of the city's most trendy and cosmopolitan. The hotel boasts 66 en suite bedrooms, tastefully decorated in the very elegant style of the 1930s. The hotel's bar, the Turks Head, is a stylish bar renowned for its extravagant design, & vibrant colours. Bistro dishes are served daily, and the bar turns into a late bar with club at the weekend. Email: info@turkshead.ie or Web: www.turkshead.ie

Bookable on www.irelandhotels.com

Room Rate from €80.00 to €240.00

Rita Barcoe
General Manager

Activities:

Member of:

Special Offer: Midweek Specials from €180.00 pps
(3 Nights B&B)

66 66

Closed 22 - 29 December

Park Plaza Tyrrelstown

Tyrrelstown,
Dublin 15

Tel: 01-703 7300 Fax: 01-662 5062
Email: info@parkplazatyrrelstown.com
Web: www.parkplazatyrrelstown.com

UNDER CONSTRUCTION - OPENING JULY 2006

HOTEL P MAP 8 O 11

Located in close proximity to both Dublin City centre and airport, this magnificent contemporary hotel features 150 bedrooms including 6 suites, with each room boasting broadband and state of the art entertainment systems. A self-contained conference area houses 12 rooms with a capacity of over 500. Our Spa and treatment rooms are available for your relaxation and our signature restaurant and bar are tailored for your enjoyment. Extensive car parking is also provided.

Member of Park Plaza Hotels & Resorts

Room Rate from €150.00 to €300.00

General Manager

150 150

Inet WiFi

Open All Year

B&B Rates are per Person Sharing per Night incl. Breakfast.
or **Room Rates** are per Room per Night - See also Page 8

Dublin City

Phoenix Park House	Plaza Hotel	Portobello Hotel & Bar

Phoenix Park House

38-39 Parkgate Street,
Dublin 8

Tel: 01-677 2870 Fax: 01-679 9769
Email: info@dublinguesthouse.com
Web: www.dublinguesthouse.com

GUESTHOUSE ★★ MAP 8 O 11

This friendly AA listed family-run guesthouse directly beside the Phoenix Park with its many facilities is ideally located 2 minutes walk from the new tram service and Heuston Station with direct bus service to ferry ports, Dublin Airport, Connolly Train Station and central bus station. Close to the Guinness Brewery, Whiskey Corner, the re-located National Museum and Kilmainham Museum of Modern Art, the popular Temple Bar and numerous pubs and restaurants. All rooms with tea/coffee making facilities.

Bookable on www.irelandhotels.com

B&B from €35.00 to €75.00

Mary Smith & Emer Smith
Proprietors

Activities:

Member of:
IRISH HOTELS FEDERATION

25 25

Closed 22 - 28 December

Plaza Hotel

Belgard Road,
Tallaght,
Dublin 24

Tel: 01-462 4200 Fax: 01-462 4600
Email: reservations@plazahotel.ie
Web: www.plazahotel.ie

HOTEL ★★★★ MAP 8 O 11

120 bedrooms, 2 suites. Convenient location on Belgard Road, just off the M50 motorway, 8 miles from the city centre. Secure underground car parking. LUAS Tallaght stop, direct tram link to the city centre is located 3 minutes from the Plaza Hotel. Extensive conference & banqueting facilities for up to 220 people. Floor One serving food from 9.00am - 10.00pm daily. Obar1 music bar. The Playhouse Nightclub. Grumpy McClafferty's traditional pub. 20 minutes from Dublin Airport.

Room Rate from €100.00 to €205.00

Jim Lavery
General Manager

Activities:

Member of:
IRISH HOTELS FEDERATION

122 122

Closed 24 - 31 December

Portobello Hotel & Bar

33 South Richmond Street,
Dublin 2

Tel: 01-475 2715 Fax: 01-478 5010
Email: portobellohotel@indigo.ie
Web: www.portobellohotel.ie

HOTEL U MAP 8 O 11

This landmark building is located in the heart of Dublin City along the Grand Canal. First opened in 1793, the Portobello Hotel & Bar boasts a long tradition in hospitality and provides guests with luxury en suite accommodation with tea/coffee making facilities, TV, radio, iron & board, direct dial phone & hairdryer. Temptation Night Club popular with all ages. A friendly welcome and service is guaranteed.

B&B from €45.00 to €140.00

Ciara Darcy
Manager

Member of:
IRISH HOTELS FEDERATION

24 24

Open All Year

B&B Rates are per Person Sharing per Night incl. Breakfast. or **Room Rates** are per Room per Night - See also Page 8

Quality Hotel Dublin

Cardiff Lane,
Sir John Rogerson's Quay,
Dublin 2
Tel: 01-6439500 Fax: 01-6439510
Email: info@qualityhoteldublin.com
Web: www.qualityhoteldublin.com

HOTEL P MAP 8 O 11

Superbly situated on Dublin's trendy South Bank, the new Quality Hotel is perfectly placed in the heart of Dublin's vibrant city centre, overlooking the River Liffey & within a short walk of main city centre shopping, Temple Bar, sightseeing & business districts. The Quality Hotel Dublin features 211 superior 3-star standard bedrooms, Lannigans Restaurant & Club Vitae Leisure Centre, all the facilities you would expect from one of Ireland's leading hotel groups.

Bookable on www.irelandhotels.com
Member of Quality Hotels

Room Rate from €89.00 to €229.00

Conor O'Kane
General Manager

🏨📶 ☎📧📺©♨CM❄🔥🎱📷🎵P
⛱️🅿️🔤 🌐 inet WiFi 🐕
211 211

Closed 23 - 27 December

Raglan Lodge

10 Raglan Road,
Ballsbridge,
Dublin 4
Tel: 01-660 6697 Fax: 01-660 6781

GUESTHOUSE ★★★★ MAP 8 O 11

Raglan Lodge is a magnificent Victorian residence dating from 1861. It is just ten minutes from the heart of Dublin in a most peaceful location. There are 7 guest rooms, all of which have bathrooms en suite, colour TV, radio/alarm, telephone & tea/coffee facilities. Several of the rooms are noteworthy for their fine proportions and high ceilings. National winner of the Galtee Irish Breakfast Award. Also, received Breakfast Award in Georgina Campbell's Jameson Guide 2001. Secure car parking facilities. Recommended by RAC, AA & Egon Ronay.

B&B from €70.00 to €80.00

Helen Moran
Proprietress

Member of:

🏨📶 ☎📺©❄♨P⛱️
7 7

Closed 18 December - 07 January

Red Cow Moran Hotel

Red Cow Complex,
Naas Road,
Dublin 22
Tel: 01-459 3650 Fax: 01-459 1588
Email: redcowres@moranhotels.com
Web: www.moranhotels.com

HOTEL ★★★★ MAP 8 O 11

4**** Red Cow Moran Hotel combines classic elegance with modern design, situated at the Gateway to the Provinces, convenient to city centre, minutes drive from Dublin Airport. Easy access into the City Centre via the LUAS Light Rail Service! Bedrooms are fully air-conditioned with colour teletext TV, direct dial phones/fax, hairdryer, trouser press & tea/coffee facilities. The complex boasts a choice of lively bars and features two superb restaurants and a carvery restaurant, conference facilities. Night Club. Free carparking. AA 4****. A Moran Hotel.

Bookable on www.irelandhotels.com
Member of Moran Hotels

B&B from €60.00 to €190.00

Tom Moran
Managing Director

Activities:

🍸

Member of:

Special Offer: Weekend Specials from €145.00 pps
(2 Nights B&B & 1 Dinner)

🏨📶 ☎📧📺©♨CM P⛱️🔤 🌐 WiFi
🐕🐈
123 123

Closed 24 - 26 December

B&B Rates are per Person Sharing per Night incl. Breakfast.
or **Room Rates** are per Room per Night - See also Page 8

Dublin & East Coast 293

Co. Dublin

Dublin City

Regency Airport Hotel	River House Hotel	Roxford Lodge Hotel

Swords Road,
Whitehall,
Dublin 9
Tel: 01-837 3544 Fax: 01-836 7121
Email: regency@regencyhotels.com
Web: www.regencyhotels.com

23/24 Eustace Street,
Temple Bar,
Dublin 2
Tel: 01-670 7655 Fax: 01-670 7650
Email: reservations@riverhousehotel.com
Web: www.riverhousehotel.com

46 Northumberland Road,
Ballsbridge,
Dublin 4
Tel: 01-668 8572 Fax: 01-668 8158
Email: reservations@roxfordlodge.ie
Web: www.roxfordlodge.ie

HOTEL ★★★ MAP 8 O 11   HOTEL ★★ MAP 8 O 11   HOTEL U MAP 8 O 11

Located 3km north of Dublin City centre on main route to Dublin Airport and Northern Ireland. The hotel's 70 executive rooms have hairdryer and trouser press as standard. The hotel features the Shanard Restaurant, the Appian Lounge, Seasons Theme Restaurant and ample parking. Opening in early 2006 is a state of the art Leisure Centre with swimming pool, children's pool, sauna, 24 spa/treatment rooms, steam room and gym.

A city centre hotel located in Dublin's colourful and exciting Temple Bar area. With its cobbled streets, shops, art galleries, bars, restaurants and lively night life, Temple Bar has become a tourist attraction itself. All of our 29 bedrooms are en suite and have tea/coffee making facilities, remote control TV, radio, hairdryer and direct dial telephone. Hotel facilities include 'The Mezz' Bar and 'The Hub' Nightclub which is sound proofed, the best live music venues in Dublin. Family-run, friendly staff.

Luxury family-run boutique style hotel located in Ballsbridge, Dublin's most exclusive area. Just 10 minutes walk from the city centre and all the major attractions such as Trinity College and Grafton Street. All of our en suite bedrooms have the added luxury of saunas, and most also have jacuzzi baths. All rooms have broadband internet access. Our executive suite offers the ultimate in luxury. Secure car parking. Public transport at front door.

Bookable on www.irelandhotels.com *Bookable on www.irelandhotels.com*

B&B from €75.00 to €140.00 *B&B from €50.00 to €80.00* *B&B from €60.00 to €125.00*

 David Kiely, Operations Manager

 Sheelagh Conway, Proprietor

 Desmond Killoran, Proprietor

Special Offer: Weekend Specials from €109.00 pps (2 Nights B&B & 1 Dinner)

Special Offer: Midweek Specials from €130.00 pps (3 Nights B&B)

Open All Year | Closed 24 - 27 December | Closed 24 - 27 December

B&B Rates are per Person Sharing per Night incl. Breakfast. or **Room Rates** are per Room per Night - See also Page 8

School House Hotel

2-8 Northumberland Road,
Ballsbridge,
Dublin 4
Tel: 01-667 5014 Fax: 01-667 5015
Email: reservations@schoolhousehotel.com
Web: www.schoolhousehotel.com

HOTEL ★★★★ MAP 8 O 11

Without doubt, one of the most unique and beautiful properties in the city. Do not miss an opportunity to stay at this charming 4**** hotel conversion. All 31 de luxe bedrooms are individually named and furnished to the highest international standard. The original classrooms now host the award-winning Canteen @ The Schoolhouse and the lively and popular Schoolhouse Bar. Just a short stroll to Grafton Street, Lansdowne Road, The RDS and all of Dublin's major visitor attractions.

Bookable on www.irelandhotels.com
Member of Sweeney Hotels

B&B from €100.00 to €150.00

Maureen Cafferkey
General Manager

Member of:

🛏️🐾 ☎️🖥️📠🇹🇨🚭CM☀️P🅿️🆔🔌 inet
31 31
WiFi

Closed 24 - 26 December

Shelbourne Hotel (The)

27 St. Stephen's Green,
Dublin 2

Tel: 01-663 4500 Fax: 01-661 6006
Email: annemarie.whelan@renaissancehotels.com
Web: www.marriott.com

UNDER REFURBISHMENT - RE-OPENING AUGUST 2006

HOTEL U MAP 8 O 11

The Shelbourne Hotel, an institution in Irish hospitality, with a distinguished address, offering the ultimate in luxury & service. Located within walking distance of Dublin's main shopping thoroughfare & cultural life. 190 rooms, 2 bars & 2 restaurants and the renowned Lord Mayor's Lounge serving afternoon tea since 1824. Shelbourne Club - 18m pool, sauna, jacuzzi, 50 pieces of gym equipment - strictly over 18s. Under restoration. Managed by Marriott International. Due to re-open August 2006. Please enquire about facilities for guests with special needs.

Member of Marriott International

Room Rate from €275.00 to €310.00

Philip Spencer
General Manager

Activities:
🎣

Member of:

🛏️🐾 ☎️🖥️📠🇹🇨🚭CM🎣🖥️🍽️🏠P🅿️🆔 inet WiFi 🐕🎣
190 190

Closed 01 January - 31 July

Sheldon Park Hotel & Leisure Centre

Kylemore Road,
Dublin 12

Tel: 01-460 1055 Fax: 01-460 1880
Email: info@sheldonpark.ie
Web: www.sheldonpark.ie

HOTEL ★★ MAP 8 O 11

The Sheldon Park is ideally situated just off the N7 and M50. City centre is just 15 minutes by bus or LUAS (Kylemore stop - 2 min walk). Liffey Valley Shopping Centre only minutes away. All rooms have tea & coffee making facilities. Relax in our superb leisure centre with fully equipped gym, sauna, steam room, 20m pool, jacuzzi and beauty salon. Extensive bar food menu in Minnie McCabes Bar all day. Award-winning Houstons Restaurant open for dinner nightly. Live entertainment Friday - Sunday. Extensive conference and banqueting facilities.

Bookable on www.irelandhotels.com

B&B from €65.00 to €85.00

Ron Marks
Deputy General Manager

Activities:
🎣

Member of:

Special Offer: Weekend Specials from €149.00 pps
(2 Nights B&B & 1 Dinner)

🛏️🐾 ☎️🖥️📠🇹🇨🚭CM🎣🖥️🏠🛁🔌♪P
104 104
S🆔🔌 inet WiFi

Closed 24 - 26 December

<u>B&B Rates</u> are per Person Sharing per Night incl. Breakfast.
or <u>Room Rates</u> are per Room per Night - See also Page 8

Co. Dublin

Dublin City

St. Aiden's Guesthouse

32 Brighton Road,
Rathgar,
Dublin 6
Tel: 01-490 2011 Fax: 01-492 0234
Email: staidens@eircom.net
Web: www.staidens.com

GUESTHOUSE ★★★ MAP 8 O 11

Charming guesthouse located in up-market village suburb of Rathgar. 10 mins from M50. Orbital link to Airport and country. 10 mins to city by bus. On excellent bus route. Several good restaurants and pubs nearby. Adjacent to lovely parks for walks and playgrounds. Discounted local health club access (swimming/gym). Car hire firm immediately adjacent. Very family friendly. Sitting room with TV / video / DVD for guest use only. Wi-Fi.

Bookable on www.irelandhotels.com

B&B from €45.00 to €57.00

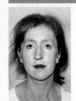

Marie Mc Donagh
Proprietress

Member of:

🛏️ 📞 ... WiFi
8   8

Closed 22 December - 02 January

Stauntons on the Green

83 St. Stephen's Green,
Dublin 2
Tel: 01-478 2300 Fax: 01-478 2263
Email: info@stauntonsonthegreen.ie
Web: www.dublincityrooms.com

GUESTHOUSE ★★★ MAP 8 O 11

Large Georgian house overlooking St. Stephen's Green, own private gardens. All rooms are en suite and fully equipped with direct dial telephone, TV and tea/coffee welcoming trays, trouser press and hairdryer. It is close to museums, galleries, Grafton Street shopping area and many other major tourist attractions. Stauntons On the Green occupies one of Dublin's most prestigious locations, close to many corporate headquarters and government buildings.

B&B from €70.00 to €95.00

Colette Saul
Manager

🛏️ 📞 ...
30 30

Closed 24 - 27 December

Stephen's Green Hotel O'Callaghan

St. Stephen's Green,
Dublin 2
Tel: 01-607 3600 Fax: 01-661 5663
Email: info@ocallaghanhotels.com
Web: www.ocallaghanhotels.com

HOTEL ★★★★ MAP 8 O 11

The O'Callaghan Stephen's Green is a warm modern boutique style hotel, located within minutes walk of Grafton Street and the main shopping and business districts. The hotel beautifully combines two refurbished Georgian houses and contemporary style with a four story glass atrium overlooking St.Stephen's Green. 75 luxurious air-conditioned bedrooms, gymnasium, business centre, fashionable Magic Glasses Bar and Pie Dish Bistro. Wired and wireless broadband throughout and excellent meeting facilities. USA toll free reservations 1800 569 9983 or www.ocallaghanhotels.com

Member of O'Callaghan Hotels

B&B from €87.50 to €189.00

Dara McEneaney
General Manager

Activities:

Member of:

🛏️ 📞 ... Inet WiFi
75 75

Closed 24 - 30 December

B&B Rates are per Person Sharing per Night incl. Breakfast. or **Room Rates** are per Room per Night - See also Page 8

Tara Towers Hotel

Merrion Road,
Dublin 4

Tel: 01-269 4666 Fax: 01-269 1027
Email: info@taratowers.com
Web: www.taratowers.com

HOTEL ★★★ MAP 8 O 11

The Tara Towers Hotel is a well-established favourite, nestled beside the sea on Merrion Road, just 3km south of Dublin's city centre. Situated along the sweeping curves of Dublin Bay you can experience breathtaking views of sea and shore. All rooms are fully appointed and cater for comfort. You can relax and unwind in PJ Branagan's Pub or have a sumptuous dinner in the Conservatory Restaurant. Guests also have the bonus of ample free car parking.

Bookable on www.irelandhotels.com
Member of Mercer Accommodation Group

Room Rate from €44.50 to €100.00

*Jim Jansen
General Manager*

Member of:

111 111

Closed 23 - 27 December

Tavistock House

64 Ranelagh Road,
Ranelagh,
Dublin 6

Tel: 01-498 8000 Fax: 01-498 8000
Email: info@tavistockhouse.com
Web: www.tavistockhouse.com

GUESTHOUSE ★★★ MAP 8 O 11

Magnificent Victorian house, tastefully converted retaining all its original plasterwork - very homely. Situated on the city side of Ranelagh Village, on the corner of Ranelagh / Northbrook Roads. We are only 7 minutes walk from Stephen's Green in the heart of Dublin, near Helen Dillon's world famous garden. All rooms have colour TV, direct dial phone, hairdryer and tea/coffee making facilities. Private parking. There is a wide variety of restaurants locally. Internet facilities.

Bookable on www.irelandhotels.com

B&B from €45.00 to €75.00

*Maureen & Brian Cusack
Co-Owners*

Member of:

6 6

Open All Year

Temple Bar Hotel

Fleet Street,
Temple Bar,
Dublin 2

Tel: 01-677 3333 Fax: 01-677 3088
Email: reservations@tbh.ie
Web: www.templebarhotel.com

HOTEL ★★★ MAP 8 O 11

A Tower Group Hotel - situated in the heart of Dublin's Temple Bar, in close proximity to theatres, shops and restaurants, the Temple Bar Hotel features 129 en suite bedrooms fully equipped with modern facilities. Restaurant. Conference and meeting room facilities for up to 70 people. The Temple Bar Hotel is within easy access of train stations, airport and Dublin Port. There is a multi storey car park nearby. Special online offers available on www.towerhotelgroup.com

Bookable on www.irelandhotels.com
Member of Tower Hotel Group

B&B from €80.00 to €130.00

*Guy Thompson
General Manager*

Activities:

Member of:

129 129

Closed 23 - 25 December

B&B Rates are per Person Sharing per Night incl. Breakfast.
or Room Rates are per Room per Night - See also Page 8

Dublin City

Trinity Capital Hotel	Uppercross House	Waterloo House

**Pearse Street,
Dublin 2**

Tel: 01-648 1000 Fax: 01-648 1010
Email: info@trinitycapitalhotel.com
Web: www.capital-hotels.com

Uppercross House

**26-30 Upper Rathmines Road,
Dublin 6**

Tel: 01-497 5486 Fax: 01-497 5361
Email: reservations@uppercrosshousehotel.com
Web: www.uppercrosshousehotel.com

Waterloo House

**8-10 Waterloo Road,
Ballsbridge,
Dublin 4**

Tel: 01-660 1888 Fax: 01-667 1955
Email: waterloohouse@eircom.net
Web: www.waterloohouse.ie

HOTEL ★★★ MAP 8 O 11

A first visit to the Trinity Capital will immediately confirm that this hotel offers something rather special indeed. At the very heart of Dublin's city centre, the striking & unique interior design will delight you in an eye-catching way & instantly you will feel relaxed, welcomed & thus pleased by your hotel choice. Opened in May 2000, this hotel features all mod cons as required by today's business & leisure guest. Accommodation is modern, spacious & of a high standard. Complimentary admission to a variety of clubs belonging to Capital Bars Group. Grafton Street, Temple Bar & Trinity College all mins away on foot.

Bookable on www.irelandhotels.com
Member of Capital Hotels

HOTEL ★★★ MAP 8 O 11

Uppercross House is a hotel providing 49 bedrooms of the highest standard of comfort. All with direct dial phone, TV, free WiFi internet access, tea/coffee maker, central heating and all bedrooms are en suite. Uppercross House has its own secure parking and is ideally situated in Dublin's south side 2km from St. Stephen's Green and R.D.S., with excellent public transport from directly outside the door. A fully licensed restaurant and bar opens nightly with a warm and friendly atmosphere.

Bookable on www.irelandhotels.com

GUESTHOUSE ★★★★ MAP 8 O 11

A warm welcome awaits you at this luxury guesthouse, in the heart of Georgian Dublin. It comprises 2 Georgian houses, refurbished to superb standard, retaining original features, offering unique atmosphere, style, elegance. Minutes from RDS, St. Stephen's Green, Grafton Street and city centre. Delicious breakfast is served in the dining room, overlooking conservatory & gardens. Lift & car park. Wireless internet connection available. Recommended: Bridgestone 100 Best Places, Alister Sawday's, Michelin Guide and Lonely Planet. AA ◆◆◆◆◆.

B&B from €60.00 to €120.00

Josephine Pepper

Member of:

Special Offer: *Midweek Specials from €139.00 pps
(3 Nights B&B)*

82 82   Inet WiFi 🐕

Closed 24 - 26 December

B&B from €49.50 to €69.50

*David Mahon
Proprietor*

Member of:

49 49   🐕

Closed 23 - 30 December

B&B from €45.00 to €95.00

*Evelyn Corcoran
Proprietor*

17 17

Closed 23 - 28 December

B&B Rates are per Person Sharing per Night incl. Breakfast.
or **Room Rates** are per Room per Night - See also Page 8

Waterloo Lodge

23 Waterloo Road,
Ballsbridge,
Dublin 4
Tel: 01-668 5380 Fax: 01-668 5786
Email: info@waterloolodge.com
Web: www.waterloolodge.com

GUESTHOUSE ★★★ MAP 8 O 11

Waterloo Lodge is centrally located in Ballsbridge on the south side of Dublin City. Just minutes walk from the city centre, Stephen's Green, Temple Bar, museums, theatres, restaurants and pubs with a bus route outside our door. Our rooms are en suite, tastefully decorated, have direct dial phone, cable TV and hairdryer. All are non-smoking. Fax and email facilities are available. We assure you of a warm welcome and a pleasant stay.

Bookable on www.irelandhotels.com

B&B from €39.50 to €80.00

Cathal Daly
Owner

Member of:

Special Offer: *Midweek Specials from €112.50 pps (3 Nights B&B)*

🐎🚶 ☎🖥🛏🚽🆃🅲♿CM✲🅿🅿💷⚓ inet 🐴
15 15

Closed 24 - 26 December

West County Hotel

Chapelizod,
Dublin 20
Tel: 01-626 4011 Fax: 01-623 1378
Email: info@westcountyhotel.ie
Web: www.westcountyhotel.ie

HOTEL ★★ MAP 8 O 11

An established family-run hotel, located in the picturesque village of Chapelizod, just off the N4, close to M50 and Dublin International Airport, is convenient to Liffey Valley and Blanchardstown shopping centres. It comprises 50 en suite bedrooms equipped to 3*** standards (AA). Secure and free car parking. Extensive conference and banqueting facilities. Part of the Colgan Group Hotels and sister of The Lucan Spa hotel. Special offers available Tel. 01 626 4647.

Bookable on www.irelandhotels.com
Member of The Colgan Group

B&B from €50.00 to €90.00

Frank Colgan
Director

Activities:

Member of:

Special Offer: *Weekend Specials from €140.00 pps (2 Nights B&B & 1 Dinner)*

🐎🚶 ☎🖥🛏🚽🆃🅲CM♪🅿🅿💷⚓•🐴
50 50

Closed 25 December

Westbury (The)

Grafton Street,
Dublin 2
Tel: 01-679 1122 Fax: 01-679 7078
Email: westbury@jurysdoyle.com
Web: www.jurysdoyle.com

HOTEL ★★★★★ MAP 8 O 11

Smartly set just off Grafton Street in the very heart of the city, The Westbury can best be described as a truly international 5-star hotel; sophisticated, stylish and at the glamorous hub of Dublin life. Luxury, impeccable service and smart contemporary surroundings with the city at your feet.

Bookable on www.irelandhotels.com
Member of Leading Hotels of the World

B&B from €140.00 to €276.00

Paraic Doyle
General Manager

Member of:

🐎🚶 ☎🖥🛏🚽🆃🅲♿CM🎥🅿🅿💷 inet WiFi
🐴🐴
205 205

Open All Year

B&B Rates are per Person Sharing per Night incl. Breakfast.
or Room Rates are per Room per Night - See also Page 8

Co. Dublin

Dublin City / Dun Laoghaire

Westin Dublin

At College Green,
Westmoreland Street,
Dublin 2
Tel: 01-645 1000 Fax: 01-645 1234
Email: reservations.dublin@westin.com
Web: www.westin.com/dublin

HOTEL ★★★★ MAP 8 O 11

Situated in the heart of the city, steps away from Grafton Street, overlooking Trinity College. One of Dublin's most luxurious five star hotels offers an ambience of warmth & Irish hospitality. Each guest room features the highly acclaimed Heavenly Bed. We also offer 17 luxurious suites. A unique array of dining experiences awaits from the stylish Exchange Restaurant to the elegant Atrium Lounge or the popular Mint Bar. Flexible air-conditioned meeting rooms offer the latest in AV technology. Our largest room The Banking Hall has been restored to its original magnificent 19th C splendour.

Bookable on www.irelandhotels.com

Room Rate from €184.00 to €409.00

Enda M Mullin
General Manager

Activities:

Member of:

163 163

Open All Year

Kingston Hotel

Adelaide St., (Off Georges St.),
Dun Laoghaire,
Co. Dublin
Tel: 01-280 1810 Fax: 01-280 1237
Email: reserv@kingstonhotel.com
Web: www.kingstonhotel.com

HOTEL ★★ MAP 8 O 11

A delightful 45 bedroomed hotel with panoramic views of Dublin Bay, approximately 15 minutes from city centre. Beside ferryport and DART line. Situated convenient to R.D.S., Point Depot, Lansdowne Road and Leopardstown Racecourse. All rooms are en suite with direct dial phone, TV, tea/coffee making facilities. A family-run hotel serving food all day in our lounge/bar and our Marconi Restaurant opened Friday and Saturday nights only. Carlisle Bar: lunch and evening dinners served 7 days a week.

Member of Countrywide Hotels - MinOtel Ireland

B&B from €70.00 to €85.00

Tom Murphy
General Manager

Member of:

45 45

Closed 24 - 26 December

Rochestown Lodge Hotel

Rochestown Avenue,
Dun Laoghaire,
Co. Dublin
Tel: 01-285 3555 Fax: 01-285 3914
Email: info@rochestownlodge.com
Web: www.rochestownlodge.com

HOTEL U MAP 8 O 11

Whether you are staying in Dublin for business or for a leisure break, Rochestown Lodge provides the perfect stylishly modern setting to work or relax in complete comfort. Rochestown Lodge Hotel 15 minutes Dublin's city centre, recently refurbished, 90 executive rooms, executive king rooms, junior suites & spacious family rooms, a stylish café bar, an intimate snug & innovative contemporary food in the restaurant. A state-of-the-art conference centre, a fully equiped gym, a health & leisure club & with ample complimentary car parking provided.

Bookable on www.irelandhotels.com

B&B from €49.00 to €159.00

Declan Meagher
General Manager

Activities:

Member of:

Special Offer: Weekend Specials from €129.00 pps (2 Nights B&B & 1 Dinner)

90 90

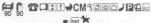

Closed 24 - 26 December

B&B Rates are per Person Sharing per Night incl. Breakfast. or Room Rates are per Room per Night - See also Page 8

Deer Park Hotel and Golf Courses

Howth,
Co. Dublin

Tel: 01-832 2624 Fax: 01-839 2405
Email: sales@deerpark.iol.ie
Web: www.deerpark-hotel.ie

HOTEL ★★★ MAP 12 P 11

14km from Dublin City/Airport on a quiet hillside overlooking the bay, Deer Park enjoys spectacular elevated sea views. Featuring Ireland's largest golf complex (5 courses), 18m swimming pool, sauna and steam room and two all-weather tennis courts. Whether on a golfing holiday or a visit to Dublin you will find Deer Park the ideal choice. Easy access to Dublin city via DART rapid rail link.

Bookable on www.irelandhotels.com
Member of Irish Country Hotels

B&B from €60.00 to €90.00

David & Antoinette Tighe Managers

Activities:
✓

Member of:
IRISH HOTELS FEDERATION

Special Offer: Weekend Specials from €160.00 pps (2 Nights B&B & 1 Dinner)

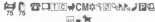
75 75

Closed 23 - 27 December

King Sitric Fish Restaurant & Accommodation

East Pier,
Howth,
Co. Dublin

Tel: 01-832 5235 Fax: 01-839 2442
Email: info@kingsitric.ie
Web: www.kingsitric.ie

GUESTHOUSE ★★★★ MAP 8 P 11

Est. 1971, Aidan and Joan MacManus have earned an international reputation for fresh seafood in their harbour-side restaurant in the picturesque fishing village of Howth. Now with 8 guest rooms, all with sea views. Wine lovers will enjoy browsing in the atmospheric wine cellar. For leisure pursuits, Howth is the perfect location for golfing, walking and sailing. Dublin City is 20 mins by DART; Dublin Airport 20 mins driving.

Member of Ireland's Blue Book

B&B from €72.50 to €102.50

Aidan & Joan MacManus

Activities:
✓

Member of:
IRISH HOTELS FEDERATION

Special Offer: Weekend Specials from €182.00 pps (2 Nights B&B & 1 Dinner)

8 8

Closed 24 - 28 December

Dún Laoghaire Rathdown County

Coastline or Countryside
Shopping or Golf
Sailing or Hill-Walking
Day-trip or Holiday

The Choice for all Seasons
An Rogha do Gach Séasúr !

Dún Laoghaire-Rathdown Tourism
Tel: +353-1-205 4855
E-mail: info@dlrtourism.com
www.dlrtourism.com

B&B Rates are per Person Sharing per Night incl. Breakfast.
or **Room Rates** are per Room per Night - See also Page 8

Fitzpatrick Castle Dublin

Killiney,
Co. Dublin

Tel: 01-230 5400 Fax: 01-230 5466
Email: dublin@fitzpatricks.com
Web: www.fitzpatrickhotels.com

HOTEL ★★★★ MAP 8 P 10

Fitzpatrick Castle Dublin is located in the fashionable surburbs of Killiney and Dalkey, over looking Dublin Bay. Over 30 years of tradition in excellence has helped to create the perfect atmosphere at this family owned 18th century castle. Relax and unwind in either PJ's Restaurant or The Dungeon Bar & Grill. The fitness centre hosts a 22m indoor pool, jacuzzi, sauna, steam room and gymnasium. Luxurious bedrooms, some featuring four posters or balcony sea views.

Bookable on www.irelandhotels.com

Room Rate from €140.00 to €270.00

Nicholas Logue
General Manager

Activities:

Member of:

Special Offer: Weekend Specials from €205.00 pps
(2 Nights B&B & 1 Dinner)

113 113

Open All Year

Becketts Country House Hotel

Cooldrinagh House,
Leixlip,
Co. Dublin / Kildare
Tel: 01-624 7040 Fax: 01-624 7072
Email: becketts@eircom.net
Web: www.becketts-leixlip.com

HOTEL ★★★ MAP 8 N 11

Becketts is situated in a quiet scenic area just off the N4 motorway at the Leixlip roundabout close to Dublin's new outer ring with easy access to Dublin Airport and all major road networks. Once home to the mother of Samuel Beckett the completely refurbished Cooldrinagh House is now home to Becketts. There are 4 suites and 6 luxury bedrooms and an elegant restaurant with a reputation for superb cuisine and full bar facilities.

B&B from €65.00 to €85.00

Colin Fitton
General Manager

Member of:

10 10

Closed 24 - 26 December

Finnstown Country House Hotel

Newcastle Road,
Lucan,
Co. Dublin
Tel: 01-601 0700 Fax: 01-628 1088
Email: manager@finnstown-hotel.ie
Web: www.finnstown-hotel.ie

HOTEL ★★★ MAP 8 N 11

One of County Dublin's finest country house hotels. Set on 45 acres of private grounds it offers privacy, peace and seclusion yet is only twenty minutes drive from the bustling city centre of Dublin. If it's good old-fashioned hospitality you're after, great food and drink, a relaxed atmosphere and stylish surroundings, you're in the right place! Leisure facilities include an 18 hole-putting course, gym, turkish bath, tennis court and indoor heated swimming pool.

Bookable on www.irelandhotels.com
Member of Distinguished Hotels

B&B from €70.00 to €115.00

Jenny Holmes
Hotel Manager

Activities:

Member of:

Special Offer: Midweek Specials from €180.00 pps
(3 Nights B&B)

53 53

Open All Year

B&B Rates are per Person Sharing per Night incl. Breakfast. or <u>Room Rates</u> are per Room per Night - See also Page 8

Lucan Spa Hotel

Lucan,
Co. Dublin

Tel: 01-628 0494 Fax: 01-628 0841
Email: info@lucanspahotel.ie
Web: www.lucanspahotel.ie

HOTEL ★★ MAP 8 N 11

Situated on the road to the West (N4) and close to the M50 and Dublin Airport, this elegant hotel offers its guests comfort and convenience in a country setting. All 70 bedrooms are equipped to 3 star standards (AA & RAC). Dine in the award-winning Honora D Restaurant (Evenings daily & Sunday lunch) or The Earl Bistro (7.30am - 9.45pm). All conference and weddings catered for. Special Offers available on 01-628 0494.

Bookable on www.irelandhotels.com
Member of The Colgan Group

B&B from €70.00 to €90.00

Frank Colgan
Director

Activities:
:/🍽

Member of:

Special Offer: Specials from €150.00 pps
(2 Nights B&B & 1 Dinner)

70 70

Closed 25 December

Moat Lodge

Newcastle Road,
Lucan,
Co. Dublin

Tel: 01-624 1584 Fax: 01-628 1356
Email: info@moatlodge.ie
Web: www.moatlodge.ie

GUESTHOUSE ★★ MAP 8 N 11

Exclusive 17th century house, convenient to buses for city centre, 200m walk to shops/pubs in the quaint Lucan Village. Ideal base for golf. Courses nearby include the K-Club, Carton House, Luttrellstown Castle, Hermitage and Lucan Golf Club. Off N4, near N7, N3 and M50. Private secure parking.

B&B from €35.00 to €50.00

Astrid Scott

Member of:

10 10

Open All Year

Grand Hotel

Malahide,
Co. Dublin

Tel: 01-845 0000 Fax: 01-845 0987
Email: booking@thegrand.ie
Web: www.thegrand.ie

HOTEL ★★★★ MAP 12 O 12

The Grand Hotel is situated by the sea in the village of Malahide. Just 10 minutes drive from Dublin Airport and 30 minutes from the city centre, the hotel is ideally situated for guests staying for business or leisure. The conference and business centre is one of Ireland's largest and most successful. All 150 bedrooms have tea/coffee making facilities and fax/broadband lines. Most bedrooms have spectacular sea views. Leisure centre includes a 21 metre swimming pool, jacuzzi, fully equipped gymnasium, sauna and steam room.

Bookable on www.irelandhotels.com

B&B from €82.50 to €145.00

Matthew Ryan
Managing Director

Activities:
:/🍽♨

Member of:

Special Offer: Weekend Specials from €140.00 pps
(2 Nights B&B & 1 Dinner)

150 150

alc ⚫ inet WiFi

Closed 24 - 27 December

B&B Rates are per Person Sharing per Night incl. Breakfast.
or Room Rates are per Room per Night - See also Page 8

Dublin & East Coast 303

Co. Dublin

Malahide / Portmarnock

Island View Hotel

Coast Road,
Malahide,
Co. Dublin
Tel: 01·845 0099 Fax: 01·845 1498
Email: info@islandviewhotel.ie
Web: www.islandviewhotel.ie

HOTEL ★★ MAP 12 O 12

Island View Hotel is ideally located for comfort and convenience and just a 10 minute drive from Dublin Airport. Our rooms are all en suite and fully equipped with modern facilities. Oscar Taylors Restaurant is an exclusive 150 seater restaurant with a panoramic view of Lambay Island and Malahide coastline. The restaurant is noted for its excellent cuisine. The menu is extensive and moderately priced.

B&B from €50.00 to €50.00

Feidhlim Hardy
General Manager

Member of:

11 11

Closed Christmas Day & Good Friday

Portmarnock Hotel & Golf Links

Strand Road,
Portmarnock,
Co. Dublin
Tel: 01·846 0611 Fax: 01·846 2442
Email: reservations@portmarnock.com
Web: www.portmarnock.com

HOTEL ★★★★ MAP 12 O 11

Once the home of the Jameson Whiskey family, the Portmarnock Hotel & Golf Links is in a prime location reaching down to the sea, with views over the 18-hole Bernhard Langer designed links golf course. The 19th C character of the ancestral home is retained in the wood panelled walls, marble fireplaces & ornate ceilings of the Jameson Bar. Just 15 mins from Dublin Airport & 25 mins from the city centre. Oceana, the newly refurbished Spa, offers the services of Beauty/Sports therapists, gym, sauna, steam room, hairdressing salon & nail bar & balneotherapy.

Bookable on www.irelandhotels.com
Member of Preferred Hotels and Resorts

B&B from €75.00 to €157.50

Philip Murphy
Conference & Banqueting Manager

Activities:

Member of:

Special Offer: Weekend Specials from €185.00 pps
(2 Nights B&B & 1 Dinner)

98 98

Open All Year

White Sands Hotel

Coast Road,
Portmarnock,
Co. Dublin
Tel: 01·866 6000 Fax: 01·866 6006
Email: sandshotel@eircom.net
Web: www.whitesandshotel.ie

HOTEL ★★★ MAP 12 O 11

De luxe 3 star family-run hotel overlooking the beautiful sandy beaches and spectacular sea views of north Co. Dublin. Within 4km of the M1 and M50 allowing easy access to Dublin Airport, Dublin City Centre and all major golf courses and tourist attractions. All superbly appointed bedrooms are en suite with tea/coffee making facilities and direct dial telephone. Non-smoking and air-conditioned rooms available. Lively Irish Bar with entertainment on selected nights, Restaurant/Carvery. Ample FREE coach and car parking. "With A View To Impress".

Bookable on www.irelandhotels.com

B&B from €70.00 to €120.00

Georgina Higgins
General Manager

Activities:

Member of:

Special Offer: Midweek Specials from €110.00 pps
(3 Nights B&B)

58 58

Closed 24 - 25 December

B&B Rates are per Person Sharing per Night incl. Breakfast. or Room Rates are per Room per Night - See also Page 8

Citywest Hotel, Conference, Leisure & Golf Resort

Saggart,
Co. Dublin

Tel: 01-401 0500 Fax: 01-401 0945
Email: sales@citywesthotel.com
Web: www.citywesthotel.com

HOTEL ★★★★ MAP 8 N 11

Ireland's premier conference, leisure and golf resort and one of Europe's most popular international conference destinations. Dublin's most popular golf resort is just 15km from the city centre. This resort offers: luxurious rooms, lively bars, choice of restaurants, superb pool and leisure facilities. Imagine two of Ireland's finest golf courses in one magnificent setting designed by Christy O'Connor Junior. Enjoy all Dublin has to offer from this beautiful and tranquil setting.

B&B from €75.00 to €140.00

John Glynn
Chief Executive

Activities:

Member of:

IRISH HOTELS FEDERATION

332 332

Open All Year

Carroll's Pierhouse Hotel

Harbour Road,
Skerries,
Co. Dublin

Tel: 01-849 1033 Fax: 01-849 4695
Email: info@pierhousehotel.ie
Web: www.pierhousehotel.ie

HOTEL U MAP 12 P 12

Carroll's Pierhouse Hotel is a family-run hotel, delightfully furnished & elegant in style. Situated on the Harbour Road of Skerries, a quaint fishing town is about 15 mins from Dublin Airport & 30 mins from Dublin City centre. The idyllic location provides its guests with a wonderful panoramic view of the Irish Sea. Each of the hotel's executive en suite rooms has Teletext TV, trouser press & tea/coffee making facilities. The restaurant provides Irish cuisine & an array of international dishes & in the main bar meals of similar content are available daily from 10am until 10pm. Our nightclub "Club Ocean" is open weekends.

B&B from €40.00 to €75.00

Michael & Mary Carroll
Proprietors

Special Offer: Midweek Specials from €180.00 pps
(3 Nights B&B plus 2 Dinners)

11 11

Closed 25 December

B&B Rates are per Person Sharing per Night incl. Breakfast.
or Room Rates are per Room per Night - See also Page 8

SKERRIES
MILLS

Located in the coastal town of Skerries just 30km north of Dublin off the M1

Two Windmills & a Watermill - Guided Tour. Watermill Café all in - house Baking & Cooking Crafts Council of Ireland recommended Craft - Shop

Open 7 days throughout the year from 10.30am Closed 20 Dec - 2 Jan (Inclusive) & Good Friday

Skerries Mills, Skerries, Co. Dublin
Tel: 353 1 8495208
Fax: 353 1 8495213
Email: skerriesmills@indigo.ie

Co. Dublin

Skerries / Sutton / Swords

Redbank House Guesthouse & Restaurant	Marine Hotel	Carnegie Court Hotel
6 & 7 Church Street, Skerries, Co. Dublin	Sutton Cross, Dublin 13	North Street, Swords, Co. Dublin
Tel: 01-849 1005 Fax: 01-849 1598	Tel: 01-839 0000 Fax: 01-839 0442	Tel: 01-840 4384 Fax: 01-840 4505
Email: info@redbank.ie	Email: info@marinehotel.ie	Email: info@carnegiecourt.com
Web: www.redbank.ie	Web: www.marinehotel.ie	Web: www.carnegiecourt.com

GUESTHOUSE ★★★ MAP 12 P 12 | HOTEL ★★★ MAP 12 P 11 | HOTEL ★★★ MAP 12 O 12

Enjoy the extended hospitality of the McCoy's in Redbank House. The world famous seafood restaurant is the dining room of Redbank House. The 18 en suite rooms have the McCoys sense of style and elegance. The area is particularly rich in golf courses and a wide variety of leisure activities includes sea fishing, boat trips, sailing and horse riding. The Chef Proprietor Terry McCoy cooks the catch of the day landed at Skerries Pier specialising in the world famous Dublin Bay prawns. Just 20 minutes from Dublin Airport on the new M1.

The Marine Hotel overlooks the north shore of Dublin Bay with its lawn sweeping down to the sea shore. All bedrooms are en suite and have trouser press, TV, direct dial phone and tea/coffee facilities. The city centre is 6km away and the airport 25 minutes drive. Close by is the DART rapid rail system. The hotel has a heated indoor swimming pool and sauna. Nearby are the Royal Dublin and Portmarnock championship golf courses.

The Carnegie Court Hotel is a luxury accommodation hotel ideally situated in the town of Swords, 5 mins from Dublin airport and 20 mins from the city centre. The newly built hotel comprising 36 beautifully decorated & spacious bedrooms and a warm welcoming atmosphere is the perfect place of rest be it business or pleasure. Enjoy our award-winning Courtyard Restaurant or indulge in a night out in one of our five bars. Other facilities include conference & banqueting services and an extensive secure car park.

Bookable on www.irelandhotels.com
Member of Premier Guesthouses

Bookable on www.irelandhotels.com

Bookable on www.irelandhotels.com

B&B from €55.00 to €70.00 | **B&B from €60.00 to €125.00** | **B&B from €65.00 to €120.00**

 Terry McCoy, Proprietor | Matthew Ryan, Managing Director |  Allen Harrington, General Manager

Special Offer: Weekend Specials from €130.00 pps (2 Nights B&B & 1 Dinner)

Special Offer: Weekend Specials from €140.00 pps (2 Nights B&B & 1 Dinner)

Open All Year	Closed 25 - 27 December	Closed 24 - 26 December

B&B Rates are per Person Sharing per Night incl. Breakfast. or Room Rates are per Room per Night - See also Page 8

Roganstown Golf & Country Club

Roganstown,
Swords,
Co. Dublin
Tel: 01-843 3118 Fax: 01-843 3303
Email: info@roganstown.com
Web: www.roganstown.com

HOTEL N MAP 12 O 12

Converted from the original Roganstown House, the spectacular Roganstown Golf & Country Club is a destination of relaxation, fine food and exceptional golf set among circa 300 acres. To compliment the magnificent 52 bedroomed hotel, facilities also include leisure club, state of the art business and conference centre, and one of Ireland's most outstanding new golf courses. Located just 5 minutes from Dublin Airport and 25 minutes from city centre. Complimentary shuttle provided from Dublin Airport.

Bookable on www.irelandhotels.com

B&B from €85.00 to €150.00

Ciaran Fogarty
General Manager

Member of:

Special Offer: Weekend Specials from €180.00 pps
(2 Nights B&B & 1 Dinner)

52 52

Open All Year

Tulip Inn Dublin Airport

Airside Retail Park,
Swords,
Co. Dublin
Tel: 01-895 7777 Fax: 01-895 7700
Email: info@tulipinndublinairport.ie
Web: www.tulipinndublinairport.ie

HOTEL P MAP 12 O 12

Stylish, comfortable, friendly and informal hotel with excellent standards of accommodation and décor. Catering for those travellers looking for a pleasant meal, relaxing drink in the bar followed by a good nights sleep all at a great price. Fully air-conditioned hotel located just 1.5km from Dublin Airport for which there is a courtesy shuttle. Being close to the motorway network makes travel around the area very easy.

Member of Golden Tulip

Room Rate from €99.00 to €139.00

Helen O'Dwyer
General Manager

Member of:

155 155

Open All Year

B&B Rates are per Person Sharing per Night incl. Breakfast.
or **Room Rates** are per Room per Night - See also Page 8

Beaufort House

Ghan Road,
Carlingford,
Co. Louth
Tel: 042-937 3879 Fax: 042-937 3878
Email: michaelcaine@beauforthouse.net
Web: www.beauforthouse.net

GUESTHOUSE ★★★ MAP 12 O 15

Beaufort House, AA ♦♦♦♦♦, listed in Bridgestone, Michelin BIB Hotel Award, Georgina Campbell, a magnificent shoreside residence with glorious sea and mountain views in mediaeval Carlingford Village. Your hosts, Michael & Glynnis Caine, Failte Ireland award winners of excellence, will ensure the highest standards. In-house activities include sailing school and yacht charter. Golfing arranged in any of five golf courses within 20 mins of Beaufort House. Private car parking. Dinner by prior arrangement. Small business conference facilities available.

Member of Premier Guesthouses

B&B from €43.00 to €43.00

Michael & Glynnis Caine

Member of:

5 5

Open All Year

Four Seasons Hotel & Leisure Club Carlingford

Carlingford,
Co. Louth
Tel: 042-937 3530 Fax: 042-937 3531
Email: info@fshc.ie
Web: www.4seasonshotel.ie

HOTEL P MAP 12 O 15

Our 59 bedroomed hotel is located in the Heritage Village of Carlingford, overlooking Carlingford Lough, and set in a backdrop of the dramatic Cooley Mountains. This is an ideal location for a relaxed short break, or adventure filled activity break. Our Conference and Banqueting facilities offer breathtaking views all with dedicated facilities. The rooms provide guests with comfortable modern surroundings and guests also have access to full leisure facilities. We look forward to welcoming you.

B&B from €55.00 to €85.00

Vincent Hoban

Activities:

Member of:

Special Offer: Midweek Specials from €235.00 pps (3 Nights B&B & 2 Evening Dinner)

59 59

Closed 25 December

McKevitt's Village Hotel

Market Square,
Carlingford,
Co. Louth
Tel: 042-937 3116 Fax: 042-937 3144
Email: villagehotel@eircom.net
Web: www.mckevittshotel.com

HOTEL ★★ MAP 12 O 15

McKevitt's Village Hotel is family owned and personally supervised by Kay & Terry McKevitt. At the hotel, pride of place is taken in the personal attention given to guests by owners and staff. Carlingford is one of Ireland's oldest and most interesting mediaeval villages. Beautifully situated on the shores of Carlingford Lough and half way between Dublin and Belfast.

B&B from €55.00 to €85.00

Terry & Kay McKevitt
Owners

Activities:

Member of:

Special Offer: Weekend Specials from €160.00 pps (2 Nights B&B & 1 Dinner)

17 17

Open All Year

B&B Rates are per Person Sharing per Night incl. Breakfast. or Room Rates are per Room per Night - See also Page 8

Bellingham Castle Hotel

Castlebellingham,
Co. Louth

Tel: 042-937 2176 Fax: 042-937 2766
Email: bellinghamcastle@eircom.net
Web: www.bellinghamcastle.com

HOTEL ★★ MAP 12 O 14

Bellingham Castle Hotel is situated close to the pleasant little village of Castlebellingham, Co. Louth, resting in countryside enveloped in history, legend and engaged in beautiful scenery. In the hotel itself, which is an elegant refurbished 17th century castle, you will find all the facilities of a modern hotel, harmonising beautifully with the antique décor and atmosphere of old world splendour.

B&B from €65.00 to €75.00

*Paschal Keenan
Manager*

Special Offer: Weekend Specials from €130.00 pps
(2 Nights B&B & 1 Dinner)

🏨🛏🐾☎️🖨📺🅣©♨CM❀☂♪🅟🔥⛄❄
19 19

Closed 24 - 26 December

Boyne Valley Hotel & Country Club

Drogheda,
Co. Louth

Tel: 041-983 7737 Fax: 041-983 9188
Email: reservations@boynevalleyhotel.ie
Web: www.boynevalleyhotel.ie

HOTEL ★★★ MAP 12 O 13

Gracious country house on 16 acres beside Drogheda: from Dublin, 35km North on M1, turn off to N1 Julianstown & Drogheda South. Only 25km from Dublin Airport. From Belfast-south on M1, turn off at Drogheda North at N1. Nearby are sites on Newgrange, Dowth, Knowth and mediaeval abbeys of Melifont, Monasterboice and Slane. Full leisure Complex, 2 tennis courts, Cellar Bistro. Large and small conference rooms available. Wireless broadband and an Intranet computer room on site.

Bookable on www.irelandhotels.com
Member of Best Western

B&B from €85.00 to €85.00

*Michael McNamara
Proprietor / Manager*

Activities:
🏊🎾♨

Member of:
IRISH
HOTELS
FEDERATION

🏨🛏☎️🖨📺🅣©♨CM❀🍴🛏🏊📷🅠∪
♪🅟🅟🅢🆀ⓐⓒ🚲 inet WiFi
72 72

Open All Year

B&B Rates are per Person Sharing per Night incl. Breakfast.
or **Room Rates** are per Room per Night - See also Page 8

Dublin & East Coast 309

Co. Louth

Drogheda

D (The)	Glenside Hotel	Westcourt Hotel

D (The)

Scotch Hall,
Drogheda,
Co. Louth
Tel: 041-987 7700 Fax: 041-987 7702
Email: reservethed@monogramhotels.ie
Web: www.monogramhotels.ie

HOTEL P MAP 12 O 13

A stylish hotel offering traditional hospitality and clean, contemporary design in the heart of one of the most historic areas of Ireland. Located on the south bank of the River Boyne in Drogheda, the d is just 25 minutes from Dublin Airport. Its 104 bedrooms are designed for guest comfort and the ground floor offers bright and spacious lounge areas and d bar and restaurant, opening onto a riverside terrace and promenade. The hotel has seven air-conditioned meeting and event suites, equipped with the latest AV technology, making it ideal as a business retreat or for a leisurely short break.

Bookable on www.irelandhotels.com
Member of Monogram Hotels

B&B from €80.00 to €140.00

Rory Scott
General Manager

Activities:

Member of:
HOTELS

Special Offer: Weekend Specials from €135.00 pps
(2 Nights B&B & 1 Dinner)

104 104 Inet WiFi

Open All Year

Glenside Hotel

Dublin Road,
Drogheda,
Co. Louth
Tel: 041-982 9185 Fax: 041-982 9049
Email: info@glensidehotel.ie
Web: www.glensidehotel.ie

HOTEL ★★ MAP 12 O 13

The recently refurbished Glenside Hotel is situated 2km south of Drogheda and 20 mins from Dublin Airport on the N1. With 15 en suite rooms fitted to an exceptionally high standard, one master suite, à la carte restaurant and lounge bar, banquet facilities for up to 200 guests. The perfect setting for a special wedding day. Ideal base for golfing enthusiasts and touring Co. Louth/Meath. Ample car parking.

B&B from €40.00 to €60.00

Ronan McAuley
Proprietor

Member of:
HOTELS

16 16

Open All Year

Westcourt Hotel

West Street,
Drogheda,
Co. Louth
Tel: 041-983 0965 Fax: 041-983 0970
Email: reservations@westcourt.ie
Web: www.westcourt.ie

HOTEL ★★★ MAP 12 O 13

Located in the heart of historical Drogheda and at the gateway of the Boyne Valley, the Westcourt Hotel is the ideal base to explore this bustling town and the many beautiful historic sites located on our doorstep. All our en suite guest rooms include TV, hairdryer and tea/coffee making facilities. Enjoy a cocktail or a perfectly poured pint @ 'Barroco', Drogheda's newest bar. Our brasserie style menu serves the finest food, both traditional and contemporary. Secure car parking available.

B&B from €65.00 to €75.00

Valerie Sherlock
General Manager

Member of:
HOTELS

27 27 WiFi

Closed 25 - 26 December

B&B Rates are per Person Sharing per Night incl. Breakfast. or **Room Rates** are per Room per Night - See also Page 8

Ballymascanlon House Hotel

Dundalk,
Co. Louth

Tel: 042-935 8200 Fax: 042-937 1598
Email: info@ballymascanlon.com
Web: www.ballymascanlon.com

HOTEL **U** MAP 12 O 14

Ballymascanlon House is a RAC 4****
Country House Hotel just 50 minutes by
motorway from Dublin and Belfast. Just
8 miles from mediaeval Carlingford, it
is set on 130 acres of parkland with its
own Ruddy & Craddock designed 18
hole golf course. The beautifully
appointed bedroom accommodation,
award-winning Restaurant and Terrace
Bar are complemented by modern
leisure facilities including 20m deck
level pool, sauna, jacuzzi, steam room,
gym and tennis courts. The perfect short
break destination.

Bookable on www.irelandhotels.com
Member of Best Western Hotels

B&B from €77.50 to €82.50

Oliver Quinn

Activities:
✓

Member of:

*Special Offer: Weekend Specials from €200.00 pps
(2 Nights B&B & 1 Dinner)*

90 90

Open All Year

Carrickdale Hotel & Leisure Complex

Carrickcarnon,
Ravensdale, Dundalk,
Co. Louth

Tel: 042-937 1397 Fax: 042-937 1740
Email: manager@carrickdale.com
Web: www.carrickdale.com

HOTEL ★★★ MAP 12 O 14

The hotel, conference, swimming and
leisure complex is situated midway
between Dublin and Belfast on the main
N1 just 10km north of Dundalk, 8km
south of Newry. Our 119 en suite
rooms include our newly open 68 de
luxe tower block rooms containing 15
fully air-conditioned executive suites
with mini bar facilities. Tastefully
decorated bar and restaurant serving
excellent food and wines. Ideal
destination for touring Cooley,
Carlingford and all of Northern Ireland's
major tourist attractions.

B&B from €65.00 to €77.50

*John McParland
Proprietor*

Member of:

119 119

Closed 25 - 26 December

Fairways Hotel & Conference Centre

Dublin Road,
Dundalk,
Co. Louth

Tel: 042-932 1500 Fax: 042-932 1511
Email: info@fairways.ie
Web: www.fairways.ie

HOTEL ★★★ MAP 12 O 14

The Fairways Hotel and Conference
Centre is situated 3 miles south of
Dundalk, approximately 45 minutes
from Dublin Airport and an hour's drive
from Belfast and 5 minutes from the
seaside. Facilities include 98 tastefully
furnished bedrooms, a new fully
equipped conference and banqueting
centre, catering for up to 1000
delegates. Carvery/grill and Modi's
Restaurant serving full meals and
snacks throughout the day.

Bookable on www.irelandhotels.com
Member of Platinum Hotels

B&B from €60.00 to €90.00

*Brian P. Quinn
Managing Director*

Activities:
✓ 🍴

Member of:

*Special Offer: Weekend Specials from €125.00 pps
(2 Nights B&B & 1 Dinner)*

98 98

Closed 24 - 25 December

B&B Rates are per Person Sharing per Night incl. Breakfast.
or Room Rates are per Room per Night - See also Page 8

Dublin & East Coast 311

Dundalk

Hotel Imperial	Keernaun House	Lismar Guesthouse & Serviced Apartments
Park Street, Dundalk, Co. Louth	Greengates, Dublin Road, Dundalk, Co. Louth	8-9 Stapleton Place, Dundalk, Co. Louth
Tel: 042-933 2241 Fax: 042-933 7909	Tel: 042-932 1795 Fax: 042-932 1795	Tel: 042-935 7246 Fax: 042-935 7247
Email: info@imperialhoteldundalk.com	Email: nmcgn@eircom.net	Email: lismar@iol.ie
		Web: www.lismar.ie

HOTEL ★★ MAP 12 O 14 | **GUESTHOUSE ★★ MAP 12 O 14** | **GUESTHOUSE P MAP 12 O 14**

40 bedroom hotel situated in the heart of Dundalk town, within walking distance to all major attractions. Under new ownership, the hotel is stylishly refurbished to the highest standard offering an exciting and stimulating atmosphere with first class customer service in its state of the art bars, nightclub, restaurant and coffee shop. Live music most nights, secure parking available, no extra cost.

A family-run guesthouse situated in the scenic village of Blackrock where you will find award-winning pubs & restaurants all overlooking the beach. Close by the Fairways Hotel and Conference Centre, DKIT and Dundalk Golf Club. 45 minutes from Dublin and Belfast Airports. Coming from Dublin come off at the 1st junction for Dundalk, at the second set of traffic lights turn right (Ritz Castle Bellingham), we are 2km up that road on the left.

An elegant Edwardian property which has been completely refurbished, retaining many of the original features. Its high ceilings, sweeping staircases flooded with natural light from the glass domed ceiling, decorative fireplace and original front door complete with fanlight, provided taste of 20th century elegance which complements the 21st century design and facilities. All bedrooms have luxurious en suites. Our Italian furniture and fittings set the perfect tone. Serviced apartments available. Lismar is centrally located in the vibrant town of Dundalk, Ireland's largest provincial town.

B&B from €50.00 to €67.50	B&B from €30.00 to €45.00	B&B from €37.50 to €42.50
Michael McCarthy General Manager	Theresa McGorrian Owner	Michael & Elizabeth Smyth

Activities:

Activities:

Member of:

Closed 25 - 26 December	Closed 23 - 31 December	Open All Year

B&B Rates are per Person Sharing per Night incl. Breakfast. or Room Rates are per Room per Night - See also Page 8

Park Inn Dundalk

Carnbeg,
Armagh Road, Dundalk,
Co. Louth
Tel: 042-939 5700 Fax: 042-938 6788
Email: info.dundalk@rezidorparkinn.com
Web: www.dundalk.parkinn.ie

HOTEL N MAP 12 O 14

A warm, friendly welcome awaits you at Park Inn Dundalk. Ideally located within easy access of M1, 1hr drive from Dublin/Belfast. With many local attractions to discover, Park Inn is surrounded by magnificent views of Carnbeg 18 hole parkland golf course and Cooley Mountains. While in Dundalk, indulge yourself at our Major's Restaurant and avail of a variety of local flavours and international dishes, complemented with our extensive selection of fine wines. Also home to a fully equipped Health & Leisure Club as well as conference facilities, unique bbq venue and a superb wedding location.

B&B from €50.00 to €60.00

Philip Uzice
General Manager

Special Offer: *Weekend Specials from €119.00 pps (2 Nights B&B & 1 Dinner)*

84 84

Closed 24 - 26 December

Broadmeadow Country House & Equestrian Centre

Bullstown,
Ashbourne,
Co. Meath
Tel: 01-835 2823 Fax: 01-835 2819
Email: info@irishcountryhouse.com
Web: www.irishcountryhouse.com

GUESTHOUSE ★★★★ MAP 12 O 12

A stunning family-run country house surrounded by mature gardens, tennis court, private parking, modern equestrian centre. Located 15 minutes from Dublin Airport, 20 minutes Dublin city. All rooms en suite and designed for maximum guest comfort. Close to numerous golf courses, race courses, clay pigeon shooting. Enjoy the tranquillity of the country side, yet minutes from the capital. Wine/supper menu available. On route R125.

Bookable on www.irelandhotels.com

B&B from €50.00 to €75.00

Sandra Duff
Owner/Manager

Member of:
IRISH
HOTELS
FEDERATION

Special Offer: *Midweek Specials from €120.00 pps (3 Nights B&B)*

8 8

Closed 24 December - 1 January

Neptune Beach Hotel & Leisure Club

Bettystown,
Co. Meath
Tel: 041-982 7107 Fax: 041-982 7412
Email: info@neptunebeach.ie
Web: www.neptunebeach.ie

HOTEL U MAP 12 O 13

Located 25 mins north of Dublin Airport with a spectacular setting overlooking Bettystown Beach. All 44 rooms are elegantly furnished to provide the comfort and facilities expected of a leading hotel. Enjoy fine dining in the restaurant, afternoon tea in the cosy Winter Garden or a relaxing drink in the Neptune Bar. The leisure club facilities include 20m swimming pool, jacuzzi, sauna and fitness suite. Local golf courses: Laytown & Bettystown, Seapoint and Co. Louth. 6 new luxury suites now available. Please contact hotel for suite rates.

B&B from €85.00 to €125.00

Nuala McDonald & Annemarina Redden
Managers

Activities:

Member of:
IRISH
HOTELS
FEDERATION

Special Offer: *Weekend Specials from €180.00 pps (2 Nights B&B & 1 Dinner)*

44 44

Open All Year

B&B Rates are per Person Sharing per Night incl. Breakfast.
or Room Rates are per Room per Night - See also Page 8

Co. Meath

Bettystown / Dunboyne / Enfield

Rannoch Guesthouse	Dunboyne Castle Hotel & Spa	Marriott Johnstown House Hotel & Spa Enfield

Rannoch Guesthouse

Coast Road,
Bettystown,
Co. Meath

Tel: 041-982 7469 Fax: 041-988 7440
Email: info@ebc.ie

GUESTHOUSE ★★ MAP 12 O 13

Spectacularly located, family-run guesthouse situated on the beach in the coastal resort of Bettystown, just 30 minutes north of Dublin City and Dublin Airport. All rooms have sea views, en suite facilities and TVs. Direct beach access from the garden, car parking and tennis facilities. Sauna available for guests use on request. A warm welcome awaits you.

B&B from €30.00 to €35.00

Nanette Kinsella

Activities:

Member of:
IRISH HOTELS FEDERATION

10 10 □△❀❄✿♫P

Open All Year

Dunboyne Castle Hotel & Spa

Dunboyne,
Co. Meath

Tel: 01-801 3500 Fax: 01-436 6801
Email: info@dunboynecastlehotel.com
Web: www.dunboynecastlehotel.com

UNDER CONSTRUCTION - OPENING APRIL 2006

HOTEL P MAP 12 N 11

Set in the historical village of Dunboyne, you will find Dunboyne Castle Hotel & Spa. One of Ireland's newest hotels built to 4**** standards, opening in April 2006, with 145 bedrooms, magnificent gardens, large conference and banquet facilities for up to 1,500 delegates and an exclusive spa spread over 3 floors. 6 bedrooms for guests with special mobility requirements. Dunboyne Castle Hotel is just 12 miles from Dublin Airport and 10 miles from Dublin City centre. The "Heritage Capital" is just on our doorstep with tours to historical Newgrange and Hill of Tara.

B&B from €70.00 to €120.00

*Shane Cookman
Director & Group General Manager*

145 145 ☎□📺↕♫C✿✈🏠🛏PS☐
aid ♿ WiFi 🐕

Open All Year

Marriott Johnstown House Hotel & Spa Enfield

Enfield,
Co. Meath

Tel: 046-954 0000 Fax: 046-954 0001
Email: info@johnstownhouse.com
Web: www.marriottjohnstownhouse.com

HOTEL N MAP 11 M 11

Located on the main Dublin to Galway road, just 40 minutes from Dublin Airport and 45 minutes from Dublin City Centre. Luxurious bedrooms, with modern features. Enjoy a choice of eating experiences - Pavilion Restaurant, Atrium Brasserie and Coach House Bar. Well equipped meeting rooms catering for 2-900 people. The spa facilities include indoor heated swimming pool, steam rooms, saunas, 12 spa therapy rooms and hot thermal suite area.

B&B from €90.00 to €200.00

*Ann Gill
General Manager*

Activities:

Member of:
IRISH HOTELS FEDERATION

*Special Offer: Weekend Specials from €129.00 pps
(2 Nights B&B & 1 Dinner)*

126 126 ☎□📺↕🚗C CM✿✈🏠🛏♫
♫PS☐ aid ♿ Inet WiFi 🐕

Open All Year

B&B Rates are per Person Sharing per Night incl. Breakfast.
or <u>Room Rates</u> are per Room per Night - See also Page 8

Hamlet Court Hotel

Johnstownbridge,
Enfield,
Co. Meath
Tel: 046-954 1200 Fax: 046-954 1704
Email: info@thehamlet.ie
Web: www.thehamlet.ie

HOTEL N MAP 11 M 11

The Hamlet Court Hotel is situated in the village of Johnstownbridge, just 1 km from Enfield and 35 minutes from Dublin. Centrally located and accessible to all mainline rail and bus links. The Hamlet Court Hotel offers style, comfort and elegance. Whether you are visiting on business or for pleasure you will find that your every need and request will be anticipated by our friendly and attentive staff.

B&B from €55.00 to €100.00

John O'Neill
Owner

Activities:

Member of:

IRISH HOTELS FEDERATION

Special Offer: *3 Nights B&B plus 2 Dinners from €189.00 pps*

30 30

Open All Year

Meath

Ireland's Heritage Capital

Just stand for a few minutes on the Hill of Tara and you'll know what we mean. Revel at the sight of Trim Castle's monumental ramparts, or the mysterious neolithic wonders of Loughcrew and Newgrange at *Brú na Bóinne*. Meath's heritage springs to life, grabbing the imagination with vivid images of the past. Discover Meath's living heritage.

For your free information pack and tourism inquiries contact Meath Tourism at:

+ 353 1 835 8022 (from abroad)
or **Callsave 1850 300 789** (within Ireland)
or email **info@meathtourism.ie**

www.meathtourism.ie

Meath
Always a visit to treasure

Headfort Arms Hotel

Kells,
Co. Meath

Tel: 046-924 0063 Fax: 046-924 0587
Email: info@headfortarms.ie
Web: www.headfortarms.ie

HOTEL **U** MAP **11 M 13**

In the Duff family for 35 years the Headfort Arms represents old and new world. Located in the heritage town of Kells only 40 km from Dublin City on the main Derry/Donegal route. Café Therese offers an array of casual food from 7.30am - 10pm, the contemporary award-winning Vanilla Pod Restaurant serving from 5.30 - late, Early Bird Menu & Sunday lunch. Conference and banqueting facilities up to 400. The wedding destination of the North East. Golfing, fishing packages available. Headfort Golf Club nearby. All rooms newly refurbished with 32 brand new de luxe rooms for business or leisure stays. Spa launching soon.

B&B from €59.00 to €99.00

*Peggy, Vincent & Olivia Duff
Proprietors*

Activities:
✓

Member of:
IRISH HOTELS FEDERATION

Special Offer: *Midweek Specials from €129.00 pps
(2 Nights B&B & 1 Dinner)*

45 45

Closed 25 December

Station House Hotel and Restaurant

Kilmessan,
Co. Meath

Tel: 046-902 5239 Fax: 046-902 5588
Email: info@thestationhousehotel.com
Web: www.thestationhousehotel.com

HOTEL **U** MAP **12 N 12**

Step off the fast track into a relaxed rural setting, where peace and tranquillity exude. Set on 12 acres of landscaped gardens and woodlands, this first class hotel offers many amenities we appreciate today, not forgetting yesterday's charm. The Signal Suite is a unique, exclusive haven with four poster bed and whirlpool bath. The Signal Restaurant which has won numerous awards, is open 7 days a week for breakfast, lunch and fine dining. Bar food served daily. 20 miles from Dublin. Special offers online: www.thestationhousehotel.com

Bookable on www.irelandhotels.com

B&B from €60.00 to €100.00

*Denise & Paul Slattery
Front Office / Banqueting Mgr*

Activities:
✓ 🍴

Member of:
IRISH HOTELS FEDERATION

Special Offer: *Midweek Specials from €165.00 pps
(3 Nights B&B)*

20 20

Open All Year

Ardboyne Hotel

Dublin Road,
Navan,
Co. Meath

Tel: 046-902 3119 Fax: 046-902 2355
Email: info@ardboynehotel.com
Web: www.ardboynehotel.com

HOTEL ★★★ MAP **12 N 13**

The Ardboyne Hotel Navan is set amidst a treasure trove of Irish historical sites in County Meath. Our warm and comfortable atmosphere coupled with our extensive gardens make the Ardboyne Hotel a perfect haven to unwind after an eventful day. Located just 2 minutes outside Navan town, and just 40 minutes from Dublin. The hotel offers guests a wide range of facilities, including 29 tastefully decorated bedrooms. The Kells Bar, La Mezzanine Restaurant and extensive conference and banqueting facilities for up to 500 people.

Bookable on www.irelandhotels.com
Member of Cusack Hotels

B&B from €65.00 to €95.00

*Mary Murphy
General Manager*

Activities:
🍴

Special Offer: *Weekend Specials from €119.00 pps
(2 Nights B&B & 1 Dinner)*

29 29

Open All Year

B&B Rates are per Person Sharing per Night incl. Breakfast. or **Room Rates** are per Room per Night - See also Page 8

Newgrange Hotel

Bridge Street,
Navan,
Co. Meath
Tel: 046-907 4100 Fax: 046-907 3977
Email: info@newgrangehotel.ie
Web: www.newgrangehotel.ie

HOTEL ★★★ MAP 12 N 13

Located in Navan, the heart of the Royal County. The Newgrange is a modern hotel, designed and inspired by the ancient history of the area. In addition to our 62 elegantly decorated en suite bedrooms, the hotel boasts extensive conference and banqueting facilities, a choice of bars, restaurant and café. Easy access to Dublin City and airport. Enjoy local attractions including Bru na Boinne, golf, angling and horse racing. One hour from Dublin on M50 and N3. Private car parking available.

Bookable on www.irelandhotels.com
Member of Cusack Hotels

B&B from €65.00 to €95.00

Noel J O'Mahony
General Manager

Activities:

Member of:

Special Offer: Weekend Specials from €119.00 pps
(2 Nights B&B & 1 Dinner)
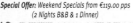

62 62

Open All Year

Castle Arch Hotel

Summerhill Road,
Trim,
Co. Meath
Tel: 046-943 1516 Fax: 046-943 6002
Email: info@castlearchhotel.com
Web: www.castlearchhotel.com

HOTEL R MAP 11 M 12

Owned by the Cusack Family, only 40 minutes from Dublin situated in the heart of the Heritage Town of Trim this charming hotel, refurbished to the highest standard hosting 22 beautifully decorated bedrooms. Take a stroll on the banks of the River Boyne and visit our famous Trim Castle where Mel Gibson filmed Braveheart (only a five minute walk). The very best of Irish cuisine and a warm and friendly welcome awaits you in our lovely bars and restaurant. The perfect venue for your dream wedding. Please contact hotel for our wedding package.

Member of Cusack Hotels

B&B from €50.00 to €65.00

Margaret Corcoran
General Manager

Activities:

Member of:

Special Offer: Weekend Specials from €99.00 pps
(2 Nights B&B & 1 Dinner)

22 22

Open All Year

Knightsbrook Hotel & Golf Resort

Dublin Road,
Trim,
Co. Meath
Tel: 046-907 4100 Fax: 046-907 3977
Email: info@cusackhotels.com
Web: www.cusackhotels.com

UNDER CONSTRUCTION - OPENING JULY 2006

HOTEL P MAP 11 M 12

Built to an exceptionally high 4**** standard, this hotel offers a unique experience in luxury and opulence combined with modern sophistication. 120 de luxe rooms, each fully air-conditioned with all the facilities a discerning guest requires. Guests will enjoy an extensive leisure centre with swimming pool, jacuzzi, sauna, steam room and health & beauty spa. 18 hole championship golf course designed by Christy O'Connor Jnr on site. Conference facilities for up to 1,000 delegates.

Member of Cusack Hotels

B&B from €80.00 to €190.00

Zoe Walsh
Marketing Manager

Activities:

120 120

Closed 24 - 25 December

B&B Rates are per Person Sharing per Night incl. Breakfast.
or **Room Rates** are per Room per Night - See also Page 8

Arklow Bay Conference and Leisure Hotel	Bridge Hotel	Clogga Bay Hotel
Arklow, Co. Wicklow	Bridge Street, Arklow, Co. Wicklow	Clogga, Arklow, Co. Wicklow
Tel: 0402-32309 Fax: 0402-32300 Email: reservations@arklowbay.com Web: www.arklowbay.com	Tel: 0402-31666 Fax: 0402-31666	Tel: 0402-39299 Fax: 0402-91910 Email: finualajameson@eircom.net

HOTEL ★★★ MAP 8 O 8	HOTEL ★★ MAP 8 O 8	HOTEL ★★ MAP 8 O 8

Nestled in the heart of Co. Wicklow, a warm welcome awaits your arrival. Overlooking Arklow Bay with panoramic views of the Garden of Ireland, the hotel boasts 92 en suite rooms. Enjoy excellent cuisine in our award-winning "Howards Dining Room" or the local craic synonymous with our Ferrybank Lounge. State of the art leisure club and superior conference facilities. Banqueting for 500 pax. Golf, fishing, hovercrafting, quad racing, horse riding & hill walking are all available locally. Sister hotel, Springhill Court Hotel Spa & Leisure Club, Kilkenny.

Bookable on www.irelandhotels.com
Member of Chara Hotel Group

The Bridge Hotel is family owned and run, with 14 en suite bedrooms, TV and car parking. The hotel is situated at the bridge in Arklow town, approximately 1 hour from Dublin and Rosslare. There is a wide choice of local golf courses as well as fine beaches nearby. Arklow is an ideal base from which to see the beautiful scenery of Wicklow.

Family owned and managed establishment situated 3km south of Arklow Town. Set on a 2 acre garden in the country by the sea, approx 60km from Rosslare and Dublin. A central location for touring Wicklow and Wexford. All rooms en suite with colour T.V. and direct dial telephone. Local attractions include golf, fishing and swimming. Our restaurant offers good traditional food.

B&B from €65.00 to €95.00	B&B from €50.00 to €60.00	B&B from €45.00 to €55.00

Tina O'Sullivan
General Manager

Activities:

Member of:

Special Offer: Golden Years Midweek Specials from €169.00 pps

92 92

Jim Hoey
Proprietor

Member of:

15 14

Fiounnuala Jameson
Proprietor

Member of:

Special Offer: Weekend Specials from €125.00 pps (2 Nights B&B & 1 Dinner)

10 10

Open All Year	Closed 25 December	Open All Year

B&B Rates are per Person Sharing per Night incl. Breakfast. or Room Rates are per Room per Night - See also Page 8

Ballyknocken Country House & Cookery School

Glenealy,
Ashford,
Co. Wicklow
Tel: 0404-44627 Fax: 0404-44696
Email: cfulvio@ballyknocken.com
Web: www.ballyknocken.com

GUESTHOUSE ★★★★ MAP 8 P 9

1850s romantic farmhouse, elegantly furnished with antiques. Charming bedrooms, some with iron beds and claw feet baths offer lovely views over gardens and forest. Relax by the Drawing Room's log fire before the splendid dinner using garden and local produce. Ballyknocken Cookery School on site. Superb breakfasts. Near to Wicklow Mountains, Glendalough, Powerscourt. Excellent golf, e.g. Druid's Glen. Lovely walks. Dublin 29 miles. Bridgestone 100 Best Places to Stay in Ireland. Gift vouchers.

Bookable on www.irelandhotels.com

B&B from €55.00 to €62.00

*Catherine Fulvio
Proprietor*

Activities:

Member of:

Special Offer: Weekend Specials from €150.00 pps
(2 Nights B&B & 1 Dinner)

7   7

Closed 15 December - 31 January

Bel-Air Hotel

Ashford,
Co. Wicklow
Tel: 0404-40109 Fax: 0404-40188
Email: belairhotel@eircom.net
Web: www.holidaysbelair.com

HOTEL U MAP 8 P 9

Bel-Air Hotel is a family-run hotel and equestrian club, situated in the centre of 81 hectares of farm and parkland. Managed by the Murphy Freeman family since 1937. The lovely gardens have a breathtaking view to the sea. The traditional family atmosphere and rich history make the hotel a popular venue, a good restaurant, rooms en suite with tea making facilities, T.V. and hairdryers. Bel Air Holiday village adjacent to hotel.

Member of Equestrian Holidays Ireland

B&B from €57.00 to €65.00

*Fidelma Freeman
Owner*

Member of:
HOTELS

Special Offer: Week Partial Board from €520.00 pps
(7 Nights B&B & 7 Dinners)

10   10

Closed 24 December - 10 January

Chester Beatty Inn

Ashford Village,
Co. Wicklow
Tel: 0404-40206 Fax: 0404-49003
Email: hotelchesterbeatty@eircom.net
Web: www.hotelchesterbeatty.ie

HOTEL U MAP 8 P 9

The Chester Beatty Inn is in the village of Ashford just off the main N11 route, 35 mins south of Dublin. Ideally situated for touring, golf (adjacent to Druids Glen and many other golf courses), fishing, hill walking and gardens (opposite Mount Usher Gardens, 15 mins from Powerscourt Gardens). Charming country inn style family-run hotel comprising 12 luxury en suite rooms, restaurant, lounge and traditional Irish bar, all with open log fires. Secure private car park. Just 1 hour from the K Club.

Bookable on www.irelandhotels.com

B&B from €49.00 to €80.00

Kitty & Paul Caprani

Activities:

Member of:
HOTELS

Special Offer: Weekend Specials from €123.00 pps
(2 Nights B&B & 1 Dinner)

12   12

Closed 23 - 26 December

B&B Rates are per Person Sharing per Night incl. Breakfast.
or Room Rates are per Room per Night - See also Page 8

Dublin & East Coast   319

BrookLodge and Wells Spa

Macreddin Village,
Near Aughrim,
Co. Wicklow
Tel: 0402-36444 Fax: 0402-36580
Email: brooklodge@macreddin.ie
Web: www.brooklodge.com

HOTEL ★★★★ MAP 8 O 8

Stunning hotel in a spectacular valley, 50 minutes from south Dublin. Home to the dramatic Strawberry Tree, Ireland's only certified organic restaurant, and "The Wells" - a truly luxurious Spa. Macreddin Village also hosts Acton's Country Pub & Brewery, The Orchard Café, an organic bakery and smokehouse, food & wine shops, an equestrian centre and 4X4 driving. A short drive from Glendalough, Ballykissangel and great golf courses. Own 18 hole course, designed by Irish Ryder Cup hero - Paul McGinley, opening for limited play September 2006.

Bookable on www.irelandhotels.com
Member of Manor House Hotels

B&B from €90.00 to €190.00

Joe Kelly & Evan Doyle
Hosts

Activities:

Member of:

🏨 50 50 ... P ...

Open All Year

Lawless's Hotel

Aughrim,
Co. Wicklow
Tel: 0402-36146 Fax: 0402-36384
Email: reservations@lawlesshotel.com
Web: www.lawlesshotel.com

HOTEL ★★★ MAP 8 O 8

Lawless's Hotel, established in 1787, is a charming country hotel which has been renovated. Over the years, the award-winning Bistro Bar & Restaurant enjoy a well established reputation for home-cooked food. Approximately one hour from Dublin, nestling in the Wicklow Hills, there is a wide choice of first class golf courses nearby as well as scenic hill walking, pony trekking and trout fishing in the adjacent river. Bar carvery daily - evening menu from 5:30 - 9:00.

Member of Irish Country Hotels

B&B from €50.00 to €77.50

Joe Whyte
Proprietor

Activities:

Member of:

🏨 14 14 ...

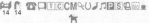
Special Offer: Sunday - Wednesday €99.00 per room (based on 2 people sharing)

Closed 24 - 26 December

Crofton Bray Head Inn

Strand Road,
Bray,
Co. Wicklow
Tel: 01-286 7182 Fax: 01-286 7182

GUESTHOUSE ★★ MAP 8 P 10

This 140 year old building is situated on the seafront, under the Bray Head Mountain. A 10 minute walk away from an excellent commuter train to Dublin, but also ideally located for touring Wicklow - The Garden of Ireland. The Bray Head Inn has ample car parking and is fully licensed. It has a lift, en suite bedrooms with TV and telephone. Our prices include full Irish breakfast.

B&B from €50.00 to €60.00

Ena Regan Cummins

Member of:

🏨 30 30 ...

Closed 02 October - 02 June

B&B Rates are per Person Sharing per Night incl. Breakfast. or **Room Rates** are per Room per Night - See also Page 8

Esplanade Hotel	Heather House Hotel	Porterhouse Inn (The)

Strand Road,
Bray,
Co. Wicklow
Tel: 01-286 2056 Fax: 01-286 6496
Email: info@esplanadehotel.ie
Web: www.esplanadehotel.ie

Strand Road,
Bray,
Co. Wicklow
Tel: 01-286 8000 Fax: 01-286 4254
Email: info@heatherhousehotel.com
Web: www.heatherhousehotel.com

Strand Road,
Bray,
Co. Wicklow
Tel: 01-286 0668 Fax: 01-286 1171
Email: bray@porterhousebrewco.com

HOTEL ★★★ MAP 8 P 10

HOTEL ★★ MAP 8 P 10

HOTEL P MAP 8 P 10

Stylish hotel with magnificent views, 12 miles from Dublin. Located on the seafront in Bray, the hotel retains many of its splendid Victorian features whilst offering modern day luxury and comfort. Comfortable lounges, excellent menu choices and exceptional value for money. Fully equipped and staffed fitness centre. Close to Bray DART station. A member of the Strandwood Hotel Group.

A family-run hotel with spectacular seaviews. Catering for the business or leisure guest, with well appointed en suite accommodation, as well as self-catering apartments. The Martello Bar offers a superb carvery and bar food menu or dine in the Tower Bistro from our select menu and fine wines. Conference and banqueting facilities. Ideally located for touring Dublin City and County Wicklow. Located 5 minutes from all public transport and N11 Motorway.

Located on Bray's seafront The Porterhouse Inn commands a panoramic view over the sea. Ideally situated for golfing (there are twelve courses within a short distance), hill walking, fishing and sightseeing, it is the ideal spot for the outdoor enthusiast. The recently renovated hotel has sixteen luxurious rooms, some available with a stunning sea view. The busy bar and restaurant serve a full range of drinks including ten of our own signature beers.

Bookable on www.irelandhotels.com
Member of Strandwood Hotel Group

B&B from €50.00 to €140.00	*B&B from €50.00 to €65.00*	*B&B from €45.00 to €70.00*

Daniel Corbett
General Manager

John Duggan
General Manager

Lyndsey Byrne

Activities:
✴️🎯

Activities:
✴️🎵

Member of:

Member of:
HOTELS

Special Offer: Weekend Specials from €125.00 pps
(2 Nights B&B & 1 Dinner)

40 40

🛏️🐕♞

25 25

16 16

Closed 24 - 26 December	Closed 24 - 26 December	Closed 24 - 25 December

B&B Rates are per Person Sharing per Night incl. Breakfast.
or **Room Rates** are per Room per Night - See also Page 8

Co. Wicklow

Bray / Dunlavin / Enniskerry

Westbourne Hotel	Rathsallagh House, Golf and Country Club	Powerscourt Arms Hotel

Westbourne Hotel

Quinsboro Road,
Bray,
Co. Wicklow
Tel: 01-286 2362 Fax: 01-204 0074

Web: www.westbournehotelbray.com

HOTEL ★★ MAP 8 P 10

The Westbourne Hotel is ideally located on the north east coast of the 'Garden of Ireland' in the charming town of Bray. Only minutes from exceptional scenery, beaches and has fast access to Dublin via the DART. Newly refurbished bedrooms en suite, direct dial phone, TV and tea/coffee making facilities. Clancy's Traditional Irish Bar, craic agus ceol. Food served all day. Dusty's contemporary style bar is recently refurbished and offers comfortable and stylish surroundings in a very relaxed atmosphere.

B&B from €40.00 to €55.00

Debbie Tiernan
General Manager

Member of:

IRISH HOTELS FEDERATION

🏨 📞 🎫 T C M U 🎵 P S 🔒 Alc
13 13

Closed 25 - 26 December

Rathsallagh House, Golf and Country Club

Dunlavin,
(West Wicklow),
Co. Wicklow
Tel: 045-403112 Fax: 045-403343
Email: info@rathsallagh.com
Web: www.rathsallagh.com

GUESTHOUSE ★★★★ MAP 8 N 9

Winner of the Supreme Irish Breakfast 2005, AA awards for Accommodation, Country House Restaurant of the year and a member of Ireland's Blue Book, Rathsallagh is a large country house one hour from Dublin Airport and close to The K Club, home of the 2006 Ryder Cup. Rathsallagh has its own 18 hole Championship Golf Course and is set in a peaceful oasis of 530 acres of rolling parkland.

Member of Ireland's Blue Book

B&B from €125.00 to €175.00

The O'Flynn Family
Proprietors

Activities:

🍸🏌️💧

Member of:

IRISH HOTELS FEDERATION

🏨 📞 🎫 T 🔧🌀 🍷 U 🎵 P 📺 🔒 Alc
29 29

inet 🐕

Open All Year

Powerscourt Arms Hotel

Enniskerry,
Co. Wicklow

Tel: 01-282 8903 Fax: 01-286 4909
Email: info@powerscourtarmshotel.com
Web: www.powerscourtarmshotel.com

HOTEL ★ MAP 8 O 10

You'll always find a warm welcome at the Powerscourt Arms Hotel, situated in the beautiful picturesque village of Enniskerry. It's an ideal base for touring expeditions, an intimate family-run hotel with 12 bedrooms furnished to include direct dial telephone, en suite bathrooms & multi channel TV, ample car parking. The restaurant seats up to 45 people, our lounge with strong features of American white ash, serves bar food daily. The public bar has its own atmosphere complete with open fire. Our exquisite and spacious refurnished lounge has a vitalising atmosphere.

B&B from €45.00 to €45.00

Charles McTernan
General Manager

Member of:

IRISH HOTELS FEDERATION

Special Offer: Weekend Specials from €110.00 pps
(2 Nights B&B & 1 Dinner)

🏨 📞 🎫 T C M J P 🔒 Alc
12 12

Closed 24 - 27 December

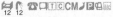

B&B Rates are per Person Sharing per Night incl. Breakfast.
or Room Rates are per Room per Night - See also Page 8

Summerhill House Hotel

Enniskerry,
Co. Wicklow

Tel: 01-286 7928 Fax: 01-286 7929
Email: info@summerhillhousehotel.com
Web: www.summerhillhousehotel.com

HOTEL ★★★ MAP 8 O 10

This charming hotel is just a short walk to the quaint village of Enniskerry, and the famous Powerscourt Gardens. Located on the N11, 19km south of Dublin City & 15km to Dunlaoire Ferryport. 57 spacious bedrooms, private free car parking, traditional Irish breakfast, hill walking & nature trails, local golf courses, family rooms (2 adults and 3 children). Enjoy a rare blend of the Wicklow countryside close to Dublin City. A member of the Strandwood Hotel Group.

Bookable on www.irelandhotels.com
Member of Strandwood Hotel Group

B&B from €100.00 to €140.00

Oonagh Cullen
General Manager

Activities:
✓

Member of:
IRISH HOTELS FEDERATION

Special Offer: Weekend Specials from €125.00 pps
(2 Nights B&B & 1 Dinner)

57 57

Closed 24 - 26 December

Glendalough Hotel

Glendalough,
Co. Wicklow

Tel: 0404-45135 Fax: 0404-45142
Email: info@glendaloughhotel.ie
Web: www.glendaloughhotel.com

HOTEL ★★★ MAP 8 O 9

The Glendalough Hotel, built in the early 1800s, is a family-run hotel situated in the heart of Wicklow's most scenic valley and within the Glendalough National Park. The hotel has recently been extended offering 40 beautifully decorated en suite bedrooms with satellite TV and direct dial phone. The hotel's restaurant offers superb cuisine and wines in a tranquil environment overlooking the Glendasan River. The Tavern Bar serves good pub food and offers entertainment at weekends.

B&B from €68.00 to €95.00

Patrick Casey

Activities:
✓ 🍴

Member of:
IRISH HOTELS FEDERATION

Special Offer: Weekend Specials from €130.00 pps
(2 Nights B&B & 1 Dinner)

40 40

Closed 01 - 31 January

B&B Rates are per Person Sharing per Night incl. Breakfast.
or **Room Rates** are per Room per Night - See also Page 8

Lynham's Hotel

Laragh,
Glendalough,
Co. Wicklow
Tel: 0404-45345 Fax: 0404-45514
Email: info@lynhamsoflaragh.ie
Web: www.lynhamsoflaragh.ie

HOTEL N MAP 8 O 9

Family owned Lynham's Hotel Laragh is situated in the heart of Wicklow National Park, just a few minutes from the beautiful historic Glendalough. The warm welcoming atmosphere of Jake's Bar lends a traditional air to Lynham's. Famous for its superb bar food, you can also enjoy candlelight dining in our old world restaurant. Lynham's also offer special concessions to the world famous Druids Glen and Druids Heath Golf Courses.

B&B from €65.00 to €85.00

John & Anne Lynham
Managers

Member of:
IRISH HOTELS FEDERATION

Special Offer: Weekend Specials from €140.00 pps
(2 Nights B&B & 1 Dinner)

16 16

Closed 21 - 28 December

Glenview Hotel

Glen-O-The-Downs,
Delgany,
Co. Wicklow
Tel: 01-287 3399 Fax: 01-287 7511
Email: sales@glenviewhotel.com
Web: www.glenviewhotel.com

HOTEL U MAP 8 O 10

Situated on a magnificent panoramic site overlooking the garden of Ireland. The Glenview Hotel offers 70 de luxe bedrooms, the unrivalled Penthouse Suite, the award-winning Woodlands Restaurant, Conservatory Bar, 8 meeting rooms for up to 220 delegates and a magnificent leisure club. From the moment you walk through the door you will experience a warm welcome, gracious hospitality and personal service. Relax and unwind in the Haven Beauty salons where calm and peace replace stress and tension.

Bookable on www.irelandhotels.com

B&B from €90.00 to €140.00

Lee Gregson
General Manager

Activities:

Member of:
IRISH HOTELS FEDERATION

Special Offer: Weekend Specials from €170.00 pps
(2 Nights B&B & 1 Dinner)

70 70

Open All Year

Marriott Druids Glen Hotel & Country Club

Newtownmountkennedy,
Co. Wicklow
Tel: 01-287 0800 Fax: 01-287 0801
Email: mhrs.dubgs.reservations@marriotthotels.com
Web: www.marriott.ie/dubgs

HOTEL **** MAP 8 P 9

Voted 'European Golf Resort of the Year 2005', Marriott Druids Glen Hotel & Country Club is located within the 400 acre Druids Glen resort and nestling between the Irish Sea and stunning Wicklow mountains. This relaxed, elegant hotel features de luxe accommodation and a choice of dining options and two championship 18 hole golf courses. AA*****.

Bookable on www.irelandhotels.com

B&B from €75.00 to €150.00

BJ Schreuder
General Manager

Activities:

Member of:
IRISH HOTELS FEDERATION

148 148

Open All Year

B&B Rates are per Person Sharing per Night incl. Breakfast.
or Room Rates are per Room per Night - See also Page 8

Hunter's Hotel

Newrath Bridge,
Rathnew,
Co. Wicklow
Tel: 0404-40106 Fax: 0404-40338
Email: reception@hunters.ie
Web: www.hunters.ie

HOTEL ★★★ MAP 8 P 9

Ireland's oldest coaching inn, its award-winning gardens along River Vartry provide a haven from the world at large. Restaurant provides the very best of Irish food, fresh fish. Local amenities include golf, tennis, horse riding and fishing. Beautiful sandy beaches and sightseeing in the Garden of Ireland. Dublin 44.8km. Rosslare 115.2km. Off N11 at Rathnew or Ashford. Irish Country Houses and Restaurant Association. Refurbished 1995-1996. 1996 new conference room added.

Member of Ireland's Blue Book

B&B from €95.00 to €105.00

*Gelletlie Family
Proprietors*

Activities:

Member of:

Special Offer: Low Season Midweek Specials (Sun - Thurs), 2 Nights B&B & 1 Dinner from €140.00 pps

16 16

Closed 24 - 26 December

Tinakilly Country House and Restaurant

Wicklow,
(Rathnew),
Co. Wicklow
Tel: 0404-69274 Fax: 0404-67806
Email: reservations@tinakilly.ie
Web: www.tinakilly.ie

HOTEL ★★★ MAP 8 P 9

This Victorian mansion was built for Captain Halpin, who laid the world's telegraph cables. The bedrooms, some with 4 posters, are furnished in period style and most overlook the Irish Sea. Award-winning cuisine is prepared from garden vegetables, local fish and Wicklow lamb. The family welcome ensures a relaxing, memorable stay. Available locally - golf, horse riding, Powerscourt, Mount Usher Gardens and Wicklow Mountains. Dublin 46km. Awarded RAC Blue Ribbon for Excellence. Blue Book member.

Bookable on www.irelandhotels.com
Member of Ireland's Blue Book

B&B from €108.00 to €134.00

*Josephine & Raymond Power
Proprietors*

Activities:

Member of:

51 51

Closed 24 - 26 December

Grand Hotel

Wicklow Town,
Co. Wicklow

Tel: 0404-67337 Fax: 0404-69607
Email: reservations@grandhotel.ie
Web: www.grandhotel.ie

HOTEL ★★★ MAP 8 P 9

This charming hotel is the perfect base for touring the beautiful Garden of Ireland. Situated in Wicklow Town, it is only a 40 minute drive from Dublin on the N11. Enjoy golf, fishing, hill walking, sandy beaches and sightseeing locally. 33 large, bright, comfortable bedrooms all en suite with direct dial telephone, multi channel TV and tea/coffee making facilities. Fine food served in the restaurant and bar all day. Lively lounge bar. Conference facilities.

B&B from €49.50 to €67.50

*Adrian Flynn
Hotel Director*

Activities:

Member of:

33 33

Closed 24 - 26 December

B&B Rates are per Person Sharing per Night incl. Breakfast.
or **Room Rates** are per Room per Night - See also Page 8

Woodenbridge

New Valley Inn	Woodenbridge Hotel	Woodenbridge Lodge
Woodenbridge, Avoca, Co. Wicklow Tel: 0402-35200 Fax: 0402-30100 Email: thenewvalleyinn@eircom.net Web: www.newvalleyinn.com	Vale Of Avoca, Arklow, Co. Wicklow Tel: 0402-35146 Fax: 0402-35573 Email: wbhotel@iol.ie Web: www.woodenbridgehotel.com	Vale Of Avoca, Arklow, Co. Wicklow Tel: 0402-35146 Fax: 0402-35573 Email: wbhotel@iol.ie Web: www.woodenbridgehotel.com

HOTEL U MAP 808

HOTEL ★★★ MAP 808

HOTEL ★★★ MAP 808

Quaint country family-run hotel. Ideally located for touring County Wicklow. 1.5 miles from Ballykissangel. 1 hour to Dublin and Rosslare. Surrounded by woodlands and forest and goldminer stream running by hotel. Walking distance to Woodenbridge Golf Club. Our restaurant offers excellent food and our bars are lively with good atmosphere. Hill walking, fishing, beaches are all within minutes of the hotel.

Family owned and run with 23 en suite rooms, including rooms with balconies overlooking Woodenbridge golf course. Dating from 1608 the hotel is the oldest in Ireland. Our restaurant and bar serve quality Irish food: Bord Bia accredited. Tourism Menu award-winner, bar food served all day. Horse riding, fishing, golfing, fine beaches and walking available locally. Near Avoca film location for Ballykissangel.

Woodenbridge Lodge is sheltered by Wicklow's rolling hills and is in the picturesque Vale of Avoca. Situated on the banks of the Aughrim River, with 40 bedrooms. A perfect setting for golfing breaks, family reunions, or relaxing, peaceful weekends for two. Il Ruscello Italian restaurant is located here, with authentic Italian cuisine recommended by Paolo Tullio.

Bookable on www.irelandhotels.com
Member of Best Western

Member of Best Western

B&B from €45.00 to €55.00	B&B from €45.00 to €80.00	B&B from €45.00 to €80.00

Gavin Moran / Sean Darcy

Esther O'Brien & Bill O'Brien
Proprietors

Esther O'Brien & Bill O'Brien
Proprietors

Activities:
✓

Member of:
IRISH
HOTELS
FEDERATION

Activities:
✓

Member of:
IRISH
HOTELS
FEDERATION

Activities:
✓

Member of:
IRISH
HOTELS
FEDERATION

Special Offer: Weekend Specials from €125.00 pps
(2 Nights B&B & 1 Dinner)

Special Offer: Midweek Specials from €120.00 pps
(3 Nights B&B)

Special Offer: Midweek Specials from €120.00 pps
(3 Nights B&B)

14 14

23 23

40 40

Open All Year	Closed 25 December	Closed 25 December

B&B Rates are per Person Sharing per Night incl. Breakfast.
or **Room Rates** are per Room per Night - See also Page 8

One source...
Endless possibilities

Map of Midlands & Lakelands Region

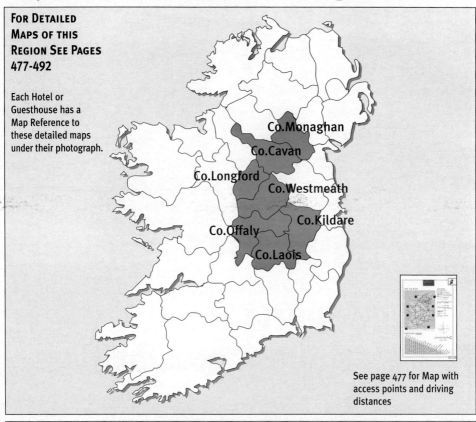

FOR DETAILED MAPS OF THIS REGION SEE PAGES 477-492

Each Hotel or Guesthouse has a Map Reference to these detailed maps under their photograph.

Co.Monaghan
Co.Cavan
Co.Longford
Co.Westmeath
Co.Kildare
Co.Offaly
Co.Laois

See page 477 for Map with access points and driving distances

Locations listing

irelandhotels.com
Official Website of the Irish Hotels Federation

INCLUDES DETAILED MAPS & GREAT VALUE SPECIAL OFFERS.

Midlands / Lakelands
East Coast and Midlands

East Coast & Midlands Tourism

Come & Discover the Undiscovered!!!

There is something for everyone in this part of Ireland - all types of activity holidays are on offer. Choose from among some of the finest parkland and links golf courses in the world, at affordable prices! Enjoy outstanding angling, both fresh water and sea, unequalled equestrian facilities including the Irish racing classics; spectacular walking routes, relaxing cruising and many exciting adventure breaks.

Visitor attractions range from ancient monuments to great houses and gardens. This area of Ireland is fortunate to have some of the very best restaurants, hotels and guesthouses in the country!

Finally Ireland is known by the warm welcome it gives to all who visit them. Come and enjoy some quality time with us in an area which is waiting to be discovered!

Ireland's Ryder Cup Region

Festival and Events: September - The Ryder Cup, The K Club, Straffan, Co. Kildare. Johnny Keenan Banjo Festival, Longford Town, Co. Longford. Oct - Wicklow Walking Festival.

The K Club, Co. Kildare will soon host one of the world's most prestigious events, Ryder Cup 2006.

Almost a quarter of the 400+ golf courses in Ireland can be found in Ireland's East Coast & Midlands, a traditional golfing region quite literally surrounding Dublin. As well as some of Europe's best known courses, you will discover a whole host of lesser known gems which combine to offer a golfing experience that for quality, choice and value is simply unbeatable!

Local upcoming events:
June - Gerald Manly Hopkins International Summer School. August - National Steam Rally, Stradbally, Co. Laois.

Many other festivals occur throughout the year, for further information please visit:
www.eastcoastmidlands.ie

Full details on all festivals and events, heritage and special interest activities from angling to walking in the East Coast and Midlands region are available from the local Tourist Information Office or from:

**East Coast and Midlands Tourism, Market House, Mullingar, Co. Westmeath.
Tel: 00 353 (0) 44-48650
Fax: 00 353 (0) 44-40413
E-mail:
info@eastcoastmidlands.ie
Web site:
www.eastcoastmidlands.ie**

 Calendar of Events

May
Nissan Irish Open, Kildare, Co. Kildare.

June
Budweiser Irish Derby, The Curragh Racecourse, Co. Kildare.

July
The Smurfit European Open, K Club, Co. Kildare.

August
Birr Vintage Week, Birr, Co. Offaly.
Tullamore Phoenix Festival, Tullamore, Co. Offaly.

Event details correct at time of going to press.
enjoy Guinness sensibly.

Co. Cavan

Arvagh / Bailieborough / Ballyconnell

Breffni Arms Hotel	Bailie Hotel	Keepers Arms

Breffni Arms Hotel

Arvagh,
Co. Cavan

Tel: 049-433 5127 Fax: 049-433 5799
Email: breffniarms@hotmail.com
Web: www.breffniarms.com

HOTEL ★★ MAP 11 K 14

The Breffni Arms is a 12 bedroomed en suite family-run licensed hotel and leisure centre. Ideally situated for a choice of golf courses, fishing, horse riding and pitch & putt, etc. Facilities include 15m indoor swimming pool, sauna, steam room, jacuzzi and fitness room. All our rooms have TV, phone, computer point and tea/coffee making facilities.

B&B from €60.00 to €85.00

Philomena & Eamonn Gray

Activities:

Special Offer: Weekend Specials from €120.00 pps (2 Nights B&B & 1 Dinner)

12 12

Open All Year

Bailie Hotel

Main Street,
Bailieborough,
Co. Cavan

Tel: 042-966 5334 Fax: 042-966 6506
Email: hotelbailie@eircom.net

HOTEL ★★ MAP 11 M 14

This newly refurbished family-run hotel is the perfect location for holiday, business or relaxation. Our 18 beautifully appointed en suite bedrooms are fitted out to the highest standard with TV, direct dial phone and tea/coffee facilities. Excellent reputation for good food with carvery lunches served daily, also à la carte and bar food. Our bar and lounge enjoy live music every weekend. Coarse fishing, golf course and mountain climbing close by. Swimming pool and leisure centre in town.

B&B from €50.00 to €70.00

Geraldine McEnaney Proprietor

Special Offer: Weekend Specials from €99.50 pps (2 Nights B&B & 1 Dinner)

18 18

Closed 24 - 26 December

Keepers Arms

Bridge Street,
Bawnboy, Ballyconnell,
Co. Cavan

Tel: 049-952 3318 Fax: 049-952 3008
Email: keepers@iol.ie
Web: www.keepersarms.com

GUESTHOUSE ★★ MAP 11 K 15

Situated in West Cavan the Village of Bawnboy boasts The Keepers Arms. It offers top of the range quality approved accommodation and fully licenced bar. Ideally based for fishing, golfing & walking holidays. All our eleven en suite rooms have been decorated and equipped with your comfort in mind. (TV'S, Tea/Coffee, DD Phone). So if you require a king, single, double, twin, or family room we are able to satisfy your needs. Our aim is to make your stay a comfortable one.

Bookable on www.irelandhotels.com

B&B from €40.00 to €50.00

Sheila McKiernan

Member of:

IRISH HOTELS FEDERATION

Special Offer: Weekend Specials from €105.00 pps (2 Nights B&B & 1 Dinner)

11 11

Closed 24 - 26 December

B&B Rates are per Person Sharing per Night incl. Breakfast.
or Room Rates are per Room per Night - See also Page 8

Slieve Russell Hotel Golf & Country Club

Ballyconnell,
Co. Cavan

Tel: 049-952 6444 Fax: 049-952 6046
Email: slieve-russell@quinn-hotels.com
Web: www.quinnhotels.com

HOTEL ★★★★ MAP 11 K 15

The Slieve Russell Hotel Golf & Country Club with Ciúin Spa and Wellness Centre is a luxury 4**** resort set amidst 300 acres of magnificently landscaped gardens, including 50 acres of lakes. Our new state of the art conference centre has enabled us to cater for conferences with up to 1,500 delegates. For the golfer, our 18 hole Championship Golf Course ensures a challenging game. Our 9 hole par 3 course and driving range are also available. Located just 90 miles from Dublin and Belfast, the Slieve Russell Hotel offers a haven of comfort and relaxation.

Bookable on www.irelandhotels.com
Member of Quinn Hotels

B&B from €125.00 to €295.00

Tony Walker
General Manager

Activities:

Member of:
IRISH HOTELS FEDERATION

Special Offer: Midweek Specials from €165.00 pps
(2 Nights B&B and 1 Dinner)

219 219

Open All Year

Cavan Crystal Hotel

Dublin Road,
Cavan Town

Tel: 049-436 0600 Fax: 049-436 0699
Email: info@cavancrystalhotel.com
Web: www.cavancrystalhotel.com

HOTEL ★★★★ MAP 11 L 14

Cavan Crystal Hotel is a contemporary new 4**** hotel. 85 superbly appointed bedrooms, 9 conference and banqueting suites, 2 bars, award-winning Opus One Restaurant, award-winning Zest Health & Fitness Club including an 18 metre deck level pool, sauna, jacuzzi, steam room & fully equipped gymnasium. Why not relax in our IBPA Salon of the Year 2005, Utopia Health & Beauty Clinic or hair salon and do a spot of shopping in our own Cavan Crystal showroom. Located on the N3, a few minutes drive from town centre, 1.5 hours Dublin / Belfast.

Bookable on www.irelandhotels.com

B&B from €80.00 to €175.00

Siobhan Smyth
General Manager

Activities:

Member of:
IRISH HOTELS FEDERATION

Special Offer: Midweek Specials from €145.00 pps
(2 Nights B&B and 1 Dinner)

85 85

Closed 24 - 26 December

B&B Rates are per Person Sharing per Night incl. Breakfast.
or Room Rates are per Room per Night - See also Page 8

Hotel Kilmore

Dublin Road,
Cavan Town

Tel: 049-433 2288 Fax: 049-433 2458
Email: info@hotelkilmore.ie
Web: www.hotelkilmore.ie

HOTEL ★★★ MAP 11 L 14

On the doorsteps of Ireland's lakelands, the charming Hotel Kilmore offers guests a perfect blend of old world charm and contemporary design. Relax and enjoy the benefits of the afternoon sun in our Victorian sunroom bar, dine in sumptuous elegance in our Annalee Restaurant or enjoy a pint and a friendly chat in our Killykeen Lounge. A vibrant venue for any conference or private function.

Bookable on www.irelandhotels.com

B&B from €65.00 to €95.00

Paul Henry
General Manager

Activities:

Member of:

Special Offer: Weekend Specials from €165.00 pps
(2 Nights B&B & 1 Dinner)

39 39

Closed 24 - 26 December

Radisson SAS Farnham Estate

Farnham Estate,
Cavan,
Co. Cavan

Tel: 049-436 5801 Fax: 049-436 5271
Email: info.farnham@radissonsas.com
Web: www.farnham.radissonsas.com

UNDER CONSTRUCTION - OPENING JUNE 2006

HOTEL P MAP 11 L 14

Home to the Farnham family for 400 years, Farnham Estate is being remodelled into a contemporary country style house, designed to focus on well being and health. Nature and nurture are key elements of the Farnham philosophy and when completed, the resort will feature the Radisson SAS Hotel, state-of-the-art Wellness Centre designed by Heinz Schletterer and a Jeff Howes designed 18-hole golf course. Other activities include angling, horse riding and walking.

Member of Radisson SAS

B&B from €65.00 to €95.00

Sheila Gray
General Manager

Activities:

158 158

Open All Year

Errigal Hotel

Cavan Road,
Cootehill,
Co. Cavan

Tel: 049-555 6901 Fax: 049-555 6902
Email: info@errigalhotel.com
Web: www.errigalhotel.com

HOTEL N MAP 11 L 15

The Errigal Hotel is a contemporary high quality hotel located just outside Cootehill town centre, deep in the heart of Cavan's Lake District. The hotel's luxurious bedrooms have been designed with the busy traveller and the relaxing holiday resident in mind, and have been furnished to a very high standard. Our award-winning Reynards Restaurant offers a superb choice menus. The hotel's gothic themed Brewery Bar provides a perfect retreat to relax with live entertainment on weekends. This small luxury hotel is the perfect destination for conferencing, golfing, business and leisure.

B&B from €62.00 to €70.00

Pat & Bernie Kelly
Proprietors

Activities:

Special Offer: Weekend Specials from €125.00 pps
(2 Nights B&B & 1 Dinner)

22 22

Open All Year

B&B Rates are per Person Sharing per Night incl. Breakfast.
or Room Rates are per Room per Night - See also Page 8

Cabra Castle Hotel

Kingscourt,
Co. Cavan

Tel: 042-966 7030 Fax: 042-966 7039
Email: sales@cabracastle.com
Web: www.cabracastle.com

HOTEL ★★★★ MAP 11 M 14

Follow in the footsteps of Oliver Cromwell and James II, and treat yourself to a stay in a Castle. Cabra Castle stands on 88 acres of gardens and parkland, with its own nine hole golf course. The bar and restaurant offer views over countryside, famous for its lakes and fishing, as well as Dun a Ri Forest Park. An ideal venue for that holiday, specialising in golfing and equestrian holidays. Member of: Manor House Hotels Tel: 01-295 8900. www.manorhousehotels.com. Sister hotel of Ballyseede Castle Hotel, Tralee, Co. Kerry.

Bookable on www.irelandhotels.com
Member of Manor House Hotels

B&B from €72.50 to €113.00

Howard Corscadden
Manager

Member of:
HOTELS

Special Offer: Weekend Specials from €185.00 pps (2 Nights B&B & 1 Dinner)

80 80

Closed 23 - 26 December

Crover House Hotel & Golf Club

Lough Sheelin,
Mountnugent,
Co. Cavan

Tel: 049-854 0206 Fax: 049-854 0356
Email: crover@iol.ie
Web: www.croverhousehotel.ie

HOTEL ★★ MAP 11 L 13

Crover House Hotel & Golf Club is a luxurious destination situated on the shores of Lough Sheelin. The hotel has 37 en suite bedrooms, with the relaxing Sailor's Bar or the more contemporary Lake View Bar. Fine dining is also available in our elegant Sheelin Room. Boats may be hired at the hotel's private jetty for those who wish to avail of the lake facilities. Enjoy a round of golf on our executive golf course or maybe stroll around our beautiful scenic gardens.

B&B from €65.00 to €80.00

Aaron Mansworth
General Manager

Activities:

Member of:
HOTELS

Special Offer: Midweek Specials from €150.00 pps (3 Nights B&B)

37 37

Closed 25 December

B&B Rates are per Person Sharing per Night incl. Breakfast. or **Room Rates** are per Room per Night - See also Page 8

Virginia

Lakeside Manor Hotel

Dublin Road,
Virginia,
Co. Cavan
Tel: 049-854 8200 Fax: 049-854 8279
Email: info@lakesidemanor.ie
Web: www.lakesidemanor.ie

HOTEL **U** MAP 11 L 13

This luxurious hotel located on the shores of scenic Lough Ramor offers something to suit everyone's taste. Relaxing in the Manor Bar with its breathtaking view of the Lake and surrounding countryside. An excellent central location for golfing and all other leisure activities. For the fisherman, boat hire is available at your request and boat trips can also be arranged. This friendly hotel with its helpful and courteous staff is an ideal venue for a relaxing weekend or just to escape the hustle and bustle of the city.

B&B from €60.00 to €75.00

Meabh & Jim Brady
Proprietors

Activities:

🐾🦆 🏌️ 🚗🍴T/🏍️🐎 🐕CM✿🍵♨👤♪♫
30 30 P🅿🆂🛗♿🚬 inet 🐎

Closed 24 - 26 December

Park Hotel

Virginia,
Co. Cavan
Tel: 049-854 6100 Fax: 049-854 7203
Email: virginiapark@eircom.net
Web: www.parkhotelvirginia.com

HOTEL ★★★ MAP 11 L 13

Beautifully restored hotel set in its own 100 acre historic estate. Located on the shores of Lough Ramor and nestled among some of the country's most beautifully landscaped gardens. Guests can avail of our 9 hole golf course, 15 miles of walking trails and excellent fishing locally. Dine in the beautiful surroundings of our AA award-winning restaurant. Our conference facilities can cater for up to 100 delegates.

Bookable on www.irelandhotels.com

B&B from €55.00 to €65.00

Michael Kelly
General Manager

Activities:

✓🏌️

Member of:

IRISH HOTELS FEDERATION

Special Offer: Weekend Specials from €125.00 pps
(2 Nights B&B & 1 Dinner)

🐾🦆 🚗🍴TCCM✿🍵🛗👤♪🅿🅿🔥
29 29

🚬

Open All Year

River Front Hotel (The)

Main Street,
Virginia,
Co. Cavan
Tel: 049-854 7561 Fax: 049-854 7761
Email: info@riverfront.ie
Web: www.riverfront.ie

HOTEL ★★ MAP 11 L 13

Nestled in the heart of the picturesque town of Virginia, this boutique hotel was tastefully transformed while upholding the traditions of seasonal fresh food and a warm welcome. Situated on the doorstep of some of Ireland's best angling and golfing, the individually appointed bedrooms enjoy all the facilities the modern traveller expects. Our recently refurbished banqueting suite boasts private landscaped gardens with exclusive frontage to the Rampart River. Private parking available.

B&B from €55.00 to €65.00

Jimmy & Antoinette Murray
Proprietors

Activities:

✓♪🏌️

Member of:

IRISH HOTELS FEDERATION

Special Offer: Weekend Specials from €115.00 pps
(2 Nights B&B & 1 Dinner)

🐾🦆 🚗🍴TC🚗CM✿🍵♨♪🎵🅿🆂🛗♿
13 13

🚬 inet

Closed 24 - 26 December

B&B Rates are per Person Sharing per Night incl. Breakfast.
or **Room Rates** are per Room per Night - See also Page 8

Bert House Hotel & Leisure Centre

Kilberry,
Athy,
Co. Kildare
Tel: 059-863 2578 Fax: 059-863 2750
Email: info@berthouse.net
Web: www.berthouse.ie

HOTEL P MAP 7 M 9

Located on the banks of the River Barrow in a secluded oasis in County Kildare, the hotel is set back one kilometre from the road giving complete privacy. It is ideal for a romantic break or a tailor-made holiday. Whether it is angling, golfing, or a more relaxed spa break you are looking for Bert House caters for all guests' need's with individual attention to detail.

B&B from €79.00 to €265.00

Eugene Hickey
Host

Activities:

Special Offer: *Weekend Specials from €165.00 pps*
(2 Nights B&B & 1 Dinner)

17 17

Inet

Open All Year

Carlton Abbey Hotel

Rathstewart,
Athy,
Co. Kildare
Tel: 059-863 0100

Web: www.carlton.ie

UNDER CONSTRUCTION - OPENING MARCH 2006

HOTEL P MAP 7 M 9

Situated in the town centre of Athy, 1 hour drive south from Dublin is the Carlton Abbey Hotel. Designed to a 4**** standard, it will open in March 2006. Originally a convent with its own private church, the building has many unique and individual features which have been maintained in the current design. The hotel comprises of 60 rooms, conference and banqueting facilities for 300 delegates and a full leisure centre and spa.

Member of Carlton Hotel Group

B&B from €65.00 to €140.00

Damien Makatarian
General Manager

Activities:

60 60

S   Inet

Closed 24 - 27 December

B&B Rates are per Person Sharing per Night incl. Breakfast.
or **Room Rates** are per Room per Night - See also Page 8

Clanard Court Hotel	Ardenode Hotel	Kilkea Castle

Dublin Road, Athy, Co. Kildare	Ballymore Eustace, Co. Kildare	Castledermot, Co. Kildare
Tel: 059-864 0666 Fax: 059-864 0888	Tel: 045-864198 Fax: 045-864139	Tel: 059-914 5156 Fax: 059-914 5187
Email: sales@clanardcourt.ie	Email: info@ardenodehotel.com	Email: kilkea@iol.ie
Web: www.clanardcourt.ie	Web: www.ardenodehotel.com	Web: www.kilkeacastle.ie

HOTEL **P** MAP 7 M 9	HOTEL **U** MAP 8 N 10	HOTEL **★★★★** MAP 7 M 8
Clanard Court Hotel is built to 4**** specifications, set in 8 acres of manicured grounds. Just 40 miles from Dublin and 1 mile from Athy. Facilities include 38 luxurious bedrooms, conference and banqueting suites catering for up to 400 delegates, Baileys Bar and Courtyard Bistro with executive head chef Aziz Joudar. Free car parking, ideal location to enjoy the charms of the Midlands and surroundings.	The ultimate holiday setting, the Ardenode Hotel takes advantage of Kildare's most convenient and beautiful setting. Views of the Wicklow Mountains and manicured grounds are enjoyed from all public rooms and outdoor areas. At the Ardenode Hotel you can be assured of graceful and relaxing surroundings with professional service from a vibrant team. Dining is a truly magical experience in our award-winning Garden Restaurant.	Kilkea Castle is the oldest inhabited Castle in Ireland. Built in 1180, offering the best in modern comfort while the charm and elegance of the past has been retained. The facilities include de luxe accommodation, a fine dining room, d'Lacy's Restaurant, restful bar/lounge area, full banqueting and conference facilities and full on-site leisure centre with an indoor heated swimming pool, sauna, jacuzzi, steam room and fully equipped gym. 18 hole golf course encircles the Castle.

Bookable on www.irelandhotels.com

Bookable on www.irelandhotels.com
Member of Manor House Hotels

B&B from €69.00 to €130.00	B&B from €65.00 to €150.00	B&B from €120.00 to €185.00

*Mary Fennin Byrne/
Diane Lynch
Managing Dir / Gen Manager*

Activities:

:/🍴

*Gary Browne
General Manager*

*Shane Cassidy
General Manager*

Member of:

HOTELS

Member of:

HOTELS

Member of:

HOTELS

Special Offer: *Weekend Specials from €129.00 pps (2 Nights B&B & 1 Dinner)*

Special Offer: *Midweek Specials from €169.00 pps (3 Nights B&B)*

38 38

17 17

36 36

Open All Year	Open All Year	Closed 23 - 27 December

B&B Rates are per Person Sharing per Night incl. Breakfast.
or Room Rates are per Room per Night - See also Page 8

Setanta House Hotel

Clane Road,
Celbridge,
Co. Kildare

Tel: 01-630 3200 Fax: 01-627 3387
Email: info@setantahousehotel.com
Web: www.setantahousehotel.com

HOTEL ★★★ MAP 8 N 11

Built in 1737, this former school situated in the historic Heritage Town of Celbridge combines elegance and tranquillity with modern facilities. Set in mature landscaped gardens with 65 newly refurbished spacious bedrooms including luxurious suites. Setanta House is ideal for business and leisure alike. Only 20 minutes from Dublin City and Airport with easy access off the N4 and M50. Renowned golf and racecourses nearby. A warm welcome is always assured.

Bookable on www.irelandhotels.com

B&B from €75.00 to €200.00

Arthur McDaniel
General Manager

Activities:

Member of:

Special Offer: *Weekend Specials from €170.00 pps*
(2 Nights B&B & 1 Dinner)

65 65

Closed 24 -26 December

Westgrove Hotel & Conference Centre

Clane,
Co. Kildare

Tel: 1800-32 42 52 Fax: 045-902597
Email: sales@westgrovehotel.com
Web: www.westgrovehotel.com

UNDER CONSTRUCTION - OPENING APRIL 2006

HOTEL P MAP 8 N 11

On the outskirts of Clane Village, this hotel combines accessibility with the feel of getting away from the bustle of the city. Flexible and comfortable conference rooms, an ideal base from which to play world class golf courses, facilities to pamper the most discerning guest and excellent value for money combine to make this a great choice whatever your requirements. 2 restaurants, bar and leisure centre with 20m pool, treatment rooms, secure parking.

B&B from €50.00 to €100.00

Ian Hyland
General Manager

Activities:

Special Offer: *Weekend Specials from €129.00 pps*
(2 Nights B&B & 1 Dinner)

104 104

Closed 23 - 27 December

B&B Rates are per Person Sharing per Night incl. Breakfast.
or **Room Rates** are per Room per Night - See also Page 8

Standhouse Hotel Leisure & Conference Centre	Curragh Lodge Hotel	Ambassador Hotel

Standhouse Hotel Leisure & Conference Centre

Curragh (The),
Co. Kildare

Tel: 045-436177 Fax: 045-436180
Email: reservations@standhousehotel.com
Web: www.standhousehotel.com

HOTEL **U** MAP 7 M 10

Standhouse Hotel has a tradition which dates back to 1700. Situated beside the Curragh Racecourse it has become synonymous with The Classics. The premises has been restored to its former elegance and offers the discerning guest a fine selection of quality restaurants, bars, leisure facilities, including 20 metre pool, state of the art gym, jacuzzi, steam room, sauna and plunge pool. Conference facilities cater for 20 to 500 delegates.

Bookable on www.irelandhotels.com

B&B from €80.00 to €150.00

George Graham
General Manager

Activities:

Member of:

IRISH HOTELS FEDERATION

Special Offer: Midweek Specials from €140.00 pps (3 Nights B&B)

63 63

Closed 25 - 26 December

Curragh Lodge Hotel

Dublin Street,
Kildare Town,
Co. Kildare

Tel: 045-522144 Fax: 045-521247
Email: clhotel@iol.ie

HOTEL **U** MAP 7 M 10

A friendly and warm welcome is assured at The Curragh Lodge Hotel, which is situated off the M7 from Dublin. Conveniently located in the town centre this popular hotel offers comfortable well equipped en suite rooms. Very close to the famous Curragh Racecourse, Japanese Gardens, also local fishing available, Mondello Park, Greyhound Racing and great golf courses including The K Club, Kilkea, Knockanally, Craddockstown, to name but a few.

Bookable on www.irelandhotels.com

B&B from €50.00 to €65.00

Bernie Cullen
General Manager

Member of:

IRISH HOTELS FEDERATION

20 20

Closed 24 - 27 December

Ambassador Hotel

Kill,
Co. Kildare

Tel: 045-877064 Fax: 045-877515
Email: reservations@ambassadorhotelkildare.com
Web: www.ambassadorhotelkildare.com

HOTEL ★★★ MAP 8 N 10

Situated just 20km from Dublin City, this 36 bedroomed hotel is ideally located for those travelling from the south or west. Our restaurants boast excellent cuisine and our bar provides music 4 nights per week. Local amenities include 3 racecourses, The Curragh, Naas and Punchestown, four golf courses, Goffs Horse Sales, (just across the road) and plenty of horse riding. The Ambassador has something for everybody.

B&B from €70.00 to €140.00

Rita Gleeson
General Manager

Member of:

IRISH HOTELS FEDERATION

36 36

Open All Year

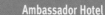

B&B Rates are per Person Sharing per Night incl. Breakfast. or **Room Rates** are per Room per Night - See also Page 8

Courtyard Hotel Leixlip (The)

Main Street,
Leixlip,
Co. Kildare
Tel: 01-629 5100 Fax: 01-629 5111
Email: info@courtyard.ie
Web: www.courtyard.ie

HOTEL P MAP 8 N 11

Opened in July 2005, The Courtyard Hotel is situated 20mins from Dublin City and approx 20mins from Dublin Airport. The hotel is situated on the site of the ancestral home of "Guinness" and features 40 tastefully appointed guest rooms. Dine in the "Riverbank Restaurant" overlooking the River Liffey and relax in "Arthur's Bar". The hotel is situated close to some of Ireland's best golf courses including the K Club and Carton House.

Member of The Moriarty Group

B&B from €39.00 to €99.00

Luke Moriarty
Owner

Activities:

Member of:
IRISH HOTELS FEDERATION

Special Offer: *Weekend Specials from €129.00 pps (2 Nights B&B & 1 Dinner)*

40 40

Inet WiFi

Open all year

B&B Rates are per Person Sharing per Night incl. Breakfast.
or Room Rates are per Room per Night - See also Page 8

Midlands & Lakelands   339

ENJOY THE LUXURY OF SPENDING LESS

OUTLET SHOPPING PRICES REDUCED BY UP TO 60% EVERY DAY ALL YEAR ROUND. A VILLAGE OF 50 BOUTIQUES, CAFÉS AND A RESTAURANT IN THE HEART OF KILDARE. OPENING SUMMER 2006.

www.KildareVillage.com
www.ChicOutletShopping.com
KILDARE VILLAGE, CO. KILDARE, IRELAND
TEL: + 353 (0) 45 520 501

KILDARE VILLAGE
OUTLET SHOPPING

Co. Kildare

Leixlip / Maynooth

Leixlip House Hotel

Captain's Hill,
Leixlip,
Co. Kildare
Tel: 01-624 2268 Fax: 01-624 4177
Email: info@leixliphouse.com
Web: www.leixliphouse.com

HOTEL ★★★ MAP 8 N 11

A most elegant Georgian house hotel built in 1772. Leixlip House is a mere 20 mins drive from Dublin City centre. The hotel has been lovingly restored and offers the discerning guest the highest standards of comfort and hospitality. It can cater for conferences of up to 70 people and our banqueting facilities can comfortably accommodate 140 people. Our signature restaurant "The Bradaun" has been awarded the prestigious AA Two Rosette 1996-2005.

B&B from €75.00 to €140.00

Christian Schmelter
General Manager

Member of:
IRISH HOTELS FEDERATION

Special Offer: Weekend Specials from €150.00 pps
(2 Nights B&B & 1 Dinner)

19 19   WiFi

Closed 24 - 27 December

Springfield Hotel

Leixlip,
Co. Kildare

Tel: 01-458 1100 Fax: 01-458 1142
Email: reception@springfieldhotel.ie
Web: www.springfieldhotel.ie

HOTEL ★★★ MAP 8 N 11

Our tastefully designed bedrooms are en suite, centrally heated with colour TV, satellite, hairdryer, tea/coffee courtesy tray, direct dial telephone, modem points, WiFi and broadband. Our restaurant offers menus to cater for all tastes. Guests return to enjoy our genuine hospitality. Our gym, which is well equipped with the latest machines, also has a sauna and steam room. Carton and Straffan golf courses within 6km. Dublin city centre 12km.

B&B from €65.00 to €185.00

Gerard Hannigan
Director / Manager

Activities:
⛳

Special Offer: 3 Nights B&B inc. Sunday & 1 Dinner
from €185.00 pps

48 48   Inet WiFi

Closed 25 - 26 December

Carton House

Maynooth,
Co. Kildare

Tel: 01-505 2000 Fax: 01-628 6555
Email: sales@cartonhouse.com
Web: www.cartonhouse.com

UNDER CONSTRUCTION - OPENING JUNE 2006

HOTEL P MAP 12 N 11

Already acclaimed for its two championship golf courses, Carton House will boast a lavish new hotel, meeting/event venues as well as a state of the art health spa and sporting activities. Carton House from Summer 2006 will have 160 bedrooms including 14 suites. Being 22kms from Dublin City and 30 minutes from Dublin Airport makes Carton House the ideal venue to book.

Room Rate from €140.00 to €360.00

James Tynan
General Manager

Activities:

Special Offer: Weekend Specials from €180.00 pps
(2 Nights B&B & 1 Dinner)

160 160   Inet WiFi

Open All Year

B&B Rates are per Person Sharing per Night incl. Breakfast.
or Room Rates are per Room per Night - See also Page 8

Glenroyal Hotel, Leisure Club & Conference Centre

Straffan Road,
Maynooth,
Co. Kildare
Tel: 01-629 0909 Fax: 01-629 0919
Email: info@glenroyal.ie
Web: www.glenroyal.ie

HOTEL ★★★ MAP 8 N 11

Located 20 minutes from Dublin off the M4, the Glenroyal Hotel has a well earned reputation for friendliness, informality and hospitality. Ideally located for the business or leisure traveller. With 112 en suite bedrooms, Saint's Bar & Bistro, Lemongrass Restaurant, extensive conference facilities, night club and free car parking. Our leisure facilities include two 20m pools, sauna, jacuzzi, steam room, solariums, gymnasium and beauty/spa. Carton and the K Club are minutes away.

Bookable on www.irelandhotels.com

B&B from €75.00 to €95.00

Helen Courtney
General Manager

Activities:

Member of:

Special Offer: Weekend Specials from €150.00 pps
(2 Nights B&B & 1 Dinner)

112 112

Closed 24 - 25 December

Moyglare Manor

Maynooth,
Co. Kildare

Tel: 01-628 6351 Fax: 01-628 5405
Email: info@moyglaremanor.ie
Web: www.moyglaremanor.ie

HOTEL ★★★ MAP 12 N 11

Ireland's nearest country house to Dublin Airport. Eighteen miles from Dublin and half a mile of tree-lined avenue leads to this unique Georgian house with its majestic exterior holding court over beautiful parklands. Enjoy the relaxed homely atmosphere of this opulent family-run Grade A hotel, which is renowned worldwide for its magnificent décor and antique furnishings.

Member of Ireland's Blue Book

B&B from €90.00 to €115.00

Annalisa Curran
Manager

Special Offer: Weekend Specials from €160.00 pps
(2 Nights B&B & 1 Dinner)

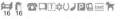

16 16

Closed 23 - 27 December

Hazel Hotel

Dublin Road,
Monasterevin,
Co. Kildare
Tel: 045-525373 Fax: 045-525810
Email: sales@hazelhotel.com
Web: www.hazelhotel.com

HOTEL ★★ MAP 7 N 10

The Hazel Hotel is a family-run country hotel on the main Dublin/Cork/Limerick road (N7). All bedrooms have bath/shower, colour TV and international direct dial telephone. The hotel's restaurant has extensive à la carte and table d'hôte menus. Ample car parking. Entertainment is provided. Ideal base for going to the Curragh, Naas or Punchestown racecourses. Several golf courses close by. National Stud and Japanese Gardens only 7 miles from hotel. No service charge.

Member of Logis of Ireland

B&B from €80.00 to €180.00

Margaret Kelly
Proprietor

Activities:

Member of:

24 24

Closed 24 - 26 December

<u>B&B Rates</u> are per Person Sharing per Night incl. Breakfast.
or <u>Room Rates</u> are per Room per Night - See also Page 8

Naas

Harbour Hotel & Restaurant

Limerick Road,
Naas,
Co. Kildare
Tel: 045-879145 Fax: 045-874002
Email: mary@harbourhotel.ie
Web: www.harbourhotel.ie

HOTEL ★★ MAP 8 N 10

Looking after the needs of our guests and providing quality service is a priority in this family-run hotel. All rooms have colour TV, direct dial telephone, hairdryer and teasmaid. We offer superb home-cooked food, extensive à la carte and table d'hôte menus and excellent wine list. Relax and enjoy a drink in our comfortable lounge. Conveniently situated to Dublin City, ferry, airport, Punchestown, The Curragh and Mondello.

B&B from €55.00 to €55.00

Mary Monaghan
Proprietor

Member of:

🐾🛏 ☎💻C CMP🅿🔔 alc 🔌 WiFi
10 10

Closed 24 - 29 December

Killashee House Hotel & Villa Spa

Killashee,
Naas,
Co. Kildare
Tel: 045-879277 Fax: 045-879266
Email: reservations@killasheehouse.com
Web: www.killasheehouse.com

HOTEL U MAP 8 N 10

Killashee House Hotel & Villa Spa is ideally located on 80 acres of gardens and parkland, 20 minutes from Dublin and 1 mile from Naas. From its winding drive to its magnificent bell tower, this Victorian house blends the dignity of a major business hotel with the casual atmosphere of a fine country resort. Killashee House Hotel & Villa Spa consists of 142 luxurious guest rooms, including executive suites, all traditionally appointed combining opulent luxury with perfect attention to detail. State of the art country club and villa spa with 18 treatment rooms and superb leisure facilities.

Bookable on www.irelandhotels.com

B&B from €90.00 to €250.00

Odhran Lawlor
General Manager

Activities:

Member of:

🐾🛏 ☎💻📺C ♥CM❄🔔💺📷🍴♪♫
142 142
P S 🔔 alc inet WiFi 🐕

Closed 24 - 25 December

Maudlins House Hotel

Dublin Road,
Naas,
Co. Kildare
Tel: 045-896999 Fax: 045-896999
Email: maudlinshousehotel@eircom.net
Web: www.maudlinshousehotel.com

UNDER CONSTRUCTION - OPENING DECEMBER 2005

HOTEL P MAP 8 N 10

Exclusive development of a 30 bedroom hotel, ideally positioned in the thoroughbred county, due to open in December 2005. Conveniently located .25km from Naas Town, 25kms from Dublin and ideal for those travelling to the South or West. The hotel combines old world charm with all the needs of the modern guest. Local amenities include golf, horse racing, Goffs Horse Sales and shopping.

B&B from €75.00 to €150.00

Teresa Harhan
Director

🐾🛏 ☎💻📺C CMU🅿🔔 alc 🔌 inet WiFi
30 30
🐕

Closed 24 - 26 December

B&B Rates are per Person Sharing per Night incl. Breakfast. or Room Rates are per Room per Night - See also Page 8

Osprey Hotel & Spa

Devoy Quarter,
Naas,
Co. Kildare
Tel: 045-881111 Fax: 045-881112
Email: info@osprey.ie
Web: www.osprey.ie

Annagh Lodge

Naas Road,
Newbridge,
Co. Kildare
Tel: 045-433518 Fax: 045-433538
Email: annaghlodge@eircom.net
Web: www.annaghlodge.ie

Gables Guesthouse & Leisure Centre

Ryston,
Newbridge,
Co. Kildare
Tel: 045-435330 Fax: 045-435355
Email: gablesguesthse@ireland.com

HOTEL N MAP 8 N 10 | **GUESTHOUSE ★★★ MAP 7 M 10** | **GUESTHOUSE ★★★ MAP 7 M 10**

The Osprey Complex, located in the heart of Kildare, is only 35 minutes from Dublin City and close to all major routes. It includes the Osprey Hotel, Osprey Spa, Life: Health & Leisure, Time: Venue, Osprey Conference Centre and Osprey Nest Crèche. Osprey Hotel is of contemporary style with 104 bedrooms including two penthouse suites, has a dramatic foyer, glazed atria, Mash: Restaurant, Statler bar and Waldorf lounge and ballroom. It has been designed to cater for an entirely new lifestyle. Complimentary wireless connectivity throughout. Suites available up to €1,000 per night.

Bookable on www.irelandhotels.com

AA ◆◆◆◆ purpose built guesthouse with private parking in a peaceful setting, ideally located beside all town amenities including hotels, restaurants, pubs and leisure centres. Annagh Lodge provides the highest standard of comfort in superior rooms and suites with all modern conveniences combined with excellent service. Dublin and the airport are 45 minutes drive. The Curragh, Naas and Punchestown Racecourses, 8 golf courses, fishing and motor racing at Mondello are a short drive. 10km from Irish National Stud and Japanese Gardens. Access for wheelchairs.

Set on the banks of the Liffey, our family-run guesthouse has 19 bedrooms with bath/shower, multi channel TV, direct dial telephone, hairdryer and teas maid. Our leisure centre includes a 14 metre indoor swimming pool, jacuzzi, steam room, large sauna, thermium, plunge pool and fully equipped gym. Horse racing, golf and fishing are well catered for locally. A warm and friendly welcome awaits you at the Gables. Brochures available on request.

B&B from €95.00 to €125.00 | *B&B from €40.00 to €80.00* | *B&B from €40.00 to €75.00*

 John O'Connell, Proprietor | Derna Wallace, Proprietor |  Ray Cribbin, Proprietor

Special Offer: Weekend Specials from €209.00 pps (2 Nights B&B & 1 Dinner)

Closed 24 - 26 December | **Open All Year** | **Closed 24 December - 02 January**

B&B Rates are per Person Sharing per Night incl. Breakfast. or **Room Rates** are per Room per Night - See also Page 8

Keadeen Hotel	Barberstown Castle	K Club (The)

Keadeen Hotel

Newbridge,
Co. Kildare

Tel: 045-431666 Fax: 045-434402
Email: keadeen@iol.ie
Web: www.keadeenhotel.ie

HOTEL ★★★★ MAP 7 M 10

Kildare's longest family-run hotel, the Keadeen is ideally located on 9 acres of magnificent landscaped gardens, just 30 minutes from Dublin off the M7. This charming 4**** hotel offers unrivalled standards of service and facilities with a variety of 75 luxurious spacious bedrooms, a superb indoor health and fitness complex and 18 metre ozone pool. An extensive range of conference/banqueting suites for up to 1000 delegates. Dining facilities include the award-winning Derby Restaurant, the new, sophisticated 'Club Bar', the Drawing Room Lounge and the Paddy Prendergast Bar.

B&B from €101.00 to €178.50

Rose O'Loughlin
Proprietor

Activities:

Member of:

HOTELS

🏌 🏌
75 75

☎ 🖥 🛁 T C ✆ CM ❄ 🍴 🌐 🛏 ♫
P S 🔊 ♿ WiFi 🐾

Closed 24 - 27 December

Barberstown Castle

Straffan,
Co. Kildare

Tel: 01-628 8157 Fax: 01-627 7027
Email: barberstowncastle@ireland.com
Web: www.barberstowncastle.ie

HOTEL N MAP 8 N 11

Dating from the 13th century, this historic castle & country house hotel located only 30 minutes from the airport and Dublin City centre provides the highest standard in comfort. Renowned for excellent food and inviting public rooms which range from the original Castle keep to the soft warmth of the tea rooms and cocktail bar. All the bedrooms are elegantly and luxuriously appointed and laden with antique furniture. A member of Ireland's Blue Book, Barberstown Castle is the ideal first or last stop on your country house tour of Ireland.

Bookable on www.irelandhotels.com
Member of Ireland's Blue Book

B&B from €115.00 to €145.00

Richard Millea, GM
Gretchen Ridgeway
Sales & Marketing Manager

Activities:

Member of:

HOTELS

🏌 🏌
59 59

☎ 🖥 🛁 T C ❄ ♫ 🍴 P 🌐 inet

Closed 24 - 26 December

K Club (The)

At Straffan,
Co. Kildare

Tel: 01-601 7200 Fax: 01-601 7297
Email: resortsales@kclub.ie
Web: www.kclub.ie

HOTEL ★★★★★ MAP 8 N 11

Ireland's only AA 5 Red Star Hotel, located 30 minutes from Dublin Airport. Leisure facilities include 2 18 hole championship golf courses designed by Arnold Palmer, home to the Smurfit European Open & venue for the Ryder Cup in 2006. Two bona fide championship courses side by side offering a distinctive and different experience for the golfer. In addition, both river & coarse fishing are available with full health & leisure club and sporting activities. Meeting & private dining facilities also available.

Bookable on www.irelandhotels.com
Member of Preferred Hotels & Worldwide Resorts

Room Rate from €265.00 to €495.00

Michael Davern
Chief Executive

Activities:

Member of:

HOTELS

🏌 🏌
92 92

☎ 🖥 🛁 C ✆ CM ❄ 🍴 🌐 🛏 ♫
P 🌐 inet

Closed 17 - 26 September

B&B Rates are per Person Sharing per Night incl. Breakfast.
or **Room Rates** are per Room per Night - See also Page 8

Abbeyleix Manor Hotel	Castle Arms Hotel	Heritage at Killenard (The)
Abbeyleix, Co. Laois	The Square, Durrow, Co. Laois	Killenard, Portarlington, Co. Laois
Tel: 057-873 0111 Fax: 057-873 0220 Email: info@abbeyleixmanorhotel.com Web: www.abbeyleixmanorhotel.com	Tel: 057-873 6117 Fax: 057-873 6566 Email: info@castlearmshotel.ie Web: www.castlearmshotel.ie	Tel: 057-864 5500 Fax: 057-864 2350 Email: info@theheritage.com Web: www.theheritage.com

HOTEL ★★★ MAP 7 L 8	HOTEL ★ MAP 7 L 8	HOTEL N MAP 7 L 10

The Abbeyleix Manor boasts a prime location, situated on the N8 halfway between Dublin and Cork, your perfect base for exploring the Midlands region. This family-run hotel has 23 luxurious bedrooms, restaurant, conference facilities and a lively bar with local artists providing traditional music every Saturday night. Already well established as a great place for breakfast, lunch or dinner, the friendly and professional staff will look forward to taking care of you. The relaxed atmosphere will revive even the most jaded traveller and with golf, fishing, walking and shopping locally, there is plenty to see and do.

The Castle Arms Hotel is a family-run hotel situated in the award-winning picturesque village of Durrow. We are situated 1.5 hours from Dublin, two hours from Cork and three hours from Belfast. Our reputation is for good food, service and friendliness. Local amenities include fishing, Granstown Lake is described as being the best coarse fishing lake in Europe. Trout can be fished from the local Rivers Erkina and Nore, horse trekking and many golf courses within easy reach. Brand Central designer outlet is 10 minutes drive away. Ideal for a weekend away shopping.

The Heritage is Ireland's newest and most comprehensive leisure and lifestyle development. Situated in the village of Killenard just off the main Dublin - Cork motorway, we are just 40 miles from Dublin. 98 rooms, world class hotel. 20 room destination Spa and Health Club, the renowned Heritage Golf Course co-designed by Seve Ballesteros, thatch pub and restaurant and the Ballesteros Natural Golf School provide a most comprehensive set of leisure and corporate offers at the highest quality. Superior, Junior & Penthouse suites available - price available upon request.

Member of Preferred Hotels & Resorts

B&B from €55.00 to €75.00	B&B from €52.50 to €52.50	B&B from €100.00 to €175.00

Ellen McDermott, Eileen O'Connor, Fern Carroll Moore, Michael Bennett
Activities:
Member of:

Seosamh Murphy
General Manager
Member of:

Eoin O'Sullivan
Managing Director
Activities:
Member of:

23 23

14 14

98 98

Closed 25 December	Open All Year	Open All Year

B&B Rates are per Person Sharing per Night incl. Breakfast.
or **Room Rates** are per Room per Night - See also Page 8

Midlands & Lakelands 345

Portlaoise / Clondra / Longford Town

Heritage Hotel Portlaoise	Richmond Inn Guesthouse	Annaly Hotel

Portlaoise,
Co. Laois

Tel: 057-867 8588 Fax: 057-867 8577
Email: res@theheritagehotel.com
Web: www.theheritagehotel.com

Clondra,
Co. Longford

Tel: 043-26126 Fax: 043-26166
Email: therichmondinn@eircom.net
Web: www.richmondinnireland.com

57 Main Street,
Longford Town

Tel: 043-42058 Fax: 043-43690
Email: annalyhotel@eircom.net
Web: www.annalyhotel.ie

HOTEL U MAP 7 L 9	GUESTHOUSE U MAP 11 J 13	HOTEL U MAP 11 J 13

The Heritage Portlaoise is the most sought after hotel in Ireland featuring superb facilities and a dedicated team. The hotel features 110 de luxe bedrooms & suites with a stylish difference, a choice of restaurants & bars, award-winning health & fitness Club with Ealu Spa & conference facilities for up to 500 delegates. A choice of 18 hole courses all within easy access of the hotel including the renowned Heritage at Killenard. Nestled in the heart of Portlaoise, the most accessible central location only 1 hour from Dublin, with direct rail access.

A family-run guesthouse and pub in the picturesque village of Clondra. 9km from Longford Town. The Richmond Inn occupies a prime position in this pretty village, standing on the banks of the Royal Canal overlooking the harbour. Your hosts are Des & Frances McPartland who assure their patrons of a warm welcome and fine home cooking. All rooms are en suite with TV, direct dial phone, tea/coffee making facilities. Local amenities include fishing, horse riding, golf, walking and cycling.

3 star standard boutique hotel located in the centre of Longford offering a modern European styled hotel and café bar in comfortable surroundings. Very competitive rates with a host of entertainment on site. 30 fully serviced stylish bedrooms. Full conference facilities. Large function room. Food available from 11am - 9pm including lunch and dinner. Full use of health and fitness centre including 22m pool.

Bookable on www.irelandhotels.com
Member of Select Hotels of Ireland

Bookable on www.irelandhotels.com

B&B from €90.00 to €120.00	B&B from €35.00 to €50.00	B&B from €55.00 to €100.00

Jacinta Naughton
General Manager

Des & Frances McPartland
Owners

James Reynolds
Manager

Activities:

Member of:
IRISH HOTELS FEDERATION

Member of:
IRISH HOTELS FEDERATION

Activities:

Member of:
IRISH HOTELS FEDERATION

Special Offer: Weekend Specials from €175.00 pps
(2 Nights B&B & 1 Dinner)

110 110

5 5

30 30

Closed 23 - 28 December	Closed 16 December - 16 January	Closed 24 - 26 December

B&B Rates are per Person Sharing per Night incl. Breakfast.
or **Room Rates** are per Room per Night - See also Page 8

Longford Arms Hotel

Main Street,
Longford Town

Tel: 043-46296 Fax: 043-46244
Email: longfordarms@eircom.net
Web: www.longfordarms.ie

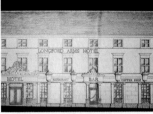

HOTEL ★★★ MAP 11 J 13

Ideally located in the heart of the midlands, this comfortable hotel, newly renovated to exacting standards has a vibrant and relaxing atmosphere. The hotel boasts a state of the art conference centre, new health and leisure centre, excellent restaurant and award-winning coffee shop where you can be assured of fine food, service and a warm welcome in relaxing convivial surroundings. Available locally: 18 hole golf course, angling, equestrian centre and watersports on the Shannon.

B&B from €80.00 to €110.00

Jim Reynolds
Proprietor

Activities:
✌️🏌️

Member of:
IRISH HOTELS FEDERATION

🛏️🐾 ☎️📺🅣🆃🅒💻CM🎿🎣⛵🚣🎵🎹🎮
60 60   aid 🚰 Inet

Closed 24 - 26 December

Nuremore Hotel & Country Club

Carrickmacross,
Co. Monaghan

Tel: 042-966 1438 Fax: 042-966 1853
Email: nuremore@eircom.net
Web: www.nuremore.com

HOTEL ★★★★ MAP 12 N 14

Set in tranquil and beautiful surroundings, amidst a championship 18-hole golf course, the Nuremore offers unrivalled standards of service and sporting, leisure and conference facilities. The Country Club boasts an 18m swimming pool, whirlpool, sauna, steam room, gymnasium, tennis courts and a beauty treatment spa. There are a wide range of spacious rooms and demi-suites on offer and our award-winning restaurant serves superb cuisine in idyllic surroundings, cooked by Ireland's Chef of the Year 2005, Raymond McArdle. Only 1 hour from Dublin, take the M1 and then the N2.

Bookable on www.irelandhotels.com

B&B from €125.00 to €160.00

Julie Gilhooly
Proprietor

Activities:
✌️🏌️💧

Member of:
IRISH HOTELS FEDERATION

Special Offer: *Weekend Specials from €225.00 pps*
(2 Nights B&B & 1 Dinner)

🛏️🐾 ☎️📺🅣🆃🅒✱CM✱🎿🎣⛵🚣Ｑ⛵
69 69   🐾🎵🎹🎮🚰🚰 WiFi 🎿

Open All Year

Castle Leslie

Glaslough,
Co. Monaghan

Tel: 047-88100 Fax: 047-88256
Email: info@castleleslie.com
Web: www.castleleslie.com

GUESTHOUSE ★★★ MAP 11 M 16

300 years of Leslie family history, roaring fires, candlelit dining, quiet corners and 20 quirky bedrooms combine to make the castle and the estate truly a home from home. You'll find no power showers or TV's, just authentic Victorian faded grandeur, wonderful food & lazy days. Choose your own company, walking or riding across our 1,000 acres, or hone your culinary skills in our new cookery school. September 2006 sees the upgraded Castle Leslie Equestrian Centre & Hunting Lodge, offering a further 30 guest rooms, bars, restaurants & spa facilities. 90 mins from Dublin or 60 mins from Belfast.

Member of Ireland's Blue Book

B&B from €145.00 to €195.00

Sir John Leslie &
Sammy Leslie
Owners

Activities:
🎿🏌️💧

Special Offer: *Midweek Specials from €300.00 pps*
(3 Nights B&B)

🛏️🐾 🅣✱🚣🎵🎹🎹
20 20

Open All Year

<u>B&B Rates</u> are per Person Sharing per Night incl. Breakfast.
or <u>Room Rates</u> are per Room per Night - See also Page 8

Co. Monaghan - Co. Offaly

Monaghan Town / Banagher

Four Seasons Hotel & Leisure Club	Hillgrove Hotel & Conference Centre	Brosna Lodge Hotel
Coolshannagh, Monaghan Town, Co. Monaghan	Old Armagh Road, Monaghan Town, Co. Monaghan	Banagher-on-the-Shannon, Co. Offaly
Tel: 047-81888 Fax: 047-83131	Tel: 047-81288 Fax: 047-84951	Tel: 057-915 1350 Fax: 057-915 1521
Email: info@4seasonshotel.ie	Email: info@hillgrovehotel.com	Email: info@brosnalodge.com
Web: www.4seasonshotel.ie	Web: www.hillgrovehotel.com	Web: www.brosnalodge.com

HOTEL ★★★ MAP 11 M 16 | **HOTEL ★★★ MAP 11 M 16** | **HOTEL ★★ MAP 7 J 10**

Elegance without extravagance!! Enjoy the excellent service, warmth and luxury of this family-run hotel. Relax by the turf fire in the Still Bar or savour the food in the informal setting of the Range Restaurant. For an alternative option we offer fine dining in Avenue Restaurant. The rooms have all modern facilities and residents have unlimited use of our leisure facilities, 18m pool, jacuzzi, steam room, sauna and gym. Also available massage and sunbed. Available locally: 18-hole golf course, angling, equestrian centre and water sports.

Minutes walk from Monaghan Town, the majestically magical Hillgrove Hotel is 1 hour from Belfast and 90 mins from Dublin. 44 beautiful bedrooms, including suites with jacuzzis. Excellent cuisine, extensive wines. Restaurant and bars. An ideal venue for weddings and conferences. Golf, rally driving, water sports, horse riding locally. A luxurious and tranquil setting awaits you. An additional 40 bedrooms, leisure club and health spa due to open July 2006.

A family owned country hotel, close to the River Shannon, welcomes guests with superb hospitality and relaxed elegance. Mature gardens surround the hotel. With unique peat bogs, mountains, the Shannon and Clonmacnois, you will delight in this gentle little known part of Ireland. Fishing, golf, pony trekking, nature and historical tours arranged locally. Enjoy beautiful food in our restaurant, The Fields and drinks in Pat's Olde Bar. Dining Pub of the Year Award 2003/2004/2005.

Bookable on www.irelandhotels.com | *Bookable on www.irelandhotels.com*

B&B from €70.00 to €110.00 | **B&B from €35.00 to €100.00** | **B&B from €40.00 to €60.00**

Frank McKenna Managing Director

Colm & Audri Herron Proprietors

Pat & Della Horan Proprietors

Activities: / Member of: IRISH HOTELS FEDERATION

Activities: / Member of: IRISH HOTELS FEDERATION

Activities: / Member of: IRISH HOTELS FEDERATION

Special Offer: Midweek Specials from €99.00 pps (3 Nights B&B)

Special Offer: Weekend Specials from €105.00 pps (2 Nights B&B & 1 Dinner)

59 59 | 44 44 | 14 14

Closed 25 - 26 December | **Closed 25 December** | **Closed 25 - 26 December**

B&B Rates are per Person Sharing per Night incl. Breakfast. or Room Rates are per Room per Night - See also Page 8

County Arms Hotel

Birr,
Co. Offaly

Tel: 057-912 0791 Fax: 057-912 1234
Email: info@countyarmshotel.com
Web: www.countyarmshotel.com

HOTEL ★★★ MAP 7 J 9

A family welcome in the Heritage Town of Birr. Completely refurbished in 2005, this 200-year-old Georgian house boasts the stunning Springs Leisure Club & Wellness Suites - indulge yourself with an Elemis Spa Treatment or plunge into our 20m pool. 70 de luxe bedrooms, family rooms and suites. 14 conference rooms for groups of all sizes. Award-winning food, atmospheric bar and well stocked wine cellar. Check our website for special offers. Lo-Call 1850 UNWIND (1850 869463).

Bookable on www.irelandhotels.com
Member of www.familyhotels.ie

B&B from €60.00 to €140.00

The Loughnane Family

Activities:

Member of:

Special Offer: Golf or Spa Packages from €159.00 pps

70 70

Open All Year

Doolys Hotel

Emmet Square,
Birr,
Co. Offaly

Tel: 057-912 0032 Fax: 057-912 1332
Email: doolyshotel@esatclear.ie
Web: www.doolyshotel.com

HOTEL U MAP 7 J 9

Doolys Hotel - a gem of a hotel in the very heart of Georgian Birr. The hotel, which has just undergone major refurbishment, is one of the oldest coaching inns in the country, dating back to 1747. Our guests receive a warm welcome and traditional hospitality and profesional service. Our coach house lounge is a favourite among locals and is very welcoming, great food served all day. Weddings are our speciality.

B&B from €60.00 to €60.00

Sharon Grant / Jo Duignan
Proprietor / General Manager

Activities:

Member of:

Special Offer: Weekend Specials from €150.00 pps
(2 Nights B&B & 1 Dinner)

18 18

Closed 25 December

Birr Castle Demesne

Ireland's Award Winning Gardens

Ireland's Historic Science Centre
Great Telescope
National Birds of Prey Centre
DISCOVER AN UNEXPLORED DIMENSION OF IRELAND

Birr, Co. Offaly, Ireland
Tel.: + 353 509 20336
Fax: + 353 509 21583
Email: mail@birrcastle.com
Website: www.birrcastle.com

B&B Rates are per Person Sharing per Night incl. Breakfast. or **Room Rates** are per Room per Night - See also Page 8

Co. Offaly

Birr / Tullamore

Kinnitty Castle Demesne

Kinnitty,
Birr,
Co. Offaly
Tel: 057-913 7318 Fax: 057-913 7284
Email: kinnittycastle@eircom.net
Web: www.kinnittycastle.com

HOTEL U MAP 7 J 9

The luxuriously refurbished castle is situated 1.5 hrs from Dublin, Galway & Limerick, 37 magnificent en suite rooms, stately reception rooms in the main castle & excellent restaurant with gourmet food & fine wines. Conference & banqueting facilities available. Moneyguyneen House on the estate with 12 en suite rooms is refurbished to exceptional country house standards. Facilities: an equestrian centre, clay pigeon shooting, falconry, gym, golf & the newly opened Gate Lodge Spa. Newly opened Monks Kitchen Bar & Restaurant. Traditional music Thursday, Friday and Saturday night.

Bookable on www.irelandhotels.com
Member of Select Hotels of Ireland

B&B from €120.00 to €160.00

Con Ryan
Proprietor

Activities:

37 37

Open All Year

Maltings Guesthouse

Castle Street,
Birr,
Co. Offaly
Tel: 057-912 1345 Fax: 057-912 2073
Email: themaltingsbirr@eircom.net

GUESTHOUSE ★★★ MAP 7 J 9

Secluded on a picturesque riverside setting beside Birr Castle, in the centre of Ireland's finest Georgian town. Built circa 1810 to store malt for Guinness, and converted in 1994 to a 13 bedroom guesthouse with full bar and restaurant. All bedrooms are comfortably furnished with bath/shower en suite, colour TV and phones.

B&B from €35.00 to €40.00

Maeve Garry
Manageress

Member of:

HOTELS

Special Offer: *Weekend Specials from €95.00 pps
(2 Nights B&B & 1 Dinner)*

13 13

Closed 24 - 27 December

Bridge House Hotel & Leisure Club

Tullamore,
Co. Offaly
Tel: 057-932 5600 Fax: 057-932 5690
Email: info@bridgehousehotel.com
Web: www.bridgehousehotel.com

HOTEL U MAP 7 K 10

A warm welcome awaits you at the Bridge House Hotel. Enjoy the best of Irish hospitality renowned for good food, service & great atmosphere. State of the art leisure club & swimming pool & a unique outdoor hot spa. Play golf in the virtual reality golf facility. Five minutes away are two of Ireland's golfing treasures, Esker Hill and Tullamore Golf Club, both 18 hole golf courses. Winner of the Best Hotel Bar in Ireland. This is one of Ireland's most luxurious hotels with 72 rooms incl. 4 executive suites and superb presidential suite. Céad Míle Fáilte, Be our guest. Reservations Lo-Call 1850 312312.

Bookable on www.irelandhotels.com

B&B from €85.00 to €160.00

Colm McCabe
Manager

Activities:

Member of:
HOTELS

Special Offer: *Midweek Specials from €145.00 pps
(2 Nights B&B & 1 Dinner)*

72 72

Closed 24 - 26 December

B&B Rates are per Person Sharing per Night incl. Breakfast. or Room Rates are per Room per Night - See also Page 8

Days Hotel Tullamore

Main Street,
Tullamore,
Co. Offaly
Tel: 1890-776 655 Fax: 057-932 0350
Email: info@dayshoteltullamore.com
Web: www.dayshoteltullamore.com

HOTEL N MAP 7 K 10

Newly opened in 2005, Days Hotel is located in the town centre, close to bars, restaurants and great shopping. 62 superior rooms, all with pay per view movies, safe, tea/coffee station, iron/ironing board. Executive rooms offer extra space with designated work desk and jacuzzi bath. Our stylish bistro and bar are open throughout the day. Conference facilities include 2 air-conditioned meeting rooms, with capacity for up to 50 delegates. Specialised audio/visual facilities on site. Hotel direct line: 057 936 0034.

Bookable on www.irelandhotels.com
Member of Days Hotels Ireland

Room Rate from €59.00 to €199.00

Brian Pierson
General Manager

Activities:

Member of:

Special Offer: Weekend Specials from €109.00 pps
(2 Nights B&B & 1 Dinner)

62 62

Closed 24 - 27 December

Grennans Country House

Aharney,
Tullamore,
Co. Offaly
Tel: 057-935 5893 Fax: 057-935 5893
Email: deirdregrennan@iol.ie
Web: www.grennanscountryhouse.ie

GUESTHOUSE N MAP 7 K 10

Situated in the heart of the Midlands 1 mile off N.80, 1.5 hours from Dublin Airport, Grennans Country House is a purpose built luxury guesthouse; golfer's paradise - 10 golf courses within 1/2 hours drive. Rural setting, ample car parking. All rooms en suite, tastefully furnished super king beds, with DD phone, TV, tea/coffee facilities, spring water, clock radio, hairdryer, iron/ironing board. Guest TV lounge, home-baking. Access for wheelchair user. Ideal touring base, golfing, fishing, equestrian, walking - your choice is our pleasure.

B&B from €40.00 to €55.00

Deirdre & Pat Grennan

Member of:

6 6

Closed 20 December - 10 January

Castle Barna Golf Club.

Daingean, Co. Offaly
Tel: 057 935 3384
Fax: 057 935 3077
Email: info@castlebarna.ie
Web: www.castlebarna.ie

A fantastic 18 hole parkland course built on the banks of the Grand Canal. Renowned for its excellent greens and lush fairways, mature trees and natural streams. It's a course that suits all levels of golfers. Castle Barna was host to the G.U.I. Pierce Purcell Shield in 2000 and 2002.

Members, Green Fees and Societies always welcome.

Located 8 miles off Dublin to Galway Road at Tyrellspass

The 19th hole is an old stone clubhouse with full bar and catering facilities and modern changing rooms.

Castle Barna is a course you would love to play again.

B&B Rates are per Person Sharing per Night incl. Breakfast.
or **Room Rates** are per Room per Night - See also Page 8

Co. Offaly

Tullamore

Moorhill House Hotel

Moorhill,
Clara Road, Tullamore,
Co. Offaly
Tel: 057-932 1395 Fax: 057-935 2424
Email: info@moorhill.ie
Web: www.moorhill.ie

HOTEL U MAP 7 K 10

Moorhill is a unique experience in the best possible ways. Combining the classic quality of a Victorian country house with the informal ambience of a modern hotel. In Moorhill, we have placed particular emphasis on marrying the elegant surroundings and atmosphere of the hotel with a warm Irish welcome and friendly efficient service. Centrally located and ideal for a relaxing break from daily life or to conduct business at a quiet and efficient pace.

B&B from €50.00 to €80.00

David & Alan Duffy

Activities:

Member of:

Special Offer: Weekend Specials from €135.00 pps
(2 Nights B&B & 1 Dinner)

10 10

Closed 24 - 26 December

Sea Dew Guesthouse

Clonminch Road,
Tullamore,
Co. Offaly
Tel: 057-935 2054 Fax: 057-935 2054
Email: enquiries@seadewguesthouse.com
Web: www.seadewguesthouse.com

GUESTHOUSE ★★★ MAP 7 K 10

Set in a mature garden of trees, Sea Dew is a purpose-built guesthouse, providing guests with a high standard of comfort, located only 5 minutes walk from the town centre. The conservatory breakfast room will give you a bright start to the day, where there is an excellent selection of fresh produce. All bedrooms are spacious with en suite facilities, TV and direct dial telephones. Golfing, fishing, horse riding and shooting are available nearby. Access for wheelchairs.

B&B from €48.00 to €50.00

Claire Gilsenan
Proprietor

Member of:

Special Offer: Midweek Specials from €42.00 pps
per night

12 12

Closed 21 December - 01 January

Tullamore Court Hotel Conference & Leisure Centre

Tullamore,
Co. Offaly

Tel: 057-934 6666 Fax: 057-934 6677
Email: info@tullamorecourthotel.ie
Web: www.tullamorecourthotel.ie

HOTEL U MAP 7 K 10

Luxury, elegance and style are the distinguishing qualities of this contemporary hotel. A wonderfully relaxed ambience in plush surroundings with friendly professional staff and superb food and wines is just the tonic you need, to enjoy your next short break. So why drive for hours when you can enjoy the superb facilities of the Midlands leading hotel and its surrounding area. Check our website regularly for last minute special offers!

Bookable on www.irelandhotels.com

B&B from €75.00 to €160.00

Joe O'Brien
Managing Director

Activities:

Member of:

Special Offer: Weekend Specials from €135.00 pps
(2 Nights B&B & 1 Dinner)

72 72

Closed 24 - 26 December

B&B Rates are per Person Sharing per Night incl. Breakfast.
or **Room Rates** are per Room per Night - See also Page 8

Creggan Court Hotel

Kilmartin N6 Centre,
N6 Roundabout, Athlone,
Co. Westmeath
Tel: 090-647 7777 Fax: 090-647 7111
Email: info@creggancourt.com
Web: www.mulcahyhotelgroup.com

HOTEL ★★★ MAP 7 J 11

The Creggan Court Hotel is located just off the N6 in Athlone, midway between Dublin and Galway. The ideal base to explore Clonmacnoise, Ely O'Carroll Country and the Shannon Basin. Athlone is a golfer's paradise, surrounded by local championship golf courses such as Glasson, Mount Temple, Esker Hills and many more. The Creggan Court Hotel offers spacious en suite rooms and ample car parking. Conference rooms also available.

Bookable on www.irelandhotels.com

B&B from €50.00 to €90.00

Patricia Flynn
General Manager

Activities:
🏌 🎣

🛏🐾 ☎🖥🖨📺C➡CM♫P🅿🎿 Inet
73 73

Closed 23 - 30 December

Glasson Golf Hotel and Country Club

Glasson,
Athlone,
Co. Westmeath
Tel: 090-648 5120 Fax: 090-648 5444
Email: info@glassongolf.ie
Web: www.glassongolf.ie

HOTEL ★★★ MAP 11 J 11

A family-owned and managed property in the heart of Ireland, set on the shores of Lough Ree 1.5 hours from Dublin, Galway and Shannon. Each of the spacious and well-appointed rooms has magnificent views over the golf course or Lough Ree. The hotel is suited to both the discerning golfer and those looking for peace and relaxation in beautiful surroundings. Designed by Christy O'Connor Jnr, the golf course has established a deserved reputation as one of Ireland's premier inland courses. "Play & Stay!"

Bookable on www.irelandhotels.com

B&B from €65.00 to €150.00

Gareth Jones & Fidelma Reid
*General Manager /
Operations Manager*

Activities:
🏌 🎣🏇

Member of:
IRISH HOTELS FEDERATION

Special Offer: *Midweek Specials from €185.00 pps
(2 Nights B&B & 1 Dinner & 1 Golf)*

🛏🐾 ☎🖥🖨📺C➡CM🌳🅿♫JPS🅰
a/c Inet 🐕 🐾
65 65

Open All Year

B&B Rates are per Person Sharing per Night incl. Breakfast.
or **Room Rates** are per Room per Night - See also Page 8

Athlone

Hodson Bay Hotel

Athlone,
Co. Westmeath

Tel: 090-644 2000 Fax: 090-644 2020
Email: info@hodsonbayhotel.com
Web: www.hodsonbayhotel.com

HOTEL ★★★★ MAP 11 J 11

Located on the picturesque shores of Lough Ree, Hodson Bay Hotel has 182 en suite bedrooms, many of which offer breathtaking views of the lake. Choose from 2 award-winning restaurants, relax in the traditional Waterfront Bar and enjoy extensive leisure facilities including 20m pool, gymnasium and thermal suite. New luxury health spa featuring relaxing and invigorating treatments. Unique Watsu Pool treatments also available.

Bookable on www.irelandhotels.com

B&B from €55.00 to €160.00

Timothy Hayes
General Manager

Activities:

Member of:

Special Offer: Weekend Specials from €129.00 pps (2 Nights B&B & 1 Dinner)

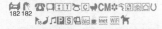

182 182

Open All Year

Prince of Wales Hotel

Church Street,
Athlone,
Co. Westmeath

Tel: 090-647 6666 Fax: 090-649 1750
Email: info@theprinceofwaleshotel.ie
Web: www.theprinceofwales.ie

HOTEL N MAP 11 J 11

Positioned in the very centre of Athlone, the new Prince of Wales Hotel offers the very highest standards of comfort & service. The hotel reopened in May 2004 with refurbished bedrooms, restaurant, conference facilities and the Prince Bar. The hotel has 46 stylish, modern rooms comprised of classic, executive and 6 junior suites. Soothingly simple in black marble, chocolate and cream, each room is a tranquil haven of understated luxury, equipped with television, DVD players, multi-port modem connection and digital climate control.

Member of Callanan Hotels

B&B from €65.00 to €75.00

Neil Cummins
Operations Manager

Activities:

Member of:

46 46

Closed 23 - 30 December

Radisson SAS Hotel

Northgate Street,
Athlone,
Co. Westmeath

Tel: 090-644 2600 Fax: 090-644 2655
Email: info.athlone@radissonsas.com
Web: www.radissonsas.com

HOTEL N MAP 11 J 11

The Radisson SAS Hotel, Athlone is centrally located overlooking the River Shannon with magnificent views of the marina, the historical cathedral and Athlone Castle. Within walking distance of the train & bus station. 128 stylish bedrooms/suites in an urban & ocean theme. Elements Restaurant offers the finest contemporary food in a trendy environment. Quayside Bar and Lounge with riverside terrace is the perfect location for guests to relax and enjoy the panoramic views across the town and the river. Synergy Health & Leisure Club offers a 16.5m indoor pool, sauna, steam room & fully equipped gym.

Bookable on www.irelandhotels.com

B&B from €72.50 to €92.50

Geir Sikko
General Manager

Activities:

Member of:

Special Offer: Weekend Specials from €160.00 pps (2 Nights B&B & 1 Dinner)

128 128

Open All Year

B&B Rates are per Person Sharing per Night incl. Breakfast. or Room Rates are per Room per Night - See also Page 8

Shamrock Lodge Hotel and Conference Centre

Clonown Road,
Athlone,
Co. Westmeath
Tel: 090-649 2601 Fax: 090-649 2737
Email: info@shamrocklodgehotel.ie
Web: www.shamrocklodgehotel.ie

HOTEL U MAP 11 J 11

Set amongst its green leafy gardens the Shamrock Lodge Hotel is highly acclaimed for its excellent food and service where a warm welcome awaits you. New development of 40 executive bedrooms and 12 apartments, several conference and banqueting rooms. Minutes walk from town centre. Free car parking with 300 spaces.

B&B from €65.00 to €85.00

Paddy McCaul
Proprietor

Activities:

Member of:

IRISH HOTELS FEDERATION

Special Offer: Weekend Specials from €155.00 pps
(2 Nights B&B & 1 Dinner)

70 70

Closed 24 - 26 December

Wineport Lodge

Glasson,
Athlone,
Co. Westmeath
Tel: 090-643 9010 Fax: 090-648 5471
Email: lodge@wineport.ie
Web: www.wineport.ie

GUESTHOUSE ★★★★ MAP 11 J 11

Wineport Lodge is blissfully located on the edge of Ireland's peaceful Inland Waterways. It is the perfect place to dine and stay, either for business or pleasure, in an easily accessible destination. In the restaurant, Eurotoques Chef Feargal O'Donnell's delicious food is matched by genuinely friendly and expert service. An always interesting menu changes seasonally, and the freshest local produce regularly appears as a daily special. If you're looking for the ideal hideaway to escape to, then Wineport Lodge is the right place to drop in and revive your jaded soul.

Member of Ireland's Blue Book

B&B from €82.50 to €125.00

Ray Byrne & Jane English

Member of:

IRISH HOTELS FEDERATION

Special Offer: Weekend Specials from €295.00 pps
(2 Nights B&B & 1 Dinner)

21 21

Closed 24 - 26 December

Austin Friar Hotel

Austin Friar Street,
Mullingar,
Co. Westmeath
Tel: 044-934 5777 Fax: 044-934 5880
Email: info@austin-friar.com

HOTEL P MAP 11 L 12

Conveniently situated in the centre of Mullingar you will find the modern and intimate Austin Friar Hotel offering warm hospitality in the best of Irish tradition. The natural light shining through the hotel creates a calm relaxing atmosphere with conference facilities for up to fifty people. Enjoy full bar facilities in the lounge. Modern Irish cuisine in The Oval Restaurant. Lunch daily from 12.00pm to 3.00pm. Early evening dinner from 5.00pm to 7.30pm Monday-Friday. Á La Carte each evening until 9.30pm - with specials available daily. A Céad Míle Fáilte awaits you.

B&B from €60.00 to €70.00

Noel Kenny
Licensee

Member of:

IRISH HOTELS FEDERATION

19 19

Closed 24 - 26 December

B&B Rates are per Person Sharing per Night incl. Breakfast.
or Room Rates are per Room per Night - See also Page 8

Mullingar

Bloomfield House Hotel

Belvedere,
Mullingar,
Co. Westmeath
Tel: 044-934 0894 Fax: 044-934 3767
Email: reservations@bloomfieldhouse.com
Web: www.bloomfieldhouse.com

HOTEL U MAP 11 L 12

Located in the beautiful countryside of central Ireland, historic Bloomfield House nestles on the shores of Lough Ennell surrounded by magnificent parkland and gently sloping meadows. Easy travelling distance from all regions and just 75 minutes from Dublin, Bloomfield House combines tradition and elegance with the latest amenities. Combining comfort, hospitality and service with an excellent leisure & spa facility, neighbouring the golf club and Belvedere House, relaxation proves effortless at Bloomfield House Hotel.

Bookable on www.irelandhotels.com
Member of Select Hotels Ireland

B&B from €85.00 to €120.00

Seamus Laffan
Managing Director

Activities:
:/🏊💧

Member of:
IRISH HOTELS FEDERATION

Special Offer: Weekend Specials from €159.00 pps
(2 Nights B&B & 1 Dinner)

111 111

Closed 23 - 26 December

Greville Arms Hotel

Mullingar,
Co. Westmeath

Tel: 044-934 8563 Fax: 044-934 8052
Email: grevillearmshotel@eircom.net
Web: www.grevillearms.com

HOTEL U MAP 11 L 12

In the heart of Mullingar town, the Greville Arms Hotel is a home from home where customers and their comfort is our main concern. Recently refurbished, the hotel offers 39 luxuriously appointed rooms. The Greville Restaurant is renowned for its cuisine and fine wines. No visit to Mullingar would be complete without a visit to our Ulysses Bar with its life - sized wax figure of James Joyce and other memorabilia. Local attractions include Belvedere House and Gardens, golf, fishing and horse riding.

B&B from €60.00 to €90.00

John Cochrane
General Manager

Activities:
:/🏊

Member of:
IRISH HOTELS FEDERATION

Special Offer: Weekend Specials from €150.00 pps
(2 Nights B&B & 1 Dinner)

39 39

Closed 25 December

Mc Cormacks Guesthouse

Old Dublin Road,
Mullingar,
Co. Westmeath
Tel: 044-934 1483
Email: info@mccormacksbandb.com
Web: www.mccormacksbandb.com

GUESTHOUSE ★★★ MAP 11 L 12

One mile from Mullingar Town and across the road from Mullingar Park Hotel. All rooms are en suite including large family rooms. The house is situated in a peaceful farm setting and yet within walking distance of town. Facilities for fishermen and tennis court and picnic area on grounds. Internet broadband access available to guests. Three specially adapted wheelchair accessible rooms. Numerous golf courses and fishing lakes nearby. Located just off Mullingar bypass (N4). Sauna and hot tub cabin available at reasonable rates.

Bookable on www.irelandhotels.com

B&B from €40.00 to €55.00

Tom & Margaret Mc Cormack
Proprietors

Member of:
IRISH HOTELS FEDERATION

Special Offer: Midweek Specials from €110.00 pps
(3 Nights B&B)

8 8

Open All Year

B&B Rates are per Person Sharing per Night incl. Breakfast.
or **Room Rates** are per Room per Night - See also Page 8

Mullingar Park Hotel

Dublin Road,
Mullingar,
Co. Westmeath
Tel: 044-933 7500 Fax: 044-933 5937
Email: info@mullingarparkhotel.com
Web: www.mullingarparkhotel.com

HOTEL N MAP 11 L 12

Contemporary in design and developed to 4**** specification, this stylish hotel is a modern classic. The hotel brings together 95 exceptional guest rooms with premium conference and banqueting facilities, the finest leisure and health spa, splendid choices for dining experiences and magnificent bars and lounges. Guests are within easy distance of championship golf courses, a range of equestrian activities, including major race meetings, and some of the best fishing in Ireland.

Bookable on www.irelandhotels.com

B&B from €80.00 to €150.00

Joesphine Hughes
Proprietor

Activities:

Member of:
IRISH HOTELS FEDERATION

Special Offer: Weekend Specials from €175.00 pps
(2 Nights B&B & 1 Dinner)

95 95

Closed 24 - 25 December

One source...
Endless possibilities

irelandhotels.com
Official Website of the Irish Hotels Federation

IRISH HOTELS FEDERATION

B&B Rates are per Person Sharing per Night incl. Breakfast.
or Room Rates are per Room per Night - See also Page 8

Map of South East Region

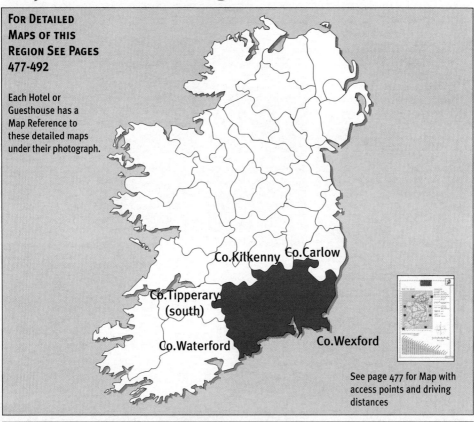

FOR DETAILED MAPS OF THIS REGION SEE PAGES 477-492

Each Hotel or Guesthouse has a Map Reference to these detailed maps under their photograph.

Co.Kilkenny   Co.Carlow

Co.Tipperary (south)

Co.Waterford

Co.Wexford

See page 477 for Map with access points and driving distances

Locations listing

irelandhotels.com
Official Website of the Irish Hotels Federation

INCLUDES DETAILED MAPS & GREAT VALUE SPECIAL OFFERS.

SOUTH EAST TOURISM

There is no better place on earth - convenient, full of interest and with that special appeal - than the Sunny South East of Ireland. Enjoy it at any time, especially in the 'Secret Season', when its many interest points and charms will be revealed at their most relaxed best. Many daytime attractions – of the more than 60 - are open and welcoming year round. Discover for yourself that elusive yet tangible difference that has made our visitor numbers grow by twenty two percent - second only to Dublin – as compared with an average of just six percent for the other five regions.

The South East is one of the best-loved holiday regions even among Irish people. It combines the tranquil elegance of historic old towns and villages with the classic splendour of mediaeval Kilkenny, Viking Wexford and regal Waterford, the Crystal City and regional capital.

The enchanting coastline offers a necklace of small, intimate, fishing villages, interspaced by safe, sandy beaches. Their charm, especially when coupled with our mild climate, all conspire to give substance to the region's age old title - The Sunny South East.

Inland, the deep and ancient river valleys of the Blackwater, Barrow, Nore, Slaney and Suir rivers still retain the dim echo of invaders and traders, merchants and early missionaries that helped shape this fascinating land. Our five great rivers, again rich in fish and wild life, have carved a patchwork of fertile valleys and plains through Carlow, Kilkenny, South Tipperary, Waterford and Wexford as they meander their majestic, unhurried way to the Celtic Sea.

There is so much to do in the South East. Our greatest activity, Golf - lauded by even Tiger Woods - is to be enjoyed on more than 30 courses, both links and parkland. Equestrian fans and racegoers, greyhound followers and anglers will each enjoy, in their own way, the wide-open spaces that beckon everywhere. Walkers and cyclists appreciate the wide range – and varied lengths – of waymarked ways. The well sign-posted touring routes for motorist appeal to a growing band of devotees. Call into any of our tourist offices at Carlow, Kilkenny, Wexford or Rosslare and pick up a wide range of literature to help you plan and secure the best possible pleasure from your visit. If you have not yet explored the South East take time to enjoy it this year. You will find a special welcome awaits you.

For all details contact:

South East Tourism,
41 The Quay,
Waterford
Tel 051 875823
Fax 051 877388
Email: info@southeasttourism.ie
Visit our website:
www.southeastireland.com

Calendar of Events

May
Carlsberg Kilkenny Rhythm & Roots Festival, Kilkenny City.
Guinness Feile na Deise, Dungarvan, Co. Waterford.

June
Smithwick's Cat Laughs Festival, Kilkenny City.

July / August
Waterford Spraoi Festival, Waterford City.
Trafest Music Festival, Tramore, Co. Waterford.

August
Guinness Dunmore East Bluegrass Festival, Dunmore East,
Co. Waterford.

October/November
Wexford Festival Opera, Wexford Town.

Event details correct at time of going to press.
enjoy Guinness sensibly.

Carlow Town

Ballyvergal House	Barrowville Town House	Carlow Guesthouse

Ballyvergal House

Dublin Road,
Carlow Town

Tel: 059-914 3634 Fax: 059-914 0386
Email: ballyvergal@indigo.ie
Web: www.ballyvergal.com

GUESTHOUSE ★★★ MAP 7 M 8

A large family-run guesthouse conveniently located just outside Carlow Town on the Dublin Road (N9), adjacent to Carlow's 18 hole championship golf course. We offer our guests en suite rooms with TV, DD phone & hairdryer, a large residents lounge & car parking. Most importantly you are assured of a warm friendly welcome. We are ideally located for golf (Carlow, Mount Wolseley, Kilkea Castle, Mount Juliet), angling, shooting, horse riding and pitch & putt. There is a restaurant next door which caters for breakfast, lunch & evening meals.

B&B from €40.00 to €45.00

Kathleen O'Toole

10 10

Open All Year

Barrowville Town House

Kilkenny Road,
Carlow Town,
Carlow

Tel: 059-914 3324 Fax: 059-914 1953
Email: barrowvilletownhouse@eircom.net
Web: www.barrowvillehouse.com

GUESTHOUSE ★★★ MAP 7 M 8

A period listed residence in own grounds, 3 minutes walk to town centre. Well appointed rooms with all facilities. Antique furnishing. Traditional or buffet breakfast served in conservatory overlooking the gardens. Ideal location for golf at Carlow, Kilkea, Mt Wolseley, touring SE, Glendalough, Kilkenny, Waterford and visiting various gardens. Orthopaedic beds, crisp linen. RAC Sparkling Diamond Award, AA RAC ◆◆◆◆◆, Bridgestone 100 Best 2005, Jameson Guide and other good guide books. German spoken. Multi Night Discount. Les Routiers Guide. Receive and send your emails.

Member of Premier Guesthouses of Ireland

B&B from €45.00 to €49.50

*Randal & Marie Dempsey
Proprietors*

Member of:
IRISH HOTELS FEDERATION

Special Offer: Apply For All Year Offers 3 Or More Days

7 7

Open All Year

Carlow Guesthouse

Green Lane,
Dublin Road,
Carlow Town

Tel: 059-913 6033 Fax: 059-913 6034
Email: info@carlowguesthouse.com
Web: www.carlowguesthouse.com

GUESTHOUSE ★★★ MAP 7 M 8

5 minutes walk north of Carlow Town centre (N9) with off street parking with CCTV monitoring. 13 en suite guest rooms equipped with tea/coffee facilities, TV, radio, telephone, hairdryer, Wi-Fi, trouser press, complimentary mineral water & toiletries, ironing board facility. A Premier Guesthouse of Ireland, we carry an AA◆◆◆◆ recommendation. Book online at www.carlowguesthouse.com. Explore Kilkenny (23 miles), Waterford (52 miles), Tipperary and numerous golf courses, race tracks & enjoy Carlow's restaurants & entertainment venues.

Bookable on www.irelandhotels.com
Member of Premier Guesthouses of Ireland

B&B from €40.00 to €80.00

*Lisa & Willie Nolan
Proprietors*

Member of:
IRISH HOTELS FEDERATION

13 13 WiFi

Open All Year

B&B Rates are per Person Sharing per Night incl. Breakfast.
or **Room Rates** are per Room per Night - See also Page 8

Dolmen Hotel and River Court Lodges

Kilkenny Road,
Carlow Town

Tel: 059-914 2002 Fax: 059-914 2375
Email: reservations@dolmenhotel.ie
Web: www.dolmenhotel.ie

HOTEL ★★★ MAP 7 M 8

Nestled along the scenic banks of the River Barrow and set in 20 acres of landscaped beauty is the Dolmen Hotel, 1.5km from Carlow. Fishing, golf, shooting and horse riding are just some of the sporting facilities surrounding the hotel. With 93 beautifully appointed rooms (81 rooms & 12 lodges) including 3 luxury suites with en suite, TV, direct dial phone, trouser press and hairdryer. Our 1 bedroomed lodges are ideal for the sporting enthusiast. One of the largest conference and banqueting facilities in the South East.

B&B from €35.00 to €80.00

Padraig Blighe
General Manager

Member of:
IRISH HOTELS FEDERATION

93 93
Inet WiFi

Closed 25 - 27 December

Redsetter Guesthouse

14 Dublin Street,
Carlow

Tel: 059-914 1848 Fax: 059-914 2837

GUESTHOUSE ★★ MAP 7 M 8

Redsetter Guesthouse is situated in Carlow's town centre. A delightful 17 bedroomed tastefully furnished residence (14 en-suite), it offers you the essence of comfort, hospitality and security (a large lock-up car park). An ideal base for touring the South East with very good public transport available. Local attractions include a variety of restaurants, Irish music, golf, angling, horse riding, swimming, museums and historical sites.

B&B from €35.00 to €45.00

Gavin Feeney
Proprietor

17 14

Closed 24 - 27 December

B&B Rates are per Person Sharing per Night incl. Breakfast.
or Room Rates are per Room per Night - See also Page 8

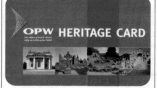

Co. Carlow

Carlow Town / Leighlinbridge

Seven Oaks Hotel

Athy Road,
Carlow Town

Tel: 059-913 1308 Fax: 059-913 2155
Email: info@sevenoakshotel.com
Web: www.sevenoakshotel.com

HOTEL ★★★ MAP 7 M 8

Ideally located just 3 mins walk to Carlow Town centre and bus/train station. We specialise in the best of Irish foods in our Oaks Bar carvery and intimate T.D. Molloy's Restaurant. Individually designed rooms, combining a selection of executive suites. Rooms are accessible by lift. Fully equipped conference facilities, with professional and friendly staff make the Seven Oaks Hotel an ideal venue for all such occasions whether large or small. Work out in our fully equipped Greenbank Health and Leisure Club with 20m swimming pool, gym, sauna and steam room.

Bookable on www.irelandhotels.com
Member of Irish Country Hotels

B&B from €70.00 to €90.00

Michael Murphy
Managing Director

Activities:

Member of:

Special Offer: Special Offers Apply

60 60

Closed 25 - 27 December

Talbot Carlow Hotel

Portlaoise Road,
Carlow

Tel: 059-915 3000 Fax: 059-915 3001
Email: sales@talbothotelcarlow.ie
Web: www.talbothotelcarlow.ie

UNDER CONSTRUCTION - OPENING DECEMBER 2005

HOTEL P MAP 7 M 8

New 4**** standard hotel in Carlow Town. 84 luxurious guest rooms. Conference & banqueting facilities for up to 300 delegates. State of the art health and leisure centre. Corries Bar and Bistro. Fine dining restaurant located on the fourth floor with stunning views of Carlow's countryside. Essence Nail and Beauty Therapy. Located beside "The Dome" children's entertainment centre.

Member of Talbot Hotel Group

B&B from €55.00 to €95.00

Michael Skehan
General Manager

Activities:

Special Offer: Weekend Specials from €155.00 pps
(2 Nights B&B & 1 Dinner)

84 84

Open All Year

Lord Bagenal Inn

Main Street,
Leighlinbridge,
Co. Carlow

Tel: 059-972 1668 Fax: 059-972 2629
Email: info@lordbagenal.com
Web: www.lordbagenal.com

HOTEL ★★★ MAP 7 M 8

Situated in the Heritage Village of Leighlinbridge along the River Barrow, with private marina and gardens, we are ideally located to explore the South East. Our en suite bedrooms are luxuriously furnished to the highest standards. Award-winning restaurant reputed for fine food and excellent wines. Locals and visitors frequent our bar where carvery lunch and bar food are served daily. Children always welcome. Weddings, conferences, banquets catered for. Gold Medal Entente Florale Floral Pride.

B&B from €55.00 to €150.00

James & Mary Kehoe

12 12

Closed 25 December - 26 December

B&B Rates are per Person Sharing per Night incl. Breakfast.
or Room Rates are per Room per Night - See also Page 8

Waterside

The Quay,
Graiguenamanagh,
Co. Kilkenny

Tel: 059-972 4246 Fax: 059-972 4733
Email: info@watersideguesthouse.com
Web: www.watersideguesthouse.com

GUESTHOUSE ★★★ MAP 7 M 7

A beautifully restored 19th century cornstore with feature wooden beams and imposing granite exterior. Riverside location, all rooms have a view of the River Barrow. Excellent base for boating, fishing, hill walking. 16km from Mount Juliet for golf. Nearby 13th century Duiske Abbey. 27km from historical Kilkenny. Superb restaurant features continental cuisine & international flavour wine list. Relaxed & friendly approach. Perfect for small groups. Guided hill walking for groups.

B&B from €39.00 to €52.50

Brian & Brigid Roberts
Managers

Member of:

Special Offer: Weekend Specials from €110.00 pps
(2 Nights B&B & 1 Dinner)

10 10

Closed 01 - 31 January

Berkeley House

5 Lower Patrick Street,
Kilkenny

Tel: 056-776 4848 Fax: 056-776 4829
Email: berkeleyhouse@eircom.net
Web: www.berkeleyhousekilkenny.com

GUESTHOUSE ★★★ MAP 7 L 7

A warm and genuine welcome awaits you here at this charming owner operated period residence, uniquely situated in the very heart of mediaeval Kilkenny City. Berkerley House boasts ample private car parking, 10 spacious & tastefully decorated rooms, all en suite with multi channel TV, direct dial phone & tea/coffee facilities. We pride ourselves on a dedicated and professional team and ensure that every effort will be made to make your stay with us a most enjoyable one.

B&B from €35.00 to €55.00

Rachael Stone & Pip Moir
Managers

10 10

Closed 23 - 28 December

B&B Rates are per Person Sharing per Night incl. Breakfast.
or **Room Rates** are per Room per Night - See also Page 8

---

carlow
through the waters of time

With soaring mountains, verdant river valleys and rich rolling countryside, Co. Carlow in Ireland's Sunny South-East, offers the perfect backdrop for golf, trekking, angling, horse riding, canoeing and quading. Take a trip and discover mystical pre-christian monuments, ancient ecclesiastical sites, grand country houses and gardens and picturesque award winning villages.

For all your tourism needs contact
CARLOW TOURISM
The Foresters' Hall,
College Street, Carlow.

Phone: +353 (0) 59 9130411
Email: info@carlowtourism.com
Website: www.carlowtourism.com

Co. Kilkenny

Kilkenny City

Brannigans Glendine Inn

Castlecomer Road,
Kilkenny

Tel: 056-772 1069 Fax: 056-777 0714
Email: branigan@iol.ie
Web: www.kilkennyaccommodation.com

GUESTHOUSE ★★ MAP 7 L 7

The Glendine Inn has been a licensed tavern for over 200 years. It consists of 7 bedrooms (all en suite), a residents' lounge, residents' dining room, and public lounge and bars serving snack or bar lunches. We are ideally located for golf (course 200m away), the railway station and the historic city of Kilkenny are only 1.5km away. We assure you of a friendly welcome.

Bookable on www.irelandhotels.com

B&B from €30.00 to €55.00

Michael Brannigan
Proprietor

Activities:

Member of:
IRISH HOTELS FEDERATION

Special Offer: Midweek Specials from €90.00 pps
(3 Nights B&B)

7 7

Open All Year

Bridgecourt House

Greensbridge,
Kilkenny

Tel: 056-776 2998 Fax: 056-776 2998
Email: anegan@eircom.net
Web: www.bridgecourtkilkenny.com

GUESTHOUSE N MAP 7 L 7

A family-run guesthouse situated in a superb city centre location with all facilities nearby. Our impressive residence has en suite rooms, colour TV, hairdryers etc. and a cosy lounge where tea/coffee making facilities are available. All our bedrooms are beautifully decorated to reach high standards. We offer all our guests a warm welcome, tasty breakfast and a friendly service all in comfortable surroundings. Private car parking.

B&B from €35.00 to €45.00

Don & Niamh Egan

9 9

Closed 24 - 26 December

Butler House

Patrick Street,
Kilkenny

Tel: 056-776 5707 Fax: 056-776 5626
Email: res@butler.ie
Web: www.butler.ie

GUESTHOUSE ★★★ MAP 7 L 7

Sweeping staircases, magnificent plastered ceilings & marble fireplaces are all features of this 16th century Dower House of Kilkenny Castle. The house is a combination of contemporary furnishings and period elegance. The larger superior rooms have graceful bow windows with lovely views of the walled Georgian garden and Kilkenny Castle. These rooms offer peace and tranquillity to the weary traveller, with the added advantage of being in the heart of the city. Conference facilities. AA ◆◆◆◆. Private car park.

B&B from €60.00 to €85.00

Gabrielle Hickey
Manager

Activities:

Member of:
IRISH HOTELS FEDERATION

Special Offer: Midweek Specials from €180.00 pps
(3 Nights B&B)

13 13

Closed 24 - 29 December

B&B Rates are per Person Sharing per Night incl. Breakfast. or **Room Rates** are per Room per Night - See also Page 8

Club House Hotel

Patrick Street,
Kilkenny

Tel: 056-772 1994 Fax: 056-777 1920
Email: clubhse@iol.ie
Web: www.clubhousehotel.com

HOTEL U MAP 7 L 7

Situated uniquely in a cultural & artistic centre & against the background of Kilkenny's mediaeval city, the magnificent 18th century Club House Hotel maintains a 200 year old tradition of effortless comfort, hospitality and efficiency. En suite rooms are decorated in both modern & period style with complimentary beverages, TV, hairdryer & phone. Food is locally sourced, cooked and presented to highest standards. Victors Bar has old world charm & luxury. Live music Saturday nights traditional Irish song & dance Tuesday nights July & August.

Bookable on www.irelandhotels.com
Member of Countrywide Hotels - MinOtel Ireland

B&B from €45.00 to €115.00

James P. Brennan
Managing Director

Member of:

Special Offer: *Weekend Specials from €165.00 pps*
(2 Nights B&B & 1 Dinner)

28 28

Closed 24 - 28 December

Days Hotel Kilkenny

Springhill,
Smithsland South,
Kilkenny

Tel: 1890-77 66 55 Fax: 01-639 1105
Email: info@dayshotelkilkenny.com
Web: www.dayshotelkilkenny.com

UNDER CONSTRUCTION - OPENING MAY 2006

HOTEL P MAP 7 L 7

Days Hotel is situated just 2km from the wonderful mediaeval city of Kilkenny, less than five minutes drive from the city centre. Boasting premium accommodation, all 80 rooms are furnished with stylish décor, offering interactive TV with pay per view movies, iron/ironing board, tea/coffee station, hairdryer and safe. Car parking is offered free of charge to all residents. Contemporary bar and restaurant open throughout the day. Meeting rooms can accommodate from 2 to 60 delegates, with excellent audio visual equipment on site.

Member of Days Hotels Ireland

Room Rate from €69.00 to €199.00

Jim Murphy
Managing Director

Activities:

Special Offer: *Weekend Specials from €109.00 pps*
(2 Nights B&B & 1 Dinner)

80 80

Closed 24 - 27 December

Fanad House

Castle Road,
Kilkenny

Tel: 056-776 4126 Fax: 056-775 6001
Email: fanadhouse@hotmail.com
Web: www.fanadhouse.com

GUESTHOUSE U MAP 7 L 7

Overlooking Kilkenny Castle Park, Fanad House is a five minute walk from the city centre. The newly built guesthouse offers all en suite rooms with complimentary beverages, multi-channel TV, hairdryer and direct dial phone. Extensive breakfast menu available. Private and secure parking provided. An ideal base for exploring the mediaeval city. We are adjacent to Kilkenny Tennis Club. Owner operated is your guarantee for an enjoyable stay.

B&B from €45.00 to €100.00

Pat Wallace
Proprietor

Member of:
HOTELS
FEDERATION

8 8

Open All Year

B&B Rates are per Person Sharing per Night incl. Breakfast.
or **Room Rates** are per Room per Night - See also Page 8

Kilkenny City

Hotel Kilkenny	Kilford Arms Hotel	Kilkenny Crest Hotel

Hotel Kilkenny

College Road,
Kilkenny

Tel: 056-776 2000 Fax: 056-776 5984
Email: kilkenny@griffingroup.ie
Web: www.griffingroup.ie

Kilford Arms Hotel

John Street,
Kilkenny

Tel: 056-776 1018 Fax: 056-776 1128
Email: info@kilfordarms.ie
Web: www.kilfordarms.ie

Kilkenny Crest Hotel

Patrick Street,
Kilkenny

Tel: 056-772 3900 Fax: 056-772 3977
Email: info@kilkennycrest.com
Web: www.kilkennycrest.com

UNDER CONSTRUCTION - OPENING DECEMBER 2005

HOTEL ★★★ MAP 7 L 7 | HOTEL U MAP 7 L 7 | HOTEL P MAP 7 L 7

Kilkenny's most accessible hotel from all major routes, yet less than ten mins stroll to the city's mediaeval heart, Hotel Kilkenny is close to the action, yet apart, allowing you to relax in comfortable and traditional surroundings after the culture and craic. 103 newly refurbished bedrooms, award-winning gardens, excellent formal and informal dining, five star Active Club with 20m pool, on-site Beauty and Wellness Lodge and an abundance of safe, complimentary parking. Excellent conference facilities for 4 - 400 delegates.

Enviably located, just minutes walk from city centre and railway station, the Kilford Arms Hotel offers a personal service and great range of facilities. The White Oak Restaurant serves fresh local produce in comfortable surroundings. PV's traditional bar has entertainment nightly, with food served daily. O'Faolain's Bar is Kilkenny's most vibrant bar, with 3 levels of stunning architecture, DJs and late bar nightly. Welcome to the Kilford Arms Hotel.

Currently under construction, the Kilkenny Crest Hotel is a modern city centre property built to a 4 **** plus standard. Sister hotel to the Kilkenny Ormonde, the Kilkenny Crest comes complete with 75 large luxurious bedrooms. Sharing extensive leisure facilities of the Kilkenny Ormonde Hotel, this stylish hotel is an ideal choice for business and leisure clients alike. Fully accessible for guests with special mobility requirements. Also offers city centre parking. Childrens' creche and playroom. Opening 1st December 2005.

Bookable on www.irelandhotels.com
Member of Griffin Hotel Group

Bookable on www.irelandhotels.com

B&B from €60.00 to €130.00 | *B&B from €45.00 to €100.00* | *B&B from €64.00 to €130.00*

Richard Butler
General Manager

Activities:

Member of:
IRISH HOTELS FEDERATION

Special Offer: *Midweek Specials from €129.00 pps (3 Nights B&B)*

103 103

Pius Phelan
Owner

Activities:

Member of:
IRISH HOTELS FEDERATION

Special Offer: *Midweek Specials from €120.00 pps (3 Nights B&B)*

50 50

Patrick Curran
General Manager/Director

Special Offer: *Weekend Specials from €226.00 pps (2 Nights B&B & 1 Dinner)*

75 75

Open All Year	Open All Year	Closed 24 - 27 December

B&B Rates are per Person Sharing per Night incl. Breakfast.
or Room Rates are per Room per Night - See also Page 8

Kilkenny Hibernian Hotel

1 Ormonde Street,
Kilkenny City

Tel: 056-777 1888 Fax: 056-777 1877
Email: info@kilkennyhibernianhotel.com
Web: www.kilkennyhibernianhotel.com

HOTEL U MAP 7 L 7

Experience old warm charm in Kilkenny's finest boutique hotel. Located in the city centre, this gracious old Victorian bank has been transformed into a unique hotel offering 46 luxury bedrooms. Guests can relax in the Black and White award-winning Hibernian Bar or sample the livelier atmosphere of Morrissons Bar. For exceptional food, Jacobs Cottage Restaurant is a must. Experience Kilkenny with us - you will find it difficult to leave!

Bookable on www.irelandhotels.com

B&B from €60.00 to €135.00

John McNena
General Manager

Member of:

Special Offer: Weekend Specials from €195.00 pps
(2 Nights B&B & 1 Dinner)

46 46

Closed 24 - 26 December

Kilkenny House Hotel

Freshford Road,
Kilkenny

Tel: 056-777 0711 Fax: 056-777 0698
Email: kilkennyhouse@eircom.net
Web: www.kilkennyhouse.com

UNDER CONSTRUCTION - OPENING MAY 2006

HOTEL P MAP 7 L 7

Kilkenny House Hotel is ideally located on the R.693 between the city's Saint Lukes and Aut Even Hospitals. A stroll into town. Newly built to a 3*** standard with spacious and tastefully decorated bedrooms. Locally produced meats and vegetables are home cooked and served daily in the bar and dining room (steaks a speciality). Situated on 2 acres with 80 car parking spaces. A patio overlooks the rear garden. Owner operated guarantees Kilkenny's best value accommodation, food and beverage.

Bookable on www.irelandhotels.com

B&B from €35.00 to €75.00

Ted & Michelene Dore
Proprietors

Member of:

Special Offer: Available Upon Request

29 29

Closed 24 - 28 December

Kilkenny Inn Hotel

15/16 Vicar Street,
Kilkenny

Tel: 056-777 2828 Fax: 056-776 1902
Email: info@kilkennyinn.com
Web: www.kilkennyinn.com

HOTEL N MAP 7 L 7

Kilkenny's newest intimate hotel located in the heart of the mediaeval city. St. Canice's Cathedral overlooks the hotel. The hotel has 30 en suite bedrooms with flat screen TV, Direct Dial telephone, tea/coffee making facilities, broadband internet access and 24 hour reception. The hotel comprises 2 bars, the Grill Room Restaurant and the Tower Suite to cater for all meetings and events. Complimentary parking is available for all residents.

Bookable on www.irelandhotels.com

Room Rate from €50.00 to €165.00

Michelle Keogh
General Manager

Activities:

30 30

Closed 25 December

B&B Rates are per Person Sharing per Night incl. Breakfast.
or **Room Rates** are per Room per Night - See also Page 8

Co. Kilkenny
Kilkenny City

Kilkenny Ormonde Hotel	Kilkenny River Court	Lacken House
Ormonde Street, Kilkenny	The Bridge, John Street, Kilkenny	Dublin Road, Kilkenny
Tel: 056-772 3900 Fax: 056-772 3977	Tel: 056-772 3388 Fax: 056-772 3389	Tel: 056-776 1085 Fax: 056-776 2435
Email: info@kilkennyormonde.com	Email: reservations@kilrivercourt.com	Email: info@lackenhouse.ie
Web: www.kilkennyormonde.com	Web: www.kilrivercourt.com	Web: www.lackenhouse.ie

HOTEL ★★★★ MAP 7 L 7 | **HOTEL ★★★★ MAP 7 L 7** | **GUESTHOUSE ★★★ MAP 7 L 7**

The new 4**** de luxe Kilkenny Ormonde Hotel is the most extensive hotel in the city. Ideally situated just off the High Street with Kilkenny Castle on its doorstep. Complete with 118 of the largest bedrooms in Kilkenny, fully equipped leisure centre with 21 metre swimming pool & 2 award-winning restaurants. A complimentary activity packed Kids Club is open throughout midterm breaks & summer season. Also offering complimentary parking. The Kilkenny Ormonde is the perfect choice for both corporate & leisure guests.

Award-winning RAC/AA 4**** hotel, leisure club and conference centre. City centre location, stunning views of Kilkenny Castle and the River Nore. Ideal as a conference venue or simply sheer relaxation. Leisure facilities, which include swimming pool, sauna, geyser pool, jacuzzi, fully equipped gymnasium and beauty salon. Limited free carparking. Within easy access of Dublin, Waterford and Cork.

Stay at Lacken House & enjoy high quality accommodation, superb food & a friendly welcome. We are a family-run guesthouse, situated in Kilkenny City, where you can enjoy exploring the mediaeval city. Superior & standard rooms available, all bedrooms are en suite with colour TV & tea/coffee facilities. Private car parking available for all residents. Our house features the home-cooking of our award-winning chefs, where fresh food is cooked to perfection. Full bar service is also available. Winners of National Feile Bia Award 2005, Best Tourism Provider Kilkenny 2005, AA Rosette Award 2005.

Bookable on www.irelandhotels.com | *Bookable on www.irelandhotels.com* Member of Spectra Group Hotels | *Bookable on www.irelandhotels.com* Member of Best Loved Hotels

B&B from €64.00 to €130.00 | **B&B from €45.00 to €160.00** | **B&B from €59.00 to €99.00**

 Patrick Curran General Manager / Director Activities: Member of:

 Peter Wilson General Manager Activities: Member of:

Jackie & Trevor Toner Owners Member of:

Special Offer: Weekend Specials from €188.00 pps (2 Nights B&B & 1 Dinner) | **Special Offer:** Midweek B&B from €45.00 pps per Night | **Special Offer:** Weekend Specials from €199.00 pps (2 Nights B&B & 1 Dinner)

| Closed 24 - 26 December | Closed 24 - 26 December | Closed 24 - 27 December |

B&B Rates are per Person Sharing per Night incl. Breakfast. or Room Rates are per Room per Night - See also Page 8

Langton House Hotel

69 John Street,
Kilkenny

Tel: 056-776 5133 Fax: 056-776 3693
Email: reservations@langtons.ie
Web: www.langtons.ie

HOTEL ★★★ MAP 7 L 7

The Langton Group, incorporating Langtons Hotel; Bar & Restaurant; The Marble City Bar; Carrigans Liquor Bar, are all located in the heart of Kilkenny City. Langtons Hotel, complete with thirty bedrooms, incorporating executive, penthouse and art-deco suites. Having won "National Pub of the Year" a record 4 times, the Langton Bar, Garden Restaurant, (member of the Kilkenny Good Food Circle) and "Club Langton" disco complete the picture that is Langtons.

B&B from €45.00 to €130.00

Eamon Langton
Proprietor

Activities:
✏️✔️

Member of:
IRISH HOTELS FEDERATION

30 30

Closed 25 December

Laragh Guest House

Smithsland North,
Waterford Road,
Kilkenny City

Tel: 056-776 4674 Fax: 056-770 3605
Email: cooneyhelen@eircom.net
Web: www.laraghhouse.com

GUESTHOUSE ★★★★ MAP 7 L 7

Laragh House is a new modern guesthouse offering luxurious, individually styled en suite rooms with TV, DD phones, tea/coffee facilities, hairdryer, power shower and/or whirlpool bath. Guests can expect a warm welcome, comfortable accommodation and an appetising breakfast. We are easily located 1 km from the city centre's shops, restaurants and historic sights, on main road to Waterford near bypass roundabout. There is off street parking for guests.

B&B from €35.00 to €45.00

Helen Cooney
Manager

Member of:
IRISH HOTELS FEDERATION

Special Offer: Please contact Manager for details

8 8

Closed 24 - 30 December

Laurels

College Road,
Kilkenny

Tel: 056-776 1501 Fax: 056-777 1334
Email: laurels@eircom.net
Web: www.thelaurelskilkenny.com

GUESTHOUSE ★★★ MAP 7 L 7

Purpose built townhouse 6-10 minutes walk from city centre and castle. Private car parking. All rooms en suite (some with whirlpool baths & super king sized beds). TV, Hairdryer, Tea/Coffee in all rooms. Some of the comments in Visitors Book: "Absolutely Wonderful", "Best B&B we had in Ireland", "First class & recommendable", "What more could one ask for, and a whirlpool bath too", "Wonderful". Opposite Hotel Kilkenny beside the famous Sceilp Pub.

Bookable on www.irelandhotels.com
Member of Premier Guesthouses

B&B from €30.00 to €50.00

Brian & Betty McHenry

Member of:
IRISH HOTELS FEDERATION

9 9

Open All Year

B&B Rates are per Person Sharing per Night incl. Breakfast.
or Room Rates are per Room per Night - See also Page 8

Kilkenny City

Lawlors Bar & Guesthouse	Lyrath Estate Hotel, Spa & Convention Centre	Metropole Hotel

Lawlors Bar & Guesthouse

42/43 John Street,
Kilkenny

Tel: 056-772 1379 Fax: 056-776 1579
Email: lawlors4243@eircom.net
Web: www.lawlorsbarandguesthouse.ie

GUESTHOUSE ★★★ MAP 7 L 7

A luxurious Victorian bar and guesthouse within walking distance of Kilkenny's mediaeval city centre (opposite railway station). Stay and relax in one of our 10 luxurious bedrooms designed for a high quality of comfort. All rooms have satellite TV, computer ports, tea/coffee making facilities, hairdryer. Visit our newly refurbished Victorian bar and restaurant which serves excellent food all day. A warm welcome awaits you.

B&B from €45.00 to €65.00

John & Miriam Lawlor

Member of:
IRISH HOTELS FEDERATION

10 10   ... WiFi

Closed 24 - 27 December

Lyrath Estate Hotel, Spa & Convention Centre

Dublin Road,
Kilkenny

Tel: 056-776 0088 Fax: 056-776 0089
Email: info@lyrath.com
Web: www.lyrath.com

UNDER CONSTRUCTION - OPENING JANUARY 2006

HOTEL P MAP 7 L 7

Lyrath is delighted to welcome its guests to a place of contemporary elegance and sophistication, where we guarantee a memorable and unique hospitality experience. Situated on 170 acres, Lyrath's 17th century house plays an integral part in the overall development. As Ireland's only ~H2O+ Spa destination, we offer you a unique and exclusive opportunity to unwind and take time out just for you. A courtesy coach is available to take you to the city centre just 5 mins away.

Bookable on www.irelandhotels.com
Member of Spectra Group Hotels

B&B from €120.00 to €200.00

*Peter Wilson
Project Manager*

Activities:

Special Offer: *Weekend Specials from €205.00 pps
(2 Nights B&B & 1 Dinner)*

137 137

Open All Year

Metropole Hotel

High Street,
Kilkenny

Tel: 056-776 3778 Fax: 056-777 0232
Email: info@metropolekilkenny.com
Web: www.metropolekilkenny.com

HOTEL ★ MAP 7 L 7

The Metropole Hotel is situated in the heart of Kilkenny City. Occupies a dominant position in Kilkenny's main shopping area (High Street). Within walking distance of all the city's mediaeval buildings e.g. Kilkenny Castle, Roth House and St. Canice's Cathedral. All bedrooms are en suite with multi channel TV, direct dial telephone and tea/coffee facilities. Live entertainment. Failte Ireland approved.

B&B from €35.00 to €75.00

*Robert Delaney
Proprietor*

Member of:
IRISH HOTELS FEDERATION

Special Offer: *Midweek Specials from €105.00 pps
(3 Nights B&B)*

12 12

Open All Year

B&B Rates are per Person Sharing per Night incl. Breakfast. or Room Rates are per Room per Night - See also Page 8

Newpark Hotel

Castlecomer Road,
Kilkenny

Tel: 056-776 0500 Fax: 056-776 0555
Email: info@newparkhotel.com
Web: www.newparkhotel.com

HOTEL ★★★ MAP 7 L 7

The newly extended and luxurious Newpark Hotel (3***, AA***), set in 40 acres of parkland in Ireland's Mediaeval City, boasts a total of 130 superior bedrooms en suite, with TV, hairdryer, telephone, trouser press and tea/coffee making facilities. Our extended leisure centre with 52ft pool, sauna, jacuzzi, steam room, gym and new health & beauty spa. Scott Dove Bar serves carvery lunch & evening meals. Enjoy fine dining in Gullivers Restaurant. Live entertainment most nights. State of the art conference and banqueting facilities.

Bookable on www.irelandhotels.com
Member of Best Western Hotels

B&B from €55.00 to €130.00

David O'Sullivan
Managing Director

Activities:

Member of:

130 130

Open All Year

Springhill Court Hotel, Spa & Leisure Club

Waterford Road,
Kilkenny

Tel: 056-772 1122 Fax: 056-776 1600
Email: reservations@springhillcourt.com
Web: www.springhillcourt.com

HOTEL ★★★ MAP 7 L 7

Located only minutes from the bustling centre of " the Marble City". We boast one of Kilkenny's most modern leisure clubs. Our facilities include a 19m deck level pool, sauna, jacuzzi, steam room and fully equipped gymnasium. Unwind in "AquaSpa" offering 7 treatment rooms including floatation therapy. This compliments our superb restaurant, friendly bar, conference centre and 85 well appointed bedrooms. Sister hotel: The Arklow Bay Conference & Leisure Hotel, Co. Wicklow.

Bookable on www.irelandhotels.com
Member of Chara Hotel Group

B&B from €65.00 to €99.00

John Hickey
General Manager

Activities:

Member of:

Special Offer: Midweek Specials from €99.00 pps
(2 Nights B&B & 1 Dinner)

85 85

Open All Year

Troysgate House

Vicar Street,
Kilkenny

Tel: 056-776 1100 Fax: 056-770 3755
Email: info@troysgatehouse.com
Web: www.troysgatehouse.com

GUESTHOUSE P MAP 7 L 7

Troysgate House formerly the Jailhouse of the Old Walled - conveniently located in the heart of the Mediaeval City of Kilkenny. With 20 en suite rooms, all individually designed & furnished to an exceptionally high standard. It is an historic & charming old world inn which has retained its character while serving the needs of the modern world. The House incorporates Bambrick's renowned traditional pub which truly has an atmosphere all of its own. Angling, horse riding & Kilkenny golf course nearby. Our mission is to create lifetime customers through excellent, friendly service. A warm welcome awaits our guests.

B&B from €35.00 to €65.00

Breda Heary

Member of:

Special Offer: Weekend Specials from €95.00 pps
(2 Nights B&B & 1 Dinner)

20 20

Open All Year

B&B Rates are per Person Sharing per Night incl. Breakfast. or **Room Rates** are per Room per Night - See also Page 8

South East 371

Kilkenny City / Knocktopher / Mullinavat

Zuni Restaurant & Townhouse	Carrolls Hotel	Rising Sun

Zuni Restaurant & Townhouse

26 Patrick Street,
Kilkenny

Tel: 056-772 3999 Fax: 056-775 6400
Email: info@zuni.ie
Web: www.zuni.ie

HOTEL U MAP 7 L 7

A family-run business in operation for five years, Zuni has earned its reputation as one of the best places to stay & eat in Ireland. Ideally located in the heart of the mediaeval city with private parking and within walking distance of all that Kilkenny has to offer.

B&B from €45.00 to €85.00

Paul Byrne
Proprietor

Special Offer: *Midweek Specials from €135.00 pps*
(2 Nights B&B and 1 Dinner)

13   13

Closed 23 - 27 December

Carrolls Hotel

Knocktopher,
Co. Kilkenny

Tel: 056-776 8082 Fax: 056-776 8290
Email: info@carrollshotel.com
Web: www.carrollshotel.com

HOTEL ★★ MAP 7 L 6

Situated on the N10 between Kilkenny and Waterford. Enjoy the excellent service, warmth and luxury of our family-run hotel. All rooms are en suite with TV and direct dial phone. Our Sionnach Sioc Restaurant has an excellent reputation for good food. The hotel provides live music 2 nights a week. Golfing, karting, fishing, horse riding and shooting are available nearby.

B&B from €40.00 to €95.00

Padraig Carroll
General Manager

Member of:
IRISH HOTELS FEDERATION

10   10

Closed 24 - 26 December

Rising Sun

Mullinavat,
Via Waterford,
Co. Kilkenny

Tel: 051-898173 Fax: 051-898435
Email: info@therisingsun.ie
Web: www.therisingsun.ie

GUESTHOUSE ★★★ MAP 4 L 6

A family-run guesthouse, 14km from Waterford City on the main Waterford-Dublin road. It has 10 luxurious bedrooms all en suite with D/D telephone, TV and tea/coffee making facilities. The Rising Sun Guesthouse is an ideal base for sports enthusiasts, surrounded by some beautiful golf courses within 15-30 minutes drive. The old world charm of stone and timberwork sets the tone of comfort and relaxation in the bar and lounge. Traditional home cooked lunches and bar food served daily. The Restaurant offers full à la carte menu and wine list.

B&B from €45.00 to €65.00

Anne Ryan
Reception

10   10

Closed 23 - 29 December

B&B Rates are per Person Sharing per Night incl. Breakfast.
or **Room Rates** are per Room per Night - See also Page 8

Mount Juliet Conrad

Thomastown,
Co. Kilkenny

Tel: 056-777 3000 Fax: 056-777 3019
Email: mountjulietinfo@conradhotels.com
Web: www.conradhotels.com

HOTEL ★★★★ MAP 7 L 6

At 1500 acres, Mount Juliet is one of the oldest surviving walled estates in the world. Guests can chose from accommodation in the carefully refurbished 18th century manor house overlooking the meandering waters of the River Nore, or in the Club Rooms at the estate's old stable yards, restored just over a decade ago. For longer stays, The Rose Garden Lodges offer privacy, flexibility & comfort. On site activities include horse riding, fishing, clay shooting & archery, golf on the 18 hole Nicklaus course or the 18 hole putting course & a luxurious spa & leisure centre.

Bookable on www.irelandhotels.com
Member of Conrad Group of Hotels

B&B from €117.00 to €237.00

Antony Treston
General Manager

Activities:

Member of:

Special Offer: Play & Stay from €199 p.p.s. (1 Nights B&B & 1 Dinner & 1 Round of Golf)

58 58

Open All Year

Cahir House Hotel

The Square,
Cahir,
Co. Tipperary

Tel: 052-43000 Fax: 052-42728
Email: info@cahirhousehotel.ie
Web: www.cahirhousehotel.ie

HOTEL ★★★ MAP 3 J 6

New health & beauty spa opened. Featuring the finest pampering facilities and treatments available. Specialty weekends. Ideal location for touring, situated where N8 meets N24. Town centre location. Golf breaks a specialty, 8 courses close by. Carvery lunch daily. Bar food available all day. Á la Carte menu served in our Butler's Pantry Restaurant. As part of the Féile Bia promotion of Irish food we serve only the finest locally produced food. Fabulous walks to the local heritage sites such as "The Swiss Cottage" and also nearby Cahir Castle, Mitchelstown Caves and the famous Rock of Cashel.

B&B from €35.00 to €70.00

Carol O'Brien

Activities:

Member of:

Special Offer: Midweek Specials from €35.00 pps (3 Nights B&B)

42 42

Open all year

Castle Court Hotel

Cashel Road,
Cahir,
Co. Tipperary

Tel: 052-43955 Fax: 052-45130
Email: info@castlecourthotelcahir.com
Web: www.castlecourthotelcahir.com

HOTEL N MAP 3 J 6

The Castle Court Hotel which boasts 18 en suite air-conditioned bedrooms is ideal for either business or a short break away. Centrally located for touring the South East. Full bar and à la carte menu. Breakfast served all day. You can also enjoy an Indian meal in Pepper's Restaurant. As part of Féile Bia and Failte Ireland we aim to provide only the best in the Castle Court Hotel.

Bookable on www.irelandhotels.com

B&B from €55.00 to €65.00

Kevin Curry
Owner / Director

Activities:

Member of:

18 18

Open All Year

B&B Rates are per Person Sharing per Night incl. Breakfast.
or **Room Rates** are per Room per Night - See also Page 8

Co. Tipperary South

Cahir / Carrick-on-Suir / Cashel

Kilcoran Lodge Hotel, Lodges & Leisure Centre	Carraig Hotel	Aulber House
Cahir, Co. Tipperary	Main Street, Carrick-on-Suir, Co. Tipperary	Deerpark, Golden Road, Cashel, Co. Tipperary
Tel: 052-41288 Fax: 052-41994	Tel: 051-641455 Fax: 051-641604	Tel: 062-63713 Fax: 062-63715
Email: kilcoran@eircom.net	Email: info@carraighotel.com	Email: beralley@eircom.net
Web: www.kilcoranlodgehotel.com	Web: www.carraighotel.com	Web: www.aulberhouse.com

HOTEL ★★★ MAP 3 J 6 | **HOTEL R MAP 3 K 5** | **GUESTHOUSE ★★★ MAP 3 J 6**

Kilcoran a former hunting lodge set in spacious grounds overlooking beautiful countryside. An ideal holiday base located equal distance (15min drive) from Tipperary, Cashel, Clonmel & Mitchelstown & 45 mins drive from Cork, Kilkenny & Limerick on the main Cork-Dublin road. The hotel has the charm of bygone days yet all the modern facilities of a 3 star hotel. Guests have free access to Shapes Leisure Centre with indoor pool etc. There are also 17 luxury detached holiday lodges, self-catering for up to 6 persons, ideal for golf, walking & fishing breaks.

The Carraig Hotel is the focal point of the town of Carrick-on-Suir. The recently refurbished hotel offers well appointed en suite bedrooms with DD telephone, TV, tea/coffee making facilities, bar/lounge, carvery lunch and bar menu served daily. Restaurant serving Irish & International cuisine. Conference meeting facilities, functions/banqueting specialists. New fitness centre from Spring 2006. Weekend entertainment. Close proximity to new marina development. Ideal base for angling, golf, walking and cycling.

Aulber House - newly built luxury guesthouse. Ideally located on the outskirts of the historic town of Cashel. Home away from home. Perfect base for touring the South. Beautiful views of the Rock of Cashel and Hoare Abbey from some rooms and lobby. All rooms are spacious with en suite, power showers, direct dial phones, TV, hairdryers and computer modems. Non-smoking guesthouse. Golf and angling facilities available locally. AA ♦♦♦♦. Wire-free internet access available.

Bookable on www.irelandhotels.com

Member of Premier Guesthouses

B&B from €65.00 to €75.00 | **B&B from €55.00 to €75.00** | **B&B from €45.00 to €65.00**

 Jacqueline Mullen, Managing Director | Bobby Carrigan, General Manager | Bernice & Sean Alley

Member of: IRISH HOTELS FEDERATION

Special Offer: Weekend Specials from €135.00 pps (2 Nights B&B & 1 Dinner) | **Special Offer:** Seasonal Special €99.00 (2 nights B&B)

22 22 | 24 24 | 12 12

| **Open All Year** | **Closed 24 - 26 December** | **Closed 23 - 29 December** |

B&B Rates are per Person Sharing per Night incl. Breakfast. or Room Rates are per Room per Night - See also Page 8

Baileys of Cashel

Main Street,
Cashel,
Co. Tipperary
Tel: 062-61937 Fax: 062-63957
Email: info@baileys-ireland.com
Web: www.baileys-ireland.com

GUESTHOUSE ★★★ MAP 3 J 6

Baileys is a beautifully restored listed Georgian house ideally situated in the town centre with private parking available. The fully licensed Cellar Restaurant serves excellent food in a cosy atmosphere with friendly service. Our elegant bedrooms are tastefully decorated with direct dial telephone, multichannel TV, and wireless broadband internet access. Guests can now enjoy our newly developed leisure centre with 20m pool, sauna, steam room, jacuzzi and spa. AA 4 ♦♦♦♦. Bridgestone recommended. Member Lucinda O'Sullivans Great Places to Stay.

Bookable on www.irelandhotels.com

B&B from €50.00 to €55.00

Phil Delaney
Manager

Member of:

IRISH HOTELS FEDERATION

🛏🛆 ☎🖥📺🌀🍴🥂🧖🅿🇵 a/c Inet WiFi
19 19

Closed 24 - 28 December

Cashel Palace Hotel

Main Street,
Cashel,
Co. Tipperary
Tel: 062-62707 Fax: 062-61521
Email: reception@cashel-palace.ie
Web: www.cashel-palace.ie

HOTEL ★★★★ MAP 3 J 6

Built in 1730 as an Archbishop's Palace, the Cashel Palace is complemented by tranquil walled gardens and a private walk to the famous Rock of Cashel. Our 23 bedrooms are all en suite with TV, phone & trouser press. Our Bishop's Buttery Restaurant is open for lunch & dinner, while the Guinness Bar is open for light snacks daily. The hotel has recently been completely restored & guests can now enjoy the finest furnishings, fabrics, art & antiques in the most elegant surroundings. AA 4**** hotel. AA Rosette Award for Culinary Excellence 2005/2006.

Bookable on www.irelandhotels.com

B&B from €112.50 to €137.50

Susan & Patrick Murphy
Proprietors

Activities:

🎿🐾

Member of:

IRISH HOTELS FEDERATION

🛏🛆 ☎🖥📺🍴♥CM☀🌀🥂🅿🇵🅂 a/c Inet
23 23
🐾

Closed 24 - 26 December

Dundrum House Hotel

Dundrum,
Cashel,
Co. Tipperary
Tel: 062-71116 Fax: 062-71366
Email: dundrumh@iol.ie
Web: www.dundrumhousehotel.com

HOTEL ★★★ MAP 3 J 7

One of Ireland's best inland resort hotels, Dundrum House Hotel is surrounded by the manicured fairways of its own 18-hole Championship course designed by Ryder Cup hero Philip Walton. The Country Club features the Venue Clubhouse Bar/Restaurant, 'White-Flag' award-winning Health & Leisure Centre with 20m indoor pool, gym, jacuzzi, sauna and steam room. Beauty treatments/massage by appointment. Eighty four elegant bedrooms with antiques, two penthouse suites and six apartments.

Bookable on www.irelandhotels.com
Member of Manor House Hotels

B&B from €90.00 to €130.00

Austin & Mary Crowe
Proprietors

Activities:

🎣🎿🏇

Member of:

IRISH HOTELS FEDERATION

Special Offer: Midweek Specials from €165.00 pps (3 Nights B&B)

🛏🛆 ☎🖥📺🇹🇨♥CM☀🌀🥂🅂🍴🏇🎵
84 84
🇵🅂🇦🌀🐾

Closed 24 - 26 December

B&B Rates are per Person Sharing per Night incl. Breakfast.
or Room Rates are per Room per Night - See also Page 8

South East 375

Hill House

Palmer's Hill,
Cashel,
Co. Tipperary
Tel: 062-61277 Fax: 062-63970
Email: hillhouse1@eircom.net
Web: www.hillhousecashel.com

GUESTHOUSE P MAP 3 J 6

Hill House is one of Ireland's most historic Georgian homes. Constructed in 1710, Hill House is overlooking the Rock of Cashel, with private car park. We are 3 minutes walk from the town centre. The house has been extensively refurbished incorporating family heirlooms and antiques. The stylish elegance in the guest bedrooms is individual, some of our rooms have 4-poster king-size beds with all modern comforts. Recommended by leading guides such as Friendly Homes of Ireland, Hidden Places of Ireland and Georgina Campbell's Ireland Guide, also a member of Les Routiers.

Bookable on www.irelandhotels.com
Member of Les Routiers

B&B from €40.00 to €60.00

Carmel Purcell Proprietor

Member of: IRISH HOTELS FEDERATION

5 5

Closed 24 - 28 December

Legends Townhouse & Restaurant

The Kiln,
Cashel,
Co. Tipperary
Tel: 062-61292
Email: info@legendsguesthouse.com
Web: www.legendsguesthouse.com

GUESTHOUSE ★★★ MAP 3 J 6

Legends is your home from home, a place to relax and unwind after your day's travelling. You can enjoy your breakfast, lunch or dinner in our comfortable surroundings with spectacular views of the Rock of Cashel. Recommended consistently by leading guides such as AA Hotel Guide, Michelin, Karen Brown, Bridgestone 100 Best and Rick Steves. An ideal base to explore Kilkenny, Waterford and Limerick or simply sit back and be inspired by the historical monument that is the Rock of Cashel. Unmissable!

Bookable on www.irelandhotels.com

B&B from €45.00 to €65.00

Grazielle & John Quinlan

Member of: IRISH HOTELS FEDERATION

Special Offer: Weekend Specials from €120.00 pps (2 Nights B&B & 1 Dinner)

7 7

Closed 07 - 30 November

Brighton House

1 Brighton Place,
Clonmel,
Co. Tipperary
Tel: 052-23665 Fax: 052-23665
Email: brighton@iol.ie
Web: www.tipp.ie/brighton.htm

GUESTHOUSE ★★ MAP 3 K 5

Family-run 3 storey Georgian guesthouse, with a hotel ambience and antique furnishings. Clonmel Town centre - the largest inland town in Ireland bridging Rosslare Harbour (132km) with Killarney (160km) and the South West. Host to Fleadh Cheoil na hEireann 2003/04. Visit the Rock of Cashel, Mitchelstown Caves, Cahir Castle etc. Golf, fishing and pony trekking arranged locally. All rooms have direct dial phones, TV, radio, hairdryer and tea/coffee making facilities. Situated opposite Dunnes Stores Oakville Shopping Centre.

B&B from €35.00 to €60.00

Bernie & Pat Morris Proprietors

Member of: IRISH HOTELS FEDERATION

Special Offer: Midweek Specials from €90.00 pps (3 Nights B&B)

6 6

Closed 24 - 29 December

B&B Rates are per Person Sharing per Night incl. Breakfast. or Room Rates are per Room per Night - See also Page 8

Clonmel Arms Hotel

Sarsfield Street,
Clonmel,
Co. Tipperary
Tel: 052-21233 Fax: 052-21526
Email: theclonmelarms@eircom.net
Web: www.theclonmelarmshotel.com

HOTEL CR MAP 3 K 5

The Clonmel Arms Hotel lies the heart of Clonmel which is situated on the north bank of the River Suir at the foot of the scenic Comeragh and Knockmealdown Mountains. It is a hotel unsurpassed in the area with excellent ground floor facilities and in easy reach of Cork, Shannon, Rosslare and Waterford. The Paddock Bar is ideal for a most enjoyable night of music every Thursday to Sunday, and delicious bar food served daily, or you can have a memorable experience in our top grade restaurant. Residential car parking.

Room Rate from €60.00 to €150.00

Rory Bates
Manager

Activities:

Member of:

30 30

Open All Year

Fennessy's Hotel

Gladstone Street,
Clonmel,
Co. Tipperary
Tel: 052-23680 Fax: 052-23783
Email: info@fennessyshotel.com
Web: www.fennessyshotel.com

HOTEL ★★ MAP 3 K 5

This beautiful Georgian building is newly restored and refurbished. Right in the centre of Clonmel, it is easily located opposite the town's main church. All bedrooms are en suite and have security safes, DD phone, multi channel TV, hairdryer, tea/coffee facilities, some with jacuzzis. Family-run hotel. Elegant ambience throughout. Main shopping area, swimming pool, leisure centre, riverside walks are a stone's throw from our front door. Golf, hill walking, fishing, pony trekking. After your visit, you will wish to return.

Bookable on www.irelandhotels.com

B&B from €35.00 to €50.00

Richard & Esther Fennessy
Proprietors

Member of:

Special Offer: Midweek Specials from €100.00 pps
(3 Nights B&B)

10 10

Open All Year

Hotel Minella & Leisure Centre

Clonmel,
Co. Tipperary

Tel: 052-22388 Fax: 052-24381
Email: frontdesk@hotelminella.ie
Web: www.hotelminella.ie

HOTEL ★★★ MAP 3 K 5

Situated on the banks of the River Suir and set amidst 9 acres of landscaped grounds, we offer a friendly welcome, warmth and hospitality. High quality bedrooms include superior rooms with spacious accommodation and either a steam room or jacuzzi. "Club Minella" has a 20m swimming pool, fully equipped gym, outdoor hot tub and tennis court. Massage and beauty treatments can be pre-booked. Newly refurbished public areas include conference facilities, the bar and restaurants. 2 RAC Dining Awards 04/05. Family-run by the Nallens.

Bookable on www.irelandhotels.com
Member of Irish Country Hotels

B&B from €90.00 to €180.00

John Nallen
Managing Director

Activities:

Member of:

Special Offer: Weekend Specials from €175.00 pps
(2 Nights B&B & 1 Dinner)

70 70

Closed 23 - 29 December

B&B Rates are per Person Sharing per Night incl. Breakfast.
or Room Rates are per Room per Night - See also Page 8

South East 377

Co. Tipperary South
Clonmel / Glen of Aherlow

Meadowvale Farm Guesthouse	**Mulcahys**	**Aherlow House Hotel and Lodges**

Meadowvale Farm Guesthouse

Meadowvale Farm,
Derrygrath, Clonmel,
Co. Tipperary
Tel: 052-38914 Fax: 052-38875
Email: info@meadowvaleguesthouse.com
Web: www.meadowvaleguesthouse.com

GUESTHOUSE ★★★ MAP 3 J 6

This family-run purpose built 3*** guesthouse provides luxury accommodation from the super king sized beds and power showers to the Chesterfield leather suites and log fires. Perfect for the quiet family getaway, romantic break or the nature lover alike. Set in a stud farm, the views are magic, with mountains on all sides. Centrally located within 1 hour of 3 airports, 10 minutes from Cashel, Cahir and Clonmel, yet it is quiet and peaceful. Mobile number: 087 2768188 - ring at any time, you are always welcome.

B&B from €45.00 to €55.00

Eithne Maher

Activities:
✓

Member of:
IRISH HOTELS FEDERATION

10 10

Open all Year

Mulcahys

47 Gladstone Street,
Clonmel,
Co. Tipperary
Tel: 052-25054 Fax: 052-24544
Email: info@mulcahys.ie
Web: www.mulcahys.ie

GUESTHOUSE ★★ MAP 3 K 5

Mulcahys is run by the Higgins family. Our bedrooms are tastefully designed, all en suite with tea/coffee making facilities, multi channel TV and hairdryer. The carvery opens for lunch from 12pm and our "East Lane" menu is served from 6pm which includes lobsters and oysters from our fish tank. "Dance the night away" at our award-winning nightclub "Dannos". Some of Ireland's best golf courses are within easy reach of Clonmel and the River Suir has been described as an "angler's paradise".

B&B from €40.00 to €80.00

Claire Harris

Member of:
IRISH HOTELS FEDERATION

10 10

Closed 24 - 28 December

Aherlow House Hotel and Lodges

Glen of Aherlow,
Co. Tipperary

Tel: 062-56153 Fax: 062-56212
Email: reservations@aherlowhouse.ie
Web: www.aherlowhouse.ie

HOTEL ★★★ MAP 3 I 6

Aherlow House Hotel and 4**** de luxe holiday homes. The hotel & lodges are set in the middle of a coniferous forest just 4 miles from Tipperary Town. Originally a hunting lodge now converted into an exquisitely furnished hotel. Aherlow House welcomes you to its peaceful atmosphere, enhanced by a fine reputation for hospitality, excellent cuisine and unique wines. Overlooks the Glen of Aherlow and has beautiful views of the Galtee Mountains. Activities can be arranged.

B&B from €69.00 to €82.00

*Ferghal & Helen Purcell
Owners*

Activities:
✓

Member of:
IRISH HOTELS FEDERATION

29 29

Open All Year

B&B Rates are per Person Sharing per Night incl. Breakfast. or <u>Room Rates</u> are per Room per Night - See also Page 8

Glen Hotel

Glen of Aherlow,
Co. Tipperary

Tel: 062-56146 Fax: 062-56152

Web: www.theglenhotel.ie

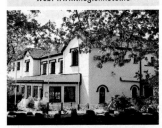

HOTEL ★★ MAP 3 I 6

The Glen Hotel set in the shadows of the majestic Galtee Mountains, amidst the splendour of the Aherlow Valley is just 5 miles from Tipperary Town. To relax, dream, reminisce or plan - this is the ideal haven. Our bedrooms are all en suite. This family owned and operated hotel has built up a fine reputation for excellent cuisine and offers friendly and efficient service. Hill walking, horse riding, fishing and golf. Musical entertainment weekly.

B&B from €55.00 to €75.00

Cormac & Joseph Rose
Proprietors

Activities:

Member of:

IRISH HOTELS FEDERATION

Special Offer: Midweek Specials from €195.00 pps
(3 Nights B&B & 2 Dinners)

20 20

Open All Year

Rathellen House

Raheen,
Bansha,
Co. Tipperary

Tel: 062-54376 Fax: 062-54376
Email: info@rathellenhouse.com
Web: www.rathellenhouse.com

UNDER CONSTRUCTION - OPENING APRIL 2006

GUESTHOUSE P MAP 3 I 6

A large Georgian style country house on 4 acres of gardens, Rathellen is located 1 mile off the N24 at Bansha with panoramic views of the Galtee Mountains. Home and locally grown produce served in the dining room. Relax by open fires in the drawing room, dining room and entrance hall. Individually decorated bedrooms classically furnished. Bathrooms have under-floor heating and heated mirrors. Experience Irish country house hospitality where the Long family will endeavour to exceed your expectations.

B&B from €50.00 to €80.00

Eamonn Long

Special Offer: Weekend Specials from €145.00 pps
(2 Nights B&B & 1 Dinner)

7 7

Open All Year

Horse and Jockey Inn

Horse and Jockey,
(Near Cashel),
Co. Tipperary

Tel: 0504-44192 Fax: 0504-44747
Email: horseandjockeyinn@eircom.net
Web: www.horseandjockeyinn.com

HOTEL ★★★ MAP 7 J 7

The Horse and Jockey Inn, located at the heartland of County Tipperary, midway between Cork and Dublin on the N8 holds great association with people from sporting, cultural and political walks of life. Our modern refurbishment includes spacious lounge and bar facilities, a high quality restaurant, de luxe accommodation and a modern conference centre. Experience the atmosphere that's steeped in tradition and share with us the real Ireland, in the comfort of our new inn. New leisure and conference facilities due for completion Autumn 2006.

B&B from €80.00 to €80.00

Tom Egan
Proprietor

Member of:

IRISH HOTELS FEDERATION

30 30

Closed 25 - 26 December

B&B Rates are per Person Sharing per Night incl. Breakfast.
or **Room Rates** are per Room per Night - See also Page 8

South East 379

Co. Tipperary South

Killenaule / Tipperary Town

Ardagh House

Killenaule,
Co. Tipperary

Tel: 052-56224 Fax: 052-56224
Email: ahouse@iol.ie
Web: www.ardaghhouse.ie

GUESTHOUSE ★ MAP 3 K 7

Fully licensed family guesthouse, piano lounge bar, residents' lounge, rooms en suite, home-cooking. Set in the shadow of romantic Slievenamon, in the area of the Derrynaflan Chalice, the famous Coolmore Stud, in the heart of the Golden Vale. Near Holycross Abbey, Cashel and Kilkenny. Central for hunting, fishing, shooting, golf, horse riding and less strenuous walks through the hills of Killenaule. Finally, just one hour from the sea.

B&B from €35.00 to €37.00

Mary & Michael McCormack Managers

Member of:
IRISH HOTELS FEDERATION

6 6

Closed 24 - 27 December

Ach Na Sheen Guesthouse

Clonmel Road,
Tipperary Town,
Co. Tipperary

Tel: 062-51298 Fax: 062-80467
Email: gernoonan@eircom.net
Web: www.achnasheen.net

GUESTHOUSE ★★ MAP 3 I 6

Family-run guesthouse, 5 minutes from the town centre with a spacious sun lounge and diningroom overlooking gardens and the beautiful Galtee Mountains. Our 8 rooms are all en suite, equipped with TV and tea/coffee making facilities. Ach-na-Sheen is adjacent to the picturesque Glen of Aherlow where fishing and hill walking can be arranged. Golf can be enjoyed at any number of nearby championship courses. G & S Noonan offer you the utmost in Irish hospitality.

B&B from €40.00 to €55.00

Sylvia & Ger Noonan Proprietors

Activities:

Member of:
IRISH HOTELS FEDERATION

8 8

Closed 18 December - 14 January

Ballyglass Country House

Glen Of Aherlow Road,
Ballyglass,
Tipperary Town

Tel: 062-52104 Fax: 062-52229
Email: info@ballyglasshouse.com
Web: www.ballyglasshouse.com

HOTEL U MAP 3 I 6

Ballyglass Country House is an 18th century country residence set in its own grounds on the outskirts of Tipperary and just 2km from the beautiful Glen of Aherlow. Here at this family-run hotel you can enjoy the best of local produce in our "Colonel's Restaurant" and relax in front of a real coal fire in our "Forge Bar". Ballyglass Country House is perfectly situated for touring Munster. Golfing, fishing, hill walking & horse riding are all available locally.

B&B from €50.00 to €60.00

Joan & Bill Byrne Proprietors

Member of:
IRISH HOTELS FEDERATION

Special Offer: *Weekend Specials from €120.00 pps (2 Nights B&B & 1 Dinner)*

10 10

Closed 24 - 26 December

380   *South East*

B&B Rates are per Person Sharing per Night incl. Breakfast. or Room Rates are per Room per Night - See also Page 8

Royal Hotel Tipperary

Bridge Street,
Tipperary Town,
Co. Tipperary
Tel: 062-33244 Fax: 062-33596

Web: www.royalhoteltipperary.com

HOTEL ★★ MAP 3 I 6

Situated in Tipperary Town, a familiar meeting place serving excellent food from 8am to 10pm daily, using finest quality local produce. Tastefully decorated rooms with all amenities. Just a few minutes from Tipperary Racecourse, 3 outstanding golf clubs (special arrangements & packages available to the hotel for Tipperary, Dundrum & Ballykisteen Clubs). Sport & Leisure Complex 3 minutes from the hotel and The Excel Theatre within a short walking distance. So if it's business or pleasure, a warm welcome awaits you.

B&B from €35.00 to €55.00

Jeremiah Iveson
Proprietor

16 16

Closed 24 - 27 December

Newtown Farm Guesthouse

Grange,
Ardmore, Via Youghal,
Co. Waterford
Tel: 024-94143 Fax: 024-94054
Email: newtownfarm@eircom.net
Web: www.newtownfarm.com

GUESTHOUSE ★★★ MAP 3 K 3

Family-run farm guesthouse in scenic location, surrounded by its own farmlands with dairying as the main enterprise, with views of the Atlantic Ocean, hills and cliff walks. All bedrooms en suite with tea/coffee making facilities, TV, DD phone and hairdryer. Grange is 6 minutes from the beach and Ardmore Round Tower and Cathedral, built in the 12th century, raises its heights to 97 feet. 2 hours drive from Port of Rosslare. Signposted on N25 turn left at Flemings Pub, 200m.

Bookable on www.irelandhotels.com
Member of Premier Guesthouses

B&B from €38.00 to €40.00

Teresa O'Connor
Proprietor

Member of:

Special Offer: Midweek Specials from €114.00 pps
(3 Nights B&B)

7 7

Closed 31 October - 01 April

Round Tower Hotel

College Road,
Ardmore,
Co. Waterford
Tel: 024-94494 Fax: 024-94254
Email: rth@eircom.net

HOTEL U MAP 3 K 3

Situated within walking distance of Ardmore's award-winning beach, the Round Tower Hotel offers 12 well appointed en suite bedrooms. Fresh local produce features prominently on both the bar and restaurant menus. The ancient monastic settlement of St. Declan & the Round Tower are situated behind the hotel. Ardmore also boasts some world famous cliff walks and breathtaking scenery. Ardmore is 21kms from Dungarvan & a 2 hour drive from the port of Rosslare on the Primary N25 route.

Bookable on www.irelandhotels.com

B&B from €45.00 to €55.00

Aidan Quirke M.I.H.C.I
Proprietor

Member of:

12 12

Closed 21 - 28 December

B&B Rates are per Person Sharing per Night incl. Breakfast.
or Room Rates are per Room per Night - See also Page 8

Ballymacarbry / Cappoquin / Cheekpoint

Hanoras Cottage	Richmond House	Three Rivers Guest House
Nire Valley, Ballymacarbry, Co. Waterford	Cappoquin, Co. Waterford	Cheekpoint, Co. Waterford
Tel: 052-36134 Fax: 052-36540	Tel: 058-54278 Fax: 058-54988	Tel: 051-382520 Fax: 051-382542
Email: hanorascottage@eircom.net	Email: info@richmondhouse.net	Email: mail@threerivers.ie
Web: www.hanorascottage.com	Web: www.richmond.house.net	Web: www.threerivers.ie

GUESTHOUSE ★★★★ MAP 3 K 5 | **GUESTHOUSE ★★★★ MAP 3 J 4** | **GUESTHOUSE ★★★ MAP 4 M 5**

A haven of peace and tranquillity in the Comeragh Mountains, Hanoras has everything for discerning guests. Relax in the sheer bliss of an adult only house with the soothing sounds of the Nire River running by. Spacious rooms with jacuzzi tubs. Superior rooms for that special occasion! Enjoy excellent cuisine from our Ballymaloe School chefs who cater for all diets. AA and RAC ◆◆◆◆. Recommended in Bridgestone Guide 100 Best Places in Ireland. National award winners Guesthouse Of The Year and Breakfast Of The Year. The Wall Family welcome you.

Delightful 18th century Georgian country house and fully licenced award-winning restaurant set in private grounds. Relax in total peace and tranquillity in front of log fires. Each room is a perfect blend of Georgian splendour combined with all modern comforts for the discerning guest. AA ◆◆◆◆◆. Recommended in the Bridgestone Guides; 100 Best Places to Stay, 100 Best Restaurants in Ireland and all leading guides. Ideal location for a short break.

3*** award-winning guesthouse, a haven of peace and tranquillity with magnificent views of Waterford Estuary. Situated on the outskirts of the historic village Cheekpoint, with its award-winning pubs and seafood restaurants. Sample the delights of breakfast in our estuary view dining room or relax over coffee in our spacious lounge. Ideal base for touring sunny South East. Close to Waterford, Dunmore East, Tramore and 2km from Faithlegg Golf Course. All rooms en suite.

B&B from €75.00 to €125.00	B&B from €75.00 to €130.00	B&B from €36.00 to €70.00

The Wall Family
Proprietors

Paul & Claire Deevy
Proprietors

Brian & Theresa Joyce

Activities:

Member of:
HOTELS

Member of:
HOTELS

Member of:
HOTELS

10 10 | 9 9 | 14 14

Closed 20 - 28 December	Closed 23 December - 10 January	Closed 20 - 28 December

B&B Rates are per Person Sharing per Night incl. Breakfast. or **Room Rates** are per Room per Night - See also Page 8

Barnawee Bridge Guesthouse

Kilminion,
Dungarvan,
Co. Waterford
Tel: 058-42074
Email: michelle@barnawee.com
Web: www.barnawee.com

Clonea Strand Hotel, Golf & Leisure

Clonea,
Dungarvan,
Co. Waterford
Tel: 058-45555 Fax: 058-42880
Email: info@clonea.com
Web: www.clonea.com

Lawlors Hotel

Bridge Street,
Dungarvan,
Co. Waterford
Tel: 058-41122 Fax: 058-41000
Email: info@lawlorshotel.com
Web: www.lawlorshotel.com

GUESTHOUSE ★★★ MAP 3 K 4

HOTEL ★★★ MAP 3 K 4

HOTEL ★★★ MAP 3 K 4

Our newly built guesthouse with fabulous sea and mountain views near all local amenities including three 18 hole golf courses, indoor swimming, sea angling, tennis, fishing and bird watching. Also various countryside walks. Food and drinks available locally, also a kitchenette for tea/coffee and snacks available for all our customers. All rooms are very spacious with en suite and color T.V., making for a very enjoyable stay. Mobile number: 087 2620269.

Clonea Strand Hotel overlooking Clonea Beach. Family-run by John and Ann McGrath. All rooms en suite with tea/coffee making facilities, hairdryer and colour TV. Indoor leisure centre with heated pool, jacuzzi, sauna, Turkish bath, gymnasium and ten pin bowling alley. Situated close by is our 18 hole golf course bordering on the Atlantic Ocean with a scenic background of Dungarvan Bay and Comeragh Mountains. Our Bay Restaurant specialises in locally caught seafood. 1 thousand sq foot children's Soft Play facility. www.playloft.net

Lawlors Hotel is family-run with 89 bedrooms, all en suite with tea/coffee making facilities, TV and direct dial phone. Lawlors is the ideal choice for your stay in the beautiful West Waterford countryside. Conferences, weddings, parties, seminars are especially catered for. Good food is a speciality at Lawlors and the friendly atmosphere of Dungarvan Town is brought to life in the Old Worlde bar surroundings. Freephone number (1800) 931 980.

Bookable on www.irelandhotels.com

B&B from €35.00 to €45.00

B&B from €34.75 to €95.00

B&B from €50.00 to €85.00

*Michelle Dwane / Gary Treen
Proprietors*

*Mark Knowles
Gen.Mgr.Group / Marketing*

*Michael Burke
Proprietor*

Activities:

Member of:

Member of:

Member of:

Special Offer: Midweek Specials from €99.00 pps (3 Nights B&B)

6   6

Special Offer: Breaks from €139.00 per couple (2 Nights B&B)

58 58

Special Offer:

89 89

Open All Year

Open All Year

Closed 24 - 26 December

B&B Rates are per Person Sharing per Night incl. Breakfast.
or **Room Rates** are per Room per Night - See also Page 8

South East 383

Dungarvan

Park Hotel	Powersfield House	Seaview

Park Hotel

Dungarvan,
Co. Waterford

Tel: 058-42899 Fax: 058-42969
Email: photel@indigo.ie
Web: www.flynnhotels.com

HOTEL ★★★ MAP 3 K 4

Overlooking the Colligan River Estuary, owned and run by the Flynn Family, whose experience in the hotel business is your best guarantee of an enjoyable and memorable stay. The hotel's spacious and comfortable bedrooms have been furnished with flair and imagination. All have private bathroom, direct dial telephone, 16 channel satellite TV. The hotel's leisure centre has a 20m swimming pool, sauna, steam room & gym.

Bookable on www.irelandhotels.com

B&B from €70.00 to €80.00

*Pierce Flynn
Manager*

Member of:

Special Offer: Weekend Specials from €135.00 pps
(2 Nights B&B & 1 Dinner)

29 29

Closed 24 - 26 December

Powersfield House

Ballinamuck,
Dungarvan,
Co. Waterford

Tel: 058-45594 Fax: 058-45550
Email: powersfieldhouse@cablesurf.com
Web: www.powersfield.com

GUESTHOUSE ★★★ MAP 3 K 4

Powersfield House is in the heart of West Waterford, one of Ireland's most beautiful locations close to the Colligan Woodland, magnificent beaches at Clonea & Helvic Head & Dungarvan's 3 golf courses. The perfect place to indulge yourself. We provide luxury accommodation with delicious breakfasts. Dinner is served to residents, advance booking is required. AA ♦♦♦♦, Bridgestone Guide 100 Best Places To Stay. Eunice's cooking described by John Mc Kenna of Bridgestone fame as "Nothing less than a triumph, a superb demonstration of cooking with a professional élan that sent us singing into the night".

Bookable on www.irelandhotels.com
Member of Les Routiers

B&B from €50.00 to €65.00

Eunice Power

Member of:

Special Offer: Midweek Specials from €150.00 pps
(3 Nights B&B)

6 6

Closed 24 - 26 December

Seaview

Windgap,
N25 / Youghal Road, Dungarvan,
Co. Waterford

Tel: 058-41583 Fax: 058-41679
Email: faheyn@gofree.indigo.ie
Web: www.amireland.com/seaview/

GUESTHOUSE ★★★ MAP 3 K 4

Want your vacation to never stop being a vacation? Enjoy breakfast overlooking the sea? Play one of Dungarvan's three 18 hole golf courses or take a bus tour of the area and let someone else do the driving. How about dinner, entertained by traditional Irish musicians, at the nearby Marine Bar? Make every ounce of your vacation count. Try Seaview on N25, 5km west of Dungarvan. Fax and e-mail facilities available. Continental and full Irish breakfast served. Laundry service available.

Bookable on www.irelandhotels.com
Member of Premier Guesthouses

B&B from €30.00 to €45.00

*Nora & Martin & Mealla
Fahey*

Member of:

8 8

Open All Year

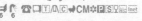

B&B Rates are per Person Sharing per Night incl. Breakfast.
or **Room Rates** are per Room per Night - See also Page 8

Beach Guest House

1 Lower Village,
Dunmore East,
Co. Waterford

Tel: 051-383316 Fax: 051-383319
Email: beachouse@eircom.net
Web: www.dunmorebeachguesthouse.com

GUESTHOUSE ★★★★ MAP 4 M 5

Newly built in a superb location overlooking Dunmore East Strand. The Beach Guesthouse provides luxury accommodation, stunning sea views and private parking. A central base from which to explore charming hidden coves, superb cliff walks and neat rows of pretty thatched cottages in this picturesque village 10 miles from Waterford, in the centre of Dunmore with excellent restaurants and sporting amenities nearby including 4 championship golf courses within 10 miles. AA/RAC ♦♦♦♦. Disabled access room available.

Bookable on www.irelandhotels.com
Member of Premier Guesthouses

B&B from €35.00 to €45.00

Breda Battles
Host

Member of:
IRISH HOTELS FEDERATION

Special Offer: Midweek Special from €100.00 pps
3 Nights B&B excluding Jul - Aug

7   7

Closed 01 November - 28 February

Haven Hotel

Dunmore East,
Co. Waterford

Tel: 051-383150 Fax: 051-383488
Email: info@thehavenhotel.com
Web: www.thehavenhotel.com

HOTEL ★★ MAP 4 M 5

The Haven Hotel is family owned and managed. Situated in Dunmore East, one of Ireland's most beautiful seaside resorts. The restaurant is renowned for its first class food and specialises in prime rib beef, steaks and locally caught seafood. The Haven is an ideal location for day trips to the many surrounding golf clubs. Children are also made especially welcome, with our motto being - the children of today are the customers of tomorrow.

B&B from €55.00 to €75.00

Jean & John Kelly
Managers / Owners

Member of:
IRISH HOTELS FEDERATION

Special Offer: Weekend Specials from €145.00 pps
(2 Nights B&B & 1 Dinner)

13   13

Closed 31 October - 01 March

Ocean Hotel

Dunmore East,
Co. Waterford

Tel: 051-383136 Fax: 051-383576
Email: oceanhotel@ireland.com
Web: www.theoceanhotel.com

HOTEL ★★ MAP 4 M 5

The Ocean Hotel 15 minutes drive from Waterford City, is situated in one of Ireland's most picturesque villages. The jewel of the sunny South East. We offer you the personal attention and service only a family-run hotel can provide. Our extensive à la carte menu is available in both dining room and bar with a strong emphasis on seafood dishes. Our menu is reasonably priced. Golf packages arranged. Our new Alfred D Snow Bar is air-conditioned with décor depicting a nautical theme. Entertainment in the bar most nights during the summer and Saturday nights all year around.

B&B from €55.00 to €75.00

Brendan Gallagher
Proprietor

Activities:

Member of:
IRISH HOTELS FEDERATION

Special Offer: Midweek Specials from €150.00 pps
(3 Nights B&B)

12   12

Closed 25 December

B&B Rates are per Person Sharing per Night incl. Breakfast.
or Room Rates are per Room per Night - See also Page 8

Co. Waterford

Faithlegg / Tramore

Faithlegg House Hotel and Golf Club	Beach Haven House	Grand Hotel
Faithlegg, Co. Waterford	Tivoli Terrace, Tramore, Co. Waterford	Tramore, Co. Waterford
Tel: 051-382000 Fax: 051-382010 Email: reservations@fhh.ie Web: www.faithlegg.com	Tel: 051-390208 Fax: 051-330971 Email: beachhavenhouse@eircom.net Web: www.beachhavenhouse.com	Tel: 051-381414 Fax: 051-386428 Email: thegrandhotel@eircom.net Web: www.grand-hotel.ie

HOTEL ★★★★ MAP 4 M 5 | **GUESTHOUSE ★★★ MAP 4 L 5** | **HOTEL ★★★ MAP 4 L 5**

A Tower Group Hotel - Faithlegg House Hotel is located on the already renowned 18-hole championship golf course, overlooking the estuary of the River Suir. This elegantly restored country house hotel incorporates 82 bedrooms, including 14 master rooms in the original house; a unique fitness, health and beauty club featuring a 17m pool; plus comprehensive meeting, conference and event management facilities. RAC ◆◆◆◆ recommended. AA and RAC 4**** approved. Special offers available on www.towerhotelgroup.com

This luxurious home in the heart of Tramore has a warm and friendly atmosphere. Newly extended and refurbished to the highest standards. Minutes walk to beach, Splashworld and racecourse with several championship golf courses in the area. All rooms are en suite with TV, phone and tea/coffee facilities. Extensive breakfast menu, family suites and private parking. AA ◆◆◆◆ accredited.

The Grand Hotel is owned and managed by the Treacy family and combines its traditional surroundings with friendly staff to create its unique atmosphere. There are 82 en suite bedrooms with tea/coffee making facilities, hairdryers, multi-channel TV and DD telephone. The award-winning Doneraile Restaurant has a panoramic view of Tramore Strand and extensive menus with something for everyone. Visit Duffy's Bar with exciting bar menus and live entertainment at weekends and every night in July and August.

Bookable on www.irelandhotels.com | *Bookable on www.irelandhotels.com* | *Bookable on www.irelandhotels.com*
Member of Tower Hotel Group | Member of Irish Guests |

B&B from €95.00 to €170.00 | **B&B from €35.00 to €40.00** | **B&B from €45.00 to €70.00**

Paul McDaid
General Manager - South East

Activities: ✓ 🛁

Member of: IRISH HOTELS FEDERATION

Avery & Niamh Coryell
Owners

Member of: IRISH HOTELS FEDERATION

Tom & Anna Treacy
Proprietors

Activities: ✓ 🛁

Member of: IRISH HOTELS FEDERATION

Special Offer: *Midweek Specials from €165.00 pps (2 Nights B&B & 1 Dinner)*

Special Offer: *Midweek Specials from €60.00 pps (2 Nights B&B)*

Special Offer: *Weekend Specials from €99.00 pps (2 Nights B&B & 1 Dinner)*

Closed 04 January - 06 February	Open All Year	Closed 24 - 26 December

B&B Rates are per Person Sharing per Night incl. Breakfast.
or Room Rates are per Room per Night - See also Page 8

Majestic Hotel

Tramore,
Co. Waterford

Tel: 051-381761 Fax: 051-381766
Email: info@majestic-hotel.ie
Web: www.majestic-hotel.ie

HOTEL ★★★ MAP 4 L 5

A warm welcome awaits you at the award-winning Majestic Hotel, overlooking Tramore Bay and its famous 5km of sandy beach. Only 10km from Waterford City. All 59 bedrooms are en suite with TV, phone, hairdryer and tea/coffee facilities. Full leisure facilities available to guests at Splashworld Health and Fitness Club near hotel. Golf packages our speciality on South East sunshine circuit. Les Routiers Gold Key Award.

Bookable on www.irelandhotels.com
Member of Kay Jay Hotels & Resorts

B&B from €50.00 to €80.00

Aoife O'Reilly
General Manager

Activities:

✔

Member of:

IRISH
HOTELS
FEDERATION

Special Offer: Weekend Specials from €99.00 pps
(2 Nights B&B & 1 Dinner)

59 59

Open All Year

Top Two Visitor Attractions
Lismore, Co. Waterford.

Lismore Castle Gardens & Art Gallery

Prince John first built a castle in Lismore in 1185, and a round tower, dating from the 13th century still stands today. Within the defensive walls of the castle, the gardens at Lismore provide spectacular views, and the herbaceous border gives an impressive show of colour throughout summer. There is also a fine selection of specimen magnolias, camellias, and rhododendrons, and a remarkable yew walk where Edward Spenser is said to have written the 'Faerie Queen'. While wandering the gardens, visitors are invited to enjoy several pieces of contemporary sculpture, and the West-Wing of the Castle has been developed as a gallery for contemporary art, providing a vibrant programme to be enjoyed by the local community and tourists alike. Visitors to the gardens are welcome to visit the gallery free of charge. Lismore Castle is the Irish home of the Duke of Devonshire and his family and, when unoccupied, the castle may be rented, fully staffed, to guests.

Tel: 058 54424 Fax: 058 54896
E-mail: lismorestates@eircom.net
Website: www.lismorecastle.com
Open daily 1.45p.m. to 4.45p.m.
from 26th. March to 2nd. October.
(11 a.m. opening during high season).
Admission charges:
€6 (adults) €3 (children)

Lismore Heritage Centre

Situated in the centre of the town, is a must for those who wish to experience the rich history of the town and its surroundings. Your host Brother Declan (alias Niall Toibin) will take you on a fascinating journey through time in "The Lismore Experience" – an exciting audio-visual presentation which tells the story of the town since St. Carthages arrival in 636AD. Also exhibition galleries on Monastic, Norman and Medieval Lismore and a science exhibition room on the life and works of Robert Boyle, 'the Father of Modern Chemistry' who was born at Lismore Castle. Guided tours of this monastic town leave the Heritage Centre at appointed times each day.

Open 9.30am – 5.30pm
Monday – Friday (year round)
10am – 5.30pm Saturday
(April – September)
12noon – 5.30pm Sunday
(April – September)

Admission charges €4 (adults)
Special rates for families and OAP's
Tel: 058 54975 Fax: 058 53009
e-mail: lismoreheritage@eircom.net

B&B Rates are per Person Sharing per Night incl. Breakfast.
or Room Rates are per Room per Night - See also Page 8

O'Shea's Hotel

Strand Street,
Tramore,
Co. Waterford
Tel: 051-381246 Fax: 051-390144
Email: info@osheas-hotel.com
Web: www.osheas-hotel.com

HOTEL ★★★ MAP 4 L 5

O'Shea's is an intimate family-run hotel, genuinely warm and welcoming to all, situated beside Tramore's safe sandy beach. Just minutes from "Splashworld Health & Fitness Club" (special discount for guests). All our rooms are en suite with TV, phone, tea/coffee making facilities. Superb restaurant, award-winning bar food, entertainment most nights. We specialise in golfing holidays - choice of excellent courses in the South East. We look forward to meeting you.

B&B from €45.00 to €85.00

Joe & Noreen O'Shea Proprietors

Activities:

Member of:

Special Offer: Weekend Specials from €125.00 pps (2 Nights B&B & 1 Dinner)

30 30

Closed 24 - 27 December

Ard Ri Hotel (The)

Ferrybank,
Waterford
Tel: 051-832111 Fax: 051-832863
Email: reservations@ardri.org
Web: www.ardri.org

HOTEL ★★★ MAP 4 L 5

The Ard Ri Hotel is newly refurbished and set on 10 acres of parkland grounds. All our rooms command stunning views of the River Suir and the historical Waterford City, which lies literally at its feet. Enjoy excellent cuisine in Bardens Restaurant or informal dinning in our Conor Bar. Extensive conference facilities to accommodate 7 to 700 delegates. The hotel also boasts a superior leisure centre. Enjoy Waterford Crystal, the old mediaeval sites and the new bustling town centre. Excellent local golf courses and Dunmore & Tramore beaches plus lots more locally.

Bookable on www.irelandhotels.com
Member of Cara Hotels

B&B from €45.00 to €80.00

Sheila Baird General Manager

Activities:

Member of:

Special Offer: Midweek Special from €179.00 pps (4 Nights B&B & 4 Dinners)

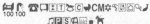

100 100

Closed 24 - 28 December

Arlington Lodge
Town House & Restaurant

John's Hill,
Waterford City
Tel: 051-878584 Fax: 051-878127
Email: info@arlingtonlodge.com
Web: www.arlingtonlodge.com

HOTEL ★★★★ MAP 4 L 5

Maurice Keller's Arlington Lodge Hotel is a gracious 18th century Georgian house, formerly the Bishop's Palace for over 200 years. Converted to a luxury town house & restaurant in 2000, it is situated in its own private grounds yet only 8 minutes walk from the city centre. The emphasis is on hospitality, good food and wine. Breakfast is a delight and should never be missed. Maurice's attention to detail and easy informality make Arlington Lodge the perfect venue for any occasion. Boardroom/meeting room facilities, complimentary broadband in all bedrooms.

Bookable on www.irelandhotels.com
Member of Les Routiers Ireland

B&B from €75.00 to €145.00

Maurice Keller Manager / Proprietor

Member of:

20 20

Closed 24 - 27 December

Athenaeum House Hotel

Christendom,
Ferrybank,
Waterford
Tel: 051-833999 Fax: 051-833977
Email: info@athenaeumhousehotel.com
Web: www.athenaeumhousehotel.com

HOTEL ★★★★ MAP 4 L 5

Athenaeum House Hotel is a 4**** boutique hotel set amidst 6 acres of parkland on the banks of the River Suir overlooking Waterford City. Offering a lifestyles elegance, with modern chic décor. Providing the ultimate in comfort and luxury for discerning travellers. Featuring Zaks Restaurant, state of the art meeting rooms, all bedrooms, including de luxe rooms & suites, are individually designed with TV, mini-hi-fi, mini-bar, voicemail and broadband.

Bookable on www.irelandhotels.com
Member of Manor House Hotels

Room Rate from €90.00 to €250.00

Mailo & Stan Power
Joint Proprietors

Activities:

Member of:

Special Offer: Available Upon Request

Closed 24 - 27 December

A Day to Remember
Welcome to Waterford. Enjoy the Experience.

Factory Tour
Retail Store
Craft & Jewellery Giftstore

Gatchell's Restaurant
World Wide Shipping
Global Refund

WATERFORD
CRYSTAL
VISITOR CENTRE™

OPENING HOURS

RETAIL STORE
Jan & Feb, Nov & Dec 7 days Mon-Sun 9.00am - 5.00pm
March to October incl. 7 days Mon-Sun 8.30am - 6.00pm

FACTORY TOUR
Jan & Feb, Nov & Dec 5 days Mon-Fri 9.00am - 3.15pm *(last tour)*
March to October incl. 7 days Mon-Sun 8.30am - 4.00pm *(last tour)*

FOR INFORMATION: T: +353 51 332500 F: +353 51 332716
E: visitorreception@waterford.ie www.waterfordvisitorcentre.com

Waterford® Crystal and the Seahorse device and all products are the Trade Marks of Waterford Wedgwood plc, Kilbarry, Waterford, Ireland. ©2004 Waterford Crystal Ltd.

B&B Rates are per Person Sharing per Night incl. Breakfast.
or **Room Rates** are per Room per Night - See also Page 8

Co. Waterford

Waterford City

Belfry Hotel

Conduit Lane,
Waterford

Tel: 051-844800 Fax: 051-844814
Email: info@belfryhotel.ie
Web: www.belfryhotel.ie

HOTEL ★★★ MAP 4 L 5

The Belfry is a family-run hotel that has a special ambience, combining traditional charm with superb modern amenities. Bedrooms are spacious and luxurious. Riada's Restaurant offers a well chosen and varied à la carte menu for dinner, while an extensive bar menu is available daily in the popular and stylish Chapter House Bar. City centre location, close to bus and rail station. Superb range of golf courses nearby. Golf packages available.

Member of Les Routiers

B&B from €50.00 to €85.00

Sharon Mansfield
General Manager

Member of:
IRISH HOTELS FEDERATION

Special Offer: Weekend Specials from €125.00 pps (2 Nights B&B & 1 Dinner)

49 49

Closed 24 - 30 December

Bridge Hotel

No 1 The Quay,
Waterford

Tel: 051-877222 Fax: 051-877229
Email: info@bridgehotelwaterford.com
Web: www.bridgehotelwaterford.com

HOTEL ★★★ MAP 4 L 5

Whether your stay in Waterford's Viking City is one of business or pleasure, you will quickly find that the Bridge Hotel, situated in the heart of this vibrant & exciting city, is exactly where you will want to stay. This 133 en suite bedroom hotel offers the finest traditions of quality & service expected from a traditional 3*** hotel. Our restaurants specialise in local seafood & succulent steaks. Relax & enjoy a drink in our Timbertoes Bar. 2 minutes walk from bus & rail stations. Entertainment 7 nights a week. The Bridge Hotel for excellence in customer care. AA ***. Golf, family, golden years & many seasonal packages available.

Bookable on www.irelandhotels.com

B&B from €49.00 to €79.00

Bridget & Jim Treacy
Proprietors

Activities:

Member of:
IRISH HOTELS FEDERATION

Special Offer: Midweek Specials from €139.00 pps (3 B&B & 1 Dinner, 4th night free)

133 133

Closed 24 - 27 December

Coach House

Butlerstown Castle,
Butlerstown, Cork Road,
Waterford

Tel: 051-384656 Fax: 051-384751
Email: coachhse@iol.ie
Web: www.iol.ie/~coachhse

GUESTHOUSE ★★★ MAP 4 L 5

Surround yourself with comfort in this elegantly restored 19th century house. Situated 3 miles from Waterford City (Waterford Crystal 5 minutes away) in an historic, tranquil, romantic setting (13th century castle in grounds). All rooms en suite. 5 golf courses within 6 mile radius. Excellent pubs, restaurants in nearby Waterford. 3*** Irish Tourist Board, AA ♦♦♦♦, Michelin recommended, Best Magazine's No.1 in Ireland. 'Crackling fires and personal attention'.

B&B from €55.00 to €55.00

Des O'Keeffe
Proprietor

Member of:
IRISH HOTELS FEDERATION

7 7

Closed 01 November - 01 April

B&B Rates are per Person Sharing per Night incl. Breakfast. or Room Rates are per Room per Night - See also Page 8

Diamond Hill Country House	Dooley's Hotel	Granville Hotel
Slieverue, Waterford	The Quay, Waterford	Meagher Quay, Waterford
Tel: 051-832855 Fax: 051-832254 Email: info@stayatdiamondhill.com Web: www.stayatdiamondhill.com	Tel: 051-873531 Fax: 051-870262 Email: hotel@dooleys-hotel.ie Web: www.dooleys-hotel.ie	Tel: 051-305555 Fax: 051-305566 Email: stay@granville-hotel.ie Web: www.granville-hotel.ie

GUESTHOUSE ★★★ MAP 4 L 5 | **HOTEL ★★★ MAP 4 L 5** | **HOTEL ★★★ MAP 4 L 5**

Situated 2km from Waterford City off the Rosslare Waterford Road N25. Convenient to ferries. A long established guesthouse of considerable charm and friendliness, set in its own national award-winning gardens. The house has been extensively refurbished incorporating family heirlooms and antiques resulting in a countryside oasis, a haven of luxury and tranquillity, yet only minutes from the bustling city of Waterford. Recommended by Frommers, Foders, Michelin, AA ◆◆◆◆. Member of Premier Guesthouses.

The waters of the River Suir swirl past the door of this renowned hotel, which is situated on The Quay in Waterford. Dooley's is an ideal choice for a centrally located hotel, close to all amenities, cultural and business centres. This family owned and managed hotel caters for the corporate/leisure traveller. The hotel has a purpose-built conference centre with full facilities - The Rita Nolan Conference and Banqueting Suite. Enjoy the style and comfort of The New Ship Restaurant and Dry Dock Bar. Dooley's Hotel serving the customer for three generations.

One of Waterford's most prestigious city centre hotels, RAC**** overlooking the River Suir. This family-run hotel is one of Ireland's oldest with significant historical connections. Justly proud of the Granville's heritage, owners Liam and Ann Cusack today vigourously pursue the Granville's long tradition of hospitality, friendliness and comfort. It has been elegantly refurbished, retaining its old world Georgian character. Award-winning Bianconi Restaurant, Thomas Francis Meagher Bar.

Bookable on www.irelandhotels.com
Member of Premier Guesthouses | Member of Holiday Ireland Hotels | Member of Best Western Hotels

B&B from €35.00 to €45.00 | **B&B from €50.00 to €100.00** | **B&B from €65.00 to €110.00**

 *Bernard Smith-Lehane Proprietor*

 Margaret & Tina Darrer Directors

Activities:

 Ann & Liam Cusack Managers / Proprietors

Activities:

Member of:
 | Member of: | Member of:

Special Offer: Weekend Specials from €125.00 pps (2 Nights B&B & 1 Dinner)

17 17	113 113	98 98

Closed 20 - 26 December	**Closed 25 - 28 December**	**Closed 24 - 27 December**

B&B Rates are per Person Sharing per Night incl. Breakfast. or Room Rates are per Room per Night - See also Page 8

Co. Waterford

Waterford City

Quality Hotel Waterford

Canada Street,
Waterford

Tel: 051-856600 Fax: 051-856605
Email: info@qualityhotelwaterford.com
Web: www.qualityhotelwaterford.com

HOTEL U MAP 4 L 5

The Quality Hotel Waterford is ideally located in the heart of Waterford City, nestled on the banks of the River Suir 5 minutes walk from Waterford City Centre. 81 superbly appointed en suite guest rooms, all offering the essentials for a comfortable stay. Relax by the river in Lannigans Restaurant or the Waterfront Bar. Other facilities include riverside terrace, conference facilities and a private underground car park.

Bookable on www.irelandhotels.com
Member of Quality Hotels

B&B from €49.00 to €109.00

Karen Dollery
General Manager

Activities:

Member of:

81 81

Closed 21 - 26 December

Rhu Glenn Country Club Hotel

Luffany,
Slieverue,
Waterford

Tel: 051-832242 Fax: 051-832242
Email: info@rhuglennhotel.com
Web: www.rhuglennhotel.com

HOTEL ★★ MAP 4 L 5

Built within its own grounds with parking for cars, coaches, etc., the hotel is family-run. Situated on the N25 Rosslare to Waterford Road, convenient to ferries, it offers a superb location whether your pleasure be golfing, fishing, or simply exploring the South East. All rooms are en suite with direct dial phone and multi-channel TV. Our Luffany Restaurant is renowned for its service of fine food. Relax and enjoy our Sliabh Mór lounge bars and the Country Club for ballroom dancing with live entertainment provided by Ireland's top artistes.

B&B from €40.00 to €70.00

Liam Mooney
Proprietor

Activities:

Member of:

*Special Offer: Midweek Specials from €115.00 pps
(3 Nights B&B)*

30 30

Closed 24 - 25 December

Rice Guesthouse & Batterberry's Bar

35 & 36 Barrack Street,
Waterford

Tel: 051-371606 Fax: 051-357013
Email: info@riceguesthouse.com
Web: www.riceguesthouse.com

GUESTHOUSE U MAP 4 L 5

Waterford's premier city centre guesthouse, located 2 minutes from Waterford's City Square Shopping Centre and Waterford Crystal Gallery. Offering our customers hotel accommodation at guesthouse prices. Purpose built in 1997, all rooms en suite with cable TV, direct dial phones & tea/coffee facilities. Full bar and resident's bar, Batterberry's Bar offers ceol and craic with live music 5 nights a week, bar food and the finest Irish hospitality. Tee times arranged for golfers. Midweek and weekend break specials available.

Bookable on www.irelandhotels.com
Member of Premier Guesthouses

B&B from €35.00 to €55.00

John & Jimmy Fitzgerald

Activities:

Member of:

20 20

Closed 23 - 27 December

B&B Rates are per Person Sharing per Night incl. Breakfast.
or **Room Rates** are per Room per Night - See also Page 8

St. Albans Guesthouse

Cork Road,
Waterford

Tel: 051-358171 Fax: 051-358171
Email: stalbansbandb@yahoo.com
Web: www.stalbanswaterford.com

GUESTHOUSE ★★ MAP 4 L 5

St. Albans is a well established family-run guesthouse. Ideally located minutes walk from Waterford City Centre and Waterford Crystal. Our very spacious superbly appointed rooms are all en suite with multi-channel TV, tea/coffee facilities and hairdryer. Secure parking at rear of premises. 4 championship golf courses in vicinity. Horse riding 3km. Tennis courts, swimming pool 2 minutes. Several local beaches and breathtaking scenery. Bus and train station a short distance.
Freephone:
UK: 0800 912 3910
USA: 0877 207 3910

B&B from €35.00 to €55.00

Tom & Helen Mullally
Proprietors

Member of:
IRISH HOTELS FEDERATION

🏠🦮 ⛛🆃🅲🆄🅿▪
8 8

Closed 18 - 28 December

Tower Hotel & Leisure Centre

The Mall,
Waterford

Tel: 051-862300 Fax: 051-870129
Email: reservations@thw.ie
Web: www.towerhotelwaterford.com

HOTEL ★★★ MAP 4 L 5

A Tower Group Hotel - with its riverside location in the heart of Waterford City and 139 guest bedrooms offering every modern amenity, the Tower Hotel is the flagship hotel of the Tower Hotel Group. The Tower Hotel is the ideal base to discover this wonderful city and county, with two restaurants - traditional carvery and award-winning Bistro, Riverside Bar, leisure centre with 20m pool, extensive conference facilities and private guest car park. Free internet access in each guest bedroom. Special online offers available on www.towerhotelgroup.com

Bookable on www.irelandhotels.com
Member of Tower Hotel Group

B&B from €50.00 to €110.00

Paul McDaid
General Manager - South East

Activities:
🏊🏋

Member of:
IRISH HOTELS FEDERATION

Special Offer: Midweek Specials from €123.00 pps
(2 Nights B&B & 1 Dinner)

🏠🦮 ☎⛛🆃↗🅲▪CM🏊🛁🌀♫♪
139 139   🅿🆂🆀🔲♨🐕🦮

Closed 24 - 28 December

Waterford Castle Hotel & Golf Club

The Island,
Ballinakill,
Waterford

Tel: 051-878203 Fax: 051-879316
Email: info@waterfordcastle.com
Web: www.waterfordcastle.com

HOTEL U MAP 4 L 5

Waterford Castle Hotel & Golf Club is uniquely situated on a 310 acre island overlooking the estuary of the River Suir, 3 miles from Waterford City. Access to the island is by a chain linked car ferry. Furnished with antiques and open fireplaces. The 15th century castle combines gracious living of an elegant past with every modern comfort, service and convenience. Own 18 hole championship golf course. Excellent dining experience.

Bookable on www.irelandhotels.com
Member of Best Loved Hotels

Room Rate from €195.00 to €450.00

Gillian Butler
General Manager

Activities:
🏊

Member of:
IRISH HOTELS FEDERATION

Special Offer: Available Upon Request

🏠🦮 ☎⛛🆃🅲↗CM🏊❄♨🍴♫🅿🔲
19 19   🆎🦮

Closed 03 January - 09 February

B&B Rates are per Person Sharing per Night incl. Breakfast.
or Room Rates are per Room per Night - See also Page 8

Co. Waterford - Co. Wexford

Waterford City / Arthurstown

Waterford Manor Hotel	Woodlands Hotel	Dunbrody Country House Hotel & Spa
Killotteran, Waterford	Dunmore Road, Waterford	Arthurstown, Co. Wexford
Tel: 051-377814 Fax: 051-354545 Email: sales@waterfordmanorhotel.ie Web: www.waterfordmanorhotel.ie	Tel: 051-304574 Fax: 051-304575 Email: info@woodlandshotel.ie Web: www.woodlandshotel.ie	Tel: 051-389600 Fax: 051-389601 Email: dunbrody@indigo.ie Web: www.dunbrodyhouse.com

HOTEL U MAP 4 L 5 — **HOTEL ★★★ MAP 4 L 5** — **HOTEL ★★★★ MAP 4 M 5**

Situated just 3 miles from Waterford City and located on 16 acres of gardens, the Waterford Manor Hotel is the ideal venue for a quiet relaxing break. It is the perfect setting for private parties and weddings and with its purpose built conference centre, it is the most sought after manor hotel in the South-East.

This contemporary hotel offers 47 stylish bedrooms, modern leisure centre (pool, sauna, jacuzzi, steam room, gym), lively bar with regular entertainment, stylish Arbutus Restaurant and air-conditioned conference and banqueting facilities. Our new addition is Caroline's Hair & Beauty Salon offering a wide variety of hair and beauty treatments. Just 3 miles from Waterford's City Centre and a short drive from local golf courses and sandy beaches.

Dunbrody Country House Hotel & Cookery School is regarded as one of Ireland's top country retreats. Offering unrivalled cuisine with a wonderfully relaxed ambience, guests return again and again. Member of both Small Luxury Hotels of the World and Ireland's Blue Book. Dunbrody is also recommended by numerous guides and is the recipient of "Restaurant of the year 2004".

Bookable on www.irelandhotels.com
Member of Select Hotels of Ireland

Member of Ireland's Blue Book

B&B from €65.00 to €80.00 — **B&B from €45.00 to €95.00** — **B&B from €125.00 to €250.00**

Pat & Kate Coughlan — Derek Andrews — Kevin & Catherine Dundon Owners

Activities:

Member of: HOTELS

Special Offer: Weekend Specials from €99.00 pps (2 Nights B&B & 1 Dinner)

Special Offer: Weekend Specials from €229.00 pps (2 Nights B&B & 1 Dinner)

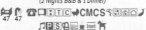

Closed 31 December - 02 January	Open All Year	Closed 22 - 27 December

B&B Rates are per Person Sharing per Night incl. Breakfast. or Room Rates are per Room per Night - See also Page 8

Stanville Lodge Hotel	Carlton Millrace Hotel (The)	Courtown Hotel

Stanville Lodge Hotel

Barntown,
Co. Wexford

Tel: 053-913 4300 Fax: 053-913 4989
Email: info@stanville.ie
Web: www.stanville.ie

HOTEL ★★★ MAP 4 N 6

Stanville Lodge is positioned in the picturesque countryside, just minutes from Wexford Town. Offering 32 finely appointed bedrooms, junior suites and executive rooms. Comprising of state of the art conference and banqueting facilities for up to 200 delegates. For the ultimate dining experience, quality & service are assured in our O' Nuaills Bistro Restaurant, lounge, daily carvery and bar. "Relish the experience".

Bookable on www.irelandhotels.com

B&B from €45.00 to €100.00

Shane Carroll
General Manager

Member of:
IRISH HOTELS FEDERATION

*Special Offer: Weekend Specials from €89.00 pps
(2 Nights B&B & 1 Dinner)*

32 32 ☎ 🖥️🍴🄣🅣🄰🄲➤CM✳🌡️♨️♪🎵🄿🅂
🅐 aid 🍺 Inet WiFi 🐕 ⛳

Closed 25 - 27 December

Carlton Millrace Hotel (The)

Carrigduff,
Bunclody,
Co. Wexford

Tel: 053-937 5100 Fax: 053-937 5124
Email: info@millrace.ie
Web: www.millrace.ie

HOTEL N MAP 8 N 7

Opened in Sept 04, this AA 4**** hotel has 60 well appointed bedrooms including family suites. Lady Lucy's fine dining rooftop restaurant overlooks the picturesque town of Bunclody. The Millrace Spa with 10 treatments suites and dedicated relaxation room with heated loungers. Bunclody is situated on the N80 between Carlow and Enniscorthy, 80 mins drive from Dublin, 45 mins from Rosslare.

Bookable on www.irelandhotels.com

B&B from €85.00 to €125.00

John Varley
Operation Director for Carlton
Group

Activities:

Member of:
IRISH HOTELS FEDERATION

*Special Offer: Midweek Specials from €99.00 pps
(2 Nights B&B and 1 Dinner)*

60 60 ☎ 🖥️🍴🄣🅣🄶➤CM✳🌡️🌀🖥️♨️♨️🍴
♪🄿🅂🅐 aid 🍺 Inet 🐕 ⛳

Closed 24 - 27 December

Courtown Hotel

Courtown Harbour,
Gorey,
Co. Wexford

Tel: 053-942 5210 Fax: 053-942 5304
Email: reservations@courtownhotel.com
Web: www.courtownhotel.com

HOTEL ★★ MAP 8 O 7

The family-run Courtown Hotel & Leisure Centre is renowned for its friendly atmosphere and excellent cuisine. This is an AA 3*** hotel and features the AA award-winning "Bradley's" Restaurant and a selection of lounge bars and beer garden. All rooms are en suite with T.V. and direct dial telephone. Residents enjoy complimentary use of our leisure facilities which include an indoor heated swimming pool, sauna, jacuzzi & steam room. Weddings and parties a speciality.

B&B from €50.00 to €90.00

Marlene Durkin
General Manager

Member of:
IRISH HOTELS FEDERATION

*Special Offer: Weekend Specials from €99.00 pps
(2 Nights B&B & 1 Dinner)*

22 22 ☎ 🖥️🍴🅣🄲➤CM✳🌀🖥️♨️🅿️🅂🄐
aid 🍺

Closed 10 November - 07 March

B&B Rates are per Person Sharing per Night incl. Breakfast.
or **Room Rates** are per Room per Night - See also Page 8

Harbour House Guesthouse	Hotel Curracloe	Lemongrove House
Courtown Harbour, Courtown, Gorey, Co. Wexford	Curracloe, Co. Wexford	Blackstoops, Enniscorthy, Co. Wexford
Tel: 053-942 5117 Fax: 053-942 5117	Tel: 053-913 7308 Fax: 053-913 7587	Tel: 053-923 6115 Fax: 053-923 6115
Email: stay@harbourhouseguesthouse.com	Email: hotelcurracloe@eircom.net	Email: lemongrovehouse@iolfree.ie
Web: www.harbourhouseguesthouse.com	Web: www.hotelcurracloe.com	Web: www.euroka.com/lemongrove

GUESTHOUSE ★★ MAP 8 O 7 | **HOTEL ★★ MAP 4 O 6** | **GUESTHOUSE ★★★ MAP 4 N 6**

Harbour House just off the main Rosslare/Dublin N11 route and only 6km from Gorey is ideally located in the renowned seaside resort of Courtown Harbour. Harbour House is the ideal base for both business and holiday travellers and is central to all amenities and only three minutes from Courtown's sandy beaches. All rooms are en suite. Private car park. Come and enjoy Courtown's new 25m swimming pool. 2 kiddies pools and a 65m water slide all set within 63 acres of woodland with beautiful river walks.

Hotel Curracloe is ideally situated, only five miles from Wexford Town, minutes from Blue/Green Flag beaches and central to golfing, angling, bird-watching, hill walking and horse riding amenities. Our 29 rooms are en suite with modern facilities and our award-winning Blake Restaurant and Tavern Pub serve the best of home produce. The Brent Banqueting Room will cater for every special occasion. Our friendly staff will ensure that Hotel Curracloe is the perfect base for your leisure time in the sunny South East.

Elegant country house 1km north of Enniscorthy just off roundabout on Dublin/Rosslare Road (N11). Lemongrove House is set in mature gardens with private parking. All rooms en suite with direct dial phone, TV, hairdryer and tea/coffee making facilities. Recommended by Guide du Routard, AA and other leading guides. Within walking distance of a choice of restaurants, pubs and new pool and leisure centre. Locally we have beaches, golf, horse riding, walking and quad track.

B&B from €37.50 to €45.00	B&B from €45.00 to €50.00	B&B from €33.00 to €40.00

Donal & Margaret O'Gorman
Proprietors

John & Margaret Hanrahan
Owners

Colm & Ann McGibney
Owners

Member of:

Member of:

Member of:

Special Offer: Room Only Per Person from €30.00

Special Offer: Weekend Specials from €95.00 pps (2 Nights B&B & 1 Dinner)

13 13

29 29

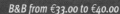
9 9

Closed 31 October - 10 April	Open All Year	Closed 20 - 29 December

B&B Rates are per Person Sharing per Night incl. Breakfast.
or Room Rates are per Room per Night - See also Page 8

Pines Country House Hotel

Camolin,
Enniscorthy,
Co. Wexford
Tel: 053-938 3600 Fax: 053-938 3588
Email: thepines@eircom.net
Web: www.pinescountryhousehotel.com

HOTEL ★★ MAP 4 N 6

Family-run hotel with award-winning resturant, European and real Indian food. Top class accommodation, state of the art gym, sauna, steam room, plunge pool, pony trekking, hill walking, birdwatching. Nearby Courtown and Curracloe beaches, historic Ferns, heritage park, quad trekking, fishing, music and on-site bouncy castle/slide, horse riding, trampolines and sunshine. Music on Saturdays.

Bookable on www.irelandhotels.com

B&B from €38.00 to €80.00

Frank Murhill
Director Manager

Activities:
✓

Member of:
IRISH HOTELS FEDERATION

Special Offer: *Weekend Specials from €115.00 pps (2 Nights B&B & 1 Dinner)*

11 11

Open All Year

Riverside Park Hotel and Leisure Club

The Promenade,
Enniscorthy,
Co. Wexford
Tel: 053-923 7800 Fax: 053-923 7900
Email: info@riversideparkhotel.com
Web: www.riversideparkhotel.com

HOTEL ★★★ MAP 4 N 6

Nestling along the scenic banks of the River Slaney, the Riverside Park Hotel and Leisure Club is an ideal base for touring the treasures of the sunny South East. With a choice of two superb restaurants, The Moorings and The Alamo, Tex-Mex at its best. A luxurious bar with spectacular views. Relax and unwind in our 15m indoor swimming pool, sauna, steam room, jacuzzi and gym.

Bookable on www.irelandhotels.com

B&B from €79.00 to €85.00

Jim Maher
General Manager

Activities:
✓ 🎾

Member of:
IRISH HOTELS FEDERATION

Special Offer: *Golden Years Over 55's from €175.00 pps (3 Nights B&B and 3 Dinners)*

60 60

Closed 24 - 26 December

Irish National Heritage Park
Ferrycarrig, Co. Wexford

Tel: +353 53 20733
Fax: +353 53 20911
Email: info@inhp.com
Web: www.inhp.com

"Over 9000 years of History"

Stroll through the park with its homesteads, places of ritual, burial modes and long forgotten remains.

Opening Times
Jan-Dec 9.30am-6.30pm
Times subject to
seasonal change.

Facilities:
- Guided Tours
- Restaurant
- Gift & Craft Shop
- Free car / coach parking

B&B Rates are per Person Sharing per Night incl. Breakfast.
or **Room Rates** are per Room per Night - See also Page 8

Treacy's Hotel	Horse and Hound Inn	Ashdown Park Hotel Conference & Leisure Centre
Templeshannon, Enniscorthy, Co. Wexford Tel: 053-923 7798 Fax: 053-923 7733 Email: info@treacyshotel.com Web: www.treacyshotel.com	Ballinaboola, Foulksmills, Co. Wexford Tel: 051-428323 Fax: 051-428471 Email: info@horseandhound.net Web: www.horseandhound.net	Coach Road, Gorey, Co. Wexford Tel: 053-948 0500 Fax: 053-948 0777 Email: info@ashdownparkhotel.com Web: www.ashdownparkhotel.com

HOTEL ★★★ MAP 4 N 6	GUESTHOUSE N MAP 4 N 5	HOTEL ★★★★ MAP 8 O 7

Situated in the heart of beautiful Enniscorthy, Treacy's Hotel has an ideal location for both excitement and relaxation. Whether it's sport, music, fine dining or a memorable night-life you desire, you need look no further. A world of choice is available including; Chang Thai - our authentic Thai resturant, Bagenal Harvey - European Continental style cuisine and in our Temple Bar we have an Italian style Bistro menu. Temple Bar and Benedicts superpub provide top Irish entertainment and our new heated all-weather beer garden is pure relaxation.

The Horse and Hound Inn Hotel is a family-run hotel in picturesque Ballinaboola, a small village on the N25 from Rosslare. Accommodation is provided in 27 tastefully decorated guest rooms. Catering for all needs - from private parties, weddings to conferences. A haven for weary tourists or busy delegate. Food served all day in our renowned restaurant. You are sure of a friendly welcome from the Murphy family and their professional staff.

On arrival at The Ashdown Park Hotel you will experience the grandeur of what we are about, 79 beautifully appointed guest rooms and suites, each have been tastefully designed. Enjoy the food on offer all day or just relax with regular live entertainment. Facilities include conference & banqueting facilities, the award-winning Rowan Tree Restaurant, Ivy & Coach Bars, Leisure Club & Beauty Studio and complimentary car park. The Ashdown Park Hotel has been awarded RAC **** AA **** ITB****.

Bookable on www.irelandhotels.com | | *Bookable on www.irelandhotels.com*

B&B from €60.00 to €120.00	B&B from €50.00 to €70.00	B&B from €80.00 to €130.00

Anton Treacy | *Christy Murphy* | *Liam Moran*
General Manager

Member of:

Activities:

Member of:

Special Offer: Weekend Specials from €110.00 pps (2 Nights B&B & 1 Dinner)

48 48

27 27

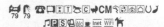

79 79

Closed 24 - 26 December	Closed 25 December	Open All Year

B&B Rates are per Person Sharing per Night incl. Breakfast. or Room Rates are per Room per Night - See also Page 8

Marlfield House Hotel	Hotel Saltees	Quay House

Marlfield House Hotel
Gorey,
Co. Wexford

Tel: 053-942 1124 Fax: 053-942 1572
Email: info@marlfieldhouse.ie
Web: www.marlfieldhouse.com

HOTEL ★★★★ MAP 8 O 7

This fine Regency period house is set in 36 acres of grounds and filled with antiques. The Bowe family opened its doors to guests in 1978 and has maintained an outstanding reputation for food, comfort and service ever since. The 20 bedrooms are filled with antiques, paintings and flowers and all have marble bathrooms. There are six sumptuous state rooms overlooking the lake. Member of Relais & Chateaux, AA Red Star and RAC Gold Ribbon. Highly acclaimed conservatory restaurant.

Bookable on www.irelandhotels.com
Member of Relais et Chateaux

B&B from €128.00 to €138.00

Mary Bowe
Proprietor

Member of:

🛏🏃 ☎📺T⏰CM❄🅿♨UP🎷🐕🐾
20 20

Closed 15 December - 25 January

Hotel Saltees
Kilmore Quay,
Co. Wexford

Tel: 053-912 9601 Fax: 053-912 9602
Email: info@hotelsaltees.ie
Web: www.hotelsaltees.ie

HOTEL ★★ MAP 4 N 5

Newly refurbished and under new management, Hotel Saltees is situated in the picturesque fishing village of Kilmore Quay. Renowned for its thatched cottages and maritime flavour, it is located just 22km from Wexford Town and 19km from the international port of Rosslare. Offering excellent accommodation, with all rooms en suite, TV, telephone and all well designed to cater for families. Le Saffron Restaurant is renowned for its relaxed atmosphere where diners can afford good food at their own leisurely pace. Eurotoque chef Dominique Dayot specialises in modern and French cuisine.

B&B from €45.00 to €65.00

Dominique Dayot
Executive Chef

Activities:
🎣

Member of:
HOTELS

🛏🏃 ☎📺T C❄CMU🎵🎶🅿♨
10 10

Closed 25 December

Quay House
Kilmore Quay,
Co. Wexford

Tel: 053-912 9988 Fax: 053-912 9808
Email: quayhome@iol.ie
Web: www.quayhouse.net

GUESTHOUSE ★★★ MAP 4 N 5

Quay House is a family-run bed and breakfast guesthouse. Deep sea fishing, miles of nature trails, sandy beaches, bird sanctuaries, near to Kilmore Quay, good position in centre of village, private car park. All facilities in rooms, en suite, TV, tea/coffee service in rooms, full Irish breakfast, guest lounge, early ferry breakfasts, 14 miles from ferry port. Spacious rooms, marina, harbour, bars, restaurants, public transport to Wexford Town daily.

B&B from €40.00 to €50.00

Siobhan McDonnell
Proprietor

Member of:

🛏🏃 ☎📺C❄UP S♨
10 10

Closed 25 December

B&B Rates are per Person Sharing per Night incl. Breakfast.
or Room Rates are per Room per Night - See also Page 8

New Ross / Newbawn

Brandon House Hotel, Health Club & Spa	Creacon Lodge Hotel	Cedar Lodge Hotel & Restaurant
New Ross, Co. Wexford	Creacon, New Ross, Co. Wexford	Carrigbyrne, Newbawn, (Near New Ross), Co. Wexford
Tel: 051-421703 Fax: 051-421567	Tel: 051-421897 Fax: 051-422560	Tel: 051-428386 Fax: 051-428222
Email: brandonhouse@eircom.net	Email: info@creaconlodge.com	Email: cedarlodge@eircom.net
Web: www.brandonhousehotel.ie	Web: www.creaconlodge.com	Web: www.prideofeirehotels.com

HOTEL ★★★ MAP 4 M 6	HOTEL ★★★ MAP 4 M 6	HOTEL ★★★ MAP 4 N 6

A de luxe country manor house set in landscaped grounds with panoramic views overlooking the River Barrow. Dine in the Gallery Restaurant or relax in the Library Bar. All rooms are elegantly furnished. Luxurious health & leisure club with 20m pool, sauna, steam room, jacuzzi, fully equipped gym, kiddies pool, hydrotherapy grotto and thalasso treatment room. Nearby golf, angling, beaches, horse riding and gardens. An ideal base for touring the sunny South East. Crèche available. Conference and banqueting for up to 400 people.

Imagine a country house covered with clematis, fuchsia, jasmine, quince, a fig tree and an exquisite rose garden . . . This is Creacon Lodge Hotel. Guests can relax in the ambient surroundings, enjoy genuine hospitality and fine food and quite simply, be pampered. Individually decorated bedrooms are en suite with DD phone and T.V. Ideally situated for touring the South-East and convenient to J.F.Kennedy Park and Homestead, Dunbrody Famine Ship and Hook Peninsula. Local amenities include golf, angling, horse riding and sandy beaches.

Charming boutique country hotel located in a picturesque setting, 30 minutes drive from Rosslare Port on the N25 New Ross Road. All bedrooms en suite with direct dial phone and TV. The restaurant, which concentrates on freshly prepared produce, is noted for its good food. Recommended by Michelin, Good Hotel Guide, RAC, AA. Forest walks nearby. Golf, horse riding, JF Kennedy Park, county museum, heritage park and sandy beaches within easy driving distance.

Bookable on www.irelandhotels.com | *Bookable on www.irelandhotels.com* | *Bookable on www.irelandhotels.com*

B&B from €65.00 to €85.00	B&B from €55.00 to €85.00	B&B from €75.00 to €100.00

Grace McPhillips
General Manager

Activities:

Member of:

Josephine Flood
Proprietor

Member of:

Tom Martin
Proprietor

Member of:

Special Offer: Weekend Specials from €145.00 pps (2 Nights B&B & 1 Dinner)

Special Offer: Weekend Specials from €135.00 pps (2 Nights B&B & 1 Dinner)

Special Offer: Weekend Specials from €185.00 pps (2 Nights B&B & 1 Dinner)

80 80

10 10

28 28

Closed 24 - 27 December	Closed 24 - 27 December	Closed 20 December - 01 February

B&B Rates are per Person Sharing per Night incl. Breakfast. or Room Rates are per Room per Night - See also Page 8

Churchtown House

Tagoat,
Rosslare,
Co. Wexford
Tel: 053-913 2555 Fax: 053-913 2577
Email: info@churchtownhouse.com
Web: www.churchtownhouse.com

GUESTHOUSE ★★★★ MAP 4 0 5

This delightful award-winning Queen Anne Country House, set in its own 8 acres; offers a peaceful escape from the bustling world. 1/2 mile from the N.25 Rosslare Harbour, Wexford, Cork, Dublin Road, 2 miles from the renowned seaside resort of Rosslare Strand. Suites, superior and ground floor rooms available. A non-smoking house. Country house style dinner offered at 7.30pm - 8pm commences with complimentary sherry. Good wines. Please book by noon. RAC Little Gem 2005, RAC ◆◆◆◆, AA 5 Red Diamonds.   Welcome to our "Special Home".

Bookable on www.irelandhotels.com
Member of Manor House Hotels

B&B from €55.00 to €65.00

Austin & Patricia Cody
Owners

Member of:
IRISH HOTELS FEDERATION

Special Offer: *Weekend Specials from €145.00 pps (2 Nights B&B & 1 Dinner)*

🏨🐾 ☎🖥️📺©❄️☀️♨️📶🅿️🛵🐕 12 12

Closed 30 November - 01 March

Crosbie Cedars Hotel

Rosslare,
Co. Wexford
Tel: 053-913 2124 Fax: 053-913 2243
Email: info@crosbiecedarshotel.com
Web: www.crosbiecedarshotel.com

HOTEL ★★★ MAP 4 0 5

In Rosslare resort, only 3 minutes from the beach, and 5 minutes from Rosslare Golf Course, Crosbie Cedars Hotel provides a warm welcome with traditional hospitality. All rooms en suite, TV, radio, direct dial telephone, hairdryer and tea/coffee facilities. Restaurant menus of excellent quality and variety. Extensive bar menu. Entertainment weekends and nightly July & August. Available nearby tennis, watersports, childrens' playground, crazy golf. 15 minutes to ferry.

Bookable on www.irelandhotels.com

B&B from €50.00 to €75.00

Donncha Crosbie
Manager

Activities:
⛳🎾

Member of:
IRISH HOTELS FEDERATION

Special Offer: *Midweek Specials from €147.00 pps (3 Nights B&B)*

🏨🐾 ☎🖥️📺©📺©❄️CM❄️☀️♨️📶🅿️🛵🐕 34 34
🆔♿🐕

Closed 03 January - 14 February

Danby Lodge Hotel

Rosslare Road,
Killinick, Rosslare,
Co. Wexford
Tel: 053-915 8191 Fax: 053-915 8191
Email: danby@eircom.net
Web: www.danbylodgehotel.com

HOTEL U MAP 4 0 5

Nestling in the heart of south county Wexford, Danby Lodge Hotel has rightfully earned for itself a reputation for excellence in cuisine and accommodation. Once the home of the painter Francis Danby, 1793-1861, this hotel bears all the hallmarks of a charming country residence. Conveniently located on main Rosslare to Wexford Road (N25). Danby Lodge Hotel offers the visitor a quiet country getaway yet just minutes drive from the port of Rosslare and the town of Wexford. RAC and AA recommended.

B&B from €45.00 to €65.00

Claire Farrell
Manager

Member of:
IRISH HOTELS FEDERATION

Special Offer: *Weekend Specials from €99.00 pps (2 Nights B&B & 1 Dinner)*

🏨🐾 ☎🖥️📺©❄️CM❄️☀️♨️📶🅿️🛵🐕 28 28
🆔♿🐕

Closed 22 - 30 December

B&B Rates are per Person Sharing per Night incl. Breakfast.
or **Room Rates** are per Room per Night - See also Page 8

Co. Wexford

Rosslare / Rosslare Harbour

Kelly's Resort Hotel	Ferryport House	Great Southern Hotel

Kelly's Resort Hotel

Rosslare,
Co. Wexford

Tel: 053-913 2114 Fax: 053-913 2222
Email: kellyhot@iol.ie
Web: www.kellys.ie

HOTEL ★★★★ MAP 4O5

Since 1895 the Kelly family have created a truly fine resort hotel. Good food, wine and nightly entertainment are very much part of the tradition. Amenities include tennis, snooker, bowls, croquet and a choice of local golf courses. Pamper yourself and relax in our new 'SeaSpa' incorporating thermal spa, 12 treatment rooms, seaweed baths and Serial Mud Chamber. Special activity midweeks in Spring & Autumn - wine tasting, cooking, gardening, painting, etc.

Bookable on www.irelandhotels.com
Member of Les Routiers

B&B from €77.00 to €94.00

William J Kelly
Manager / Director

Activities:

Member of:

Special Offer: (Spring or Autumn) 3 Nights B&B, Dinner & Lunch from €396.00 pps

118 118

Closed 11 December - 17 February

Ferryport House

Rosslare Harbour,
Co. Wexford

Tel: 053-913 3933 Fax: 053-916 1707
Email: info@ferryporthouse.com
Web: www.ferryporthouse.com

GUESTHOUSE ★★★ MAP 4O5

400m from Rosslare Euro Port & train station.16 beautifully appointed newly refurbished en suite bedrooms. Fantastic new restaurant opened July 2005 boasts fresh fish dishes from Kilmore Quay and fuses authentic cooking from the Far East. Fusion Restaurant is a unique dining experience. Local amenities include Blue Flag Beach, local golf courses, horse riding and fishing.

B&B from €30.00 to €50.00

Billy & Patrica Roche
Proprietors

16 16

Open All Year

Great Southern Hotel

Rosslare Harbour,
Co. Wexford

Tel: 053-913 3233 Fax: 053-913 3543
Email: res@rosslare-gsh.com
Web: www.greatsouthernhotels.com

HOTEL ★★★ MAP 4O5

In Rosslare, a favourite resort, the Great Southern Hotel provides a warm welcome with traditional hospitality. The hotel is beautifully situated on a cliff-top overlooking Rosslare Harbour. All rooms are en suite with TV, radio, hairdryer and tea/coffee facilities. Enjoy the leisure centre with indoor swimming pool, jacuzzi, steam room, the comfortable lounges and excellent food of the Mariner's Restaurant. Central reservations Tel: 01-214 4800 or UTELL.

Bookable on www.irelandhotels.com

Room Rate from €79.00 to €160.00

Eoin O'Sullivan
General Manager

Activities:

Member of:

Special Offer: Weekend Specials from €140.00 pps
(2 Nights B&B & 1 Dinner)

100 100

Closed 01 January - 28 February

B&B Rates are per Person Sharing per Night incl. Breakfast.
or Room Rates are per Room per Night - See also Page 8

Harbour View Hotel	Hotel Rosslare	Faythe Guest House

Harbour View Hotel

Rosslare Harbour,
Co. Wexford

Tel: 053-916 1450 Fax: 053-916 1455
Email: info@harbourviewhotel.ie
Web: www.harbourviewhotel.ie

HOTEL ★★★ MAP 405

Overlooking Rosslare Euro Port, this charming hotel is situated ideally on the N25 within walking distance of the ferry terminal, train and bus stations. It boasts 24 beautifully appointed guest rooms, all en suite with TV, coffee/tea making facilities, hairdryer, telephone and safe. You can enjoy the finest Asian and European cuisine in the exquisite surroundings of the Seasons Chinese Restaurant or the warm atmosphere of the Mail Boat Bar. Local amenities include golf, angling, horse riding and sandy beaches.

Bookable on www.irelandhotels.com

B&B from €45.00 to €75.00

James & Grace Chan

Member of:
IRISH HOTELS FEDERATION

24 24 ☎️📋T C CM🎵🎵P S🔒🍴

Open All Year

Hotel Rosslare

Rosslare Harbour,
Co. Wexford

Tel: 053-913 3110 Fax: 053-913 3386
Email: reservations@hotelrosslare.ie
Web: www.hotelrosslare.ie

HOTEL ★★★ MAP 405

Situated on the cliff-top overlooking Rosslare Harbour, Hotel Rosslare boasts stunning views of the bay and Irish Sea. 25 en suite bedrooms, many with sea views and private balconies located 2 minutes from Rosslare Europort, ideal for ferry travel. The historic town of Wexford with its quaint streets, boutiques and arts & crafts outlets is only 15 minutes away. Hotel Rosslare offers the perfect location for business, leisure and family breaks all year round.

Bookable on www.irelandhotels.com

B&B from €55.00 to €65.00

Dean Diplock
General Manager

Member of:
IRISH HOTELS FEDERATION

Special Offer: *Midweek Specials from €135.00 pps*
(3 Nights B&B)

25 25 ☎️📋T C⬛CM☎️🎵🎵P S🔒🍴
🐕

Closed 24 - 25 December

Faythe Guest House

The Faythe,
Swan View,
Wexford

Tel: 053-912 2249 Fax: 053-912 1680
Email: faythhse@iol.ie
Web: www.faytheguesthouse.com

GUESTHOUSE ★★★ MAP 406

Family-run guesthouse in a quiet part of the town centre, is built on the grounds of a former castle of which one wall remains today. All rooms refurbished recently to the highest standard. Some of our rooms overlook Wexford Harbour. All rooms have bathroom en suite, colour TV, DVD player, direct dial phone, clock radios and tea/coffee facilities. Rosslare Ferry Port is only 15 minutes drive (early breakfast on request). We also have a large private car park.

Bookable on www.irelandhotels.com
Member of Premier Guesthouses

B&B from €28.50 to €50.00

Damian & Siobhan Lynch
Proprietors

Member of:
IRISH HOTELS FEDERATION

10 10 ☎️📋T⬛✳️J P S🍴

Closed 25 - 27 December

B&B Rates are per Person Sharing per Night incl. Breakfast.
or Room Rates are per Room per Night - See also Page 8

South East 403

Wexford Town

Ferrycarrig Hotel	Newbay Country House	Quality Hotel & Leisure Wexford

Ferrycarrig Hotel

Ferrycarrig Bridge,
Wexford

Tel: 053-912 0999 Fax: 053-912 0982
Email: ferrycarrig@ferrycarrighotel.com
Web: www.ferrycarrighotel.ie

HOTEL ★★★★ MAP 4 N 6

Renowned Ferrycarrig Hotel has one of the most spectacular locations of any hotel in Ireland, with every room providing memorable views of the River Slaney Estuary. Offers contemporary luxurious, spacious bedrooms, award-winning service, excellent waterfront dining, award-winning waterfront bar, 5***** health and fitness club with 20m pool, on site Beauty and Wellness Lodge and hairdresser. Abundance of historic, cultural and sporting amenities, including golf are nearby. Excellent conference facilities for 4 - 400 delegates.

Bookable on www.irelandhotels.com

B&B from €65.00 to €160.00

Jeanette O'Keeffe
General Manager

Activities:

Member of:

Special Offer: *Midweek Specials from €180.00 pps
(3 Nights B&B, Nov - Feb)*

102 102

Open All Year

Newbay Country House

Newbay,
Wexford

Tel: 053-914 2779 Fax: 053-914 6318
Email: newbay@newbayhouse.com
Web: www.newbaycountryhouse.com

GUESTHOUSE ★★★ MAP 4 O 6

Charming Georgian house, set in magnificent gardens, including a wood. 12 en suite bedrooms many with 4 poster beds with garden views. Boasting a spectacular bridal suite. For casual dining, the Cellar Bistro and Courtyard are open 7 days for lunch and dinner. Now fully licensed and serving bar food all day, everyday.

B&B from €45.00 to €85.00

Alex Scallan
Sales & Marketing Manager

Member of:

Special Offer: *Weekend Specials from €129.00 pps
(2 Nights B&B & 1 Dinner)*

12 12

Open All Year

Quality Hotel & Leisure Wexford

New Ross Roundabout,
Wexford

Tel: 053-917 2000 Fax: 053-917 2001
Email: info@qualityhotelwexford.com
Web: www.qualityhotelwexford.com

HOTEL N MAP 4 O 6

New to Wexford superb new 3*** standard hotel with every comfort. With 108 generously sized guest rooms, including a number of family rooms for up to 2 children. Great menu at Lannigan's Restaurant and great atmosphere in the Glenville Bar & Lounge. Club Vitae health and fitness club and beauty suites for complete pampering. Supervised crèche and outdoor playground on site. The most modern in conference and meeting facilities also available.

Bookable on www.irelandhotels.com
Member of Quality Hotels

B&B from €49.00 to €109.00

Anthony Spencer
General Manager

Activities:

Member of:

108 108

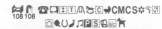

Closed 25 - 26 December

B&B Rates are per Person Sharing per Night incl. Breakfast. or <u>Room Rates</u> are per Room per Night - See also Page 8

Riverbank House Hotel

The Bridge,
Wexford

Tel: 053-912 3611 Fax: 053-912 3342
Email: info@riverbankhousehotel.com
Web: www.riverbankhousehotel.com

HOTEL ★★★ MAP 4 O 6

The Riverbank House Hotel commands magnificent views of the old Viking town, the River Slaney and the miles of golden beach surrounding Wexford. The hotel boasts an excellent à la carte menu, delicious bar food together with an exciting wine list. Benefiting from its own private car park, the hotel offers easy access to five of the best golf courses in the South East, sea angling sites and shooting - ensuring that whatever your stay, business or leisure, it will be most enjoyable. Conference facilities available.

Bookable on www.irelandhotels.com

B&B from €40.00 to €115.00

Colm Campbell
General Manager

Member of:
IRISH HOTELS FEDERATION

Special Offer: Weekend Specials from €89.00 pps
(2 Nights B&B & 1 Dinner - Jan-Apr)

23 23

Closed 25 December

Talbot Hotel Conference and Leisure Centre

On The Quay,
Wexford Town

Tel: 053-912 2566 Fax: 053-912 3377
Email: sales@talbothotel.ie
Web: www.talbothotel.ie

HOTEL ★★★ MAP 4 O 6

The Talbot Hotel provides the perfect backdrop for relaxing with friends or family. The hotel is situated in the heart of Wexford town on the waters edge, ideal for savouring the beautiful maritime views. Luxuriously appointed guest rooms, Ballast Bank Bar & Grill, Oyster Lane Restaurant, Conference & Banqueting Centre, Quay Leisure Centre, Essence Nail & Beauty Therapy. In the dawning of a new era, The Talbot Hotel still retains it's reputation for old world charm and a friendly atmosphere.

Bookable on www.irelandhotels.com
Member of Talbot Hotel Group

B&B from €55.00 to €95.00

Philip Gavin
Group General Manager

Activities:

Member of:
IRISH HOTELS FEDERATION

Special Offer: Midweek Specials from €115.00 pps
(2 Nights B&B & 1 Dinner)

109 109

Closed 24 - 26 December

Whitford House Hotel Health & Leisure Club

New Line Road,
Wexford

Tel: 053-914 3444 Fax: 053-914 6399
Email: info@whitford.ie
Web: www.whitford.ie

HOTEL ★★★ MAP 4 N 5

One of Irelands leading family-run hotels situated 2 Km from Wexford. Renowned for hospitality, luxury accommodation, "Footprints" award-winning restaurant and superb new health and leisure club boasting 20m pool, gym jacuzzi, sauna and steam room, massage, reflexology and beauty treatments. Locally there is golf, fishing, horse riding and Blue Flag beaches. Attractions include National Heritage Park, Johnstown Castle and Wexford Wildfowl Reserve. AA, RAC and Michelin recommended. Treat your loved ones to a most remarkable hotel.

Bookable on www.irelandhotels.com

B&B from €55.00 to €98.00

The Whitty Family

Member of:
IRISH HOTELS FEDERATION

Special Offer: Midweek Specials from €119.00 pps
(2 Nights B&B & 1 Dinner)

36 36

Closed 24 - 26 December

B&B Rates are per Person Sharing per Night incl. Breakfast.
or Room Rates are per Room per Night - See also Page 8

*H*AVEN'T DONE A TAP TODAY?

OUR QUALITY TEAM DO 7,000 EVERY DAY.

NO WONDER THE GUINNESS IS GREAT

enjoy GUINNESS *sensibly*   The GUINNESS word and the HARP device are registered trade marks.

We invite you to sample the golf, the countryside and the friendship of the Irish people and then to stay in some of Ireland's most charming accommodation. We have listed a range of hotels and guesthouses which are either situated on or close to a golf course. Your host will assist you if necessary in arranging your golfing requirements including tee reservations and green fee charges. A full description of the hotels and guesthouses can be had by looking up the appropriate page number.

Premises are listed in Alphabetical Order in each County.

South West

Co. Cork

Actons Hotel
Kinsale, Co. Cork
Tel: 021-477 9900......................Page 60
Arrangements with Golf Courses:
Kinsale, Old Head of Kinsale, Fota Island, Bandon, Harbour Point, Little Island
Facilities available:

Ambassador Hotel
Cork City, Co. Cork
Tel: 021-455 1996 ....Page 47
Arrangements with Golf Courses:
Fota Island, Little Island, Harbour Point, Douglas, Cork, Water Rock
Facilities available:

Ashlee Lodge
Blarney, Co. Cork
Tel: 021-438 5346......................Page 40
Arrangements with Golf Courses:
Lee Valley, Harbour Point, Fota Island, Muskerry, Cork, Mallow
Facilities available:

Ballymaloe House
Shanagarry, Co. Cork
Tel: 021-465 2531 ....Page 68
Arrangements with Golf Courses:
Wate Rock Golf Course, Fota Golf Course
Facilities available:
TA GC AT AB CH TC HC

Blarney Castle Hotel
Blarney, Co. Cork
Tel: 021-438 5116 ....Page 40
Arrangements with Golf Courses:
Muskerry, Lee Valley, Fota Island, Harbour Point, Mallow, Monkstown
Facilities available:
GP TA GC AT AB CH TC PG HC

Blue Haven Hotel and Restaurant
Kinsale, Co. Cork
Tel: 021-477 2209......................Page 60
Arrangements with Golf Courses:
Kinsale Golf Club, Old Head Golf Club
Facilities available:
GP TA GC AT AB CH TC PG HC

Celtic Ross Hotel Conference & Leisure Centre
Rosscarbery, Co. Cork
Tel: 023-48722 ....Page 67
Arrangements with Golf Courses:
Skibbereen, Bandon, Lisselan, Bantry, Kinsale, Dunmore
Facilities available:
GP TA GC AT AB CH TC PG HC

Commodore Hotel
Cobh, Co. Cork
Tel: 021-481 1277 ....Page 45
Arrangements with Golf Courses:
East Cork, Midleton - 18 Hole Course, Cobh - 9 Hole Course
Facilities available:
GP AT AB PG

Dunmore House Hotel
Clonakilty, Co. Cork
Tel: 023-33352 ....Page 43
Golf Course(s) On Site:
9 Hole Golf Course
Arrangements with Golf Courses:
Macroom, Bandon, Skibbereen, Old Head of Kinsale, The Island and Fota Island
Facilities available:
GP GC AT AB CH TC HC

Emmet Hotel
Clonakilty, Co. Cork
Tel: 023-33394 ....Page 43
Arrangements with Golf Courses:
Dunmore, Lisselan Estate, Bandon, Skibbereen
Facilities available:
GP TA GC AT AB CH TC PG HC

Fernhill Carrigaline Accommodation, Golf & Health Club
Carrigaline, Co. Cork
Tel: 021-437 2226......................Page 42
Golf Course(s) On Site:
18 Hole Golf Course
Arrangements with Golf Courses:
Douglas, Monkstown, Harbour Point, Kinsale - Old Head, Cork, Fota
Facilities available:
GP TA GC AT AB CH TC PG HC

Fernhill House Hotel
Clonakilty, Co. Cork
Tel: 023-33258 ....Page 44
Golf Course(s) On Site:
Par 3 Golf Course
Arrangements with Golf Courses:
Skibbereen, Bandon, Lisselan, Bantry Bay, Lee Valley, Dunmore
Facilities available:
GP TA GC AT AB CH TC PG HC

Glengarriff Eccles Hotel
Glengarriff, Co. Cork
Tel: 027-63003 ....Page 59
Arrangements with Golf Courses:
Bantry Bay, Glengarriff, Ring of Kerry
Facilities available:
GP AB PG

Gresham Metropole
Cork City, Co. Cork
Tel: 021-464 3789 ....Page 51
Arrangements with Golf Courses:
Fota Island, Little Island, Harbour Point, Muskerry, Kinsale
Facilities available:
TA GC AT AB CH TC PG HC

Hibernian Hotel and Leisure Centre
Mallow, Co. Cork
Tel: 022-21588 ....Page 64
Arrangements with Golf Courses:
Mallow, Lee Valley, Charleville, Doneraile, Fota Island, Kanturk
Facilities available:
GP AB PG HC

GP All inclusive Golf Package TA Tuition Available GC Golf Cart / Pull Cart AT Arrange Tee Off Times HC Hire Of Caddy
AB Advance Golf Booking Made CH Hire Of Clubs TC Transport To Course PG Preferential Green Fees
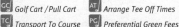

Hotel Isaacs
Cork City, Co. Cork
Tel: 021-450 0011 ....Page 52
Arrangements with Golf Courses:
Lee Valley, Fota Island, Harbour Point, Old Head, Muskerry
Facilities available:

Imperial Hotel with Lifestyle Salon and Spa
Cork City, Co. Cork
Tel: 021-427 4040......................Page 52
Arrangements with Golf Courses:
Fota Island, Douglas, Cork, Muskerry, Lee Valley, Monkstown, Old Head Golf Links
Facilities available:

Lee Valley Hotel
Macroom, Co. Cork
Tel: 026-41082 ....Page 64
Arrangements with Golf Courses:
Lee Valley GC, Macroom GC
Facilities available:

Maryborough House Hotel
Cork City, Co. Cork
Tel: 021-436 5555......................Page 55
Arrangements with Golf Courses:
Douglas, Fota Island, Cork, Kinsale Old Head, Harbour Point, Monkstown
Facilities available:

Old Bank House
Kinsale, Co. Cork
Tel: 021-477 4075......................Page 62
Arrangements with Golf Courses:
Old Head of Kinsale, Kinsale - Farrangalway, Fota Golf Course
Facilities available:

Oriel House Hotel & Leisure Centre
Ballincollig, Co. Cork
Tel: 021-487 0888......................Page 36
Arrangements with Golf Courses:
Lee Valley, Killarney, Muskerry, Fota Island, Cork, Harbour Point
Facilities available:

Quality Hotel & Leisure Centre Clonakilty
Clonakilty, Co. Cork
Tel: 023-36400..........................Page 45
Arrangements with Golf Courses:
Lisselan, Dunmore, Kinsale, Bandon, Skibbereen, Bantry
Facilities available:

Quality Hotel and Leisure Centre Youghal
Youghal, Co. Cork
Tel: 024-93050 ....Page 69
Arrangements with Golf Courses:
Youghal, West Waterford, Dungarvan, Water Rock, Little Island, Fota
Facilities available:

Radisson SAS Hotel & Spa, Cork
Cork City, Co. Cork
Tel: 021-429 7000......................Page 55
Arrangements with Golf Courses:
Fota Island GC, Harbour Point GC
Facilities available:

Rochestown Park Hotel
Cork City, Co. Cork
Tel: 021-489 0800......................Page 56
Arrangements with Golf Courses:
Fota Island, Harbour Point (Little Island), Mahon Golf Club, Douglas G.C, Lee Valley, Monkstown
Facilities available:

Silver Springs Moran Hotel
Cork City, Co. Cork
Tel: 021-450 7533......................Page 57
Arrangements with Golf Courses:
Old Head of Kinsale, Harbour Point GC, Blarney GC, Water Rock GC, Fota Island GC, Bantry GC
Facilities available:

Trident Hotel
Kinsale, Co. Cork
Tel: 021-477 9300......................Page 63
Arrangements with Golf Courses:
Old Head Golf Links, Kinsale Golf Club, Lisselan Golf Club, Fota Island, Lee Valley
Facilities available:

Vienna Woods Hotel
Cork City, Co. Cork
Tel: 021-482 1146 ....Page 57
Arrangements with Golf Courses:
Cork, Harbour Point, Fota, Old Head of Kinsale, Water Rock
Facilities available:

Walter Raleigh Hotel
Youghal, Co. Cork
Tel: 024-92011 ....Page 70
Arrangements with Golf Courses:
Youghal GC, Fota Island GC, Water Rock GC, West Waterford GC, Harbour Point GC, Little Island
Facilities available:

WatersEdge Hotel
Cobh, Co. Cork
Tel: 021-481 5566 ....Page 46
Arrangements with Golf Courses:
Fota Island, Harbour Point, Cobh, Water Rock, East Cork, Old Head of Kinsale, Cork
Facilities available:

West Cork Hotel
Skibbereen, Co. Cork
Tel: 028-21277 ....Page 68
Arrangements with Golf Courses:
Skibbereen, West Carbery
Facilities available:

Westlodge Hotel
Bantry, Co. Cork
Tel: 027-50360..........................Page 40
Arrangements with Golf Courses:
Arrangement with Bantry Bay Golf Club - guaranteed times, 18 hole Championship Course
Facilities available:

White House
Kinsale, Co. Cork
Tel: 021-477 2125 ....Page 63
Arrangements with Golf Courses:
Kinsale (18 Hole) and (9 Hole), Old Head, Bandon, Carrigaline, Muskerry
Facilities available:

 All inclusive Golf Package    Tuition Available   Golf Cart / Pull Cart   Arrange Tee Off Times   Hire Of Caddy
 Advance Golf Booking Made   Hire Of Clubs    Transport To Course   Preferential Green Fees

409

Co. Kerry

Aghadoe Heights Hotel & Spa
Killarney, Co. Kerry
Tel: 064-31766 ....Page 88
Arrangements with Golf Courses:
*Waterville, Ballybunion, Kenmare,
Killarney, Beaufort, Tralee, Dooks*
Facilities available:

Arbutus Hotel
Killarney, Co. Kerry
Tel: 064-31037 ....Page 89
Arrangements with Golf Courses:
*Killarney, Ballybunion, Waterville, Dooks,
Tralee, Ring of Kerry*
Facilities available:

Ard-Na-Sidhe
Caragh Lake, Co. Kerry
Tel: 066-976 9105.......................Page 73
Arrangements with Golf Courses:
*Dooks, Killorglin, Waterville, Beaufort,
Killarney, Tralee*
Facilities available:

Ashville Guesthouse
Killarney, Co. Kerry
Tel: 064-36405 ....Page 89
Arrangements with Golf Courses:
*Killarney, Ross, Dunloe, Beaufort,
Waterville, Dooks, Ballybunion*
Facilities available:

Bianconi
Killorglin, Co. Kerry
Tel: 066-976 1146 ....Page 108
Arrangements with Golf Courses:
*Killarney, Beaufort, Dunloe, Killorglin,
Dooks, Waterville*
Facilities available:

Brehon (The)
Killarney, Co. Kerry
Tel: 064-30700.........................Page 90
Arrangements with Golf Courses:
Killarney, Ross, Beaufort
Facilities available:

Brook Lane Hotel
Kenmare, Co. Kerry
Tel: 064-42077 ....Page 84
Arrangements with Golf Courses:
Ring of Kerry GC, Kenmare GC, Dooks GC
Facilities available:
GP AT PG

Brookhaven Country House
Waterville, Co. Kerry
Tel: 066-947 4431 ....Page 115
Arrangements with Golf Courses:
*Skellig Bay Links, Waterville Links
Course, Ring of Kerry, Dooks*
Facilities available:
TC HC

Butler Arms Hotel
Waterville, Co. Kerry
Tel: 066-947 4144 ....Page 116
Arrangements with Golf Courses:
*Waterville, Dooks, Killarney, Tralee,
Ballybunion, Ring of Kerry, Skellig Bay*
Facilities available:

Carrig Country House
Caragh Lake, Co. Kerry
Tel: 066-976 9100......................Page 74
Arrangements with Golf Courses:
*Dooks, Killarney, Beaufort, Killorglin,
Waterville, Tralee*
Facilities available:

Cashen Course House
Ballybunion, Co. Kerry
Tel: 068-27351 ....Page 71
Arrangements with Golf Courses:
*Ballybunion Old Course, Ballybunion
Cashen Course, Listowel GC, Tralee
(Barrow), Lahinch GC, Doonbeg GC*
Facilities available:
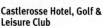

Castlerosse Hotel, Golf &
Leisure Club
Killarney, Co. Kerry
Tel: 064-31144 ....Page 91
Golf Course(s) On Site:
9 Hole Golf Course
Arrangements with Golf Courses:
*Killarney, Beaufort, Dooks,
Mahony's Point, Lackabane, Killorglin*
Facilities available:
GP TA GC AT AB CH PG HC

Derrynane Hotel
Caherdaniel, Co. Kerry
Tel: 066-947 5136......................Page 72
Arrangements with Golf Courses:
*Ring of Kerry, Kenmare, Waterville,
Parknasilla, Beaufort, Dooks, Skellig Bay*
Facilities available:
AT AB PG

Dingle Benners Hotel
Dingle (An Daingean), Co. Kerry
Tel: 066-915 1638 ....Page 78
Arrangements with Golf Courses:
*Dingle Golf Links, Ceann Sibéal,
Castlegregory Golf Club*
Facilities available:
GP GC AT AB CH PG

Dingle Skellig Hotel
& Peninsula Spa
Dingle (An Daingean), Co. Kerry
Tel: 066-915 0200......................Page 78
Arrangements with Golf Courses:
*Dingle Golf Links, Ceann Sibéal,
Castlegregory*
Facilities available:
GP GC AT AB CH PG

Dromhall Hotel
Killarney, Co. Kerry
Tel: 064-39300.........................Page 92
Arrangements with Golf Courses:
*Killarney Golf & Fishing Club, Tralee,
Ballybunion, Waterville, Dooks,
Ring of Kerry*
Facilities available:
GP TA GC AT AB CH TC PG HC

Earls Court House
Killarney, Co. Kerry
Tel: 064-34009.........................Page 93
Arrangements with Golf Courses:
*Killarney, Waterville, Ballybunion, Tralee,
Beaufort, Dooks, Old Head*
Facilities available:
TA GC AT AB CH TC HC

Eviston House Hotel
Killarney, Co. Kerry
Tel: 064-31640 ....Page 93
Arrangements with Golf Courses:
*Ballybunion, Beaufort, Killarney,
Waterville, Dooks, Tralee*
Facilities available:
GP TA GC AT AB CH TC PG HC

 GP All inclusive Golf Package   **TA** Tuition Available   **GC** Golf Cart / Pull Cart   **AT** Arrange Tee Off Times   **HC** Hire Of Caddy
AB Advance Golf Booking Made   **CH** Hire Of Clubs   **TC** Transport To Course   **PG** Preferential Green Fees

Failte Hotel
Killarney, Co. Kerry
Tel: 064-33404 ....Page 94
Arrangements with Golf Courses:
*Lackabane, O'Mahony's Point, Beaufort,
Ross, Castlerosse, Killeen*
Facilities available:
 GC / AT / AB / CH / TC / HC

Fairview Guesthouse
Killarney, Co. Kerry
Tel: 064-34164 ....Page 94
Arrangements with Golf Courses:
*Killarney, Waterville, Tralee, Dooks,
Ballybunion, Beaufort*
Facilities available:
 GP / TA / GC / AT / AB / CH / TC / PG / HC

Foley's Townhouse
Killarney, Co. Kerry
Tel: 064-31217 ....Page 94
Arrangements with Golf Courses:
*Killarney, Barrow, Beaufort, Dooks,
Ballybunion, Waterville*
Facilities available:
 AT / AB

Fuchsia House
Killarney, Co. Kerry
Tel: 064-33743 ....Page 95
Arrangements with Golf Courses:
*Killarney, Tralee, Ballybunion, Waterville,
Dooks, Beaufort*
Facilities available:
 TA / GC / AT / AB / CH / TC / HC

Gleann Fia Country House
Killarney, Co. Kerry
Tel: 064-35035 ....Page 95
Arrangements with Golf Courses:
*Killarney, Beaufort, Tralee, Ballybunion,
Dooks, Waterville, Ring of Kerry Golf
Course, Kenmare, Old Head, Kinsale*
Facilities available:
 GP / TA / GC / AT / AB / CH / TC / PG / HC

Gleneagle Hotel
Killarney, Co. Kerry
Tel: 064-36000 ....Page 96
Arrangements with Golf Courses:
*Killarney, Ross, Beaufort, Ring of Kerry,
Dooks, Ballybunion*
Facilities available:
 GP / AT / TC / PG

Grand Hotel
Tralee, Co. Kerry
Tel: 066-712 1499 ....Page 113
Arrangements with Golf Courses:
*Tralee, Ballybunion, Waterville, Dingle,
Dooks, Killarney*
Facilities available:
 GP / TA / GC / AT / AB / CH / TC / PG / HC

Grove Lodge Riverside Guesthouse
Killorglin, Co. Kerry
Tel: 066-976 1157 ....Page 108
Arrangements with Golf Courses:
*Waterville, Tralee, Ballybunion, Beaufort,
Killarney, Killorglin, Dooks,
Gap of Dunloe, Dingle*
Facilities available:
TA / GC / AT / AB / CH / TC / PG

Harty Costello Town House
Ballybunion, Co. Kerry
Tel: 068-27129 ....Page 71
Arrangements with Golf Courses:
*Ballybunion, Tralee, Listowel,
Ballyheigue, Killarney, Waterville*
Facilities available:
 GP / TA / GC / AT / AB / CH / TC / PG / HC

Hotel Dunloe Castle
Killarney, Co. Kerry
Tel: 064-44111 ....Page 97
Golf Course(s) On Site:
9 Hole Golf Course
Arrangements with Golf Courses:
*Dunloe, Dooks, Beaufort, Killarney, Ross,
Killorglin*
Facilities available:
 GP / TA / GC / AT / AB / CH / TC / HC

Hotel Europe
Killarney, Co. Kerry
Tel: 064-71300 ....Page 97
Golf Course(s) On Site:
18 Hole Golf Course
Arrangements with Golf Courses:
*Killarney, Mahony's Point, Killeen,
Lackabane, Beaufort, Dooks, Killorglin*
Facilities available:
TA / GC / AT / AB / CH / TC / HC

Inveraray Farm Guesthouse
Killarney, Co. Kerry
Tel: 064-44224 ....Page 98
Arrangements with Golf Courses:
*Beaufort, Dunloe, Killarney, Ross,
Killorglin, Dooks*
Facilities available:
TA / GC / AT / AB / CH / TC / HC

Kathleens
Country House
Killarney, Co. Kerry
Tel: 064-32810 ....Page 99
Arrangements with Golf Courses:
*Killarney, Waterville, Tralee, Dooks,
Ballybunion, Beaufort*
Facilities available:
TA / GC / AT / AB / CH / TC / PG / HC

Killarney Avenue Hotel
Killarney, Co. Kerry
Tel: 064-32522 ....Page 99
Arrangements with Golf Courses:
*Killarney, Ballybunion, Tralee, Waterville,
Beaufort, Castleisland*
Facilities available:
 GP / TA / GC / AT / AB / CH / TC / PG / HC

Killarney Lodge
Killarney, Co. Kerry
Tel: 064-36499 ....Page 100
Arrangements with Golf Courses:
*Killarney GC, Tralee, Waterville, Dooks,
Old Head, Beaufort*
Facilities available:
TA / GC / AT / AB / CH / TC / PG / HC

Killarney Park Hotel
Killarney, Co. Kerry
Tel: 064-35555 ....Page 100
Arrangements with Golf Courses:
*Killarney, Ballybunion, Tralee, Waterville,
Dooks, Ring of Kerry*
Facilities available:
 TA / GC / AT / AB / CH / TC / PG

Killarney Plaza Hotel & Spa
Killarney, Co. Kerry
Tel: 064-21111 ....Page 101
Arrangements with Golf Courses:
*Killarney Golf & Fishing Club, Waterville,
Ballybunion, Dooks, Tralee, Old Head of
Kinsale*
Facilities available:
 GP / AT / AB / CH / TC / HC

Killarney Royal
Killarney, Co. Kerry
Tel: 064-31853 ....Page 101
Arrangements with Golf Courses:
*Killarney, Tralee, Dooks, Waterville,
Beaufort, Ross*
Facilities available:
TA / GC / AT / AB / CH / TC / PG

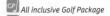  GP All inclusive Golf Package   TA Tuition Available   GC Golf Cart / Pull Cart   AT Arrange Tee Off Times   HC Hire Of Caddy
  AB Advance Golf Booking Made   CH Hire Of Clubs   TC Transport To Course   PG Preferential Green Fees

411

Co. Kerry Continued

Killarney Valley Hotel & Suites
Killarney, Co. Kerry
Tel: 064-23600 ....Page 101
Arrangements with Golf Courses:
Killarney GC, Dooks GC, Beaufort GC
Facilities available:

Kingfisher Lodge Guesthouse
Killarney, Co. Kerry
Tel: 064-37131 ....Page 102
Arrangements with Golf Courses:
Beaufort, Killarney, Killorglin, Waterville, Ballybunion, Tralee
Facilities available:

Lake Hotel
Killarney, Co. Kerry
Tel: 064-31035 ....Page 102
Arrangements with Golf Courses:
Killarney (3 courses), Beaufort, Dooks, Ballybunion, Waterville, Tralee, Ross, Castlerosse, Ring of Kerry
Facilities available:

Lansdowne Arms Hotel
Kenmare, Co. Kerry
Tel: 064-41368 ....Page 84
Arrangements with Golf Courses:
Ring of Kerry Golf Club, Kenmare Golf Club
Facilities available:

McSweeney Arms Hotel
Killarney, Co. Kerry
Tel: 064-31211.........................Page 103
Arrangements with Golf Courses:
Killarney, Waterville, Tralee, Ballybunion, Ring of Kerry, Dooks
Facilities available:

Meadowlands Hotel
Tralee, Co. Kerry
Tel: 066-718 0444 ....Page 114
Arrangements with Golf Courses:
Ballybunion, Tralee (Barrow), Killarney, Dooks, Killorglin, Waterville
Facilities available:

Moorings (The)
Portmagee, Co. Kerry
Tel: 066-947 7108 ....Page 109
Arrangements with Golf Courses:
Waterville Golf Links
Facilities available:

Muckross Park Hotel
Killarney, Co. Kerry
Tel: 064-31938 ....Page 104
Arrangements with Golf Courses:
Beaufort, O'Mahony's Point, Killeen, Ross, Tralee, Ballybunion, Waterville, Dooks
Facilities available:

O'Donnabhain's
Kenmare, Co. Kerry
Tel: 064-42106 ....Page 85
Arrangements with Golf Courses:
Ring of Kerry, Kenmare, Bantry, Waterville
Facilities available:

Old Weir Lodge
Killarney, Co. Kerry
Tel: 064-35593 ....Page 104
Arrangements with Golf Courses:
Killarney, Waterville, Ballybunion, Tralee, Dooks, Beaufort
Facilities available:

Parknasilla Great Southern Hotel
Sneem, Co. Kerry
Tel: 064-45122 ....Page 109
Golf Course(s) On Site:
9 Hole Golf Course
Arrangements with Golf Courses:
Ring of Kerry, Waterville, Killarney, Dooks
Facilities available:

Randles Court Clarion Hotel
Killarney, Co. Kerry
Tel: 064-35333 ....Page 105
Arrangements with Golf Courses:
Killarney, Tralee, Beaufort, Dooks, Ring of Kerry, Ballybunion, Waterville
Facilities available:

Rivermere
Killarney, Co. Kerry
Tel: 064-37933 ....Page 105
Arrangements with Golf Courses:
Killarney (O'Mahony's Point and Killeen), Dooks, Ballybunion, Waterville, Tralee, Ring of Kerry
Facilities available:

Sheen Falls Lodge
Kenmare, Co. Kerry
Tel: 064-41600 ....Page 86
Arrangements with Golf Courses:
Kenmare, Ring of Kerry
Facilities available:

Smerwick Harbour Hotel
Dingle (An Daingean), Co. Kerry
Tel: 066-915 6470....................Page 82
Arrangements with Golf Courses:
Dingle Golf Course (18 hole golf links, par 72)
Facilities available:

Smugglers Inn
Waterville, Co. Kerry
Tel: 066-947 4330 ....Page 116
Arrangements with Golf Courses:
Waterville, Killarney, Dooks, Tralee, Ballybunion, Kenmare, Parknasilla
Facilities available:

Towers Hotel
Glenbeigh, Co. Kerry
Tel: 066-976 8212....................Page 82
Arrangements with Golf Courses:
Dooks, Beaufort, Killorglin, Killarney, Waterville, Ballybunion, Tralee
Facilities available:

Tuscar Lodge
Killarney, Co. Kerry
Tel: 064-31978 ....Page 107
Arrangements with Golf Courses:
Killarney Golf Club, Beaufort, Dooks, Killorglin, Waterville, Tralee
Facilities available:
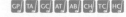

 All inclusive Golf Package   *Tuition Available* 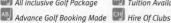 *Golf Cart / Pull Cart*   *Arrange Tee Off Times*  *Hire Of Caddy*
Advance Golf Booking Made *Hire Of Clubs* *Transport To Course* *Preferential Green Fees*

...where to stay when you play!

Waterville Lodge Hotel
Waterville, Co. Kerry
Tel: 066-947 4436 ....Page 117
Arrangements with Golf Courses:
Waterville New Golf & Leisure Club
Facilities available:

Shannon

Co. Clare

Aran View House Hotel & Restaurant
Doolin, Co. Clare
Tel: 065-707 4061 ....Page 124
Arrangements with Golf Courses:
Lahinch Links Course, Lahinch Castle Course, Doonbeg Greg Norman Course, Woodstock, Ennis Golf Club
Facilities available:

Auburn Lodge Hotel
Ennis, Co. Clare
Tel: 065-682 1247 ....Page 126
Arrangements with Golf Courses:
Ennis GC, Dromoland GC, Lahinch GC, Woodstock GC, East Clare GC, Doonbeg GC
Facilities available:

Ballinalacken Castle Country House & Restaurant
Doolin, Co. Clare
Tel: 065-707 4025 ....Page 124
Arrangements with Golf Courses:
Lahinch, Lahinch Castle, Woodstock, Galway Bay, Dromoland Castle, Doonbeg
Facilities available:

Bellbridge House Hotel
Milltown Malbay, Co. Clare
Tel: 065-708 4038 ....Page 138
Arrangements with Golf Courses:
Spanish Point, Lahinch, Doonbeg
Facilities available:

Bunratty Manor Hotel
Bunratty, Co. Clare
Tel: 061-707984 ....Page 123
Arrangements with Golf Courses:
Dromoland, Adare Manor, Shannon, Lahinch, Doonbeg, Ballybunion
Facilities available:

Dough Mor Lodge
Lahinch, Co. Clare
Tel: 065-708 2063....................Page 132
Arrangements with Golf Courses:
Lahinch Golf Club (36 holes), Doonbeg Golf Club, Kilrush, Kilkee
Facilities available:

Falls Hotel Spa & Leisure Centre
Ennistymon, Co. Clare
Tel: 065-707 1004 ....Page 129
Arrangements with Golf Courses:
Lahinch, Doonbeg, Woodstock, Dromoland
Facilities available:

Greenbrier Inn Guesthouse
Lahinch, Co. Clare
Tel: 065-708 1242 ....Page 133
Arrangements with Golf Courses:
Lahinch Championship Links, Lahinch Castle Links, Doonbeg Championship Links, Woodstock (Ennis), Dromoland Castle GC
Facilities available:

Grovemount House
Ennistymon, Co. Clare
Tel: 065-707 1431 ....Page 129
Arrangements with Golf Courses:
Lahinch, Spanish Point, Doonbeg, Ennis, Dromoland
Facilities available:

Halpin's Townhouse Hotel
Kilkee, Co. Clare
Tel: 065-905 6032....................Page 130
Arrangements with Golf Courses:
Ballybunion, Lahinch, Kilkee, Doonbeg, Woodstock, Shannon
Facilities available:

Kilkee Bay Hotel
Kilkee, Co. Clare
Tel: 065-906 0060....................Page 130
Arrangements with Golf Courses:
Kilkee, Kilrush, Doonbeg
Facilities available:

Lahinch Golf & Leisure Hotel
Lahinch, Co. Clare
Tel: 065-708 1100 ....Page 133
Arrangements with Golf Courses:
Lahinch Golf Course, Doonbeg Golf Course, Spanish Point
Facilities available:

Magowna House Hotel
Ennis, Co. Clare
Tel: 065-683 9009....................Page 128
Arrangements with Golf Courses:
Woodstock, Ennis, Lahinch, Dromoland Castle, Shannon, Doonbeg
Facilities available:

Mountshannon Hotel
Mountshannon, Co. Clare
Tel: 061-927162 ....Page 139
Arrangements with Golf Courses:
Bodyke - East Clare Golf Club, Portumna
Facilities available:

Old Ground Hotel
Ennis, Co. Clare
Tel: 065-682 8127 ....Page 128
Arrangements with Golf Courses:
Doonbeg, Lahinch, Woodstock, Ennis, Dromoland, Shannon, East Clare
Facilities available:

Sancta Maria Hotel
Lahinch, Co. Clare
Tel: 065-708 1041 ....Page 134
Arrangements with Golf Courses:
Lahinch Championship Golf Links, Lahinch Castle, Doonbeg, Woodstock, Dromoland, Spanish Point
Facilities available:

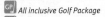 

Co. Clare Continued

Temple Gate Hotel
Ennis, Co. Clare
Tel: 065-682 3300....................Page 128
Arrangements with Golf Courses:
*Woodstock, Ennis, Lahinch, East Clare,
Doonbeg, Dromoland*
Facilities available:

Co. Limerick

**Adare Manor Hotel
& Golf Resort**
Adare, Co. Limerick
Tel: 061-396566 ....Page 140
Golf Course(s) On Site:
18 Hole Golf Course
Facilities available:

Carrabawn House
Adare, Co. Limerick
Tel: 061-396067 ....Page 141
Arrangements with Golf Courses:
*Adare Manor Golf Resort, Limerick Golf &
Country Club, Newcastle West,
Ballybunion, Lahinch*
Facilities available:

Courtenay Lodge Hotel
Newcastle West, Co. Limerick
Tel: 069-62244 ....Page 146
Arrangements with Golf Courses:
*Newcastle West, Adare Manor Golf &
Country Club, Adare Golf Club,
Ballybunion, Charleville, Dingle (Ceann
Sibeal)*
Facilities available:

**Fitzgeralds Woodlands House
Hotel, Health and Leisure Spa**
Adare, Co. Limerick
Tel: 061-605100 ....Page 142
Arrangements with Golf Courses:
*Adare Manor Golf Club, Adare Golf Club,
Newcastle West, Charleville, Limerick
County Golf Club, Castletroy Golf Club*
Facilities available:

Rathkeale House Hotel
Rathkeale, Co. Limerick
Tel: 069-63333 ....Page 147
Arrangements with Golf Courses:
*Adare, Adare Manor, Newcastle West,
Charleville, Ballybunion*
Facilities available:

Co. Tipperary North

**Abbey Court Hotel and
Trinity Leisure Club**
Nenagh, Co. Tipperary North
Tel: 067-41111 ....Page 147
Arrangements with Golf Courses:
*Nenagh, Roscrea, Birr, Portumna,
Thurles, Castletroy*
Facilities available:

Anner Hotel & Leisure Centre
Thurles, Co. Tipperary North
Tel: 0504-21799 ....Page 149
Arrangements with Golf Courses:
Thurles, Dundrum, Templemore
Facilities available:

Grant's Hotel
Roscrea, Co. Tipperary North
Tel: 0505-23300 ....Page 148
Arrangements with Golf Courses:
*Roscrea, Birr, Thurles, Nenagh,
Portumna, Mountrath*
Facilities available:

**Racket Hall Country House
Golf & Conference Hotel**
Roscrea, Co. Tipperary North
Tel: 0505-21748 ....Page 148
Arrangements with Golf Courses:
*Roscrea, Birr, Mountrath, Rathdowney,
Portumna, The Heritage*
Facilities available:

West

Co. Galway

Adare Guest House
Galway City, Co. Galway
Tel: 091-582638 ....Page 163
Arrangements with Golf Courses:
Galway Bay, Oughterard
Facilities available:

Alcock and Brown Hotel
Clifden, Co. Galway
Tel: 095-21206 ....Page 157
Arrangements with Golf Courses:
*Connemara GC, Oughterard GC,
Westport GC*
Facilities available:

Anno Santo Hotel
Galway City, Co. Galway
Tel: 091-523011......................Page 163
Arrangements with Golf Courses:
*Glenlo, Athenry, Galway, Oughterard,
Galway Bay, Barna*
Facilities available:

Ardagh Hotel & Restaurant
Clifden, Co. Galway
Tel: 095-21384 ....Page 157
Arrangements with Golf Courses:
Connemara Championship Links
Facilities available:

Ben View House
Clifden, Co. Galway
Tel: 095-21256 ....Page 158
Arrangements with Golf Courses:
Connemara
Facilities available:

Carrown Tober House
Oughterard, Co. Galway
Tel: 091-552166......................Page 181
Arrangements with Golf Courses:
*Oughterard, Galway, Connemara,
Westport*
Facilities available:

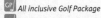 All inclusive Golf Package Tuition Available Golf Cart / Pull Cart Arrange Tee Off Times Hire Of Caddy
 Advance Golf Booking Made Hire Of Clubs Transport To Course Preferential Green Fees

Cashel House Hotel
Cashel, Co. Galway
Tel: 095-31001 ....Page 155
Arrangements with Golf Courses:
Ballyconneely (Clifden)
Facilities available:

Clifden Station House Hotel
Clifden, Co. Galway
Tel: 095-21699 ....Page 159
Arrangements with Golf Courses:
Connemara Chamionship Links
Facilities available:
GP

Connemara Country Lodge
Clifden, Co. Galway
Tel: 095-22122 ....Page 159
Arrangements with Golf Courses:
*Connemara GC, Ballyconneely,
Hazel Wood, Oughterard, Westport*
Facilities available:

Connemara Gateway Hotel
Oughterard, Co. Galway
Tel: 091-552328 ....Page 182
Arrangements with Golf Courses:
Oughterard, Barna Golf and Country Club
Facilities available:

Dun Ri Guesthouse
Clifden, Co. Galway
Tel: 095-21625 ....Page 160
Arrangements with Golf Courses:
Connemara, Westport, Oughterard
Facilities available:

Fairhill House Hotel
Clonbur (An Fháirche), Co. Galway
Tel: 094-954 6176 ....Page 161
Arrangements with Golf Courses:
*Ballinrobe 18 Hole GC (15 mins),
Westport 18 Hole GC (25 mins),
Claremorris 18 Hole GC (25 mins),
Galway 18 Hole GC (40 mins)*
Facilities available:

Forster Court Hotel
Galway City, Co. Galway
Tel: 091-564111 ....Page 168
Arrangements with Golf Courses:
*Galway, Barna, Galway Golf & Country,
Athenry*
Facilities available:

Galway Bay Hotel, Conference & Leisure Centre
Galway City, Co. Galway
Tel: 091-520520 ....Page 168
Arrangements with Golf Courses:
*Galway, Galway Bay, Athenry, Bearna,
Gort*
Facilities available:
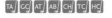

Glenlo Abbey Hotel
Galway City, Co. Galway
Tel: 091-526666 ....Page 169
Golf Course(s) On Site:
18 Hole Golf Course
Arrangements with Golf Courses:
*Glenlo Abbey, Galway, Bearna,
Oughterard, Galway Bay, Connemara*
Facilities available:

Inishmore Guesthouse
Galway City, Co. Galway
Tel: 091-582639 ....Page 170
Arrangements with Golf Courses:
*Barna, Galway Bay, Oughterard, Athenry,
Galway, Gort*
Facilities available:
GP TA GC AT AB CH TC PG HC

Lady Gregory Hotel
Gort, Co. Galway
Tel: 091-632333 ....Page 177
Arrangements with Golf Courses:
Gort
Facilities available:
GP TA GC AT AB CH TC PG HC

Mountain View Guest House
Oughterard, Co. Galway
Tel: 091-550306 ....Page 183
Arrangements with Golf Courses:
*Oughterard, Galway, Connemara,
Westport*
Facilities available:

O'Deas Hotel
Loughrea, Co. Galway
Tel: 091-841611 ....Page 180
Arrangements with Golf Courses:
Loughrea, Curragh, Gort, Galway Bay
Facilities available:

Peacockes Hotel & Complex
Maam Cross, Co. Galway
Tel: 091-552306 ....Page 180
Arrangements with Golf Courses:
*Oughterard, Ballyconneely,
Glenlo Abbey, Barna, Westport*
Facilities available:

Rock Glen Country House Hotel
Clifden, Co. Galway
Tel: 095-21035 ....Page 161
Arrangements with Golf Courses:
Connemara GC
Facilities available:

Rockbarton Park Hotel
Galway City, Co. Galway
Tel: 091-522 018 ....Page 173
Arrangements with Golf Courses:
*Glenlo Abbey, Barna, Athenry, Galway,
Galway Bay, Oughterard*
Facilities available:

Shannon Oaks Hotel & Country Club
Portumna, Co. Galway
Tel: 090-974 1777 ....Page 184
Arrangements with Golf Courses:
*Portumna, Galway Bay, Birr, Glasson,
Gort, Lahinch*
Facilities available:
GP TA GC AT AB CH TC PG HC

St. Clerans Manor House
Craughwell, Co. Galway
Tel: 091-846555 ....Page 162
Arrangements with Golf Courses:
*Galway Bay Golf & Country Club, Athenry,
Lahinch*
Facilities available:

 All inclusive Golf Package    Tuition Available   GC Golf Cart / Pull Cart   AT Arrange Tee Off Times   HC Hire Of Caddy
AB Advance Golf Booking Made   CH Hire Of Clubs   Transport To Course   Preferential Green Fees

Co. Galway Continued

Westwood House Hotel
Galway City, Co. Galway
Tel: 091-521442 ....Page 176
Arrangements with Golf Courses:
Barna, Oughterard, Ballyconneely,
Galway Bay Golf and Country Club
Facilities available:

Co. Mayo

Ashford Castle
Cong, Co. Mayo
Tel: 094-954 6003 ....Page 191
Golf Course(s) On Site:
9 Hole Golf Course
Arrangements with Golf Courses:
Ballyconneely GC, Ballinrobe GC, Galway
Bay GC, Rosses Point GC, Enniscrone GC,
Westport GC
Facilities available:

Atlantic Coast Hotel
Westport, Co. Mayo
Tel: 098-29000 ....Page 195
Arrangements with Golf Courses:
Westport, Enniscrone, Carne,
Ballyconneely, Castlebar, Ballinrobe
Facilities available:

Augusta Lodge
Westport, Co. Mayo
Tel: 098-28900 ....Page 195
Arrangements with Golf Courses:
Westport, Castlebar, Ballinrobe, Carne
Facilities available:

Castlecourt Hotel Conference and Leisure Centre
Westport, Co. Mayo
Tel: 098-55088 ....Page 196
Arrangements with Golf Courses:
Westport, Ballinrobe, Castlebar,
Belmullet, Clew Bay, Enniscrone
Facilities available:

Downhill House Hotel
Ballina, Co. Mayo
Tel: 096-21033 ....Page 188
Arrangements with Golf Courses:
Ballina, Enniscrone, Carne (Belmullet),
Rosses Point, Strandhill, Westport,
Claremorris, Ballinrobe, Castlebar
Facilities available:

Healys Restaurant & Country House Hotel
Pontoon, Co. Mayo
Tel: 094-925 6443....................Page 194
Arrangements with Golf Courses:
Castlebar, Ballina, Westport, Enniscrone,
Carne, Swinford, Ballinrobe, Mulranny
Facilities available:

Hotel Westport, Leisure, Spa, Conference
Westport, Co. Mayo
Tel: 098-25122 ....Page 197
Arrangements with Golf Courses:
Westport, Castlebar, Ballinrobe, Carne
Facilities available:

JJ Gannons Bar, Restaurant & Hotel
Ballinrobe, Co. Mayo
Tel: 094-954 1008 ....Page 189
Arrangements with Golf Courses:
Ballinrobe GC, Carne GC, Westport GC,
Enniscrone GC, Castlebar GC,
Ballyconneely GC
Facilities available:

Knockranny House Hotel & Spa
Westport, Co. Mayo
Tel: 098-28600 ....Page 197
Arrangements with Golf Courses:
Westport, Castlebar, Ballinrobe, Clew
Bay, Mulranny
Facilities available:

Olde Railway Hotel
Westport, Co. Mayo
Tel: 098-25166 ....Page 198
Arrangements with Golf Courses:
Westport Championship 18 Hole,
Castlebar, Ballinrobe, Carne, Connemara,
Rosses Point, Enniscrone
Facilities available:

Ostan Oilean Acla
Achill Island, Co. Mayo
Tel: 098-45138 ....Page 188
Arrangements with Golf Courses:
Achill, Mulranny, Westport, Castlebar,
Ballinrobe, Carne
Facilities available:

Park Inn Mulranny
Mulranny, Co. Mayo
Tel: 098-36000 ....Page 194
Arrangements with Golf Courses:
Westport, Carne, Ballinrobe, Mulranny
Facilities available:

Ryan's Hotel
Cong, Co. Mayo
Tel: 094-954 6243....................Page 192
Arrangements with Golf Courses:
Ballinrobe GC, Claremorris GC,
Ballyconneely GC, Ashford GC,
Castlebar GC
Facilities available:

Stella Maris Country House Hotel
Ballycastle, Co. Mayo
Tel: 096-43322 ....Page 189
Arrangements with Golf Courses:
Carne/Belmullet, Enniscrone,
Bartra Island, Ballina, Rosses Point,
Westport, Castlebar
Facilities available:

Teach Iorrais
Geesala, Co. Mayo
Tel: 097-86888 ....Page 193
Arrangements with Golf Courses:
Carne Links Golf Course, Ballina,
Enniscrone, Westport, Castlebar
Facilities available:

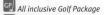 All inclusive Golf Package 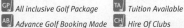 Tuition Available Golf Cart /Pull Cart   Arrange Tee Off Times   Hire Of Caddy
Advance Golf Booking Made Hire Of Clubs Transport To Course Preferential Green Fees

TF Royal Hotel & Theatre
Castlebar, Co. Mayo
Tel: 094-902 3111 ....Page 191
Arrangements with Golf Courses:
Castlebar, Westport, Three Oaks, Ballinrobe, Belmullet, Enniscrone
Facilities available:

Western Strands Hotel
Belmullet, Co. Mayo
Tel: 097-81096 ....Page 190
Arrangements with Golf Courses:
Carne Golf Course
Facilities available:

Westport Plaza Hotel
Westport, Co. Mayo
Tel: 098-51166 ....Page 199
Arrangements with Golf Courses:
Westport, Ballinrobe, Belmullet, Clew Bay, Enniscrone, Castlebar
Facilities available:

Westport Woods Hotel & Spa
Westport, Co. Mayo
Tel: 098-25811 ....Page 199
Arrangements with Golf Courses:
Westport, Castlebar, Ballinrobe, Clew Bay, Carne (Belmullet)
Facilities available:

Wyatt Hotel
Westport, Co. Mayo
Tel: 098-25027 ....Page 199
Arrangements with Golf Courses:
Westport Golf Club, Castlebar Golf Club, Ballinrobe Golf Club, Carne Golf Links
Facilities available:

Co. Roscommon

Abbey Hotel, Conference and Leisure Centre
Roscommon Town, Co. Roscommon
Tel: 090-662 6240 ....Page 200
Arrangements with Golf Courses:
Glasson 18 hole, Carrick-on-Shannon 18 hole, Ballinasloe 18 hole, Longford 18 hole, Roscommon 18 hole
Facilities available:
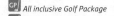

Gleesons Townhouse & Restaurant
Roscommon Town, Co. Roscommon
Tel: 090-662 6954.....................Page 201
Arrangements with Golf Courses:
Roscommon, Ballinasloe, Athlone, Carrick-on-Shannon, Longford, Glasson
Facilities available:

O'Gara's Royal Hotel
Roscommon Town, Co. Roscommon
Tel: 090-662 6317 ....Page 201
Arrangements with Golf Courses:
Roscommon, Glasson, Longford, Athlone
Facilities available:

North West

Co. Donegal

Arnolds Hotel
Dunfanaghy, Co. Donegal
Tel: 074-913 6208 ....Page 211
Arrangements with Golf Courses:
Dunfanaghy 18 Hole Links, Cloughaneely 9 Hole, Parkland, Rosapenna 36 Hole Links, St. Patricks 36 Hole Links, Portsalon 18 Hole Links, Letterkenny 18 Hole Parkland
Facilities available:

Bay View Hotel & Leisure Centre
Killybegs, Co. Donegal
Tel: 074-973 1950 ....Page 212
Arrangements with Golf Courses:
Murvagh (Donegal), Narin, Portnoo, Castle Hume
Facilities available:

Carlton Redcastle Hotel & Thalasso Spa
Moville, Co. Donegal
Tel: 074-938 5555.....................Page 217
Golf Course(s) On Site:
9 Hole Golf Course
Facilities available:

Castle Grove Country House Hotel
Letterkenny, Co. Donegal
Tel: 074-915 1118 ....Page 213
Arrangements with Golf Courses:
Portsalon, Letterkenny, Rosapenna, Ballyliffin
Facilities available:

Dorrians Imperial Hotel
Ballyshannon, Co. Donegal
Tel: 071-985 1147 ....Page 206
Arrangements with Golf Courses:
Murvagh (Donegal), Bundoran
Facilities available:

Downings Bay Hotel
Letterkenny, Co. Donegal
Tel: 074-915 5586 ....Page 214
Arrangements with Golf Courses:
Rosapenna Links, St. Patricks Carrigart Links, Dunfanaghy, Portsalon
Facilities available:

Fort Royal Hotel
Rathmullan, Co. Donegal
Tel: 074-915 8100 ....Page 218
Golf Course(s) On Site:
Par 3 Golf Course
Arrangements with Golf Courses:
Portsalon, Letterkenny, Otway
Facilities available:

Great Northern Hotel
Bundoran, Co. Donegal
Tel: 071-984 1204 ....Page 208
Golf Course(s) On Site:
18 Hole Golf Course
Arrangements with Golf Courses:
Donegal, Strandhill, Rosses Point
Facilities available:

Highlands Hotel
Glenties, Co. Donegal
Tel: 074-955 1111 ....Page 212
Arrangements with Golf Courses:
Narin Portnoo Golf Club
Facilities available:

 All inclusive Golf Package   Tuition Available Golf Cart / Pull Cart Arrange Tee Off Times   Hire Of Caddy
Advance Golf Booking Made Hire Of Clubs Transport To Course Preferential Green Fees

Co. Donegal Continued

Inishowen Gateway Hotel
Buncrana, Co. Donegal
Tel: 074-936 1144 .... Page 208
Arrangements with Golf Courses:
Buncrana, North West Golf Course,
Ballyliffin Old Course, Ballyliffin Glashedy
Course
Facilities available:

Malin Hotel
Malin, Co. Donegal
Tel: 074-937 0606.................... Page 216
Arrangements with Golf Courses:
Ballyliffin Golf Club - Glashedy Links, The
Old Course, Greencastle Golf Club, North
West Golf Club
Facilities available:

McGrorys of Culdaff
Culdaff, Co. Donegal
Tel: 074-937 9104.................... Page 209
Arrangements with Golf Courses:
Ballyliffin Golf Club
Facilities available:

Milford Inn Hotel
Milford, Co. Donegal
Tel: 074-915 3313 .... Page 216
Arrangements with Golf Courses:
Portsalon, Rosapenna, Letterkenny,
Dunfanaghy, Ballyliffin
Facilities available:

Ostan Na Tra (Beach Hotel)
Downings, Co. Donegal
Tel: 074-915 5303 .... Page 211
Arrangements with Golf Courses:
Rosapenna Hotel (2 courses - 36 Holes),
Carrigart Hotel St.Patricks (2 courses - 36
Holes)
Facilities available:

Portsalon Golf Hotel
Portsalon, Co. Donegal
Tel: 074-915 9806 .... Page 217
Golf Course(s) On Site:
18 Hole Golf Course
Arrangements with Golf Courses:
Portsalon, Dunfanaghy, Ballyliffin,
Rosapenna
Facilities available:
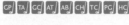

Rosapenna Hotel and Golf Links
Downings, Co. Donegal
Tel: 074-915 5301 .... Page 211
Golf Course(s) On Site:
2 x 18 Hole Golf Courses
Arrangements with Golf Courses:
Old Tom Morris Course, Sandy Hills Links
Facilities available:

Sandhouse Hotel
Rossnowlagh, Co. Donegal
Tel: 071-985 1777 .... Page 218
Arrangements with Golf Courses:
Donegal Murvagh, Bundoran,
Rosses Point, Castle Hume, Ballyliffin,
Portnoo
Facilities available:

Silver Tassie Hotel
Letterkenny, Co. Donegal
Tel: 074-912 5619 .... Page 216
Arrangements with Golf Courses:
Portsalon, Letterkenny, Rosapenna,
Dunfanaghy, Ballyliffin
Facilities available:

Co. Leitrim

Leitrim Marina Hotel
Leitrim Village, Co. Leitrim
Tel: 071-962 2262.................... Page 220
Arrangements with Golf Courses:
Carrick-On-Shannon, Rosses Point,
Ballyconnell
Facilities available:

Shannon Key West Hotel
Rooskey, Co. Leitrim
Tel: 071-963 8800 .... Page 221
Arrangements with Golf Courses:
Longford, Carrick-on-Shannon,
Roscommon
Facilities available:

Co. Sligo

Kingsfort Country House
Ballintogher, Co. Sligo
Tel: 071-911 5111 .... Page 221
Arrangements with Golf Courses:
Co. Sligo, Strandhill, Enniscrone,
Murvagh, Bundoran
Facilities available:

Sligo City Hotel
Sligo Town, Co. Sligo
Tel: 071-914 4000 .... Page 225
Arrangements with Golf Courses:
Strandhill (Sligo), Rosses Point (Sligo),
Murvagh (Donegal)
Facilities available:

Sligo Southern Hotel & Leisure Centre
Sligo Town, Co. Sligo
Tel: 071-916 2101 .... Page 226
Arrangements with Golf Courses:
Rosses Point, Strandhill, Bundoran,
Enniscrone
Facilities available:

Yeats Country Hotel, Spa & Leisure Club
Rosses Point, Co. Sligo
Tel: 071-917 7211 .... Page 223
Arrangements with Golf Courses:
Co. Sligo, Strandhill, Enniscrone,
Bundoran
Facilities available:

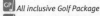 All inclusive Golf Package
 Tuition Available
 Golf Cart / Pull Cart
 Arrange Tee Off Times
 Hire Of Caddy
Advance Golf Booking Made
Hire Of Clubs
Transport To Course
 Preferential Green Fees

North

Co. Antrim

Bayview Hotel
Bushmills, Co. Antrim
Tel: 028-2073 4100..................Page 230
Arrangements with Golf Courses:
Royal Portrush, Portstewart, Castlerock, Ballycastle, Bushfoot, Gracehill, Galgorm Castle
Facilities available:

`GP` `TA` `GC` `AT` `AB` `CH` `TC` `PG` `HC`

Bushmills Inn Hotel
Bushmills, Co. Antrim
Tel: 028-2073 3000 ....Page 230
Arrangements with Golf Courses:
Royal Portrush, Portstewart, Castlerock, Ballycastle, Bushfoot, Gracehill
Facilities available:

`GP` `TA` `GC` `AT` `AB` `CH` `TC` `HC`

Comfort Hotel Portrush
Portrush, Co. Antrim
Tel: 028-7082 6100..................Page 232
Arrangements with Golf Courses:
Royal Portrush, Portstewart, Castlerock, Ballycastle, Bushfoot, Gracehill, Galgorm Castle
Facilities available:
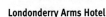
`GP` `TA` `GC` `AT` `AB` `CH` `TC` `PG` `HC`

Londonderry Arms Hotel
Carnlough, Co. Antrim
Tel: 028-2888 5255..................Page 231
Arrangements with Golf Courses:
Cairndhu GC (18 Hole, 7 miles), Galgorm GC (18 Hole, 14 miles), Ballycastle (18 Hole, 26 miles), Cushendall (9 Hole, 12 miles)
Facilities available:

`AT`

Belfast City

Malone Lodge Hotel & Apartments
Belfast City, Belfast City
Tel: 028-9038 8000 ....Page 237
Arrangements with Golf Courses:
Malone Golf Club
Facilities available:

`GP` `TA` `GC` `AT` `AB` `CH` `TC` `PG` `HC`

Co. Derry

Radisson SAS Roe Park Resort
Limavady, Co. Derry
Tel: 028-7772 2222 ....Page 240
Golf Course(s) On Site:
18 Hole Golf Course
Arrangements with Golf Courses:
Roe Park Golf Club, Radisson SAS Roe Park Resort
Facilities available:

`GP` `TA` `GC` `AT` `AB` `CH` `TC` `PG` `HC`

Co. Down

Burrendale Hotel and Country Club
Newcastle, Co. Down
Tel: 028-4372 2599 ....Page 242
Arrangements with Golf Courses:
Royal County Down, Kilkeel, Downpatrick, Ardglass, Spa, Bright
Facilities available:
`AT` `AB`

Clandeboye Lodge Hotel
Bangor, Co. Down
Tel: 028-9185 2500..................Page 241
Arrangements with Golf Courses:
Blackwood Golf Centre (adjacent to hotel)
Facilities available:

`GP` `TA` `AT` `AB` `CH` `PG`

Royal Hotel
Bangor, Co. Down
Tel: 028-9127 1866 ....Page 241
Arrangements with Golf Courses:
Bangor, Clandeboye, Blackwood
Facilities available:

`GP`

Dublin & East Coast

Co. Dublin

Aberdeen Lodge
Dublin City, Co. Dublin
Tel: 01-283 8155 ....Page 254
Arrangements with Golf Courses:
St. Margaret's, Portmarnock, K Club, Elm Park, Carton House, Druids Glen
Facilities available:
`GP` `TA` `GC` `AT` `AB` `CH` `TC` `PG` `HC`

Best Western Academy Hotel
Dublin City, Co. Dublin
Tel: 01-878 0666......................Page 262
Arrangements with Golf Courses:
Portmarnock, Royal Dublin, K Club, St. Margaret's, The Island, St. Anne's
Facilities available:
`GP` `TA` `GC` `AT` `AB` `TC` `HC`

Bracken Court Hotel
Balbriggan, Co. Dublin
Tel: 01-841 3333 ....Page 248
Arrangements with Golf Courses:
Balbriggan, Seapoint, Co. Louth, Bellewstown, Rush, Portmarnock
Facilities available:
`GP` `AT` `AB` `CH` `TC` `PG`

Castleknock Hotel and Country Club
Dublin City, Co. Dublin
Tel: 01-640 6300......................Page 266
Golf Course(s) On Site:
18 Hole Golf Course
Arrangements with Golf Courses:
Luttrellstown, Carton House, Citywest, Castleknock Golf Course
Facilities available:
`GP` `GC` `AT` `AB` `CH` `PG` `HC`

Charleville Lodge
Dublin City, Co. Dublin
Tel: 01-838 6633......................Page 268
Arrangements with Golf Courses:
St. Margaret's, Luttrellstown, The Links, Portmarnock, The Island Golf Links
Facilities available:
`GP` `TA` `GC` `AT` `AB` `CH` `TC` `PG` `HC`

Citywest Hotel, Conference, Leisure & Golf Resort
Saggart, Co. Dublin
Tel: 01-401 0500 ....Page 305
Golf Course(s) On Site:
18 Hole Golf Course
Facilities available:
`GP` `GC` `AT` `AB` `CH` `PG`

Clontarf Castle Hotel
Dublin City, Co. Dublin
Tel: 01-833 2321......................Page 270
Arrangements with Golf Courses:
Royal Dublin, St. Margarets, Portmarnock, St. Anne's, Clontarf, Malahide
Facilities available:
`GP` `TA` `GC` `AT` `AB` `CH` `TC` `PG` `HC`

 `GP` All inclusive Golf Package   `TA` Tuition Available   `GC` Golf Cart / Pull Cart   `AT` Arrange Tee Off Times   `HC` Hire Of Caddy
 `AB` Advance Golf Booking Made   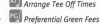 `CH` Hire Of Clubs   `TC` Transport To Course   `PG` Preferential Green Fees 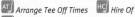

419

Co. Dublin Continued

Deer Park Hotel and Golf Courses
Howth, Co. Dublin
Tel: 01-832 2624 ....Page 301
Golf Course(s) On Site:
18 Hole Golf Course, 9 Hole Golf Course,
Par 3 Golf Course
Facilities available:

Egan's Guesthouse
Dublin City, Co. Dublin
Tel: 01-830 3611 ....Page 274
Arrangements with Golf Courses:
St. Margarets 5 Star Golf Course near
Dublin Airport
Facilities available:

Grand Hotel
Malahide, Co. Dublin
Tel: 01-845 0000.....................Page 303
Arrangements with Golf Courses:
Portmarnock GC, Malahide GC, The Island
GC, Swords GC, St. Margaret's, Royal
Dublin
Facilities available:

Gresham (The)
Dublin City, Co. Dublin
Tel: 01-874 6881 ....Page 277
Arrangements with Golf Courses:
Royal Dublin, Portmarnock, St.
Margaret's, The Island, St. Anne's,
Malahide
Facilities available:

Hilton Dublin Airport
Dublin Airport, Co. Dublin
Tel: 01-866 1800 ....Page 252
Arrangements with Golf Courses:
St. Margaret's, Donabate, Malahide
Facilities available:

Holiday Inn Dublin City Centre
Dublin City, Co. Dublin
Tel: 01-670 3666.....................Page 279
Arrangements with Golf Courses:
Elm Park, Clontarf, St. Margaret's,
Royal Dublin, The Island, Portmarnock
Links
Facilities available:

King Sitric Fish Restaurant & Accommodation
Howth, Co. Dublin
Tel: 01-832 5235 ....Page 301
Arrangements with Golf Courses:
Deerpark, Howth, Royal Dublin,
Portmarnock, St. Margaret's, The Island
Facilities available:

Lansdowne Hotel
Dublin City, Co. Dublin
Tel: 01-668 2522.....................Page 284
Arrangements with Golf Courses:
St. Annes, Deerpark, Elmgreen,
Leopardstown
Facilities available:

Lucan Spa Hotel
Lucan, Co. Dublin
Tel: 01-628 0494.....................Page 303
Arrangements with Golf Courses:
Carton House, Hermitage, Citywest,
Lucan, The K Club
Facilities available:

Marine Hotel
Sutton, Co. Dublin
Tel: 01-839 0000.....................Page 306
Arrangements with Golf Courses:
Portmarnock Hotel & Golf Links, Howth
GC, Sutton GC, Royal Dublin GC,
St. Anne's
Facilities available:

Merrion Hall
Dublin City, Co. Dublin
Tel: 01-668 1426 ....Page 287
Arrangements with Golf Courses:
Portmarnock, Royal Dublin, Elm Park,
Castle, K Club, Druid's Glen
Facilities available:

Phoenix Park House
Dublin City, Co. Dublin
Tel: 01-677 2870.....................Page 292
Arrangements with Golf Courses:
Carton House GC
Facilities available:

Portmarnock Hotel & Golf Links
Portmarnock, Co. Dublin
Tel: 01-846 0611 ....Page 304
Golf Course(s) On Site:
18 Hole Golf Course
Arrangements with Golf Courses:
Portmarnock, St. Margaret's, Royal
Dublin, Malahide, The Island
Facilities available:

Redbank House Guesthouse & Restaurant
Skerries, Co. Dublin
Tel: 01-849 1005 ....Page 306
Arrangements with Golf Courses:
Skerries, Laytown, Bettystown, Baltray,
Portmarnock, St. Margaret's, Donabate
Facilities available:

Regency Airport Hotel
Dublin City, Co. Dublin
Tel: 01-837 3544.....................Page 294
Arrangements with Golf Courses:
Malahide, Clontarf, Hollystown,
St. Anne's, Royal Dublin
Facilities available:

Rochestown Lodge Hotel
Dun Laoghaire, Co. Dublin
Tel: 01-285 3555.....................Page 300
Arrangements with Golf Courses:
Powerscourt GC, Woodbrook GC,
Druids Glen GC, The European GC
Facilities available:

Waterside Hotel
Donabate, Co. Dublin
Tel: 01-843 6153 ....Page 249
Arrangements with Golf Courses:
Donabate, Turvey, Beaverstown,
Balcarrick, The Island, Corballis
Facilities available:

White Sands Hotel
Portmarnock, Co. Dublin
Tel: 01-866 6000.....................Page 304
Arrangements with Golf Courses:
Malahide, St. Margaret's, Royal Dublin,
Portmarnock Golf Links, Donabate,
Balcarrick
Facilities available:

 All inclusive Golf Package   Tuition Available   Golf Cart / Pull Cart   Arrange Tee Off Times   Hire Of Caddy
 Advance Golf Booking Made   Hire Of Clubs   Transport To Course   Preferential Green Fees

Co. Louth

Ballymascanlon House Hotel
Dundalk, Co. Louth
Tel: 042-935 8200 ....Page 311
Golf Course(s) On Site:
18 Hole Golf Course
Facilities available:

Boyne Valley Hotel & Country Club
Drogheda, Co. Louth
Tel: 041-983 7737.....................Page 309
Arrangements with Golf Courses:
Baltray - Seapoint, Laytown/Bettystown, Dundalk, Headfort (2 courses), Kells, Ardee, St. Margarets
Facilities available:

Fairways Hotel & Conference Centre
Dundalk, Co. Louth
Tel: 042-932 1500 ....Page 311
Arrangements with Golf Courses:
Ballymascalon, Carnbeg, Killeen, Dundalk, Seapoint, Greenore
Facilities available:

Hotel Imperial
Dundalk, Co. Louth
Tel: 042-933 2241 ....Page 312
Arrangements with Golf Courses:
Ballymascanlon, Dundalk, Greenore, Carnbeg
Facilities available:

Keernaun House
Dundalk, Co. Louth
Tel: 042-932 1795 ....Page 312
Arrangements with Golf Courses:
Dundalk, Killeen, Greenore, Mannan Castle
Facilities available:

McKevitt's Village Hotel
Carlingford, Co. Louth
Tel: 042-937 3116 ....Page 308
Arrangements with Golf Courses:
Greenore
Facilities available:

Co. Meath

Castle Arch Hotel
Trim, Co. Meath
Tel: 046-943 1516 ....Page 317
Arrangements with Golf Courses:
Trim, Keegans, Glebe, Royal Tara Golf Club
Facilities available:

Hamlet Court Hotel
Johnstownbridge, Co. Meath
Tel: 046-954 1200 ....Page 315
Arrangements with Golf Courses:
Knockanally GC, Rathcore GC, Carton House, K Club, Highfield, Edenderry
Facilities available:

Headfort Arms Hotel
Kells, Co. Meath
Tel: 046-924 0063.....................Page 316
Arrangements with Golf Courses:
Headfort Golf Course - 36 Holes, Royal Tara, Navan Race Course, Delvin Castle, Ballinbugh Castle
Facilities available:

Knightsbrook Hotel & Golf Resort
Trim, Co. Meath
Tel: 046-907 4100 ....Page 317
Golf Course(s) On Site:
18 Hole Golf Course
Arrangements with Golf Courses:
Headfort GC, Co. Meath GC, Navan GC
Facilities available:

Neptune Beach Hotel & Leisure Club
Bettystown, Co. Meath
Tel: 041-982 7107 ....Page 313
Arrangements with Golf Courses:
Laytown & Bettystown, Sea Point, County Louth/Baltray, Royal Tara
Facilities available:

Rannoch Guesthouse
Bettystown, Co. Meath
Tel: 041-982 7469 ....Page 314
Arrangements with Golf Courses:
Bettystown & Laytown GC, Baltray GC
Facilities available:

Station House Hotel and Restaurant
Kilmessan, Co. Meath
Tel: 046-902 5239.....................Page 316
Arrangements with Golf Courses:
Royal Tara, Blackbush, Headfort
Facilities available:

Co. Wicklow

Arklow Bay Conference and Leisure Hotel
Arklow, Co. Wicklow
Tel: 0402-32309 ....Page 318
Arrangements with Golf Courses:
European, Arklow, Woodenbridge, Blainroe, Seafield
Facilities available:

Ballyknocken Country House & Cookery School
Ashford, Co. Wicklow
Tel: 0404-44627 ....Page 319
Arrangements with Golf Courses:
Druid's Glen, European Club, Woodenbridge, Wicklow Town, Blainroe, Powerscourt
Facilities available:

Chester Beatty Inn
Ashford, Co. Wicklow
Tel: 0404-40206 ....Page 319
Arrangements with Golf Courses:
Druid's Glen, Woodenbridge, Blainroe, European, Glen of the Downs, Charlesland
Facilities available:

Glendalough Hotel
Glendalough, Co. Wicklow
Tel: 0404-45135 ....Page 323
Arrangements with Golf Courses:
The European Club, Woodenbridge, Charlesland, Druid's Glen, Blainroe, Roundwood
Facilities available:

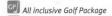 

Co. Wicklow Continued

Glenview Hotel
Glen-O-The-Downs, Co. Wicklow
Tel: 01-287 3399......................Page 324
Arrangements with Golf Courses:
Glen O' The Downs, Powerscourt, Druid's Glen, The European Club, Charlesland, Delgany, Greystones
Facilities available:

Grand Hotel
Wicklow Town, Co. Wicklow
Tel: 0404-67337 ....Page 325
Arrangements with Golf Courses:
Blainroe, Wicklow, Druid's Glen, European Golf Course
Facilities available:

Heather House Hotel
Bray, Co. Wicklow
Tel: 01-286 8000 ....Page 321
Arrangements with Golf Courses:
Bray, Woodbrook, Old Conna, Powerscourt, Greystones, Druid's Glen
Facilities available:

Hunter's Hotel
Rathnew, Co. Wicklow
Tel: 0404-40106 ....Page 325
Arrangements with Golf Courses:
Druid's Glen, European, Blainroe, Powerscourt, Woodenbridge, Delgany
Facilities available:

Lawless's Hotel
Aughrim, Co. Wicklow
Tel: 0402-36146 ....Page 320
Arrangements with Golf Courses:
Woodenbridge, Coollattin, European, Blainroe, Arklow, Druid's Glen, Tulfarris
Facilities available:

Marriott Druids Glen Hotel & Country Club
Newtownmountkennedy, Co. Wicklow
Tel: 01-287 0800......................Page 324
Golf Course(s) On Site:
2 x 18 Hole Golf Courses
Arrangements with Golf Courses:
Druid's Glen, Druid's Heath
Facilities available:

New Valley Inn
Woodenbridge, Co. Wicklow
Tel: 0402-35200 ....Page 326
Arrangements with Golf Courses:
Woodenbridge, Arklow, European Club, Blainroe, Seafield, Coollattin
Facilities available:

Porterhouse Inn (The)
Bray, Co. Wicklow
Tel: 01-286 0668 ....Page 321
Arrangements with Golf Courses:
Bray Golf Club, Druid's Glen G.C., Glen of the Downs G.C., Woodbrook G.C., Powerscourt G.C. and European Club
Facilities available:

Rathsallagh House, Golf and Country Club
Dunlavin, Co. Wicklow
Tel: 045-403112 ....Page 322
Golf Course(s) On Site:
18 Hole Golf Course
Arrangements with Golf Courses:
Mount Juliet, K Club, Druid's Glen, Powerscourt, Portmarnock, Carton, The Heritage
Facilities available:

Summerhill House Hotel
Enniskerry, Co. Wicklow
Tel: 01-286 7928......................Page 323
Arrangements with Golf Courses:
Powerscourt, Druid's Glen, Kilternan, Old Conna
Facilities available:

Tinakilly Country House and Restaurant
Rathnew, Co. Wicklow
Tel: 0404-69274 ....Page 325
Arrangements with Golf Courses:
European Club, Druid's Glen, Blainroe, Woodenbridge, Wicklow, Delgany
Facilities available:

Woodenbridge Hotel
Woodenbridge, Co. Wicklow
Tel: 0402-35146 ....Page 326
Arrangements with Golf Courses:
Woodenbridge, Blainroe, Arklow, European Club, Coollattin, Seafield
Facilities available:

Woodenbridge Lodge
Woodenbridge, Co. Wicklow
Tel: 0402-35146 ....Page 326
Arrangements with Golf Courses:
Woodenbridge GC, Arklow GC, Seafield GC, Coollattin GC, Blainroe GC, European Club
Facilities available:

Midlands & Lakelands

Co. Cavan

Breffni Arms Hotel
Arvagh, Co. Cavan
Tel: 049-433 5127....................Page 330
Arrangements with Golf Courses:
Cavan, Longford, Carrick on Shannon, Slieve Russell
Facilities available:

Cavan Crystal Hotel
Cavan Town, Co. Cavan
Tel: 049-436 0600....................Page 331
Arrangements with Golf Courses:
Co. Cavan Golf Club, Clones, Headfort Golf Club, Kells
Facilities available:

 All inclusive Golf Package Tuition Available Golf Cart / Pull Cart Arrange Tee Off Times Hire Of Caddy
 Advance Golf Booking Made Hire Of Clubs Transport To Course Preferential Green Fees

Crover House Hotel & Golf Club
Mountnugent, Co. Cavan
Tel: 049-854 0206 ....Page 333
Golf Course(s) On Site:
9 Hole Golf Course
Arrangements with Golf Courses:
Headfort GC
Facilities available:

Park Hotel
Virginia, Co. Cavan
Tel: 049-854 6100.....................Page 334
Golf Course(s) On Site:
9 Hole Golf Course
Arrangements with Golf Courses:
Cavan Golf Club, Headfort Golf Club, Kells
Facilities available:

River Front Hotel (The)
Virginia, Co. Cavan
Tel: 049-854 7561.....................Page 334
Arrangements with Golf Courses:
Headfort, Slieve Russell, Park Virginia
Facilities available:

Slieve Russell Hotel Golf & Country Club
Ballyconnell, Co. Cavan
Tel: 049-952 6444.....................Page 331
Golf Course(s) On Site:
18 Hole Golf Course, 9 Hole Golf Course, Par 3 Golf Course
Facilities available:

Co. Kildare

Barberstown Castle
Straffan, Co. Kildare
Tel: 01-628 8157 ....Page 344
Arrangements with Golf Courses:
K Club, Carton House, Rathsallagh House
Facilities available:

Bert House Hotel & Leisure Centre
Athy, Co. Kildare
Tel: 059-863 2578 ....Page 335
Arrangements with Golf Courses:
Kilkea Castle, The Heritage, Athy, Mount Juliet, Rathsallagh, The K Club
Facilities available:

Carlton Abbey Hotel
Athy, Co. Kildare
Tel: 059-863 0100.....................Page 335
Arrangements with Golf Courses:
Coollattin, Killerig
Facilities available:

Carton House
Maynooth, Co. Kildare
Tel: 01-505 2000.....................Page 340
Golf Course(s) On Site:
2 x 18 Hole Golf Courses
Arrangements with Golf Courses:
The K Club, Royal Dublin, Portmarnock, The Island, Portmarnock Links, Luttrellstown
Facilities available:

Clanard Court Hotel
Athy, Co. Kildare
Tel: 059-864 0666 ....Page 336
Arrangements with Golf Courses:
Athy Golf Club, Cardenton Par 3
Facilities available:

Courtyard Hotel Leixlip (The)
Leixlip, Co. Kildare
Tel: 01-629 5100 ....Page 339
Arrangements with Golf Courses:
K Club - 2 x 18 Hole Courses, Carton - 2 x 18 Hole Courses, Heritage - 18 Hole Course, Lucan - 18 Hole Course
Facilities available:

Glenroyal Hotel, Leisure Club & Conference Centre
Maynooth, Co. Kildare
Tel: 01-629 0909 ....Page 341
Arrangements with Golf Courses:
Knockanally, K Club, Killeen, Castlewarden, Bodenstown, Citywest, Carton
Facilities available:

Hazel Hotel
Monasterevin, Co. Kildare
Tel: 045-525373 ....Page 341
Arrangements with Golf Courses:
Cill Dara, Portarlington, Curragh, The Heath, Athy, The Heritage at Killenard
Facilities available:

K Club (The)
Straffan, Co. Kildare
Tel: 01-601 7200 ....Page 344
Golf Course(s) On Site:
2 x 18 Hole Golf Courses
Arrangements with Golf Courses:
Luttrellstown Castle, Druid's Glen, Portmarnock Links, Rathsallagh, Hermitage, Heritage
Facilities available:

Setanta House Hotel
Celbridge, Co. Kildare
Tel: 01-630 3200.....................Page 337
Arrangements with Golf Courses:
Carton House GC, K Club, Citywest GC, Millicent GC
Facilities available:

Standhouse Hotel Leisure & Conference Centre
Curragh (The), Co. Kildare
Tel: 045-436177 ....Page 338
Arrangements with Golf Courses:
Killeen, Cill Dara, The Curragh, Castlewarden, Naas, Craddockstown
Facilities available:

Westgrove Hotel & Conference Centre
Clane, Co. Kildare
Tel: 1800-32 42 52 ....Page 337
Arrangements with Golf Courses:
The K Club, Carton House GC, Millicent GC
Facilities available:

Co. Laois

Heritage at Killenard (The)
Killenard, Co. Laois
Tel: 057-864 5500 ....Page 345
Golf Course(s) On Site:
18 Hole Golf Course, 9 Hole Golf Course, Par 3 Golf Course
Facilities available:

GP All inclusive Golf Package   TA Tuition Available   GC Golf Cart / Pull Cart   AT Arrange Tee Off Times   HC Hire Of Caddy
AB Advance Golf Booking Made   CH Hire Of Clubs   TC Transport To Course   PG Preferential Green Fees

423

Co. Laois Continued

Heritage Hotel Portlaoise
Portlaoise, Co. Laois
Tel: 057-867 8588 ....Page 346
Arrangements with Golf Courses:
*The Heritage at Killenard - Portarlington,
The Heath, Abbeyleix*
Facilities available:

Co. Longford

Annaly Hotel
Longford Town, Co. Longford
Tel: 043-42058 ....Page 346
Arrangements with Golf Courses:
*Longford, Ballyconnell, Glasson,
Mullingar, Roscommon*
Facilities available:

Longford Arms Hotel
Longford Town, Co. Longford
Tel: 043-46296 ....Page 347
Arrangements with Golf Courses:
*Longford, Glasson, Ballyconnell,
Carrick-on-Shannon, Roscommon,
Mullingar*
Facilities available:

Co. Monaghan

**Four Seasons Hotel &
Leisure Club**
Monaghan Town, Co. Monaghan
Tel: 047-81888 ....Page 348
Arrangements with Golf Courses:
*Rossmore, Nuremore, Armagh, Clones,
Slieve Russell*
Facilities available:

**Hillgrove Hotel &
Conference Centre**
Monaghan Town, Co. Monaghan
Tel: 047-81288 ....Page 348
Arrangements with Golf Courses:
*Rossmore GC, Clones GC, Nuremore
Country Club, Castle Hume GC, Mannan
Castle GC, Co. Armagh GC*
Facilities available:
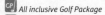

Nuremore Hotel & Country Club
Carrickmacross, Co. Monaghan
Tel: 042 -966 1438 ....Page 347
Golf Course(s) On Site:
18 Hole Golf Course
Arrangements with Golf Courses:
*Nuremore, Baltray, Headfort, Dundalk,
Greenore, Royal County Down*
Facilities available:

Co. Offaly

**Bridge House Hotel
& Leisure Club**
Tullamore, Co. Offaly
Tel: 057-932 5600 ....Page 350
Arrangements with Golf Courses:
*Esker Hills & Tullamore Golf Club both
5 minutes away, Castlebarna Golf Club
12km away, Virtual Reality Golf Facility on
site*
Facilities available:

Brosna Lodge Hotel
Banagher, Co. Offaly
Tel: 057-915 1350 ....Page 348
Arrangements with Golf Courses:
*Birr, Esker Hills, Tullamore, Glasson,
Portumna, Ballinasloe*
Facilities available:

County Arms Hotel
Birr, Co. Offaly
Tel: 057-912 0791 ....Page 349
Arrangements with Golf Courses:
*Birr, Portumna, Roscrea, Glasson,
Tullamore, Esker Hills*
Facilities available:

Days Hotel Tullamore
Tullamore, Co. Offaly
Tel: 1890-776 655 ....Page 351
Arrangements with Golf Courses:
Esker Hills GC, Tullamore GC, Glasson GC
Facilities available:

Doolys Hotel
Birr, Co. Offaly
Tel: 057-912 0032 ....Page 349
Arrangements with Golf Courses:
*Birr, Roscrea, Esker Hills, Mount Temple,
Tullamore*
Facilities available:

Moorhill House Hotel
Tullamore, Co. Offaly
Tel: 057-932 1395 ....Page 352
Arrangements with Golf Courses:
*Esker Hills, Tullamore, Daingean,
Mount Temple, Birr, Glasson*
Facilities available:

**Tullamore Court Hotel
Conference & Leisure Centre**
Tullamore, Co. Offaly
Tel: 057-934 6666 ....Page 352
Arrangements with Golf Courses:
*Tullamore, Esker Hills, Castle Barna,
Mount Temple, Glasson, Birr,
The Heritage at Killenard*
Facilities available:

Co. Westmeath

Bloomfield House Hotel
Mullingar, Co. Westmeath
Tel: 044-934 0894 ....Page 356
Arrangements with Golf Courses:
*Mullingar, Glasson, Mount Temple,
Esker Hills, Athlone, Tullamore*
Facilities available:

Creggan Court Hotel
Athlone, Co. Westmeath
Tel: 090-647 7777 ....Page 353
Arrangements with Golf Courses:
*Glasson, Mount Temple, Esker Hills,
Athlone, Mullingar*
Facilities available:

 All inclusive Golf Package Tuition Available Golf Cart / Pull Cart Arrange Tee Off Times Hire Of Caddy
Advance Golf Booking Made   Hire Of Clubs   Transport To Course   Preferential Green Fees

Glasson Golf Hotel and Country Club
Athlone, Co. Westmeath
Tel: 090-648 5120....................Page 353
Golf Course(s) On Site:
18 Hole Golf Course
Arrangements with Golf Courses:
*Glasson Golf Hotel and Country Club,
Athlone Golf Club,
Mount Temple Golf Club, Esker Hills,
Moate Golf Club, Tullamore*
Facilities available:

Greville Arms Hotel
Mullingar, Co. Westmeath
Tel: 044-934 8563 ....Page 356
Arrangements with Golf Courses:
*Mullingar, Glasson, Mount Temple,
Tullamore, Longford, Esker Hills*
Facilities available:

Hodson Bay Hotel
Athlone, Co. Westmeath
Tel: 090-644 2000 ....Page 354
Golf Course(s) On Site:
18 Hole Golf Course
Arrangements with Golf Courses:
*Athlone, Glasson, Mount Temple,
Ballinasloe, Roscommon, Esker Hills*
Facilities available:

Mullingar Park Hotel
Mullingar, Co. Westmeath
Tel: 044-933 7500 ....Page 357
Arrangements with Golf Courses:
*Mullingar, Glasson, Tullamore, Delvin,
Mount Temple, Athlone, Highfield,
Rathcore*
Facilities available:

Prince of Wales Hotel
Athlone, Co. Westmeath
Tel: 090-647 6666 ....Page 354
Arrangements with Golf Courses:
*Glasson Golf, Mount Temple, Athlone,
Esker Hills, Tullamore, Birr*
Facilities available:

Radisson SAS Hotel
Athlone, Co. Westmeath
Tel: 090-644 2600 ....Page 354
Arrangements with Golf Courses:
*Glasson Golf Club, Athlone Golf Club,
Esker Hills, Moate Golf Club,
Mullingar GC, Tullamore GC*
Facilities available:

Shamrock Lodge Hotel and Conference Centre
Athlone, Co. Westmeath
Tel: 090-649 2601....................Page 355
Arrangements with Golf Courses:
*Glasson, Athlone, Moate, Esker Hills,
Tullamore, Roscommon*
Facilities available:

South East

Co. Carlow

Seven Oaks Hotel
Carlow Town, Co. Carlow
Tel: 059-913 1308 ....Page 362
Arrangements with Golf Courses:
*Mount Wolseley, Kilkea Castle,
Killerig Castle, Carlow, Gowran Park*
Facilities available:

Co. Kilkenny

Brannigans Glendine Inn
Kilkenny City, Co. Kilkenny
Tel: 056-772 1069....................Page 364
Arrangements with Golf Courses:
*Kilkenny, Mount Juliet, Callan,
Castlecomer, Pococke, Gowran*
Facilities available:

Butler House
Kilkenny City, Co. Kilkenny
Tel: 056-776 5707 ....Page 364
Arrangements with Golf Courses:
*Kilkenny, Mount Juliet, Carlow,
Killerig Castle,Kilkea Castle, Gowran Park*
Facilities available:

Kilford Arms Hotel
Kilkenny City, Co. Kilkenny
Tel: 056-776 1018 ....Page 366
Arrangements with Golf Courses:
*Mount Juliet, Kilkenny, Callan, Gowran,
Castlecomer, Borris*
Facilities available:

Kilkenny River Court
Kilkenny City, Co. Kilkenny
Tel: 056-772 3388 ....Page 368
Arrangements with Golf Courses:
*Gowran Park, Mount Juliet, Kilkenny,
Callan, Castlecomer, Carlow*
Facilities available:

Langton House Hotel
Kilkenny City, Co. Kilkenny
Tel: 056-776 5133....................Page 369
Arrangements with Golf Courses:
*Mount Juliet, Kilkenny, Callan,
Mountain View, Ballyhale, Castlecomer*
Facilities available:

Lyrath Estate Hotel, Spa & Convention Centre
Kilkenny City, Co. Kilkenny
Tel: 056-776 0088 ....Page 370
Arrangements with Golf Courses:
*Gowran Park, Mount Juliet, Kilkenny,
Callan, Castlecomer, Carlow*
Facilities available:

Mount Juliet Conrad
Thomastown, Co. Kilkenny
Tel: 056-777 3000 ....Page 373
Golf Course(s) On Site:
*18 Hole Golf Course and
18 Hole Putting Course*
Facilities available:

Springhill Court Hotel, Spa & Leisure Club
Kilkenny City, Co. Kilkenny
Tel: 056-772 1122 ....Page 371
Arrangements with Golf Courses:
Castlecomer, Callan, Gowran
Facilities available:

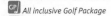 **GP** *All inclusive Golf Package*  **TA** *Tuition Available* **GC** *Golf Cart / Pull Cart* **AT** *Arrange Tee Off Times*   **HC** *Hire Of Caddy*
AB *Advance Golf Booking Made* **CH** *Hire Of Clubs* **TC** *Transport To Course* **PG** *Preferential Green Fees*

Co. Tipperary South

Ach Na Sheen Guesthouse
Tipperary Town, Co. Tipperary South
Tel: 062-51298 ....Page 380
Arrangements with Golf Courses:
Tipperary, Ballykisteen, Cahir, Dundrum
Facilities available:

Aherlow House Hotel and Lodges
Glen Of Aherlow, Co. Tipperary South
Tel: 062-56153 ....Page 378
Arrangements with Golf Courses:
Tipperary GC, Ballykisteen GC, Dundrum House Hotel
Facilities available:

Cahir House Hotel
Cahir, Co. Tipperary South
Tel: 052-43000 ....Page 373
Arrangements with Golf Courses:
Cahir Park, Carrick-on-Suir, Clonmel, Ballykisteen, Dundrum, Tipperary, Thurles
Facilities available:

Dundrum House Hotel
Cashel, Co. Tipperary South
Tel: 062-71116 ....Page 375
Golf Course(s) On Site:
18 Hole Golf Course
Facilities available:

Glen Hotel
Glen Of Aherlow, Co. Tipperary South
Tel: 062-56146 ....Page 379
Arrangements with Golf Courses:
Tipperary Golf Club, Ballykisteen Golf & Country Club, Co. Tipperary Golf & Country Club, Dundrum Golf & Country Club
Facilities available:

Meadowvale Farm Guesthouse
Clonmel, Co. Tipperary South
Tel: 052-38914 ....Page 378
Arrangements with Golf Courses:
Cahir Park GC, Clonmel GC, Dundrum GC, Slievenamon Golf Club, Carrick-on-Suir GC, Thurles GC
Facilities available:

Co. Waterford

Ard Ri Hotel (The)
Waterford City, Co. Waterford
Tel: 051-832111......................Page 388
Arrangements with Golf Courses:
Waterford Golf Club, Faithlegg Golf Club, Waterford Castle Golf Club
Facilities available:

Athenaeum House Hotel
Waterford City, Co. Waterford
Tel: 051-833999 ....Page 389
Arrangements with Golf Courses:
Waterford, Faithlegg, Waterford Castle, Tramore, Mount Juliet
Facilities available:

Bridge Hotel
Waterford City, Co. Waterford
Tel: 051-877222 ....Page 390
Arrangements with Golf Courses:
Waterford Castle, Faithlegg, Waterford Golf Club, Dunmore East, Gold Coast Golf
Facilities available:

Dooley's Hotel
Waterford City, Co. Waterford
Tel: 051-873531 ....Page 391
Arrangements with Golf Courses:
Waterford, Tramore, Faithlegg, Waterford Castle, Dunmore, Carrick-on-Suir
Facilities available:

Faithlegg House Hotel and Golf Club
Faithlegg, Co. Waterford
Tel: 051-382000 ....Page 386
Golf Course(s) On Site:
18 Hole Golf Course
Arrangements with Golf Courses:
Waterford Castle, Tramore, Waterford Golf Club, Faithlegg Golf Course, Mount Juliet
Facilities available:

Grand Hotel
Tramore, Co. Waterford
Tel: 051-381414 ....Page 386
Arrangements with Golf Courses:
Tramore, Dunmore East, Faithlegg, Waterford Castle, Mount Juliet, Dungarvan Gold Coast Golf Course
Facilities available:

Granville Hotel
Waterford City, Co. Waterford
Tel: 051-305555 ....Page 391
Arrangements with Golf Courses:
Waterford, Faithlegg, Waterford Castle, Tramore, Dunmore East
Facilities available:

Lawlors Hotel
Dungarvan, Co. Waterford
Tel: 058-41122 ....Page 383
Arrangements with Golf Courses:
Dungarvan, West Waterford, Gold Coast
Facilities available:

Majestic Hotel
Tramore, Co. Waterford
Tel: 051-381761 ....Page 387
Arrangements with Golf Courses:
Tramore, Waterford, Faithlegg, Waterford Castle, Mount Juliet, Dunmore East
Facilities available:

Ocean Hotel
Dunmore East, Co. Waterford
Tel: 051-383136 ....Page 385
Arrangements with Golf Courses:
Waterford, Waterford Castle, Faithlegg, Dunmore East, Tramore
Facilities available:

O'Shea's Hotel
Tramore, Co. Waterford
Tel: 051-381246 ....Page 388
Arrangements with Golf Courses:
Tramore, Faithlegg, Waterford Castle, Waterford, Dungarvan
Facilities available:

GP All inclusive Golf Package   **TA** Tuition Available   **GC** Golf Cart / Pull Cart   **AT** Arrange Tee Off Times   **HC** Hire Of Caddy
AB Advance Golf Booking Made   **CH** Hire Of Clubs   **TC** Transport To Course   **PG** Preferential Green Fees

Rhu Glenn Country Club Hotel
Waterford City, Co. Waterford
Tel: 051-832242 ....Page 392
Arrangements with Golf Courses:
*Waterford, New Ross, Faithlegg,
Waterford Castle, Tramore,
Dunmore East*
Facilities available:

Rice Guesthouse &
Batterberry's Bar
Waterford City, Co. Waterford
Tel: 051-371606 ....Page 392
Arrangements with Golf Courses:
*Dunmore East, Faithlegg, Waterford
Castle, Tramore, Waterford*
Facilities available:

Three Rivers Guest House
Cheekpoint, Co. Waterford
Tel: 051-382520 ....Page 382
Arrangements with Golf Courses:
*Faithlegg, Dunmore East, Tramore,
Waterford Castle, Waterford,
Mount Juliet*
Facilities available:

Tower Hotel & Leisure Centre
Waterford City, Co. Waterford
Tel: 051-862300 ....Page 393
Arrangements with Golf Courses:
*Waterford Castle, Waterford, Faithlegg,
Tramore*
Facilities available:

Waterford Castle Hotel
& Golf Club
Waterford City, Co. Waterford
Tel: 051-878203 ....Page 393
Golf Course(s) On Site:
18 Hole Golf Course
Arrangements with Golf Courses:
*Waterford Castle Golf Club, Faithlegg,
Tramore, Waterford Golf Club,
Mount Juliet*
Facilities available:

Co. Wexford

Ashdown Park Hotel Conference
& Leisure Centre
Gorey, Co. Wexford
Tel: 053-948 0500 ....Page 398
Arrangements with Golf Courses:
*Seafield, Courtown, Ballymoney,
Coollattin, Enniscorthy, Woodenbridge*
Facilities available:

Carlton Millrace Hotel (The)
Bunclody, Co. Wexford
Tel: 053-937 5100....................Page 395
Arrangements with Golf Courses:
*Enniscorthy Golf Club, Seafield Golf Club,
Killerig Golf Course*
Facilities available:

Crosbie Cedars Hotel
Rosslare, Co. Wexford
Tel: 053-913 2124 ....Page 401
Arrangements with Golf Courses:
*Rosslare 18 Hole Links, Rosslare 12 Hole
Links, St. Helen's Golf & Country Club,
Wexford Golf Course*
Facilities available:

Pines Country House Hotel
Enniscorthy, Co. Wexford
Tel: 053-938 3600 ....Page 397
Arrangements with Golf Courses:
Ballymoney Golf Club, Courtown, Seafield
Facilities available:

Quality Hotel & Leisure
Wexford
Wexford Town, Co. Wexford
Tel: 053-917 2000....................Page 404
Arrangements with Golf Courses:
*St Helen's GC, Wexford GC, Rosslare GC,
Scarke GC*
Facilities available:

Riverside
Park Hotel and
Leisure Club
Enniscorthy, Co. Wexford
Tel: 053-923 7800 ....Page 397
Arrangements with Golf Courses:
*Enniscorthy Golf Club, Rosslare Golf Club,
Wexford Golf Club, New Ross Golf Club,
Seaview Golf Club,
St. Helens Golf Club*
Facilities available:

Talbot Hotel Conference
and Leisure Centre
Wexford Town, Co. Wexford
Tel: 053-912 2566....................Page 405
Arrangements with Golf Courses:
*St. Helens, Wexford, Rosslare,
Enniscorthy, Courtown*
Facilities available:

 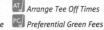

IRELAND 2006
ANGLING

Ireland is accepted as being the outstanding angling holiday resort in Europe. Whether you are a competition angler, a serious specimen hunter, or just fishing while on holiday, you are sure to enjoy yourself here. With over 14,000km of rivers feeding over 4,000 lakes and with no part of Ireland over 112km from the sea, Ireland can, in truth, be called an angler's dream!

.....*So come on and get hooked!*

irelandhotels.com

Official Website of the Irish Hotels Federation

IRISH
HOTELS
FEDERATION

One source - Endless possibilities

We invite you to sample the fishing, the countryside and the friendship of the Irish people and then to stay in some of Ireland's most charming accommodation. We have listed a range of hotels and guesthouses which are either situated with or near angling facilities. Your host will assist you in arranging your angling itinerary. A full description of the hotels and guesthouses can be had by looking up the appropriate page number.
Premises are listed in Alphabetical Order in each County.

South West

Co. Cork

Blue Haven Hotel and Restaurant
Kinsale, Co. Cork
Tel: 021-477 2209
Game Angling:
Salmon, Brown Trout
Sea Angling:
Sea Trout, Ling, Blue Shark, Sea Bass, Conger, Cod
Facilities available:
 ....Page 60

Celtic Ross Hotel Conference & Leisure Centre
Rosscarbery, Co. Cork
Tel: 023-48722
Coarse Angling:
Bream, Roach, Tench
Game Angling:
Trout, Salmon
Sea Angling:
Cod, Shark, Wrasse, Flat Fish
Facilities available:
 ......Page 67

Commodore Hotel
Cobh, Co. Cork
Tel: 021-481 1277
Sea Angling:
Ling, Cod, Pollock, Conger, Blue Shark
Facilities available:
 ....Page 45

Coolcower House
Macroom, Co. Cork
Tel: 026-41695
Coarse Angling:
Bream, Rudd, Pike, Perch
Game Angling:
Trout
Facilities available:
 ....Page 64

Dunmore House Hotel
Clonakilty, Co. Cork
Tel: 023-33352
Sea Angling:
Bass, Cod, Mackerel, Skate, Whiting, Ling
Facilities available:
 ....Page 43

Hibernian Hotel and Leisure Centre
Mallow, Co. Cork
Tel: 022-21588
Coarse Angling:
Bream, Pike, Perch, Tench
Game Angling:
Trout, Salmon
Facilities available:
 ....Page 64

Innishannon House Hotel
Innishannon, Co. Cork
Tel: 021-477 5121
Game Angling:
Salmon, Brown Trout
Sea Angling:
Sea Trout, Shark, Cod, Ling, Skate
Facilities available:
 ....Page 59

Lee Valley Hotel
Macroom, Co. Cork
Tel: 026-41082
Coarse Angling:
Bream, Hybrids, Roach, Dace, Tench, Carp
Game Angling:
Trout
Facilities available:
 ....Page 64

Maryborough House Hotel
Cork City, Co. Cork
Tel: 021-436 5555
Coarse Angling:
Bream, Perch, Pike, Trout, Rudd, Eel
Game Angling:
Salmon
Sea Angling:
Shark, Ling, Conger, Pollock, Cod, Ray, Wrasse
Facilities available:
 ....Page 55

Trident Hotel
Kinsale, Co. Cork
Tel: 021-477 9300
Sea Angling:
Shark, Ling, Conger Eels, Mackerel, Pollock
Facilities available:
 ....Page 63

Walter Raleigh Hotel
Youghal, Co. Cork
Tel: 024-92011
Sea Angling:
Mackerel, Salmon, Bass, Whiting, Conger Eels
Facilities available:
 ....Page 70

Whispering Pines Hotel
Crosshaven, Co. Cork
Tel: 021-483 1843
Sea Angling:
Blue Shark, Conger, Ling, Pollock, Coalfish
Facilities available:
 ....Page 58

BT Bait & Tackle | BH Boats For Hire | DR Drying Room | PL Packed Lunches Available On Request
GI Gillie | TR Tackle Room | FR Freezer For Storage Of Catch | PR Permits Required

Co. Kerry

19th Green (The)
Killarney, Co. Kerry
Tel: 064-32868
Coarse Angling:
Pike, Perch, Roach

Game Angling:
Salmon, Trout

Sea Angling:
Pollock, Blue Shark, Ling, Ray

Facilities available:
 Page 87

Ard-Na-Sidhe
Caragh Lake, Co. Kerry
Tel: 066-976 9105
Game Angling:
Salmon, Trout

Facilities available:
 ....Page 73

Butler Arms Hotel
Waterville, Co. Kerry
Tel: 066-947 4144
Game Angling:
Salmon, Trout

Sea Angling:
Bass, Pollock, Cod, Shark, Mackerel, Whiting

Facilities available:
 ......Page 116

Derrynane Hotel
Caherdaniel, Co. Kerry
Tel: 066-947 5136
Game Angling:
Salmon

Sea Angling:
Mackerel, Pollock, Shark, Bass, Cod, Whiting, Wrasse

Facilities available:
 ......Page 72

Dingle Benners Hotel
Dingle (An Daingean), Co. Kerry
Tel: 066-915 1638
Game Angling:
Salmon, Trout

Sea Angling:
Pollock, Garfish, Blue Shark, Tope, Dogfish, Ling, Whiting, Ray

Facilities available:
 ....Page 78

Dingle Skellig Hotel & Peninsula Spa
Dingle (An Daingean), Co. Kerry
Tel: 066-915 0200
Sea Angling:
Pollock, Garfish, Blue Shark, Tope, Dogfish, Ling, Whiting, Ray

Facilities available:
 ....Page 78

Hotel Dunloe Castle
Killarney, Co. Kerry
Tel: 064-44111
Game Angling:
Salmon, Trout

Facilities available:
............Page 97

Inveraray Farm Guesthouse
Killarney, Co. Kerry
Tel: 064-44224
Game Angling:
Brown Trout, Salmon

Sea Angling:
Sea Trout

Facilities available:
..................Page 98

Killarney Avenue Hotel
Killarney, Co. Kerry
Tel: 064-32522
Coarse Angling:
Perch, Tench

Game Angling:
Wild Brown Trout

Sea Angling:
Sole, Cod, Mackerel

Facilities available:
..................Page 99

Killarney Plaza Hotel & Spa
Killarney, Co. Kerry
Tel: 064-21111
Coarse Angling:
Perch, Tench

Game Angling:
Wild Brown Trout, Wild Salmon

Sea Angling:
Sole, Mackerel, Cod

Facilities available:
................Page 101

Killarney Royal
Killarney, Co. Kerry
Tel: 064-31853
Game Angling:
Brown Trout, Salmon

Facilities available:
 Page 101

Lake Hotel
Killarney, Co. Kerry
Tel: 064-31035
Game Angling:
Salmon, Trout

Facilities available:
....Page 102

Lakelands Farm Guesthouse
Waterville, Co. Kerry
Tel: 066-947 4303
Game Angling:
Salmon

Sea Angling:
Sea Trout

Facilities available:
 Page 116

Lansdowne Arms Hotel
Kenmare, Co. Kerry
Tel: 064-41368
Game Angling:
Salmon, Wild Brown Trout, Stocked Rainbow Trout

Sea Angling:
Sea Trout, Sole, Mackerel, Plaice, Pollock

Facilities available:
......Page 84

Moorings (The)
Portmagee, Co. Kerry
Tel: 066-947 7108
Game Angling:
Salmon, Trout

Sea Angling:
Cod, Pollock, Mackerel, Shark, Turbot, Sea Trout, Plaice

Facilities available:
 Page 109

 Bait & Tackle
 Boats For Hire
Drying Room
Packed Lunches Available On Request
Gillie
 Tackle Room
 Freezer For Storage Of Catch
Permits Required

Co. Kerry Continued

Muckross Park Hotel
Killarney, Co. Kerry
Tel: 064-31938
Coarse Angling:
Perch, Tench
Game Angling:
Wild Brown Trout, Wild Salmon
Facilities available:
 ....Page 104

Sheen Falls Lodge
Kenmare, Co. Kerry
Tel: 064-41600
Game Angling:
Salmon, Trout
Sea Angling:
Shark, Mackerel, Pollock, Skate,
Conger Eel, Dogfish
Facilities available:
 Page 86

Tuscar Lodge
Killarney, Co. Kerry
Tel: 064-31978
Coarse Angling:
Pike, Perch
Game Angling:
Salmon, Trout
Sea Angling:
Bass, Herring, Whiting, Cod
Facilities available:
Page 107

Waterville Lodge Hotel
Waterville, Co. Kerry
Tel: 066-947 4436
Game Angling:
Sea Trout, Salmon
Sea Angling:
Sea Bass, Pollock
Facilities available:
 Page 117

Shannon

Co. Clare

Ardilaun Guesthouse
Ennis, Co. Clare
Tel: 065-682 2311
Coarse Angling:
Pike, Perch, Trout
Game Angling:
Trout, Salmon
Facilities available:
 ....Page 126

Grovemount House
Ennistymon, Co. Clare
Tel: 065-707 1431
Coarse Angling:
Roach
Game Angling:
Trout
Facilities available:
 ....Page 129

Kilkee Bay Hotel
Kilkee, Co. Clare
Tel: 065-906 0060
Game Angling:
Trout
Sea Angling:
Mackerel, Pollock, Cod, Herring, Bass
Facilities available:
 ....Page 130

Mountshannon Hotel
Mountshannon, Co. Clare
Tel: 061-927162
Coarse Angling:
Bream, Perch, Pike
Game Angling:
Salmon, Trout
Facilities available:
Page 139

Co. Limerick

Adare Manor Hotel & Golf Resort
Adare, Co. Limerick
Tel: 061-396566
Game Angling:
Salmon, Trout
Facilities available:
 ....Page 140

Fitzgeralds Woodlands House Hotel, Health and Leisure Spa
Adare, Co. Limerick
Tel: 061-605100
Coarse Angling:
Pike
Game Angling:
Trout, Salmon
Facilities available:
 ....Page 142

Co. Tipperary North

Grant's Hotel
Roscrea, Co. Tipperary North
Tel: 0505-23300
Coarse Angling:
Pike, Perch, Tench, Bream
Game Angling:
Salmon, Trout
Facilities available:
 ....Page 148

Racket Hall Country House Golf & Conference Hotel
Roscrea, Co. Tipperary North
Tel: 0505-21748
Coarse Angling:
Pike, Perch, Roach, Bream, Tench
Game Angling:
Salmon, Trout
Facilities available:
 ....Page 148

BT Bait & Tackle   BH Boats For Hire   DR Drying Room   PL Packed Lunches Available On Request
GI Gillie   TR Tackle Room   FR Freezer For Storage Of Catch   PR Permits Required

West

Co. Galway

Alcock and Brown Hotel
Clifden, Co. Galway
Tel: 095-21206
Coarse Angling:
Perch, Pike, Tench, Roach
Game Angling:
Trout, Salmon, Brown Trout
Sea Angling:
Pollock, Cod, Seabass, Mackerel
Facilities available:
 ....Page 157

Ballynahinch Castle Hotel
Ballynahinch, Co. Galway
Tel: 095-31006
Game Angling:
Salmon, Brown Trout, Sea Trout
Sea Angling:
Charter Available
Facilities available:
 Page 154

Ben View House
Clifden, Co. Galway
Tel: 095-21256
Game Angling:
Salmon, Trout
Sea Angling:
Cod, Herring, Whiting, Pollock, Plaice
Facilities available:
 ....Page 158

Carrown Tober House
Oughterard, Co. Galway
Tel: 091-552166
Coarse Angling:
Pike, Perch
Game Angling:
Trout, Salmon
Facilities available:
 ....Page 181

Cashel House Hotel
Cashel, Co. Galway
Tel: 095-31001
Coarse Angling:
Pike
Game Angling:
Trout, Salmon
Facilities available:
 ....Page 155

Clifden Station House Hotel
Clifden, Co. Galway
Tel: 095-21699
Game Angling:
Trout
Sea Angling:
Cod, Pollock, Halibut, Mackerel, Whiting
Facilities available:
 ....Page 159

Connemara Gateway Hotel
Oughterard, Co. Galway
Tel: 091-552328
Coarse Angling:
Pike, Perch
Game Angling:
Salmon, Trout
Sea Angling:
Mackerel
Facilities available:
 ....Page 182

Corrib Wave Guest House
Oughterard, Co. Galway
Tel: 091-552147
Coarse Angling:
Pike, Perch
Game Angling:
Brown Trout, Salmon
Facilities available:
....Page 182

Day's Inishbofin House Hotel
Inishbofin Island, Co. Galway
Tel: 095-45809
Sea Angling:
Pollock, Ray, Plaice, Mackerel, Gurnard, Tope
Facilities available:
................Page 177

Eldons Hotel
Roundstone, Co. Galway
Tel: 095-35933
Sea Angling:
Shark, Pollock, Cod, Mackerel
Facilities available:
 ....Page 185

Fairhill House Hotel
Clonbur (An Fháirche), Co. Galway
Tel: 094-954 6176
Coarse Angling:
Pike, Roach, Perch, Bream, Eel
Game Angling:
Salmon, Wild Brown Trout
Sea Angling:
Dogfish, Cod, Ray, Shark, Pollock
Facilities available:
......Page 161

Galway Bay Hotel, Conference & Leisure Centre
Galway City, Co. Galway
Tel: 091-520520
Coarse Angling:
Bream, Roach, Perch, Rudd
Game Angling:
Salmon, Brown Trout
Sea Angling:
Blue Shark, Cod, Ling, Pollock, Ray
Facilities available:
..........Page 168

Glenlo Abbey Hotel
Galway City, Co. Galway
Tel: 091-526666
Coarse Angling:
Pike, Bream, Roach
Game Angling:
Trout, Salmon
Sea Angling:
Shark, Cod, Mackerel
Facilities available:
..........Page 169

Lough Inagh Lodge
Recess, Co. Galway
Tel: 095-34706
Game Angling:
Salmon, Brown Trout
Sea Angling:
Sea Trout
Facilities available:
 Page 184

 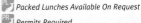

…where to stay when you're Angling!

Co. Galway Continued

Mountain View Guest House
Oughterard, Co. Galway
Tel: 091-550306
Coarse Angling:
Pike, Perch, Bream
Game Angling:
Salmon, Trout
Facilities available:
 ....Page 183

O'Deas Hotel
Loughrea, Co. Galway
Tel: 091-841611
Coarse Angling:
Pike, Perch
Game Angling:
Trout
Facilities available:
 ....Page 180

Peacockes Hotel & Complex
Maam Cross, Co. Galway
Tel: 091-552306
Game Angling:
Salmon
Sea Angling:
Sea Trout, Shark, Cod, Pollock, Mackerel, Ray
Facilities available:
 ....Page 180

Rosleague Manor Hotel
Letterfrack, Co. Galway
Tel: 095-41101
Game Angling:
Salmon, Sea Trout, Brown Trout, Rainbow Trout
Sea Angling:
Mackerel, Pollock, Cod, Shark, Tuna
Facilities available:
 ....Page 179

Shannon Oaks Hotel & Country Club
Portumna, Co. Galway
Tel: 090-974 1777
Coarse Angling:
Pike, Bream, Eel, Roach, Perch
Facilities available:
 ....Page 184

Co. Mayo

Achill Cliff House Hotel
Achill Island, Co. Mayo
Tel: 098-43400
Sea Angling:
Tuna, Pollock, Skate, Shark, Cod, Conger Eel
Facilities available:
 ....Page 187

Ashford Castle
Cong, Co. Mayo
Tel: 094-954 6003
Coarse Angling:
Perch, Pike
Game Angling:
Trout, Salmon
Sea Angling:
Pollock, Mackerel
Facilities available:
 Page 191

Atlantic Coast Hotel
Westport, Co. Mayo
Tel: 098-29000
Coarse Angling:
Eel, Pike, Perch
Game Angling:
Salmon, Trout
Sea Angling:
Sea Trout, Brill, Mackerel, Ling, Pollock, Ray, Shark, Herring
Facilities available:
 ....Page 195

Castlecourt Hotel Conference and Leisure Centre
Westport, Co. Mayo
Tel: 098-55088
Coarse Angling:
Pike, Perch, Roach, Bream, Tench, Hybrids
Game Angling:
Trout, Salmon
Sea Angling:
Cod, Shark, Pollock, Plaice, Dog Fish, Conger Eels, Whiting, Monkfish
Facilities available:
....Page 196

Healys Restaurant & Country House Hotel
Pontoon, Co. Mayo
Tel: 094-925 6443
Coarse Angling:
Pike, Perch
Game Angling:
Salmon, Brown Trout
Sea Angling:
Sea Trout, Rainbow Trout, Shark, Pollock, Cod, Sole
Facilities available:
Page 194

Hotel Westport, Leisure, Spa, Conference
Westport, Co. Mayo
Tel: 098-25122
Coarse Angling:
Pike, Perch, Bream
Game Angling:
Salmon, Trout
Sea Angling:
Pollock, Dog Fish, Cod, Whiting, Blue Shark, Ling, Tope, Skate
Facilities available:
Page 197

JJ Gannons Bar, Restaurant & Hotel
Ballinrobe, Co. Mayo
Tel: 094-954 1008
Coarse Angling:
Bream, Roach, Perch, Pike
Game Angling:
Brown Trout, Salmon
Sea Angling:
Eel, Cod, Herring, Mackerel, Pollock, Sea Trout
Facilities available:
....Page 189

Knockranny House Hotel & Spa
Westport, Co. Mayo
Tel: 098-28600
Game Angling:
Salmon, Trout
Sea Angling:
Sea Trout, Cod, Whiting, Skate, Ray, Monkfish
Facilities available:
....Page 197

 BT Bait & Tackle
 BH Boats For Hire
 DR Drying Room
PL Packed Lunches Available On Request

GI Gillie
TR Tackle Room
FR Freezer For Storage Of Catch
PR Permits Required

Ostan Oilean Acla
Achill Island, Co. Mayo
Tel: 098-45138
Game Angling:
Trout
Sea Angling:
*Cod, Ling, Conger Eel, Shark, Mackerel,
Sea Trout, Brill, Whiting, Ray, Tuna*
Facilities available:
 ....Page 188

Ryan's Hotel
Cong, Co. Mayo
Tel: 094-954 6243
Coarse Angling:
Perch, Pike
Game Angling:
Salmon, Trout
Facilities available:
 Page 192

**Stella Maris
Country House Hotel**
Ballycastle, Co. Mayo
Tel: 096-43322
Game Angling:
Trout, Salmon
Sea Angling:
Cod, Sole, Shark, Pollock, Mackerel
Facilities available:
 ....Page 189

Teach Iorrais
Geesala, Co. Mayo
Tel: 097-86888
Game Angling:
Salmon, Trout
Sea Angling:
Cod, Mackerel
Facilities available:
 ....Page 193

Western Strands Hotel
Belmullet, Co. Mayo
Tel: 097-81096
Sea Angling:
*Mackerel, Pollock, Glasson, Turbot,
Halibut*
Facilities available:
 ....Page 190

Westport Plaza Hotel
Westport, Co. Mayo
Tel: 098-51166
Coarse Angling:
*Pike, Perch, Roach, Bream, Tench,
Hybrids*
Sea Angling:
*Cod, Shark, Pollock, Plaice, Dog Fish,
Conger Eels, Whiting, Monkfish*
Facilities available:
 ....Page 199

Co. Roscommon

**Abbey Hotel, Conference and
Leisure Centre**
Roscommon Town, Co. Roscommon
Tel: 090-662 6240
Coarse Angling:
Pike, Perch, Bream, Roach, Eel
Game Angling:
Trout, Salmon
Facilities available:
 ....Page 200

**Gleesons Townhouse &
Restaurant**
Roscommon Town, Co. Roscommon
Tel: 090-662 6954
Coarse Angling:
*Pike, Rudd, Tench, Roach, Bream,
Perch, Eel*
Game Angling:
Trout
Facilities available:
 ....Page 201

Whitehouse Hotel
Ballinlough, Co. Roscommon
Tel: 094-964 0112
Coarse Angling:
Pike, Perch, Rudd, Bream, Tench
Game Angling:
Brown Trout
Facilities available:
 ....Page 200

North West

Co. Donegal

Arnolds Hotel
Dunfanaghy, Co. Donegal
Tel: 074-913 6208
Game Angling:
Brown Trout, Salmon
Sea Angling:
*Sea Trout, Mackerel, Pollock, Haddock,
Cod, Ling*
Facilities available:
 ....Page 211

Arranmore House Hotel
Arranmore Island, Co. Donegal
Tel: 074-952 0918
Game Angling:
Brown Trout, Rainbow Trout
Sea Angling:
*Pollock, Cod, Plaice, Ling, Conger Eel,
Wrasse*
Facilities available:
 ....Page 204

Bay View Hotel & Leisure Centre
Killybegs, Co. Donegal
Tel: 074-973 1950
Game Angling:
Salmon, Brown Trout
Sea Angling:
*Sea Trout, Tuna, Shark, Pollock, Cod,
Ling*
Facilities available:
 ....Page 212

Dorrians Imperial Hotel
Ballyshannon, Co. Donegal
Tel: 071-985 1147
Coarse Angling:
Bream, Pike, Eel
Game Angling:
Trout, Salmon
Sea Angling:
Cod, Sea Trout, Sole
Facilities available:
 ....Page 206

 Bait & Tackle   *Boats For Hire*   *Drying Room*   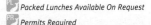 *Packed Lunches Available On Request*

 *Gillie*   *Tackle Room*   *Freezer For Storage Of Catch*   *Permits Required*

Co. Donegal *Continued*

Downings Bay Hotel
Letterkenny, Co. Donegal
Tel: 074-915 5586
Sea Angling:
Pollock, Mackerel, Tuna, Ling, Skate, Cod, Haddock
Facilities available:
BH PL ....Page 214

Great Northern Hotel
Bundoran, Co. Donegal
Tel: 071-984 1204
Coarse Angling:
Pike, Perch
Game Angling:
Salmon, Trout
Sea Angling:
Pollock, Cod, Ling, Plaice, Shark, Sole
Facilities available:
BT BH DR PL GI TR FR PR Page 208

Malin Hotel
Malin, Co. Donegal
Tel: 074-937 0606
Sea Angling:
Cod, Trout, Salmon, Garnet, Whiting
Facilities available:
BT BH PL ....Page 216

Milford Inn Hotel
Milford, Co. Donegal
Tel: 074-915 3313
Game Angling:
Brown Trout, Salmon
Sea Angling:
Sea Trout, Shark, Tope, Ling, Mackerel
Facilities available:
BT BH PL GI FR PR ....Page 216

Ostan Na Tra (Beach Hotel)
Downings, Co. Donegal
Tel: 074-915 5303
Sea Angling:
Shark, Cod, Haddock, Conger, Tuna
Facilities available:
BT BH DR PL FR ....Page 211

Silver Tassie Hotel
Letterkenny, Co. Donegal
Tel: 074-912 5619
Game Angling:
Brown Trout, Salmon
Sea Angling:
Sea Trout, Shark, Tope, Ling, Mackerel
Facilities available:
BT BH PL GI FR PR ....Page 216

North

Co. Down

Royal Hotel
Bangor, Co. Down
Tel: 028-9127 1866
Sea Angling:
Cod, Skate, Mackerel, Haddock, Whiting
Facilities available:
BT BH PL FR ....Page 241

Dublin & East Coast

Co. Meath

Castle Arch Hotel
Trim, Co. Meath
Tel: 046-943 1516
Game Angling:
Trout, Salmon
Facilities available:
PL FR PR ....Page 317

Hamlet Court Hotel
Johnstownbridge, Co. Meath
Tel: 046-954 1200
Coarse Angling:
Tench, Bream, Pike, Roach, Carp
Game Angling:
Trout, Salmon
Facilities available:
BT BH PL GI FR ....Page 315

Co. Wicklow

Arklow Bay Conference and Leisure Hotel
Arklow, Co. Wicklow
Tel: 0402-32309
Game Angling:
Trout
Facilities available:
BT PL ....Page 318

Lawless's Hotel
Aughrim, Co. Wicklow
Tel: 0402-36146
Game Angling:
Wild Brown Trout, Rainbow Trout
Sea Angling:
Codling, Dab, Bass, Dogfish
Facilities available:
PL PR ....Page 320

Porterhouse Inn (The)
Bray, Co. Wicklow
Tel: 01-286 0668
Coarse Angling:
Pike, Perch
Game Angling:
Salmon, Brown Trout
Sea Angling:
Sea Trout, Cod, Mackerel, Sea Bass, Pollock
Facilities available:
BT PL FR PR ....Page 321

Midlands & Lakelands

Co. Cavan

Breffni Arms Hotel
Arvagh, Co. Cavan
Tel: 049-433 5127
Coarse Angling:
Bream, Tench, Pike, Roach, Hybrids
Game Angling:
Trout
Facilities available:
BT BH DR PL TR FR ....Page 330

436

 Bait & Tackle   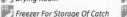 **Boats For Hire**   **Drying Room**    **Packed Lunches Available On Request**
Gillie   **Tackle Room**   **Freezer For Storage Of Catch**   **Permits Required**

Crover House Hotel & Golf Club
Mountnugent, Co. Cavan
Tel: 049-854 0206
Coarse Angling:
Pike
Game Angling:
Trout
Facilities available:
 ....Page 333

Errigal Hotel
Cootehill, Co. Cavan
Tel: 049-555 6901
Coarse Angling:
Pike, Perch, Roach, Bream
Facilities available:
 ....Page 332

Lakeside Manor Hotel
Virginia, Co. Cavan
Tel: 049-854 8200
Coarse Angling:
Bream, Hybrids, Roach, Perch, Pike
Game Angling:
Trout
Facilities available:
 ....Page 334

River Front Hotel (The)
Virginia, Co. Cavan
Tel: 049-854 7561
Coarse Angling:
Bream, Perch, Hybrid
Facilities available:
.........Page 334

Co. Kildare

Bert House Hotel & Leisure Centre
Athy, Co. Kildare
Tel: 059-863 2578
Coarse Angling:
Pike, Bream, Perch, Tench, Rudd
Game Angling:
Trout, Salmon
Facilities available:
 ....Page 335

Carton House
Maynooth, Co. Kildare
Tel: 01-505 2000
Game Angling:
Trout, Salmon
Facilities available:
..........Page 340

Hazel Hotel
Monasterevin, Co. Kildare
Tel: 045-525373
Coarse Angling:
Pike, Rudd, Roach, Eel, Tench, Perch
Game Angling:
Salmon, Trout
Facilities available:
.....................Page 341

Co. Monaghan

Castle Leslie
Glaslough, Co. Monaghan
Tel: 047-88100
Coarse Angling:
Pike, Tench, Bream, Perch, Rudd
Facilities available:
.....................Page 347

Co. Offaly

Brosna Lodge Hotel
Banagher, Co. Offaly
Tel: 057-915 1350
Coarse Angling:
Bream, Tench, Rudd, Roach, Perch, Pike
Game Angling:
Brown Trout, Salmon
Facilities available:
Page 348

Moorhill House Hotel
Tullamore, Co. Offaly
Tel: 057-932 1395
Coarse Angling:
Bream, Roach, Perch, Brown Trout, Pike
Facilities available:
...............Page 352

Co. Westmeath

Glasson Golf Hotel and Country Club
Athlone, Co. Westmeath
Tel: 090-648 5120
Coarse Angling:
Pike, Perch, Roach, Bream
Game Angling:
Brown Trout
Facilities available:
....Page 353

Hodson Bay Hotel
Athlone, Co. Westmeath
Tel: 090-644 2000
Coarse Angling:
Bream, Perch, Pike
Game Angling:
Brown Trout
Facilities available:
..........Page 354

South East

Co. Carlow

Seven Oaks Hotel
Carlow Town, Co. Carlow
Tel: 059-913 1308
Coarse Angling:
Bream, Perch, Roach, Pike, Eel
Game Angling:
Salmon, Trout
Facilities available:
..........Page 362

Co. Kilkenny

Butler House
Kilkenny City, Co. Kilkenny
Tel: 056-776 5707
Game Angling:
Brown Trout, Salmon
Facilities available:
....Page 364

 Bait & Tackle
 Boats For Hire
 Drying Room
 Packed Lunches Available On Request
Gillie
Tackle Room
Freezer For Storage Of Catch
Permits Required
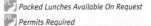

Co. Kilkenny continued

Kilkenny River Court
Kilkenny City, Co. Kilkenny
Tel: 056-772 3388
Game Angling:
Trout, Salmon

Facilities available:
...................................Page 368

Lyrath Estate Hotel, Spa & Convention Centre
Kilkenny City, Co. Kilkenny
Tel: 056-776 0088
Coarse Angling:
Shad, Bream

Game Angling:
Salmon, Trout

Facilities available:
Page 370

Mount Juliet Conrad
Thomastown, Co. Kilkenny
Tel: 056-777 3000
Game Angling:
Salmon, Trout

Facilities available:
..........Page 373

Co. Tipperary South

Cahir House Hotel
Cahir, Co. Tipperary South
Tel: 052-43000
Coarse Angling:
Perch, Pike

Game Angling:
Trout, Salmon

Facilities available:
..........Page 373

Cashel Palace Hotel
Cashel, Co. Tipperary South
Tel: 062-62707
Coarse Angling:
Perch

Game Angling:
Salmon, Brown Trout, Grilse

Facilities available:
Page 375

Co. Wexford

Carlton Millrace Hotel (The)
Bunclody, Co. Wexford
Tel: 053-937 5100
Game Angling:
Small Wild Brown Trout

Sea Angling:
Bass, Sea Trout

Facilities available:
......................Page 395

Hotel Saltees
Kilmore Quay, Co. Wexford
Tel: 053-912 9601
Sea Angling:
Tope, Cod, Pollock, Ray, Ling

Facilities available:
......................Page 399

 Bait & Tackle   Boats For Hire   Drying Room   Packed Lunches Available On Request
Gillie   Tackle Room   Freezer For Storage Of Catch   Permits Required

IRELAND 2006 CONFERENCE

Small meetings or large conferences are part and parcel of life in Irish hotels and guesthouses. What makes Ireland special as a venue is the warmth of the welcome you will receive, coupled with excellent facilities which can be tailored to your needs.

.....Our venues will tick all your boxes!

We will be glad to see you and work with you to make your meeting or conference a successful one. Choose from the wide selection of special facilities throughout the country as shown here. A full description of the hotels and guesthouses can be had by looking up the appropriate page number.

Premises are listed in Alphabetical Order in each County.

South West

Co. Cork

Actons Hotel
Kinsale, Co. Cork
Tel: 021-477 9900 ....Page 60
Contact Person:
Kate Howey
Seating Capacity of Meeting Rooms:
+300: **1** -50: **2**
Facilities available:

Aherne's Townhouse & Seafood Restaurant
Youghal, Co. Cork
Tel: 024-92424 ....Page 69
Contact Person:
John Fitzgibbon
Seating Capacity of Meeting Rooms:
-50: **2**
Facilities available:

Ambassador Hotel
Cork City, Co. Cork
Tel: 021-455 1996 ....Page 47
Contact Person:
Sile Ni Dhonaile / Dudley Fitzell
Seating Capacity of Meeting Rooms:
+200: **1** +100: **2** +50: **2** -50: **1**
Facilities available:

Ballymaloe House
Shanagarry, Co. Cork
Tel: 021-465 2531 ....Page 68
Contact Person:
Natasha Harty
Seating Capacity of Meeting Rooms:
-50: **2**
Facilities available:

Blarney Park Hotel and Leisure Centre
Blarney, Co. Cork
Tel: 021-438 5281.....................Page 41
Contact Person:
Josephine Noonan
Seating Capacity of Meeting Rooms:
+200: **1** +50: **3** -50: **2**
Facilities available:

Celtic Ross Hotel Conference & Leisure Centre
Rosscarbery, Co. Cork
Tel: 023-48722 ....Page 67
Contact Person:
Peter McDermott
Seating Capacity of Meeting Rooms:
+200: **1** +50: **1** -50: **1**
Facilities available:

Clarion Hotel
Cork City, Co. Cork
Tel: 021-422 4900 ....Page 49
Contact Person:
Miriam Casey
Seating Capacity of Meeting Rooms:
+300: **1**
Facilities available:

Commodore Hotel
Cobh, Co. Cork
Tel: 021-481 1277.....................Page 45
Contact Person:
Robert Fitzpatrick
Seating Capacity of Meeting Rooms:
+300: **1** -50: **1**
Facilities available:

Commons Inn
Cork City, Co. Cork
Tel: 021-421 0300 ....Page 49
Contact Person:
Ashley Colson
Seating Capacity of Meeting Rooms:
+300: **1** +50: **1** -50: **3**
Facilities available:

Glengarriff Eccles Hotel
Glengarriff, Co. Cork
Tel: 027-63003 ....Page 59
Contact Person:
Geraldine Owens
Seating Capacity of Meeting Rooms:
+300: **1** +50: **1** -50: **1**
Facilities available:

Great Southern Hotel
Cork Airport, Co. Cork
Tel: 021-494 7500 ....Page 46
Contact Person:
Agnes Hennessy
Seating Capacity of Meeting Rooms:
+200: **1** -50: **5**
Facilities available:

Gresham Metropole
Cork City, Co. Cork
Tel: 021-464 3789 ....Page 51
Contact Person:
Fiona Keohane
Seating Capacity of Meeting Rooms:
+500: **1** +400: **1** +300: **1** +200: **2** +100: **2** +50: **6** -50: **11**
Facilities available:

 440

BO Black Out Facilities
IEH Interpreting Equipment (Can Arrange Hire)
AC Air-Conditioning
AVO Audio Visual (Available On Premises)
IEO Interpreting Equipment (Available On Premises)
AVH Audio Visual (Can Arrange Hire)

Hibernian Hotel and Leisure Centre
Mallow, Co. Cork
Tel: 022-21588..........................Page 64
Contact Person:
Catherine Gyves
Seating Capacity of Meeting Rooms:
+300: **1** +100: **1** +50: **2** -50: **4**
Facilities available:
BO AC IEH AVO

Hotel Isaacs
Cork City, Co. Cork
Tel: 021-450 0011.......................Page 52
Contact Person:
Paula Lynch
Seating Capacity of Meeting Rooms:
-50: **2**
Facilities available:
BO AC IEH AVH

Imperial Hotel with Lifestyle Salon and Spa
Cork City, Co. Cork
Tel: 021-427 4040 ....Page 52
Contact Person:
Jodi Cronin
Seating Capacity of Meeting Rooms:
+300: **1** +200: **1** +100: **2** +50: **5**
-50: **1**
Facilities available:
BO AC IEH AVH

Inchydoney Island Lodge & Spa
Clonakilty, Co. Cork
Tel: 023-33143...........................Page 44
Contact Person:
Peter Lehoybe
Seating Capacity of Meeting Rooms:
+300: **1** -50: **4**
Facilities available:
BO AC IEH AVO

Kingsley Hotel & Residence
Cork City, Co. Cork
Tel: 021-480 0500 ....Page 53
Contact Person:
Anne Cahill / Aoife Brennan
Seating Capacity of Meeting Rooms:
+200: **1** +100: **1** +50: **1** -50: **7**
Facilities available:
BO AC IEH AVO

Maryborough House Hotel
Cork City, Co. Cork
Tel: 021-436 5555 ....Page 55
Contact Person:
Mary Bernard
Seating Capacity of Meeting Rooms:
+400: **1** +300: **1** +100: **2** +50: **2**
-50: **5**
Facilities available:
BO AC IEH AVO

Oriel House Hotel & Leisure Centre
Ballincollig, Co. Cork
Tel: 021-487 0888 ....Page 36
Contact Person:
Sales Manager
Seating Capacity of Meeting Rooms:
+300: **2** +100: **2** -50: **2**
Facilities available:
BO AC IEH AVO

Quality Hotel & Leisure Centre Clonakilty
Clonakilty, Co. Cork
Tel: 023-36400 ....Page 45
Contact Person:
Raymond Kelleher
Seating Capacity of Meeting Rooms:
+100: **1** +50: **1** -50: **1**
Facilities available:
BO AVH

Quality Hotel and Leisure Centre Youghal
Youghal, Co. Cork
Tel: 024-93050 ....Page 69
Contact Person:
Raymond Kelleher
Seating Capacity of Meeting Rooms:
+50: **1** -50: **1**
Facilities available:
BO IEH AVO

Radisson SAS Hotel & Spa, Cork
Cork City, Co. Cork
Tel: 021-429 7000 ....Page 55
Contact Person:
Linda Schnadt
Seating Capacity of Meeting Rooms:
+400: **1** +200: **2** -50: **11**
Facilities available:
BO AC IEH AVO

Rochestown Park Hotel
Cork City, Co. Cork
Tel: 021-489 0800 ....Page 56
Contact Person:
Liam Lally/Jim Casey
Seating Capacity of Meeting Rooms:
+500: **2** +400: **2** +300: **2** +200: **2**
+100: **4** +50: **9** -50: **9**
Facilities available:
BO AC IEH AVH

Silver Springs Moran Hotel
Cork City, Co. Cork
Tel: 021-450 7533 ....Page 57
Contact Person:
Sales & Conference Co-Ordinator
Seating Capacity of Meeting Rooms:
+500: **2** +300: **4** +200: **4** +100: **4**
+50: **4** -50: **7**
Facilities available:
BO AC IEH AVH

Springfort Hall Hotel
Mallow, Co. Cork
Tel: 022-21278..........................Page 65
Contact Person:
Mags Brazzill
Seating Capacity of Meeting Rooms:
+300: **1** +200: **1** +100: **1** +50: **1**
-50: **3**
Facilities available:
IEH AVO

Trident Hotel
Kinsale, Co. Cork
Tel: 021-477 9300 ....Page 63
Contact Person:
Hal McElroy/Una Wren
Seating Capacity of Meeting Rooms:
+200: **1** -50: **5**
Facilities available:
BO AC IEH AVO

Walter Raleigh Hotel
Youghal, Co. Cork
Tel: 024-92011 ....Page 70
Contact Person:
Eoin Daly
Seating Capacity of Meeting Rooms:
+300: **1** +200: **1** +100: **1** +50: **1**
-50: **2**
Facilities available:
BO AC IEH AVH

Co. Cork Continued

Westlodge Hotel
Bantry, Co. Cork
Tel: 027-50360 ....Page 40
Contact Person:
Eileen M. O'Shea

Seating Capacity of Meeting Rooms:
+300: 1 +200: 1 +100: 1 +50: 1
-50: 1
Facilities available:
BO AC IEH AVH

Co. Kerry

Abbey Gate Hotel
Tralee, Co. Kerry
Tel: 066-712 9888 ....Page 110
Contact Person:
Kieran Murphy

Seating Capacity of Meeting Rooms:
+300: 1 +100: 1 +50: 2 -50: 2
Facilities available:
BO AC AVO

Aghadoe Heights Hotel & Spa
Killarney, Co. Kerry
Tel: 064-31766 ....Page 88
Contact Person:
Emma Phillips

Seating Capacity of Meeting Rooms:
+100: 1 -50: 2
Facilities available:
BO AC AVO

Ballygarry House Hotel
Tralee, Co. Kerry
Tel: 066-712 3322 ....Page 111
Contact Person:
Patricia Hourihane

Seating Capacity of Meeting Rooms:
+300: 1 +200: 1 -50: 5
Facilities available:
BO AC IEH AVO

Ballyroe Heights Hotel
Tralee, Co. Kerry
Tel: 066-712 6796 ....Page 111
Contact Person:
Mark Sullivan

Seating Capacity of Meeting Rooms:
+400: 1 +300: 1 +200: 1 +100: 2
+50: 2 -50: 1
Facilities available:
BO AC IEH AVO

Brandon Hotel Conference and Leisure Centre
Tralee, Co. Kerry
Tel: 066-712 3333 ....Page 112
Contact Person:
Aine Brosnan

Seating Capacity of Meeting Rooms:
+500: 1 +400: 1 +300: 2 +200: 3
+100: 4 +50: 7 -50: 8
Facilities available:
BO AC IEH AVO

Brehon (The)
Killarney, Co. Kerry
Tel: 064-30700 ....Page 90
Contact Person:
Cara Fuller

Seating Capacity of Meeting Rooms:
+200: 1 -50: 4
Facilities available:
BO AC IEH AVO

Castlerosse Hotel, Golf & Leisure Club
Killarney, Co. Kerry
Tel: 064-31144 ....Page 91
Contact Person:
Michael O'Sullivan

Seating Capacity of Meeting Rooms:
+200: 1 +50: 1
Facilities available:
BO IEH AVH

Dingle Skellig Hotel & Peninsula Spa
Dingle (An Daingean), Co. Kerry
Tel: 066-915 0200 ....Page 78
Contact Person:
Karen Byrnes

Seating Capacity of Meeting Rooms:
+200: 1 -50: 2
Facilities available:
BO AC IEH AVO

Dromhall Hotel
Killarney, Co. Kerry
Tel: 064-39300 ....Page 92
Contact Person:
Bernadette Randles

Seating Capacity of Meeting Rooms:
+300: 1 +200: 1 +100: 1 +50: 1
-50: 1
Facilities available:
BO AC IEH AVH

Gleneagle Hotel
Killarney, Co. Kerry
Tel: 064-36000 ....Page 96
Contact Person:
Cara Fuller

Seating Capacity of Meeting Rooms:
+500: 2 +400: 2 +300: 3 +200: 3
+100: 4 +50: 4 -50: 4
Facilities available:
BO AC IEH AVO

Grand Hotel
Tralee, Co. Kerry
Tel: 066-712 1499 ....Page 113
Contact Person:
Eileen Egan

Seating Capacity of Meeting Rooms:
+200: 1 +100: 1 +50: 6 -50: 6
Facilities available:
BO AC IEH AVH

Hotel Dunloe Castle
Killarney, Co. Kerry
Tel: 064-44111 ....Page 97
Contact Person:
Suzanne Ennis

Seating Capacity of Meeting Rooms:
+200: 1 +100: 2 +50: 2 -50: 2
Facilities available:
BO IEH AVH

Hotel Europe
Killarney, Co. Kerry
Tel: 064-71300 ....Page 97
Contact Person:
Suzanne Ennis

Seating Capacity of Meeting Rooms:
+400: 1 +300: 1 +200: 1 +100: 3
+50: 2
Facilities available:
BO IEO AVH

BO Black Out Facilities
IEH Interpreting Equipment (Can Arrange Hire)
AC Air-Conditioning
AVO Audio Visual (Available On Premises)
IEO Interpreting Equipment (Available On Premises)
AVH Audio Visual (Can Arrange Hire)

Killarney Great Southern Hotel
Killarney, Co. Kerry
Tel: 064-38000 ....Page 99
Contact Person:
Emer Smyth
Seating Capacity of Meeting Rooms:
👤+500: **1** 👤+200: **1** 👤+50: **2** 👤-50: **2**
Facilities available:

Killarney Park Hotel
Killarney, Co. Kerry
Tel: 064-35555.........................Page 100
Contact Person:
Marie Carmody/ Aoife Hickey
Seating Capacity of Meeting Rooms:
👤+100: **1** 👤+50: **1** 👤-50: **3**
Facilities available:

Killarney Plaza Hotel & Spa
Killarney, Co. Kerry
Tel: 064-21111..........................Page 101
Contact Person:
Mary Hartnett
Seating Capacity of Meeting Rooms:
👤+200: **1** 👤+50: **2**
Facilities available:

Killarney Royal
Killarney, Co. Kerry
Tel: 064-31853 ....Page 101
Contact Person:
Nicola Duggan
Seating Capacity of Meeting Rooms:
👤+50: **1**
Facilities available:

Lake Hotel
Killarney, Co. Kerry
Tel: 064-31035 ....Page 102
Contact Person:
Catherine Ryan / Eileen O'Sullivan
Seating Capacity of Meeting Rooms:
👤+50: **1** 👤-50: **2**
Facilities available:

Manor West Hotel, Spa & Leisure Club
Tralee, Co. Kerry
Tel: 066-719 4500....................Page 114
Contact Person:
Ruth O'Reilly / Hazel Boyle
Seating Capacity of Meeting Rooms:
👤+200: **1** 👤+50: **1** 👤-50: **2**
Facilities available:

Meadowlands Hotel
Tralee, Co. Kerry
Tel: 066-718 0444.....................Page 114
Contact Person:
Pamela Lucey
Seating Capacity of Meeting Rooms:
👤+200: **1** 👤+100: **2** 👤+50: **1** 👤-50: **2**
Facilities available:

Muckross Park Hotel
Killarney, Co. Kerry
Tel: 064-31938 ....Page 104
Contact Person:
Susan Whelan
Seating Capacity of Meeting Rooms:
👤+400: **1** 👤+300: **1** 👤+200: **1** 👤+50: **4**
Facilities available:

Parknasilla Great Southern Hotel
Sneem, Co. Kerry
Tel: 064-45122 ....Page 109
Contact Person:
Andrew Rees
Seating Capacity of Meeting Rooms:
👤+50: **1** 👤-50: **1**
Facilities available:

Randles Court Clarion Hotel
Killarney, Co. Kerry
Tel: 064-35333.........................Page 105
Contact Person:
Tom Randles
Seating Capacity of Meeting Rooms:
👤+100: **1** 👤+50: **1**
Facilities available:

Sheen Falls Lodge
Kenmare, Co. Kerry
Tel: 064-41600..........................Page 86
Contact Person:
Marianne Wiley
Seating Capacity of Meeting Rooms:
👤+100: **1** 👤+50: **1** 👤-50: **2**
Facilities available:

Smerwick Harbour Hotel
Dingle (An Daingean), Co. Kerry
Tel: 066-915 6470 ....Page 82
Contact Person:
Brendan Houlihan
Seating Capacity of Meeting Rooms:
👤+100: **1** 👤+50: **1** 👤-50: **1**
Facilities available:

Waterville Lodge Hotel
Waterville, Co. Kerry
Tel: 066-947 4436 ....Page 117
Contact Person:
Patrick Fahy
Seating Capacity of Meeting Rooms:
👤+400: **1**
Facilities available:

Shannon

Co. Clare

Bunratty Castle Hotel
Bunratty, Co. Clare
Tel: 061-478700 ....Page 122
Contact Person:
Marguerite Curran
Seating Capacity of Meeting Rooms:
👤+100: **1** 👤+50: **1** 👤-50: **2**
Facilities available:

Falls Hotel Spa & Leisure Centre
Ennistymon, Co. Clare
Tel: 065-707 1004 ....Page 129
Contact Person:
Joanne Clancy
Seating Capacity of Meeting Rooms:
👤+300: **1** 👤+200: **1** 👤+100: **1** 👤+50: **2**
👤-50: **4**
Facilities available:

 Black Out Facilities
 Interpreting Equipment (Can Arrange Hire)
 Air-Conditioning
Audio Visual (Available On Premises)
 Interpreting Equipment (Available On Premises)
Audio Visual (Can Arrange Hire)

Co. Clare Continued

Great Southern Hotel
Shannon Airport, Co. Clare
Tel: 061-471122 ....Page 140
Contact Person:
Louise O'Hara
Seating Capacity of Meeting Rooms:
+200: 1 -50: 3
Facilities available:

Kilkee Bay Hotel
Kilkee, Co. Clare
Tel: 065-906 0060 ....Page 130
Contact Person:
Stephanie Smyth
Seating Capacity of Meeting Rooms:
+100: 1 +50: 1
Facilities available:

Mountshannon Hotel
Mountshannon, Co. Clare
Tel: 061-927162 ....Page 139
Contact Person:
Pauline Madden
Seating Capacity of Meeting Rooms:
+200: 1
Facilities available:

Temple Gate Hotel
Ennis, Co. Clare
Tel: 065-682 3300 ....Page 128
Contact Person:
Paul Madden
Seating Capacity of Meeting Rooms:
+200: 1 +100: 1 +50: 2 -50: 1
Facilities available:

Co. Limerick

Adare Manor Hotel & Golf Resort
Adare, Co. Limerick
Tel: 061-396566 ....Page 140
Contact Person:
Yvette Kennedy
Seating Capacity of Meeting Rooms:
+200: 1 +100: 1 +50: 1 -50: 4
Facilities available:

Castletroy Park Hotel
Limerick City, Co. Limerick
Tel: 061-335566 ....Page 142
Contact Person:
Ursula Cullen
Seating Capacity of Meeting Rooms:
+400: 1 +300: 2 +200: 2 +100: 2
+50: 2 -50: 9
Facilities available:

Clarion Hotel Limerick
Limerick City, Co. Limerick
Tel: 061-444100 ....Page 143
Contact Person:
Veronica Edwards
Seating Capacity of Meeting Rooms:
+100: 1 +50: 2 -50: 9
Facilities available:

Fitzgeralds Woodlands House Hotel, Health and Leisure Spa
Adare, Co. Limerick
Tel: 061-605100 ....Page 142
Contact Person:
David or Michael
Seating Capacity of Meeting Rooms:
+400: 1 +300: 1 +200: 1 +100: 2
+50: 3 -50: 3
Facilities available:

Greenhills Hotel Conference/Leisure
Limerick City, Co. Limerick
Tel: 061-453033 ....Page 143
Contact Person:
Maura Shine
Seating Capacity of Meeting Rooms:
+500: 1 +400: 1 +300: 1 +200: 1
+100: 2 +50: 3 -50: 4
Facilities available:

Kilmurry Lodge Hotel
Limerick City, Co. Limerick
Tel: 061-331133 ....Page 144
Contact Person:
Ciara Hogan
Seating Capacity of Meeting Rooms:
+300: 1 +100: 1 +50: 2 -50: 3
Facilities available:

Old Quarter Lodge
Limerick City, Co. Limerick
Tel: 061-315320 ....Page 144
Contact Person:
Carole Kelly
Seating Capacity of Meeting Rooms:
-50: 1
Facilities available:

Rathkeale House Hotel
Rathkeale, Co. Limerick
Tel: 069-63333......................Page 147
Contact Person:
Gerry O'Connor
Seating Capacity of Meeting Rooms:
+300: 1 +100: 1 -50: 1
Facilities available:

Woodfield House Hotel
Limerick City, Co. Limerick
Tel: 061-453022 ....Page 146
Contact Person:
Ken or Majella
Seating Capacity of Meeting Rooms:
+50: 1 -50: 1
Facilities available:

Co. Tipperary North

Abbey Court Hotel and Trinity Leisure Club
Nenagh, Co. Tipperary North
Tel: 067-41111 ....Page 147
Contact Person:
Clodagh McDonnell
Seating Capacity of Meeting Rooms:
+400: 1 +300: 1 +200: 1 +100: 2
+50: 6 -50: 4
Facilities available:

Anner Hotel & Leisure Centre
Thurles, Co. Tipperary North
Tel: 0504-21799 ....Page 149
Contact Person:
Joan Brett-Moloney
Seating Capacity of Meeting Rooms:
+400: 1 +300: 1 +200: 1 +100: 2
+50: 3
Facilities available:

BO Black Out Facilities

IEH Interpreting Equipment (Can Arrange Hire)

AC Air-Conditioning

AVO Audio Visual (Available On Premises)

IEO Interpreting Equipment (Available On Premises)

AVH Audio Visual (Can Arrange Hire)

Grant's Hotel
Roscrea, Co. Tipperary North
Tel: 0505-23300......................Page 148
Contact Person:
Liam Grimes
Seating Capacity of Meeting Rooms:
👤+500: **1** 👤+400: **1** 👤+300: **1** 👤+200: **2**
👤+100: **2** 👤+50: **2** 👤-50: **3**
Facilities available:
BO AC IEH AVO

Racket Hall Country House Golf & Conference Hotel
Roscrea, Co. Tipperary North
Tel: 0505-21748 ....Page 148
Contact Person:
Belinda McSpadden
Seating Capacity of Meeting Rooms:
👤+300: **1** 👤+200: **1** 👤+100: **2** 👤+50: **4**
👤-50: **3**
Facilities available:
BO AC IEH AVO

Templemore Arms Hotel
Templemore, Co. Tipperary North
Tel: 0504-31423 ....Page 149
Contact Person:
Julie Tarrant
Seating Capacity of Meeting Rooms:
👤+200: **1** 👤+50: **1** 👤-50: **1**
Facilities available:
AC AVH

West

Co. Galway

Ardilaun House Hotel, Conference Centre & Leisure Club
Galway City, Co. Galway
Tel: 091-521433 ....Page 164
Contact Person:
Orla Dolan
Seating Capacity of Meeting Rooms:
👤+400: **1** 👤+300: **1** 👤+200: **1** 👤+100: **2**
👤+50: **4** 👤-50: **6**
Facilities available:
AC IEH AVO

Best Western Flannery's Hotel
Galway City, Co. Galway
Tel: 091-755111......................Page 165
Contact Person:
Siobhan Farragher
Seating Capacity of Meeting Rooms:
👤+100: **1** 👤+50: **1** 👤-50: **1**
Facilities available:
BO AC IEH AVH

Clifden Station House Hotel
Clifden, Co. Galway
Tel: 095-21699 ....Page 159
Contact Person:
Daniel Loosley
Seating Capacity of Meeting Rooms:
👤+100: **1**
Facilities available:
AC AVO

Connemara Coast Hotel
Furbo, Co. Galway
Tel: 091-592108 ....Page 162
Contact Person:
Karl Reinhardt
Seating Capacity of Meeting Rooms:
👤+400: **1** 👤+300: **1** 👤+200: **2** 👤+100: **2**
👤+50: **5** 👤-50: **8**
Facilities available:
BO IEH AVO

Corrib Great Southern Hotel
Galway City, Co. Galway
Tel: 091-755281 ....Page 166
Contact Person:
Anne Nangle
Seating Capacity of Meeting Rooms:
👤+500: **1** 👤+200: **2** 👤+50: **1** 👤-50: **3**
Facilities available:
BO AC IEH AVO

Courtyard By Marriott
Galway City, Co. Galway
Tel: 091-513200 ....Page 166
Contact Person:
The Conference Organiser
Seating Capacity of Meeting Rooms:
👤+100: **2** 👤+50: **4** 👤-50: **1**
Facilities available:
BO AC IEH AVO

Days Hotel Galway
Galway City, Co. Galway
Tel: 1890-776655 ....Page 167
Contact Person:
Laurie Clothier
Seating Capacity of Meeting Rooms:
👤+50: **6**
Facilities available:
BO AC IEH AVO

Doonmore Hotel
Inishbofin Island, Co. Galway
Tel: 095-45804......................Page 178
Contact Person:
Aileen Murray
Seating Capacity of Meeting Rooms:
👤+50: **2**
Facilities available:
BO IEH AVH

Fairhill House Hotel
Clonbur (An Fháirche), Co. Galway
Tel: 094-954 6176 ....Page 161
Contact Person:
Edward Lynch
Seating Capacity of Meeting Rooms:
👤+50: **1**
Facilities available:
BO AC IEH AVH

G (The)
Galway City, Co. Galway
Tel: 091-865200 ....Page 168
Contact Person:
Karen Jones
Seating Capacity of Meeting Rooms:
👤+50: **1** 👤-50: **5**
Facilities available:
BO AC IEH AVO

Galway Bay Hotel, Conference & Leisure Centre
Galway City, Co. Galway
Tel: 091-520520 ....Page 168
Contact Person:
Virginia Connolly
Seating Capacity of Meeting Rooms:
👤+500: **1** 👤+400: **1** 👤+300: **2** 👤+200: **2**
👤+100: **2** 👤+50: **5** 👤-50: **5**
Facilities available:
BO AC IEH AVO

 BO Black Out Facilities
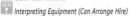 **IEH** Interpreting Equipment (Can Arrange Hire)
AC Air-Conditioning
AVO Audio Visual (Available On Premises)
 IEO Interpreting Equipment (Available On Premises)
AVH Audio Visual (Can Arrange Hire)

445

Co. Galway *Continued*

Glenlo Abbey Hotel
Galway City, Co. Galway
Tel: 091-526666 ....Page 169
Contact Person:
Brian Bourke
Seating Capacity of Meeting Rooms:
+100: **1** +50: **2** -50: **9**
Facilities available:
BO AC IEH AVH

Great Southern Hotel
Galway City, Co. Galway
Tel: 091-564041 ....Page 169
Contact Person:
Tina Kelly
Seating Capacity of Meeting Rooms:
+200: **1** +100: **1** -50: **3**
Facilities available:
BO AC IEH AVO

Harbour Hotel
Galway City, Co. Galway
Tel: 091-569466 ....Page 169
Contact Person:
Victoria Joyce
Seating Capacity of Meeting Rooms:
+50: **1** -50: **4**
Facilities available:
BO AC IEH AVO

Kilmurvey House
Aran Islands, Co. Galway
Tel: 099-61218 ....Page 152
Contact Person:
Treasa Joyce
Seating Capacity of Meeting Rooms:
+50: **1**
Facilities available:
BO IEH AVH

Lady Gregory Hotel
Gort, Co. Galway
Tel: 091-632333 ....Page 177
Contact Person:
Brian Morrissey
Seating Capacity of Meeting Rooms:
+300: **1** -50: **2**
Facilities available:
BO AC IEH AVO

Meadow Court Hotel
Loughrea, Co. Galway
Tel: 091-841051 ....Page 179
Contact Person:
Tom Corbett Jnr
Seating Capacity of Meeting Rooms:
+300: **1** -50: **1**
Facilities available:
BO AC AVH

Oranmore Lodge Hotel, Conference & Leisure Centre
Oranmore, Co. Galway
Tel: 091-794400 ....Page 180
Contact Person:
Mary O'Higgins/ Shirley Kilduff
Seating Capacity of Meeting Rooms:
+300: **1** +100: **1** +50: **1** -50: **1**
Facilities available:
BO AC IEH AVH

Peacockes Hotel & Complex
Maam Cross, Co. Galway
Tel: 091-552306 ....Page 180
Contact Person:
Eimear Killian
Seating Capacity of Meeting Rooms:
+500: **1** +200: **1** +100: **1**
Facilities available:
BO AC IEH AVO

Radisson SAS Hotel & Spa Galway
Galway City, Co. Galway
Tel: 091-538300 ....Page 173
Contact Person:
Fiona Keys
Seating Capacity of Meeting Rooms:
+500: **1** +100: **3** -50: **8**
Facilities available:
BO AC IEH AVO

Salthill Court Hotel
Galway City, Co. Galway
Tel: 091-522711 ....Page 174
Contact Person:
Pauline Griffin
Seating Capacity of Meeting Rooms:
+200: **1** +100: **1**
Facilities available:
BO AC IEH AVO

Shannon Oaks Hotel & Country Club
Portumna, Co. Galway
Tel: 090-974 1777 ....Page 184
Contact Person:
Mary Broder
Seating Capacity of Meeting Rooms:
+500: **1** +100: **1** +50: **1** -50: **2**
Facilities available:
BO AC IEH AVO

Victoria Hotel
Galway City, Co. Galway
Tel: 091-567433 ....Page 175
Contact Person:
Reception
Seating Capacity of Meeting Rooms:
-50: **1**
Facilities available:
AC IEH AVH

Westwood House Hotel
Galway City, Co. Galway
Tel: 091-521442 ....Page 176
Contact Person:
Declan Curtis
Seating Capacity of Meeting Rooms:
+300: **1** +200: **1** +100: **1** +50: **3**
-50: **3**
Facilities available:
BO AC IEH AVO

Co. Mayo

Ashford Castle
Cong, Co. Mayo
Tel: 094-954 6003 ....Page 191
Contact Person:
Regina O'Donoghue
Seating Capacity of Meeting Rooms:
+100: **1**
Facilities available:
IEH AVH

Atlantic Coast Hotel
Westport, Co. Mayo
Tel: 098-29000......................Page 195
Contact Person:
Suzanne O'Brien
Seating Capacity of Meeting Rooms:
+100: **1** -50: **3**
Facilities available:
BO AC IEH AVO

BO Black Out Facilities
IEH Interpreting Equipment (Can Arrange Hire)
AC Air-Conditioning
AVO Audio Visual (Available On Premises)
IEO Interpreting Equipment (Available On Premises)
AVH Audio Visual (Can Arrange Hire)

Castlecourt Hotel Conference and Leisure Centre
Westport, Co. Mayo
Tel: 098-55088.........................Page 196
Contact Person:
Ciara Joyce
Seating Capacity of Meeting Rooms:
+500: **1** +400: **1** +300: **2** +200: **3**
+100: **4** +50: **6** -50: **8**
Facilities available:
BO AC IEH AVO

Downhill House Hotel
Ballina, Co. Mayo
Tel: 096-21033 ....Page 188
Contact Person:
Kay Devine / Rachael Moylett
Seating Capacity of Meeting Rooms:
+400: **1** +300: **1** +200: **1** +100: **1**
+50: **2** -50: **4**
Facilities available:
AC IEH AVO

Hotel Westport, Leisure, Spa, Conference
Westport, Co. Mayo
Tel: 098-25122   Page 197
Contact Person:
Gerry Walshe / Ruth Farrell / Rhona Chambers
Seating Capacity of Meeting Rooms:
+300: **1** +100: **1** +50: **3** -50: **1**
Facilities available:
BO AC IEH AVO

JJ Gannons Bar, Restaurant & Hotel
Ballinrobe, Co. Mayo
Tel: 094-954 1008 ....Page 189
Contact Person:
Niki Gannon
Seating Capacity of Meeting Rooms:
+500: **1**
Facilities available:
BO AC IEO AVO

Knock House Hotel
Knock, Co. Mayo
Tel: 094-938 8088 ....Page 193
Contact Person:
Brian Crowley
Seating Capacity of Meeting Rooms:
+100: **1** +50: **1** -50: **1**
Facilities available:
AVO

Knockranny House Hotel & Spa
Westport, Co. Mayo
Tel: 098-28600.........................Page 197
Contact Person:
Patricia Crowley / Fergal Harte
Seating Capacity of Meeting Rooms:
+500: **1** +400: **1** +300: **1** +200: **1**
+100: **2** +50: **3** -50: **3**
Facilities available:
BO AC IEH AVO

Ostan Oilean Acla
Achill Island, Co. Mayo
Tel: 098-45138 ....Page 188
Contact Person:
Michael McLoughlin
Seating Capacity of Meeting Rooms:
+300: **1** +50: **1** -50: **1**
Facilities available:
BO AC IEO AVO

Park Inn Mulranny
Mulranny, Co. Mayo
Tel: 098-36000.........................Page 194
Contact Person:
Tara O'Brien
Seating Capacity of Meeting Rooms:
+300: **1** +50: **2**
Facilities available:
BO AC IEH AVO

Pontoon Bridge Hotel
Pontoon, Co. Mayo
Tel: 094-925 6120 ....Page 194
Contact Person:
Breeta Geary / Sean McLinden
Seating Capacity of Meeting Rooms:
+200: **1** +100: **1** +50: **1** -50: **3**
Facilities available:
AC IEH AVH

Teach Iorrais
Geesala, Co. Mayo
Tel: 097-86888.........................Page 193
Contact Person:
Sean Gaughan
Seating Capacity of Meeting Rooms:
+200: **2**
Facilities available:
BO AC IEH AVH

TF Royal Hotel & Theatre
Castlebar, Co. Mayo
Tel: 094-902 3111 ....Page 191
Contact Person:
Donnacha Roache
Seating Capacity of Meeting Rooms:
+500: **1** +400: **1** +300: **2** +200: **2**
+100: **3** +50: **3** -50: **4**
Facilities available:
BO AC IEH AVO

Westport Plaza Hotel
Westport, Co. Mayo
Tel: 098-51166 ....Page 199
Contact Person:
Sinead Hopkins
Seating Capacity of Meeting Rooms:
+50: **1**
Facilities available:
BO AC IEH AVO

Westport Woods Hotel & Spa
Westport, Co. Mayo
Tel: 098-25811 ....Page 199
Seating Capacity of Meeting Rooms:
+400: **1** +300: **1** +200: **1** +100: **2**
+50: **1** -50: **2**
Facilities available:
BO AC IEH AVH

Wyatt Hotel
Westport, Co. Mayo
Tel: 098-25027.........................Page 199
Contact Person:
Chris McGauley / Maire Brid Ni Ghionnain
Seating Capacity of Meeting Rooms:
+400: **1** +100: **2** +50: **3**
Facilities available:
BO AC AVO

Co. Roscommon

Abbey Hotel, Conference and Leisure Centre
Roscommon Town, Co. Roscommon
Tel: 090-662 6240 ....Page 200
Contact Person:
Rachel Moran
Seating Capacity of Meeting Rooms:
+200: **2** +50: **1** -50: **3**
Facilities available:
BO AC AVH

BO Black Out Facilities
IEH Interpreting Equipment (Can Arrange Hire)
AC Air-Conditioning
AVO Audio Visual (Available On Premises)
IEO Interpreting Equipment (Available On Premises)
AVH Audio Visual (Can Arrange Hire)

447

Co. Roscommon Continued

O'Gara's Royal Hotel
Roscommon Town, Co. Roscommon
Tel: 090-662 6317 ....Page 201
Contact Person:
Larry O'Gara
Seating Capacity of Meeting Rooms:
+500: 1 +400: 1 +300: 1 +200: 1
+100: 1 +50: 2 -50: 1
Facilities available:
BO AC AVO

Whitehouse Hotel
Ballinlough, Co. Roscommon
Tel: 094-964 0112 ....Page 200
Contact Person:
Conference Co-Ordinator
Seating Capacity of Meeting Rooms:
+300: 1 -50: 2
Facilities available:
BO AC IEO AVO

North West

Co. Donegal

Arranmore House Hotel
Arranmore Island, Co. Donegal
Tel: 074-952 0918 ....Page 204
Contact Person:
Manager
Seating Capacity of Meeting Rooms:
+200: 1 -50: 1
Facilities available:
BO IEH AVH

Carlton Redcastle Hotel & Thalasso Spa
Moville, Co. Donegal
Tel: 074-938 5555 ....Page 217
Contact Person:
Cathryn Baldrick
Seating Capacity of Meeting Rooms:
+200: 1 +100: 2 -50: 2
Facilities available:
BO AC IEH AVO

Castle Grove Country House Hotel
Letterkenny, Co. Donegal
Tel: 074-915 1118 ....Page 213
Contact Person:
Mary Sweeney
Seating Capacity of Meeting Rooms:
-50: 1
Facilities available:
AVH

Clanree Hotel Conference & Leisure Centre
Letterkenny, Co. Donegal
Tel: 074-912 4369 ....Page 214
Contact Person:
Marie Gallagher
Seating Capacity of Meeting Rooms:
+500: 1 +400: 2 +50: 1 -50: 2
Facilities available:
BO AC IEH AVH

Dorrians Imperial Hotel
Ballyshannon, Co. Donegal
Tel: 071-985 1147 ....Page 206
Contact Person:
Mary Dorrian
Seating Capacity of Meeting Rooms:
+200: 1 +50: 1 -50: 1
Facilities available:
BO AC AVH

Downings Bay Hotel
Letterkenny, Co. Donegal
Tel: 074-915 5586 ....Page 214
Contact Person:
Eileen Rock
Seating Capacity of Meeting Rooms:
+300: 1 +100: 1 +50: 1 -50: 1
Facilities available:
AC IEH AVO

Great Northern Hotel
Bundoran, Co. Donegal
Tel: 071-984 1204 ....Page 208
Contact Person:
Philip McGlynn
Seating Capacity of Meeting Rooms:
+500: 1 +400: 1 +300: 1 +200: 1
+100: 1 +50: 1 -50: 1
Facilities available:
BO IEH AVO

Jackson's Hotel, Conference & Leisure Centre
Ballybofey, Co. Donegal
Tel: 074-913 1021...................Page 205
Contact Person:
Marie Di Bartolo
Seating Capacity of Meeting Rooms:
+500: 3 +200: 1 +50: 1 -50: 5
Facilities available:
BO AC IEH AVO

Malin Hotel
Malin, Co. Donegal
Tel: 074-937 0606 ....Page 216
Contact Person:
Jacqueline Byrnes
Seating Capacity of Meeting Rooms:
+200: 1
Facilities available:
BO IEH AVO

McGrorys of Culdaff
Culdaff, Co. Donegal
Tel: 074-937 9104 ....Page 209
Contact Person:
Anne Doherty
Seating Capacity of Meeting Rooms:
+100: 1 +50: 1
Facilities available:
BO IEH AVO

Milford Inn Hotel
Milford, Co. Donegal
Tel: 074-915 3313...................Page 216
Contact Person:
Denise Forrest
Seating Capacity of Meeting Rooms:
+500: 1 +400: 1 +50: 1 -50: 3
Facilities available:
BO IEH AVO

Mill Park Hotel, Conference Centre & Leisure Club
Donegal Town, Co. Donegal
Tel: 074-972 2880 ....Page 210
Contact Person:
Claire McDermott
Seating Capacity of Meeting Rooms:
+300: 1 -50: 4
Facilities available:
BO AC IEO AVO

BO Black Out Facilities
IEH Interpreting Equipment (Can Arrange Hire)
AC Air-Conditioning
AVO Audio Visual (Available On Premises)
IEO Interpreting Equipment (Available On Premises)
AVH Audio Visual (Can Arrange Hire)

Radisson SAS Hotel
Letterkenny, Co. Donegal
Tel: 074-919 4444 ....Page 215
Contact Person:
Siobhán Barrett
Seating Capacity of Meeting Rooms:
+400: **1** +50: **1** -50: **4**
Facilities available:

Ramada Encore - Letterkenny
Letterkenny, Co. Donegal
Tel: 074-912 3100....................Page 215
Contact Person:
General Manager
Seating Capacity of Meeting Rooms:
+200: **1** -50: **3**
Facilities available:

Sandhouse Hotel
Rossnowlagh, Co. Donegal
Tel: 071-985 1777....................Page 218
Contact Person:
Paul Diver
Seating Capacity of Meeting Rooms:
+50: **1** -50: **3**
Facilities available:

Silver Tassie Hotel
Letterkenny, Co. Donegal
Tel: 074-912 5619....................Page 216
Contact Person:
Rose Blaney
Seating Capacity of Meeting Rooms:
+300: **1** +200: **1** +100: **1** +50: **2**
-50: **3**
Facilities available:

Co. Leitrim

Bush Hotel
Carrick-on-Shannon, Co. Leitrim
Tel: 071-967 1000 ....Page 220
Contact Person:
Joseph Dolan
Seating Capacity of Meeting Rooms:
+300: **1** +100: **2** +50: **3** -50: **5**
Facilities available:

Shannon Key West Hotel
Rooskey, Co. Leitrim
Tel: 071-963 8800 ....Page 221
Contact Person:
Anne Marie Frisby
Seating Capacity of Meeting Rooms:
+300: **1** -50: **1**
Facilities available:

Co. Sligo

Clarion Hotel Sligo
Sligo Town, Co. Sligo
Tel: 071-911 9000....................Page 224
Contact Person:
Patricia Prendergast
Seating Capacity of Meeting Rooms:
+500: **1**
Facilities available:

Sligo City Hotel
Sligo Town, Co. Sligo
Tel: 071-914 4000 ....Page 225
Contact Person:
Edel McPartland
Seating Capacity of Meeting Rooms:
+200: **1** +100: **1** -50: **2**
Facilities available:

Sligo Park Hotel & Leisure Centre
Sligo Town, Co. Sligo
Tel: 071-919 0400 ....Page 225
Contact Person:
Seamus Preston
Seating Capacity of Meeting Rooms:
+500: **1** +400: **1** +300: **1** +200: **1**
+100: **2** +50: **3** -50: **3**
Facilities available:

Sligo Southern Hotel & Leisure Centre
Sligo Town, Co. Sligo
Tel: 071-916 2101 ....Page 226
Contact Person:
Kevin McGlynn
Seating Capacity of Meeting Rooms:
+300: **1** +200: **1** +100: **1** +50: **2**
-50: **4**
Facilities available:

Yeats
Country Hotel, Spa & Leisure Club
Rosses Point, Co. Sligo
Tel: 071-917 7211 ....Page 223
Contact Person:
Breda O'Dwyer
Seating Capacity of Meeting Rooms:
+100: **1** +50: **2** -50: **3**
Facilities available:

North

Co. Antrim

Ballymac
Stoneyford, Co. Antrim
Tel: 028-9264 8313 ....Page 233
Contact Person:
Cathy Muldoon
Seating Capacity of Meeting Rooms:
+100: **1** -50: **1**
Facilities available:

Bayview Hotel
Bushmills, Co. Antrim
Tel: 028-2073 4100 ....Page 230
Contact Person:
Mary O'Neill
Seating Capacity of Meeting Rooms:
+50: **1** -50: **1**
Facilities available:

Comfort Hotel Portrush
Portrush, Co. Antrim
Tel: 028-7082 6100 ....Page 232
Contact Person:
Mary O'Neill
Seating Capacity of Meeting Rooms:
+50: **1** -50: **1**
Facilities available:

BO Black Out Facilities
IEH Interpreting Equipment (Can Arrange Hire)
AC Air-Conditioning
AVO Audio Visual (Available On Premises)
IEO Interpreting Equipment (Available On Premises)
AVH Audio Visual (Can Arrange Hire)

Co. Antrim Continued

Londonderry Arms Hotel
Carnlough, Co. Antrim
Tel: 028-2888 5255 ....Page 231
Contact Person:
Frank O'Neill
Seating Capacity of Meeting Rooms:
+100: **1** +50: **2** -50: **2**
Facilities available:

Co. Armagh

Armagh City Hotel
Armagh City, Co. Armagh
Tel: 028-3751 8888 ....Page 233
Contact Person:
Gary Hynes
Seating Capacity of Meeting Rooms:
+500: **2** +400: **2** +300: **2** +200: **4**
+100: **4** +50: **5** -50: **10**
Facilities available:

Belfast City

Dunadry Hotel and Country Club
Belfast City
Tel: 028-9443 4343 ....Page 235
Contact Person:
Sheree Davis
Seating Capacity of Meeting Rooms:
+300: **1** +200: **1** +100: **1** +50: **3**
-50: **4**
Facilities available:

La Mon Hotel & Country Club
Belfast City
Tel: 028-9044 8631 ....Page 237
Contact Person:
Duty Manager
Seating Capacity of Meeting Rooms:
+500: **1** +400: **1** +300: **1** +200: **3**
+100: **4** +50: **5** -50: **5**
Facilities available:

Malone Lodge Hotel & Apartments
Belfast City
Tel: 028-9038 8000 ....Page 237
Contact Person:
Conference Co-Ordinator
Seating Capacity of Meeting Rooms:
+100: **1** +50: **1** -50: **4**
Facilities available:

Park Avenue Hotel
Belfast City
Tel: 028-9065 6520 ....Page 237
Contact Person:
Angela Reid
Seating Capacity of Meeting Rooms:
+500: **1** +400: **1** +300: **1** +200: **3**
+100: **4** +50: **8** -50: **11**
Facilities available:

Wellington Park Hotel
Belfast City
Tel: 028-9038 1111 ....Page 238
Contact Person:
Gerardo Jimenez
Seating Capacity of Meeting Rooms:
+400: **1** +300: **1** +200: **2** +100: **3**
+50: **4** -50: **9**
Facilities available:

Co. Derry

City Hotel
Derry City, Co. Derry
Tel: 028-7136 5800 ....Page 239
Contact Person:
Colette Brennan
Seating Capacity of Meeting Rooms:
+400: **1** +300: **1** +200: **1**
Facilities available:

Tower Hotel Derry
Derry City, Co. Derry
Tel: 028-7137 1000 ....Page 239
Contact Person:
Elaine Ferguson
Seating Capacity of Meeting Rooms:
+300: **1** +200: **1** +50: **2** -50: **1**
Facilities available:

Co. Down

Burrendale Hotel and Country Club
Newcastle, Co. Down
Tel: 028-4372 2599 ....Page 242
Contact Person:
Fiona O'Hare
Seating Capacity of Meeting Rooms:
+200: **1** +100: **1** -50: **6**
Facilities available:

Canal Court Hotel
Newry, Co. Down
Tel: 028-3025 1234 ....Page 242
Contact Person:
Conference & Banqueting Office
Seating Capacity of Meeting Rooms:
+400: **1** +300: **1** +200: **2** +100: **2**
+50: **5** -50: **4**
Facilities available:

Clandeboye Lodge Hotel
Bangor, Co. Down
Tel: 028-9185 2500 ....Page 241
Contact Person:
Melanie Orr / Donna Wilson
Seating Capacity of Meeting Rooms:
+300: **1** +100: **2** +50: **4** -50: **7**
Facilities available:

Royal Hotel
Bangor, Co. Down
Tel: 028-9127 1866 ....Page 241
Contact Person:
Glenda Feeney
Seating Capacity of Meeting Rooms:
+100: **1** -50: **2**
Facilities available:

BO Black Out Facilities
IEH Interpreting Equipment (Can Arrange Hire)
AC Air-Conditioning
AVO Audio Visual (Available On Premises)
IEO Interpreting Equipment (Available On Premises)
AVH Audio Visual (Can Arrange Hire)

Dublin & East Coast

Co. Dublin

Airport View
Blakes Cross, Co. Dublin
Tel: 01-843 8756 ....Page 249
Contact Person:
Gerry / Annie
Seating Capacity of Meeting Rooms:
👤+50: **1** 👤-50: **2**
Facilities available:

Alexander Hotel O'Callaghan
Dublin City, Co. Dublin
Tel: 01-607 3700 ....Page 256
Contact Person:
Laura Mulvaney
Seating Capacity of Meeting Rooms:
👤+400: **1** 👤+300: **1** 👤+200: **2** 👤+100: **4**
👤+50: **5** 👤-50: **1**
Facilities available:

Ashling Hotel
Dublin City, Co. Dublin
Tel: 01-677 2324 ....Page 260
Contact Person:
Lynsey
Seating Capacity of Meeting Rooms:
👤+200: **1** 👤+100: **1** 👤+50: **1** 👤-50: **5**
Facilities available:

Best Western Academy Hotel
Dublin City, Co. Dublin
Tel: 01-878 0666 ....Page 262
Contact Person:
Peter Collins
Seating Capacity of Meeting Rooms:
👤-50: **5**
Facilities available:

Bracken Court Hotel
Balbriggan, Co. Dublin
Tel: 01-841 3333 ....Page 248
Contact Person:
Mary Atherton
Seating Capacity of Meeting Rooms:
👤+200: **1** 👤-50: **3**
Facilities available:

Brooks Hotel
Dublin City, Co. Dublin
Tel: 01-670 4000 ....Page 264
Contact Person:
Stephanie Hayes
Seating Capacity of Meeting Rooms:
👤-50: **3**
Facilities available:

Buswells Hotel
Dublin City, Co. Dublin
Tel: 01-614 6500 ....Page 265
Contact Person:
Julie McCole
Seating Capacity of Meeting Rooms:
👤+50: **1** 👤-50: **5**
Facilities available:

Camden Court Hotel
Dublin City, Co. Dublin
Tel: 01-475 9666 ....Page 265
Contact Person:
Denise Corboy
Seating Capacity of Meeting Rooms:
👤+100: **1** 👤+50: **1** 👤-50: **3**
Facilities available:

Carlton Dublin Airport Hotel
Dublin Airport, Co. Dublin
Tel: 01-866 7500 ....Page 250
Contact Person:
Conference Co-Ordinator
Seating Capacity of Meeting Rooms:
👤+300: **1** 👤+200: **1** 👤+100: **2** 👤+50: **3**
👤-50: **2**
Facilities available:

Carnegie Court Hotel
Swords, Co. Dublin
Tel: 01-840 4384 ....Page 306
Contact Person:
Teresa Long
Seating Capacity of Meeting Rooms:
👤+200: **1** 👤+100: **1** 👤+50: **1** 👤-50: **2**
Facilities available:

Castleknock Hotel and Country Club
Dublin City, Co. Dublin
Tel: 01-640 6300 ....Page 266
Contact Person:
Mark Howell, Conference and
Banqueting Manager
Seating Capacity of Meeting Rooms:
👤+500: **1** 👤+400: **1** 👤+300: **1** 👤+200: **2**
👤+100: **4** 👤+50: **4** 👤-50: **6**
Facilities available:

Chief O'Neill's Hotel
Dublin City, Co. Dublin
Tel: 01-817 3838 ....Page 268
Contact Person:
Triona Thornton
Seating Capacity of Meeting Rooms:
👤+200: **1** 👤+100: **2** 👤+50: **3** 👤-50: **2**
Facilities available:

Citywest Hotel, Conference, Leisure & Golf Resort
Saggart, Co. Dublin
Tel: 01-401 0500 ....Page 305
Contact Person:
Fiona Killilea / Gillian Murphy
Seating Capacity of Meeting Rooms:
👤+500: **4** 👤+400: **5** 👤+300: **5** 👤+200:
9 👤+100: **12** 👤+50: **16** 👤-50: **9**
Facilities available:

Clarence (The)
Dublin City, Co. Dublin
Tel: 01-407 0800 ....Page 269
Contact Person:
Linda Storey
Seating Capacity of Meeting Rooms:
👤+50: **1** 👤-50: **3**
Facilities available:

BO Black Out Facilities
IEH Interpreting Equipment (Can Arrange Hire)
AC Air-Conditioning
AVO Audio Visual (Available On Premises)
IEO Interpreting Equipment (Available On Premises)
AVH Audio Visual (Can Arrange Hire)

451

Co. Dublin Continued

Clarion Hotel Dublin Airport
Dublin Airport, Co. Dublin
Tel: 01-808 0500 ....Page 251
Contact Person:
Joanne Fleming
Seating Capacity of Meeting Rooms:
+100: **1** +50: **1** -50: **8**
Facilities available:
BO AC IEH AVO

Clarion Hotel Dublin Liffey Valley
Dublin City, Co. Dublin
Tel: 01-625 8000 ....Page 269
Contact Person:
Tara Byrne
Seating Capacity of Meeting Rooms:
+300: **1** +200: **2** +50: **2** -50: **7**
Facilities available:
BO AC IEH AVO

Clontarf Castle Hotel
Dublin City, Co. Dublin
Tel: 01-833 2321 ....Page 270
Contact Person:
Valerie Burns
Seating Capacity of Meeting Rooms:
+500: **1** +100: **3** +50: **2** -50: **1**
Facilities available:
BO AC IEH AVH

Conrad Dublin
Dublin City, Co. Dublin
Tel: 01-602 8900 ....Page 271
Contact Person:
Breffne Costello
Seating Capacity of Meeting Rooms:
+200: **1** +100: **1** +50: **4** -50: **9**
Facilities available:
BO AC IEH AVH

Crowne Plaza, Dublin Airport
Dublin Airport, Co. Dublin
Tel: 01-862 8888 ....Page 251
Contact Person:
Judith Graham
Seating Capacity of Meeting Rooms:
+200: **1** -50: **12**
Facilities available:
BO AC IEH AVH

Davenport Hotel O'Callaghan
Dublin City, Co. Dublin
Tel: 01-607 3500 ....Page 271
Contact Person:
Karen Wright
Seating Capacity of Meeting Rooms:
+300: **1** +200: **2** +100: **2** +50: **2** -50: **7**
Facilities available:
BO AC IEH AVO

Dublin Skylon Hotel
Dublin City, Co. Dublin
Tel: 01-837 9121......................Page 273
Contact Person:
Andrew Hyland
Seating Capacity of Meeting Rooms:
+50: **1** -50: **1**
Facilities available:
BO AC IEH AVH

Finnstown Country House Hotel
Lucan, Co. Dublin
Tel: 01-601 0700 ....Page 302
Contact Person:
Edwina King
Seating Capacity of Meeting Rooms:
+300: **1** +200: **1** +100: **1** +50: **2** -50: **4**
Facilities available:
BO IEH AVO

Fitzpatrick Castle Dublin
Killiney, Co. Dublin
Tel: 01-230 5400 ....Page 302
Contact Person:
Brenda Killeen
Seating Capacity of Meeting Rooms:
+500: **1** +400: **2** +300: **2** +200: **2** +100: **4** +50: **6** -50: **14**
Facilities available:
BO AC IEH AVO

Fitzwilliam Hotel
Dublin City, Co. Dublin
Tel: 01-478 7000 ....Page 275
Contact Person:
Orna Eiffe, Events Manager
Seating Capacity of Meeting Rooms:
+50: **1** -50: **2**
Facilities available:
BO AC IEH AVO

Four Seasons Hotel Dublin
Dublin City, Co. Dublin
Tel: 01-665 4000 ....Page 276
Contact Person:
Helen Graham
Seating Capacity of Meeting Rooms:
+500: **1** +200: **1** +50: **3** -50: **1**
Facilities available:
BO AC IEH AVH

Grand Canal Hotel
Dublin City, Co. Dublin
Tel: 01-646 1000 ....Page 277
Contact Person:
Rebecca Sloper
Seating Capacity of Meeting Rooms:
+100: **1** +50: **1** -50: **3**
Facilities available:
BO AC IEH AVH

Grand Hotel
Malahide, Co. Dublin
Tel: 01-845 0000 ....Page 303
Contact Person:
Hilary Fogarty
Seating Capacity of Meeting Rooms:
+400: **1** +200: **1** +100: **1** +50: **6** -50: **6**
Facilities available:
BO AC IEH AVO

Great Southern Hotel
Dublin Airport, Co. Dublin
Tel: 01-844 6000 ....Page 252
Contact Person:
Caroline Fitzsimons
Seating Capacity of Meeting Rooms:
+300: **1** +200: **1** +100: **3** -50: **8**
Facilities available:
BO AC IEH AVO

Gresham (The)
Dublin City, Co. Dublin
Tel: 01-874 6881 ....Page 277
Contact Person:
Ian Craig
Seating Capacity of Meeting Rooms:
+300: **1** +200: **2** +100: **3** +50: **8** -50: **22**
Facilities available:
BO AC IEH AVH

 BO Black Out Facilities
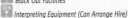 IEH Interpreting Equipment (Can Arrange Hire)
 AC Air-Conditioning
 AVO Audio Visual (Available On Premises)
 IEO Interpreting Equipment (Available On Premises)
AVH Audio Visual (Can Arrange Hire)

Herbert Park Hotel
Dublin City, Co. Dublin
Tel: 01-667 2200 ....Page 279
Contact Person:
Sorcha Moore
Seating Capacity of Meeting Rooms:
+100: **2** +50: **1** -50: **2**
Facilities available:

Hilton Dublin Airport
Dublin Airport, Co. Dublin
Tel: 01-866 1800 ....Page 252
Contact Person:
Ruth Kelly
Seating Capacity of Meeting Rooms:
+300: **1** -50: **9**
Facilities available:

Holiday Inn Dublin City Centre
Dublin City, Co. Dublin
Tel: 01-670 3666 ....Page 279
Contact Person:
Stephanie Howard
Seating Capacity of Meeting Rooms:
+400: **1** +300: **1** +200: **1** +100: **2**
+50: **5** -50: **6**
Facilities available:

Hotel Isaacs
Dublin City, Co. Dublin
Tel: 01-813 4700 ....Page 279
Contact Person:
Justin Lowry
Seating Capacity of Meeting Rooms:
+100: **1** -50: **4**
Facilities available:

IMI Residence
Dublin City, Co. Dublin
Tel: 01-207 5900 ....Page 280
Contact Person:
Adrienne Hughes
Seating Capacity of Meeting Rooms:
+300: **1** +200: **2** +100: **3** +50: **10**
-50: **30**
Facilities available:

Lansdowne Hotel
Dublin City, Co. Dublin
Tel: 01-668 2522 ....Page 284
Contact Person:
George Hook
Seating Capacity of Meeting Rooms:
+100: **1** +50: **1**
Facilities available:

Lucan Spa Hotel
Lucan, Co. Dublin
Tel: 01-628 0494 ....Page 303
Contact Person:
Betty Dolan / Stephen Foran
Seating Capacity of Meeting Rooms:
+500: **1** +400: **1** +300: **1** +200: **1**
+100: **1** +50: **1** -50: **2**
Facilities available:

Lynch Green Isle Hotel Spa & Suites
Dublin City, Co. Dublin
Tel: 01-459 3406 ....Page 285
Seating Capacity of Meeting Rooms:
+500: **1** +200: **1**
Facilities available:

Maples House Hotel
Dublin City, Co. Dublin
Tel: 01-830 4227 ....Page 286
Contact Person:
Kathleen Fitzpatrick
Seating Capacity of Meeting Rooms:
+50: **1** -50: **1**
Facilities available:

Marine Hotel
Sutton, Co. Dublin
Tel: 01-839 0000 ....Page 306
Contact Person:
Emma Connolly
Seating Capacity of Meeting Rooms:
+100: **1** -50: **6**
Facilities available:

Merrion Hall
Dublin City, Co. Dublin
Tel: 01-668 1426 ....Page 287
Contact Person:
Pat Halpin
Seating Capacity of Meeting Rooms:
-50: **2**
Facilities available:

Mont Clare Hotel O'Callaghan
Dublin City, Co. Dublin
Tel: 01-607 3800 ....Page 288
Contact Person:
Claire Walker
Seating Capacity of Meeting Rooms:
+100: **1** +50: **2** -50: **9**
Facilities available:

Morgan Hotel
Dublin City, Co. Dublin
Tel: 01-643 7000 ....Page 289
Contact Person:
Reservations
Seating Capacity of Meeting Rooms:
+50: **1** -50: **5**
Facilities available:

Morrison (The)
Dublin City, Co. Dublin
Tel: 01-887 2400 ....Page 289
Contact Person:
Sharon Shevlin
Seating Capacity of Meeting Rooms:
+200: **1** +100: **2** +50: **2** -50: **4**
Facilities available:

Mount Herbert Hotel
Dublin City, Co. Dublin
Tel: 01-668 4321 ....Page 289
Contact Person:
Toni Walsh
Seating Capacity of Meeting Rooms:
+50: **2** -50: **2**
Facilities available:

BO Black Out Facilities
IEH Interpreting Equipment (Can Arrange Hire)

AC Air-Conditioning
AVO Audio Visual (Available On Premises)

IEO Interpreting Equipment (Available On Premises)
AVH Audio Visual (Can Arrange Hire)

Co. Dublin Continued

Paramount Hotel
Dublin City, Co. Dublin
Tel: 01-417 9900 ....
Contact Person:
Bernadette Monaghan
Seating Capacity of Meeting Rooms:
-50: **1**
Facilities available:
AC AVH

Plaza Hotel
Dublin City, Co. Dublin
Tel: 01-462 4200 ....
Contact Person:
Claire Coleman
Seating Capacity of Meeting Rooms:
+200: **1** +100: **2** +50: **2** -50: **11**
Facilities available:
IEH AVH

Portmarnock Hotel & Golf Links
Portmarnock, Co. Dublin
Tel: 01-846 0611 ....
Contact Person:
Nicola Cassidy
Seating Capacity of Meeting Rooms:
+300: **1** +50: **1** -50: **6**
Facilities available:
BO AC IEH AVH

Radisson SAS St Helen's Hotel
Blackrock, Co. Dublin
Tel: 01-218 6000 ....
Contact Person:
Jennifer Patton
Seating Capacity of Meeting Rooms:
+200: **1** +50: **6** -50: **5**
Facilities available:
BO AC IEH AVH

Red Cow Moran Hotel
Dublin City, Co. Dublin
Tel: 01-459 3650 ....
Contact Person:
Karen Moran
Seating Capacity of Meeting Rooms:
+500: **1** +400: **1** +300: **1** +200: **2**
+100: **5** +50: **10** -50: **16**
Facilities available:
BO AC IEH AVO

Regency Airport Hotel
Dublin City, Co. Dublin
Tel: 01-837 3544 ....
Contact Person:
Catherine McGettigan
Seating Capacity of Meeting Rooms:
+300: **2** +50: **1** -50: **3**
Facilities available:
BO AC IEH AVO

Rochestown Lodge Hotel
Dun Laoghaire, Co. Dublin
Tel: 01-285 3555 ....
Contact Person:
Lisa Bradshaw
Seating Capacity of Meeting Rooms:
+100: **1** +50: **1** -50: **6**
Facilities available:
BO AC IEH AVO

Shelbourne Hotel (The)
Dublin City, Co. Dublin
Tel: 01-663 4500 ....
Contact Person:
Anne-Marie Whelan
Seating Capacity of Meeting Rooms:
+400: **1** +100: **2** +50: **2** -50: **6**
Facilities available:
BO AC IEH AVH

Sheldon Park Hotel & Leisure Centre
Dublin City, Co. Dublin
Tel: 01-460 1055 ....
Contact Person:
Sue Anne Haskett
Seating Capacity of Meeting Rooms:
+300: **1** +200: **1** +100: **1** +50: **6**
-50: **10**
Facilities available:
BO AC IEH AVO

Stephen's Green Hotel O'Callaghan
Dublin City, Co. Dublin
Tel: 01-607 3600 ....
Contact Person:
Laura Mulvaney
Seating Capacity of Meeting Rooms:
-50: **6**
Facilities available:
BO AC IEH AVO

Stillorgan Park Hotel
Blackrock, Co. Dublin
Tel: 01-288 1621 ....
Contact Person:
Cailin Keaney
Seating Capacity of Meeting Rooms:
+500: **1** +400: **1** +300: **1** +200: **3**
+100: **6** +50: **7** -50: **12**
Facilities available:
BO AC IEH AVO

Temple Bar Hotel
Dublin City, Co. Dublin
Tel: 01-677 3333 ....
Contact Person:
Ciara Delaney
Seating Capacity of Meeting Rooms:
+50: **1** -50: **4**
Facilities available:
BO IEH AVH

Waterside Hotel
Donabate, Co. Dublin
Tel: 01-843 6153 ....
Contact Person:
Paula Baldwin
Seating Capacity of Meeting Rooms:
+200: **1** +100: **1** +50: **1** -50: **3**
Facilities available:
AC IEH AVH

West County Hotel
Dublin City, Co. Dublin
Tel: 01-626 4011 ....
Contact Person:
Aine Grogan
Seating Capacity of Meeting Rooms:
+100: **1** +50: **1** -50: **2**
Facilities available:
BO AC IEH AVO

Westin Dublin
Dublin City, Co. Dublin
Tel: 01-645 1000 ....
Contact Person:
Jane O'Donnell
Seating Capacity of Meeting Rooms:
+200: **1** +100: **2** +50: **2** -50: **8**
Facilities available:
BO AC IEH AVO

BO Black Out Facilities
IEH Interpreting Equipment (Can Arrange Hire)
AC Air-Conditioning
AVO Audio Visual (Available On Premises)
IEO Interpreting Equipment (Available On Premises)
AVH Audio Visual (Can Arrange Hire)

Co. Louth

Boyne Valley Hotel & Country Club
Drogheda, Co. Louth
Tel: 041-983 7737 ....Page 309
Contact Person:
Noel Comer
Seating Capacity of Meeting Rooms:
+500: **2** +400: **2** +300: **1** +200: **2**
+100: **1** +50: **2** -50: **4**
Facilities available:

D (The)
Drogheda, Co. Louth
Tel: 041-987 7700 ....Page 310
Contact Person:
Martina Hannigan
Seating Capacity of Meeting Rooms:
+100: **2** -50: **5**
Facilities available:

Fairways Hotel & Conference Centre
Dundalk, Co. Louth
Tel: 042-932 1500 ....Page 311
Contact Person:
Ken Byrne / Karen Taggart
Seating Capacity of Meeting Rooms:
+500: **1** +400: **1** +300: **2** +200: **2**
+100: **2** +50: **5** -50: **10**
Facilities available:

Four Seasons Hotel & Leisure Club Carlingford
Carlingford, Co. Louth
Tel: 042-937 3530 ....Page 308
Contact Person:
Collette / Rachel
Seating Capacity of Meeting Rooms:
+300: **1** +200: **2** +100: **2** +50: **3**
-50: **2**
Facilities available:

Hotel Imperial
Dundalk, Co. Louth
Tel: 042-933 2241 ....Page 312
Contact Person:
Conference Co-Ordinator
Seating Capacity of Meeting Rooms:
-50: **1**
Facilities available:

McKevitt's Village Hotel
Carlingford, Co. Louth
Tel: 042-937 3116 ....Page 308
Contact Person:
Terry and Kay McKevitt
Seating Capacity of Meeting Rooms:
+100: **1** -50: **1**
Facilities available:

Co. Meath

Ardboyne Hotel
Navan, Co. Meath
Tel: 046-902 3119 ....Page 316
Contact Person:
Joanne O'Brien
Seating Capacity of Meeting Rooms:
+300: **1** +100: **2** +50: **3** -50: **4**
Facilities available:

Hamlet Court Hotel
Johnstownbridge, Co. Meath
Tel: 046-954 1200 ....Page 315
Contact Person:
Denise Kelly
Seating Capacity of Meeting Rooms:
+300: **1** +200: **1** +100: **2** +50: **2**
Facilities available:

Knightsbrook Hotel & Golf Resort
Trim, Co. Meath
Tel: 046-907 4100 ....Page 317
Contact Person:
Conference & Banqueting Manager
Seating Capacity of Meeting Rooms:
+500: **2** +400: **2** +300: **2** +200: **4**
+100: **6** +50: **10** -50: **10**
Facilities available:

Marriott Johnstown House Hotel & Spa Enfield
Enfield, Co. Meath
Tel: 046-954 0000 ....Page 314
Contact Person:
Patsy Mooney
Seating Capacity of Meeting Rooms:
+500: **1** +400: **1** +300: **2** +200: **2**
+100: **2** +50: **2** -50: **13**
Facilities available:

Neptune Beach Hotel & Leisure Club
Bettystown, Co. Meath
Tel: 041-982 7107 ....Page 313
Contact Person:
Barth O'Connor
Seating Capacity of Meeting Rooms:
+200: **1** -50: **2**
Facilities available:

Newgrange Hotel
Navan, Co. Meath
Tel: 046-907 4100 ....Page 317
Contact Person:
Lorraine Cunningham
Seating Capacity of Meeting Rooms:
+500: **1** +200: **2** +100: **1** +50: **1**
-50: **3**
Facilities available:

Station House Hotel and Restaurant
Kilmessan, Co. Meath
Tel: 046-902 5239 ....Page 316
Contact Person:
Paul Slattery / Denise Slattery
Seating Capacity of Meeting Rooms:
+400: **1** +300: **1** +200: **1** +100: **1**
+50: **1** -50: **1**
Facilities available:

BO Black Out Facilities
IEH Interpreting Equipment (Can Arrange Hire)

AC Air-Conditioning
AVO Audio Visual (Available On Premises)

IEO Interpreting Equipment (Available On Premises)
AVH Audio Visual (Can Arrange Hire)

Conference Facilities
...Select A Venue For your Agenda!

Co. Wicklow

Arklow Bay Conference and Leisure Hotel
Arklow, Co. Wicklow
Tel: 0402-32309......................Page 318
Contact Person:
Sabine Luedke
Seating Capacity of Meeting Rooms:
👤+500: **1** 👤+400: **1** 👤+300: **1** 👤+200: **2**
👤+100: **2** 👤+50: **4** 👤-50: **5**
Facilities available:
[BO] [AC] [IEH] [AVO]

Glendalough Hotel
Glendalough, Co. Wicklow
Tel: 0404-45135......................Page 323
Contact Person:
Cormac O'Sullivan
Seating Capacity of Meeting Rooms:
👤+100: **1** 👤-50: **2**
Facilities available:
[BO] [AC] [IEH] [AVO]

Glenview Hotel
Glen-O-The-Downs, Co. Wicklow
Tel: 01-287 3399 ....Page 324
Contact Person:
Fiona O'Regan
Seating Capacity of Meeting Rooms:
👤+200: **1** 👤+100: **1** 👤+50: **2** 👤-50: **4**
Facilities available:
[BO] [AC] [IEH] [AVO]

Heather House Hotel
Bray, Co. Wicklow
Tel: 01-286 8000 ....Page 321
Contact Person:
Frances Lamb / Donal Byrne
Seating Capacity of Meeting Rooms:
👤+50: **1**
Facilities available:
[BO] [AVH]

Hunter's Hotel
Rathnew, Co. Wicklow
Tel: 0404-40106......................Page 325
Contact Person:
Tom Gelletlie
Seating Capacity of Meeting Rooms:
👤-50: **3**
Facilities available:
[BO] [IEH] [AVH]

Lawless's Hotel
Aughrim, Co. Wicklow
Tel: 0402-36146......................Page 320
Contact Person:
Paul Kinsella (or Duty Manager)
Seating Capacity of Meeting Rooms:
👤+200: **1** 👤-50: **1**
Facilities available:
[BO] [AVO]

Marriott Druids Glen Hotel & Country Club
Newtownmountkennedy, Co. Wicklow
Tel: 01-287 0800 ....Page 324
Contact Person:
Aileen Strachan
Seating Capacity of Meeting Rooms:
👤+400: **1** 👤+200: **2** 👤+100: **1** 👤-50: **7**
Facilities available:
[BO] [AC] [IEH] [AVO]

Rathsallagh House, Golf and Country Club
Dunlavin, Co. Wicklow
Tel: 045-403112......................Page 322
Contact Person:
Catherine Lawlor
Seating Capacity of Meeting Rooms:
👤+100: **1** 👤-50: **4**
Facilities available:
[BO] [IEH] [AVO]

Tinakilly Country House and Restaurant
Rathnew, Co. Wicklow
Tel: 0404-69274 ....Page 325
Contact Person:
Brenda Gilmore
Seating Capacity of Meeting Rooms:
👤+50: **1** 👤-50: **3**
Facilities available:
[BO] [AC] [IEH] [AVO]

Midlands & Lakelands

Co. Cavan

Breffni Arms Hotel
Arvagh, Co. Cavan
Tel: 049-433 5127 ....Page 330
Contact Person:
Eamon Gray
Seating Capacity of Meeting Rooms:
👤+500: **1**
Facilities available:
[BO] [AC] [AVO]

Cavan Crystal Hotel
Cavan Town, Co. Cavan
Tel: 049-436 0600 ....Page 331
Contact Person:
Lorraine Meegan
Seating Capacity of Meeting Rooms:
👤+500: **1** 👤+400: **2** 👤+300: **2** 👤+200: **2**
👤+100: **2** 👤+50: **6** 👤-50: **8**
Facilities available:
[BO] [AC] [IEH] [AVO]

Crover House Hotel & Golf Club
Mountnugent, Co. Cavan
Tel: 049-854 0206 ....Page 333
Contact Person:
Pauline Kehoe
Seating Capacity of Meeting Rooms:
👤+500: **1** 👤+50: **1** 👤-50: **2**
Facilities available:
[AC] [AVO]

Errigal Hotel
Cootehill, Co. Cavan
Tel: 049-555 6901 ....Page 332
Contact Person:
Conference Co-Ordinator
Seating Capacity of Meeting Rooms:
👤+200: **1** 👤+50: **1** 👤-50: **1**
Facilities available:
[BO] [AC] [IEO] [AVO]

[BO] *Black Out Facilities*
[IEH] *Interpreting Equipment (Can Arrange Hire)*

[AC] *Air-Conditioning*
[AVO] *Audio Visual (Available On Premises)*

[IEO] *Interpreting Equipment (Available On Premises)*
[AVH] *Audio Visual (Can Arrange Hire)*

456

Hotel Kilmore
Cavan Town, Co. Cavan
Tel: 049-433 2288 ....Page 332
Contact Person:
Deborah Egan
Seating Capacity of Meeting Rooms:
+500: **1** +200: **2** +100: **2** +50: **3**
-50: **4**
Facilities available:

Lakeside Manor Hotel
Virginia, Co. Cavan
Tel: 049-854 8200 ....Page 334
Contact Person:
Meabh Brady
Seating Capacity of Meeting Rooms:
+400: **1** +200: **1** +50: **1** -50: **2**
Facilities available:

Park Hotel
Virginia, Co. Cavan
Tel: 049-854 6100 ....Page 334
Contact Person:
Michael Kelly
Seating Capacity of Meeting Rooms:
+50: **2** -50: **2**
Facilities available:

Radisson SAS Farnham Estate
Cavan Town, Co. Cavan
Tel: 049-436 5801 ....Page 332
Contact Person:
Vari McGreevy
Seating Capacity of Meeting Rooms:
+400: **1** +100: **4** +50: **7** -50: **8**
Facilities available:

River Front Hotel (The)
Virginia, Co. Cavan
Tel: 049-854 7561 ....Page 334
Contact Person:
Caroline McQuaid
Seating Capacity of Meeting Rooms:
+300: **1** +200: **1** +100: **1** +50: **1**
-50: **3**
Facilities available:

Slieve Russell Hotel
Golf & Country Club
Ballyconnell, Co. Cavan
Tel: 049-952 6444 ....Page 331
Contact Person:
Clodagh Seberry
Seating Capacity of Meeting Rooms:
+500: **2** +400: **2** +300: **3** +200: **4**
+100: **4** +50: **4** -50: **7**
Facilities available:

Co. Kildare

Barberstown Castle
Straffan, Co. Kildare
Tel: 01-628 8157 ....Page 344
Contact Person:
Gretchen Ridgeway
Seating Capacity of Meeting Rooms:
+200: **1** +100: **1** +50: **1** -50: **2**
Facilities available:

Carlton Abbey Hotel
Athy, Co. Kildare
Tel: 059-863 0100 ....Page 335
Contact Person:
Damien Makatarian
Seating Capacity of Meeting Rooms:
+300: **1** +200: **1** +100: **1** +50: **1**
-50: **4**
Facilities available:

Carton House
Maynooth, Co. Kildare
Tel: 01-505 2000 ....Page 340
Contact Person:
Events Manager
Seating Capacity of Meeting Rooms:
+300: **1** +200: **2** +100: **5** +50: **10**
-50: **8**
Facilities available:

Clanard
Court Hotel
Athy, Co. Kildare
Tel: 059-864 0666 ....Page 336
Contact Person:
Diane Lynch
Seating Capacity of Meeting Rooms:
+400: **1** +200: **1** +100: **1** +50: **1**
-50: **3**
Facilities available:

Courtyard Hotel Leixlip (The)
Leixlip, Co. Kildare
Tel: 01-629 5100 ....Page 339
Contact Person:
Gavin O'Shea
Seating Capacity of Meeting Rooms:
+100: **2** +50: **4** -50: **5**
Facilities available:

Glenroyal Hotel, Leisure Club &
Conference Centre
Maynooth, Co. Kildare
Tel: 01-629 0909 ....Page 341
Contact Person:
Clare Lyons
Seating Capacity of Meeting Rooms:
+500: **1** +400: **2** +300: **4** +200: **4**
+100: **6** +50: **6** -50: **12**
Facilities available:

Hazel Hotel
Monasterevin, Co. Kildare
Tel: 045-525373 ....Page 341
Contact Person:
John Kelly
Seating Capacity of Meeting Rooms:
+300: **1** +200: **1** +100: **1** +50: **1**
-50: **1**
Facilities available:

Keadeen Hotel
Newbridge, Co. Kildare
Tel: 045-431666 ....Page 344
Contact Person:
Pauline Barry
Seating Capacity of Meeting Rooms:
+500: **1** +400: **1** +300: **1** +200: **1**
+100: **3** +50: **4** -50: **7**
Facilities available:

 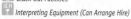 

BO Black Out Facilities   AC Air-Conditioning   IEO Interpreting Equipment (Available On Premises)
IEH Interpreting Equipment (Can Arrange Hire)   AVO Audio Visual (Available On Premises)   AVH Audio Visual (Can Arrange Hire)

Co. Kildare Continued

Killashee House Hotel & Villa Spa

Naas, Co. Kildare

Tel: 045-879277 ....Page 342

Contact Person:

Anne-Marie Hayes

Seating Capacity of Meeting Rooms:

+500: 1 +400: 2 +300: 2 +200: 2
+100: 3 +50: 4 -50: 20

Facilities available:

BO AC IEH AVO

Osprey Hotel & Spa

Naas, Co. Kildare

Tel: 045-881111 ....Page 343

Contact Person:

Sharon Deegan

Seating Capacity of Meeting Rooms:

+300: 1 +100: 1

Facilities available:

BO AC AVH

Setanta House Hotel

Celbridge, Co. Kildare

Tel: 01-630 3200 ....Page 337

Contact Person:

Arthur McDaniel

Seating Capacity of Meeting Rooms:

+500: 1 +400: 1 +300: 1 +200: 2
+100: 2 +50: 2 -50: 6

Facilities available:

BO AC IEH AVO

Springfield Hotel

Leixlip, Co. Kildare

Tel: 01-458 1100..................Page 340

Contact Person:

Barry, Kathleen or Padraig

Seating Capacity of Meeting Rooms:

+300: 1 +200: 1 +100: 1 +50: 2
-50: 3

Facilities available:

AC IEH AVO

Standhouse Hotel Leisure & Conference Centre

Curragh (The), Co. Kildare

Tel: 045-436177..................Page 338

Contact Person:

Helen O'Donnell / Jennifer O'Dwyer

Seating Capacity of Meeting Rooms:

+500: 1 +400: 1 +300: 2 +200: 3
+100: 4 +50: 4 -50: 7

Facilities available:

BO AC IEH AVO

Westgrove Hotel & Conference Centre

Clane, Co. Kildare

Tel: 1800-32 42 52 ....Page 337

Contact Person:

Ian Hyland

Seating Capacity of Meeting Rooms:

+400: 2 +50: 5 -50: 6

Facilities available:

BO AC IEH AVO

Co. Laois

Abbeyleix Manor Hotel

Abbeyleix, Co. Laois

Tel: 057-873 0111..................Page 345

Contact Person:

Eileen O'Connor

Seating Capacity of Meeting Rooms:

+200: 1 +50: 1 -50: 2

Facilities available:

BO AC IEH AVH

Heritage at Killenard (The)

Killenard, Co. Laois

Tel: 057-864 5500 ....Page 345

Contact Person:

Grainne O'Malley

Seating Capacity of Meeting Rooms:

+400: 1 +50: 2 -50: 4

Facilities available:

BO AC IEH AVO

Heritage Hotel Portlaoise

Portlaoise, Co. Laois

Tel: 057-867 8588 ....Page 346

Contact Person:

Nollaig Baker

Seating Capacity of Meeting Rooms:

+500: 1 +400: 2 +300: 2 +200: 1
+100: 1 +50: 1 -50: 9

Facilities available:

BO AC IEH AVO

Co. Longford

Longford Arms Hotel

Longford Town, Co. Longford

Tel: 043-46296 ....Page 347

Contact Person:

Duty Manager

Seating Capacity of Meeting Rooms:

+500: 1 +100: 2 +50: 3

Facilities available:

BO AC IEH AVH

Co. Monaghan

Castle Leslie

Glaslough, Co. Monaghan

Tel: 047-88100..................Page 347

Contact Person:

Maggie McKernan

Seating Capacity of Meeting Rooms:

+50: 1 -50: 1

Facilities available:

BO IEH AVH

Four Seasons Hotel & Leisure Club

Monaghan Town, Co. Monaghan

Tel: 047-81888..................Page 348

Contact Person:

Orla McKenna

Seating Capacity of Meeting Rooms:

+400: 2 +300: 3 +200: 3 +100: 3
+50: 7 -50: 7

Facilities available:

BO AC IEH AVO

BO Black Out Facilities
IEH Interpreting Equipment (Can Arrange Hire)
AC Air-Conditioning
AVO Audio Visual (Available On Premises)
IEO Interpreting Equipment (Available On Premises)
AVH Audio Visual (Can Arrange Hire)

Hillgrove Hotel & Conference Centre
Monaghan Town, Co. Monaghan
Tel: 047-81288........................Page 348
Contact Person:
Fiona Gilsenan
Seating Capacity of Meeting Rooms:
+500: **2** +400: **2** +300: **3** +200: **3**
+100: **5** +50: **8** -50: **15**
Facilities available:

Nuremore Hotel & Country Club
Carrickmacross, Co. Monaghan
Tel: 042 -966 1438..................Page 347
Contact Person:
Sinead Rock
Seating Capacity of Meeting Rooms:
+500: **1** +100: **2** +50: **3** -50: **4**
Facilities available:

Co. Offaly

Bridge House Hotel & Leisure Club
Tullamore, Co. Offaly
Tel: 057-932 5600 ....Page 350
Contact Person:
Colm McCabe
Seating Capacity of Meeting Rooms:
+500: **1** +400: **1** +300: **2** +200: **2**
+100: **3** +50: **4** -50: **9**
Facilities available:

County Arms Hotel
Birr, Co. Offaly
Tel: 057-912 0791 ....Page 349
Contact Person:
Barry Loughnane
Seating Capacity of Meeting Rooms:
+400: **1** +300: **1** +200: **1** +100: **1**
+50: **4** -50: **6**
Facilities available:

Days Hotel Tullamore
Tullamore, Co. Offaly
Tel: 1890-776 655 ....Page 351
Contact Person:
Brian Pierson
Seating Capacity of Meeting Rooms:
+50: **1** -50: **1**
Facilities available:

Kinnitty Castle Demesne
Birr, Co. Offaly
Tel: 057-913 7318 ....Page 350
Contact Person:
Sales & Marketing Dept.
Seating Capacity of Meeting Rooms:
+100: **1** -50: **1**
Facilities available:

Moorhill House Hotel
Tullamore, Co. Offaly
Tel: 057-932 1395 ....Page 352
Contact Person:
David Duffy / Alan Duffy
Seating Capacity of Meeting Rooms:
+50: **1** -50: **3**
Facilities available:

Tullamore Court Hotel Conference & Leisure Centre
Tullamore, Co. Offaly
Tel: 057-934 6666 ....Page 352
Contact Person:
Ann Lynch
Seating Capacity of Meeting Rooms:
+500: **1** +400: **1** +300: **2** +200: **2**
+100: **3** +50: **4** -50: **8**
Facilities available:

Co. Westmeath

Bloomfield House Hotel
Mullingar, Co. Westmeath
Tel: 044-934 0894 ....Page 356
Contact Person:
Conference & Banqueting Co-Ordinator
Seating Capacity of Meeting Rooms:
+300: **1** +200: **2** +100: **4** +50: **5**
-50: **8**
Facilities available:

Creggan Court Hotel
Athlone, Co. Westmeath
Tel: 090-647 7777 ....Page 353
Contact Person:
Marilyn Peters
Seating Capacity of Meeting Rooms:
+50: **1** -50: **4**
Facilities available:

Glasson Golf Hotel and Country Club
Athlone, Co. Westmeath
Tel: 090-648 5120 ....Page 353
Contact Person:
Gareth Jones / Fidelma Reid
Seating Capacity of Meeting Rooms:
+100: **1** +50: **1** -50: **2**
Facilities available:

Greville Arms Hotel
Mullingar, Co. Westmeath
Tel: 044-934 8563 ....Page 356
Contact Person:
John Cochrane
Seating Capacity of Meeting Rooms:
+200: **1** +100: **2** +50: **1** -50: **2**
Facilities available:

Hodson Bay Hotel
Athlone, Co. Westmeath
Tel: 090-644 2000 ....Page 354
Contact Person:
Christina Melican
Seating Capacity of Meeting Rooms:
+500: **1** +400: **1** +300: **1** +200: **2**
+100: **3** +50: **6** -50: **13**
Facilities available:

Mullingar Park Hotel
Mullingar, Co. Westmeath
Tel: 044-933 7500 ....Page 357
Contact Person:
Ita Kerrigan
Seating Capacity of Meeting Rooms:
+500: **2** +400: **2** +300: **3** +200: **4**
+100: **7** +50: **14** -50: **9**
Facilities available:

 Black Out Facilities
 *Interpreting Equipment (Can Arrange Hire)*
 Air-Conditioning *Audio Visual (Available On Premises)*
 *Interpreting Equipment (Available On Premises)* *Audio Visual (Can Arrange Hire)*

459

Co. Westmeath Continued

Prince of Wales Hotel
Athlone, Co. Westmeath
Tel: 090-647 6666 ....Page 354
Contact Person:
Neil Cummins
Seating Capacity of Meeting Rooms:
+100: 1 +50: 3 -50: 1
Facilities available:

Radisson SAS Hotel
Athlone, Co. Westmeath
Tel: 090-644 2600 ....Page 354
Contact Person:
Meetings and Events Department
Seating Capacity of Meeting Rooms:
+500: 1 +400: 1 +300: 1 +200: 2
+100: 4 +50: 4 -50: 7
Facilities available:

Shamrock Lodge Hotel and Conference Centre
Athlone, Co. Westmeath
Tel: 090-649 2601 ....Page 355
Contact Person:
Fiona Claffey / Pamela Egan
Seating Capacity of Meeting Rooms:
+200: 1 +100: 2 +50: 3 -50: 3
Facilities available:

South East

Co. Carlow

Seven Oaks Hotel
Carlow Town, Co. Carlow
Tel: 059-913 1308 ....Page 362
Contact Person:
Kathleen Dooley / Michael Walsh
Seating Capacity of Meeting Rooms:
+400: 1 +200: 1 +50: 1 -50: 2
Facilities available:

Talbot Carlow Hotel
Carlow Town, Co. Carlow
Tel: 059-915 3000 ....Page 362
Contact Person:
Deirdre Kavanagh
Seating Capacity of Meeting Rooms:
+300: 1
Facilities available:

Co. Kilkenny

Butler House
Kilkenny City, Co. Kilkenny
Tel: 056-776 5707 ....Page 364
Contact Person:
Gabrielle Hickey
Seating Capacity of Meeting Rooms:
+100: 1 +50: 2 -50: 2
Facilities available:

Days Hotel Kilkenny
Kilkenny City, Co. Kilkenny
Tel: 1890-77 66 55 ....Page 365
Contact Person:
Mary Daly
Seating Capacity of Meeting Rooms:
+50: 1 -50: 4
Facilities available:

Hotel Kilkenny
Kilkenny City, Co. Kilkenny
Tel: 056-776 2000 ....Page 366
Contact Person:
Catriona Loughrey
Seating Capacity of Meeting Rooms:
+300: 2 +100: 1 +50: 1 -50: 3
Facilities available:

Kilkenny Inn Hotel
Kilkenny City, Co. Kilkenny
Tel: 056-777 2828 ....Page 367
Contact Person:
Michelle Keogh
Seating Capacity of Meeting Rooms:
-50: 1
Facilities available:

Kilkenny Ormonde Hotel
Kilkenny City, Co. Kilkenny
Tel: 056-772 3900 ....Page 368
Contact Person:
Sheena McCanny
Seating Capacity of Meeting Rooms:
+500: 1 +300: 1 +50: 2 -50: 6
Facilities available:

Kilkenny River Court
Kilkenny City, Co. Kilkenny
Tel: 056-772 3388 ....Page 368
Contact Person:
Stephanie Gahan
Seating Capacity of Meeting Rooms:
+200: 1 +50: 1 -50: 2
Facilities available:

Lyrath Estate Hotel, Spa & Convention Centre
Kilkenny City, Co. Kilkenny
Tel: 056-776 0088 ....Page 370
Contact Person:
Stephanie Gahan
Seating Capacity of Meeting Rooms:
+500: 2 +400: 3 +300: 3 +200: 3
+100: 4 +50: 6 -50: 10
Facilities available:

Mount Juliet Conrad
Thomastown, Co. Kilkenny
Tel: 056-777 3000 ....Page 373
Contact Person:
Lisa Dunphy
Seating Capacity of Meeting Rooms:
+100: 1 +50: 3 -50: 2
Facilities available:

Newpark Hotel
Kilkenny City, Co. Kilkenny
Tel: 056-776 0500 ....Page 371
Contact Person:
Sinead Corcoran
Seating Capacity of Meeting Rooms:
+500: 1 +400: 1 +100: 1 +50: 2
-50: 9
Facilities available:

 BO Black Out Facilities
IEH Interpreting Equipment (Can Arrange Hire)
AC Air-Conditioning
AVO Audio Visual (Available On Premises)
IEO Interpreting Equipment (Available On Premises)
AVH Audio Visual (Can Arrange Hire)

Springhill Court Hotel, Spa & Leisure Club
Kilkenny City, Co. Kilkenny
Tel: 056-772 1122 ....Page 371
Contact Person:
Eimear O'Farrell
Seating Capacity of Meeting Rooms:
+500: 1 +100: 2 -50: 2
Facilities available:

Co. Tipperary South

Cahir House Hotel
Cahir, Co. Tipperary South
Tel: 052-43000 ....Page 373
Contact Person:
Carol O'Brien
Seating Capacity of Meeting Rooms:
+400: 1 +300: 1 +200: 1 +100: 1
+50: 1 -50: 3
Facilities available:

Cashel Palace Hotel
Cashel, Co. Tipperary South
Tel: 062-62707 ....Page 375
Contact Person:
Susan Murphy
Seating Capacity of Meeting Rooms:
+50: 1 -50: 2
Facilities available:

Castle Court Hotel
Cahir, Co. Tipperary South
Tel: 052-43955 ....Page 373
Contact Person:
Kevin Curry / Rita Carr
Seating Capacity of Meeting Rooms:
+200: 1
Facilities available:

Clonmel Arms Hotel
Clonmel, Co. Tipperary South
Tel: 052-21233........................Page 377
Contact Person:
Management on Duty
Seating Capacity of Meeting Rooms:
+300: 1 +200: 2 +50: 3 -50: 4
Facilities available:

Dundrum House Hotel
Cashel, Co. Tipperary South
Tel: 062-71116 ....Page 375
Contact Person:
Dolores Thornton
Seating Capacity of Meeting Rooms:
+400: 1
Facilities available:

Glen Hotel
Glen Of Aherlow, Co. Tipperary South
Tel: 062-56146........................Page 379
Contact Person:
Cormac Rose
Seating Capacity of Meeting Rooms:
+300: 1 +200: 1 +100: 2 +50: 2
-50: 1
Facilities available:

Hotel Minella & Leisure Centre
Clonmel, Co. Tipperary South
Tel: 052-22388 ....Page 377
Contact Person:
John Nallen
Seating Capacity of Meeting Rooms:
+500: 1 +200: 2 +100: 2 +50: 4
-50: 5
Facilities available:

Co. Waterford

Ard Ri Hotel (The)
Waterford City, Co. Waterford
Tel: 051-832111 ....Page 388
Contact Person:
John Hornby
Seating Capacity of Meeting Rooms:
+500: 1 +100: 2 +50: 2 -50: 2
Facilities available:

Dooley's Hotel
Waterford City, Co. Waterford
Tel: 051-873531 ....Page 391
Contact Person:
Margaret Darrer
Seating Capacity of Meeting Rooms:
+300: 1 +200: 1 +100: 2 +50: 1
-50: 3
Facilities available:

Faithlegg House Hotel and Golf Club
Faithlegg, Co. Waterford
Tel: 051-382000......................Page 386
Contact Person:
Suzanne Molloy
Seating Capacity of Meeting Rooms:
+200: 1 +50: 1 -50: 3
Facilities available:

Grand Hotel
Tramore, Co. Waterford
Tel: 051-381414 ....Page 386
Contact Person:
Mary Power
Seating Capacity of Meeting Rooms:
+200: 1 +100: 1 +50: 1 -50: 1
Facilities available:

Granville Hotel
Waterford City, Co. Waterford
Tel: 051-305555 ....Page 391
Contact Person:
Richard Hurley
Seating Capacity of Meeting Rooms:
+100: 1 +50: 2 -50: 1
Facilities available:

Lawlors Hotel
Dungarvan, Co. Waterford
Tel: 058-41122 ....Page 383
Contact Person:
Lucy McEnery
Seating Capacity of Meeting Rooms:
+400: 1 +200: 2 +100: 3 +50: 4
-50: 5
Facilities available:

Quality Hotel Waterford
Waterford City, Co. Waterford
Tel: 051-856600......................Page 392
Contact Person:
Linda Bennett
Seating Capacity of Meeting Rooms:
-50: 3
Facilities available:

 Black Out Facilities
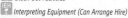 Interpreting Equipment (Can Arrange Hire)
 Air-Conditioning
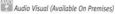 Audio Visual (Available On Premises)
 Interpreting Equipment (Available On Premises)
Audio Visual (Can Arrange Hire)

461

Co. Waterford Continued

Rhu Glenn Country Club Hotel
Waterford City, Co. Waterford
Tel: 051-832242......................Page 392
Contact Person:
Anne / Rita
Seating Capacity of Meeting Rooms:
+400: **1** +300: **1** +200: **1** +100: **1**
+50: **2** -50: **2**
Facilities available:

Tower Hotel & Leisure Centre
Waterford City, Co. Waterford
Tel: 051-862300......................Page 393
Contact Person:
Catherina Hurley
Seating Capacity of Meeting Rooms:
+400: **1** +100: **3** +50: **1** -50: **2**
Facilities available:

Co. Wexford

Ashdown Park Hotel Conference & Leisure Centre
Gorey, Co. Wexford
Tel: 053-948 0500 ....Page 398
Seating Capacity of Meeting Rooms:
+500: **1** +50: **1** -50: **2**
Facilities available:

Brandon House Hotel, Health Club & Spa
New Ross, Co. Wexford
Tel: 051-421703 ....Page 400
Contact Person:
Sharon Boland
Seating Capacity of Meeting Rooms:
+300: **1** -50: **3**
Facilities available:

Carlton Millrace Hotel (The)
Bunclody, Co. Wexford
Tel: 053-937 5100 ....Page 395
Contact Person:
Frank Morris
Seating Capacity of Meeting Rooms:
+300: **1** +200: **1** +100: **1** -50: **2**
Facilities available:

Crosbie Cedars Hotel
Rosslare, Co. Wexford
Tel: 053-913 2124....................Page 401
Contact Person:
Liz Sinnott
Seating Capacity of Meeting Rooms:
+200: **1** +50: **1** -50: **2**
Facilities available:

Ferrycarrig Hotel
Wexford Town, Co. Wexford
Tel: 053-912 0999 ....Page 404
Contact Person:
Siobhán O'Rourke
Seating Capacity of Meeting Rooms:
+300: **1**
Facilities available:

Great Southern Hotel
Rosslare Harbour, Co. Wexford
Tel: 053-913 3233 ....Page 402
Contact Person:
Eoin O'Sullivan
Seating Capacity of Meeting Rooms:
+200: **1** -50: **1**
Facilities available:

Quality Hotel & Leisure Wexford
Wexford Town, Co. Wexford
Tel: 053-917 2000 ....Page 404
Contact Person:
Vivian Delgado
Seating Capacity of Meeting Rooms:
-50: **4**
Facilities available:

Riverside Park Hotel and Leisure Club
Enniscorthy, Co. Wexford
Tel: 053-923 7800 ....Page 397
Contact Person:
Barbara Bailey - Conference & Banqueting Manager
Seating Capacity of Meeting Rooms:
+500: **1** +200: **1** +100: **1** +50: **2**
-50: **1**
Facilities available:

Talbot Hotel Conference and Leisure Centre
Wexford Town, Co. Wexford
Tel: 053-912 2566 ....Page 405
Contact Person:
Niamh Lambert
Seating Capacity of Meeting Rooms:
+300: **1** +200: **1** +100: **2** +50: **3**
-50: **8**
Facilities available:

BO Black Out Facilities
IEH Interpreting Equipment (Can Arrange Hire)
AC Air-Conditioning
AVO Audio Visual (Available On Premises)
IEO Interpreting Equipment (Available On Premises)
AVH Audio Visual (Can Arrange Hire)

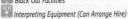

IRELAND 2006
SPA & LEISURE

Ireland is rapidly developing its spa market, with a selection of destination, day, health and resort spas to choose from, as well as superb leisure facilities - all in the wonderful surroundings that make Ireland a unique holiday destination. The following pages will provide a flavour of some of the facilities and treatments on offer in many of the hotels and guesthouses featured in this guide.

.....So come on and get pampered!

Official Website of the Irish Hotels Federation

One source - Endless possibilities

We invite you to Ireland to enhance your precious leisure time. Relax in the perfect sanctuary of the oasis that is Ireland! Our philosophy is to enable you to leave us fully refreshed and restored by experiencing some of the wonderful spa & leisure treatments available in the unique and warm facilities on offer in the hotels and guesthouses listed in this section. A full description of the hotels and guesthouses can be had by looking up the appropriate page number.
Premises are listed in Alphabetical Order in each County.

South West

Co. Cork

Clarion Hotel
Cork City, Co. Cork
Tel: 021-422 4900 ....Page 49
Name of Spa:
SenoVitae
Treatments:36 ......Treatment Rooms:5

Type of Treatments:
Rénovateur Lift Fermeté, Hot Stone Massage, Massotherm-Detox Tunnel, Aroma Enveloppement, Aroma Man, Rénovateur Revitalisant Corps

Type of Facilities:
18m Pool, Sauna, Steam Room, Jacuzzi, Gymnasium, Aerobic Suite, Spa

Imperial Hotel with Lifestyle Salon and Spa
Cork City, Co. Cork
Tel: 021-427 4040 ....Page 52
Name of Spa:
Aveda Lifestyle Salon & Spa @ The Imperial Hotel
Treatments:80 ....Treatment Rooms:10

Type of Treatments:
Full range of Aveda Signature Salon, Spa & Beauty Treatments, Facials, Massages, Body Treatments, Body Wraps, Everyday Essentials for Hands & Feet, Aveda Make-Up, Spa Rituals

Type of Facilities:
Relaxation Lounge, Evian Hydrotherapy Pool, Experience Showers, Dry Floatation Tank, Rasul, Couple Suites

Inchydoney Island Lodge & Spa
Clonakilty, Co. Cork
Tel: 023-33143..........................Page 44
Treatments:25   Treatment Rooms:17

Type of Treatments:
Algotherapy, Balneotherapy, Brumisation, Japanese Silk Facial, Luxury Manicure & Pedicure, Cryotherapy, Reiki, Reflexology

Type of Facilities:
Thalassotherapy Pool, Hammam, Sauna, Relaxation Room, Gymnasium

Kingsley Hotel & Residence
Cork City, Co. Cork
Tel: 021-480 0500 ....Page 53
Name of Spa:
Yauvana Spa
Treatments:60 ....Treatment Rooms:14

Type of Treatments:
Hydrating Facials, Swedish Massage, Deep Cleansing Facials, Aromatherapy Massage, Specific Facials for Man, Reflexology, Facials for Mums-to-be, Indian Head Massage, Deep Bath Cleanse, Targeted Eye Treatments, Ayurvedic Treatments

Type of Facilities:
20m Swimming Pool, Sauna, Steam Room, Jacuzzi, Outdoor Hot Tub, Gymnasium, Aerobic Suite, Spa

Lough Mahon House
Cork City, Co. Cork
Tel: 021-450 2142 ....Page 54
Treatments:8   Treatment Rooms:3

Type of Treatments:
Integrated Energy Therapy (healing with the energy of angels), Reiki, Massage, Reflexology, Indian Head Massage, Body Wraps, Facials

Quality Hotel and Leisure Centre Youghal
Youghal, Co. Cork
Tel: 024-93050 ....Page 69
Name of Spa:
La Spa Vitae
Treatments:30 ......Treatment Rooms:4

Type of Treatments:
Eye Care, Make Up, Pamper Package, Waxing, Mens Grooming Treatments, Therapeutic Treatments, Body Treatments, Facials, Hand & Foot Treatments

Type of Facilities:
Treatment Rooms, Hydrotherapy Bath Suite, Relaxation Area with Sea View

Radisson SAS Hotel & Spa, Cork
Cork City, Co. Cork
Tel: 021-429 7000 ....Page 55
Name of Spa:
The Retreat Spa
Treatments:11........Treatment Rooms:9

Type of Treatments:
Balneotherapy, Algae Wraps, Body Polish, Presso Therapy, Vichy Massage, Elemis Deep Tissue Massage, Classic Rasul, Advanced Elemis Facials, Jessica Manicure, Jessica Pedicure

Type of Facilities:
9 Treatment Rooms, Rasul, Relaxation Suite, Hydrotherapy Pool

Rochestown Park Hotel
Cork City, Co. Cork
Tel: 021-489 0800 ....Page 56
Name of Spa:
Rochestown Park Hotel Thalasso Therapy Centre
Treatments:30 ....Treatment Rooms:15

Type of Treatments:
Seaweed Wraps, Seaweed Baths, Massage, Reflexology, Circulation Treatments, Hot Stone Therapy, Hydrojets, Full Range of Beauty Treatments

Type of Facilities:
20m Swimming Pool, Sauna, Steam Room, Jacuzzi, Hydro Massage Pool, Solarium, Gymnasium

Westlodge Hotel
Bantry, Co. Cork
Tel: 027-50360 ....Page 40
Treatments:7   Treatment Rooms:2

Type of Treatments:
Reflexology, Full Body Massage, Aromatherapy Massage, Indian Head Massage, Sports Massage, Reiki, Top'n'Tail

Type of Facilities:
Heated Swimming Pool, Sauna, Steam Room, Jacuzzi, Fully equipped Gym, Squash Courts

Co. Kerry

Aghadoe Heights Hotel & Spa
Killarney, Co. Kerry
Tel: 064-31766..........................Page 88
Name of Spa:
The Spa at The Heights
Treatments: 58 ....Treatment Rooms: 12

Type of Treatments:
Aveda Elemental Facial Treatments & Body Massage, Fusion Stone Massage, Aqua Polish, Aveda Aqua Polish, Ayurvedic Treatments - Himalayan Rejuvenation & Aveda Wellness Treatment, Elemental Precious Stone Therapy, Reiki, Hammam Massage, Aromatherapy Steam Serail

Type of Facilities:
Hammam, Rock Sauna, Laconium, Aroma Grotto, Tropical Rain Shower, Cold Fog Shower, Heated Loungers, Relaxation Room, Slipper Bath, Serail, Swimming Pool, Jacuzzi, Fitness Suite, Tennis Court, Yoga, Pilates, Hair Salon

Ballygarry House Hotel
Tralee, Co. Kerry
Tel: 066-712 3322 ....Page 111
Name of Spa:
Nádúr
Treatments: 40 ......Treatment Rooms: 7

Type of Treatments:
Hydrotherapy, Amboo & Ginseng Body Polish, USPA Concept Face Treatments, Holistic Therapy, Herbal & Mud Body Wrap, Hot Stone Massage, Ritual Body Massage, Beauty, many other treatments available

Type of Facilities:
Beauty Suite, Relaxing Room, Glass Sauna, Crystal Steam Room, Outdoor Canadian Hot Tub, Vitality Showers, Tanning Suite, Hydrotherapy Suite

Brandon Hotel Conference and Leisure Centre
Tralee, Co. Kerry
Tel: 066-712 3333 ....Page 112
Name of Spa:
The Sanctuary Spa
Treatments: 15 ......Treatment Rooms: 8

Type of Treatments:
Decleor Facials (Aromaplasty, Harmonie & Evidence), Exfoliating Body Polish, Sea Algae Body Wraps, Aromaceane Sea Mud & Sea Salt Wrap, Marine Prelude, Balneotherapy, Aroma Spa Envelopment Programme, Body Massage, Carita Hot Stone Therapy Massage, Carita Progressive Lift Facial, Olys Anti Aging Facial, Endermologie, Ellipse Light Hair Removal, Photorejuvenation, Manicures, Pedicures, All Grooming Treatments

Type of Facilities:
17m Indoor Swimming Pool, Sauna, Steam Room, Jacuzzi, Full Gym, Hydrobath, Solarium and Laser Treatments

Brehon (The)
Killarney, Co. Kerry
Tel: 064-30700 ....Page 90
Name of Spa:
Angsana Spa
Treatments: 23 ......Treatment Rooms: 6

Type of Treatments:
Rain Shower, Massage, Body Polish, Facial, Foot Soak, Rasul, Indian Head Massage, Skin Enhancer, Signature Angsana Massage, Manicure

Type of Facilities:
Herb Sauna, Crystal Steam Room, Salt Grotto, Rasul, Foot Spa, Tropical Shower, Ice Fountain, Kubeldusche, Vitality Pool, Hot & Cold Spa

Dingle Skellig Hotel & Peninsula Spa
Dingle (An Daingean), Co. Kerry
Tel: 066-915 0200 ....Page 78
Name of Spa:
The Peninsula Spa
Treatments: 55 ......Treatment Rooms: 7

Type of Treatments:
Yon-ka Aroma Stone, Yon-ka Face & Body Treatments, Peninsula Spa Face & Body Treatments, Massage, Holistic Treatments, Hydrotherapy, Body Wraps, Sports Injury, Tanning, Nail Treatments, Makeovers, Selection of unique "Irish" treatments from local organic products & ingredients

Type of Facilities:
Outdoor Hot Tub overlooking Dingle Harbour, Relaxation Suite, Hydrotherapy Suite, Sauna, Steam Room, Solarium, Beauty Salon, Outdoor Relaxation Balcony, Disabled Facility and Access, Refreshments Bar

Killarney
Great Southern Hotel
Killarney, Co. Kerry
Tel: 064-38000 ....Page 99
Name of Spa:
Innisfallen Spa
Treatments: 20 ......Treatment Rooms: 3

Type of Treatments:
Hydrotherapy Baths, Hand and Feet Treatments, Waxing Treatments, Massage (various), Seaweed Treatments (various), Aromatherapy, Body Polishing

Type of Facilities:
Relaxation Room, Hydrotherapy Baths, Indoor Heated Swimming Pool, Jacuzzi, Steam Room, Monsoon Shower, Gym

Killarney Park Hotel
Killarney, Co. Kerry
Tel: 064-35555 ....Page 100
Name of Spa:
The Spa at the Killarney Park Hotel
Treatments: 45 ......Treatment Rooms: 8

Type of Treatments:
Eve Lom Facial, Elemis Aroma Stone Therapy, Elemis Japanese Silk Booster Facial, Elemis Well Being Massage, Elemis Fennel Cleansing Cellulite and Colon Therapy, Healing Bath Ceremony, Elemis Aromapure Facial, Reflexology, Elemis Musclean Aroma Spa Ocean Wrap

Type of Facilities:
8 custom built private treatment suites, A specially designed Relaxation Room, Hydrotherapy Suite, Caldarium, Couples Suite, Juice Bar

Killarney Plaza Hotel & Spa
Killarney, Co. Kerry
Tel: 064-21111 ....Page 101
Name of Spa:
Molton Brown Spa
Treatments: 20 ......Treatment Rooms: 8

Type of Treatments:
Spring, Summer, Autumn and Winter Facial and Massage, Cloud Walking, Palm Pressure, Earth, Fire and Water Serail, Gulf Stream Pool

Type of Facilities:
Gulf Stream Pool, Sauna, Steam Room, Jacuzzi

Co. Kerry Continued

Lake Hotel
Killarney, Co. Kerry
Tel: 064-31035 ....Page 102
Name of Spa:
Muckross Fitness Centre
Type of Treatments:
Relaxing Moments Facial, Firm Your Face Facial, Shape Your Face Firming Facial, Relaxing Moments Body Massage, Firm Your Body Massage, Shape Your Body Detox Treatment, Refresh Your Feet Treatment, Aroma Herbal Treatment Facial, Aroma Herbal Body Treatment

Type of Facilities:
Gym, Sauna, Steam Room, Outdoor Hot Tub, Spa Sensations Treatment Centre

**Manor West Hotel,
Spa & Leisure Club**
Tralee, Co. Kerry
Tel: 066-719 4500 ....Page 114
Name of Spa:
**Harmony Spa & Leisure Club
(Opening Early 2006)**
Treatments:20 ......Treatment Rooms:5
Type of Treatments:
Selection of Treatments from the Elemis range

Type of Facilities:
Laconium, 18m Swimming Pool, Razul, Sauna, Steam Room, Aromatherapy Room, Jacuzzi, State of the Art Gymnasium

Park Hotel Kenmare
Kenmare, Co. Kerry
Tel: 064-41200..........................Page 86
Name of Spa:
SAMAS
Treatments:78 ......Treatment Rooms:8
Type of Treatments:
Full Spa Facilities with Treatments - Ayurvedic, Deep Tissue, Aromatherapy etc.

Type of Facilities:
Laconium, Rock Sauna, Steam, Tropical Mist Showers, Vitality Pool, Relaxation Rooms, Tai Chi

Parknasilla Great Southern Hotel
Sneem, Co. Kerry
Tel: 064-45122 ....Page 109
Treatments:10   Treatment Rooms:2

Type of Treatments:
Massage - 1 hour & 1/2 hour, Reflexology - 45 minutes, Aromatherapy - 1 hour, Hydrotherapy Baths

Type of Facilities:
Outdoor Canadian Hot Tub, Hydrotherapy Baths, Jacuzzi, Sauna, Steam Room, Indoor Heated Swimming Pool, Organised Walks

Ross (The)
Killarney, Co. Kerry
Tel: 064-31855 ....Page 106
Name of Spa:
The Spa at The Killarney Park Hotel (Adjacent - Sister Hotel)
Treatments:45 ......Treatment Rooms:8

Type of Treatments:
Eve Lom Facial, Elemis Aroma Stone Therapy, Elemis Japanese Silk Booster Facial, Elemis Well Being Massage, Elemis Fennel Cleansing Cellulite and Colon Therapy, Healing Bath Ceremony, Elemis Aromapure Facial, Reflexology, Elemis Musclease Aroma Spa Ocean Wrap

Type of Facilities:
8 custom built private treatment suites, A specially designed Relaxation Room, Hydrotherapy Suite, Caldarium, Couples Suite, Juice Bar

Sheen Falls Lodge
Kenmare, Co. Kerry
Tel: 064-41600..........................Page 86
Name of Spa:
The Sheen Spa
Treatments:30 ......Treatment Rooms:3

Type of Treatments:
Facial, Body Wrap, Manicure, Massage, Aromastone, Pedicure, Indian Head Massage, Reiki, Body Detox Wrap, Seaweed Wrap

Type of Facilities:
Jacuzzi, Sauna, Steam Room, Swimming Pool, Gymnasium, Sun Deck, Tennis, Jogging Trail

Shannon

Co. Clare

Auburn Lodge Hotel
Ennis, Co. Clare
Tel: 065-682 1247 ....Page 126

Name of Spa:
**Auburn Lodge Hotel Leisure Centre
(Opening late 2006)**
Type of Treatments:
Various treatments available - please enquire

Type of Facilities:
Swimming Pool, Sauna, Jacuzzi, Steam Room, Gymnasium, Treatment Rooms

**Falls Hotel Spa
& Leisure Centre**
Ennistymon, Co. Clare
Tel: 065-707 1004 ....Page 129
Name of Spa:
Falls Hotel Spa
Treatments:5 ......Treatment Rooms:10

Type of Treatments:
Elemis Treatments, Hot Stone Therapy Massage, Elemis Facials, Rasul Signature Treatment, Hammam Signature Treatment

Type of Facilities:
Sabbia Sun Suite, Tanning Suite, Double Hydro, 20m Swimming Pool, Jacuzzi, Steam Room, Outdoor Hot Tub, Sauna, Gymnasium

Thomond Guesthouse & Kilkee Thalassotherapy Centre
Kilkee, Co. Clare
Tel: 065-905 6742 ....Page 131
Name of Spa:
Kilkee Thalassotherapy Centre
Treatments:18 ......Treatment Rooms:6

Type of Treatments:
Natural Seaweed Baths, Balneotherapy, Swedish Massage, Body Scrub, Seaweed Body Wrap, Frigi-Thalgo, Facials, Manicures, Pedicures, Aromatherapy, Massage

Type of Facilities:
Sauna, Steam Room, Manicure/Pedicure room, 6 Treatment rooms. Relaxation area. Winner, Best Day Spa 2004 (Irish Beauty Industry)

Co. Limerick

**Adare Manor Hotel
& Golf Resort**
Adare, Co. Limerick
Tel: 061-396566 ....Page 140
Name of Spa:
The Spa at Adare Manor
Treatments:24 ......Treatment Rooms:6

Type of Treatments:
Elemis Deep Tissue Massage, Elemis Aromatherapy Massage, Elemis Skin Specific Facials, Elemis Visible Brilliance Facial, Elemis Pro Collagen Facial, Lime & Ginger Salt Glow, Elemis Coconut & Milk Body Wrap, Frangipani Body Nourish Wrap, Elemis Pregnancy Massage, Elemis Hydrotherapy Baths

Type of Facilities:
Guest Shower Rooms, Hydrotherapy Bath

Fitzgeralds Woodlands House Hotel, Health and Leisure Spa
Adare, Co. Limerick
Tel: 061-605100 .... Page 142
Name of Spa:
Revas Hair Salon, Beauty & Relaxation Spa
Treatments:100 .... Treatment Rooms:10

Type of Treatments:
Plantogen Hot Stone Massage Therapy, Thalgo Body Polish, Platinum Detox, Non-Surgical Lyposculpture, Ocean Chleir Seaweed Envelopment Wrap, Genesis Inch Loss Wrap, Stimulating & Oxygenerating Facial, Lifting with Vitamin C, Acadespa Light Legs Treatment, Acadespa Tonic Treatment

Type of Facilities:
Spray Tan, Balneotherapy, Hair Salon

Co. Tipperary North

Abbey Court Hotel and Trinity Leisure Club
Nenagh, Co. Tipperary North
Tel: 067-41111 .... Page 147
Name of Spa:
The Spa Health and Beauty Sanctuary
Treatments:20 ...... Treatment Rooms:8

Type of Treatments:
Swedish Massage, Decleor Facials, Jessica Pedicure, Manicure, Make-up, Waxing, Self-Tan, Universal Contour Wrap

Type of Facilities:
Stand Up Balneotherapy Bath, Sunroom

West

Co. Galway

Clifden Station House Hotel
Clifden, Co. Galway
Tel: 095-21699 .... Page 159
Name of Spa:
Renew
Treatments:10 ...... Treatment Rooms:4

Type of Treatments:
Mud Wrap, Waxing, Reflexology, Salt Scrub, Aromatherapy, Detox Hydro, Sunbeds

Type of Facilities:
Pool, Baby Pool, Sauna, Steam Room, Jacuzzi, Sunbeds

Day's Inishbofin House Hotel
Inishbofin Island, Co. Galway
Tel: 095-45809 .... Page 177
Treatment Rooms:5

Type of Treatments:
Variety of Treatments and Beauty Therapy available

Type of Facilities:
Outdoor Canadian Tub

Great Southern Hotel
Galway City, Co. Galway
Tel: 091-564041 .... Page 169
Name of Spa:
The Square Spa and Health Club
Treatments:20 ...... Treatment Rooms:3

Type of Treatments:
Hydrotherapy Baths, Waxing Treatments (various), Massage (various), Facials (various), Hand & Feet Treatments, Aromatherapy

Type of Facilities:
Fitness Suite, Steam Room, Jacuzzi, Outdoor Canadian Hot Tub, Hydrotherapy Baths

Harbour Hotel
Galway City, Co. Galway
Tel: 091-569466 .... Page 169
Name of Spa:
Haven Health and Beauty
Treatments:21 ...... Treatment Rooms:2

Type of Treatments:
The Repechage Four Layer Facial, Seaweed "on the go" Facial, Aromatherapy Purifying Facial, Back Facial, Repechage Sea Body Treat, Repechage New York Experience, Peppermint Sea Twist, Seaweed Body Treatment, Honey & Almond Body Polish, Manicure/Pedicure

Type of Facilities:
Jacuzzi, Gym, Steam Room

Radisson SAS Hotel & Spa Galway
Galway City, Co. Galway
Tel: 091-538300 .... Page 173
Name of Spa:
Spirit One Spa
Treatments:60 .... Treatment Rooms:16

Type of Treatments:
Massage, Facials, Hand Treatments, Foot Treatments, Floats, Wraps, Waxing, Reflexology, Exfoliation, Eye Teatments

Type of Facilities:
Indoor Swimming Pool, Hot Tub, Gym, Slipper Bath, Laconium, Sabia Med, Heated Loungers, Rock Sauna, Hammam, Snail Showers

Shannon Oaks Hotel & Country Club
Portumna, Co. Galway
Tel: 090-974 1777 .... Page 184
Treatments:20   Treatment Rooms:3

Type of Treatments:
Aroma Spa Relax, Aroma Spa Tonic, Nutrivital, Oxygenating, Revitalising, Nutri Soie, Evidence

Co. Mayo

Atlantic Coast Hotel
Westport, Co. Mayo
Tel: 098-29000 .... Page 195
Name of Spa:
Elysium Health and Beauty Spa
Treatments:25 ...... Treatment Rooms:4

Type of Treatments:
Holistic/Swedish Massage Therapy, Reflexology, Reiki Therapy, Aromatherapy, Indian Head Massage, Facials, Seaweed Bath, Enzymatic Sea Mud Pack Treatment

Type of Facilities:
Swimming Pool, Steam Room, Sauna, Gymnasium, Childrens' Pool

Co. Mayo Continued

Belmont Hotel
Knock, Co. Mayo
Tel: 094-938 8122 ....Page 193
Name of Spa:
The Health Suite
Treatments:9 ....Treatment Rooms:3

Type of Treatments:
Reiki, Aromatherapy, Reflexology,
Swedish Massage, Indian Head Massage,
Stress Management, Hydrotherapy Bath

Type of Facilities:
Sauna, Steam Room, Sunbed, Gym,
Hydrotherapy Bath

Hotel Westport, Leisure, Spa, Conference
Westport, Co. Mayo
Tel: 098-25122 ....Page 197
Name of Spa:
Ocean Spirit Spa
Treatments:35 ....Treatment Rooms:10

Type of Treatments:
Cleopatra Bath, Serail Mud Treatment,
Turkish Hammam Massage,
Aromatherapy Massage, Swedish &
Holistic Massage, Body Exfoliant
Treatments, Body Moisturising
Treatments, Facials, Pedicure/Manicure

Type of Facilities:
Cleopatra Bath, Serail Mud Chamber,
Hammam Wet Massage, Relaxation
Suite, 20 Metre Pool, Lounger Pool,
Jacuzzi, Steam Room, Sauna, Gym

Knockranny House Hotel & Spa
Westport, Co. Mayo
Tel: 098-28600........................Page 197
Name of Spa:
Spa Salveo
Treatments:30 ....Treatment Rooms:12

Type of Treatments:
Elemis Deep Tissue Muscle Massage,
Elemis Deep Tissue Back Massage,
Elemis Oxygen SkinCalm Facial, Elemis
S.O.S. Purifying Facial, Elemis Absolute
Spa Ritual, Elemis Pro-Collagen Marine
Facial - many other treatments available

Type of Facilities:
Vitality Pool, Thermal Suite, Gym, 12
Treatment Rooms, Serail, Hammam
Massage, Dry Floatation, Relaxation
Areas

Westport Woods Hotel & Spa
Westport, Co. Mayo
Tel: 098-25811 ....Page 199
Name of Spa:
Westport Woods Hotel & Spa
Treatments:36 ......Treatment Rooms:5

Type of Treatments:
Swedish Massage, Aromatherapy
Massage, Reiki, Reflexology, Indian Head
Massage, La Grand Classique Facial,
Hydralessence Visage, Optimizer, Plaisir
D'Arômes, Phyto-Marine (Mud and
Seaweed)

Type of Facilities:
Sauna, Steam Room, Jacuzzi, Relaxation
Suite, Outdoor Hot Tub

Co. Roscommon

Abbey Hotel, Conference and Leisure Centre
Roscommon Town, Co. Roscommon
Tel: 090-662 6240 ....Page 200
Name of Spa:
Abbey House & Fitness
Treatments:4 ....Treatment Rooms:2

Type of Treatments:
Massage, Reflexology, Indian Head
Massage

Type of Facilities:
Sauna, Jacuzzi, Steam Room, Plunge
Pool, 20m Swimming Pool, Fully
Equipped Gymnasium

North West

Co. Donegal

Carlton Redcastle Hotel & Thalasso Spa
Moville, Co. Donegal
Tel: 074-938 5555 ....Page 217
Name of Spa:
Thalasso Therapy Spa
Treatments:11........Treatment Rooms:9

Type of Treatments:
Chromotherapy Bath, Rasul,
Balneotherapy Bath, Affusion Shower,
Hydrojet Massage, Pressotherapy,
Cryotherapy, Thalasso Body Wrapping,
Marine Body Polish, Massage

Type of Facilities:
Gymnasium, Thalasso Spa Boutique,
Thalasso Spa Relaxation Room,
Thalassotherapy Pool

Downings Bay Hotel
Letterkenny, Co. Donegal
Tel: 074-915 5586 ....Page 214
Name of Spa:
Secrets Beauty Salon
Treatments:25 ......Treatment Rooms:2

Type of Treatments:
Manicure/pedicure, Waxing, Eye
Treatments, Nail Extensions, Facials -
Absolute Hydrating Facial, Cold Marine
Facial, Body Treatments - Marine Prelude
Treatment, Thalgobodytherm Wrap,
Spray Tan

Type of Facilities:
Beauty Salon

Inishowen Gateway Hotel
Buncrana, Co. Donegal
Tel: 074-936 1144 ....Page 208
Name of Spa:
Seagrass Wellbeing Centre
Treatments:50 ......Treatment Rooms:6

Type of Treatments:
Aroma Stone Massage, Body Wraps,
Hydrotherapy, Indian Head Massage,
Reiki, Aromatherapy Massage, Facials,
Pedicures, Manicures, Reflexology

Type of Facilities:
Relaxation Room, Herbal Teas & Juice
Bar, Showers & Changing Rooms,
Towelling Robes and Slippers provided,
Hydrotherapy Bath

Malin Hotel
Malin, Co. Donegal
Tel: 074-937 0606 ....Page 216

Type of Treatments:
Variety of Treatments available on
request

Type of Facilities:
Fully equipped gymnasium

Mill Park Hotel, Conference Centre & Leisure Club
Donegal Town, Co. Donegal
Tel: 074-972 2880 ....Page 210
Treatments:20   Treatment Rooms:4

Type of Treatments:
Massage, Waxing, Make up, Manicure,
Pedicure, Facials, Body Wraps

Type of Facilities:
Massage Room, Beauty Treatment
Room, Nail Bar

Sandhouse Hotel
Rossnowlagh, Co. Donegal
Tel: 071-985 1777 ....Page 218
Name of Spa:
The Marine Spa & Wellness Centre
Treatments:25 ......Treatment Rooms:5

Type of Treatments:
Manicure, Pedicure, Facials, Massage, Hydrotherapy, Body Wraps, Tinting, Waxing, Electrolysis, Tanning

Type of Facilities:
Jacuzzi, Steam Room

Shandon Hotel
Spa and Wellness
Letterkenny, Co. Donegal
Tel: 074-913 6137 ....Page 215
Name of Spa:
Shandon Spa and Wellness
Treatments:41 ......Treatment Rooms:8

Type of Treatments:
Balneotherapy, Dry Floatation, Hot & Cold Stone Therapy, Swedish Massage, Reflexology, Aromatherapy, Indian Head Massage & many more

Type of Facilities:
10,000sq feet of Total Spa with Executive Lounge, Male & Female Changing Rooms, Relaxation Room, Exercise Room, Vitality Pool, Heated Slabs, Foot Spa, Outdoor Hot Tub, Salt Grotto, Ice Fountain, Aromatherapy Showers

Co. Leitrim

Shannon Key West Hotel
Rooskey, Co. Leitrim
Tel: 071-963 8800 ....Page 221

Type of Treatments:
Pamper Packages Available, Full Beauty Salon in-house

Type of Facilities:
Steam Room, Jacuzzi, Sunbed, Fully Equipped Gym, Tennis & Basketball Courts

Co. Sligo

Clarion Hotel Sligo
Sligo Town, Co. Sligo
Tel: 071-911 9000....................Page 224
Name of Spa:
SanoVitae Health & Spa
Treatment Rooms:7

Type of Treatments:
Hydrotherapy Baths, Massages, Facials, Body Wrap, Detox Tunnel, Nail Treatments, Full Body Tan, Manicure, Pedicure

Type of Facilities:
Steam Chamber, Water Jet Massage Bath, Relaxation Room, Sauna, Jacuzzi, Steam Room, 20m Pool, Kiddies Pool, Aerobics Studio

Yeats Country Hotel, Spa & Leisure Club
Rosses Point, Co. Sligo
Tel: 071-917 7211 ....Page 223
Name of Spa:
Eros Health Spa
Treatments:35 ......Treatment Rooms:6

Type of Treatments:
Seaweed Baths, Hydrotherapy Bath, Reiki, Reflexology, Aromatherapy, Swedish Massage, Hot Stone Treatments, Yon-ka Paris Beauty Treatments, Manicure, Waxing

Type of Facilities:
Relaxation Suite, Double Treatment Room, Single Treatment Room, Double Seaweed Bath Suite, Single Seaweed Bath Suite, Hydrotherapy Suite, Day Packages & Vouchers available

Dublin & East Coast

Co. Dublin

Castleknock Hotel and Country Club
Dublin City, Co. Dublin
Tel: 01-640 6300 ....Page 266
Treatments:19   Treatment Rooms:4

Type of Treatments:
Facials, Massage, Reflexology, Body Treatments, Manicures, Pedicures, Waxing, False Tan Application, Beauty Treatments

Type of Facilities:
Sauna, Steam Room, Spa Jacuzzi, 18m Swimming Pool, Gymnasium, Aerobics Studio, Childrens' Pool

Clarence (The)
Dublin City, Co. Dublin
Tel: 01-407 0800 ....Page 269
Name of Spa:
Therapy
Treatments:10 ....Treatment Rooms:1

Type of Treatments:
Ladies & Gents Facials & 8 Essential Body Treatments

Type of Facilities:
Fitness Room with running machine, cross-trainer & cycling machine

Clarion Hotel Dublin Liffey Valley
Dublin City, Co. Dublin
Tel: 01-625 8000 ....Page 269
Name of Spa:
SanoVitae Health & Fitness (Opening Spring 2006)
Treatments:10 ......Treatment Rooms:3

Type of Treatments:
Beauty Treatments, Massage

Type of Facilities:
Please contact hotel for full details or email:
sanovitae@clarionhotelliffeyvalley.com

Fitzwilliam Hotel
Dublin City, Co. Dublin
Tel: 01-478 7000 ....Page 275
Name of Spa:
Free Spirit @ The Fitzwilliam
Treatment Rooms:3

Type of Treatments:
Dermalogica Aromatherapy Massage, Aromastone Massage, Ultra-calming Facial, Dermalogica Total Eyecare Treatment, Men's Facial, Toning Body Wrap

Type of Facilities:
3 Treatment Rooms, Nail Bar, Hair Salon, Mist Tanning

Four Seasons Hotel Dublin
Dublin City, Co. Dublin
Tel: 01-665 4000 ....Page 276
Name of Spa:
The Spa
Treatments:45 ......Treatment Rooms:4

Type of Treatments:
La Prairie Facial, Holistic Foot/Hand Treatment, Detoxifying Algae Wrap, Caviar Energising Stone Therapy, Four Seasons Massage

Type of Facilities:
Whirlpool, Sauna, Steam Room, Indoor Swimming Pool, Fitness Facilities

Co. Dublin Continued

Grand Hotel
Malahide, Co. Dublin
Tel: 01-845 0000 .... Page 303
Name of Spa:
Arena Health & Fitness Centre
Treatments:9 ....Treatment Rooms:5

Type of Treatments:
4 Repêchage Facials, Swedish Massage, Reflexology, Hot Stone Full Body & Scrub

Type of Facilities:
Jacuzzi, Steam Room, Sauna, Treatment Rooms

Merrion Hall
Dublin City, Co. Dublin
Tel: 01-668 1426 .... Page 287
Name of Spa:
Merrion Hall & Spa (Opening Spring 2006)
Treatments:6 ....Treatment Rooms:2

Type of Treatments:
Massage, Facial & Various Body Treatments

Type of Facilities:
Fitness Room, Relaxation Area, Sauna & Steam Room

Morrison (The)
Dublin City, Co. Dublin
Tel: 01-887 2400 .... Page 289
Name of Spa:
Headspace (Opening February 2006)
Type of Treatments:
Various treatments available - please enquire

Type of Facilities:
Yoga, Reiki, Turkish Bath, Jacuzzi, Massage & Meditation Facilities available on site

Portmarnock Hotel & Golf Links
Portmarnock, Co. Dublin
Tel: 01-846 0611...................... Page 304
Name of Spa:
Oceana
Treatments:10 ......Treatment Rooms:3

Type of Treatments:
Facials, Body Treatments, Tanning, Nails, Pedicures, Waxing, De-stressing and Sports Physiotherapy, Balneotherapy

Type of Facilities:
Sauna, Gym, Steam Shower, Hairdressing, Nail Bars, Treatment Rooms

Co. Louth

Boyne Valley Hotel & Country Club
Drogheda, Co. Louth
Tel: 041-983 7737 .... Page 309
Name of Spa:
Boyne Valley Health & Beauty Spa
Treatments:30 ......Treatment Rooms:2

Type of Treatments:
Hot Stone Full Body/Back Massage, Botox Facials, Royal Jelly Facials, Solglo Spray Tan, Spa Manicures, Spa Pedicures, Indian Head Massage, Make Up, Waxing, Inch Loss Wraps

Type of Facilities:
20m Swimming Pool with Jacuzzi, Sauna & Steam Room Facilities, Aerobic & Spinning Studios with Aqua, Body Board, Body Bar, Yoga and Boxercise, Powerplate, Lifestyle Checks, CV and Weight Equipment

Co. Meath

Marriott Johnstown House Hotel & Spa Enfield
Enfield, Co. Meath
Tel: 046-954 0000 .... Page 314
Name of Spa:
The Spa at Marriott Johnstown House
Treatments:24 ....Treatment Rooms:12

Type of Treatments:
Aromapure Taster Facial, Aromapure Facial, Japanese Silk Booster Facial, Japanese Silk Eye Zone Therapy, Well-Being Massage, Well Being Back Massage, Absolute Spa Ritual, Indian Head Massage

Type of Facilities:
Indoor Heated Swimming Pool, Gymnasium, Retail Outlets, Steam Rooms, Saunas, 12 Spa Therapy Rooms and Hot Thermal Suite

Co. Wicklow

Arklow Bay Conference and Leisure Hotel
Arklow, Co. Wicklow
Tel: 0402-32309..................... Page 318
Name of Spa:
Rivendell Body & Beauty Spa
Treatments:50 ......Treatment Rooms:6

Type of Treatments:
Aromatherapy & Hot Stone Massage, Dermalogica Facials, Nail Bar, Pedicure, Waxing, Holistic Treatments, Fake Bake Tan Spray, Make-up for all occasions, Spa Packages

Type of Facilities:
6 treatment rooms plus Sauna, Steam Room, Jacuzzi, 20 metre level-deck swimming pool

BrookLodge and Wells Spa
Aughrim, Co. Wicklow
Tel: 0402-36444 .... Page 320
Name of Spa:
The Wells Spa at The BrookLodge Hotel
Treatments:45 ....Treatment Rooms:14

Type of Treatments:
Decleor body and Facials including Envelopment, Carita Body and Facials including Renovateur, Floatation Therapy, Hammam Massage, Cleopatra and Thalassotherapy Baths, Mud Chamber

Type of Facilities:
Indoor to Outdoor Swimming Pool, Floatation Room, Serail Mud Chamber, Aroma Steam Room, Finnish Baths, Outdoor Hot Tub, Jacuzzi, Hammam Massage Room

Glenview Hotel
Glen-O-The-Downs, Co. Wicklow
Tel: 01-287 3399 .... Page 324
Name of Spa:
The Haven
Treatments:26 ......Treatment Rooms:3

Type of Treatments:
Specialised Hot Stone Massage, Aromaplastie Facial, Tranquillity Back Massage, Vital Eyes Treatment, Aroma Relax Envelopment, De luxe French Manicure & Pedicure, Perfect Contour, Swedish Massage, Reflexology

Type of Facilities:
Swimming Pool, Sauna, Steam Room, Jacuzzi, Outdoor Hot Tub, Fully Equipped Gymnasium

Marriott Druids Glen Hotel & Country Club
Newtownmountkennedy, Co. Wicklow
Tel: 01-287 0800 .... Page 324
Name of Spa:
The Spa
Treatment Rooms:4

Type of Treatments:
Irish Hot Stone Experience, Reiki, Toning Body Wrap, The Body Booster, Body Polish, Abolute Rehydrating Facial, Really Grand Hands, Reflexology

Type of Facilities:
18 metre Pool, Aroma Steam Pool, Wet Steam Pool, Plunge Pool, Sauna, Hydrotherapy Pool, Gym, Sunbed, Ladies and Gents Locker Rooms, Solarium

Rathsallagh House, Golf and Country Club
Dunlavin, Co. Wicklow
Tel: 045-403112 ....Page 322
Treatments:5   Treatment Rooms:2

Type of Treatments:
Full Body Massage, Back and Leg Massage, Hand and Feet Massage, Anti-Cellulite Massage, All Beauty Treatments

Type of Facilities:
Jacuzzi, Steam Room, Sauna

Midlands & Lakelands

Co. Cavan

Radisson SAS Farnham Estate
Cavan Town, Co. Cavan
Tel: 049-436 5801 ....Page 332
Name of Spa:
Farnham Wellness Centre (Opening June 2006)
Treatments:100 ....Treatment Rooms:18

Type of Treatments:
Various treatments available - please enquire

Type of Facilities:
Gymnasium, Indoor/Outdoor Infinity Pool, Glazed Meditation Garden, Herbal Aroma Bath, Salad & Juice Bar, Relaxation Room with Waterbeds and Soft Lighting, Hot & Cold Water Splash Pools with Light Therapy

Slieve Russell Hotel Golf & Country Club
Ballyconnell, Co. Cavan
Tel: 049-952 6444 ....Page 331
Name of Spa:
Ciúin Spa and Wellness Centre
Treatments:24 ....Treatment Rooms:17

Type of Treatments:
Wide selection of Yon-ka Aromatic Face and Body Treatments available, along with other Beauty Treatments

Type of Facilities:
Rasul Room, Hammam Traditional Turkish Bath, Herb Sauna, Salt Grotto, Floatation Tank, Relaxation Rooms

Co. Kildare

Bert House Hotel & Leisure Centre
Athy, Co. Kildare
Tel: 059-863 2578 ....Page 335
Name of Spa:
Bert House Health & Beauty Retreat
Treatment Rooms:3

Type of Treatments:
Holistic Massage, Manicures, Aromatherapy, Facials, Reflexology, Waxing, Hopi Ear Candling, Colonic Irrigation, Indian Head Massage

Type of Facilities:
Sauna, Steam Room, Hot Tub, Massage Therapy Room, Cellar Juice Bar, Private Spa Day Suites

Carlton Abbey Hotel
Athy, Co. Kildare
Tel: 059-863 0100 ....Page 335
Treatment Rooms:7

Type of Treatments:
Hydro Bath, Sports Massage, Full Body Wraps, Anti-stress Package, Manicure & Pedicure, Body & Facial Massage, Gentlemen's Well-being Treatments

Type of Facilities:
Relaxation Room, Hydrotherapy Bath Pool, Sauna, Gym, Jacuzzi

Carton House
Maynooth, Co. Kildare
Tel: 01-505 2000 ....Page 340
Name of Spa:
(Opening Summer 2006)
Treatment Rooms:10

Type of Treatments:
Various treatments available - please enquire

Glenroyal Hotel, Leisure Club & Conference Centre
Maynooth, Co. Kildare
Tel: 01-629 0909 ....Page 341

Name of
Spa:
Ealú Spa
Treatment Rooms:6

Type of Treatments:
Body Wraps, Hot Stone Massage, Waxing, Facials, Manicures, Pedicures, Spray Tans, Indian Head Massage, Tinting, Make up

Type of Facilities:
2 x 20m Pools, Sauna, Jacuzzi, Steam Room, Solariums, Hydro Spa, Gymnasium, Aerobics Studio, Spinning Room

K Club (The)
Straffan, Co. Kildare
Tel: 01-601 7200 ....Page 344
Name of Spa:
The K Spa
Treatments:100 ....Treatment Rooms:13

Type of Treatments:
Body Wraps, Hot Stone Therapy, Waxing, Facials, Massage, Hair Salon, Reflexology, Manicure, Pedicure, Rasul, Pilates

Type of Facilities:
Rasul, Swimming Pool, Hot Tub, Hair Beauty & Pedicure Salon, Tanning System, Kings Bath, Vichy Shower, Hammam, Hot Stone

Killashee House Hotel & Villa Spa
Naas, Co. Kildare
Tel: 045-879277 ....Page 342
Name of Spa:
The Villa Spa
Treatments:65 ....Treatment Rooms:18

Type of Treatments:
Algotherapy, Rasul, Balneotherapy, Massage, Pedicure, Balinese Treatment Rooms, Cellcosmet Treatment Rooms, Hammam, Elemis Hot Stone Massage

Type of Facilities:
Therapeutic Pool, Mud Chamber, Hair Salon, Juice Bar, Relaxation Rooms, Hydrojets, Floatation Rooms

Co. Kildare Continued

Osprey Hotel & Spa
Naas, Co. Kildare
Tel: 045-881111 ....Page 343
Name of Spa:
Osprey Spa
Treatments:76 ......Treatment Rooms:8

Type of Treatments:
Hydrofloat, Aqualux, Rasul Bath,
Reflexology, Sports Massage, Hot Stone
Massage, Aromatherapy, La Phyto Facial,
Salt Brushing, Pedicure

Type of Facilities:
Swimming Pool, Footbaths, Sanarium,
Relaxation Room, Salt Grotto, Snow
Paradise, Hydro Jet Pool, Fitness Studio,
Steam Room, Family Changing Room

Standhouse Hotel Leisure &
Conference Centre
Curragh (The), Co. Kildare
Tel: 045-436177 ....Page 338
Name of Spa:
Decleor Beauty Salon
Type of Treatments:
Aromatherapy Facials, Body Massage,
Reflexology, Dermalogica Treatments

Type of Facilities:
Sauna, Steam Room, Jacuzzi, Plunge
Pool, Swimming Pool, Gymnasium

Westgrove Hotel & Conference
Centre
Clane, Co. Kildare
Tel: 1800-32 42 52 ....Page 337
Name of Spa:
(Opening April 2006)
Treatments:12 ......Treatment Rooms:5

Type of Treatments:
Various treatments available - please
enquire

Type of Facilities:
Fully Equipped Gym, 20m Pool, Sauna,
Steam Room, Jacuzzi, Kids Pool, Aerobics
Suite

Co. Laois

Heritage at Killenard (The)
Killenard, Co. Laois
Tel: 057-864 5500 ....Page 345
Name of Spa:
The Spa at the Heritage
Treatments:75 ....Treatment Rooms:20

Type of Treatments:
Massage, Wraps, Hydrotherapy, Facials,
Mud Wraps, Stone Therapy, Manicure,
Sports & Body Therapy, Mens
Treatments, Eye/Lip Treatments

Type of Facilities:
Sanarium, Tepadarium, Hydrotherapy
Pool, Tropical Showers, Hammam, Steam
Bath, Sauna, Foot Bath, Mud Chamber,
Ice Fountain

Heritage Hotel Portlaoise
Portlaoise, Co. Laois
Tel: 057-867 8588 ....Page 346
Name of Spa:
The Heritage Beauty Spa
Treatments:25 ......Treatment Rooms:9

Type of Treatments:
Full Body Wraps, Massages, Nail
Treatments, Reflexology, Waxing,
Footcare, Make-up, False Tan, General
Grooming, Electrolysis, Skin Exfoliation
Treatments, Slimming Treatments, Body
Toning

Type of Facilities:
Swimming Pool, Sauna, Steam Room,
Jacuzzi, Gymnasium, Relaxation Room,
Balneotherapy Room

Co. Monaghan

Castle Leslie
Glaslough, Co. Monaghan
Tel: 047-88100 ....Page 347
Name of Spa:
The Spa @ Castle Leslie (Opening
Sept 2006)
Type of Treatments:
Various treatments available - please
enquire

Hillgrove Hotel &
Conference Centre
Monaghan Town, Co. Monaghan
Tel: 047-81288 ....Page 348
Name of Spa:
Hillgrove Leisure & Spa
Treatments:25 ......Treatment Rooms:8

Type of Treatments:
Facials, Massage, Body Wraps,
Exfoliation, Water Treatments,
Alternative Therapies, Tanning
Treatments, Beauty Treatments, Nail Bar
& Hair Salon

Type of Facilities:
Swimming Pool, Jacuzzi, Steam Room,
Sauna, Hot Tub, Gym, Thermal Spa Area,
Hammam & Rasul, Nail Bar, Hair Salon

Nuremore Hotel & Country Club
Carrickmacross, Co. Monaghan
Tel: 042 -966 1438 ....Page 347
Name of Spa:
Vida
Treatments:40 ......Treatment Rooms:4

Type of Treatments:
Aromatherapy, Full Body Massage,
Detoxifying Algae Wrap, Reflexology,
Indian Head Massage, Golfers Tonic,
Luxury Eye Treatment, Sports and Fitness
Massage, Facials

Type of Facilities:
Sauna, Steam Room, Whirlpool
Swimming Pool, Gym, Tennis Courts

Co. Offaly

Bridge House Hotel
& Leisure Club
Tullamore, Co. Offaly
Tel: 057-932 5600 ....Page 350
Treatments:5   Treatment Rooms:1

Type of Treatments:
Swedish Holistic Massage, Solarium,
Sports Massage, Indian Head Massage,
Pilates

Type of Facilities:
Sauna, Steam Room, Jacuzzi, Outdoor
Hydrotherapy Pool, Swimming Pool,
Gymnasium

County Arms Hotel
Birr, Co. Offaly
Tel: 057-912 0791 ....Page 349
Name of Spa:
Springs Wellness Suites
Treatments:30 ......Treatment Rooms:7

Type of Treatments:
Elemis Spa Treatments Exclusively. Anti-
Ageing Facials, Aromapure Facials,
Absolute Spa Ritual, Aroma Spa Ocean
Wrap, Well-Being Massage, Hot Stone
Therapy, Spray Tanning, Manicure,
Pedicure

Type of Facilities:
Hot Tub, Jacuzzi, Kids Pool, Sauna,
Steam Room, 20m Pool, Hydrotherapy
Pool, Air-Conditioned Gym

Kinnitty Castle Demesne
Birr, Co. Offaly
Tel: 057-913 7318 ....Page 350
Name of Spa:
The Gate Lodge Spa at Kinnitty Castle
Treatments:40 ......Treatment Rooms:3

Type of Treatments:
Hot Stone Massage, Aromatic Facials, Massor Exotic Wrap, Nails by Design, MAC Make-Up Design, Eye Treatments, Tanning Treatments

Type of Facilities:
Outdoor Hot Tub, Massor Hydrotherapy Baths, Sauna, Steam, Exotic Wrap, Redken Hair Salon

Co. Westmeath

Bloomfield House Hotel
Mullingar, Co. Westmeath
Tel: 044-934 0894 ....Page 356
Name of Spa:
Zoi Spa - Beauty
Treatments:30 ......Treatment Rooms:8

Type of Treatments:
Facials, Massage, Spa Wraps, Exfoliation, Nourishing Wraps, Pedicures, Manicures, Full Range of Grooming Treatments, and Complimentery Therapies

Type of Facilities:
Relaxation Room, Solarium, Sauna, Steam Room, Swimming Pool, Gymnasium, Jacuzzi, Aerobics Studio

Hodson Bay Hotel
Athlone, Co. Westmeath
Tel: 090-644 2000 ....Page 354
Name of Spa:
The Spa at Hodson Bay - (Opening Early 2006)
Treatments:20 ....Treatment Rooms:12

Type of Treatments:
Aromatherapy Massage, Reflexology, Aroma Stone Therapy, Reiki, Full Body Polish, Watsu Treatments, Jet Douche Treatments, Bath Ceremony, Vichy Shower, Seaweed Body Wraps

Type of Facilities:
Thermal Suite, Outdoor Hot Tub overlooking lake shore, Hair & Beauty Studios, Aerobics & Fitness Studios, Watsu Pool, Jet Douche, Rasul, Laconiums, 20m Pool with Hydrotherapy Features, Relaxation Suites

Mullingar Park Hotel
Mullingar, Co. Westmeath
Tel: 044-933 7500 ....Page 357
Name of Spa:
Azure Leisure and Spa
Treatments:36 ......Treatment Rooms:7

Type of Treatments:
Aromatherapy, Swedish Body Massage, Body Wraps, Facials, Paraffin Wax, Manicures, Pedicures, Fake Tan, Eye Masks and Tinting, Body Wax, La Stone Therapy

Type of Facilities:
Shower facility for Body Treatments, Massage Room, Relaxation Room, Nail Bar, Linen Facility - Towels, Duvet etc.

South East
Co. Carlow

Seven Oaks Hotel
Carlow Town, Co. Carlow
Tel: 059-913 1308 ....Page 362
Name of Spa:
Greenbank Health and Leisure Club
Treatments:10 ......Treatment Rooms:2

Type of Treatments:
Indian Head Massage, Aerobics, Massage, Reflexology

Type of Facilities:
20m Deck Level Pool, Childrens' Pool, Jacuzzi, Steam Room & Sauna, Solarium, Massage & Sports Injury Clinic, Gynasium - Cardiovascular Resistance, Free Weights, Aerobic Studio, Disabled Facilities

Talbot Carlow Hotel
Carlow Town, Co. Carlow
Tel: 059-915 3000 ....Page 362
Name of Spa:
Essence Nail & Beauty Therapy
Treatments:25 ......Treatment Rooms:5

Type of Treatments:
Dermalogica Customised Facial, Multi-Vitamin Power Facial, Multi-Vitamin Power Plus Facial, Skin Brightening Treatment, Intensive Moisture Facial, Revitalising Eye Rescue Treatment

Type of Facilities:
Treatment Rooms, Nail Bar, Make Up Room, Sauna, Spa Pool, Steam Room

Co. Kilkenny

Hotel Kilkenny
Kilkenny City, Co. Kilkenny
Tel: 056-776 2000 ....Page 366
Name of Spa:
Lilac Lodge Spa
Treatments:40 ......Treatment Rooms:4

Type of Treatments:
Dermalogica Facial Treatments, Yon-ka Facial Treatments, Aroma Hot Stone Massage, Phyto-Marine Swimming Treatment, Reflexology, Sports Therapy Massage

Type of Facilities:
Luxury Relaxation Room, Nail Technology, Waxing, Tanning, Complimentary off-street Parking

Kilkenny River Court
Kilkenny City, Co. Kilkenny
Tel: 056-772 3388 ....Page 368
Name of Spa:
~H2o+ Oasis (@Kilkenny River Court Leisure Club)
Treatments:10 ......Treatment Rooms:4

Type of Treatments:
H2o+ Aromaplasty, H2o+ Nutri-Gain Moisture, H2o+ Harmony Epidermis, H2o+ Anti-Ageing Eye Treatment, H2o+ Fitness Essential Massage, Reiki, Reflexology

Type of Facilities:
Treatment Rooms, Gymnasium, 17m Swimming pool, Geyser Pool, Jacuzzi, Sauna

Lyrath Estate Hotel, Spa & Convention Centre
Kilkenny City, Co. Kilkenny
Tel: 056-776 0088 ....Page 370
Name of Spa:
~H2o+ Spa & Wellness Centre (Opening Jan 2006)
Treatments:12 ......Treatment Rooms:10

Type of Treatments:
Body Massage, Aromatherapy Facial, Body Wraps, Hot Stone Massage, Rasul, Hydrofloat

Type of Facilities:
Male Relaxtion Area, Female Relaxation Area, Hydro Pool - both indoor + outdoor, Sauna, Steam Room, Gym

Co. Kilkenny Continued

Mount Juliet Conrad
Thomastown, Co. Kilkenny
Tel: 056-777 3000 ....Page 373

Name of Spa:
The Spa at Mount Juliet Conrad
Treatments:70 ......Treatment Rooms:7

Type of Treatments:
*Reiki, La Stone Therapy, Floatation
Therapy Treatment, Reflexology,
Radiance Facial, Body Polish, Deep
Cleansing Back Treatment, ESPA Facials,
Matis Facials*

Type of Facilities:
*Swimming pool, Steam Room, Sauna,
Gym, Floatation Tank, Relaxation rooms*

Newpark Hotel
Kilkenny City, Co. Kilkenny
Tel: 056-776 0500 ....Page 371
Treatments:30   Treatment Rooms:6

Type of Treatments:
*Swedish Body Massage, Hot Stone
Therapy, Seaweed Body Wraps, Collagen
Hydro Lifting Facial, Hydrotherapy
Massage Bath, Hand and Foot
Treatments, Nails/Manicures, all Related
Beauty Treatments*

Type of Facilities:
*Six Wet & Dry Treatment Rooms, Nail &
Manicure Bar, Hydrotherapy Massage
Bath, Relaxation Area &
Kieran O' Gorman Hair Salon*

**Springhill Court Hotel, Spa &
Leisure Club**
Kilkenny City, Co. Kilkenny
Tel: 056-772 1122 ....Page 371
Name of Spa:
AquaSpa
Treatments:50 ......Treatment Rooms:7

Type of Treatments:
*Floatation Therapy, Balneotherapy,
Dermalogical Facials & Body Wraps,
Phytomer Body Wraps, Luxury Spa
Pedicure & Manicure, Mens Skincare &
De luxe Body Treaments*

Type of Facilities:
*Relaxation Room, Sauna, Steam Room,
Floatation Therapy, Chromatherapy Bath*

Co. Tipperary South

Cahir House Hotel
Cahir, Co. Tipperary South
Tel: 052-43000 ....Page 373
Name of Spa:
**Cahir House Hotel Health & Beauty
Spa**
Treatments:36 ......Treatment Rooms:4

Type of Treatments:
*Facials, Manicure, Pedicure, Hot Stone
Massage, Hydrotherapy Bath, Ear
Candling, Body Treatments, Sunbeds,
Multi Gym, Pamper Days*

Type of Facilities:
*Steam Room,Treadmill, Multi Gym,
Sauna, Air Strider, Exercise Bike,
Sunbeds*

Dundrum House Hotel
Cashel, Co. Tipperary South
Tel: 062-71116 ....Page 375
Name of Spa:
The Beauty Suite
Treatments:20 ......Treatment Rooms:3

Type of Treatments:
*Full range of "Matis" Beauty & Body
Treatments, also Holistic & Massage
Therapies*

Type of Facilities:
*Swimming Pool, Sauna, Steam Room,
Jacuzzi, Solarium, Fitness Suite*

Hotel Minella & Leisure Centre
Clonmel, Co. Tipperary South
Tel: 052-22388 ....Page 377
Name of Spa:
Club Minella
Treatments:14 ......Treatment Rooms:2

Type of Treatments:
*Massage, Reflexology, Micronized Marine
Algae Wrap, Toning Body Wrap, Marine
Facial, Waxing, Manicure, Body Polish*

Type of Facilities:
*Treatment Rooms, Jacuzzi, Relaxaton
Room, Outdoor Hot Tub, 20m Pool,
Outdoor Tennis Court, Sauna, Steam
Room, Gym, Gardens*

Co. Waterford

**Faithlegg House Hotel and
Golf Club**
Faithlegg, Co. Waterford
Tel: 051-382000......................Page 386
Name of Spa:
Estuary Club
Treatments:40 ......Treatment Rooms:5

Type of Treatments:
*Aromatherapy Massage, Reflexology,
Reiki, Deep Sea Mud Treatment, Facials*

Type of Facilities:
*Swimming Pool, Jacuzzi, Steam Room,
Gym, Sauna*

Woodlands Hotel
Waterford City, Co. Waterford
Tel: 051-304574......................Page 394
Name of Spa:
Carolines Hair & Beauty
Treatments:25 ......Treatment Rooms:6

Type of Treatments:
*Facials, Body Treatments, Pedicures,
Manicures, Electrolysis, Waxing, Tinting,
Eyebrow Shaping, Make Up, Nail Art*

Type of Facilities:
*Hair Salon, Pool, Jacuzzi, Steam Room,
Sauna, Beauty and Health Treatment
Rooms*

Co. Wexford

**Brandon House Hotel,
Health Club & Spa**
New Ross, Co. Wexford
Tel: 051-421703 ....Page 400
Treatments:55   Treatment Rooms:3

Type of Treatments:
*Reiki, Reflexology, Marine Algae
Bodywrap, Cold Marine, La Stone
Massage, The Energiser, Swedish
Massage*

Type of Facilities:
*20m Swimming Pool, Swimming
Lessons, Sauna, Aerobics, Gym, Hydro
Therapy Grotto, Kids Swimming Pool*

Carlton Millrace Hotel (The)
Bunclody, Co. Wexford
Tel: 053-937 5100 ....Page 395
Name of Spa:
The Millrace Spa
Treatments:30 ....**Treatment Rooms:**10

Type of Treatments:
Facials, Massage, Hydrotherapy Bath, Body Wrap, Rasul, Relaxation Room with Heated Loungers

Type of Facilities:
Relaxation Room, Whirlpool, Sauna, Steam Room, 18m Indoor Pool, Gym

Ferrycarrig Hotel
Wexford Town, Co. Wexford
Tel: 053-912 0999 ....Page 404
Name of Spa:
Lodge Spa
Treatments:45 ......**Treatment Rooms:**4

Type of Treatments:
Facials, Aromatherapy, Massage, Reflexology, Hot Stone Therapy, Indian Head Massage, Manicures & Pedicures, Makeovers, Body Treatments

Type of Facilities:
Intense Pulsed Light, Platinum Detox, Relaxation and Reception Area, Pamper Days, Bridal Packages

Kelly's Resort Hotel
Rosslare, Co. Wexford
Tel: 053-913 2114 ....Page 402
Name of Spa:
SeaSpa
Treatments:34 ....**Treatment Rooms:**12

Type of Treatments:
Aromatherapy & Holistic Massages, Body Wraps, Facials, Ayurvedic Hot Stone Treatments, Reflexology, Reiki, Sports Therapy Massage, Manicure & Pedicure, Thai Massage, Candling

Type of Facilities:
Serail Mud Room, Seaweed Baths, Rock Sauna, Heated Loungers, Sea Water Vitality Pool, Rain Forest Showers, Pebble Walk Way, Salt Infused Steam Rooms, Relaxation Rooms, Laconium Sauna

Quality Hotel & Leisure Wexford
Wexford Town, Co. Wexford
Tel: 053-917 2000 ....Page 404

Treatments:30   **Treatment Rooms:**2

Type of Treatments:
Body Therapy Treatments, Skin Therapy Treatments, Facial Treatments, Nail Care, Grooming Treatments

Type of Facilities:
20m Swimming Pool, Sauna, Steam Room, Jacuzzi, Fitness Gym, Aerobics Studio, Dedicated Kids Pool

Talbot Hotel Conference and Leisure Centre
Wexford Town, Co. Wexford
Tel: 053-912 2566 ....Page 405
Name of Spa:
Essence Nail & Beauty Therapy
Treatments:44 ......**Treatment Rooms:**3

Type of Treatments:
Dermalogica Customised Facial, Multi Vitamin Power Plus Facial, Ultimate Spa Experience, Hydro-Mineral Salt Scrub, Enzymatic Sea Mudwrap

Type of Facilities:
Treatment Rooms, Nail Bar, Tanning Booth, Make Up Room, Sports Massage Therapist

Planning a Visit to Ireland?

For information on over 80 of Ireland's leading Visitor Attractions and Heritage Towns, sample touring itineraries and news of what's on there really is only one choice:

WWW.HERITAGEISLAND.COM

Present this page at any Heritage Island centre to receive discount on admission price.

For a full listing of Heritage Island centres please visit www.heritageisland.com Discounts should be confirmed when booking is made. Discounts not valid for groups. Heritage Island cannot accept responsibility for any errors, omissions or misinformation.

KEY TO MAPS

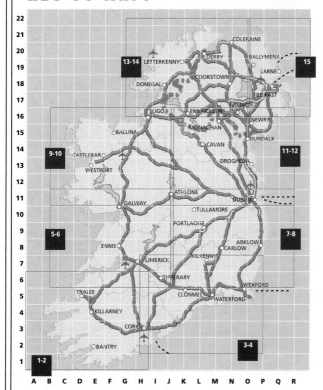

LEGEND

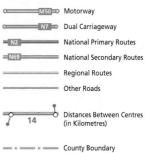

M50	Motorway
N7	Dual Carriageway
N2	National Primary Routes
N69	National Secondary Routes
	Regional Routes
	Other Roads
14	Distances Between Centres (in Kilometres)
	County Boundary
	Northern Ireland/ Republic of Ireland Border

SHANNON AIRPORT — Airports

Holyhead — Ferries

Derrynane House — Heritage Sites

DISTANCE CHART
in Kilometres

	ARMAGH	ATHLONE	BELFAST	CARLOW	CLIFDEN	CORK	DERRY	DUBLIN	DUNDALK	ENNISKILLEN	GALWAY	KILKENNY	KILLARNEY	LARNE	LIMERICK	PORTLAOISE	ROSSLARE HARBOUR	SHANNON AIRPORT	SLIGO	TRALEE	WATERFORD	WEXFORD
ATHLONE	159																					
BELFAST	66	224																				
CARLOW	211	108	248																			
CLIFDEN	316	171	370	256																		
CORK	380	219	423	187	287																	
DERRY	114	225	118	309	303	460																
DUBLIN	129	124	167	82	296	256	233															
DUNDALK	45	142	82	166	314	340	158	84														
ENNISKILLEN	81	127	135	240	237	346	98	175	101													
GALWAY	238	92	303	177	79	206	277	216	233	192												
KILKENNY	245	121	282	39	248	148	335	114	200	242	169											
KILLARNEY	388	229	430	235	295	89	480	303	348	356	214	196										
LARNE	105	264	40	287	411	462	122	206	121	174	343	320	470									
LIMERICK	279	119	320	138	184	101	369	192	238	245	105	114	109	356								
PORTLAOISE	208	71	250	37	229	174	287	82	167	192	150	50	221	285	109							
ROSSLARE HARBOUR	282	201	320	93	348	206	385	151	237	324	269	100	272	356	204	130						
SHANNON AIRPORT	293	134	345	163	172	126	357	216	261	261	93	138	134	380	24	134	229					
SLIGO	148	116	203	224	167	336	134	213	171	68	142	237	345	240	235	187	319	224				
TRALEE	382	222	423	242	288	121	472	296	341	349	208	216	32	460	103	213	291	127	338			
WATERFORD	285	167	324	74	296	126	383	156	240	290	217	48	192	359	124	97	81	148	283	211		
WEXFORD	264	184	301	76	330	187	365	132	219	306	250	81	254	338	187	113	19	209	272	61		
WICKLOW	185	138	222	61	311	256	293	56	140	221	232	100	303	259	193	82	118	216	238	296	135	100

0	5	10	15	20	25km
0	5		10		15miles

SCALE 1 : 625 000

N

Variation 10°40' (1990)

MAPS

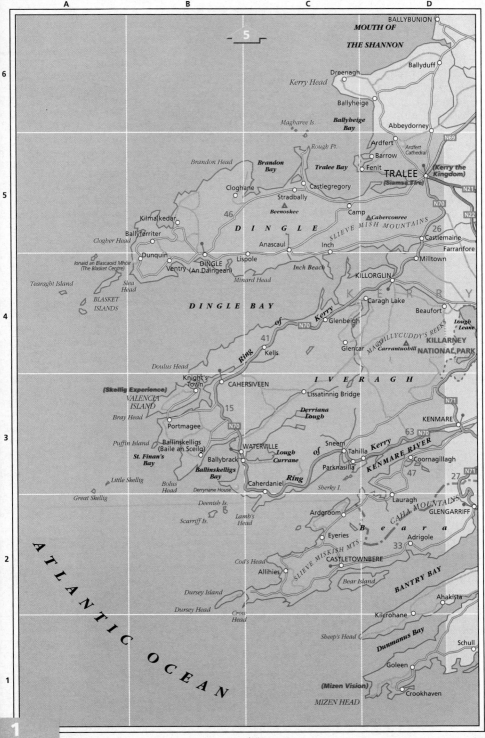

MOUTH OF

THE SHANNON

BALLYBUNION

Dreenagh

Kerry Head

Ballyduff

Ballyheige

Abbeydorney

Magharee Is.

Ballyheige Bay

Ardfert

Rough Pt.

Ardfert Cathedral

Barrow

N69

Brandon Head

Brandon Bay

Tralee Bay

Fenit

TRALEE (Siamsa Tíre)

(Kerry the Kingdom)

Cloghane

Castlegregory

Camp

N21

Stradbally

46

Beenoskee

D I N G L E

Caherconree

SLIEVE MISH MOUNTAINS

26

N70

N22

Kilmalkedar

Ballyferriter

Clogher Head

Anascaul

Inch

Castlemaine

Farranfore

Dunquin

DINGLE (An Daingean)

Lispole

Milltown

Ionaid an Blascaoid Mhóir (The Blasket Centre)

Ventry

Minard Head

Inch Beach

KILLORGLIN

Tearaght Island

Slea Head

D I N G L E   B A Y

of

Kerry

K   E   R   R   Y

Caragh Lake

Beaufort

Lough Leane

BLASKET ISLANDS

Ring

41

N70

Glenbeigh

Kells

KILLARNEY NATIONAL PARK

MACGILLYCUDDY'S REEKS

Doulus Head

Glencar

Carrantuohill

Knight's Town

CAHERSIVEEN

I V E R A G H

(Skellig Experience)

Lissatinnig Bridge

VALENCIA ISLAND

Bray Head

15

N70

Derriana Lough

KENMARE

N71

Portmagee

of

Sneem

Kerry

63

N70

Puffin Island

Ballinskelligs (Baile an Sceilg)

WATERVILLE

Lough Currane

Tahilla

Coornagillagh

St. Finan's Bay

Ballybrack

Parknasilla

KENMARE RIVER

47

27

N71

Little Skellig

Ballinskelligs Bay

Ring

Caherdaniel

Sherky I.

Lauragh

Great Skellig

Bolus Head

Derrynane House

GLENGARRIFF

Deenish Is.

Ardgroom

CAHA MOUNTAINS

B e a r a

Scarriff Is.

Lamb's Head

Eyeries

Adrigole

33

Cod's Head

SLIEVE MISKISH MTS.

CASTLETOWNBERE

Allihies

Bear Island

BANTRY BAY

Ahakista

Dursey Island

Dursey Head

Crow Head

Kilcrohane

Sheep's Head

Dunmanus Bay

Schull

A T L A N T I C   O C E A N

Goleen

(Mizen Vision)

Crookhaven

MIZEN HEAD

478

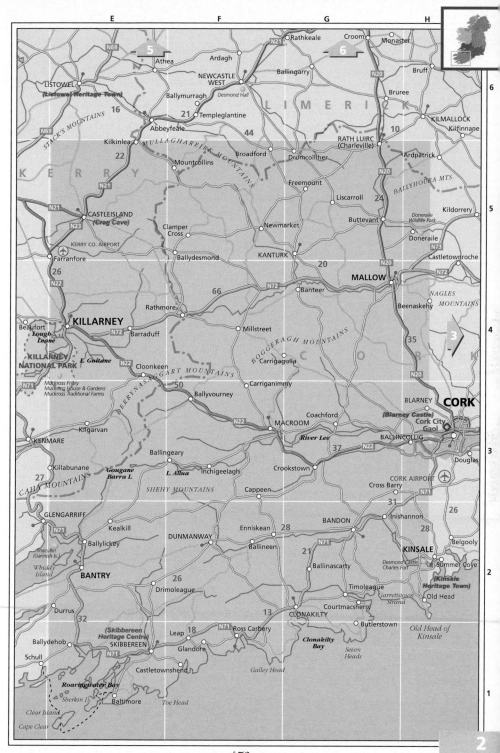

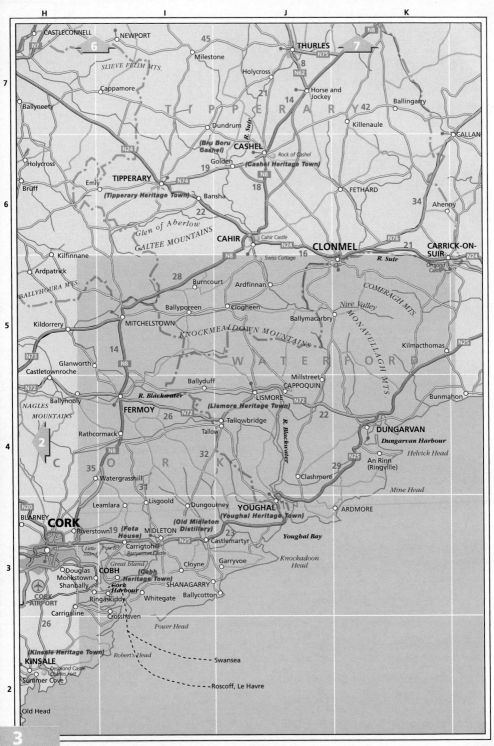

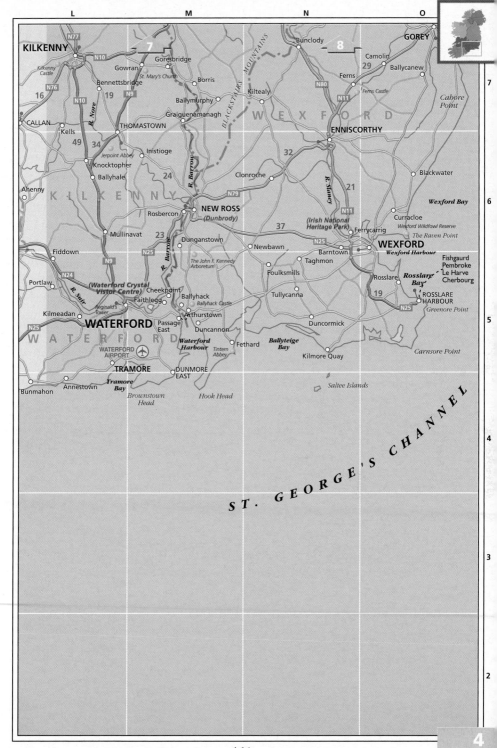

KILKENNY
N77
N10
Kilkenny Castle
16
N76
N10
19
N9
CALLAN
Kells
49
34
Ahenny
KILKENNY
Fiddown
Portlaw
N24
N9
Kilmeadan
N25
WATERFORD
WATERFORD
WATERFORD AIRPORT
TRAMORE
Tramore Bay
Bunmahon
Annestown
Brownstown Head

7
Goresbridge
Gowran
St. Mary's Church
Bennettsbridge
Borris
Ballymurphy
Graiguenamanagh
THOMASTOWN
Inistioge
Jerpoint Abbey
Knocktopher
24
Ballyhale
R. Nore
R. Barrow
N79
Rosbercon
NEW ROSS
(Dunbrody)
Mullinavat
23
N25
Dunganstown
R. Barrow
The John F. Kennedy Arboretum
Cheekpoint
Faithlegg
Ballyhack
Ballyhack Castle
Reginald's Tower
Arthurstown
Passage East
Duncannon
Waterford Harbour
Tintern Abbey
Fethard
DUNMORE EAST
Hook Head

BLACKSTAIRS MOUNTAINS
Bunclody
8
Kiltealy
WEXFORD
Clonroche
32
R. Slaney
Newbawn
37
(Irish National Heritage Park)
Foulksmills
Tullycanna
Ballyteige Bay
Kilmore Quay
Saltee Islands

GOREY
Camolin
Ferns
29
Ballycanew
N80
Ferns Castle
N11
Cahore Point
ENNISCORTHY
21
Blackwater
Wexford Bay
Curracloe
Wexford Wildfowl Reserve
The Raven Point
Ferrycarrig
N25
Barntown
WEXFORD
Wexford Harbour
Taghmon
Rosslare
Rosslare Bay
Fishgaurd
Pembroke
Le Harve
Cherbourg
ROSSLARE HARBOUR
19
N25
Greenore Point
Duncormick
Carnsore Point

ST. GEORGE'S CHANNEL

7
6
5
4
3
2

4

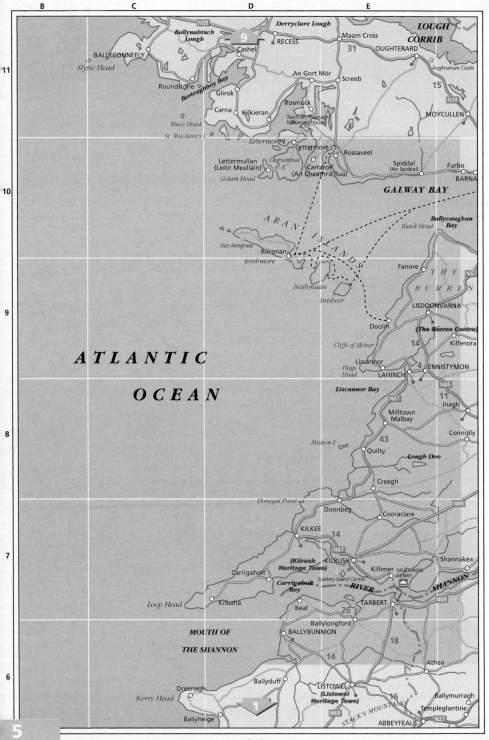

ATLANTIC

OCEAN

LOUGH
CORRIB

GALWAY BAY

Derryclare Lough

Ballynahinch
Lough

BALLYCONNEELY
Slyne Head

Roundstone
Bertraghboy Bay
Glinsk
Carna
Kilkieran
Mace Head
St. Macdara's I.

Cashel

RECESS

Maam Cross

OUGHTERARD

An Gort Mór

Screeb

Aughnanure Castle

Rosmuck

Teach an Phiarsaigh
(Pearse's House)

MOYCULLEN

Lettermore I.
Gorumna
I.

Lettermore

Rossaveel

Spiddal
(An Spidéal)

Furbo
BARNA

Lettermullan
(Leitir Meallain)
Golam Head

Carraroe
(An Cheathrú Rua)

A R A N

I S L A N D S

Ballyvaughan
Bay

Black Head

Dún Aonghasa

Kilronan
Inishmore

Fanore

T H E
B U R R E N

Inishmaan

Inisheer

LISDOONVARNA

(The Burren Centre)

Doolin

14

Kilfenora

Cliffs of Moher

Hags
Head

Liscannor

LAHINCH

4

ENNISTYMON

Liscannor Bay

Milltown
Malbay

11

Inagh

Mutton I.

Quilty

43

Lough Doo

Connolly

Creegh

Donegal Point

Doonbeg

Cooraclare

KILKEE

14

Carrigaholt

(Kilrush
Heritage Town)

KILRUSH

Killimer

SHANNON
FERRY

Shannakea

Loop Head

Kilbaha

Carrigaholt
Bay

Scattery Island Centre

RIVER

SHANNON

Beal

TARBERT

Dreenagh
Kerry Head

Ballyduff

MOUTH OF

THE SHANNON

Ballylongford

BALLYBUNNION

26

18

Athea

14

Ballyheige

LISTOWEL
(Listowel
Heritage Town)

16

Ballymurragh

STACK'S MOUNTAINS

Templeglantine

ABBEYFEALE

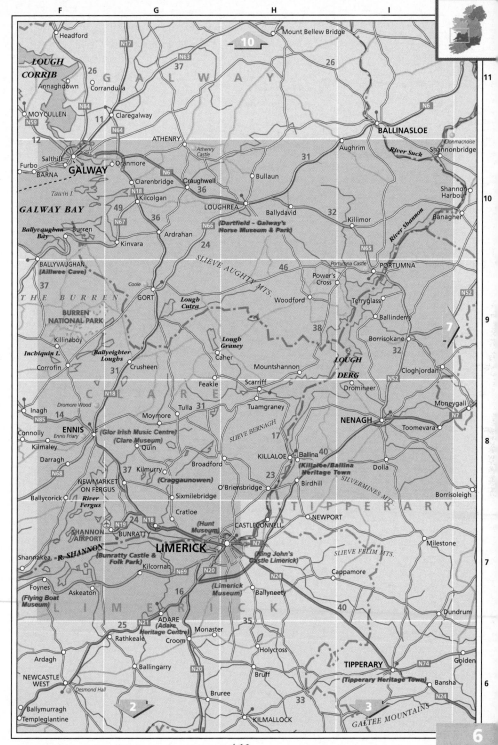

F G H I

11

LOUGH CORRIB

Headford
Mount Bellew Bridge

N17
10
N63
37
26

26
Annaghdown
Corrandulla
GALWAY
N84

MOYCULLEN
11
Claregalway
N6
N59
N64
BALLINASLOE
Clonmacnoise
River Suck
Shannonbridge

12
ATHENRY
Salthill
Oranmore
Athenry Castle
31
Aughrim
Shannon Harbour
GALWAY
Furbo
BARNA
Clarenbridge
Craughwell
N6
Bullaun
Shannon Harbour

Tawin I.
Kilcolgan
36
LOUGHREA
32
Killimor
Banagher
N18

GALWAY BAY
49
36
Ballydavid
River Shannon

N67
Ardrahan
(Dartfield - Galway's Horse Museum & Park)
24
N66

Ballyvaughan Bay
Burren
Kinvara
SLIEVE AUGHTY MTS.
46
Portumna Castle
PORTUMNA

BALLYVAUGHAN (Aillwee Cave)
Coole
Power's Cross
Terryglass
N52

37
THE BURREN
GORT
Lough Cutra
Woodford
38
Ballinderry
9

BURREN NATIONAL PARK
Killinaboy
Lough Graney
Caher
Borrisokane
32
7

Inchiquin L.
Ballyeighter Loughs
Crusheen
Mountshannon
LOUGH
Cloghjordan

Corrofin
31
Feakle
Scarriff
DERG
N52
Moneygall
N7

Dromore Wood
Tulla
31
Tuamgraney
Dromineer
NENAGH
Toomevara

Inagh
14
Moymore
SLIEVE BERNAGH
17
8
N85

Connolly
ENNIS
Ennis Friary
(Glor irish Music Centre)
(Clare Museum)
KILLALOE
Ballina
40
(Killaloe/Ballina Heritage Town)
Dolla

Kilmaley
Quin
Broadford
23
Birdhill
SILVERMINES MTS.
Borrisoleigh

Darragh
37
Kilmurry
O'Briensbridge
N68

NEWMARKET ON FERGUS
(Craggaunowen)
Sixmilebridge
TIPPERARY

Ballycorick
River Fergus
Cratloe
(Hunt Museum)
CASTLECONNELL
NEWPORT
Milestone

SHANNON AIRPORT
N19
24
N18
7
N7

Shannakea
BUNRATTY
LIMERICK
King John's Castle Limerick
SLIEVE FELIM MTS.

R. SHANNON
(Bunratty Castle & Folk Park)
Kilcornan
N69
N20
Cappamore

Foynes
Askeaton
16
(Limerick Museum)
Ballyneety
40
Dundrum

(Flying Boat Museum)
LIMERICK
ADARE (Adare Heritage Centre)
Monaster
35

25
N21
Croom
Holycross
TIPPERARY
N74
Golden

Rathkeale
N20
Bruff
(Tipperary Heritage Town)
Bansha

Ardagh
Ballingarry
TIPPERARY
6
N24

NEWCASTLE WEST
Desmond Hall
Bruree
33
GALTEE MOUNTAINS

Ballymurragh
Templeglantine
Kilmallock

2

3

483

6

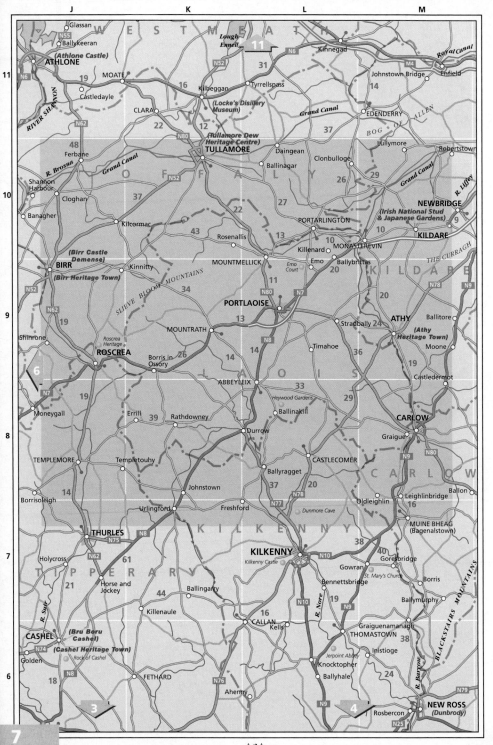

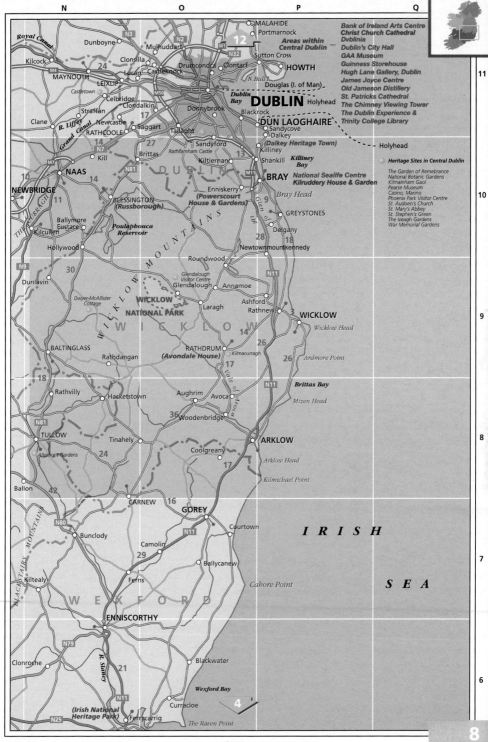

N O P Q

MALAHIDE
Portmarnock

Dunboyne
Mulhuddart
Sutton Cross

Kilcock
Clonsilla
Drumcondra
Clontarf
HOWTH

MAYNOOTH
Lucan
Castleknock
N. Bull I.

LEIXLIP
Castletown
Douglas (I. of Man)

Celbridge
Clondalkin
Dublin Bay
DUBLIN
Holyhead

Straffan
Newcastle
Donnybrook
Blackrock

Clane
Saggart
Tallaght
DÚN LAOGHAIRE

RATHCOOLE
Sandycove
Dalkey

Sandyford
(Dalkey Heritage Town)
Killiney

Brittas
Kiltiernan
Shankill
Killiney Bay

Kill
DUBLIN
Enniskerry
(Powerscourt House & Gardens)
BRAY
National Sealife Centre
Kilruddery House & Garden

NEWBRIDGE
BLESSINGTON
(Russborough)
Bray Head

Ballymore Eustace
Poulaphouca Reservoir
GREYSTONES

Kilcullen
Delgany

Hollywood
Newtownmountkennedy

Dunlavin
Roundwood

WICKLOW MOUNTAINS

Glendalough Visitor Centre
Glendalough
Annamoe

Dwyer-McAllister Cottage
WICKLOW NATIONAL PARK
Laragh
Ashford
Rathnew
WICKLOW
Wicklow Head

BALTINGLASS
WICKLOW
Rathdangan

RATHDRUM
(Avondale House)
Kilmacurragh
Ardmore Point

Rathvilly
Hacketstown
Aughrim
Avoca
Brittas Bay
Mizen Head

TULLOW
Woodenbridge

Altamont Gardens
Tinahely
ARKLOW

Ballon
Coolgreany
Arklow Head

Kilmichael Point

CARNEW
GOREY

Bunclody
Courtown

Camolin
IRISH

Kiltealy
Ferns
Ballycanew
SEA

WEXFORD
Cahore Point

ENNISCORTHY

Clonroche
R. Slaney
Blackwater

Wexford Bay

(Irish National Heritage Park)
Curracloe
Ferrycarrig
The Raven Point

Areas within Central Dublin
Bank of Ireland Arts Centre
Christ Church Cathedral
Dvblinia
Dublin's City Hall
GAA Museum
Guinness Storehouse
Hugh Lane Gallery, Dublin
James Joyce Centre
Old Jameson Distillery
St. Patricks Cathedral
The Chimney Viewing Tower
The Dublin Experience &
Trinity College Library

Holyhead

Heritage Sites in Central Dublin

The Garden of Remebrance
National Botanic Gardens
Kilmainham Gaol
Pearse Museum
Phoenix Park Visitor Centre
Casino, Marino
St. Audoen's Church
St. Mary's Abbey
St. Stephen's Green
The Iveagh Gardens
War Memorial Gardens

12
11
10
9
8
7
6
8

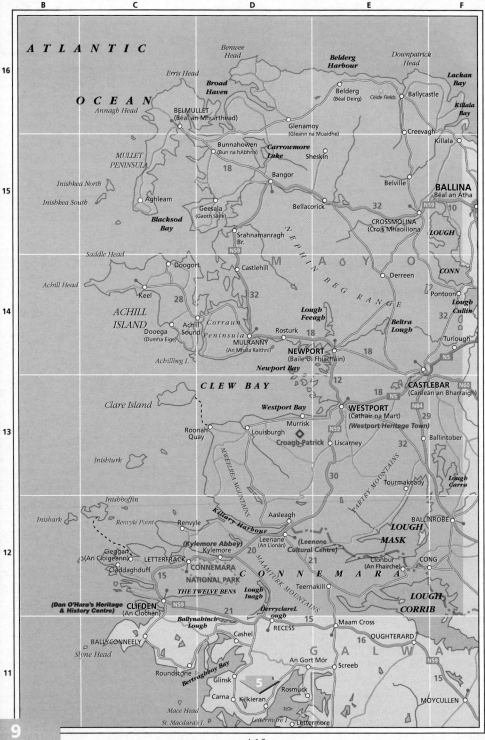

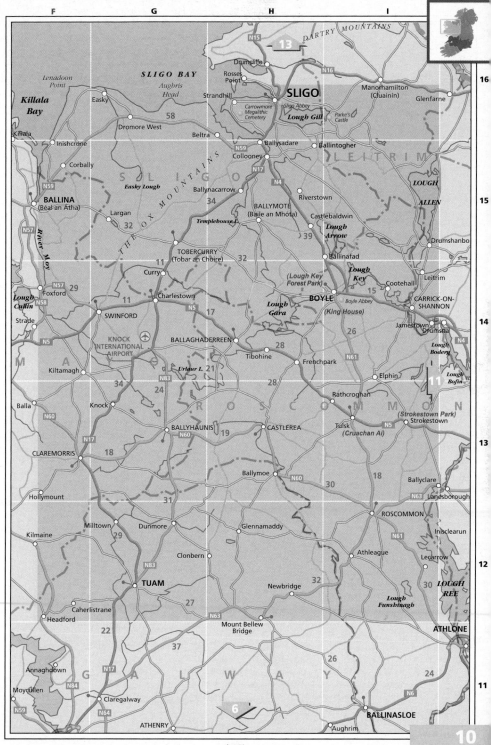

DARTRY MOUNTAINS

N15 **13**

Drumcliffe

Rosses Point N16

SLIGO BAY
Aughris Head

Strandhill Manorhamilton
(Cluainin) Glenfarne

SLIGO

Lenadoon Point

Easky

Carrowmore Megalithic Cemetery Sligo Abbey
Parke's Castle

Killala Bay *Lough Gill*

58

Dromore West Beltra Ballysadare Ballintogher

Killala Inishcrone LEITRIM

Corbally Colooney N59

S L I G O N17 N4 *LOUGH*

Easky Lough Ballynacarrow Riverstown *ALLEN*

BALLINA
(Béal an Átha) N59 34 **BALLYMOTE**
(Baile an Mhóta) Castlebaldwin Drumshanbo

Largan 32 *Templehouse L.* 39 *Lough Arrow*

N57 29 *THE OX MOUNTAINS* **TOBERCURRY**
(Tobar an Choire) 32 Ballinafad Leitrim

River Moy 11 Curry *Lough Key* Cootehall

N58 Foxford 11 Charlestown 17 *Lough Gara* **BOYLE** 15 Drumsna

Lough Cullin 29 **SWINFORD** N5 (Lough Key Forest Park) **CARRICK-ON-SHANNON**

Strade KNOCK INTERNATIONAL AIRPORT *Lough Gara* Boyle Abbey Jamestown
(King House) N4

N5 **BALLAGHADERREEN** 28 26 *Lough Boderg*

Kiltamagh *Urlaur L.* 21 Tibohine Frenchpark N61 Elphin *Lough Bofin*

M A 34 24 N83 28 Ráthcroghan **11**

Balla N60 Knock R O S C O M M O N (Strokestown Park)

N17 18 **BALLYHAUNIS** 19 **CASTLEREA** Tulsk N5 Strokestown
(Cruachan Ai)

CLAREMORRIS N60 Ballymoe N60 30 18 Ballyclare

Hollymount 31 **ROSCOMMON** N63 Lanesborough

Milltown Dunmore Glennamaddy N61 Inisclearun

Kilmaine 29 Clonbern Athleague Lecarrow

N83 Newbridge 32 *LOUGH REE*

TUAM 27 *Lough Funshinagh* 30

Caherlistrane 22 Mount Bellew Bridge **ATHLONE**

Headford 37 N63 26

Annaghdown N17 G A L W A Y 24

Moycullen N84 **6**

N59 Claregalway N64 **BALLINASLOE**

ATHENRY Aughrim N6

16
15
14
13
12
11

10

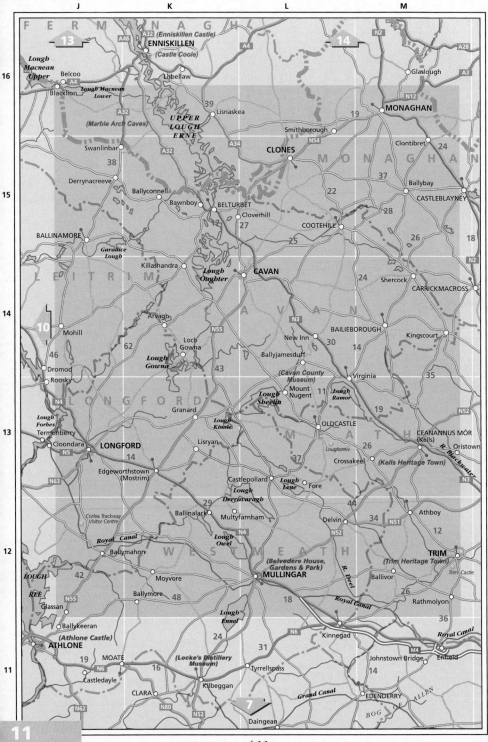

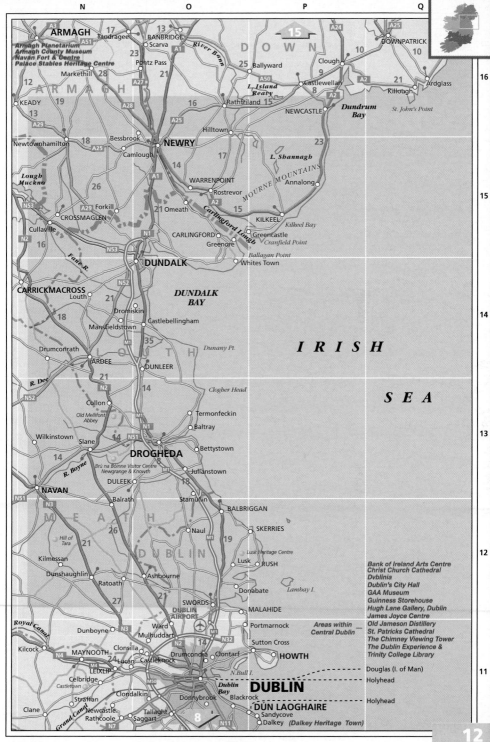

ARMAGH
Armagh Planetarium
Armagh County Museum
Navan Fort & Centre
Palace Stables Heritage Centre

A3
A51
17 Tandragee
13
BANBRIDGE
Scarva
Pontz Pass
Markethill 28
A27
21

DOWN
15
A24
10
25 Ballyward
A50
Clough
9
Castlewellan
8
A2
21
Killough
Ardglass
St. John's Point

DOWNPATRICK
10

12
A R M A G H
KEADY 19
13
A29
18 Bessbrook
Newtownhamilton
A25
Camlough
NEWRY
A1
14
16 Rathfriland 15
Hilltown
17
WARRENPOINT
Rostrevor
A2
15
Omeath
21
KILKEEL
NEWCASTLE
Dundrum
Bay
23
L. Shannagh
MOURNE MOUNTAINS
Annalong
Kilkeel Bay

Lough
Muckno
26
N53
Forkill
A29
CROSSMAGLEN
Cullaville
N2
16
Fane R.
N53
N1
CARLINGFORD
Greenore
Carlingford Lough
Greencastle
Cranfield Point
Ballagan Point
Whites Town

DUNDALK
CARRICKMACROSS
Louth 21
18
Dromiskin
Mansfieldstown
Castlebellingham
N52
M1
35
**DUNDALK
BAY**
Dunany Pt.

I R I S H

Drumconrath
N2
ARDEE 21
DUNLEER
R. Dee
14
Clogher Head
N52
N1
Collon
Old Mellifont
Abbey
Termonfeckin
Baltray

S E A

Wilkinstown
Slane 14
N51
M1
DROGHEDA
Bettystown
14
R. Boyne
Brú na Bóinne Visitor Centre
Newgrange & Knowth
DULEEK
Julianstown
8
M1
18
NAVAN
N51
N3
Balrath
Stamullin
BALBRIGGAN
M E A T H
Hill of
Tara
21
26
Naul
SKERRIES
M1
19
Kilmessan
D U B L I N
Lusk Heritage Centre
Lusk
RUSH
Dunshaughlin
Ratoath
Ashbourne
Donabate
Lambay I.
27
21
SWORDS
MALAHIDE
DUBLIN
AIRPORT
Portmarnock
Dunboyne
N3
Ward
Mulhuddart
N32
Sutton Cross
HOWTH
Kilcock
Royal Canal
MAYNOOTH
Clonsilla
Drumcondra
Clontarf
N4
M4
Lucan
Castleknock
N. Bull I.
LEIXLIP
M50
Celbridge
Castletown
Clondalkin
DUBLIN
Clane
Straffan
Grand Canal
Tallaght
Saggart
Donnybrook
Blackrock
DÚN LAOGHAIRE
Newcastle
Rathcoole
N7
8
N11
Sandycove
Dalkey (Dalkey Heritage Town)

Bank of Ireland Arts Centre
Christ Church Cathedral
Dvblinia
Dublin's City Hall
GAA Museum
Guinness Storehouse
Hugh Lane Gallery, Dublin
James Joyce Centre
Old Jameson Distillery
St. Patricks Cathedral
The Chimney Viewing Tower
The Dublin Experience &
Trinity College Library

Areas within
Central Dublin

Douglas (I. of Man)
Holyhead
Holyhead

16
15
14
13
12
11

12

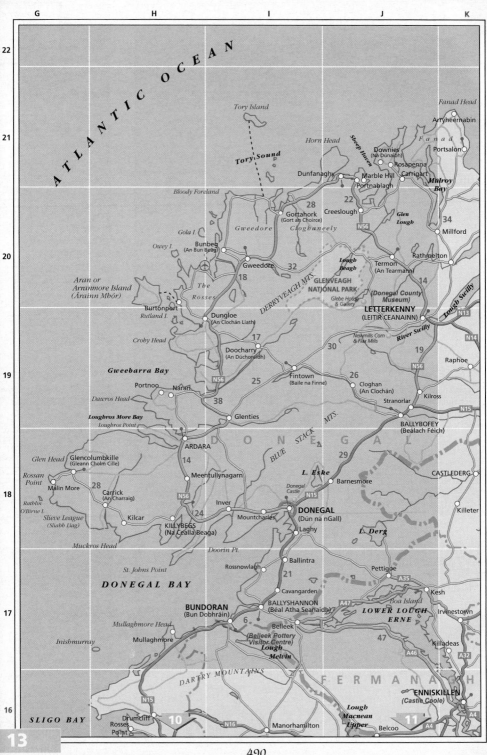

ATLANTIC OCEAN

Tory Island

Tory Sound

Horn Head   *Sheep Haven*   Fanad Head
Arryheernabin

Fanad   Portsalon

Downies
(Na Dúnaibh)   Rosapenna
Marble Hill   Carrigart   *Mulroy*
Dunfanaghy   Portnablagh   *Bay*

Bloody Foreland

28   Creeslough   22
Gortahork
(Gort an Choirce)   *Glen*   34
Lough   Millford

Gola I.   N56

Owey I.   Bunbeg
(An Bun Beag)   Rathmelton

Gweedore   *Cloghaneely*

Aran or   Gweedore   32   *Lough*   Termon   14
Arranmore Island   18   *Beagh*   (An Tearmann)
(Árainn Mhór)   *The*   GLENVEAGH
Rosses   DERRYVEAGH MTS.   NATIONAL PARK   (Donegal County
Burtonport   Glebe House   Museum)
Rutland I.   Dungloe   & Gallery   LETTERKENNY
(An Clochán Liath)   (LEITIR CEANAINN)   N13

Croby Head   17   Newmills Corn   *River Swilly*   N14
Doocharry   & Flax Mills   19
(An Dúchoraidh)   30   Raphoe
Gweebarra Bay   25   Fintown   26   N56
Portnoo   Naran   (Baile na Finne)   Cloghan   Kilross
(An Clochán)   N15
Dawros Head   38   Stranorlar
Glenties   BALLYBOFEY
Loughros More Bay   (Bealach Féich)   L
Loughros Point   D   O   N   E   G   A   L

Glen Head   Glencolumbkille   ARDARA   29   CASTLEDERG
Rossan   (Gleann Cholm Cille)   14   BLUE STACK MTS.
Point   Meentullynagarn   *L. Eske*
Malin More   28   Barnesmore
Rathlin   Carrick   *Donegal*   Killeter
O'Birne I.   (An Charraig)   N56   *Castle*
Slieve League   24   Inver   N15   DONEGAL
(Sliabh Liag)   Kilcar   Mountcharles   (Dún na nGall)
KILLYBEGS   Laghy   *L. Derg*
Muckros Head   (Na Cealla Beaga)

Doorin Pt.   Ballintra
St. Johns Point   Rossnowlagh   21   Pettigoe   Kesh
DONEGAL BAY   Cavangarden   A35
Mullaghmore Head   BUNDORAN   A47   *LOWER LOUGH*   Irvinestown
Inishmurray   (Bun Dobhráin)   BALLYSHANNON   *ERNE*   *Boa Island*
Mullaghmore   6   (Béal Átha Seanaidh)   47   Killadeas
Belleek   A46   A32
(Belleek Pottery   *Lough*
Visitor Centre)   *Melvin*
DARTRY MOUNTAINS   F   E   R   M   A   N   A   G   H
Lough   ENNISKILLEN
N15   *Macnean*   (Castle Coole)
SLIGO BAY   10   *Upper*   11   A4
Rosses   Drumcliff   N16   Manorhamilton   Belcoo   A4
Point

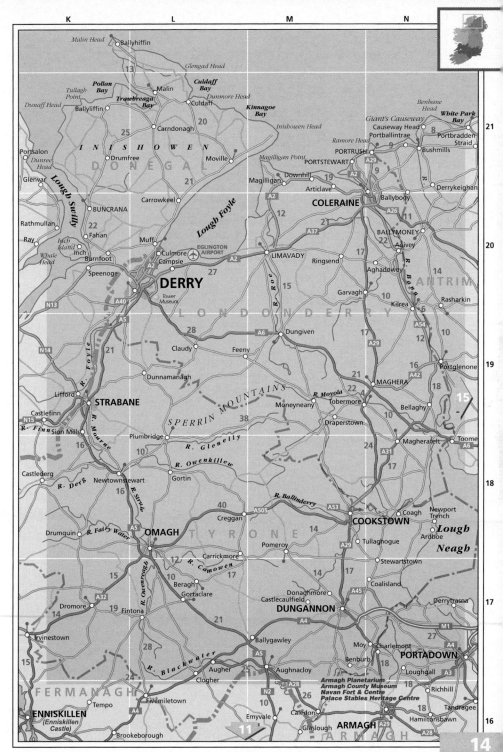

14

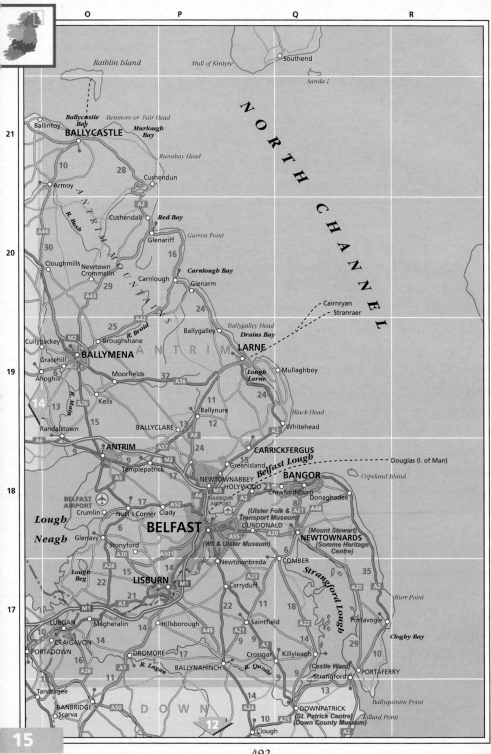

Rathlin Island

Mull of Kintyre

Southend

Sanda I.

NORTH CHANNEL

Ballintoy

Ballycastle Bay   Benmore or Fair Head

BALLYCASTLE   *Murlough Bay*

21

10

Armoy

28

Cushendun

Runabay Head

A2

Cushendall   *Red Bay*

A44

Glenariff   *Garron Point*

30

16

Cloughmills   Newtown Crommelin

20

Carnlough Bay

Carnlough   Glenarm

A43

29

24

Cairnryan

Stranraer

Cullybackey   A42   R. Braid

25

Ballygalley

Ballygalley Head

Drains Bay

Broughshane

M2

LARNE

Gracehill

BALLYMENA

Lough Larne

Mullaghboy

19

Ahoghill

6

Moorfields

32

A36

24

14

13

R. Main

A26

Kells

11

Ballynure

Black Head

Randalstown

15

12

Whitehead

A6

BALLYCLARE

13

A2

ANTRIM

A57

24

A8

CARRICKFERGUS

M2

Greenisland

15

Douglas (I. of Man)

Templepatrick

17

NEWTOWNABBEY

Belfast Lough

BANGOR

A5

HOLYWOOD

Crawfordsburn

Copeland Island

18

BELFAST AIRPORT

17

A52

A6

HARBOUR AIRPORT

8

Donaghadee

Crumlin

Nutt's Corner   Clady

(Ulster Folk & Transport Museum)

A48

Lough

6

DUNDONALD

A20

NEWTOWNARDS

Neagh

Glenavy   Stonyford

BELFAST

A55

(W5 & Ulster Museum)

(Mount Stewart)

(Somme Heritage Centre)

A30

A501

Newtownbreda

COMBER

35

Lough Beg

A26

22

14

LISBURN

M1

Carryduff

A23

Strangford Lough

A20

A2

Burr Point

17

21

A3

22

11

18

M1

LURGAN

Magheralin

14

Hillsborough

Saintfield

A22

Portavogie

10

A49

A21

A7

9

29

Cloghy Bay

CRAIGAVON

14

9

Crossgar

Killyleagh

10

PORTADOWN

16

DROMORE

17

R. Lagan

BALLYNAHINCH

R. Quoile

9

(Castle Ward)

PORTAFERRY

A26

A1

Strangford

Tandragee

11

14

13

Ballyquintin Point

BANBRIDGE

A50

DOWN

A24

DOWNPATRICK

Scarva

12

10

(St. Patrick Centre)

(Down County Museum)

Killard Point

A25

Clough

A2

15

INDEX OF HOTELS & GUESTHOUSES GUINNESS.

BLUE HAVEN HOTEL AND RESTAURANT
Kinsale, Co. Cork............................60
☎ 021-477 2209

BOAT INN (THE)
Oughterard, Co. Galway 181
☎ 091-552196

BOFFIN LODGE
Westport, Co. Mayo 196
☎ 098-26092

BOLAND'S GUESTHOUSE
Dingle (An Daingean), Co. Kerry ..77
☎ 066-915 1426

BOYNE VALLEY HOTEL & COUNTRY CLUB
Drogheda, Co. Louth..................309
☎ 041-983 7737

BRACKEN COURT HOTEL
Balbriggan, Co. Dublin 248
☎ 01-841 3333

BRANDON HOTEL CONFERENCE AND LEISURE CENTRE
Tralee, Co. Kerry 112
☎ 066-712 3333

BRANDON HOUSE HOTEL, HEALTH CLUB & SPA
New Ross, Co. Wexford 400
☎ 051-421703

BRANDON INN
Tralee, Co. Kerry 112
☎ 066-712 9666

BRANNIGANS GLENDINE INN
Kilkenny City, Co. Kilkenny 364
☎ 056-772 1069

BRASS LANTERN
Kenmare, Co. Kerry......................83
☎ 064-42600

BREFFNI ARMS HOTEL
Arvagh, Co. Cavan 330
☎ 049-433 5127

BREHON (THE)
Killarney, Co. Kerry 90
☎ 064-30700

BRENNANS YARD HOTEL
Galway City, Co. Galway............165
☎ 091-568166

BRIDGE HOTEL
Waterford City, Co. Waterford....390
☎ 051-877222

BRIDGE HOTEL
Arklow, Co. Wicklow 318
☎ 0402-31666

BRIDGE HOUSE HOTEL & LEISURE CLUB
Tullamore, Co. Offaly..................350
☎ 057-932 5600

BRIDGECOURT HOUSE
Kilkenny City, Co. Kilkenny 364
☎ 056-776 2998

BRIGHTON HOUSE
Clonmel, Co. Tipperary South 376
☎ 052-23665

BROADMEADOW COUNTRY HOUSE & EQUESTRIAN CENTRE
Ashbourne, Co. Meath 313
☎ 01-835 2823

BROOK LANE HOTEL
Kenmare, Co. Kerry......................84
☎ 064-42077

BROOK LODGE HOTEL
Killarney, Co. Kerry 90
☎ 064-31800

BROOK MANOR LODGE
Tralee, Co. Kerry 113
☎ 066-712 0406

BROOKFIELD HOTEL
Cork City, Co. Cork 48
☎ 021-480 4700

BROOKHAVEN COUNTRY HOUSE
Waterville, Co. Kerry 115
☎ 066-947 4431

BROOKLODGE AND WELLS SPA
Aughrim, Co. Wicklow 320
☎ 0402-36444

BROOKS HOTEL
Dublin City, Co. Dublin 264
☎ 01-670 4000

BROSNA LODGE HOTEL
Banagher, Co. Offaly 348
☎ 057-915 1350

BROWN TROUT GOLF & COUNTRY INN
Aghadowey, Co. Derry 238
☎ 028-7086 8209

BUNRATTY CASTLE HOTEL
Bunratty, Co. Clare 122
☎ 061-478700

BUNRATTY GROVE
Bunratty, Co. Clare 122
☎ 061-369579

BUNRATTY MANOR HOTEL
Bunratty, Co. Clare 123
☎ 061-707984

BUNRATTY WOODS COUNTRY HOUSE
Bunratty, Co. Clare 123
☎ 061-369689

BURKES ARMADA HOTEL
Milltown Malbay, Co. Clare........138
☎ 065-708 4110

BURLINGTON (THE)
Dublin City, Co. Dublin 264
☎ 01-660 5222

BURRENDALE HOTEL AND COUNTRY CLUB
Newcastle, Co. Down 242
☎ 028-4372 2599

BUSH HOTEL
Carrick-on-Shannon, Co. Leitrim 220
☎ 071-967 1000

BUSHMILLS INN HOTEL
Bushmills, Co. Antrim 230
☎ 028-2073 3000

BUSWELLS HOTEL
Dublin City, Co. Dublin 265
☎ 01-614 6500

BUTLER ARMS HOTEL
Waterville, Co. Kerry 116
☎ 066-947 4144

BUTLER HOUSE
Kilkenny City, Co. Kilkenny 364
☎ 056-776 5707

BUTLERS TOWN HOUSE
Dublin City, Co. Dublin 265
☎ 01-667 4022

BUTTERMILK LODGE
Clifden, Co. Galway....................158
☎ 095-21951

BYRNE MAL DUA HOUSE
Clifden, Co. Galway....................159
☎ 095-21171

C

CABRA CASTLE HOTEL
Kingscourt, Co. Cavan................333
☎ 042-966 7030

CAHERNANE HOUSE HOTEL
Killarney, Co. Kerry 90
☎ 064-31895

CAHIR HOUSE HOTEL
Cahir, Co. Tipperary South..........373
☎ 052-43000

CAIRN BAY LODGE
Bangor, Co. Down......................240
☎ 028-9146 7636

CAMDEN COURT HOTEL
Dublin City, Co. Dublin 265
☎ 01-475 9666

CANAL COURT HOTEL
Newry, Co. Down 242
☎ 028-3025 1234

CAPPABHAILE HOUSE
Ballyvaughan, Co. Clare 120
☎ 065-707 7260

CAPTAINS QUARTERS
Kinsale, Co. Cork............................60
☎ 021-477 4549

496 SEE ALSO INDEX TO LOCATIONS

CROFTON BRAY HEAD INN
Bray, Co. Wicklow......................320
☎ 01-286 7182

CROSBIE CEDARS HOTEL
Rosslare, Co. Wexford................401
☎ 053-913 2124

CROVER HOUSE HOTEL
& GOLF CLUB
Mountnugent, Co. Cavan 333
☎ 049-854 0206

CROWNE PLAZA, DUBLIN AIRPORT
Dublin Airport, Co. Dublin..........251
☎ 01-862 8888

CRUTCH'S HILLVILLE HOUSE HOTEL
Castlegregory, Co. Kerry 74
☎ 066-713 8118

CRYSTAL SPRINGS
Killarney, Co. Kerry 92
☎ 064-33272

CULLINAN'S SEAFOOD
RESTAURANT & GUESTHOUSE
Doolin, Co. Clare........................125
☎ 065-707 4183

CURRAGH LODGE HOTEL
Kildare Town, Co. Kildare 338
☎ 045-522144

CURRAREVAGH HOUSE
Oughterard, Co. Galway 183
☎ 091-552312

CUSTOMS HOUSE COUNTRY INN
Belcoo, Co. Fermanagh 243
☎ 028-6638 6285

D

D (THE)
Drogheda, Co. Louth..................310
☎ 041-987 7700

DANBY LODGE HOTEL
Rosslare, Co. Wexford................401
☎ 053-915 8191

DARBY O'GILLS COUNTRY HOUSE
HOTEL
Killarney, Co. Kerry 92
☎ 064-34168

DAVENPORT HOTEL
O'CALLAGHAN
Dublin City, Co. Dublin 271
☎ 01-607 3500

DAVITTS
Kenmare, Co. Kerry......................84
☎ 064-42741

DAYS HOTEL, BELFAST
Belfast City 234
☎ 028-9024 2494

DAYS HOTEL GALWAY
Galway City, Co. Galway 167
☎ 1890-776655

DAYS HOTEL KILKENNY
Kilkenny City, Co. Kilkenny 365
☎ 1890-77 66 55

DAYS HOTEL RATHMINES
Dublin City, Co. Dublin 272
☎ 1890-776 655

DAYS HOTEL TULLAMORE
Tullamore, Co. Offaly..................351
☎ 1890-776 655

DAY'S INISHBOFIN HOUSE HOTEL
Inishbofin Island, Co. Galway 177
☎ 095-45809

DAYS INN TALBOT STREET
Dublin City, Co. Dublin 272
☎ 1890-776 655

DEER PARK HOTEL AND
GOLF COURSES
Howth, Co. Dublin 301
☎ 01-832 2624

DERGVALE HOTEL
Dublin City, Co. Dublin 272
☎ 01-874 4753

DERRYNANE HOTEL
Caherdaniel, Co. Kerry 72
☎ 066-947 5136

DIAMOND HILL COUNTRY HOUSE
Waterford City, Co. Waterford....391
☎ 051-832855

DINGLE BAY HOTEL
Dingle (An Daingean), Co. Kerry ..78
☎ 066-915 1231

DINGLE BENNERS HOTEL
Dingle (An Daingean), Co. Kerry ..78
☎ 066-915 1638

DINGLE SKELLIG HOTEL
& PENINSULA SPA
Dingle (An Daingean), Co. Kerry ..78
☎ 066-915 0200

DOBBINS INN HOTEL
Carrickfergus, Co. Antrim 232
☎ 028-9335 1905

DOHERTY'S POLLAN BEACH HOTEL
Ballyliffin, Co. Donegal 206
☎ 074-937 8840

DOLMEN HOTEL AND
RIVER COURT LODGES
Carlow Town, Co. Carlow 361
☎ 059-914 2002

DONEGAL MANOR
Donegal Town, Co. Donegal 210
☎ 074-972 5222

DONNYBROOK LODGE
Dublin City, Co. Dublin 273
☎ 01-283 7333

DOOLEY'S HOTEL
Waterford City, Co. Waterford....391
☎ 051-873531

DOOLYS HOTEL
Birr, Co. Offaly 349
☎ 057-912 0032

DOONMACFELIM HOUSE
Doolin, Co. Clare........................125
☎ 065-707 4503

DOONMORE HOTEL
Inishbofin Island, Co. Galway 178
☎ 095-45804

DORRIANS IMPERIAL HOTEL
Ballyshannon, Co. Donegal 206
☎ 071-985 1147

DOUGH MOR LODGE
Lahinch, Co. Clare......................132
☎ 065-708 2063

DOWNHILL HOUSE HOTEL
Ballina, Co. Mayo 188
☎ 096-21033

DOWNHILL INN
Ballina, Co. Mayo 189
☎ 096-73444

DOWNINGS BAY HOTEL
Letterkenny, Co. Donegal 214
☎ 074-915 5586

DOYLES SEAFOOD BAR &
TOWN HOUSE
Dingle (An Daingean), Co. Kerry ..79
☎ 066-915 1174

DROMHALL HOTEL
Killarney, Co. Kerry 92
☎ 064-39300

DROMOLAND CASTLE
Newmarket-on-Fergus, Co. Clare139
☎ 061-368144

DRUMCREEHY HOUSE
Ballyvaughan, Co. Clare 120
☎ 065-707 7377

DRURY COURT HOTEL
Dublin City, Co. Dublin 273
☎ 01-475 1988

DUBLIN SKYLON HOTEL
Dublin City, Co. Dublin 273
☎ 01-837 9121

DUKES HOTEL
Belfast City, Belfast City..............235
☎ 028-9023 6666

DUN RI GUESTHOUSE
Clifden, Co. Galway....................160
☎ 095-21625

DUNADRY HOTEL AND
COUNTRY CLUB
Belfast City, Belfast City..............235
☎ 028-9443 4343

FUCHSIA HOUSE
Killarney, Co. Kerry 95
☎ 064-33743

FULLERTON ARMS
Ballintoy, Co. Antrim..................230
☎ 028-2076 9613

G

G (THE)
Galway City, Co. Galway 168
☎ 091-865200

GABLES GUESTHOUSE &
LEISURE CENTRE
Newbridge, Co. Kildare..............343
☎ 045-435330

GALWAY BAY HOTEL,
CONFERENCE & LEISURE CENTRE
Galway City, Co. Galway 168
☎ 091-520520

GARNISH HOUSE
Cork City, Co. Cork 51
☎ 021-427 5111

GARRYVOE HOTEL
Shanagarry, Co. Cork...................68
☎ 021-464 6718

GEORGE FREDERIC HANDEL HOTEL
Dublin City, Co. Dublin 276
☎ 01-670 9400

GLASSON GOLF HOTEL AND
COUNTRY CLUB
Athlone, Co. Westmeath............353
☎ 090-648 5120

GLEANN FIA COUNTRY HOUSE
Killarney, Co. Kerry 95
☎ 064-35035

GLEBE HOUSE
Mohill, Co. Leitrim 221
☎ 071-963 1086

GLEESONS TOWNHOUSE &
RESTAURANT
Roscommon Town, Co. Roscommon ..201
☎ 090-662 6954

GLEN HOTEL
Glen of Aherlow, Co. Tipperary South 379
☎ 062-56146

GLENA GUESTHOUSE
Killarney, Co. Kerry 96
☎ 064-32705

GLENDALOUGH HOTEL
Glendalough, Co. Wicklow 323
☎ 0404-45135

GLENDUFF HOUSE
Tralee, Co. Kerry 113
☎ 066-713 7105

GLENEAGLE HOTEL
Killarney, Co. Kerry 96
☎ 064-36000

GLENEANY HOUSE
Letterkenny, Co. Donegal 214
☎ 074-912 6088

GLENGARRIFF BLUE POOL LODGE
Glengarriff, Co. Cork 58
☎ 027-63000

GLENGARRIFF ECCLES HOTEL
Glengarriff, Co. Cork 59
☎ 027-63003

GLENLO ABBEY HOTEL
Galway City, Co. Galway 169
☎ 091-526666

GLENMORE HOUSE
Dublin Airport, Co. Dublin..........251
☎ 01-840 3610

GLENOGRA HOUSE
Dublin City, Co. Dublin 276
☎ 01-668 3661

GLENROYAL HOTEL, LEISURE CLUB
& CONFERENCE CENTRE
Maynooth, Co. Kildare 341
☎ 01-629 0909

GLENSIDE HOTEL
Drogheda, Co. Louth..................310
☎ 041-982 9185

GLENVIEW GUESTHOUSE
Ballinamore, Co. Leitrim 219
☎ 071-964 4157

GLENVIEW HOTEL
Glen-O-The-Downs, Co. Wicklow324
☎ 01-287 3399

GLENWOOD HOUSE
Carrigaline, Co. Cork 42
☎ 021-437 3878

GOLF VIEW
Newmarket-on-Fergus, Co. Clare139
☎ 061-368095

GORMAN'S CLIFFTOP HOUSE
AND RESTAURANT
Dingle (An Daingean), Co. Kerry ..79
☎ 066-915 5162

GOUGANE BARRA HOTEL
Gougane Barra, Co. Cork..............59
☎ 026-47069

GRAFTON CAPITAL HOTEL
Dublin City, Co. Dublin 277
☎ 01-648 1100

GRAND CANAL HOTEL
Dublin City, Co. Dublin 277
☎ 01-646 1000

GRAND CENTRAL HOTEL
Bundoran, Co. Donegal 208
☎ 071-984 2722

GRAND HOTEL
Malahide, Co. Dublin 303
☎ 01-845 0000

GRAND HOTEL
Wicklow Town, Co. Wicklow......325
☎ 0404-67337

GRAND HOTEL
Tralee, Co. Kerry 113
☎ 066-712 1499

GRAND HOTEL
Tramore, Co. Waterford..............386
☎ 051-381414

GRANT'S HOTEL
Roscrea, Co. Tipperary North......148
☎ 0505-23300

GRANVILLE HOTEL
Waterford City, Co. Waterford....391
☎ 051-305555

GRAYS GUEST HOUSE
Achill Island, Co. Mayo 187
☎ 098-43244

GREAT NORTHERN HOTEL
Bundoran, Co. Donegal 208
☎ 071-984 1204

GREAT SOUTHERN HOTEL
Shannon Airport, Co. Clare 140
☎ 061-471122

GREAT SOUTHERN HOTEL
Dublin Airport, Co. Dublin..........252
☎ 01-844 6000

GREAT SOUTHERN HOTEL
Rosslare Harbour, Co. Wexford ..402
☎ 053-913 3233

GREAT SOUTHERN HOTEL
Cork Airport, Co. Cork..................46
☎ 021-494 7500

GREAT SOUTHERN HOTEL
Galway City, Co. Galway 169
☎ 091-564041

GREENBRIER INN GUESTHOUSE
Lahinch, Co. Clare 133
☎ 065-708 1242

GREENHILLS HOTEL
CONFERENCE/LEISURE
Limerick City, Co. Limerick 143
☎ 061-453033

GREENMOUNT HOUSE
Dingle (An Daingean), Co. Kerry ..80
☎ 066-915 1414

GREGANS CASTLE HOTEL
Ballyvaughan, Co. Clare 121
☎ 065-707 7005